Gender and Peacebuilding

Peace and Conflict Studies

Series Editors: Thomas G. Matyók, Sean Byrne, Jessica Senehi, Maureen P. Flaherty, and Hamdesa Tuso

Within a global context, this interdisciplinary series advances the work of recognized scholars in the field of Peace and Conflict Studies (PACS) as well as emerging and marginalized voices. Peacebuilding and conflict transformation are activities that address the world's wicked problems—a task that requires a broad range of global actors. The series seeks a balance of Western and non-Western approaches to peacebuilding and conflict resolution practice, and a wide range of theoretical and methodological approaches to peace and conflict studies is encouraged. Particular interest is placed on scholarship and practice developing in the Two-Thirds World. As an integrated field of study and practice it incorporates a substantial number of subdisciplines: alternative dispute resolution, conflict analysis and resolution, peacebuilding, human rights, social justice, reconciliation and forgiveness, narrative and peacemaking, indigenous peacemaking, gender, and religion, among others.

Recent Titles

Transformative Change: An Introduction to Peace and Conflict Studies, edited by Laura E. Reimer, Cathryne L. Schmitz, Emily M. Janke, Ali Askerov, Barbara T. Strahl, and Thomas G. Matyók

Gender and Peacebuilding: All Hands Required, edited by Maureen P. Flaherty, Thomas G. Matyók, Sean Byrne, and Hamdesa Tuso

Gender and Peacebuilding

All Hands Required

Edited by
Maureen P. Flaherty, Thomas G. Matyók,
Sean Byrne, and Hamdesa Tuso

LEXINGTON BOOKS
Lanham • Boulder • New York • London

Published by Lexington Books
An imprint of The Rowman & Littlefield Publishing Group, Inc.
4501 Forbes Boulevard, Suite 200, Lanham, Maryland 20706
www.rowman.com

Unit A, Whitacre Mews, 26-34 Stannary Street, London SE11 4AB

British Library Cataloguing in Publication Information Available

Library of Congress Control Number: 2015949008
ISBN: 978-0-7391-9260-3 (cloth : alk. paper)
eISBN: 978-0-7391-9261-0

∞™ The paper used in this publication meets the minimum requirements of American National Standard for Information Sciences—Permanence of Paper for Printed Library Materials, ANSI/NISO Z39.48-1992.

Printed in the United States of America

For our children and grandchildren

Contents

Acknowledgments xi

Introduction xiii

PART I: CHALLENGES AND RESPONSES: CASE STUDIES AND EXAMPLES 1

1 Barbara Deming: Feminism and Nonviolence 3
Celia Cook-Huffman

2 Afghan Women: Subjects of Peace and Objects of Violence 17
Elham Atashi

3 Healing the Wounds of Genocide Rape: The Experiences of Two Women in Rwanda 35
Regine Uwibereyeho King

4 Mothers at the Tree of Frustration: Locating Healing in Liberia 53
Angela J. Lederach

5 Inclusion-Exclusion of Women in Local Peacemaking Systems in the Kaffa Society of Ethiopia 69
Federica De Sisto

6 A Positive Peace Initiative with Rural Women in China 83
Maria Cheung and Tuula Heinonen

7 The Role of Oromo Women in Peacemaking: Perspectives from an Indigenous System 99
Hamdesa Tuso

8 Remaining Human: Ukrainian Women's Experiences of Constructing "Normal Life" in the Gulag 121
Oksana Kis

9 One Step Forward, Two Steps Back? Developing a Women's Peace Agenda in Post-Soviet Armenia and Azerbaijan 139
Sinéad Walsh

10 Black Tradeswomen Building: Toward Pragmatic Peacebuilding for Personal, Cultural, and Institutional Change 157
Roberta Hunte

11 Karen Women Resettling in Canada: Exploring the Challenges of Transnational Networks for Peace 175
Anna Snyder

12 "It's Not Just the Icing, It's the Glue": Rural Women's Volunteering in Manitoba, Canada 195
Robin Neustaeter

13 Militarization and Gender in Israel 213
Galia Golan

14 Women at the Peace Table: The Gender Dynamics of Peace Negotiations 229
Monica McWilliams

15 (Re)Examining Women's Role in Peacebuilding: Assessing the Impact of the International Fund for Ireland (IFI) and the European Union (EU) PEACE III Funding on Women's Role in Community Development, Peacebuilding, and Reconciliation in Northern Ireland and the Border Counties 245
Patlee Creary and Sean Byrne

16 Women Peacekeepers: Gender Discourses on "Equal but Different" Among Irish Peacekeepers 263
Shirley Graham

PART II: PEACE EDUCATION 279

17 Peace Studies and Feminism: Debates, Linkages, and Intersections 281
Lisa McLean and María Lucía Zapata

18 Cultural Violence and Gender: Peacebuilding via Peace Education 299
Katerina Standish

19 Peacebuilding without Western Saviors? An Approach to Teaching African Gender and Sexuality Politics to American students 321
Robin L. Turner

PART III: MOVING FORWARD 339

20 Gender, Violence, and Dehumanization: No Peace with Patriarchy 341
Franke Wilmer

21 Queer Theory and Peace and Conflict Studies: Some Critical Reflections 359
Robert C. Mizzi and Sean Byrne

22 (Dis)ability, Gender, and Peacebuilding: Natural Absences Present but Invisible 375
Maureen Flaherty and Nancy Hansen

23 Getting It Right: Some Advice from Feminist Methodologists 391
Joey Sprague

Index 409

Contributor Biographies 421

Acknowledgments

This book is a labor of love and commitment by not only the writers/contributors who participated so generously in this project, but also those dear ones who have surrounded and supported us throughout the process, particularly Fred and Renee, who behind the scenes have gone above and beyond. We thank you all from the bottom of our hearts. Another unsung hero is the eagle-eyed and patient Jennifer Ham, editorial assistant from the Arthur V. Mauro Centre for Peace and Justice who, with great accommodation and energy, devoted her considerable talent and many painstaking hours to sifting through the commas and periods and much more consolidating this tome. Thank you Annette Jones for your efficiency and professionalism assisting with those pesky details that can stop people in their tracks. Thank you also to our wonderful publishers, including Geoffrey Zokal and particularly Justin Race, for your patience, encouragement, judgment, and much appreciated humor. We would also like to thank all the peacebuilders, some of whom are mentioned in this book, who do their work every day often without notice or acknowledgment, and who are the foundations and glue of the communities in which they live.

Introduction

Why this book and why now? Why is a text that uses a gendered lens to focus on peacebuilding needed? Gender roles are different in various cultures and settings; how does the intersection of gender and culture, gender and power, gender and anything influence the ways people interact in building peaceful communities? How can Peace and Conflict Studies (PACS) represent gendered experiences in conversations that will facilitate peacebuilding rather than conflate any conflicts that might exist? These are some of our original questions in designing this text.

Clearly, there are peacebuilding tasks for everyone;[1] however until very recently, the scholarship interested in peacebuilding focused largely on heterosexual male aspects as if they represented all of humanity. Our own collective experience tells us that others, for example, people identifying as women, are engaged daily in peacebuilding at the interpersonal, community, national, and regional levels. People who identify on a continuum of gender are involved in peacebuilding work. As citizens of a shared world, as peace scholars, we realize that in order to work together for a truly peaceful planet, we must look to each and every individual as co-citizen, learning to be much more open with each other, widening our world, acknowledging that we are all in this work together. This is an ongoing effort.

The twenty-first century has brought with it a shift from the notion that human security is located in secure national borders to a focus on the need to facilitate and protect the safety and development, the freedom and dignity of all.[2] This has led to the theories underpinning humanitarian intervention in conflicts around the world. Following Kosovo in 1999, Responsibility-to-Protect (R2P) has become prevalent in discussions focusing on intervention. Sovereignty is being redefined. Within this change is the need for a next-level discussion of the role of not only women, but also of all people engaged in peacebuilding and stability. A focus on women's peacebuilding work opens that conversation to more complex perspectives.

Despite efforts to equalize women's status in the world evidenced by changes in many international projects requiring a gender focus, we have realized that gender mainstreaming must be a norm in conflict analysis and in broader peacebuilding efforts. Women and men inhabit their worlds in very different ways related to their gender identification and appearance, the way their gender is performed, experienced and perceived internally and externally. The United Nations Development Programme has been instrumental in providing training and tools to assist communities to understand and work with the enormous and fundamental challenge of gender analysis in development and community-building.[3]

Further, the reality is that humans who do not all fall neatly into the category of male or female, or for that matter in the binary of heterosexual male or female, often find themselves further challenged. Our understanding of the complexity of being human continues to evolve. And the growing realization of this complexity suggests that any discussion of gender needs to be viewed as ever changing, and where we are today, vis-à-vis gender, is not where we believe we will be, or where we need to be, tomorrow. This book is our contribution to an ongoing dialogue regarding gender and its place in peacebuilding as a unique dimension of theory and practice.

While gender studies have been popular for some time, it was not until the 1980s, that PACS first began to acknowledge and study the different experiences males and females have during war and peace.[4] Since, there have been books about women and war,[5] women working at the grassroots to build peace,[6] women and transitional justice,[7] women and peace education,[8] and a different view of human security,[9] all much needed contributions to the discourse that should influence our changing world. Still, we know this work must go far beyond acknowledgment of heterosexual men and women and their differing involvement and needs.

The relatively new focus on gender considerations in peacebuilding and PACS has meant that those interested in the area are challenged to find materials that deal with issues across the spectrum from practical grassroots examples, to theory related to the study and research of gender and peacebuilding, and the rainbow of challenges not often as yet reflected in the related literature.

This book brings together some of those themes and voices and adds more with the final product being more than the sum of its parts. We want to add to the gender and peacebuilding conversations a book that considers foundational/fundamental issues that span from the interpersonal to the global, and areas in between. The writers are a collection of experts in their own fields of study and practice, many well-known, well-reputed and often cited, but never have they all been together in one volume. Joining these voices are some newer ones who have engaged with PACS, and the larger world, in a variety of ways and now add their own thoughts and experiences to the discussion. Many of the chapters describe empirical research completed with author and community, only now being shared with the world.

Certainly, it is our belief that all people, irrespective of gender and identity, can evolve once they think about their position. Each of us has the capacity to experience the world through lenses we design and create. For example, "male" and "female" and places in between are points of identity and behavior, not end states.

INTERSECTIONALITY

Each of the chapters in this book tells a tale of individuals or groups who engage with their community and in some way improve the quality of their own and others' lives. This is the purpose of PACS, to achieve nonviolent, constructive social change that includes rather than excludes. Important, too, is the recognition that we do not assume a linear approach to conflict transformation; rather, we look to improve conflicts, to make them better. Our mental frame is one of a spiral, continuously moving conflict upward into a qualitatively better condition.

We recognize that all conflict analysis is inherently inadequate, and that more information is always desirable. Our world is complex. And, as PACS scholars and practitioners we must embrace complexity at every opportunity. Adding gender as a dimension of analysis leads to a broader, deeper, and more nuanced understanding of the conflicts we are engaging and the peacebuilding that takes place on an everyday basis on a variety of domains in so many communities.

Many of our contributors address these complexities through their research and reflections related not only to gender and power, the most common consideration, but also the interaction of gender and ethnicity, gender and class, gender and ability. Again, one of the few assumptions we can make is that we can assume nothing at all about individuals' and groups' experiences of conflict and peacebuilding.

Our goal is not to contribute to a fragmentation of peacebuilding, separating out unique subdivisions or domains of influence. We view peacebuilding as a holistic enterprise. The holistic approach we suggest requires peacebuilders to develop a balanced understanding of the many "parts" of the process. An understanding of gender contributes to individuals' awareness of the many ways people make sense of their worlds and the many ways the world may impact a variety of individuals who, on the surface, may be sharing the same experience. Acknowledging difference is part of building true empathy and inclusion, a continual effort required for building peace.

OVERVIEW OF THIS BOOK

Earlier, we noted the progression of the focus on gender in PACS originating from the acknowledgment that gender is indeed something to consider when analyzing the dynamics of peaceful living and of conflict. Our field has come a long way to name gender issues. Still, with all the work that has been done in the academy and at the grassroots level, we are only beginning to take the time to notice the challenges and triumphs at local levels to actually document these challenges. While there are principles that can be shared across cultures, peacebuilding is not a "one size fits all" process. For example, much of the peacebuilding and conflict transformation work that is being conducted by women on a daily basis goes unnoticed, possibly because it is at the grassroots level, and often appears to be routine; this work can easily be overlooked as unimportant. On the contrary, the day-to-day peacebuilding efforts of grassroots actors, wherever they occur are often the backbone of sustenance and resilience for a community.

The first part of this book shares specific examples of work that is and has been done in different cultures and contexts by women of various ages and stages of building and keeping community. We share examples from the Middle East, from countries in Africa, from Eastern Europe, Western Europe, and from North America. Part II focuses on peace education, examining not only what is being taught, but also what should be taught. Part II critiques today's efforts at teaching PACS and provides suggestions and examples of how this important work might be shared in more open and equitable ways. Part III enters into territory that is found even less in the PACS literature. In this section our authors confront patriarchy head on, engage in a discussion about the contribution queer theory makes to PACS, and tussle with the notion of inclusivity with considerations of not only gender, but also disability and then end with a discussion about the contribution feminist methodologies make to PACS. Some of our contributors did not consider themselves to be peace scholars; we believe that they are and that their voices are much needed to open the discussion even wider.

We invite the reader to engage with the contributors to this book. Have a conversation with them as you read and challenge and add to what has been written. We see this book as a small step toward a more considerate, equitable world.

NOTES

1. Elise Boulding, *Cultures of Peace: The Hidden Side of History* (New York, NY: Syracuse University Press, 2000).

2. United Nations Office for the Coordination of Humanitarian Affairs (OCHA), "Thematic Areas: Transition from Relief to Development," accessed April 30, 2015, http://www.unocha.org/what-we-do/policy/thematic-areas/transition-from-relief-to-development#.

3. UN Women, *Advancing Gender Equality and Women's Empowerment: An Assessment of Gender Mainstreaming in UN Operational Activities for Development*, June 15, 2012, accessed April 30, 2015, http://www.un.org/esa/coordination/pdf/qcpr_final_report_6-15.pdf.

4. Christine Sylvester, "Patriarchy, Peace, and Women Warriors," in *A Peace Reader: Essential Readings on War, Justice, Non-Violence, and World Order*, edited by Joseph Fahey and Richard Armstrong (Nahwah, NJ: Paulist Press, 1992).

5. See, for example, Cynthia Enloe, *Bananas, Beaches and Bases: Making Feminist Sense of International Politics* (Berkely, CA: University of California Press, 2000/1989); Cyntia Enloe, *Nimo's War, Emma's War: Making Feminist Sense of the Iraq War* (Berkely, CA: University of California Press, 2010); Janie L. Leatherman, *Sexual Violence and Armed Conflict* (Cambridge, England: Polity Press, 2011); Betty Reardon, *Sexism and the War System* (Syracuse, NY: Syracuse University Press, 1985); Betty Reardon, *Women and Peace: Feminist Visions of Global Security* (Albany, NY: State University of New York Press, 1993).

6. See, for example, Boulding, *Cultures of Peace*; Peggy Chinn, *Peace and Power: Creative Leadership for Building Community*, 6th ed. (Mississauga, ON: Jones and Bartlett, 2004); Leymah Gbowee, *Mighty Be Our Powers: How Sisterhood, Prayer, and Sex Changed a Nation at War* (New York, NY: Beast Books, 2011).

7. Fionnuala Ní Aoláin, Dina Francesca Haynes, and Naomi Cahn, *On the Frontlines: Gender, War, and the Post-Conflict Process* (Oxford, UK: Oxford University Press, 2011).

8. Betty Reardon, *Educating for a Culture of Peace in a Gender Perspective* (Paris, France: UNESCO, 2001).

9. See, for example, Betty Reardon, "Women and Human Security: A Feminist Framework and Critique of the Prevailing Patriarchal Security System," in *The Gender Imperative: Human Security vs State Security*, edited by Betty Reardon and Asha Hans (New York, NY: Routledge, 2010); Laura Sjoberg, ed., *Gender and International Security: Feminist Perspectives* (London, England: Routledge, 2010).

BIBLIOGRAPHY

Chinn, Peggy. *Peace and Power: Creative Leadership for Building Community*. 6th ed. Mississauga, ON: Jones and Bartlett, 2004.

Boulding, Elise. *Cultures of Peace: The Hidden Side of History*. Syracuse, NY: Syracuse University Press, 2000.

Enloe, Cynthia. *Bananas, Beaches and Bases: Making Feminist Sense of International Politics.* Berkely, CA: University of California Press, 2000/1989.

———. *Nimo's War, Emma's War: Making Feminist Sense of the Iraq War.* Berkely, CA: University of California Press, 2010.

Gbowee, Leymah. *Mighty Be Our Powers: How Sisterhood, Prayer, and Sex Changed a Nation at War.* New York, NY: Beast Books, 2011.

Leatherman, Janie L. *Sexual Violence and Armed Conflict.* Cambridge, England: Polity Press, 2011.

Ní Aoláin, Fionnuala, Dina Francesca Haynes, and Naomi Cahn. *On the Frontlines: Gender, War, and the Post-Conflict Process.* Oxford, England: Oxford University Press, 2011.

Reardon, Betty. *Educating for a Culture of Peace in a Gender Perspective.* Paris, France: UNESCO, 2001.

———. *Sexism and the War System.* Syracuse, NY: Syracuse University Press, 1985.

———. "Women and Human Security: A Feminist Framework and Critique of the Prevailing Patriarchal Security System." In *The Gender Imperative: Human Security vs State Security*, edited by Betty Reardon and Asha Hans, 7–37. New York, NY: Routledge, 2010.

———. *Women and Peace: Feminist Visions of Global Security.* Albany, NY: State University of New York Press, 1993.

Sjoberg, Laura, ed. *Gender and International Security: Feminist Perspectives.* London, England: Routledge, 2010.

Sylvester, Christine. "Patriarchy, Peace, and Women Warriors." In *A Peace Reader: Essential Readings on War, Justice, Non-Violence, and World Order*, edited by Joseph Fahey and Richard Armstrong, 33–49. Nahwah, NJ: Paulist Press, 1992.

United Nations Office for the Coordination of Humanitarian Affairs (OCHA). "Thematic Areas: Transition from Relief to Development." Accessed April 30, 2015. http://www.unocha.org/what-we-do/policy/thematic-areas/transition-from-relief-to-development#.

UN Women. *Advancing Gender Equality and Women's Empowerment: An Assessment of Gender Mainstreaming in UN Operational Activities for Development*, June 15, 2012. Accessed April 30, 2015. http://www.un.org/esa/coordination/pdf/qcpr_final_report_6-15.pdf.

PART I

CHALLENGES AND RESPONSES: CASE STUDIES AND EXAMPLES

Chapter 1

Barbara Deming

Feminism and Nonviolence

Celia Cook-Huffman

In his "Agenda for Peace,"[1] Boutros Boutros-Ghali describes peacebuilding as actions that strive to strengthen and stabilize conditions of peace in order to avoid the re-escalation of conflicts. The language of peacebuilding has been adopted into the vocabulary and structures of organizations, local and global. Around the world, and across diverse conflicts, actors engage in a wide range of peacebuilding activities.

And yet, despite more than half a century of work to "mainstream" gender to include women and women's voices more centrally in the work of peacebuilding, negotiations, peace accords, political policies, economic institutions, post-conflict reconstruction efforts, elections continue to exclude women around the globe.

As peace theorists and practitioners, we understand that "including women and applying a gender lens are part of a broader transformation of social power relations towards positive peace."[2] As Tony Jenkins and Betty Reardon argue, gender can in fact "serve as an organizing concept" for the exploration of gender equality and peace, and "as the potential core of a systematic inquiry into the possibilities for the transformation of the present violent world order."[3]

This chapter seeks to illuminate a voice that makes a significant contribution to a feminist theory of peacebuilding. Writing in the 1960s through to her death in the 1984, Barbara Deming explored the intersections of war, structural violence, racial inequality, and gender oppression, offering the field both a theoretical frame for a feminist peace, and a model for feminist nonviolent action. For Deming, gender is a core construct informing her understanding of violence, and the way out. Gender is the basic opposition, the first dichotomy that creates "other," and thus, is a foundational source of violence. To end violence we must challenge the patriarchal lie that "men and women are of different natures," and embrace the truth, "that no human being should be thought of as The Other."[4]

> . . . men and women—and women and women, and men and men—should finally learn to come together simply as human beings, *no more* and *no less*, then love would no longer draw women backward by the hair, away from themselves; and it would no longer drive men to seek themselves where they will never find themselves, in despoiling others, and in despoiling the earth itself.[5]

Deming's journey, her story, and her developing consciousness as a political activist and a feminist, is the story of the peace movement in the United States from the 1960s to the 1980s. Her writings reveal the "masculinist" culture of the peace movement, and the struggles of women to be full participants in that movement. Her own increasing awareness of oppression led her to re-imagine the concerns of the antiwar movement linking them to other struggles against injustice and to an increasingly deeper understanding of the connections between personal and political violence.

Ira Chernus calls Barbara Deming "the least well known of all the great theorists on nonviolence in US history."[6] Her place as one of the key theorists of nonviolence is unquestionably true. Her understanding of the practice of nonviolence and her theoretical insights into why and how nonviolence works as a form of social change are grounded in personal experience, reflective practice, experience in civil disobedience, and extensive dialogue with others who were at the forefront of American nonviolent movements from the 1960s onward.

Her invisibility is the legacy of nonviolent movements that come of age in the midst of patriarchy. The radical pacifist movements in which Deming was involved were highly masculinized. Men within these movements did not want to be seen as weak or unmanly. Maintaining privileged leadership positions, and a narrative that identified them as the protectors of those who needed to be protected, allowed them to preserve masculine identities. The narratives of nonviolent actions often used a frame that positioned women in essentialized, supporting roles. Mothers protecting their children, women supporting their men, were acceptable stories, a kind of nonviolence both visible and celebrated, but a lesbian feminist on a hunger fast in jail still struggled to find visibility. The generic male voice is a voice that Deming herself did not overcome until late in her own writing.[7]

And yet, what she offers us is a comprehensive, clearly articulated theory of nonviolence as action that creates change and that is informed by feminist politics and a gendered analysis of power relations. She was interested in the ability of the oppressed to resist and alter the injustices of the systems in which they live using methods that are able to create the kind of just world they desire. She called nonviolence "the most practical discipline"[8] with the capacity to bring about radical social change, and create a world where people "treat each other with true respect."[9]

SEARCHING FOR THE TRUTH

Deming was born in 1917 in New York City. She grew up in a middle/upper class family, attended Quaker Schools, good colleges, and spent a year traveling in Europe. She worked in theater as a stage manager and director, was an editor, taught, and in 1954 became a full-time writer.[10]

Deming came to the nonviolent movements of the 1960s through a series of events, which brought about both a political awakening and a commitment to nonviolence as a way to bring about a more just world. Two significant events that contributed to her awakening include a trip to India in 1959, which led to an interest in the writings of Gandhi, and a trip to Cuba in 1960 in which a personal meeting with Castro forced her to question the US story that was being told about Cuba and Castro's governance.[11]

Her interest in Gandhi, a growing sense of distrust in the US portrayal of its enemies, and a growing concern with the realities of nuclear weapons led her to participate in a sixteen-day training on nonviolence put together by The Peacemakers in New London, Connecticut in August 1960. At the training she met a number of folks from the Committee for Nonviolent Action (CNVA). She wrote of this event: "It never occurred to me that there were any other people in the US who had the same nonviolent vision."[12] Here finally was a way to take action that recognized the complexity of human nature and thus refused to call anyone "the enemy," a way to turn from her "private search for her personal, individual truth to a public effort to find and implement the political truths"[13] she had begun to see. Within this group she found a community: "The pacifists are the only freely active people I have met in a long time. Coming face to face with them was, in fact, like entering a new world."[14]

Deming's life as a nonviolent activist included well-known movements as well as lesser studied actions and campaigns. When she joined the CNVA she became involved in protests against the Polaris submarine, as well as other actions like the San Francisco to Moscow Walk for Peace and the Quebec-Washington-Guantanamo Walk for Peace (QWGWP), an interracial walk for peace.

She was involved in the War Resisters League, actions opposing nuclear tests and for unilateral disarmament,[15] the 1961 Beirut conference to establish a World Peace Brigade for Nonviolent Action, and Women Strike for Peace. She became involved in the civil rights movement when the QWGWP reached the south and the integrated nature of the event forced the group to take the issues of segregation and structural violence as seriously as they had the threat of militarization and nuclear war. In 1966 Vietnam became a specific focus of her work and she traveled with AJ Muste, Brad Lyttle, and others to Saigon and to North Vietnam to see for themselves the realities of the war.[16]

Deming's political journey was central to her experience of nonviolence. Her insights about nonviolence were also inextricably linked to and informed by her personal journey. From a very young age she knew she was a lesbian. She did not however come out publically until she was in her fifties. When she publically came out, she developed a radical feminist consciousness, and began to work specifically from a feminist point of view on feminist issues. She joined the antipornography campaign, helped to organize a branch of Women Against Violence Against Women, worked with Women's Encampment for a Future of Peace and Justice, and began to write about women's and lesbian issues.[17]

Her understanding of the power of nonviolence and the importance of "clinging to truth," trusting one's own experiences, was informed by the need to bridge her personal struggles with her sexuality and her experience of herself as a lesbian woman and public political struggles to end violence and oppression. Her own struggles to be truthful with herself and to find an equilibrium with who she was and the society she was born into, clearly informed her feminist understanding of peacebuilding and her theorizing about the importance of nonviolence as a mechanism for social change.[18]

FEMINIST PEACEBUILDING

Deming first began to articulate a feminist gender-informed perspective on peacebuilding in the encounters between pacifists and civil rights activists and actions. In "On Anger"[19] she recounted a discussion of whether or not pacifists should participate in civil rights actions—what was the "right" way to expend one's energies? Wasn't the threat of nuclear war the more pressing problem? For the pacifist it was obvious that for the black man to be consistent in his nonviolence he must be opposed to war, "but it wasn't obvious to a lot of pacifists that they were inconsistent in their nonviolence if they didn't act against racism."[20] Deming rejected these hierarchies of struggle, arguing that there is only one struggle, which is to create a "world in which no person exploits another, abuses, dominates another. . ."[21]

She recognized and named the similarity in all violence, the "will to dominate,"[22] as the central core of the problem. In this understanding of the foundation of violence her work resonates with bell hooks' argument that it is the belief that it is "acceptable to maintain power by coercion or force"[23] that sustains violence in all its forms, and that ending violence requires challenging the idea that it is acceptable to maintain control of others through the use of coercive domination.[24]

In locating the roots of violence in the ideology of domination Deming built a bridge that many radical feminists of the time rejected, and again foreshadowed hooks, arguing that we may all be oppressors at some point in time.

> If the complicated truth is that many of the oppressed are also oppressors, and many of the oppressors are also oppressed, nonviolent confrontation is the only form of confrontation that allows us to respond realistically to such complexity. In this kind of struggle we address ourselves always both to that which we can respect in them, have in common with them, however much or little that may be.[25]

Deming explored this understanding of being oppressor and oppressed openly in a series of letters she exchanged with Ray Robinson and his wife, civil rights activists living in Selma, Alabama.[26] Deming understood her place of privilege as a middle class white woman, an identity that allowed her to walk away from the south, to find places and times of rest from the "struggle." At the same time she understood the link between the struggles of the blacks of the south and her own struggles as a lesbian. She understood that the struggle against racism was her struggle too, because she knew what it was to be labeled a degenerate, "I didn't walk out of some sense that it would be nice of me to help the downtrodden; I walked because I am a nigger too. And no one should be a nigger."[27]

It is this articulation of the links between the personal and the political that makes Deming's understanding of peacebuilding work distinctly feminist. Key to her analysis is the need to identify the particular differences in men and women's experiences of exploitation. She challenged those in the movement who want to focus on economic exploitation to examine more deeply "the ways in which people subsist upon one another."[28] For her, the violence of patriarchy must be understood, articulated, and challenged if the violence of war and poverty and segregation are to be successfully challenged. This violence is both material and cultural. War is oppressive, it challenges "moral well-being" in the injustices perpetrated in one's name, and it challenges "our very right to be" in the case of nuclear war. What Deming adds, is the specific, personal oppression that exists for the "woman—or black, or chicano, or gay." This oppression "calls into question one's right to be oneself, fully oneself. It touches one's pride in the deepest sense."[29] This oppression, which makes some people secondary, a "second self," a second-class citizen, must be named and challenged.[30]

This oppression ends, she believed, when the notion that there is a duality of masculine/feminine natures, ends.

> Manliness has been defined as assertion of the self. Womanliness has been defined as the nurturing of selves other than our own. . . but every individual person is born *both* to assert herself or himself *and* to act out a sympathy for others trying to find themselves.[31]

Deming believed that it is this split, assigning assertiveness to men and sympathy to women that is at the core of violence. She also understood this split is perpetuated by men and women. Yes, men need to see women as fully constituted human beings, but women also need to take the "step of perceiving themselves as human beings, each with a consciousness distinct from the consciousness of any man."[32]

For Deming the world that she wanted to create was an inclusive world, and she believed ending sexism would free both men and women.[33] For Deming, no one should be an "enemy," including men. She believed that it was as critical to create space for men to set aside the societal constraints imposed upon them, as it was and is for women: "Men, in succumbing to all the pressures put upon them from an early age to dominate, lose the chance to be freely themselves, too—to follow all kinds of contrary impulses."[34]

FEMINIST NONVIOLENCE

Deming brought her personal and political analysis together, and in this synthesis developed "the philosophy of feminist nonviolence."[35] Deming saw the need for a social change strategy that is revolutionary, that is courageous, uncompromising, non-patriarchal, that challenges, resists, uses force to compel change, and at the same time:

> . . . abandons the concept of naming enemies and adopts a concept familiar to the nonviolent tradition: naming behavior that is oppressive, naming abuse of power. . . but naming no person whom we are willing to destroy.[36]

When asked during an argument about nonviolence if she chose nonviolence because it was her desire to remain pure, Deming said no. The reason to engage in nonviolent action is not to remain pure; rather, it is so that one can escape becoming "dizzy."[37] Deming argued "violence makes men dizzy."[38] She was fundamentally interested in ending oppression, stopping violence, and challenging the nation-state's ability to wage war. The end goal was a just society and the question for Deming was "what are the best means for changing our lives?"[39] Chernus argued that one of Deming's most significant contributions was that she made a purely secular argument for the use of nonviolence.[40] Deming assessed nonviolence on its ability to achieve practical results—could nonviolence be used to improve society?

Her answer was and is, "yes." In one of her most widely read essays, "On Revolution and Equilibrium,"[41] she articulated her theory of the power of nonviolence as the means by which the present conditions that do not allow people to be fully human, can be changed.[42]

Deming did not shy away from the notion that nonviolence is about force. The radical pacifist movement of the 1950s and 1960s, coming from a pacifist perspective, struggled to articulate the complex relationship between violence, force, and power, often choosing to articulate nonviolence as a moral force—something that depended on appealing to the good in people—a prayer, calling on those in "power to be good to us."[43] Deming made a different argument about nonviolence. She argued:

> The most effective nonviolent action resorts to power and engages conscience. Nonviolent action does not have to beg others to "be nice." It can in effect force them to consult their consciences—or to pretend to have them. Nor does it have to petition those in power to do something about a situation. I can face the authorities with a new fact and say: Accept this new situation, which we have created.[44]

For Deming nonviolence was clearly about force. "One cannot simply petition those in power for change—expect to touch the consciences of men. One has to confront those in power with power on our part."[45] The difference between violence and nonviolence is not the refusal to use force, but the refusal to do harm—the refusal to "injure the antagonist."[46]

Deming acknowledged that this distinction is complicated by the reality that those whose privilege and power is being challenged will feel injured by the force of the movement. She had two responses to this concern. First, she argued that the difference is that with violence one forces the other do one's own will, which "tears the other away from himself"[47] and in nonviolence one insists upon acting out one's own will—"not tearing him away from himself but tearing from him only that which is not properly his own—the strength loaned to him by all those who have been giving him obedience."[48] She further argued that some freedoms are basic freedoms and some are not. One can frustrate another's actions without doing injury, for example if one interferes with another's freedom to kill, or to help kill, or to recruit to kill.

The power of radical nonviolence for Deming relied on two kinds of pressure. The first is the refusal to cooperate. The system needs us; so by refusing labor, money, bodies, by obstructing the system wherever possible one makes "business as usual, simply impossible for our antagonists."[49]

Here is where nonviolence must become action, *satyagraha*, which she understood to mean clinging to truth. "One has to cling with one's entire weight."[50] The action is not speaking the truth, *we have the right to sit here*, but sitting; or we should be hired here if we shop here—*stop shopping*; I don't believe in this war, *then don't put on the uniform, or pay war taxes*. Economic weight, physical weight, psychological weight, political weight—this weight goes beyond moral appeal—it is force that challenges current power structures through direct action.[51]

The second pressure is reassurance—reassurance that one's rights will be respected, that one is safe, that the goal is not destruction of the person, but justice. This pressure forces the opponent to think "about the nature of our actions and our grievance, about the real issues involved, about what others watching the struggle will think, about where his real long term interests lie—whether they don't lie in adjusting himself to change."[52]

To explain why nonviolence works she used the imagery of two hands. "They have as it were two hands upon him, the one calming him, making him ask questions and the other makes him move."[53] One hand reflects the first kind of pressure, refusing the adversary by making it "impossible to continue as he has been."[54] The second hand is used to calm and to control by acknowledging the humanity of the other.

The result is a limit on the adversary's capacity to escalate the struggle. The nonviolent activist gains control by interrupting the typical routine in a way that limits the response to the disruption "making it impossible for him to simply strike back without thought and with all his strength."[55] If the adversary escalates unreasonably he/she loses allies and supporters. She argued that just as guerilla warfare makes it impossible for the other side to use its weaponry in full force—this too is the genius of nonviolence. One force works on the other's ability to take action, and the other force works on their will to act.

Equally important for Deming was that the combination of these dual actions, the active, stubborn interference combined with human concern, the refusal to objectify the "other," or treat them as an enemy, allows for nonviolent activists to exercise control and avoid dizziness.

What is it that gives the nonviolent actor power? In part it is poise. Poise rooted in the conviction that all people have value (there is something about any person that can be loved even if we don't feel it) and the action that accompanies this truth. Poise "calls equally for the strengthening of two impulses," assertion, speaking and acting "aggressively the truth as we see it," ". . . and for restraint towards others."[56] It is "this equilibrium between self-assertion and respect for others,"[57] the refusal to "treat them as nothing," the insistence on "treating them not as part of a machine but as men capable of thought and change"[58] that is the power of nonviolence. Deming's commitment to nonviolence was in part a means and ends argument.

> It is my stubborn faith if, as revolutionaries, we will wage battle without violence, we can remain very much more in control—of our own selves, of the responses to us which our adversaries make, of the battle as it proceeds, and of the future we hope will issue from it.[59]

Violence as means makes the actor dizzy, confused, out of control. The way to regain balance, equilibrium, is to connect means and ends. Nonviolence is the method.

In articulating this theory of nonviolence Deming circled back to her belief in the power of truth arguing in "battle we rely on truth."[60] It is not just that we speak the truth or that we don't lie, but that we insist upon telling truths that the opponent does not want to hear—revealing the truth about the injustice being committed.

CONCLUSIONS

Deming articulated a theory of nonviolence informed by a feminist understanding of oppression, using her personal experience to inform her understanding of the political world she sought to change. She focused on the need to end dualistic, dichotomous notions of gender in order to liberate both men and women. In doing so, she articulated a feminist theory of peacebuilding that used the power of nonviolence as a social change strategy. For Deming nonviolence is a strategy that relies on the power of truth, and the strength found in acting from a place of equilibrium—equilibrium, which is rooted in remembering that every human has the right to exist as a subjective self, and not as a objectified other, and in doing so compels change.

Her journey from peace movement, to civil rights movement, to feminism, exploring, theorizing, and practicing nonviolence at each step along the journey, led her to one clear truth: we are all part of one another.[61] This is a truth of feminism, and nonviolence lets this truth live not only in words, but also in our actions.

NOTES

1. Boutros Boutros-Ghali, "An Agenda for Peace: Preventive Diplomacy, Peacemaking and Peace-Keeping," Report of the Secretary-General pursuant to the

statement adopted by the Summit Meeting of the Security Council, January 31, 1992, retrieved from http://www.un.org/en/peacebuilding/doc_sg.shtml.

2. Evelyn Thornton and Tobie Whitman, "Gender and Peacebuilding," in *Integrated Peacebuilding: Innovative Approaches to Transforming Conflict*, ed. Craig Zelizer (Boulder, CO: Westview, 2013), 104.

3. Tony Jenkins and Betty A. Reardon, "Gender and Peace: Towards a Gender-Inclusive, Holistic Perspective," in *Peace and Conflict Studies: A Reader*, ed. Charles Webel and Johan Galtung (London, England: Routledge, 2012), 209.

4. Barbara Deming, "Two Perspectives on Women's Struggle," *Liberation*, June 1973, in *We are All Part of One Another: A Barbara Deming Reader*, ed. Jane Meyerding (Philadelphia, PA: New Society, 1984), 289.

5. Ibid., 231.

6. Ira Chernus, *American Nonviolence: The History of an Idea* (New York, NY: Orbis Books, 2004), 182.

7. Barbara Deming, "New Men, New Women: Some Notes on Nonviolence," *WIN*, May 1, 1971 (titled "Pacifism"), in *We Cannot Live Without Our Lives*, ed. Barbara Deming (New York, NY: Grossman, 1974); Jane Meyerding, *We are All Part of One Another: A Barbara Deming Reader* (Philadelphia, PA: New Society, 1984).

8. Barbara Deming, "Nonviolence and Radical Social Change," in *On Revolution and Equilibrium*, ed. Barbara Deming (New York, NY: Grossman, 1971), 222.

9. Ibid.

10. Chernus, *American Nonviolence*; Donna McCabe, "Barbara Deming: An Activist Life" (Troy, NY: Rensselaer Polytechnic Institute, 1995), last modified October 2, 2013, http://archive.today/LQK60.

11. Barbara Deming, *On Revolution and Equilibrium* (New York, NY: Grossman, 1971).

12. Mab Segrest, "Feminism and Disobedience: Conversations with Barbara Deming," in *Reweaving the Web of Life*, ed. Pam Mcallister (Philadelphia, PA: New Society, 1982), 48.

13. Meyerding, *Part of One Another*, 3.

14. Barbara Deming, "The Peacemakers," *The Nation*, December 17, 1960, in *We Are All Part of One Another: A Barbara Deming Reader*, ed. Jane Meyerding (Philadelphia, PA: New Society, 1984), 79.

15. McCabe, "Barbara Deming."

16. Ibid.; Meyerding, *Part of One Another*.

17. Ibid.

18. McCabe, "Barbara Deming"; Meyerding, *Part of One Another.*

19. Barbara Deming, "On Anger," *Liberation*, November 1971, in *We are All Part of One Another: A Barbara Deming Reader*, ed. Jane Meyerding (Philadelphia, PA: New Society, 1984).

20. Ibid., 209.

21. Ibid.

22. Ibid., 207.

23. bell hooks, *Feminist Theory: From Margin to Center* (Boston, MA: South End, 1984), 119.

24. Ibid.

25. Barbara Deming, "Remembering Who We Are," *Quest*, Summer, 1977, in *We Are All Part of One Another: A Barbara Deming Reader*, ed. Jane Meyerding (Philadelphia, PA: New Society, 1984), 289.

26. Barbara Deming, *We Cannot Live Without Our Lives* (New York, NY: Grossman, 1974).

27. Ibid., 130. Deming is referring to the Quebec-Washington-Guantanamo Walk for Peace.

28. Barbara Deming, "Love Has Been Exploited Labor," in *We Are All Part of One Another: A Barbara Deming Reader*, ed. Jane Meyerding (Philadelphia, PA: New Society, 1984), 263.

29. Deming, "On Anger," 214.

30. Ibid., 215.

31. Deming, "Two Perspectives on Women's Struggle," 226.

32. Deming, "Love Has Been Exploited," 249.

33. McCabe, "Barbara Deming."

34. Deming, "On Anger," 217.

35. Meyerding, *Part of One Another*, 13.

36. Barbara Deming, "To Fear Jane Alpert is to Fear Ourselves: A letter to Susan Sherman," *WIN*, May 22, 1975, in *We Are All Part of One Another: A Barbara Deming Reader*, ed. Jane Meyerding (Philadelphia, PA: New Society, 1984), 271.

37. Barbara Deming, "On Revolution and Equilibrium," *Liberation*, February 1968, in *We Are All Part of One Another: A Barbara Deming Reader*, ed. Jane Meyerding (Philadelphia, PA: New Society, 1984), 169.

38. Deming, "On Revolution and Equilibrium," 181.

39. Ibid.,169.

40. Chernus, *American Nonviolence*.

41. Deming, "On Revolution and Equilibrium."

42. Ibid.,168.

43. Deming, "Nonviolence and Radical Social Change," 222.

44. Deming, "On Revolution and Equilibrium," 175.

45. Deming, "Nonviolence and Radical Social Change," 223.

46. Deming, "On Revolution and Equilibrium," 177.

47. Ibid.

48. Ibid.

49. Deming, "Nonviolence and Radical Social Change," 223.

50. Deming, "On Revolution and Equilibrium," 176.

51. Ibid.

52. Deming, "Nonviolence and Radical Social Change," 224.

53. Deming, "On Revolution and Equilibrium," 178.

54. Deming, "Nonviolence and Radical Social Change," 224.

55. Deming, "On Revolution and Equilibrium," 178.

56. Ibid.,188.

57. Ibid.

58. Ibid., 183.

59. Ibid., 169.
60. Ibid., 176.
61. Meyerding, *Part of One Another.*

BIBLIOGRAPHY

Boutros-Ghali, Boutros. "An Agenda for Peace: Preventive Diplomacy, Peacemaking and Peace-Keeping." Report of the Secretary-General pursuant to the statement adopted by the Summit Meeting of the Security Council, January 31, 1992. Retrieved from http://www.un.org/en/peacebuilding/doc_sg.shtml.

Chernus, Ira. *American Nonviolence: The History of an Idea.* New York, NY: Orbis Books, 2004.

Deming, Barbara. "Love Has Been Exploited Labor." In *We Are All Part of One Another: A Barbara Deming Reader,* edited by Jane Meyerding, 248–65. Philadelphia, PA: New Society, 1984. Originally published in *Women and Revolution: A Dialogue,* a pamphlet of the National Interim Committee for a Mass Party of the People, April 1975.

———. "New Men, New Women: Some Notes on Nonviolence." *WIN,* May 1, 1971 (titled "Pacifism"). In *We Cannot Live Without Our Lives,* edited by Barbara Deming, 3–13. New York, NY: Grossman, 1974.

———. "Nonviolence and Radical Social Change." In *On Revolution and Equilibrium,* edited by Barbara Deming, 222–25. New York, NY: Grossman, 1971. Originally published in *The New Left,* edited by Priscilla Long. Boston, MA: P. Sargent, 1969.

———. "On Anger." *Liberation,* November 1971. In *We Are All Part of One Another: A Barbara Deming Reader,* edited by Jane Meyerding, 207–17. Philadelphia, PA: New Society, 1984.

———. "On Revolution and Equilibrium." *Liberation,* February 1968. In *We Are All Part of One Another: A Barbara Deming Reader,* edited by Jane Meyerding, 168–88. Philadelphia, PA: New Society, 1984.

———. *On Revolution and Equilibrium.* New York, NY: Grossman, 1971.

———. "Remembering Who We Are." *Quest,* Summer, 1977. In *We Are All Part of One Another: A Barbara Deming Reader,* edited by Jane Meyerding, 274–95. Philadelphia, PA: New Society, 1984.

———. "The Peacemakers." *The Nation,* December 17, 1960. In *We Are All Part of One Another: A Barbara Deming Reader,* edited by Jane Meyerding, 77–88. Philadelphia, PA: New Society, 1984.

———. "To Fear Jane Alpert is to Fear Ourselves: A Letter to Susan Sherman." *WIN,* May 22, 1975. In *We Are All Part of One Another: A Barbara Deming Reader,* edited by Jane Meyerding, 267–72. Philadelphia, PA: New Society, 1984.

———. "Two Perspectives on Women's Struggle." *Liberation,* June 1973. In *We Are All Part of One Another: A Barbara Deming Reader,* edited by Jane Meyerding, 220–31. Philadelphia, PA: New Society, 1984.

———. *We Cannot Live Without Our Lives.* New York, NY: Grossman, 1974.

hooks, bell. *Feminist Theory: From Margin to Center*. Boston, MA: South End, 1984.

Jenkins, Tony and Betty A. Reardon."Gender and Peace: Towards a Gender-Inclusive, Holistic Perspective." In *Peace and Conflict Studies: A Reader*, edited by Charles Webel and Johan Galtung, 209–31. London, England: Routledge, 2012.

McCabe, Donna. "Barbara Deming: An Activist Life." Troy, NY: Rensselaer Polytechnic Institute, 1995. Last modified October 2, 2013. http://archive.today/LQK60.

Meyerding, Jane. *We Are All Part of One Another: A Barbara Deming Reader*. Philadelphia, PA: New Society, 1984.

Segrest, Mab. "Feminism and Disobedience: Conversations with Barbara Deming." In *Reweaving the Web of Life*, edited by Pam Mcallister, 45–62. Philadelphia, PA: New Society, 1982.

Thornton, Evelyn and Tobie Whitman. "Gender and Peacebuilding." In *Integrated Peacebuilding: Innovative Approaches to Transforming Conflict*, edited by Craig Zelizer, 103–26. Boulder, CO: Westview, 2013.

Chapter 2

Afghan Women

Subjects of Peace and Objects of Violence

Elham Atashi

From the launch of the US military intervention in Afghanistan, oppression and violence against women has been central in the war against the Taliban. The overthrow of the Taliban was followed by peacebuilding measures aimed at transforming women's position in Afghan society. The solid international support and commitment to gender-inclusive policies has positioned women directly, as subjects of peace. This was not surprising given that women played a critical role in legitimizing the US-led military intervention in the liberation of Afghanistan. To catalyze change, democratic reforms with aid from the international community were to take place in areas of statebuilding. Yet the top-down approach to the implementation of such measures was in direct contradiction to promises of a new democratic era since they took place without the consensus of the Afghan people. The inherent paradox has led to the dichotomy of inclusion and participatory practices in terms of gender-based peacebuilding and exclusion, regulation and control in terms of statebuilding.

On the ground the combined approach to peacebuilding and statebuilding was exigent. Most evident was the strong backlash against the discourse on women's rights. Despite peacebuilding measures directed at programs and institutions with the goal of empowerment to advance women's position, progress was constrained. Women were vulnerable to participation constructed along the lines of betrayal and cooperation with external actors. Even when peacebuilding measures have been effectively organized by women the close association to Western models of imposed change has undermined the potential for promoting women's rights. This has weakened women's ability to advocate for rights at the local level. In turn, external interventions perceived as promoting a liberal ideology have strengthened the harsh response as well as authoritarian control over women. In this context women's transformation from subjects to objects of peace has remained stagnant. In many instances, "local" power holders have increasingly gained legitimacy in using violence against women as a protective response to imposed "global" measures that seek to infiltrate Western cultural values intended to destroy local traditions. As a consequence, the platform and salience for change becomes synonymous with infiltration by outsiders, an artificial imposition. Discourse on rights and equality remain contested and imposed rather than genuine and legitimate.

This chapter explores the tension between the local and global for authenticity and legitimacy in promoting gender-based peacebuilding in the post-Taliban period. It is not intended to provide a comprehensive history, evaluation of peacebuilding programs or typology of gender-based interventions and outcomes. Rather it contextualizes the term *local* by highlighting the competing agendas that have led to the binary position of women, as subjects of peace while enduring the objects of violence. It begins by locating Afghan women in the context of perpetual political transitions, wars, and external interventions. It argues that the transnational gender agenda that has placed Afghan women at the locus of peacebuilding has not led to sustainable change or increased agency at the local level. Local mobilization for strategies to combat what has largely been perceived as foreign liberalization has gained legitimacy as a way to reassert ownership, control, and social order lost to the global. Such tensions have ultimately limited women's spaces in contexts that have already placed numerous challenges in negotiating change. This has at times escalated to increasing violence directed at women and widening of gender gaps. While focused on Afghanistan, the analysis offers important linkages to other cases particularly concerned about whether global efforts to address violence and oppression of women with internationalization and external support can hinder or advance women's rights at the local level.

CONTEXTUALIZATION OF WOMEN

Providing a profile of Afghan women is challenging given the intricate dynamics that differentiate experiences among the 14 different ethnic groups spread over 34 provinces. The concept of identity, a more fluid terrain compared to rigid categories inherent in some Western systems, is located in a complex web of contrasting and often contradictory layers that move along autonomous units of family and community. Each community stands by a set of norms and customary laws that are followed collectively but differ depending on various factors. There are, for example, vast differences along the urban and rural divide that determine loyalty as well as family, clan, tribal, and patriarchal influences. In relation to women, strategies aimed at influencing and altering lives at the state level have been typically met by uproar from local leaders united in opposition to external intervention. Political leaders at the central national level have surrendered to such demands given the complexity of power relations, requiring alliances in return for security and stability.

The history of Afghan woman is one of struggle at the forefront of resistance and confrontation. Some of the longest established women's organizations demonstrate a continuous effort to place the discourse on gender rights as rooted within patriarchal domination and fundamentalism. For many around the world, images of oppressed victims, suffering under the brutality of the Taliban, has come to symbolize understanding of Afghan women. However, the roots of exclusion and violence endured by women did not begin and will not likely end with the Taliban. Oppressive practices arise from the complex relationship between power and other dynamics such as class, economic status, demographics, culture, and politics. Gender is one, but not the only lens that exclaims such relations. The analysis of women in terms of binary contradictions defined by practices external to the gaze of the global, fail to contextualize women's active interaction within social contexts. Too often, this depiction has been constructed by the peripheral or in what Ann Russo terms as "orientalist benevolence," which simply affirms the continuation of power over women.[1] This constricted lens produces a shadow of women, reducing agency and the vast space of identity.

Women and the spaces they inhabit have historically served as a space to negotiate power throughout Afghanistan's political transitions. Under King Zahir Shah, the 1964 constitution ensured women basic rights such as universal suffrage and equal pay. This period, often looked back upon nostalgically as the progressive glory days, provided women with freedom of movement as well as economic opportunities to secure jobs as doctors, civil servants, teachers, and nurses. Women's visible presence in public without a head covering and miniskirts were linked with modernity. Despite strong opposition from tribal and religious leaders, many women in urban areas benefited from these measures and gained access to prominent roles in society including government positions. The most direct and rapid campaign for social reform took place following the Soviet invasion of Afghanistan in 1979. According to Leila Ahmed, under the banner of socialism, women were openly encouraged to abandon the veil, attend compulsory education, attain jobs, and increase public participation.[2] These new but artificially given freedoms were leading to changes in relation to family matters, a highly private and guarded unit. State-imposed policies aimed at improving opportunities for women in areas of education such as eradication of illiteracy in the rural areas led to thousands of teachers participating in educational campaigns. Women were now out of seclusion and forced to attend mandatory education. Fashima Vorgetts stresses that these changes were met with resistance by local communities where their imposition was considered threatening to family life, tradition, and identity.[3] New laws regulated domestic lives while attempting to modernize women by eradicating what was now believed to be old traditions. Such policies led to increasing crackdowns and intolerance for customary practices challenging tribal and religious leaders.[4]

Although the harsh enforcement of these policies under the banner of gender equality led to improvements and basic freedoms, women were increasingly subjects of state violence.[5] According to Weeda Mansoor, Afghan women were now free to pursue rights but their husbands, fathers and brothers were in jail or killed, accused of anti-Soviet resistance.[6] In response, women became active participants of the national resistance movement with some taking up arms and fighting alongside the men. For many, the struggle for national liberation from foreign occupation remained a priority and therefore a precondition to the imposed Soviet campaign for gender equality. Women's activism, as argued by Deborah Ellis, was the largest organized resistance movement at the grassroots level.[7] In retaliation, the Soviet army was particularly brutal in rural areas targeting civilians where much of the resistance was rooted. Female students active in protests were regularly the objects of violence, particularly in universities.

The decade-long Soviet invasion had a significant impact in shaping the political landscape and transition of power to the Mujahideen, leading to another brutal civil war. The highly polarized climate of the post-Soviet period was focused on regaining national pride. As with previous transitions, women were once again the object of reform under the banner of purification, a return to honor, tradition, and a glorious past.[8]

THE TALIBAN'S WAR ON WOMEN AND THE WAR WITH THE TALIBAN

For many around the world, the introduction to the Taliban's takeover of Afghanistan in 1996 was also the first time they learned of the plight of Afghan women.[9] With the US-led military invasion of Afghanistan, the gender policies of the Taliban were suddenly at the center of international attention. Instantly, Afghan women were transformed from objects of violence to subjects of liberation ready to be rescued. The Taliban were up to that point largely ignored despite the suffering inflicted on the Afghan people.[10] Huma Ahmed Ghosh warns of the tendency to attribute the suffering of women to a sole perpetrator and the inherent dangers that isolate the causes of inequality.[11] The rise of the Taliban must be explored within the context of instability, chaos, and tensions between the different ethnic and tribal groups as well as regional and international power rivalries at the end of the Soviet withdrawal. The Taliban's campaign to restore harmony and peace to the country by bringing back honor associated with women initially gained much local support. The message was appealing, particularly to the majority of Pashtuns devastated and desperate for some order and security. The Taliban were able to take advantage of instability to emerge as a traditional reform movement able to promote a specific ideology on a platform of an idealized Islamic society, with force if necessary. It was not long before another war, brutality, and violence once again plunged the country into devastation.

The Taliban were in many ways reintroducing rather than initiating patriarchal and fundamentalist policies to control women. A return to authenticity was interpreted in extreme practices such as forcing men to wear beards, mandatory prayers and religious instruction for young boys in Taliban-authorized schools. Women were banned from employment, receiving education, and appearing in public spaces without spouses or male relatives. These measures were justified as necessary to reclaim respect for women's virtue and honor particularly in urban areas. As a measure of protection, women were now forced to re-veil their bodies and faces as well as cover their eyes with what has come to symbolize their anguish to the international community, the Burqa.

The September 11 attacks and subsequent US-led military intervention in Afghanistan officially marked the end of Taliban rule. The war against the Taliban was soon transformed to a US campaign of peacebuilding, reconstruction, and development. Afghan women were now the frequent subjects of concern, draped on the front cover of magazines, and the highlight of mainstream news stories. While the violence of the civil war brought about during Taliban rule had an equal impact on all civilians, including men, accounts of Western media remained exclusively focused on women. Jiwani's analysis of contrasting news in the post–September 11 period demonstrates an increased focus on Afghan women as victims in need of intervention and protection from the alleged dangers of violent local men.[12] While the US military intervention led to the political downfall of the Taliban, it did not end their power and influence. Afghanistan once again plunged into another period of violence and war.

In the post-Taliban period, the need to include women as key actors with recognition of full rights and the guarantee of basic freedoms was centralized. Little was done to address the obstacles in women's achievement of equality within the context of insecurity and increasing militarization. The oppression of and discrimination against women were considered to be rooted in

Islam and therefore incompatible with empowering women. In the United States, this discourse was backed by a softer feminist agenda for the justification of US military intervention. In a radio address to the nation in 2001, Laura Bush focused on the brutality and violence against Afghan women and children by the Taliban, therefore perpetuating gendered violence. This message was appealing to Western audiences to prompt a proactive stance as the protectors of the helpless Afghan women and in support of the military intervention as a moral strategy.[13] Charles Hirschkind and Saba Mahmood argue that the plight of women gained celebrity backing as a result of the emotional role played by organizations such as the Feminist Majority Campaign to end Taliban's gender apartheid in Afghanistan.[14] The portrayal framed a symbolic separation between Western women as liberal and free and Afghan women as in need of liberation. Carol Stabile and Deepa Kumar acknowledge this position by arguing that US military operation was constructed to reposition the West as the beacon of civilization with an obligation to tame the Islamic world and liberate its women.[15]

WOMEN AS SUBJECTS OF PEACE

In Afghanistan, the implementation and emphasis on peacebuilding with the goal of delivering institutions and policies to enhance women's rights and status were evident very early on. Yet despite the momentum for what promised to be a more open and democratic state, a number of contradictory processes were in place. First, the Taliban were defeated and the end of war had come about as a result of victory for the US military rather than inclusive peace negotiations.[16] The Taliban would continue and eventually regain power with a campaign of resistance to foreign occupation. Military intervention and the continuous presence of foreign troops provided the fertile ground for rebellion. In such circumstances the legitimacy of initiatives aimed at empowering and strengthening local populations are likely to be compromised.

Afghanistan would embark on the transitional phase with a democratically elected government, a new constitution to guarantee women's rights, an independent judiciary to protect and strengthen rule of law, and political inclusion. In the initial stages leading up to the 2004 constitution, women's participation, at least symbolically, remained strong with 100 representatives from the 502 delegates at the traditional form of assembly, the Loya Jirga.[17] The new constitution is an impressive document that guarantees women's rights in all areas including a quota for representation in parliament. New institutions such as the Ministry of Women's Affairs and the Afghanistan Independent Human Rights Commission were to monitor and directly address women's marginalization in society. Despite a strong agenda, the issue of women's rights remains highly contested and controversial. While women have gained political positions and symbolic representation, they have little influence. Debates in parliament regarding laws against gender violence or issues such as electoral rights have typically been met with increasing hostility, at times escalating to wide-scale national protests. This has affirmed the culture of impunity as many women in parliament and government positions fear retaliatory violent attacks and targeted assassinations. The local leaders continue to hold political power while also benefiting from a new level of support from the international community that has legitimized their position. This has led to a two-tier system, one at the national level empowering women while ignoring the local leaders with a zero tolerance policy for what they considered as change imposed from the state. Conservative parliamentary representatives have successfully framed the women's rights agenda as closely linked to a Western liberation strategy and therefore incompatible with Afghan culture and tradition. At the local level, many leaders have pressed for even tighter control over women as a guard against foreign influences.

The drafting of the constitution was followed by what is often framed as the universal blue print for international interventions placed under the broader umbrella of democratic reform, similar to other postwar societies such as Kosovo and Iraq. This model is based on international intervention and the radical transition of postwar failed states into liberal democracies with market economies.[18] What typically follows is the strengthening of external influence in a number of processes including drafting a constitution, holding elections, strengthening judiciary, enacting new laws, and the promotion of a market economy to catalyze growth in the private sector.[19] However, what made Afghanistan different in the direction of external intervention was the significance placed on addressing and prioritizing gender. Peacebuilding measures were directed at securing the right to representation, education, jobs, and health care as significant components in integrating women into the future of Afghanistan. The timing was ripe as the gendered approach to peacebuilding had come at a significant period calling for greater participation of women in peace and security.[20]Foreign assistance in terms of donor funding was directed at local organizations that would help champion causes aimed at empowerment, capacity building, and leadership to improve women's lives. Soon, as argued by Miriam Arghandiwal, Kabul was home to some 170 non-governmental organizations (NGOs), with more than half receiving funding from the United States, involved in some form of gender-based peacebuilding.[21] Matsumoto notes that the impact of foreign aid could be seen directly with rapid availability of jobs in the NGO sector for women.[22] Kabul was experiencing an economic boost and transformation in terms of public visibility of Afghan women and opening of restaurants, hotels, and shops catering to the growing international aid workers.

Despite the increased focus on gender, achieving legitimacy and ownership at the local level has been challenging from the start. Drafting new laws and policies aimed at bringing about change at the local level and encouraging women's participation are not necessarily the same as localized peacebuilding. Since many of the measures impacting women's rights had not been achieved as a result of consensus or localized advocacy, policies were often rejected as part of the international community's agenda to impose change. Valentine Moghadam points out that despite the rapid growth in the number of NGO's and foreign gender specialists in Kabul, promoting women's rights has remained a mere formality.[23] Julie Billaud's evaluation of women's empowerment training programs implemented by the Ministry of Women's Affairs, points to the inherent tensions resulting from what many locals feared as a social change model.[24] According to Isabell Coleman, programs were often misguided, generating widespread resistance among both male and female employees.[25] There were also concerns that the international community conceived of Afghanistan as a project in Westernization while ignoring socioeconomic problems that were the cause of much suffering among ordinary Afghans, including men.

Many Afghans were alienated from the focus of peacebuilding measures and questioned the prioritization of women's rights against the backdrop of devastating poverty, unemployment, and daily realities focused on survival. It was not necessarily the case that Afghan people did not care about women's rights or education; they had little access to inclusion and decision making as they were being told what they need and how to achieve it.[26] The promotion of women's rights along the macro intervention plan involving all aspects of governance had led to increasing mistrust. Astri Suhrke considers the broader measures of statebuilding attached to a war of conquest as accountable for undermining the legitimacy of peacebuilding as well as local participation.[27] Afghan women were in a difficult position to mobilize the community in favor of changes that could benefit them. Such efforts were immediately linked to the external mission for control rather than genuine advocacy to improve women's situation. This has weakened the local capacity to address genuine community grievances. It has also promoted incentives to resist the international agenda for reforms as Western, and not fitting with local ways.[28] Shahrbanou Tadjkbakhsh and Michael Schoiswohl point to the top-down approach of these measures responsible for local resentment and frustration as programs were disconnected from the core issues faced by women.[29] For many Afghans, this approach to fixing the country and tensions around the international military occupation contradicted the goals of peacebuilding projects that were taking place simultaneously.

GENDER, PEACEBUILDING, AND SECURITY

Peacebuilding measures have focused on strengthening women's position in society with an emphasis on local participation and ownership as key in determining the sustainability of such measures. Yet, the challenges in defining the term local and women in the local remain largely overlooked.[30] There are, for example, significant gaps in the level of participation for peacebuilding implemented at the national level and impacting local levels. Peacebuilding measures may be directed with a view to government-supported policies to affect the status of women at the national level. These include laws and institutions to support the agenda of gendered peacebuilding. Many women may participate in such measures but this may lead to elitism and selection biases by the international community. In Afghanistan, peacebuilding measures have worked well to mediate a relationship between a global agenda and women's empowerment at the national level framed in terms of setting up non-government organizations, policies, and legal frameworks. The translation of such representation in influencing women's lives on the ground and at the local has been more challenging. First, the local is not homogenous, but rather dispersed and decentralized. At the national level, policies may receive popular support, but historically there has been little spill over. Furthermore, the local remains isolated with pockets of smaller and scattered self-governed communities each with diverse sets of actors and complex leadership. Afghanistan has rarely demonstrated a strong linkage between the centralized, national policies and the local. The latter has historically considered intervention efforts directed from the national as an external challenge to sovereignty and removal of autonomy. Given that such efforts were also perceived at promoting Western values and norms has further increased the likelihood of resistance. For many Afghans family is among the most honored and a unit protected from the outside gaze. Women's power is often negotiated in the complex layers of identity within an interactive relationship with spaces they inhabit. It would be difficult to assign imposed meanings such as empowerment to spaces defined externally with little relevance to the subject. Local communities may, for example, interpret power as freedom from external influence. Some women may consider it shameful to work outside of their home due to poor socioeconomic status or lack of opportunity for male members. More significantly, given the level of mistrust toward external actors, women participating in agendas of Western intervention models may be subject to threats and intimidation by local communities. As such, peacebuilding approaches can focus on improving women's positions while ignoring the context of insecurity as a result of growing hostility toward foreign intervention.

Enhancing education for girls backed with international funding is a good example of this pattern. Louise Hancock and Orzala Ashraf Nemat argue that education has been a central focus of peacebuilding projects with the goal of addressing gender inequalities by allowing access to previously denied opportunity.[31] Yet in terms of peacebuilding, education is interconnected to security, cultural, political, and social factors. Implementation and outcome as far as the construction of physical spaces and the number of girls attending school have in many ways been successful. However, there are challenges in linking peacebuilding at the local level to transforming women's lives from the bottom-up and in bringing about change. The lack of security, increasing violence, and expansion in the number of militant factions has placed women in a vulnerable situation. Despite state-level policies and adequate funding aimed at improving education for girls, deteriorating security has led to school closures. In certain provinces, many girls have been pulled out of their schools because of concerns with safety. They are at risk of attacks by Taliban forces, local private armies funded by warlords, Afghan government security forces and the US military. The Taliban are just one, but not the only faction responsible for constraints over women's security. The presence of foreign military troops can strengthen local hegemony to place a greater grip on ensuring the protection of women. The recognition of Afghan women as subjects of peace must rest on a comprehensive and inclusive understanding of empowerment, in which security is a significant component.

In terms of education as a tool of empowerment, there are also challenges for some who see women as the sole beneficiary. The increased attention on women and girls as recipients of education can marginalize men. According to Huma Ahmed Ghosh, attempts to empower women by isolating them from the men have only reinforced traditional kinships.[32] Young boys are left with few choices as argued by Simi Wali since they lack access to development opportunities with many attending free religious education offered by the Taliban.[33] This is counterproductive to progress as it makes it easier to indoctrinate young men to perceive control and protection of women as their rightful duty in the name of honor and in taking back the women from the grip of foreign intervention. Furthermore, the promotion and implementation of education for women and girls have taken place under the careful eye and auspices of international organizations. In such cases, women's participation in international agendas ranging from education to capacity building can appear in contrast to local and traditional efforts to safeguard women. Violence directed at women as recipients of foreign aid money is justified for self-preservation and security of the community against intervention. Framed in such a way, local mobilization in support of violence leaves women vulnerable as objects of violence.

Equity in terms of distribution of donor funds directed at projects that are gender-specific can also be a divisive factor. Local organizations focused on easing poverty and improving economic and living conditions for all Afghans may be left out of funding. Competition among organizations with agendas supported by international funding can hinder unity and community-building at the local level. Reliance on external experts and funding can impact accountability as well as the ability of local women's organizations to lobby and mobilize around issues that may not be of interest to the international community. Resistance to international support in achieving rights may be based on the perception that bottom-up approaches mobilized locally may be the best option in achieving change.[34] Throughout the decades of conflicts and wars, Afghan women have demonstrated the capacity to organize collectively without external funding or support. This can be seen in the unity among women that led to an intricate system of hidden local networks during the Taliban period. Sally Armstrong describes the resistance movement that organized a complex web of clandestine schools for young girls and health care facilities for women.[35] These movements formed organically and as a creative response to the Taliban's harsh policies and strict ban on education. Despite the restrictions and threats of punishment women successfully formed close to 2000 fully functional underground schools in Kabul. Fahima Gaheez considers the efforts of the underground school system as pivotal in ensuring education for girls that would otherwise be part of an illiterate generation.[36] For many Afghan women these schools were the foundation of the education system that simply resurfaced openly in the post-Taliban period. Since the US-led military intervention many Western-funded schools have been the target of Taliban attacks in stronghold areas that have retaliated against girls attending by forbidding education. Local communities have met such challenges by once again offering informal clandestine schooling. According to Kevin Seiff, volunteer teachers provide education for young girls as well as men and women.[37]

The inclination to frame issues of equality based on a platform of gender rights may isolate the discourse on human rights to favor women. For example, two prominent local organizations, the Afghan Women's Mission and the Revolutionary Association of the Women of Afghanistan, maintain the need for demilitarization, disarmament of all insurgents and the end of war. This campaign has been ignored in highlighting the negative impact of US military presence and air attacks that target Afghan men.[38] These organizations have been critical of the international community's programs that focus on teaching Afghan students peace education with the goal of promoting a culture of nonviolence, while increasing militarization.[39] There has been little effort to address the structures of violence that impact communities outside the boundaries of gender. This ignores addressing foreign military forces conducting security raids into Afghan homes that have been the cause of much resentment and hostility. For example, upon entering homes shared among several family generations in rural and remote areas, US soldiers would routinely separate female and male residents before searching and questioning the men. This practice dishonored men and made them feel powerless as the protectors of women who were left under the gaze of foreign male soldiers, bringing shame to the family and the community.[40] Local women activists and organizations that lobby on the platform of universal rights have received little attention in calling for an end to the use of violence. Civilians in Pashtun communities of Pakistan and Taliban-controlled areas of Afghanistan have increasingly been the target of arbitrary arrest, detention, and well-documented crimes perpetrated by unmanned drones. The internationalization of women's rights in Afghanistan has weakened the ability of local organizations to lobby on issues that are not considered as significant to external actors. The human rights agenda has been increasingly dispersed and dominated by women's rights.[41]

The need for the protection and liberation of Afghan women has been framed to popularize and construct the enemy as Afghan men. This reinforces a culture of fear and mistrust that pivots Afghans against each other. Gayatri Chakravorty Spivak and Rosalind Morris have framed this tendency as the brown women being saved from the local men by the heroic white man.[42] Cynthia Enloe warns of the dangers in the normalization of violence as a means to address power rivalries including domestic politics as well as practices of foreign governments leading to military occupations.[43] Since the US-led military intervention, violence directed at women, has grown considerably.[44] This has taken place despite the international community's support for legislation and commitment to gender equality.[45] In 2009, the Elimination of Violence against Women (EVAW) was established with a presidential decree and support from the Ministry of Women's Affairs. This landmark legislation would for the first time criminalize domestic violence with punishment for the perpetrators. Yet, on the ground few women are aware of such legislation with nominal execution by the Afghan judicial and law enforcement forces.[46] Such laws as part of the legal framework written and perceived as products of the international community are not likely to gain legitimacy, particularly at the local level.[47] Given the majority of laws that govern gender relations in Afghanistan take place well outside of the formal legal system, the provisions made by the international community have virtually no impact as they are not widely accepted practices. Negative and at times violent backlashes have gained more momentum as local resentments and anger have often been directed at any effort to gain control over "our" women. The issue of women's rights has become an ideological battlefield and increasingly politicized, making it easier to mobilize local support for violence. This has further jargonized women as objects of violence.

CONCLUSION

The impact of peacebuilding measures aimed at centralization of gender rights must be explored in interaction with local experiences and perceptions of the long history of futile models of social change. In Afghanistan the implementation of peacebuilding measures amidst a military campaign aimed at liberation of the country and its women has led to a dichotomy. It set in motion a number of contradictory processes that profoundly shaped the negative landscape that can work against improving women's position in society. Local resistance to such measures has placed women in increasingly vulnerable positions, as objects of violence. The association of women's rights to Western liberation models is likely to empower actors that justify mobilization at the local level against such measures as a way to protest intervention. As a result, women's advocacy and agency at the local level may remain stagnant against agendas of peacebuilding, dependent on the direction and supervision of the international community. This is evident in the plea of Afghan women to ensure that the departure of US troops in 2014 does not lead to international indifference toward their situation. For local peacebuilding to become a tool in the transformation of women from subjects to objects of peace, change has to become localized to be sustainable. Without a comprehensive peace agreement to end war and violence as a way to establish security, women are unlikely to create an environment where consensus regarding their rights can be localized and negotiated internally. As objects of peace, women should be able to stand in the locality of their own narrative to define agency and create the conditions necessary for sustainable peace.

NOTES

1. Ann Russo, "The Feminist Majority Foundation's Campaign to Stop Gender Apartheid," *International Feminist Journal of Politics* 8.4 (2006).

2. Leila Ahmed, "Western Ethnocentrism and Perceptions of the Harem," *Feminist Studies* 8.3 (1982).

3. Fahima Vorgetts, "A Vision of Justice, Equality and Peace," in *Women for Afghan Women: Shattering Myths and Claiming the Future*, ed. Sunita Mehta (New York, NY: Palgrave Macmillan, 2002), 96.

4. For more on this see Nancy Hatch Dupree, "Afghan Women under the Taliban," in *Fundamentalism Reborn? Afghanistan and the Taliban*, ed. William Maley (New York, NY: New York University Press, 1998).

5. Hafizullah Emadi, *Repression, Resistance, and Women in Afghanistan* (Westport, CT: Praeger, 2002), 110.

6. Weeda Mansoor, "The Mission of RAWA," in *Women for Afghan Women*, ed. Sunita Mehta (New York, NY: Palgrave Macmillan), 70.

7. Deborah Ellis, *Women of the Afghan War* (Westport, CT: Praeger, 2000), 8.

8. Posters depict this campaign to detoxify women. See Mathew Trevithick, "The Not so Funny Papers, Exclusive Cartoons from the Afghan Mujahideen," *Foreign Policy*, October 26, 2012.

9. See, for example, Vincent Lacopino and Zohra Rakesh, "The Taliban's War on Women: A Health and Human Rights Crisis in Afghanistan," Boston, MA and Washington, DC: Physicians for Human Rights, August 1998; "Report on the Taliban's War against Women," Bureau of Democracy, Human Rights and Labor, US Department of State, November 17, 2001; "Background—Feminist Majority Foundation's Campaign to Stop Gender Apartheid," Feminist Majority Foundation, last modified June 14, 2014, http://www.feminist.org/afghan/aboutcampaign.asp.

10. For more on this see Mary Anne Franks, "Obscene Undersides: Women and Evil between the Taliban and the United States," *Hypatia* 18.1 (2003).

11. Huma Ahmed Ghosh, "A History of Women in Afghanistan: Lessons Learnt for the Future or Yesterdays and Tomorrow: Women in Afghanistan," *Journal of International Women's Studies* 4.3 (2003): 2.

12. Yasmin Jiwani, "Mediations of Domination: Gendered Violence Within and Across Borders," in *Feminist Intervention in International Communication: Minding the Gap*, ed. Katherine Sarikakis and Leslie Regan Shade (Lanham, MD: Rowman & Littlefield, 2008).

13. Dana L. Cloud, "To Veil the Threat of Terror: Afghan Women and the Clash of Civilizations in the Imagery of the U.S. War on Terrorism," *Quarterly Journal of Speech* 90.3 (2004).

14. Charles Hirschkind and Saba Mahmood, "Feminism, the Taliban, and Politics of Counter Insurgency," *Anthropological Quarterly* 75.2 (2002).

15. Carol Stabile and Deepa Kumar, "Unveiling Imperialism: Media, Gender and the War on Afghanistan," *Media, Culture & Society* 27.5 (2005).

16. Elham Atashi, "Afghanistan: Transitional Justice in the Midst of War," *Nationalities Papers: The Journal of Nationalism and Ethnicity* 41.6 (2013).

17. 1,500 delegates were selected as representatives at the Loya Jirga, a traditional gathering of tribal leaders.

18. Ronald Paris, *At War's End: Building Peace after Civil Conflict* (Cambridge, MA: Cambridge University Press, 2006).

19. Timothy Donais, "Empowerment or Imposition? Dilemmas of Local Ownership in Post-Conflict Peacebuilding Processes," *Peace and Change* 34.1 (2009).

20. The 1325 resolution was adopted by the United Nations Security Council in October 2000.

21. For more on this see Miriam Arghandiwal, "As Foreign Aid Dries up, Afghan NGOs Fight to Survive," *Reuters*, July 5, 2012.

22. Yukitoshi Matsumoto, "Young Afghans in Transition: Towards Afghanistan, Exit or Violence?" *Conflict, Security & Development* 11.5 (2011).

23. Valentine M. Moghadam, "Peacebuilding and Reconstruction with Women: Reflections on Afghanistan, Iraq and Palestine," *Development* 48.3 (2005).

24. Julie Billaud, "The Making of Modern Afghanistan: Reconstruction, Transnational Governance and Gender Politics in the New Islamic Republic," *Anthropology of the Middle East* 7.1 (2012).

25. For more on this see Isabell Coleman, "The Payoff of Women's Rights," *Foreign Affairs*, May/June 2004.

26. Author's Interview with representative of the Ministry of Afghan Women, Bamyan, Afghanistan, January 26, 2013.

27. Astri Suhrke, "Reconstruction as Modernisation: The 'Post-Conflict' Project in Afghanistan," *Third World Quarterly* 28.7 (2007).

28. Author's Interview with Nasrin, Education Program Adviser in Kabul, Washington, DC, February 9, 2013.

29. Shahrbanou Tadjbakhsh and Michael Schoiswohl, "Playing with Fire? The International Community's Democratization Experiment in Afghanistan," *International Peacekeeping* 15.2 (2008).

30. Elham Atashi, "Challenges to Conflict Transformation from the Streets," in *Conflict Transformation and Peacebuilding: Moving from Violence to Sustainable Peace*, ed. Bruce Dayton and Louis Kriesberg (London, England: Routledge, 2009), 55–56.

31. Louise Hancock and Orzala Ashraf Nemat, "A Place at the Table: Safeguarding Women's Rights in Afghanistan," Oxfam International Briefing Paper 153, October 3, 2011.

32. Huma Ahmed Ghosh, "A History of Women in Afghanistan."

33. Sima Wali, "Afghanistan Truth and Mythology," forward to *Women for Afghan Women: Shattering Myths and Claiming the Future*, ed. Sunita Mehta (New York, NY: Palgrave Macmillan, 2002), 6–7.

34. Author's Interview with Fahima Gaheez, Director of Afghan Women's Fund, Washington, DC, February 26, 2014.

35. Sally Armstrong, *Veiled Threats: The Hidden Power of the Women of Afghanistan* (New York, NY: Four Walls Eight Windows, 2003).

36. Author's Interview with Fahima Gaheez, Director of Afghan Women's Fund, Washington, DC, February 26, 2014.

37. Kevin Seiff, "In Afghanistan, Underground Girls School Defies Taliban Edict, Threats," *Washington Post*, April 24, 2012.

38. Carlotta Gall, "British Criticize Air Attacks in Afghan Region," *New York Times*, August 9, 2007.

39. Interview with a member of RAWA, undisclosed location, July 6, 2012.

40. General Lt. Barno describes this practice as lack of understanding for Afghan culture and life. Christopher N. Koontz, ed., *Enduring Voices: Oral Histories of the U.S. Army Experience in Afghanistan, 2003–2005* (Washington, DC: Center for Military History, United States Army, 2008), 36–38.

41. Author's Interview with Huma, an Afghan Women's Advocate, Washington, DC, September 18, 2012.

42. See Gayatri Chakravorty Spivak and Rosalind C. Morris, *Can the Subaltern Speak? Reflections on the History of an Idea* (New York, NY: Columbia University Press, 2002).

43. Cynthia Enloe, *Maneuvers: the International Politics of Militarizing Women's Lives* (Berkeley, CA: University of California Press, 2000).

44. Jessica Donati, "Violence against Afghan Women more Frequent, Brutal in 2013," *Reuters*, January 4, 2014.

45. World Report 2013: Afghanistan, Human Rights Watch, last modified June 11, 2014, http://www.hrw.org/world-report/2013/country-chapters/afghanistan.

46. "A Long Way to Go: Implementation of the Elimination of Violence Against Women Law in Afghanistan," Kabul, Afghanistan: UNAMA, November 2011.

47. See Susanna Campbell, David Chandler, and Meera Sabaratnam, eds., *A Liberal Peace: The Problems and Practices of Peacebuilding* (London, England: Zed Books, 2011).

BIBLIOGRAPHY

Ahmed Ghosh, Huma. "A History of Women in Afghanistan: Lessons Learnt for the Future or Yesterdays and Tomorrow: Women in Afghanistan." *Journal of International Women's Studies* 4.3 (2003): 1–14.

Ahmed, Leila. "Western Ethnocentrism and Perceptions of the Harem." *Feminist Studies* 8.3 (1982): 521–34.

"A Long Way to Go: Implementation of the Elimination of Violence against Women Law in Afghanistan." Kabul, Afghanistan: UNAMA, November 2011.

Arghandiwal, Miriam. "As Foreign Aid Dries up, Afghan NGOs Fight to Survive." *Reuters*, July 5, 2012.

Armstrong, Sally. *Veiled Threats: The Hidden Power of the Women of Afghanistan*. New York, NY: Four Walls Eight Windows, 2003.

Atashi, Elham. "Afghanistan: Transitional Justice in the Midst of War." *Nationalities Papers: The Journal of Nationalism and Ethnicity* 41.6 (2013): 1049–64.

———. "Challenges to Conflict Transformation from the Streets." In *Conflict Transformation and Peacebuilding: Moving from Violence to Sustainable Peace*, edited by Bruce Dayton and Louis Kriesberg, 45–60. London, England: Routledge, 2009.

"Background—Feminist Majority Foundation's Campaign to Stop Gender Apartheid." Feminist Majority Foundation. Last modified June 14, 2014. http://www.feminist.org/afghan/aboutcampaign.asp.

Billaud, Julie. "The Making of Modern Afghanistan: Reconstruction, Transnational Governance and Gender Politics in the New Islamic Republic." *Anthropology of the Middle East* 7.1 (2012): 18–37.

Campbell, Susanna, David Chandler, and Meera Sabaratnam, eds. *A Liberal Peace: The Problems and Practices of Peacebuilding*. London, England: Zed Books, 2011.

Cloud, Dana L. "To Veil the Threat of Terror: Afghan Women and the Clash of Civilizations in the Imagery of the U.S. War on Terrorism." *Quarterly Journal of Speech* 90.3 (2004): 285–306.

Coleman, Isabell. "The Payoff of Women's Rights." *Foreign Affairs*, May/June 2004.

Donais, Timothy. "Empowerment or Imposition? Dilemmas of Local Ownership in Post-Conflict Peacebuilding Processes." *Peace and Change* 34.1 (2009): 3–26.

Donati, Jessica. "Violence against Afghan Women more Frequent, Brutal in 2013." *Reuters*, January 4, 2014.

Dupree, Nancy Hatch. "Afghan Women under the Taliban." In *Fundamentalism Reborn? Afghanistan and the Taliban*, edited by William Maley, 140–68. New York, NY: New York University Press, 1998.

Ellis, Deborah. *Women of the Afghan War*. Westport, CT: Praeger, 2000.

Emadi, Hafizullah. *Repression, Resistance, and Women in Afghanistan*. Westport, CT: Praeger, 2002.

Enloe, Cynthia. *Maneuvers: The International Politics of Militarizing Women's Lives*. Berkeley, CA: University of California Press, 2000.

Franks, Mary Anne. "Obscene Undersides: Women and Evil between the Taliban and the United States." *Hypatia* 18.1 (2003): 135–56.

Gall, Carlotta. "British Criticize Air Attacks in Afghan Region." *New York Times*, August 9, 2007.

Hancock, Louise and Orzala Ashraf Nemat. "A Place at the Table: Safeguarding Women's Rights in Afghanistan." Oxfam International Briefing Paper 153, October 3, 2011.

Hirschkind, Charles and Saba Mahmood. "Feminism, the Taliban, and Politics of Counter-Insurgency." *Anthropological Quarterly* 75.2 (2002): 339–54.

Jiwani, Yasmin. "Mediations of Domination: Gendered Violence Within and Across Borders." In *Feminist Intervention in International Communication: Minding the Gap*, edited by Katherine Sarikakis and Leslie Regan Shade, 129–45. Lanham, MD: Rowman & Littlefield, 2008.

Koontz, Christopher N., ed. *Enduring Voices: Oral Histories of the U.S. Army Experience in Afghanistan, 2003–2005*. Washington, DC: Center of Military History, United States Army, 2008.

Lacopino, Vincent and Zohra Rakesh. "The Taliban's War on Women: A Health and Human Rights Crisis in Afghanistan." Boston, MA and Washington, DC: Physicians for Human Rights, August 1998.

Mansoor, Weeda. "The Mission of RAWA." In *Women for Afghan Women: Shattering Myths and Claiming the Future*, edited by Sunita Mehta, 68–83. New York, NY: Palgrave Macmillan, 2002.

Matsumoto, Yukitoshi. "Young Afghans in 'Transition': Towards Afghanistan, Exit or Violence?" *Conflict, Security & Development* 11.5 (2011): 555–78.

Moghadam, Valentine M. "Peacebuilding and Reconstruction with Women: Reflections on Afghanistan, Iraq and Palestine." *Development* 48.3 (2005): 63–72.

Paris, Ronald. *At War's End: Building Peace after Civil Conflict*. Cambridge, MA: Cambridge University Press, 2006.

"Report on the Taliban's War against Women." Bureau of Democracy, Human Rights and Labor." US Department of State, November 17, 2001.

Russo, Ann. "The Feminist Majority Foundation's Campaign to Stop Gender Apartheid." *International Feminist Journal of Politics* 8.4 (2006): 557–80.

Seiff, Kevin. "In Afghanistan, Underground Girls School Defies Taliban after Earlier Efforts Failed." *Washington Post*, April 24, 2012.

Spivak, Gayatri Chakravorty and Rosalind C. Morris. *Can the Subaltern Speak? Reflections on the History of an Idea*. New York, NY: Columbia University Press, 2002.

Stabile, Carol A. and Deepa Kumar. "Unveiling Imperialism: Media, Gender and the War on Afghanistan." *Media, Culture & Society* 27.5 (2005): 765–82.

Suhrke, Astri. "Reconstruction as Modernisation: The 'Post-Conflict' Project in Afghanistan." *Third World Quarterly* 28.7 (2007): 1291–308.

Tadjbakhsh, Shahrbanou and Michael Schoiswohl. "Playing with Fire? The International Community's Democratization Experiment in Afghanistan." *International Peacekeeping* 15.2 (2008): 252–67.

Trevithick, Matthew. "The Not so Funny Papers, Exclusive Cartoons from the Afghan Mujahideen." *Foreign Policy*, October 26, 2012.

Vorgetts, Fahima. "A Vision of Justice, Equality and Peace." In *Women for Afghan Women: Shattering Myths and Claiming the Future*, edited by Sunita Mehta, 93–101. New York, NY: Palgrave Macmillan, 2002.

Wali, Sima. "Afghanistan Truth and Mythology." Forward to *Women for Afghan Women: Shattering Myths and Claiming the Future*, edited by Sunita Mehta, 6–7. New York, NY: Palgrave Macmillan, 2002.

"World Report 2013: Afghanistan." *Human Rights Watch*. Last modified June 11, 2014. http://www.hrw.org/world-report/2013/country-chapters/afghanistan.

Chapter 3

Healing the Wounds of Genocide Rape

The Experiences of Two Women in Rwanda

Regine Uwibereyeho King

The experience of sexual violence in ethnic conflicts creates deep and lasting wounds to the physical, psychological, and social well-being of wartime rape survivors, their families, and communities.[1] Some women are killed immediately after being raped; others are kept alive for further sexual humiliation and torture and left to live with the personal and social devastation caused by their tormentors. Unfortunately, there is a lack of legal, political, health, and social supports for these women, their families, and commununities to overcome the negative biopsychosocial effects of sexual violence in contemporary wars waged against civilians.

This chapter describes one promising intervention, the Healing of Life Wounds (HLW) program, which invites Hutu and Tutsi men and women, young and old, to come together and share personal stories of suffering for mutual healing. This chapter draws on my PhD dissertation research in Rwanda, which investigated the role and impact of sharing personal stories through HLW. I focus specifically on the experiences of two Tutsi women who were raped during the 1994 genocide and later participated in my doctoral research. The challenges and possibilities of integrating recovery from genocide rape into day-to-day struggles are explored.

WARTIME RAPE AND ITS IMPACT

Rape is historically known to be an integral part of war and other forms of mass violence. While war impacts men and women, women are more likely to be the target of rape and other forms of sexual violence at the hands of men.[2] Historian Niall Ferguson describes rape in civil conflicts as a politically calculated behavior designed to shame, humiliate, and degrade an entire ethnic group.[3] There is a growing consensus that rape is a weapon of war and a crime of genocide.[4] Unfortunately, the exact number of rape cases remains unknown, either because women are killed after being raped or because they do not report experiences of rape to avoid stigma.

Rape and sexual assault can result in long-lasting physical, psychological, and social damage. Robin Lay Schott indicates that wartime rape can physiologically and psychologically prevent women from engaging in intimate sexual activity and conceiving.[5] Frequently the rape experience is coupled with other complex traumatizing events, such as exposure to the murder of loved ones. Women and girls who have been raped tend to suffer alone and in silence because of the fear of further marginalization. For instance, men may separate from their wives if they learn that they were raped. Those who give birth to children from rape are particularly vulnerable because they can be rejected by their own families.[6] Research is lacking on the impact of the interaction of these factors on the psychosocial well-being of women survivors, their families, and their communities. As a result, the short and long-term impacts of wartime rape are relegated to the categories of personal and social wounds that are largely unacknowledged and unaddressed.[7]

Over the past two decades, critical feminists and activists have begun to document women's experiences of wartime rape and to demand legal and political action from the international community. This collective work has challenged old stereotypes that silenced women and considered rape as some form of inevitable collateral damage of war. This advocacy forced the international community to consider issues of gender relations and sociopolitical meanings of war rape.[8] UN Security Council Resolution 1820, passed in 2008, recognized rape as a tactic of war, constituting it as a crime against humanity and an act of genocide[9] because of its unique intent, through the use of women's bodies, not only to annihilate a people, but also to systematically destroy a nation's culture and the cohesiveness of group and community.[10]

Different scholars have suggested integrating gender mainstreaming into government policies and strategies, and civil society programming.[11] Some local governments, including the government of Rwanda, took legal and political measures to recognize and punish war and genocide. However, many of these measures have not translated into practical interventions that could address the specific needs of women.[12] The international and national courts have tended to conflate rape with other crimes against humanity. For example, by 2008 the International Court Tribunal for Rwanda in Arusha completed 45 trials of males accused of genocide crimes. Only five men were charged with sexual violence, although there was evidence of such violence in 15 cases. These charges were later dropped in all five cases in exchange for guilty pleas for other crimes.[13] In addition, the individual experiences of rape and their impact on bodies and social structures have been particularly ignored.[14] These observations suggest that existing legal responses through the judicial system are insufficient in responding to the complex needs of those affected.

After mass violence has ended, goverments give priority to state security, infrastructure and economic development and push women back into their traditional roles as mothers and wives.[15] This push silences rape experiences and their impact on the lives of women and their families. Even when legal solutions are suggested, there are no programs adequately equipped to address wartime rape.[16] This gap has been observed in many truth commissions and non-government organizations (NGOs) that take a gender-neutral approach.[17]

The particular needs of women survivors of wartime rape are often overlooked. The lack of action indirectly communicates the message that women can continue to be abused without protection or redress. Tristan Borer[18] explains that even within families, men may turn against the women in their lives in order to reestablish and retain control. Various forms of violence against women have been found to increase after mass violence due to a lack of strong structures and mechanisms to protect women.[19] This is particularly the case in post-conflict, low-income states.

GENOCIDE RAPE AND ITS AFTERMATH IN RWANDA

During the 100 days of the 1994 genocide in Rwanda, an estimated 250,000 to 500,000 women were raped with the estimated average number being approximately 354,440.[20] Rape targeted mainly Tutsi women and involved the widespread participation of Hutu males.[21] Women were raped repeatedly, sometimes over extended periods, either by individuals or gangs.[22] They were intentionally infected with the HIV virus so that they would suffer a slow and painful death.[23] A significant number of women died before they could tell their stories. Those who survived endured complex consequences that are indescribable.[24] They have all had to contend with poverty, caring for orphans and people disabled by the genocide, and often suffer continued abuse and threats from the very people who violated them and killed their loved ones. The collective impact of sexual violence and its ongoing consequences on survivors of rape and their families remains largely unstudied.

While emerging research recognizes that women survivors have distinct psychosocial problems,[25] there are also suggestions that rape should be treated as a societal issue impacting immediate victims, perpetrators, families, communities, and future generations.[26] Unfortunately, local government programs and humanitarian agencies have dealt with the effects of rape inadequately.[27] Existing interventions, such as rural health centers, are not equipped to address the traumatic crises and psychosomatic disorders related to genocide and rape memories.[28] Women's organizations such as the Association of Widows of Genocide (AVEGA) in Rwanda provide valuable assistance to many widows[29] and encourage them to mutually support one another. However, they find it difficult to integrate these women back into their communities and to reach those who are most vulnerable. Women members of such organizations can be marginalized by other community members. Women who live with the stigma of rape in isolated rural areas may also refuse to connect with others, fearing further violence. Opportunities to address the impact of genocide rape at the community level are still rare, undocumented, and understudied.

My study investigated HLW, a program that has made attempts to engage in discussions various community members, including women survivors of rape. HLW was introduced to Rwanda in 1995 by Dr. Simon Gasibirege, a former Rwandan refugee in Belgium. Dr. Gasibirege decided to return to Rwanda in order to participate in the healing of wounded hearts and spirits. HLW invites individuals, and at times couples, who recognize personal and/or community suffering and are willing to come together and share the stories of their personal experiences. The healing groups are heterogeneous in terms of gender, age, and social background. HLW comprises three main modules: (a) dealing with bereavement and living together, (b) managing emotions, and (c) dealing with forgiveness. Each module alternates plenary sessions with a series of guided exercises that facilitate the sharing of personal stories and ideas through small group activities. The content combines both Western and non-Western theories and practices. The sharing of personal experiences is guided by a series of open-ended exercises that encourage participants to choose stories they feel comfortable sharing. In the next section I present the methods and results of the study.

THE STUDY

In this chapter I provide only a summary description of the study methods described in more detail elsewhere.[30] The study's aim was to gain understanding of the experiences of people living in post-genocide Rwanda and to assess the role and impact of sharing personal stories through the HLW program. After obtaining ethics approvals from the University of Toronto (PhD home institution) and the Rwandan National Ethics Committee (RNEC), the study was conducted in a district of the southern province of Rwanda.

Participants were a list of people who had expressed an interest in the healing workshop after completing a three-day sensitization session on issues encountered in their community. A total of twenty-three participants, nineteen women and four men, between twenty-six and eighty years of age, completed one five-day workshop per month over a period of three months. All sessions took place in a residential retreat center.

Data reported in this chapter includes individual interviews and notes from participant observation and self-reflexivity. Individual interviews were conducted with ten participants both before and after the HLW intervention. In the first series of interviews, questions focused on participants' experiences of living in post-genocide Rwanda and how they coped with stress. In the second interview series, participants were asked about their experiences of sharing personal stories during the HLW workshops, and the lessons learned in the process. All interviews were conducted in the Kinyarwanda language. The onsite and offsite notes were primarily taken in English.

The presented data were analyzed and interpreted using dialogic performance analysis. This method is an interpretive approach that helps to analyze oral narratives as people perform their different identities through interactions with others and their environment.[31] According to Riessman[32] the telling of a story has immediacy as the audience experiences the unfolding of events as active actors who participate in the meaning-making of the event and the shaping of new identities. Thus the participants, the facilitator in the HLW intervention, and I (as the interviewer) participated in meaning-making through stories shared during this investigation. In this chapter, I focus on the experiences of two women who reported having been raped during the genocide. I use a storytelling approach to report the findings. Storytelling is a form of communication that allows a researcher to enter into conversations with the narratives of the participants as they engage in interpreting and making sense of their experiences[33] while honoring their stories as they are told. I recognize and respect that ultimately the stories shared in this chapter belong to the speakers and cannot be appropriated.

Rosa and Bernadette (pseudonyms) were assigned to the small group I had decided to observe during the HLW intervention. The stories of their lives and the pathways they followed during the HLW intervention were very different and yet aligned in some ways. The HLW intervention gave participants someone to talk with, raised their consciousness, and challenged them to reconnect with others inside and outside the group. I start with summaries of the genocide rape experience of the two women.

ROSA AND BERNADETTE'S EXPERIENCES OF GENOCIDE RAPE

Rosa was in her early twenties when the genocide started. She was visiting with relatives in another city when their home was attacked. She tried to run away, but was caught by a group of killers. She collapsed after one of them hit her on her shoulder with a club. When she regained consciousness, an unknown old man offered to protect her. His offer turned into an ordeal of sexual enslavement that lasted three months. He repeatedly raped her and threatened to kill her if she attempted to escape. He used degrading language about owning her and testing sex with a Tutsi woman. In addition, Rosa was traumatized by the screams of Tutsi who were thrown in a pit outside the house of her rapist. When she could not bear her ordeals she attempted suicide with a chlorine disinfectant. However, she did not die. She managed to escape only when, in the last days of the genocide, her captor decided to flee the country as the Rwandan Patriotic Army (RPF) approached his community. She settled in another village after she learned that her family had been exterminated. A few years later, Rosa was diagnosed with HIV, a condition she attributed to her genocide rape.

Bernadette was also in her early twenties when the genocide started. As a child of a mixed marriage with a Hutu mother and a Tutsi father, following Rwanda's patrilineal social norms, she was automatically classified as Tutsi. Bernadette and her mother hid at her maternal uncle's house. Her refuge proved to be unsafe when her cousin started to threaten that he would take her to the killers if she refused to have sex with him. Bernadette knew that he had AIDS, but did not want to be cut with machetes. He picked her up, raped her and returned her to her so-called hiding place any time he wanted during the three months of the genocide. After the genocide, she could not bear the fear that she had contracted HIV and was to give birth to an ill child. Her menstrual cycle had stopped and she strongly believed she was pregnant. She began a series of pregnancy and HIV tests which had negative results. However, because she did not trust the medical team that administered the tests and was suspicious of the results, Bernadette continued to ask for further tests. In the meantime she developed persistent headaches, high blood pressure, and asthma. Although she strongly associated her physical symptoms with her rape experience, she never informed the doctors that she had been a victim of sexual violence. At times she refused to take her prescribed medication, especially if any doctor attempted to inquire about her psychological well-being. She resented anyone who seemed to treat her as a "crazy" person.

Silence and Social Isolation

Both Rosa and Bernadette hid their experience of genocide rape from other people. They both reported that before the HLW intervention they were very lonely, socially isolated, and helpless. Rosa, like many other survivors, suffered from genocide losses and their consenquences:

> Not having something to eat, not having family who could be there for you, all these things were very overwhelming to the point that they could make you

> crazy, a crazy person who runs outside in the public. When I felt this way at first, I kept quiet and I stayed in bed for days.

However, the issue that troubled her the most was her experience of rape. During my first interview with her, she stated:

> After the genocide, life was very meaningless and I did not care whether I lived or not. The world seemed to have ended . . .. Personally, I did not want to talk about it or to remember what had happened to me, and I begged God to turn me mute.

For Rosa, rape was not only about the sexual violation by an older man, but also about the circumnstances in which it occurred. She was vulnerable and powerless to the point that she could not even take her own life or do anything to stop the horrifying noises coming from outside. The memories of the events haunted her and overwhelmed her. She described her memories as being "an unstoppable television show" of her problems. She had not been able to share her story of rape with anyone including other survivors. She feared that her pain would be increased through the gossip of others. She said that she was unable to even tell her husband about this incident. When he died of HIV/AIDS, she blamed herself, as she believed that she must be the one who had infected him. She was sick due to AIDS-related infectious diseases and the injury to her shoulder. She feared that her children would end up orphaned at a young age. All of these internal and external factors of the past, present, and the projected future overwhelmed and silenced her.

Bernadette's social world started to shrink as her physical problems intensified. She did not want to interact with people in her neighborhood. She never shared her painful experiences with other survivors. She reported: "When I spoke with those who went through the genocide like me, there were things I did not talk about." She developed suspicions about people, including friends and family members. She imagined that they were talking about her or seeking to harm her. Her day-to-day life was increasingly characterized by silence and isolation:

> When I felt well I did my chores without interacting with other people . . . I could spend days without talking and my family accepted it as such . . . I didn't visit people . . . I walked through our farm land, and then sat under one avocadoe tree, . . . remained silent when passing people attempted to greet me . . . I wore one skirt and people did not know I had any other clothes . . . I wore it on the farm and wore it when I went to places.

Rape stained Rosa's and Bernadette's self-image and deprived them of social interactions. They assumed that talking about their rape experience would single them out and make them feel ashamed and vulnerable. Rosa stated: "I thought that if I talked about it, people would be pointing at me and telling others that 'that one was raped during the war [genocide],' I felt ashamed to even think about it." Bernadette thought that sharing her pain could render her crazy and make others believe she was crazy. Both women reported suffering in silence.

Rosa and Bernadette concurred that existing interventions had not given attention to the issue of rape. One example they shared was the *gacaca* community trials, in which the offended were able to bring their complaints and testimonies about acts of genocide committed against them. Both women did not find *gacaca* to be an appropriate and safe place in which they could bring their rapists to justice. Rather, they felt further silenced and more deeply entrenched in the injustice of their suffering. Rosa reported:

> When we went to *gacaca*, we found that the judges did not give any importance to rape experiences. They did not want to waste their time on it. They implicitly encouraged people to not talk about it . . . they did not want us to ask questions about it . . . even though they kept saying that rape was in the first category of genocide crimes.

Rosa was not only distressed by the fact the *gacaca* courts did not value her rape experience, but also terrified by the idea of what she could say if given an opportunity to speak. She asked herself many questions about how she could be able to speak up:

> How will I dare standing in front of more than 100 people gathered and start telling them I was raped during the genocide? How will I bring it [rape] to justice? Is the person who raped me going to admit it? When they ask me about it, where will I start?

She wondered what would become of her if the rapist or the judges questioned the validity of her testimony or rejected it. Like Rosa, Bernadette chose to stay mute because she did not find her story fitting with the common testimonies that were shared at *gacaca* hearings. Neither their homes, nor the circle of survivors or of former friends, nor the programs such as *gacaca* that aimed to address past wounds and reconcile people, offered a safe environment in which these women could share the most painful experience of their lives.

The Healing Journey Through the HLW

Rosa and Bernadette decided to attend the HLW with others who were recruited in this study. Like other participants, they initially seemed more confortable talking about the dominant narratives of what was happening in their neighborhoods and in the country. Rosa was particularly eloquent in telling the stories of loved ones who died in 1994. At times she was surprisingly confrontational. She asked why the Hutu participants were not forthcoming about what they knew or saw during the genocide. Her body also became an active participant in her quests. On the second day of the first workshop she developed severe hiccups. At times she was forced to leave the group in order to vomit, but made sure she returned to the group activities.

Bernadette's participation was more guarded. She said little about herself and wept when others shared their stories. She turned her back to others when she spoke and struggled with tears. She expressed cynicism about survivors who made themselves vulnerable in public places. She stated, "When I hear that so and so were traumatized, I say to myself, 'they have treasures [unique things] to display! Why do they go [to public events about the genocide] in the first place?' " At times she seemed lost in her own thoughts. When she shared, her words were carefully measured. This was quite puzzling to me as an observer. During the first one-on-one interview she had stared at me with piercing eyes, clapped her hands and repeated the expression "let me tell you! . . . " as if she was seeking to convince me about the truthfulness of her story. These reactions contrasted with the ones she exibited in her interactions with others in the group.

When Rosa returned for the second session, her hiccups had stopped. She looked stronger and healthier. On the second day of the second session, she and other participants were asked to reflect on a written text entitled "Accepting" that described things people are able or unable to accept in life. In the large group Rosa revealed that she had been raped, without providing further details. Later, in the small group, she did not offer to start the exercise as was her custom. She waited and listened carefully to what others had to say about the theme of accepting. When it came to her turn to talk she smiled nervously and then stated:

> The worst thing that I haven't been able to accept is the rape I touched upon this morning [in the big group]. He [the man who raped her] did many things to me and said many horrible things that I cannot repeat here. Then, he started assuming I was his wife even though I continued to be locked inside his house. When I sit down at home . . . all I can think of is life in his house and the noises that came from the pit behind his house. It is as if I get removed from being in the present and on the face of the earth.

She explained that these memories escalated into a chain reaction that made her feel as if her inside organs were being cut into pieces and urged her to rush out and run away without knowing exactly where she was heading.

The combination of memories of her rape along with other genocide experiences resulted in regular traumatic crises.

Rosa appreciated the opportunity to share her pain and was able to put her trust in other participants with their promise of confidentiality. After the intervention, I asked her what would happen if other participants breached that confidentiality. She responded that many women who wish to tell their stories of rape do not have someone with whom they can talk. She added, "I do not have that problem anymore because I had people who listened to what I had to say and I was able to express myself."[34] For Rosa, having people to talk to, people who listened carefully to what she had to say, was all she needed—at least until the time of my last interview with her. She was very pleased and strengthened by the ways other participants responded to her.

When Rosa shared her story of rape, Bernadette was crying profusely. This time she did not turn her back to others in her group. Other participants offered Rosa words of encouragement. Although Bernadette participated in this group activity, mostly through her tears and other nonverbal behaviors, she did not share her own experience. It was not until the end of the second individual interview with her after the intervention that she revealed that she had been raped repeatedly by her cousin. Even during this one-on-one conversation, her story of rape did not come easily. She first talked about related stories, such as experiencing disruptions of her menstruation after she heard Rosa's story, regretting the wasted years she spent stuck in the past and in hospitals, feeling envious of Rosa's courage and progress, and so on. As I nodded, she finally said in a very low voice: "I was also raped." She then explained how it happened.

Although Bernadette did not feel the courage to tell her own story during the HLW workshops she reported benefiting from what she was able to share:

> I learned to never get stuck in my own suffering and think that I am the only one who suffered . . . there are others who have suffered more than I have . . . I learned how I can manage my own problems. After listening to others, you feel sorry for them, which changes the way you view your own issues.

Bernadette explained that she had started to understand her personal life and the world around her differently. This new understanding helped her to become less suspicious. The revelation of her genocide rape experience was an indication of her emerging trust. Physically she reported feeling healthier, with no hospitalization since she started the HLW workshops. Socially, she had made personal resolutions about renewing old friendships with people she had not seen for a long time and staying connected with other group members. She also decided to engage in the activities of helping those who continued to experience traumatic crises in the community. She reported that people around her were asking her to explain what had changed her life.

DISCUSSION

This study shows how the painful stories of sexual violence experienced by Rosa and Bernadette were intertwined with the genocide event. One of the questions that arose for me during this study was: "What factors encouraged and facilitated Rosa to speak about her experience while Bernadette chose to remain silent?" In this section, I discuss possible assumptions based on existing literature and my personal reflections. I particularly focus on the common issue of silence and its parameters and the possibility HLW offers to help overcome genocide rape.

Rosa and Bernadette shared many similarities. They were young adult women at the time of the genocide in 1994. They were each repeatedly raped by one man, and over an extended period of time. Rosa was kept inside the house of her rapist while Bernadette was picked up and dropped off any time her rapist desired her. Both women adopted a strategy of silence after the genocide in order to avoid stigma and other related emotions. In addition, it appears to me the women did not or could not find an appropriate setting in which to tell their stories in ways that would benefit them. Living in silence after rape is not unique to Rosa and Bernadette. Many survivors of rape opt for silence in patriarchal societies that attribute shame to the victim rather than to the perpetrator.[35] The internalized sense of humiliation[36] and "the reluctance of victims to come forward"[37] have led many women to impose silence upon themselves.

Silence and isolation from others in the community and self-imposed silence are damaging because they prevent women from seeking help. In addition, they destroy important social relations and marginalize women survivors further. The energy these women utilize to hold it all together must be enormous. Programs and policies working to support women survivors of wartime rape need to pay special attention to personal and sociocultural aspects that silence the victims in order to help them regain voice and reconnect both with their inner and social worlds.

In addition to the structures that impose silence, the contextual realities in which Rosa and Bernadette were raped seem to have shaped the subsequent patterns of interaction between the two women and their environments. Rosa was raped away from her village, by a stranger. After the genocide, she decided not to resettle in the town of her rapist or her hometown. She moved to another district where she could associate with other survivors. By all appearances, she had resumed a normal life. She had married and become the mother of three children. Bernadette, in contrast, continued to live in her village and seemed to have been trapped by her experience of rape. She never married and was socially isolated. As time passed, she became bitter and cynical. Based on the stories of these two women, the ability to trust and the timing of sharing rape stories can be viewed as a case of individual differences. Differences in personality may explain variations in behaviors after experiences of violence. While this position may hold some truth, viewing rape in the context of only one's personality type is very limiting and fails to take into account these other complex realities surrounding their experience.

Rosa's and Bernadette's overall health and well-being were impacted by the knowledge and beliefs they had or developed about their rape experience. Rosa described feeling as if her internal organs were being cut into pieces as she remembered her ordeal. This internal turmoil appeared to be linked with her hiccups and vomiting during the intervention. Bernadette had a strong belief that she had contracted HIV and been impregnated through rape. Her physical reactions, her understanding of the experience, and her emotions became wrapped up in the event of rape. The fact that she was raped by a close relative who she hoped would offer protection and who she knew lived with AIDS complicated her problems. She developed physiological and emotional reactions that continued to trouble her after the genocide. She was hospitalized frequently. These intertwined issues confirm the suggested bio[psycho]social[38] hypothesis that seeks to explain the complexity of wartime rape and its negative impacts. At the same time, Bernadette's body appears to have been very resilient and acted as a protective barrier. Her body blocked off the channels of reproduction and infection. During the HLW intervention, her body, like Rosa's, seemed to be going through its own healing process. She experienced menstrual disruptions, but this did not seem to trouble her. Her asthmatic crises seemed to improve over the course of the intervention. Further research is needed on the bio-psychosocial functioning of those who experience mass violence and wartime rape in particular. The connections between the risk and protective factors during and after experiencing traumatic events, such as rape, will be useful for holistic healing programs.

The HLW allowed participants to share what they felt confortable revealing and to go through the healing process at their own pace. People like Rosa seized the moment to share stories about the most troubling issues in their lives while others like Bernadette were able to participate without being coerced to reveal things that they were not ready to handle in a group context. The flexibility of the HWL workshops enriched the shared understanding of participants through stories that probed the contours of life's negative and positive experiences. Participants who felt constrained were able to observe and learn from others in the group while internally exploring the meanings of their personal experiences and related reactions. Bernadette is a good example of one who learned from others in the group. She and other participants appreciated the HLW flexibility, the shared stories, especially Rosa's story, and drew some personal lessons from it.

The factors that facilitate healing and learning during the HLW workshops have been discussed elsewhere.[39] The HLW workshops are conducted over a period of three months with time in between that allows participants to process the stories heard and reassess their personal involvement. This approach seems to allow participants to put into practice the lessons learned. It was during the gaps between sessions that Rosa and Bernadette tried to reconnect socially. With other participants they both made a commitment to participate in the sixteenth annual commemoration of the genocide as strong women who felt able to help community members who continued to experience traumatic crises at these events. This community action seemed to have its own positive impact on the two. They both reported feeling accepted and empowered because, for the first time, they were on the helping side and not among those receiving support. These social activities moved Rosa and Bernadette from the margins to the center of the community and allowed them to claim their sense of belonging. They were able to break the isolation and begin the process of accepting the past and living at greater ease in the present.

CONCLUSION

Psychosocial interventions for survivors of rape, both in times of peace and in times of war, have focused on the individual survivors and the act of sexual violence alone. Emerging practice-based literature on sexual violence in the context of post-conflict, low-income countries suggests a new paradigm of understanding rape within actions of civil conflict and its lasting impact on individual victims, families and communities.[40] Dr. Gasibirege, a practitioner-researcher on issues of sexual violence in the Great Lakes Region of Africa, argues that the psychosocial impact of wartime rape and sexual violence goes beyond the woman's body and person to affect entire communities, including the family of the victim, the perpetrators, and even their families. Gasibirege[41] advocates for addressing psychosocial wounds through community-based interventions that bring together diverse members to share different aspects of pain and to seek mutual healing. Such inteventions focus not only on recognizing the harm done directly to victims of rape but also on the environments in which rape occurred and in which the victim and perpetrator live. This perspective is rooted in the collective nature of wartime rape experiences and their impact. The community group-based approach helps those affected by rape directly and indirectly to determine new protective factors that can facilitate their reintegration into the community. Developing new understandings about suffering, and rape in particular, in a group-context allows participants to challenge issues of stigma, isolation, and other forms of continuing violence by acting together and nurturing a new sense of community belonging. Further systematic research and evaluation is needed on community-based programs like the HLW and their biopsychosocial impact on affected individuals and communities in order to shape future interventions for the survivors of wartime rape.

NOTES

1. Simon Gasibirege, *Comprendre les Violences Sexuelles Massive and* Répetitives, vol. 1, Manuels d'Initiation (Kigali, Rwanda: Publications de l'Institut Africain pour la Psychologie Integrale, 2013), 36–38; Robin Lay Schott, "War Rape, Natality and Genocide," *Journal of Genocide Research* 13.1–2 (2011): 9.

2. Tristan A. Borer, "Gendered War and Gendered Peace: Truth Commissions and Postconflict Gender Violence: Lessons From South Africa," *Violence Against Women* 15.10 (2009); Lisa Sharlach, "Rape as Genocide: Bangladesh, the Former Yugoslavia, and Rwanda," *New Political Science* 22.1 (2010): 90–92.

3. Niall Ferguson, *The War of the World: Twentieth-Century Conflict and the Descent of the West* (New York, NY: Penguin, 2006), 478–79.

4. Doris E. Buss, "Rethinking 'Rape as a Weapon of War,'" *Feminist Legal Studies* 17.2 (2009): 151; Lisa Sharlach, "Rape as Genocide," 395–96; Bronwyn Winter, "International Versus Transnational? The Politics of Prefixes in Feminist International Relations," in *Conflict-Related Sexual Violence: International Law, Local Responses*, ed. Tonia Germain and Susan Dewey (Sterling,VA: Kumarian, 2012), 15–16.

5. Schott, "War Rape," 9.

6. Padmasayee Papineni, "Children of Bad Memories," *Lancet* 362.9386 (2003): 825.

7. Katharina Lee Koo, "Confronting a Disciplinary Blindness: Women, War and Rape in the International Politics of Security," *Australian Journal of Political Science* 37.3 (2002): 526–27.

8. Christine Sylvester, "War Experiences/War Practices/War Theory," *Millenium - Journal of International Studies* 40.3 (2012): 496.

9. Sara Meger, "Rape in Contemporary Warfare: The Role of Globalization in Sexual Violence," *African Conflict and Peacebuilding Review* 1.1 (2011): 103.

10. Ruth Seifert, "The Second Front: The Logic of Sexual Violence in Wars," *Women's Studies International Forum* 19.1–2 (1996): 39.

11. Borer, "Gendered War and Gendered Peace," 1185; Julius Omona and Jennifer R. Aduo, "Gender Issues during Post-Conflict Recovery: The Case of Nwoya District, Northern Uganda," *Journal of Gender Studies* 22.2 (2013): 132.

12. Sally Hargreaves, "Rape as a War Crime: Putting Policy into Practice," *The Lancet* 357.9268 (2001): 737.

13. Buss, "Rethinking 'Rape,'" 151.

14. Sylvester, "War Experiences," 496.

15. Borer, "Gendered War and Gendered Peace," 1171–72; Elaine Zuckerman, Suzana Dennis, and Marcia E. Greenberg, *The Gender Dimensions of Post-Conflict Reconstruction: The World Bank Track Record* (Washington, DC: Gender Action, 2007), 19.

16. Borer, "Gendered War and Gendered Peace," 1183.

17. Ibid., 1170.

18. Ibid., 1172.

19. Rashida Manjoo and Calleigh MacRaith, "Gender-Based Violence and Justice in Conflict and Post-Conflict Areas," *Cornell International Law Journal* 44.1 (2011): 26–28.

20. Anne-Marie de Brouwer and Sandra K. H. Chu, *The Men Who Killed Me: Rwandan Survivors of Sexual Violence* (Vancouver, BC: Douglas & McIntyre, 2009), 11, citing Organisation of African Unity (OAU), *Rwanda: The Preventable Genocide* (Addis Ababa, Ethiopia: OAU, 2000), para. 16.20; Catrien Bijleveld, Aafke Morssinkhof, and Alette Smeulers, "Counting the Countless: Rape Victimization during the Rwandan Genocide," *International Criminal Justice Review* 19.2 (2009): 216.

21. Buss, "Rethinking 'Rape,'" 155; Petra Seawell, "Rape as a Social Construct: A Comparative Analysis of Rape in the Bosnian and Rwandan Genocides and US Domestic Law," *National Black Law Journal* 18.1 (2004): 186.

22. Alison Des Forges, *Leave None to Tell the Story: Genocide in Rwanda* (New York, NY: Human Rights Watch, 1999), 215; Christopher W. Mullins, "He Would Kill Me with His Penis: Genocidal Rape in Rwanda as a State Crime," *Critical Criminology* 17.1 (2009): 23–26.

23. de Brouwer and Chu, *The Men Who Killed Me*; Paula Donovan, "Rape and HIV/AIDS in Rwanda," *The Lancet* 360 (2002): S17.

24. de Brouwer and Chu, *The Men Who Killed Me*, 145–48.

25. Maggie Zraly, Julia Rubin-Smith, and Theresa Betancourt, "Primary Mental Health Care for Survivors of Collective Sexual Violence in Rwanda," *Global Public Health* 6.3 (2011): 258.

26. Cassandra Clifford, "Rape as a Weapon of War and It's Long-Term Effects on Victims and Society," *7th Global Conference: Violence and the Contexts of Hostility*, Budapest, Hungary, 2008, 7–8.

27. Zraly, Rubin-Smith, and Betancourt, "Primary Mental Health Care," 266.

28. Ibid.

29. Ibid., 266.

30. Regine Uwibereyeho King, "Factors that facilitate intergroup dialogue and psychosocial healing in post-genocide Rwanda," *Intervention: Journal of Mental Health and Psychosocial Support in Conflict Affected Areas*, forthcoming, 8–10.

31. Catherine K. Riessman, *Narrative Methods for Human Sciences* (Thousand Oaks, CA: Sage, 2008), 136–37.

32. Ibid., 137.

33. Mary Maynes, Jennifer L. Pierce, and Barbara Laslett, *Telling Stories: The Use of Personal Narratives in the Social Sciences and History* (Ithaca, NY: Cornell University Press, 2008).

34. King, "Factors that Facilitate Intergroup Dialogue." This paragraph has also been cited in another upcoming publication of the journal *Intervention: Journal of Mental Health and Psychosocial Support in Conflict Affected Areas.*

35. Koo, "Confronting a Disciplinary Blindness," 526; Sharlach, "Rape as Genocide," 90.

36. Keith V. Bletzer, "Review Symposium: A Voice for Every Woman and the Travesties of War," *Violence Against Women* 12.7 (2006): 700.

37. Jonathan Gottschall, "Explaining Wartime Rape," *The Journal of Sex Research* 41.2 (2010): 129.

38. Ibid., 134–35.

39. King, "Factors that Facilitate Intergroup Dialogue," 12–16.

40. Gasibirege, *Comprendre les Violences Sexuelles Massive and Répetitives*, 36–40.

41. Ibid., 47.

BIBLIOGRAPHY

Bijleveld, Catrien, Aafke Morssinkhof, and Alette Smeulers. "Counting the Countless: Rape Victimization during the Rwandan Genocide." *International Criminal Justice Review* 19.2 (2009): 208–24.

Bletzer, Keith V. "Review Symposium: A Voice for Every Woman and the Travesties of War." *Violence Against Women* 12.7 (2006): 700–05.

Borer, Tristan A. "Gendered War and Gendered Peace: Truth Commissions and Post-conflict Gender Violence: Lessons from South Africa." *Violence Against Women* 15.10 (2009): 1169–93.

Buss, Doris E. "Rethinking 'Rape as a Weapon of War.'" *Feminist Legal Studies* 17.2 (2009): 145–63.

Clifford, Cassandra. "Rape as a Weapon of War and it's Long-Term Effects on Victims and Society." *7th Global Conference: Violence and the Contexts of Hostility*. Budapest, Hungary, 2008.

de Brouwer, Anne-Marie and Sandra K. H. Chu. *The Men Who Killed Me: Rwandan Survivors of Sexual Violence*. Vancouver, BC: Douglas & McIntyre, 2009.

Des Forges, Alison. *Leave None to Tell the Story: Genocide in Rwanda*. New York, NY: Human Rights Watch, 1999.

Donovan, Paula. "Rape and HIV/AIDS in Rwanda." *The Lancet* 360 (2002): S17–18.

Ferguson, Niall. *The War of the World: Twentieth-Century Conflict and the Descent of the West*. New York, NY: Penguin, 2006.

Gasibirege, Simon. *Comprendre les Violences Sexuelles Massive and Répetitives*. Vol. 1. Manuels d'Initiation. Kigali, Rwanda: Publications de l'Institut Africain pour la Psychologie Integrale, 2013.

Gottschall, Jonathan. "Explaining Wartime Rape." *The Journal of Sex Research* 41.2 (2010): 129–36.

Hargreaves, Sally. "Rape as a War Crime: Putting Policy into Practice." *The Lancet* 357.9258 (2001): 737.

King, Regine Uwibereyeho. "Factors that Facilitate Intergroup Dialogue and Psychosocial Healing in Post-Genocide Rwanda." *Intervention: Journal of Mental Health and Psychosocial Support in Conflict Affected Areas*, forthcoming.

Koo, Katharina Lee. "Confronting a Disciplinary Blindness: Women, War and Rape in the International Politics of Security." *Australian Journal of Political Science* 37.3 (2002): 525–36.

Manjoo, Rashida and Calleigh MacRaith. "Gender-Based Violence and Justice in Conflict and Post-Conflict Areas." *Cornell International Law Journal* 44.1 (2011): 11–31.

Maynes, Mary, Jennifer L. Pierce, and Barbara Laslett. *Telling Stories: The Use of Personal Narratives in the Social Sciences and History.* Ithaca, NY: Cornell University Press, 2008.

Meger, Sara. "Rape in Contemporary Warfare: The Role of Globalization in Sexual Violence." *African Conflict and Peacebuilding Review* 1.1 (2011): 100–32.

Mullins, Christopher W. "He Would Kill Me With His Penis: Genocidal Rape in Rwanda as a State Crime." *Critical Criminology* 17.1 (2009): 15–33.

Omona, Julius, and Jennifer R. Aduo. "Gender Issues during Post-Conflict Recovery: The Case of Nwoya District, Northern Uganda." *Journal of Gender Studies* 22.2 (2013): 119–36.

Papineni, Padmasayee. "Children of Bad Memories." *Lancet* 362.9386 (2003): 825–26.

Riessman, Catherine K. *Narrative Methods for Human Sciences.* Thousand Oaks, CA: Sage, 2008.

Schott, Robin Lay. "War Rape, Natality and Genocide." *Journal of Genocide Research* 13.1–2 (2011): 5–21.

Seawell, Petra. "Rape as a Social Construct: A Comparative Analysis of Rape in the Bosnian and Rwandan Genocides and US Domestic Law." *National Black Law Journal* 18.1 (2004): 180–200.

Seifert, Ruth. "The Second Front: The Logic of Sexual Violence in Wars." *Women's Studies International Forum* 19.1–2 (1996): 35–43.

Sharlach, Lisa. "Rape as Genocide: Bangladesh, the Former Yugoslavia, and Rwanda." *New Political Science* 22.1 (2010): 89–102.

Sylvester, Christine. "War Experiences/War Practices/War Theory." *Millenium - Journal of International Studies* 40.3 (2012): 483–503.

Winter, Bronwyn. "International versus Transnational? The Politics of Prefixes in Feminist International Relations." In *Conflict-Related Sexual Violence: International Law, Local Responses*, edited by Tonia Germain and Susan Dewey, 15–32. Sterling,VA: Kumarian, 2012.

Zraly, Maggie, Julia Rubin-Smith, and Theresa Betancourt. "Primary Mental Health Care for Survivors of Collective Sexual Violence in Rwanda." *Global Public Health* 6.3 (2011): 257–70.

Zuckerman, Elaine, Suzanna Dennis, and Marcia E. Greenberg. *The Gender Dimensions of Post-Conflict Reconstruction: The World Bank Track Record.* Washington, DC: Gender Action, 2007.

Chapter 4

Mothers at the Tree of Frustration

Locating Healing in Liberia

Angela J. Lederach

In traditional telling of war stories, women are always in the background. . .. This is not a traditional war story. You have not heard it before, because it is an African woman's story and our stories rarely are told.[1]

THE LIBERIAN CIVIL WAR: AN INTRODUCTION

Political and economic tensions in Liberia date back to the late 1800s when Liberia became the primary destination to resettle freed slaves from North America. The colonial resettlement project drove a wedge of inequality between the indigenous Liberians and the resettled "Americo-Liberians," who emerged as the ruling elite, systematically marginalizing the indigenous tribes of Liberia.[2] In response to growing inequality and increased poverty among indigenous Liberians, Samuel Doe led a *coup d'état* in 1980, and rose to power as Liberia's new leader.[3] Unfortunately, Doe's regime brought little change and continued political unrest gave rise to the National Patriotic Front of Liberia (NPFL), a rebel movement led by Charles Taylor.[4] In 1989, civil war erupted across the small West African nation. Characterized by brutality, torture, and rape, the civil war killed an estimated 200,000 people between 1989 and 1996.[5] In 1996, the Abuja II peace agreement was signed and Charles Taylor emerged as Liberia's new president.[6] Repeated violations of the peace agreement and the continued presence of corruption and violence under Taylor's regime soon reignited the war. The Liberians United for Reconciliation and Democracy (LURD) challenged Taylor's leadership, claiming the northern territory, while the Movement for Democracy in Liberia (MODEL), in opposition to both LURD and the Taylor regime, asserted military control over the southeastern region of Liberia.[7]

The brutality that characterized the previous civil war continued to ravage the countryside. Over 70 percent of all the warring factions were comprised of children under the age of 15.[8] Torture, systematic gang rape, and gender-based violence, carried out primarily by young children, disintegrated the social fabric of Liberian society and left the country in ruins. Finally, in 2003, as Taylor's control over Liberia faltered, the fighting factions agreed to meet in Accra for peace negotiations. On August 18, 2003, the warring factions in Liberia signed the Comprehensive Peace Agreement in Accra, Ghana. Over a decade of war left 250,000 dead, 500,000 refugees, and more than one million internally displaced people within Liberia.[9]

In the background of this war story are women. Women lined the streets of Monrovia, wearing white t-shirts, and demanded an end to war. Women united across political, ethnic, religious, and economic divisions to face the challenges confronting Liberia. Women stripped naked and declared a sex strike, reclaiming their broken and violated bodies as sites of resistance and protest. Women danced, sang, and wept their communities toward healing.

In this chapter I seek to bring these women, who too-often remain in the background of the stories of war, to the foreground by highlighting the lessons learned from the experience and strategies of the Liberian Women's Mass Action for Peace (LWMAP). First, I focus on the methods employed by LWMAP to end the civil war in Liberia. Next, I highlight the movement's participation in the reintegration of child soldiers and community reconciliation in the aftermath of war. By following the work of these Liberian women in the midst and aftermath of armed conflict, this chapter seeks to provide a comprehensive understanding of women's participation in grassroots peacebuilding as well as their gender-specific experiences with violence. Rather than confine these women to the stagnant category of victim, this chapter underscores Liberian women as key actors in building peace. Their imaginative strategies critically engage traditional approaches to conflict resolution and offer a new paradigm for peacebuilding practitioners.

THE LIBERIAN WOMEN'S MASS ACTION FOR PEACE CAMPAIGN

At the height of the Liberian civil war, women began to talk. Late night conversations in small kitchens, after a full day of work, planted and nurtured the seeds of peace. These women had watched their brothers, sisters, husbands, sons, and daughters killed and raped. And they were struck by their shared experience of war, violence, and exclusion. "We all suffered," Leymah Gbowee reflected, "If you were illiterate: you were a target of rape; if you were a market woman: you were a target of rape; if you were active in civil society and politics: you were a target of rape. We were all victims. And we all had a voice."[10] They began meeting regularly and expanded their network by targeting places "inhabited by women."[11] Marketplaces. Refugee camps. Homes and street stalls. Mosques and churches. The leaders of the movement intentionally worked across the same divisive barriers that gave birth to the civil war. They were market women and political elites, "Americo-Liberians" and members of indigenous tribes. They were refugees, educators, politicians, police officers, and street vendors. Within a month, the first meeting of four women grew to more than 500 and the LWMAP was formed.[12]

They organized a sustained, mass protest in the streets of Monrovia. For weeks on end, they lined the streets, wearing bright white t-shirts. Their message was simple: "We Want Peace, No More War."[13] They declared a sex strike. Their bodies, once violated and vulnerable, were transformed into sites of resistance and power. The sex strike also made visible and public the silenced reality of women's lives and garnered international attention and support. Their presence continued to grow daily, as they gained support from the Liberian public who were amazed at their willingness to risk their lives for the nation.[14] After months of protest, President Taylor agreed to meet with the women. They lined the halls of parliament in white t-shirts as Leymah Gbowee's voice rang out: "The women of Liberia, including the Internally Displaced People are tired of war. We are tired of the killing of our people and we, the women of Liberia, want peace now."[15]

The LURD rebels also demanded to speak with the women. And so the women traveled, unarmed into the bush, and began engaging in shuttle diplomacy in an effort to promote peace negotiations.[16] Finally, in June 2003, Charles Taylor and the fighting factions agreed to meet in Accra, Ghana to begin peace talks.[17] Although the women were excluded from the negotiation table, this did not stop them from organizing to make their demands heard. This time, they reached across the barriers of nation-state and combined their efforts with the Mano River Union Women's Peace Network (MARWOPNET) and the Women in Peacebuilding Network (WIPNET). Women from Sierra Leone, Nigeria, and Cote d'Ivoire flew to Ghana to participate in the mass action for peace. They lined the streets in white t-shirts, this time in Accra, and surrounded the hotel where the negotiations were held.[18]

In the midst of the ongoing peace talks, the Special Court for Sierra Leone (SCSL) announced the indictment of President Charles Taylor for war crimes in Sierra Leone. Charles Taylor fled and soon after a bomb exploded in a refugee camp in Monrovia.[19] As the negotiations began to crumble, the women united, publicly mourning the loss of life and the violation of the ceasefire. A powerful coalition of more than 200 women gathered outside the hotel in Accra, Ghana. Fatura, a thin, strong woman from the north of Ghana recalled the day:

> We were dressed in our white t-shirts. We all wanted peace. We were Liberian Women. We were Ghanaian Women. We were Nigerian women. And we were weeping and dancing and it was raining and we were in the rain dancing and singing and weeping.[20]

Through their collective and public expressions of grief, they made the suffering of ordinary Liberians visible. Their public mourning once again drew international attention, and carved out a space for their voices to be heard around the negotiating table. They also increased their presence. Hundreds of women spilled into the hotel, blockading the doors of the negotiating room.[21] When the men inside attempted to leave, Leymah Gbowee began to publicly strip naked, a serious taboo in Liberian culture, used by mothers on rare occasions to punish their sons.[22] By stripping naked, Leymah Gbowee effectively manipulated traditional notions of masculinity to publicly shame the generals and commanders into continuing their negotiations. The men returned, defeated, to the negotiating room. Several weeks later, the Government of Liberia along with LURD, and the MODEL signed the Comprehensive Peace Agreement.[23]

GENDER AND THE LIBERIAN WOMEN'S MASS ACTION FOR PEACE CAMPAIGN

The LWMAP campaign drew on the gender-specific dimensions of violence to inform their actions of protest and resistance. Carol Cohn defines gender as "a way of categorizing, ordering, and symbolizing power, of hierarchically structuring relationships among different categories of people, and different human activities symbolically associated with masculinity or femininity."[24] She argues that organized violence cannot be "fruitfully understood, or changed, without a gender analysis."[25] Cohn's definition of "gender," which moves beyond a limited focus on women, to include socially constructed understandings of masculinity and femininity, provides an important framework to analyze the gendered dimensions of the Liberian civil war. Definitions of gender that are limited to women's experience have, as Anu Pillay asserts, "a tendency to focus on victimhood."[26] In the Liberian civil war, women and girls accounted for 30 to 40 percent of all armed factions.[27] While some women were kidnapped and forced to join, others joined by choice, viewing their participation with the armed groups as a form of survival.[28] Furthermore, 8 percent of the reported rapes were committed against men, a low estimate, given the high stigmatization and silencing of male rape in Liberia.[29]

Understanding the ways that gender "hierarchically structured relationships"[30] in Liberia also serves to expose the unjust structures that limited women's access to economic and political power. Traditional inheritance and land rights excluded women from primary ownership, making them utterly dependent on men for economic survival. This caused disproportionate suffering for internally displaced women, in particular, who had no land to return to and no economic alternatives to meet their basic needs.[31] In the final analysis of the Liberian Truth and Reconciliation Commission (LTRC), the authors determined that women were indeed the "most marginalized, economically, socially, and politically in Liberia."[32]

The underlying gender inequality coupled with the operative hypermasculinity used to train and recruit rebels, gave rise to widespread rape and gender-based violence in Liberia. Young boys who gang raped women old enough to be their grandmothers utterly destroyed the gerontocracy that defined traditional social structures in Liberia before the war. Pregnant women had their stomachs split open and were buried alive, symbolizing the loss of not only life, but also lineage. Power and domination were inscribed on women's bodies, which became the new frontlines of war. Nancy Scheper-Hughes and Philippe Bourgois write,

> Violence can never be understood solely in terms of its physicality . . .. Violence also includes assaults on the personhood, dignity, sense of worth or value of the victim. The social and cultural dimensions of violence are what gives violence its power and meaning.[33]

The use of gender-based violence in Liberia had specific meaning and power, rooted in notions of femininity, masculinity, and motherhood. LWMAP strategically subverted these culturally constructed notions of gender and in doing so made visible the structural violence that afflicted their lives before, during, and after the war. They transformed the "private" spheres of women's lives into political spaces for action and resistance: marketplaces, food stalls, and homes became places of political mobilization and protest. "Motherhood" became a powerful organizing framework, which both exposed and undermined gender-based violence that specifically targeted mothers during war. By reclaiming ownership over their bodies and publicly denying sex, they transformed their bodies from sites of violence into sites of resistance. Vulnerability became power. The private became political.

Ironically, a peace accord often entails the loss of voice and leadership for women as life returns to "normalcy," translating too often to a return to patterns of male-dominated leadership.[34] Liberian women actually experienced an increase in domestic violence, prostitution, and human trafficking in the aftermath of the Liberian civil war.[35] As Carolyn Nordstrom writes,

> Somewhere between the girls raped in war and prostituted in peace, I have lost the clear distinction dividing war and peace. I think this is a positive step, a

> useful ambiguity. It is a step that leads us into questions of who profits from war, from silence, and from the lives . . . of girls on a global scale.[36]

It was perhaps their ability, to blur the lines between the false dichotomy of war and peace that made LWMAP so effective. Their intimate understanding of this "ambiguity" allowed the women's movement to address the immediate crisis of the war while simultaneously working toward a long-term vision that addressed the structural and cultural roots of the violence.[37] To this end, the leaders of the movement not only organized mass protests aimed at ending the war, they also developed training to provide women with new skills in trauma healing, reconciliation, and reintegration.[38] They understood that violence does not end at the signing of the peace accord, and worked tirelessly to build capacity and vision for lasting peace in their country.[39] From previous experience, they also recognized that the key to lasting peace began with a successful Disarmament, Demobilization, and Reintegration (DDR) process. Understanding that much more was needed than the promise of money to sustain disarmament, Gbowee and the women's movement developed a "rehumanizing" approach to the reintegration of child soldiers.[40]

THE REINTEGRATION OF CHILD SOLDIERS: A RE-HUMANIZING APPROACH

Child soldiering posed particular challenges in the aftermath of the Liberian civil war. First, child soldiering dismantled common Western notions of warfare that assumed a separation of victim and perpetrator. In Liberia, children experienced the seamlessness of being victim-perpetrators that created and sustained a complex system of violation and destruction.[41] Second, child soldiers consistently faced a de- and re-construction of identity and place. The act of destroying an old identity was for many literal: they were sent to wipe out their own villages and family members as an act of breaking their former ties and reconstituting dependence and allegiance to their new identity.[42] These initiation rites also frequently coincided with naming ceremonies where the young soldiers took on new "bush" names like "Rambo" and "Superman."[43] Third, security and belonging were renegotiated around surrogate, parent-like figures. Weapons and commanders became their new form of survival. For girl soldiers, this often meant becoming a "bush wife." Seeking security from gang rape, young girls chose to "marry" rebel commanders.[44] With young infants slung over their backs and AK-47s nestled in their arms, these young women embodied the everyday reality for many child soldiers, a reality that demanded they hold and move between identities and social spaces like victim–perpetrator, between rituals of violence and community, powerlessness and Rambo, separation and belonging, motherlessness and mother.

Successful disarmament, then, required not only the removal of weapons, but also the healing of individuals by reconstituting identity and belonging. As Morris, a former child combatant and commander in both the Liberian and Sierra Leonean wars explained, "Your mind is the weapon, and all you have in your mind is violence. It is embedded in you. And it is creative. You can do unimaginable things, terrible things with this creativity."[45] Where is healing located in the aftermath of such devastating violence, which utterly destroys a sense of personhood and belonging? For Leymah Gbowee, the answer lies in a rehumanizing approach to community reconciliation.

> We had to re-humanize them in their powerlessness. We had to take away not only their guns but also their vulnerability. We had to give them a new kind of power. We took away their fear and gave them a new kind of boldness through love.[46]

One example of this re-humanizing approach is found in the story of the "Mothers at the Tree of Frustration."

MOTHERS OF THE TREE OF FRUSTRATION: LOCATING HEALING IN THE AFTERMATH OF WAR

With the war officially "over," young soldiers began to return to their villages. Outside one small village, former child soldiers started to appear, gathering under the shade of a large tree that was located on the border of the village. From the tree, they could see their homes, but remained outside the village boundaries. With no guns, little food, ragged clothes and a decade of matted hair down their backs, they had nowhere to go, but did not know how to enter the village they had destroyed. Day in and day out they lived under the tree. They named it the "Tree of Frustration."[47]

Most people avoided the tree, not wanting to see the young children who reminded them of their painful war experiences. However, several women who had participated in LWMAP began to visit the former combatants. Every day they brought food. Little by little they built a relationship. They told traditional stories, sang the village songs, and prayed together. Months passed. Finally the women invited the children to return to the village. In preparation for the reintegration ceremony, the women decided to perform a "haircutting" ritual. The children's wild unkempt hair, which served as a powerful reminder of the war, had to go. Haircutting was also a mundane task traditionally performed by mothers. As Veena Das writes, life is "recovered not through some grand gestures in the realm of the transcendent but through a descent into the ordinary."[48] Through their descent into the ordinary, the women found a way to re-constitute their relationship with the young combatants. They worked to rebuild their identities as mother and child, recreating the social institutions that the war had destroyed. When the haircutting ritual ended, the mothers, dressed in white, a color symbolic of childbirth, lined up two-by-two: one woman, one child. They took the hand of the child next to them and, side-by-side, they began to walk toward the village center. As they walked, they sang. They began by singing traditional songs of lamentation, mourning, and loss. But as they reached the threshold of the village, their voices erupted in songs of celebration and new life.[49]

The haircutting ritual touched a memory of life and relationship that seamlessly linked the past and present. Women reestablished a sense of self and place for the former combatants, rekindling their shared living history and connectedness after a devastating separation. As Gbowee writes in her memoir, *Mighty Be Our Powers*, peacebuilding is "healing those victimized by war . . . bringing them back to the people they once were. It's helping victimizers rediscover their humanity."[50] This understanding of peacebuilding seeks to combine the "inner and outer" experiences of healing, which is both, and at once, intimately individual and deeply collective.[51] Such an approach to social healing has the capacity to create "an intermediary space that touches on the idiosyncrasies of individual healing and the ephemeral promise of fully restored relationships."[52]

Unfortunately, the reintegration efforts of LWMAP received very little recognition from international organizations, like the United Nations (UN). The women were once again excluded, this time from the formal DDR efforts spearheaded by the UN. They were not taken seriously as qualified peace practitioners. Cohn argues that the systematic exclusion of women from leadership positions in peacebuilding efforts often stems from a lack of awareness and recognition of the "masculinist assumptions built into . . . conceptions of 'qualified.' "[53] This was certainly the case in Liberia. "When I talked with the men," Gbowee explained,

> I would tell them that you are only comfortable with empowerment and with women's leadership as long as it doesn't involve your own social structure. So during the war, women could engage in peacebuilding because it did not interfere with the immediate social structures. But, when the war ended and communities started to come back together, women recognized that they could continue leading, but that is when the men tried to take away the voice of the women again. So the question then became, do we sit down again, or do we push this leadership so that it is sustained?[54]

Sustainable change required not only the restoration of relationships at the community level, but also a transformation in the high-level political processes in Liberia. To address their repeated exclusion from political and social leadership in Liberia, LWMAP joined the Liberian Women's Initiative (LWI) in a campaign to register women to vote with the hope of electing the first woman president in Liberia, Ellen Johnson Sirleaf.[55] Recognizing that the privilege of voting was often not afforded to women who were constrained by their obligations of work, they offered childcare and tended market stands to ensure women's participation.[56] Eventually, more than 7000 women registered. And on November 8, 2005, Ellen Johnson Sirleaf became Liberia's first woman president.[57]

LESSONS FROM THE LIBERIAN WOMEN'S MASS ACTION FOR PEACE

"This is not a traditional war story," Leymah Gbowee writes, "You have not heard it before, because it is an African woman's story and our stories are rarely told."[58] The painful truth is that the tireless efforts of women to build peace remain on the margins of peacebuilding literature and theory. Carolyn Nordstrom poignantly writes, "unseen is to unexist."[59] Many of the approaches to community-based peacebuilding like those documented in this chapter remain unseen. Both the static confines of "victimhood" placed on women's experience, as well as essentialist views of women as *inherently* peaceful reinforce this invisibility. As Nancy Scheper-Hughes asserts:

> In the end, it's simply not the case that men make wars and women make peace, or that mothering "naturally" opposes militarism . . . Only by intentional design, rather than by a natural predisposition, do women devote the thinking and practices of motherhood to peacekeeping and world repair rather than to war making and world destruction.[60]

Too much of the peacebuilding technical literature takes an essentialist perspective that scarcely accounts for or simply fails to give credit to women who have, by intentional design, imagined a way to work for the healing of their communities. The Liberian women's movement offers a critical engagement with traditional conflict resolution practices and provides several important insights for the practice of peacebuilding.

First, the Liberian women embraced a holistic approach, weaving what John Paul Lederach calls "a web of relationships" that connected high-level policies to local, community-based peacebuilding efforts.[61] They mobilized women across the deeply embedded social divisions that initially gave rise to civil war. In cultivating a strong "horizontal capacity"[62] that unified women across these divisions, they worked to transform the root causes of civil war and unrest in Liberia. They also worked to mobilize an effective "vertical capacity,"[63] linking market women with some of the most powerful leaders in Liberia, eventually leading to the election of Ellen Johnson Sirleaf. They embraced a holistic approach that recognized the importance of connecting high-level processes with the work of rebuilding relationships at the local, community level.

Second, the Liberian women rooted their peacebuilding strategies within their own cultural context. As Leymah Gbowee suggests in the quote at the beginning of this chapter, the lack of recognition for the diverse experience of women in war stems not only from gender inequality, but also from the tendency to privilege Western notions of peacebuilding over local approaches. Lasting peace demands that international efforts embrace "a preferential option for the local community."[64] This asks that we not only interrogate the masculinist assumptions built into Western notions of what constitutes "qualified peacebuilders," but also recognizes how such assumptions intersect with multiple forms of oppression like racism, nationalism, and classism. In the conclusion of her memoir Leymah Gbowee argues that

> It's insulting when outsiders come in and tell a traumatized people what it will take for them to heal . . . . People who have lived through a terrible conflict . . . often have very good ideas about how peace can evolve, and they need to be asked.[65]

The Mothers at the Tree of Frustration provide an important example of the critical and unique role the local community plays in building peace. They drew upon the ordinary, but deeply rooted, practices of their village to bring the children "back to their humanity," reestablishing their connectedness and shared living history. Similarly, the protests organized by LWMAP's campaign clearly demonstrate the meaningful uses of cultural traditions and understandings in the work of peace and effective social change processes.

The women also used a multidimensional and multidirectional approach to building peace.[66] The work of restoring individuals and communities in the aftermath of sustained and devastating violence is not easily understood exclusively by the sequential and linear views of negotiation and conflict resolution prevalent in much of the Western-based literature. For the Liberian women, a "singular" peace process represented a misnomer that ignored their experience of violence both before and after war. As a result, they chose to employ significant nonlinear elements in their approach to peace, addressing multiple aspects of the challenges facing local communities. Their "re-humanizing" approach to reintegration called to a past life in order to pave the way toward reconciliation, simultaneously evoking the past, present, and future in their approach to peacebuilding. Rather than ignore emotions associated with past grievances, the Liberian women created rituals that allowed space for both memory and hope to operate simultaneously, serving to re-root communities and deepen reconciliation efforts.[67]

Finally, the Liberian women addressed the immediate crisis of the war, while simultaneously engaging in processes that promoted long-term change. The techniques they used during their mass demonstrations repeatedly built upon and subverted culturally constructed notions of gender. By making visible the gendered dimensions of violence, the Liberian women highlighted the operative cultural and structural violence that constituted the root causes of the war. They did so, in part, by effectively transforming "motherhood" into a political space. There has been wide debate in feminist literature about the use of "motherhood" in peace activism, with some scholars arguing that maternalist politics only serve to deepen essentialist views of women.[68] However, the politicization of "motherhood" in the Liberian context represented a powerful subversion of gender-based violence that specifically targeted mothers during the war. The Liberian women politicized "motherhood" not only to restore their own dignity and reconstitute relationships at the community level, but also as way to transform the patriarchal structures that defined political culture in Liberia. Motherhood represented a new way of doing politics, one that privileged compassion and equality over greed and domination. By making the "private" realm of motherhood political, the Liberian women sought to unify the country across the dividing lines of gender, ethnicity, and class. The politics of motherhood provided a strategic approach that addressed the root causes of the civil war, recreating a world that made lasting peace possible.

In *Life and Words*, Veena Das documents the devastating violence women experienced during partition in India, writing,

> The terror of the violation . . . was precisely that the victims *knew* their perpetrators to be human: that is what puts life itself into question. There is a deep moral energy in the refusal to represent some violations of the human body, for these violations are seen as being "against nature," as defining the limits of life itself.[69]

The Liberian women, who suffered violation of body and personhood at the hands of their own children, reached the "limits of life." In response, they reclaimed power in their relationships with one another and shared experiences as women. Peace became their form of survival. They overturned the vulnerability of being "woman" by subverting culturally constructed understandings of gender. And they engaged in the difficult task of rebuilding their communities in the midst of rubble and devastation. Today, they continue on their journey toward social healing in Liberia. This is not a linear journey, with the finality of an "end," but rather, an iterative journey founded on the daily work of nurturing relationships that shelter and protect the fragile borders of life.

NOTES

1. Leymah Gbowee, *Mighty Be Our Powers: How Sisterhood, Prayer, and Sex Changed a Nation at War* (New York, NY: Beast Books, 2011), ix–x.

2. Filomina Chioma Steady, *Women and Leadership in West Africa: Mothering the Nation and Humanizing the State* (New York, NY: Palgrave Macmillan, 2011); African Women and Peace Support Group, *Liberian Women Peacemakers: Fighting for the Right to be Seen, Heard and Counted* (Trenton, NJ: Africa World Press, 2004), 2; Gbowee, *Mighty Be Our Powers*; Mary H. Moran and M. Anne Pitcher, "The 'Basket Case' and the 'Post Child': Explaining the End of Civil Conflicts in Liberia and Mozambique," *Third World Quarterly* 25.3 (2004): 505.

3. Ibid., 505.

4. Ibid.

5. African Women and Peace Support Group, *Liberian Women*, 40.

6. Ibid., xi.

7. Ibid., x–xi.

8. Ibid., 53.

9. Ibid., 39.

10. Leymah Gbowee, personal communication, Harrisonburg, VA, 2006.

11. Gbowee, *Mighty Be Our Powers*, 127.

12. John Paul Lederach and Angela Jill Lederach, *When Blood and Bones Cry Out: Journeys through the Soundscape of Healing and Reconciliation* (New York, NY: Oxford University Press, 2010); Gbowee, personal communication.

13. Ibid.

14. William Saa, personal communication, Accra, Ghana, 2006; Gbowee, personal communication.

15. Gini Reticker (Director) and Abigail Disney (Producer), *Pray the Devil Back to Hell* (New York, NY: Fork Films, 2008).

16. Etweda "Sugars" Cooper, personal communication, Accra, Ghana, 2006.

17. African Women and Peace Support Group, *Liberian Women*.

18. Gbowee, personal communication.

19. Ibid.; Saa, personal communication.

20. Fatura, personal communication, Accra, Ghana, 2006.

21. Gbowee, personal communication.

22. Ibid.

23. United Nations Security Council, "Peace Agreement Between the Government of Liberia (GOL), the Liberians United for Reconciliation and Democracy (LURD),

the Movement for Democracy and the Political Parties (MODEL)," Accra, Ghana, August 18, 2003; Lederach and Lederach, *When Blood and Bones.*

24. Carol Cohn, ed. *Women and Wars: Contested Histories* (Cambridge, England: Polity Press, 2013), 3.

25. Ibid., 29.

26. Anu Pillay, "Truth Seeking and Gender: The Liberian Experience," *African Journal of Conflict Resolution* 9.2 (2009): 97.

27. AI International Secretariat, *Liberia: A Flawed Process Discriminates against Women and Girls*, Amnesty International, March 31, 2008, http://www.amnesty.org/en/library/info/AFR34/004/2008/en.

28. Mats Utas, "Victimcy, Girlfriending, Soldiering: Tactic Agency in a Young Woman's Social Navigation of the Liberian War Zone," *Anthropological Quarterly* 78.2 (2005).

29. Pillay, "Truth Seeking," 98.

30. Cohn, *Women and Wars*, 3.

31. Helen Liebling-Kalifani et al., "Women War Survivors of the 1989-2003 Conflict in Liberia: The Impact of Sexual and Gender-Based Violence," *Journal of International Women's Studies* 12.1 (2011): 14.

32. Ibid., 7.

33. Nancy Scheper-Hughes and Philippe Bourgois, *Violence in War and Peace: An Anthology* (Malden, MA: Blackwell, 2004), 1.

34. Sheila Meintjes, Anu Pillay, and Meredeth Turshen, eds., *The Aftermath: Women in Post-Conflict Transformation* (London, England: Zed Books, 2002).

35. Liebling-Kalifani et al., "Women War Survivors," 3.

36. Carolyn Nordstrom, "Visible Wars & Invisible Girls, Shadow Industries, and the Politics of Not-Knowing," *International Feminist Journal of Politics* 1.1 (1999): 16.

37. John Paul Lederach, *The Moral Imagination: The Art and Soul of Building Peace* (New York, NY: Oxford University Press, 2005).

38. Emmanuel Bombande, personal communication, Accra, Ghana, 2006.

39. Coopers, personal communication; Gbowee, personal communication.

40. Ibid.

41. Michael Wessells, *Child Soldiers: From Violence to Protection* (Cambridge, MA: Harvard University Press, 2006).

42. Ibid; David Rosen, *Armies of the Young: Child Soldiers in War and Terror* (New Brunswick, NY: Rutgers University Press, 2005); Alcinda Honwana, *Child Soldiers in Africa* (Philadelphia, PA: University of Pennsylvania Press, 2006); Bombande, personal communication; Lederach and Lederach, *When Blood and Bones.*

43. Wessells, *Child Soldiers*; Rosen, *Armies of the Young*; Honwana, *Child Soldiers in Africa*; Bombande, personal communication; Lederach and Lederach, *When Blood and Bones.*

44. Utas, "Victimcy, Girlfriending."

45. Morris Matadi, personal communication, Budaburam Refugee Camp, Ghana, 2006.

46. Gbowee, personal communication.

47. Ibid; Lederach and Lederach, *When Blood and Bones.*

48. Veena Das, *Life and Words: Violence and the Descent into the Ordinary* (Berkeley, CA: University of California Press), 7.

49. Gbowee, personal communication; Lederach and Lederach, *When Blood and Bones.*

50. Gbowee, *Mighty Be Our Powers*, 82.

51. Lederach and Lederach, *When Blood and Bones*, 234.

52. Ibid.

53. Cohn, *Women and Wars*, 18.

54. Gbowee, personal communication.

55. Ibid.

56. Cooper, personal communication.

57. Gbowee, *Mighty Be Our Powers*, 183–84.

58. Ibid., xi.

59. Nordstrom, "Visible Wars," 15.

60. Nancy Scheper-Hughes, "Maternal Thinking and the Politics of War," in *The Women and War Reader*, ed. Lois Ann Lorentzen and Jennifer Turpin (New York, NY: New York University Press, 1998), 228.

61. Lederach, *The Moral Imagination*, 80.

62. Ibid., 78–79.

63. Ibid.

64. Lederach and Lederach, *When Blood and Bones*, 210.

65. Gbowee, *Mighty Be Our Powers*, 171.

66. Lederach and Lederach, *When Blood and Bones.*

67. Ibid.

68. Scheper-Hughes, "Maternal Thinking"; Cohn, *Women and Wars*; Steady, *Women and Leadership*; *The Women and War Reader*, eds. Lois Ann Lorentzen and Jennifer Turpin (New York, NY: New York University Press, 1998); Steady, *Women and Leadership*; Malathi De Alwis, "Motherhood as a Space of Protest," in *Appropriating Gender: Women's Activism and Politicized Religion in South Asia*, ed. Patricia Jeffery and Amrita Basu (New York, NY: Routledge, 1998), 185–202.

69. Das, *Life and Words*, 90.

BIBLIOGRAPHY

African Women and Peace Support Group. *Liberian Women Peacemakers: Fighting for the Right to be Seen, Heard and Counted.* Trenton, NJ: Africa World Press, 2004.

AI International Secretariat. "Liberia: A Flawed Process Discriminates against Women and Girls." Amnesty International, March 31, 2008. http://www.amnesty.org/en/library/info/AFR34/004/2008/en.

Bombande, Emmanuel. Personal communication. Accra, Ghana, 2006.

Cohn, Carol, ed. *Women and Wars: Contested Histories, Uncertain Futures.* Cambridge, England: Polity Press, 2013.

Cohn, Carol and Ruth Jacobson. "Women and Political Activism in the Face of War and Militarization." In *Women and Wars: Contested Histories, Uncertain Futures*, edited by Carol Cohn, 102–23. Cambridge, England: Polity Press, 2013.

Cooper, Etweda. "Sugars." Personal communication. Accra, Ghana, 2006.

Das, Veena. *Life and Words: Violence and the Descent into the Ordinary*. Berkeley, CA: University of California Press, 2007.

De Alwis, Malathi. "Motherhood as a Space of Protest." In *Appropriating Gender: Women's Activism and Politicized Religion in South Asia*, edited by Patricia Jeffrey and Amrita Basu, 185–202. New York, NY: Routledge, 1998.

Fatura. Personal communication. Accra, Ghana, 2006.

Gbowee, Leymah. *Mighty Be Our Powers: How Sisterhood, Prayer, and Sex Changed a Nation at War*. New York, NY: Beast Books, 2011.

———. Personal communication. Harrisonburg, VA, 2006.

Honwana, Alcinda. *Child Soldiers in Africa*. Philadelphia, PA: University of Pennsylvania Press, 2006.

Lederach, John Paul. *The Moral Imagination: The Art and Soul of Building Peace*. New York, NY: Oxford University Press, 2005.

Lederach, John Paul and Angela Jill Lederach. *When Blood and Bones Cry Out: Journeys through the Soundscape of Healing and Reconciliation*. New York, NY: Oxford University Press, 2010.

Liebling-Kalifani, Helen, Victoria Mwaka, Ruth Ojiambo-Ochieng, Juliet Were-Oguttu, Eugene Kinyanda, Deddeh Kwekwe, Lindora Howard, and Cecilia Danuweli. "Women War Survivors of the 1989–2003 Conflict in Liberia: The Impact of Sexual and Gender-Based Violence." *Journal of International Women's Studies* 12.1 (2011): 1–21.

Lorentzen, Lois Ann and Jennifer Turpin, eds. *The Women and War Reader*. New York, NY: New York University Press, 1998.

Matadi, Morris. Personal communication. Budaburam Refugee Camp, Ghana, 2006.

Meintjes, Sheila, Anu Pillay, and Meredeth Turshen, eds. *The Aftermath: Women in Post-Conflict Transformation*. London, England: Zed Books, 2002.

Moran, Mary H. and M. Anne Pitcher. "The 'Basket Case' and the 'Post Child': Explaining the End of Civil Conflicts in Liberia and Mozambique." *Third World Quarterly* 25.3 (2004): 501–19.

Nordstrom, Carolyn. "Visible Wars and Invisible Girls, Shadow Industries, and the Politics of Not-Knowing." *International Feminist Journal of Politics* 1.1 (1999): 14–33.

Pillay, Anu. "Truth Seeking and Gender: The Liberian Experience." *African Journal of Conflict Resolution* 9.2 (2009): 91–99.

Reticker, Gini (Director) and Abigail Disney (Producer). *Pray the Devil Back to Hell*. New York, NY: Fork Films, 2008.

Rosen, David. *Armies of the Young: Child Soldiers in War and Terror*. New Brunswick, NY: Rutgers University Press, 2005.

Saa, William. Personal Communication. Accra, Ghana, 2006.

Scheper-Hughes, Nancy. "Maternal Thinking and the Politics of War." In *The Women and War Reader*, edited by Lois Ann Lorentzen and Jennifer Turpin, 229–33. New York, NY: New York University Press, 1998.

Scheper-Hughes, Nancy and Philippe Bourgois. *Violence in War and Peace: An Anthology*. Malden, MA: Blackwell, 2004.

Steady, Filomina Chioma. *Women and Leadership in West Africa: Mothering the Nation and Humanizing the State*. New York, NY: Palgrave Macmillan, 2011.

United Nations Security Council. "Peace Agreement Between the Government of Liberia (GOL), the Liberians United for Reconciliation and Democracy (LURD), the Movement for Democracy and the Political Parties (MODEL)." Accra, Ghana, August 13, 2003.

Utas, Mats. "Victimcy, Girlfriending, Soldiering: Tactic Agency in a Young Woman's Social Navigation of the Liberian War Zone." *Anthropological Quarterly* 78.2 (2005): 403–30.

Wessells, Michael. *Child Soldiers: From Violence to Protection*. Cambridge, MA: Harvard University Press, 2006.

Chapter 5

Inclusion-Exclusion of Women in Local Peacemaking Systems in the Kaffa Society of Ethiopia

Federica De Sisto

The late legal historian Aberra Jembere,[1] in describing customary law in Ethiopia, stated that it is "made by the people and not the state" and finds its legitimacy in the "participation and consensus of the community." In the Ethiopian context, local systems to make peace are widespread and have worked historically in the absence of, or together with the state justice system. Based on ethnographic fieldwork in the Kaffa society of South Western Ethiopia, this chapter briefly outlines mechanisms, processes, rules, and characteristics of the most widespread peace-making systems in use in the area vis-à-vis women.

This chapter is part of a more comprehensive research project carried out for a total of 10 months in 2008 in the Kaffa zone of South Western Ethiopia. The project focused on discriminatory practices and policies affecting a minority group in that part of the country and looked in particular at the cultural roots of discrimination and ways of addressing it. Fieldwork took place in two different *woreda*, administrative divisions managed by a local government and equivalent to a district. The *woreda* are typically collected together into zones and are divided into *kebele* or neighborhood associations, which are the smallest unit of local government in Ethiopia.

The *woreda* selected were Decha and Gimbo. Kaja Raba *kebele* in Gimbo *woreda* was the site most visited. It was chosen because of its proximity to Bonga, the principal administrative and political center of the Kaffa zone. Being also an important trading center, Bonga has attracted people from all over Ethiopia and for this reason the level of discrimination against women is believed to be lower than in other areas of Kaffa. Due to its proximity to the town, Kaja Raba can also be considered an urban environment. The study focused on the Kaja Raba *kebele* village of Baho, about a 30-minute walk off the main road to Bonga.

Decha *woreda*, on the other hand, was chosen for its rural enviroment. In Decha *woreda* the research mainly focused on the rural *kebele* of Ermo, about six kilometers south of Chiri, the administrative center of the district. Within this *kebele* the site most visited was the village of Copi Cocho. There are hardly any shops, government organizations, or community-based services in Ermo *kebele*.

To ensure optimum coverage, fieldwork was not limited to the above-mentioned areas; rather, intermittent visits were made to other sites in Kaffa as part of an effort to obtain a comprehensive picture of the socio-cultural-political scene in the area. The work was carried out using an ethnographic methodology consisting largely of semi-structured interviews and participant observation.

Based on the approach and objectives, the following criteria were elaborated for the definition of the sample:

- Small size: to acquire more detailed information;
- Variety of views: informants should be from different social groups;
- Representatives of the social setting (e.g., prominent members of the Church and traditional institutions as well as youth);
- Representatives of the various formal and nonformal institutions shaping the local context;
- Gender sensitivity.

In addition, the research was based on the key idea that the sample should be stratified in order to record differences in views and social status. To assure the sample would be rich in information, informants who were better at expressing themselves, reflecting, and articulating their knowledge were selected.[2] This argument affected the balance of the well-being and gender criteria as information in the end was mainly collected where it was the most comprehensible for the research. Overall, the process yielded 63 formal interviews, of which 21 were women (two divorced, 14 married, and five unmarried).

Along with interviews, the research made use of participant observation. As underlined by a conspicuous number of scholars,[3] the ethnographic approach allows involvement in participants' activities and the study of people in their natural settings instead of under the experimental circumstances created by the researcher. More specifically for this research, observation was mainly carried out at local houses, markets, on the road, in community gatherings such as religious congregations, political meetings, and workshops. Due to my insufficient knowledge of the local language of Kaffa the assistance of translators was also essential during fieldwork.[4]

THE KAFFA ZONE

The Kaffa zone of Southern Ethiopia consists of rugged hills and terrains, several rivers, steep valleys and thick heterogeneous forests. Locals explain the ecological features of the area through the use of myths, most notably the interaction between the male sky god and female earth goddess.[5] Myths like this, embedded in the local oral traditions, are central to the life of the inhabitants of Kaffa. In the introduction to Arthur Maurice Hocart's book *The Life-giving Myth* Lord Raglan notices that myth, ritual and social organizations are interconnected:

> Social organization originated to perform rituals and it is also dependent on myth "which purports to tell how the kinship, classes, castes, clans and so on came to be instituted, and thereby explains and justifies the part which they play in the life of community.[6]

Myths are thus inheritably linked to social organization and the mechanisms through which it works.

In Kaffa, oral tradition is in many cases used to justify an unequal redistribution of power and inclusion/exclusion from power administration of certain categories of people. To a considerable extent, local ways to administer justice reflect existing societal structures: they tend to be controlled by elderly men and reproduce unequal rights, notably with regard to women, children, and occupational minorities.[7] Women often receive unfair treatment in a number of ways that include: not being selected as mediators, facing discrimination in verdicts, and receiving less compensation than men.

The following paragraphs provide an overview of the peacemaking systems in use in the area, the leading principles upon which they are based, the dynamics that make them work, and their ways of administering justice vis-à-vis women.

RELEVANT PRINCIPLES IN PEACEMAKING SYSTEMS

According to Alula Pankhurst and Getachew Assefa[8] local systems to make peace in Ethiopia are organized under three main principles: locality, spiritual authority, and kinship.

Locality

Throughout the country, Ethiopian people who are called upon to mediate and settle disputes are well-known in the community and generally live in the same village/area as the disputants. In the Kaffa society as in other Ethiopian societies, there are ritual spaces for assemblies that consider, among other things, disputes. The venue hosting these events may be located at the periphery of the villages/communities under big trees that grant shade during lengthy sessions.

Kinship

Kinship is a strong means of promoting peace, stability, and conflict management in families and entire communities in Ethiopia as well as all across the African continents. The titles of relationship are titles of responsibilities, obligations, and duties: the roles of aunts and uncles, mothers and elderly are seen as societal roles or positions of authority.[9] The structures of kinship put in place by locals in Kaffa have often proved to be effective in maintaining security and restoring a status quo after troubled times. Kinship is thus another key principle in local systems to make peace, often complementary to territorial organization.[10] Mediators, in fact, are often selected among kin of the disputants, even in the absence of clan systems.

Spiritual Authority

Spiritual authority is another overarching principle of local systems to make peace. Spiritual authority is always present during sessions, even when it seems not to be the main component. It often assumes the form of the following recurrent rituals that are present during processes: blessing, cursing, and oath taking.

- Blessing: Peacemaking sessions are often opened and concluded with blessings by the elders or the spiritual leaders.
- Cursing: Cursing is intimately connected to blessing as its negative counterpart. It may also be used in the event that litigants fail to comply with the decision or swear falsely.
- Oath taking: This is a very important spiritual ritual in use in many peacemaking systems. Oaths are taken by all actors participating in a process: by the accused if there is no proof; by the witnesses to confirm that they will not lie; by both disputants to promise that they will comply with the decision or judgment; and by the elders to state that they will be fair in their judgment. In Kaffa, all these actors solemnly swear in front of the village in the name of their ancestors. The supernatural is invoked to witness, as speakers call upon it.

The principles of locality, kinship, and spiritual authority are common features of the three main and overlapping forms of local justice in use in the research sites.

LOCAL JUSTICE IN KAFFA

The use of local systems of making peace have a long history of successfully resolving disputes, including those which could be described as civil, criminal, commercial, and individual disputes. They are backed with legitimacy from the community and this explains why they are still widely used today despite the spread of formal judicial structures.

In Kaffa the main local systems to make peace are:

- Elders' moot, locally known as *kabechino*;
- Religious leaders, especially leaders of the traditional belief;
- Self-help associations, notably funeral, which can become involved in dispute settlements among members.

The *Kabechino*: Mechanism, Rules, and the Gender Question

The most common peacemaking system in both research sites is known as *kabechino* which means a group of elders ad hoc selected and involved in mediation. The term finds its roots in the word *kabecho* a term in the local language referring to an aged person. In practice, though, elders tend to be those who have the time, experience, respect, and standing to engage in reconciling litigants. The term is also inherently linked to patriarchal notions as it refers to male elders. In fact, women are not selected as elders and according to research participants the reason for this exclusion is to be found in characteristics generally ascribed to them: temperamental and too emotional, thus not fitted for the role.

The number of elders in a *kabechino* varies according to the importance of the issues. Once cases are referred to the elders, they fix the place and time for meetings. Deliberation is through consultation with the contenders. Normally the session is held in the morning and under a big tree. The process of dispute settlements takes place by first hearing the cases of the involved parties individually, then jointly in a public session. This gives the elders the opportunity to concentrate on points of disagreement between parties and assist in fact-finding and reconciliation. The role of witnesses is kept to a minimum because the disputants are forewarned to speak the truth and are trusted to do so, in most cases for fear of the harsh social consequences (threat of expulsion).

As this institution tends to reflect patriarchal values, it is also often discriminatory in its judgments toward women. Women are excluded from the selection procedure to become a member of *kabechino*, and although in the vast majority of the cases they are able to represent themselves at judicial processes, discrimination by elders against women often becomes evident in judgments. Pankhurst and Assefa[11] note that in family conflicts between husbands and wives elders would tendencially try to persuade women to return to their husbands, occasionally asking only for an excuse by the husband or, for reparation, the provision of an item such as a dress, for example. In cases of divorce, "elders may not ensure that women obtain their portion of the property so that divorced women are among the poorest and most disadvantaged."[12] Similarly, in cases of inheritance, women may face discrimination in the form of receiving less or being "inherited" themselves and remarried against their will to a brother of their deceased husband.

In land disputes, which are very common in Kaffa, widows' claims are often challenged by more powerful contenders. A widow recounted how her neighbor stole her portion of bordering land after her husband died.

> I was shocked to realize that a few days after my beloved husband passed away, my neighbor moved the fence that separated my property from his and stole a portion of my land. I went to his house to complain and he shouted at me. I then referred the case to the *kabechino* and they agreed on hearing my case but when the judgment was made I had to give up a small part of my land for the sake of good relationships with my neighbor. I was also told that I had to comply with the judgment and not to complain anymore.

In terms of judgment, domestic violence, abruption, and rape may be condemned but not necessarily punished. Elders may simply try to arrange marriages after an act of abruption. Overall, this system of making peace seems to work toward a restoration of stability and maintenance of patriarchal control rather then securing positive peace and social justice.

Spirit-based Dispute Resolution

Religious leaders, notably leaders of the local traditional belief, play a key role in the process of making peace in Kaffa. From unknown time, the vast majority of the people of Kaffa believe in the possession spirit known as *eko*, which comes to a person after his/her father's death. Once the person is chosen by an *eko*, he/she becomes an *alamo* (one who can communicate with ancestral spirits) and the spirit will appear through the person until death. In ordinary life, before a spirit possesses the *alamo*, they lead a life like anyone else in the community, but when possessed, they become a changed personality and do not exercise their own actions anymore but those of the spirit.[13]

Among the Kaffa people, possession cults have always played a central role and the *alamo* or medium can be of assistance in solving conflicts. In many cases, this form of dispute resolution is used when issues cannot be solved by local elders, or where there is no final proof but just suspicion on the part of the victim. The latter generally approaches the spirit medium who will call upon the counterpart; failure to appear before the medium is said to result in bad luck, death, or illness. When both parties are present they may be questioned and the medium will enter a trance to obtain the verdict from the spirit. The final settlement may, however, involve elders who finalize the agreement and reconciliation. It is believed that through the threat of invoking the spirits mediums can make those who are guilty come forward, confess, and agree on reconciliation.

The medium can be either male or female, although males are superior in number. Even if the figure of the *alamo* has played a significant role in projecting an image of social structure and supporting the power of the existing male elite, according to female research participants, the *alamo* nowadays tend to be less discriminatory than in the past when it comes to compensation for harm caused to women by their male contenders. Research participants attribute this gender opening to the presence of female *alamo* who tend to be more fair in their judgments toward members of their same sex and, in doing so, might have positively influenced their male colleagues.

The *Iddir*

The last peacemaking systems examined in this paper are indigenous voluntary mutual help associations known as *iddir*. Alula Pankhurst and Damen Haile Mariam[14] define *iddir* as "indigenous voluntary associations established primarily not only to provide mutual aid in burial matters but also to address other community concerns." They can be found throughout Ethiopia, in rural as well as more urban settings. Initially born with the aim of taking care of activities linked to burial ceremonies and supporting its members in time of grievances, the *iddir* ensures a payout in cash and in kind at the time of a funeral for a deceased member of the family and of the group.[15] Generally, a tent and goods are lent to the member's family in mourning time. This traditional funeral association is strictly organized with leaders democratically elected. The *iddir* members live in a geographically defined area, and every month or every two weeks contribute a certain amount of money to offset the expenses of burial cost.[16] They, however, have progressively expanded their range of activities and have now become multifunctional institutions able to provide mutual help and financial assistance in emergency situations for their members.[17] The composition of an *iddir*, the number of members, its functions and organizations, may vary from one *iddir* to another, but they are all based on a voluntary, mutual agreement between community members that collaborate when one of them or one of their direct relatives faces a serious shock. Thus the *iddir* are based on strong bonds among its members.[18]

In Kaffa, the *iddir* are often consulted through their leaders to solve disputes. The disputants refer the matter of dispute to the *iddir* leaders and the leaders enquire into it by checking all evidence at their disposal. Disputants must present detailed evidence and introduce their witnesses. *Iddir* leaders assess and evaluate the evidence, questioning and probing the witnesses and the disputants. They then discuss the aspects of the evidence among themselves in order to reach a decision and pass judgment; the decision is usually announced by the chairman of the *iddir* and written copies are distributed to the victim, the wrongdoer, and to the secretary.

The outcome of the judgment may be an apology with or without reparation of the damages. In the case of an apology, the victim must express willingness to accept it. In a case where reparation is needed, the reparation should take into account the economic status of the wrongdoer. Reparation can be in the form of medical expenses, of a sheep to be slaughtered as a sacrifice for blood-reparation, or some other financial expenses related to the dispute. To reinforce the decision, sanctions including financial penalties and informal enforcement mechanisms such as the decision to remove the disputant from *iddir* membership might be used. Refusal to comply with the decision may in fact result in refusal of community members to participate at social events involving the disputant, such as funerals and weddings.

Iddir membership is open to all regardless of gender. It should however be noted that *iddir* members who are considered to have full membership are often males, meaning husbands or the head of the family. Wives are generally seen as indirect members, with exception made for widows who become the head of a household if their male children are not of the age to take over their father's role.

Women perform specific services in *iddir*, such as preparation of food or coffee during funeral ceremonies. They can also form their own subcommittee that functions like the general community *iddir*. The women's subcommittee is self-directed with a board of women leaders elected by other female members. As it happens with all subcommittees, they report to the community *iddir* during meetings. Written rules exist as well as registration books that are used to record the involvement of every woman in the *iddir*.

In cases where a quarrel arises within members of the women's *iddir*, the women's *iddir* board will try to solve it. If it is not possible to reach an agreement, the case will then be referred to the community *iddir*.

When the dispute sees opponents of a different gender, then the community *iddir* is considered competent to solve it. In this case, the local rule-based system applied by the community *iddir* leaders (all males) shows the enduring practice that reinforces gender inequality through "community harmony." As for *kabechino*, this is particularly evident as women try to maintain control over land and efforts are challenged by village males.

One research participant recounted the case of a friend, who after divorcing her husband, met another man and invited him to live in her house. She later married him in a traditional marriage. The man then became head of the household. A few years after marriage the new husband decided to divorce the woman on the basis of a mental disease he allegedly said she suffered from. The woman, in shock, referred the case to the *iddir*. The *iddir* members, after hearing the case, agreed on the divorce and obliged her to sign the divorce agreement. Eventually, the woman's inability to read and write brought her to sign an agreement whereby her land was released to the man who was better able to expose his case and was favored by social rules.

THE CULTURAL DIMENSION OF GENDER INEQUALITY

Improving literacy and fostering education is a key step on the path to promoting gender empowerment and a more gender-balanced society. Women's restricted access to education and the incapability of many in rural areas to read and write has also affected their vulnerability to the traditional peacemaking institutions. Formal education however, is not sufficient in the attempt to reach gender equality, especially in the presence of a male-dominant society. In fact, the women interviewed pointed at the inability to receive a fair hearing as the main cause of inequality during judgment. The same problem was identified in a study by Tihut Asfaw and Terre Satterfield, who looked at gender relations in local-level dispute settlements in North Western Ethiopia.[19]

On the whole, despite all the transformations happening in the Kaffa society, discrimination against women has a strong social and cultural impact that is far more complex than can be dealt with through only economics or law. The assumption that gender imbalance is merely the lack of economic power and fair distribution of resources and therefore can be solved by economic packages and political reforms, is in fact one-sided. Such an analysis fails to understand the complex social formation, attachments, interaction, and structure found in this traditional society in the same way that it fails to understand the power of culture. Embedded and internalized social norms based on sets of values and beliefs nurture divisions and are responsible for social closure by restricting access to resources and opportunity to women. While the transformation of society encompasses many layers and dimensions of intervention, this process is guaranteed to fail if the cultural dimension of violence remains unaddressed.

Johan Galtung[20] argues that the achievement of peace in a society is a more complex process than the mere absence of direct violence (negative peace). While attempts to stop events that kill or harm members of a society are certainly key, such efforts will be useless if the belief/value system that vindicates the direct and structural violence is not challenged.[21] It is only when overt and covert aspects of violence are tackled that social justice through equal opportunity, a fair distribution of power and resources, equal protection, and impartial enforcement of law can be reached. Indeed, the concept of peace involves breaking down the structures of exploitation, marginalization and fragmentation of people and groups, the preservation and defense of human rights, the elimination of structural discrimination, the development of more just and equitable systems, the encouragement and appreciation of diversity through community dialogue and cultural exchange, and the conscious effort to build a society which reflects these commitments.[22]

In Kaffa, the cultural dimension of discrimination against women has not yet been addressed. Culture is indeed used to describe ideologies, convictions, traditions, and systems of legitimacy with whose help direct or structural violence is made possible, justified, and *de facto* legitimatized. Throughout this study those who denied, officially or unofficially, that women should have the same rights as men claimed to be defending the local tradition. A potent shaper of individual's and group's behavior, the mainstream culture of Kaffa is considered by local communities as the root of discrimination against women and its grounds for justification.

In this scenario, local peacemaking institutions that stem from local culture seem to bring a peace that has the connotations of a ceasefire in the sense that it only refers to the absence of direct violence. These systems can thus only work in the framework of the *status quo*, or restoration of the old order. They are difficult to apply with regard to conflicts against the community, conflicts that challenge the framework of values and relations of the traditional order.

CONCLUSION

During fieldwork in the Kaffa zone of South Western Ethiopia, three main local systems to make peace were identified: the *kabechino*, belief-based systems, and self-help associations. The first term refers to a group of elders defined by age, experience, and love for peace. The elders function as a court with broad and flexible powers to interpret evidence, impose judgments, and manage the process of reconciliation. Statements are followed by open deliberation that may integrate listening to witnesses, holding private consultations, and considering solutions. The elders use their judgment and position of moral ascendancy to find an acceptable solution. Decisions may be based on consensus within the elders' or chiefs' council and may be rendered on the spot. Resolution may involve forgiveness and mutual formal release of the problem, and, if necessary, the arrangement of restitution.

The second, belief-based systems, refers to the justice administered by leaders of the traditional *eko* belief. Contenders bring the case in front of the religious leader who reaches a decision after having heard what the parties have to say.

Under the third category of local peacemaking systems fall the self-help associations. Among them, this research looked at the role of the *iddir*. When a dispute arises, the contenders call on the *iddir* leaders for justice. The leaders will pass judgments after an enquiry into the matter and following discussion with other members of the *iddir*.

All these institutions are built on cultural rules linked to local belief systems, and are based on localized trust among people who know each other and have face-to-face contact within the community.

With regard to gender issues, the research findings showed a clear problem of inequality. Embedded ideas and negative stereotypes about women permeate the society to such an extent that all societal institutions reflect this asymmetry. Hence, despite their wide coverage, local systems of making peace are quintessentially serving particular groups. They reflect existing hierarchies and reproduce unequal rights.

Whether based on religious leaders (*alamo*), elderly wisdom (*kabechino*) or funeral associations (*iddir*), the laws and procedures that apply during judgment have their basis in the idea of male superiority. The peace that these institutions in Kaffa are able to bring seems then to be limited to the restoration of the traditional order in the society. They are not able to produce positive peace filled with constructive content such as the creation of social systems that serve the needs of the whole population, the achievement of more balanced gender relationships, and the constructive resolution of conflict.

NOTES

1. Aberra Jembere, "Customary Law," vol. 1 of *Encyclopaedia Aethiopica*, ed. Siegbert Uhlig (Wiesbaden, Germany: Harrassowitz Verlag, 2003).

2. Burke Johnson and Larry B. Christensen, *Educational Research: Quantitative, Qualitative and Mixed Approaches*, 3rd ed. (Thousand Oaks, CA: Sage, 2008), 221–50.

3. Paul Atkinson and Martyn Hammersley, "Ethnography and Participant Observation," in *Handbook of Qualitative Research*, ed. Norman K. Denzin and Yvonna S. Lincoln (Thousand Oaks, CA: Sage, 1994); Fredrik Barth, *Balinese Worlds* (Chicago, IL: University of Chicago Press, 1993), 23; Bernard H. Russell, *Research Methods in Anthropology: Qualitative and Quantitative Approaches*, 4th ed. (Oxford, England: AltaMira Press, 2006), 342–86.

4. When a researcher needs the help of a translator to carry out the work, it is assumed that the interpreter must be neutral. However, the interviewer can never be a depersonalized data collecting instrument purified of the bias, as stated by Ian Macpherson in "Some Questions and Answers for External Researchers Attempting to Conduct Ethnographic Case Studies in Developing Countries," MA Thesis, Oxford University, 2002. He argues that even the best approximation of a translation of a sentence into another language may be difficult in the heat of an unstructured interview.

More than simply interpreters, the translators were considered as "research assistants." Their experience in fact was invaluable for the research. However, they showed a tendency to control the interview, as described by Maria Birbili in "Translating from One Language to Another," *Social Research Update* no. 31, 2000, accessed February 18, 2014, http://www.sru.soc.surrey.ac.uk. In these cases, it is important to take into account some factors that influence the quality of the translation. Three main factors were identified by Bogusia Temple in "Watch Your Tongue: Issues in Translation and Cross-Cultural Research," *Sociology* 31.3 (1997).

1. The interpreter's effect on the communication process;
2. The interpreter's effect on the translation (English competence of the translator);
3. The interpreter's effect on the informant.

The first two of these three factors had some limiting effect on this research. I worked with four different research assistants and in three out of four cases the research assistants were found to be persons used to explaining things and adding particulars rather than listening "neutrally" and reporting only what has been said by the participants. Once, for instance, during an interview the participant was asked if he was familiar with any peacemaking systems and was also asked to list them. While the participant mentioned only two systems and named them, in translating from local language into English, the research assistant added explanations on how these systems worked. Additionally, with English language competencies of the research assistants somewhat limited, it is probable that some important information was lost in translation.

5. Gezahen Petros, "Differentiation and Integration: Craft-Workers and Manjo in the Social Stratification of Kaffa, Southwest Ethiopia," MA Thesis, University of Berger, 2003.

6. Arthur Maurice Hocart, *The Life-Giving Myth, and Other Essays* (London, England: Mathuen, 1952); Lord Raglan, Introduction to *The Life-Giving Myth, and Other Essays* by Arthur Maurice Hocart (London, England: Methuen, 1952), 6.

7. Occupational minorities are marginalized minority groups who are defined by occupation or notional occupation. The dominant farming population articulates the social and cultural exclusion of craftworkers by giving them different labels and considering that their profession is polluting. In South Western Ethiopia members of occupational groups are known for being potters, tanners, smiths, weavers, woodworkers, and hunters.

8. Alula Pankhurst and Getachew Assefa, eds., *Ethiopia at a Justice Crossroads: the Challenge of Customary Dispute Resolution* (Unpublished manuscript, Addis Ababa, Ethiopia: Centre Français des Études Éthiopiennes, 2008), 43–48.

9. Faith Sibanda, Lindiwe Ndlovu, and Beatrice Lntern, "Ndebele Kinship Structures: A Solid Base for Conflict Management, Peace and Security in Our Communities," *Humanities and Social Sciences Letters* 2.2 (2014): 108–19.

10. Pankhurst and Assefa, *Ethiopia at a Justice Crossroads*, 44–45.

11. Ibid., 61.

12. Ibid.

13. Petros, "Differentiation and Integration."

14. Alula Pankhurst and Damen Haile Mariam, "The *Iddir* in Ethiopia: Historical Development, Social Function, and Potential Role in HIV/AIDS Prevention and Control," *Northeast African Studies* 7.2 (2000).

15. Stefan Dercon et al., "Group-Based Funeral Insurance in Ethiopia and Tanzania," *World Development* 34.4 (2006).

16. Bart Van Halteren, "The Socio-Cultural and Socio-Economic Position of the Manjo of Kaffecho-Shekacho Zone" (Unpublished report, Bonga, Ethiopia: Government of Kaffa Zone, 1996).

17. Dirk Bustorf and Charles G. H. Schaefer, "Edder," vol. 2 of *Encyclopaedia Aethiopica*, ed. Siegbert Uhlig (Wiesbaden, Germany: Harrassowitz Verlag, 2005).

18. Dejene Aredo, "The Informal and Semiformal Financial Sectors in Ethiopia: A Study of the *Iqqub*, *Iddir* and Savings and Credit Co-operatives," Research Paper 21 (Nairobi, Kenya: AERC, 1993), 29.

19. Tihut Asfaw and Terre Satterfield, "Gender Relations in Local-Level Dispute Settlement in Ethiopia's Zeghie Peninsula," *Research in Human Ecology* 17.2 (2010).

20. Johan Galtung, "Cultural Violence," *Journal of Peace Research* 27.3 (1990).

21. Johan Galtung, *Peace by Peaceful Means: Peace, Conflict, Development and Civilization* (London, England: Sage, 1996).

22. Johan Galtung, "Violence, Peace and Peace Research," *Journal of Peace Research* 6.3 (1969): 167–91.

BIBLIOGRAPHY

Aredo, Dejene. "The Informal and Semiformal Financial Sectors in Ethiopia: A Study of the *Iqqub*, *Iddir* and Savings and Credit Co-operatives." Research Paper 21. Nairobi, Kenya: African Economic Research Consortium (AERC), 1993.

Asfaw, Tihut and Terre Satterfield. "Gender Relations in Local-Level Dispute Settlement in Ethiopia's Zeghie Peninsula." *Research in Human Ecology* 17.2 (2010): 160–74.

Atkinson, Paul and Martyn Hammersley. "Ethnography and Participant Observation." In *Handbook of Qualitative Research*, edited by Norman K. Denzin and Yvonna S. Lincoln, 248–61. Thousand Oaks, CA: Sage, 1994.

Barth, Fredrik. *Balinese Worlds*. Chicago, IL: University of Chicago Press, 1993.

Birbili, Maria. "Translating from One Language to Another." *Social Research Update* no. 31, 2000. Accessed February 18, 2014. http://www.sru.soc.surrey.ac.uk.

Bustorf, Dirk and Charles G. H. Schaefer. "Edder." Vol. 2 of *Encyclopaedia Aethiopica*, edited by Siegbert Uhlig, 225–27. Wiesbaden, Germany: Harrassowitz Verlag, 2005.

Dercon, Stefan, Tessa Bold, Joachim De Weerdt, and Alula Pankhurst. "Group-Based Funeral Insurance in Ethiopia and Tanzania." *World Development* 34.4 (2006): 685–703.

Galtung, Johan. "Cultural Violence." *Journal of Peace Research* 27.3 (1990): 291–305.

———. *Peace by Peaceful Means: Peace, Conflict, Development and Civilization.* London, England: Sage, 1996.

———. "Violence, Peace and Peace Research." *Journal of Peace Research* 6.3 (1969): 167–91.

Hocart, Arthur Maurice. *The Life-Giving Myth, and Other Essays.* London, England: Methuen, 1952.

Jembere, Aberra. "Customary Law." Vol. 1 of *Encyclopaedia Aethiopica*, edited by Siegbert Uhlig, 839–41. Wiesbaden, Germany: Harrassowitz Verlag, 2003.

Johnson, Burke and Larry B. Christensen. *Educational Research: Quantitative, Qualitative, and Mixed Approaches.* 3rd ed. Thousand Oaks, CA: Sage, 2008.

Macpherson, Ian. "Some Questions and Answers for External Researchers Attempting to Conduct Ethnographic Case Studies in Developing Countries." MA Thesis, Oxford University, 2002.

Pankhurst, Alula and Damen Haile Mariam. "The *Iddir* in Ethiopia: Historical Development, Social Function, and Potential Role in HIV/AIDS Prevention and Control." *Northeast African Studies* 7.2 (2000): 35–57.

Pankhurst, Alula and Getachew Assefa, eds. *Ethiopia at a Justice Crossroads: The Challenge of Customary Dispute Resolution.* Unpublished manuscript. Addis Ababa, Ethiopia: Centre Français des Études Éthiopiennes, 2008.

Petros, Gezahen. "Differentiation and Integration: Craft-Workers and Manjo in the Social Stratification of Kaffa, Southwest Ethiopia." MA Thesis, University of Berger, 2003.

Raglan, Lord. Introduction to *The Life-Giving Myth, and Other Essays* by Arthur Maurice Hocart, 6–8. London, England: Methuen, 1952.

Russell, Bernard H. *Research Methods in Anthropology: Qualitative and Quantitative Approaches.* 4th ed. Oxford, England: AltaMira, 2006.

Sibanda, Faith, Lindiwe Ndlovu and Beatrice Lntern. "Ndebele Kinship Structures: A Solid Base for Conflict Management, Peace and Security in Our Communities." *Humanities and Social Sciences Letters* 2.2 (2014): 108–19.

Temple, Bogusia. "Watch Your Tongue: Issues in Translation and Cross-Cultural Research." *Sociology* 31.3 (1997): 607–18.

Van Halteren, Bart. "The Socio-Cultural and Socio-Economic Position of the Manjo of Kaffecho-Shekacho Zone." Unpublished report. Bonga, Ethiopia: Government of Kaffa Zone, 1996.

Chapter 6

A Positive Peace Initiative with Rural Women in China

Maria Cheung and Tuula Heinonen

In this chapter, writing from outside China, we use a peacebuilding framework to reflect on a collaborative social work project completed from 2004 to 2010 in China. Since experience and knowledge are shaped by and within national social institutions, we do not claim to represent the views of anyone else involved in the project. The women whose words are included in the chapter have not been part of this exploration of peacebuilding nor do we know if they have or could have similar sentiments to those expressed in this chapter.

According to Johan Galtung, "peace is the absence/reduction of violence of all kinds." He elaborates, "peace work is work to reduce violence by peaceful means."[1] Galtung further defines *negative peace* and *positive peace*, where negative peace refers to "the absence of violence of all kinds."[2] On the other hand, positive peace refers to transformations within and across institutions that rectify structural inequities. Positive peace involves actions that prevent violence.

In many settings, positive peace efforts take place at the grassroots level through experiences that change values and attitudes and, subsequently, behavior. In this chapter we describe the outcomes of a project that employed participatory training methods to develop a climate of inclusivity, egalitarian relations and local innovation with and for rural women in China. We will also describe changes that occurred by drawing on the accounts of those who work for the Communist Party at the All China Women's Federation and the rural women in the villages in which they provided services.

WOMEN AND PEACE

Peace processes have not often included women at the formal meetings of decision-making bodies. This may be because peacebuilding has occurred in the context of negotiations during conflicts or in post-conflict situations that have involved military personnel and national leaders who are primarily men. However, there are good reasons why women need to be included in such processes. A publication of the International Association for Humanitarian Policy and Conflict Resolution states: "[W]omen involved in these processes will help design a lasting peace that will be advantageous to the empowerment, inclusion and protection of women."[3]

Based on her peace work with women in Hong Kong, mainland China and Taiwan, Shun Hing Chan conceptualizes positive peace as a holistic concept that includes gender equality, education, and sustainable livelihood. She articulates that peacebuilding takes place in "the everyday," which includes actions taken at the individual, group, and community levels to promote peace.[4] Building a peace process involves cultural values related to hard work, persistence, and harmony, qualities that women bring to bear in the face of a harsh environment and struggles to sustain a livelihood. Chan wrote:

> Whether as elected officials, members of worker cooperatives, or environmental entrepreneurs, women use their different positioning and tactics to exercise power and sustain their work, which indirectly subverts unequal power relationships while building a balanced cultural ecology. Securing the rights of indigenous people, defending the livelihoods of low-income workers, and cultivating cultural values and sustainable environments are new kinds of peacemaking that require persistence, creativity and intensive negotiation.[5]

Julie Drolet and Tuula Heinonen find that in some traditional rural settings and localities women's engagement with family and household, including home-based economic production and animal-raising, in comparison to men's involvement in wage earning away from the household, represents different needs, interests, and priorities[6] and, thus, the meaningful inclusion of women's experiences and perspectives in discussions of peacebuilding are required. However, shifts in roles and responsibilities may occur due to social and economic change, processes and effects related to violence and conflict, and these will be accompanied by resultant and often differential effects on women's and men's lives.

We embarked on a six-year international project in partnership with academic institutions and a number of All China Women's Federations (ACWF) from several provinces to work in three regions of rural China with the aim of building capacity in over 500 front line ACWF cadres employed by the Chinese Communist Party.[7] The purpose of the project was to promote gender equality and human rights.[8] We adopted participatory methods in a series of social work training courses in five counties of the project areas, including two counties in Sichuan (southwestern China), two in Inner Mongolia and a smaller county in Shandong. Twenty-six townships and 73 villages from the five counties were involved in the project. The three provinces in which the project was implemented represented different developmental stages in economic development and marketization as a result of Deng Xiaoping's reform strategies since 1978.[9]

Although structural oppression and violence are not easily discussed by people in China, there has, however, been some latitude in discussion and activities around women's human rights and entitlements. During this six-year project, our university partners designed and delivered participatory training programs for the Women's Federation in each project site and enabled cross-site learning between them. We collaborated to conduct workshops for students and non-governmental organizations (NGOs) that work with rural migrants in Beijing and participated in an annual exchange program for faculty members, students, and leaders in the ACWF and local governments. We also trained three Master of Social Work students who graduated and later applied their newly acquired knowledge in the project sites.

In this chapter, we examine the project's outcome and critically discuss how our project contributed to building a culture of peace that transcended what might be seen as an otherwise rigid and hierarchical context that structurally oppresses rural women. During the years of this project, we witnessed a change of culture in the everyday lives of women and their respective communities that contributed toward a process of peacebuilding.

WOMEN'S WORK IN CHINA

In rural China, the role of organizing women is monopolized by the ACWF. Nonparty state-controlled NGOs are nearly nonexistent in our project sites. ACWF is a mass organization formed under the Chinese Communist Party to carry out the Party's political work.[10] Since economic reforms in 1978, the Women's Federation has assumed a more active role in mobilizing women to participate in economic development. The ACWF is the main actor in organizing activities and services for local women, including matters of domestic dispute. The Women's Federation also serves as the main resource for mobilizing women in economic production and carrying out centralized policies.

The ACWF structure starts at the national level and terminates at the township level in rural areas. At the village level, a nominal honorarium is given to a local woman resident (called *funu zhuren*) appointed by the ACWF to carry out officially prescribed duties in mobilizing grassroots women to support party policies. Although most of the paid cadres were university trained, they were not prepared or specifically trained for *women's work* (as social services with women are referred to in the ACWF organization). Those at the township level need to fulfill duties other than women's work and have limited external resources and support to do so.[11] With its top-down, party-oriented approach to management and communication, the ACWF has had difficulty gaining the trust or support of rural women over the years.[12]

Without any formal structure for NGOs in the rural project sites, our project's main partner was the ACWF in each respective site. We conducted social work training with the ACWF local women leaders and cadres on gender equality, and social work skills based on humanistic principles and practice that were adapted to suit Chinese indigenous cultures. The social work training was grounded in participatory and interactive methods,[13] which focused on relationship building underscored by principles of *power-with* and *power-to-empower* others.[14] Western knowledge was adapted to local culture and context and trainers from Chinese university partners drew on local knowledge and experiences of rural women. We used participatory rural appraisal (PRA) to work with rural women to identify needs in their local communities.[15] The main idea of PRA is that by using a participatory method and seeing villagers as local experts, the villagers can work together to resolve local issues collectively and on their own. PRA often involves the use of appropriate and available technology from the local environment, such as pebbles, grains, and beans, to represent information. Villagers who are very familiar with these local materials can participate by using them, even if limited by low literacy or numeracy, to cast votes on their views or priorities of concern. During project training, cadre trainees worked together in small groups on the floor to draw community maps and voice their perceived needs and dreams for improvement in their villages. The PRA methods were widely used in project sites not only to conduct needs assessments, but also to democratically make community decisions. For example, a democratic method was used to select a model family in the village, which sharply contrasted with the conventional method in which only the local authority was designated to choose. The result of encouraging rural women to express their own opinions was more local participation that reflected the rural women's interests. The ACWF cadres promoted a greater variety of activities for rural women and their families.

At the beginning our project partners were worried about the use of community organizing due to the sensitivity of grassroots organizing as a method in China. Without naming it as such, the end result of employing participatory methods was similar to some community organizing strategies and outcomes from outside of China.[16] In the project sites during PRA workshops, women identified issues such as poor water resources, lack of road infrastructure to support their economic activities, inadequate health care facilities and few women's voices in community leadership. The most common need identified in all sites was for technical knowledge about agriculture and animal-raising for income generation. At the end of the six-year project, through mutual aid projects and learning ways to access and negotiate resources with local authorities, water pumps were installed and roads were built in local communities. A small number of women won local elections and had more say in community and political affairs. Women's needs, particularly in health care, were better addressed. Women led their households by engaging in new economic activities. As a result, women's status in social and economic domains was raised in their families and communities.

MAJOR ACHIEVEMENTS FOSTERING A CULTURE OF PEACE

1. Accessing Traditional Cooperative Values which Humanized the *Other* and Built Trust

At the beginning of project training for ACWF cadres, the trainees were skeptical of the participatory approaches, which were unfamiliar to them. The approaches adopted by the project contrasted with the conventional top-down, didactic approach imposed by the upper hierarchy. With some skill development and practice, the trainees tried out their new methods as they sat in circles, a format which generated interaction and learning in a way they had not experienced before. Into the second year of the project training, the cadres started reporting a change in their own lives such as an increase in communication with their children and families and, hence, improved relationships. In their everyday work encounters they noticed how a different approach could bring about positive engagement with the rural women they served. They welcomed this new approach and adapted the knowledge to their practice in local cultural contexts.

> In the first couple of training sessions, I resisted [social work ideas], considering them practically useless.
>
> During the course of training, when we heard about these, we were all so excited, it's like butterflies in the stomach. We just think, after we come back, we would like to do something when we go back.

The change required disciplined action, constant self-observation and reflection, as well as feedback from and exchange with other cadres who found this change equally challenging. The positive response of cadres, especially among the village directors, and the remarkable increase in local women's participation in the various community projects confirmed that these changes in method were indeed bearing positive results. Seeing results from applying these methods reinforced their continued use among the cadres and led to further evolution of their participatory approach within the practicum context. The participatory interaction and collective reflection created an alternative way of knowing that was flexible and interpersonally connected.

In our project's outcome study, the trained participants provided evidence of remarkable changes as a result of the social work training. One of the greatest achievements of the project was that the ACWF cadres began to work more collaboratively with rural women who came for help. They no longer saw these women in the category of *other* or as women inferior to them. Many cadres spoke about the contrast between the newly learned and applied bottom-up approach with the previously applied judgmental, top-down and rigid approach. Instead of using the old mode of giving orders to rural women, the cadres learned to listen to their service recipients and built their own capacity for empathy toward their rural service recipients. One of the greatest achievements was removing some of the hierarchies imposed by the system. A more egalitarian relationship emerged in the cadres' relationships with those they served.

After training, many trained Women's Federation cadres noted greater trust and respect for the rural women and families to whom they provided services:

> After we learned this social work method, we now approach things from bottom to top, to know about their needs; then we will launch the services in an appropriate way [according to people's needs]. I think this is much better.
>
> The clients we are dealing with are all socially vulnerable people. I used to think that they were all incapable. But, after the training, I believe that those people are also respectable and capable. Thirdly, my work attitudes have changed a lot. I used to only do the work that was assigned by others. Now, I try my best to find the work by myself in order to help others better.

Following training on gender equality, PRA, and social work methods, cadres learned and tried to apply principles such as respect for privacy, self-determination, being nonjudgmental, and helping others so they could help themselves, as contrasted with earlier top-down methods.

> After this project, we learned to respect each other and to keep their information confidential. . . . [In the past] we helped them make the decision, but now they make the decision by themselves. We are no longer their leader. Instead . . . we give women some references and comments, and we do not impose our own ideas but let them make a decision by themselves. The results are better than what they were in the past.

Respect for the individual, understanding, and genuine regard for the right to self-determination were developed through training as reflected in the following scenario about a domestic dispute shared by a cadre:

> Previously, when I tried to resolve family disputes such as fights and quarrels between husband and wife, I was also very *angry* when they came to me for help. I would usually directly give them my opinions and comments regarding their dispute. After they both agreed to my comments, I asked them to write and sign a contract indicating commitment to prevent future similar disputes from happening again. But this method was not effective enough and could only solve problems temporarily. After a while, they started to quarrel and fight again.
>
> When the same couple came to my office again, this time I listened to their complaints carefully and asked the woman to decide how she really wanted to solve the dispute. She decided to sue her husband, take him to court, and divorce him. Generally, a court hearing does not result in the immediate approval of a divorce. The judge took a short period of time to try to resolve their dispute first before divorcing them. During this period, her husband realized how serious it was this time. So he stopped drinking alcohol and started to work really hard like he had before. Then the wife slowly changed her mind and expressed concern to her husband. Later on the husband moved back to the house and lived together again with his wife. She withdrew her divorce application from the court, so the problem was resolved. I don't have to force them to sign the contract and become their guarantor.

In the outcome study conducted in 2010, project participants reported that conflicts with in-laws had been reduced. Family communication and relations improved. Women learned and applied various methods in handling conflicts that resulted in less occurrence of domestic violence. Many mothers-in-law became more supportive of their daughters-in-law when they saw the younger women become economically active and bringing additional income to the family. The shift in women's economic status at home changed gender relationships in the household. Women were treated with more respect at home. Decision-making patterns changed. The women's husbands listened to their views more and they became more supportive, taking on household tasks such as cooking and housework that were traditionally assigned to women. The spouses were proud of their wives' newly acquired role in leading the family in economic achievement and sustainable livelihoods.[17] In the agricultural project areas, women were engaged in producing high-value cash crops, and sideline electronic production work, while in pastoral areas women acquired the skills to raise chickens and goats. Both women leaders and cadres reported increased self-esteem and confidence, and greater awareness of needs and their own potential. The knowledge acquired by ACWF cadres equipped them with a new approach in working with rural women. The new training they offered to rural women helped local women increase their self-confidence, hence, realizing greater self-esteem and better self-care.

2. Building Social Capital and Caring Communities through Cooperation

In Sichuan and Inner Mongolia, over 100 mutual aid groups were formed in local villages during the six years of the project. In the villages where we conducted outcome studies women were mobilized and took the lead in negotiating resources with local government to build pumping stations to relieve them of the heavy labor of increasing farm work. In one village, in a joint, practical effort with men, women worked toward more sustainable livelihood for the village by opening up a canal so that water pumped from a lower level could run through the canal and irrigate their farmland.[18]

Women formed themselves into different self-help groups to support one another socially and economically. Some formed micro-credit groups to obtain small-scale loans to support new economic activities. With financial help to start up local businesses, some women became entrepreneurs by opening hardware or other shops or engaging in recycling businesses. The social work practice methods that the cadres had learned taught them how to coordinate different kinds of available resources to enable the women to start these local businesses. Following is a story told by a cadre at the end of the project:

> When [the rural woman] originally came to us, she told us she was motivated to start the business, but was afraid of losing money and did not have the capital she needed. We helped her get a loan from the *Rural Credit Co-operatives* but, as this loan was not sufficient, we also loaned her some through micro-credit groups. We no longer only sought social assistance from the local civil affairs department, which would have been our previous approach. This change in approach was more effective. As the old Chinese proverb tells us: "It is better to teach one how to fish than to give one a fish, for the one who is taught will eat for a lifetime, not only for a day."

The following story told by a trainee in a photovoice session (involving photography as a data collection strategy) is representative of many village women's stories of achievement that captures the process of building social capital:

> Originally, she was the only *left behind* woman in the village who had become rich by raising pigs. Then she started a mutual aid group in the community to teach group members pig-raising techniques and experiences. Because of her efforts, more than 30 women followed her example and started to raise pigs. This has been done exclusively by this *left behind* woman.
>
> In some of the villages, we heard from women about their dreams of having a concrete road so that they could transport their fresh produce to the market on time. During the outcome study we heard that, in some project sites, roads were built and the women's incomes had increased. Since most of their spouses

> migrated to work in urban centres, the women organized themselves to repair the road. In other villages, women told us that some had to wait to participate in such projects as all were enthusiastic and wanted to help but not all could be accommodated.

Women who participated utilized their newly acquired skills not only to generate income, but also to provide care for persons who were disabled or pregnant women and whose husbands had migrated to work. In their respective mutual aid groups, the rural women helped one another during harvest season when someone was sick or needed additional help so they could tend to their in-laws.

Ervin Staub remarked on the values of cooperation and community that aptly describe the results of our project:

> Values of cooperation and community, an appreciation of others' humanity and worth that is not based on their material possessions but on their character, capacity for positive relationships, and contribution to their neighbour's lives and community, would make the evolution of violence less likely.[19]

3. A Change in Culture

In one of the northern project counties, a group of women took up singing and dancing as a means to express themselves. Yangko dance was performed publicly despite the conventional male-dominant view that such practices took women away from household chores and was a waste of time. The women wanted to sing and dance together and worked with the village women directors, subsequently forming a group of over 80 women dancers who practiced and performed publicly. Some more conservative members believed that women who appeared in public to perform in this way would encourage the corruption of village morals. The dancers were sometimes subject to gossip and ridicule that prevented some from taking part, however, the dancing activities flourished and the women soon performed at cultural activities with community support. The role of dance was important for the women because, as Julia Anwar McHenry notes, the arts can represent both social and civic engagement; dance and other arts are "a means of communicating meaning and emotion . . . and are used to make a statement, for pleasure and the creation of beauty."[20] In rural China, these activities opened up for the women the possibility of building networks and communal expression. Dancing also promoted harmonious activities and relations among village women, instilling in them a sense of common purpose and effort.

As a result of the project more women participated in community affairs and decision making. For example, there was an increase in the number of women and men who participated in community activities initiated by women. With regard to local political decision making, men had previously dominated village leadership and women had seldom voted. At the end of the project, it was reported in many villages that 70 to 80 percent of villagers who came to vote were rural women. Women voted for the people they wanted to support, which resulted in more women being selected as village representatives and taking up political positions.

After the social work training, the cadres developed abilities in resource mobilization and acquired the knowledge and skills to tap into available resources to meet the needs of villagers. With increased ability of cadres to write their own funding proposals and reports, they began to experience some success in soliciting funds for a variety of local projects aimed at improving the lives of rural women and their communities. Through learning how to apply participatory approaches and generate positive support from local governments, rural women's capacities were also built, as well as awareness of their needs. The following account was given during focus group interviews of the evaluation study:

> I think this project has been a big influence. Before, our work was all arranged by the government; each department was responsible for its own business. Before, we carried out tasks by using that approach. But now it is different, according to women's wishes; they know we focus on them too. Their awareness has been improved. This project pays more attention to women, and the government does as well—and other working methods have also changed. Now, even if their husbands are not at home or the government doesn't initiate any projects, women would look for work and develop their own projects. Their awareness of self-empowerment has improved. It is because the local government now pays attention to the work of rural women, and this project has played some role in that, too.

One of the major achievements as a result of trainees' local initiatives in Inner Mongolia was the establishment of centers for women and for children who were left behind in the villages as men migrated to work in city centers. With minimal start-up funds from the project itself, the Women's Federation cadres convinced the county government to finance the infrastructure of the centers. These are also important gathering places for women who can share experiences and concerns. Regular discussions were held on topics such as women's health and parent-child relationships. Both in Sichuan and Inner Mongolia, several project townships obtained over 100,000 *renminbi* (approximately 17,000 Canadian dollars) to build irrigation projects and roads. One trainee recounted the following:

> This time our whole village completed an application form, so it was clear how many people were participating in this project and experiencing this water

> issue. After completing this form, they submitted it to our leaders, and they felt it was very good, as it reflected the need and the size of the community. Before the government didn't know which *Kacha* [*village*, in Mongolian] needed this project, but now with the submitted application, they know what the needs are and have a better understanding.

According to Johan Galtung, a condition for peace is an equitable relationship.[21] The changes in cadres' attitudes and work methods not only had a tremendous impact on the women in the villages but also resonated with their superiors in the ACWF, contributing to the creation of institutional change. Some cadres who went through the social work training shifted from a submissive stance to one in which they challenged their local government supervisors and brought forward ideas from the grassroots to the local authorities. As local authorities witnessed concrete results from the changes, they became more supportive of the Women's Federation cadres' work and more affirming of the gender initiatives they proposed. The transformation that took place in trainees' attitudes and methods led to ripple effects of change evident in a less hierarchical organizational management in the ACWF institution and outreach to the grassroots. There was also more consultation with women in local villages, rather than direct orders from front line cadres.

In the past, county leaders seldom traveled to the countryside to participate in local village activities. The participatory approach adopted by trained local township and village cadres motivated the county leaders to visit the townships. For the first time, rather than separating themselves on the higher points of the podium as in the past, leaders sat with the local women during their public engagement activities. A cadre recounted how this action moved many local women to tears:

> We held an activity for these *left-behind* populations that involved us going into the front level, riding a long way to the towns and villages. The most impressive thing was that those *left-behind* rural women in the village held our hands and cried. One said, "I am in my 40s. This is the first time that Women's Federation has come to us to hold this activity and we can sit together and enjoy the activity." Because before, during our activities, we would sit on the platform (top), while village women would sit off-stage. We gave them lectures, and sometimes announced orders from upper levels of governments or bills passed in conferences. But now we joined their activities.

4. Praxis in Relation to Transformation

During the six years of the China project, the ACWF trainees experienced praxis during a process of change as a result of active learning in the social work training program. This process resembles what Stephen Kemmis describes as "action, practice and change."[22] From the cadres' accounts in reports and their written stories, we see seeds of praxis that developed as the cadres learned, tried out what they learned, reflected on their actions and results and revised their course of action to fit better with the local situation and context. In their everyday lives and work, the cadres reported that they often revisited ideas and questioned their assumptions. Reflection and further practice enabled them to re-evaluate existing values and premises in the light of their developing new practices.

> Through the training, I started to wonder if I really hold the assumption that every woman has the capability. So, for the recent New Year's celebration party, I changed my approach. I asked them what I could do for them. They offered lots of good suggestions, such as playing games, dancing and talk shows, etc. We tried them out. Everyone had a good time as a result of the varieties of the activities.

The praxis process encouraged trainees to examine and challenge their notions related to gender, for example, the perception that men are superior and women inferior, and to explore the structural issues related to such gender assumptions. Thus, after taking part in gender awareness training, cadres started to question these notions and wanted to address the structural issues that lead to gender inequity. The following reflection characterizes a shift from an individual to a structural level of problem analysis:

> The techniques that we learn are not sufficient to solve problems on a larger scale. Moreover, as societies evolve there will be all kinds of new problems and dilemmas. If we just work with our clients in terms of individual cases, it will not get us very far. In order to solve a problem from the root, we need to raise the awareness of gender equality in the whole society, and with the mutual support of other social benefit policies. This is a piece of my thoughts about the deep problems.[23]

According to Malcolm Payne, reflection is a cognitive process influenced by emotions and bodily reactions, which are also regarded as important sources of knowledge.[24] From the outcome data, we found that cadres had a subjective experience as they took action through reflection and further action, which had evoked a great deal of emotion. In the process of learning social work in class and practice settings, the authors (also occasional trainers) witnessed the trainees going through stages of confusion, challenge, and reflection on what they were taught in social work, deconstructing old concepts and modes of action, and finally embracing the appropriate ones to develop their base of informed practice. During the praxis process, trainees used an indigenous term, *thought collision*, to describe the arguments and reciprocal challenges that occurred between trainers and trainees as they strove to find the practice modes most relevant to local rural practice. Their practicum experiences offered an opportunity to immediately apply theory to practice, and supported learning from the bottom-up and from grassroots practice experiences.

The positive response of cadres, especially among the village directors, and the remarkable increase in local women's participation in the various community projects confirmed that these changes in method were indeed bearing positive results. Seeing results from applying these methods reinforced their continued use among the cadres and led to further evolution of their participatory approach within the practicum context. The participatory interaction and collective reflection created an alternative way of knowing that was flexible and interpersonally connected. Such a process is an example of effective social work practice that makes use of a thoughtful and critical approach where different ideas and concepts generate reflection and action and lead to a new conceptualization of practice. Ultimately, practice is transformed, as reflected in the accounts of front-line experience of both the cadres and the rural women.

Michael Edwards and Gita Sen suggest that deep-rooted personal transformation fuels a search for more humane social systems founded upon more collaborative, egalitarian principles. The potential for change is made possible when the wishes of people at the grassroots level can be expressed and realized.[25] We saw such a possibility occurring as cadres strove to understand the needs of rural women and work more collaboratively with them and as they reflected these needs to their superiors. For their efforts, they experienced some good responses from the authorities. In their exploration of how transformation of human relationships may lead to social change, Edwards and Sen also argue that change requires a fundamental shift in values. This shift needs to be freely chosen in order to be sustainable, and such choice is more likely to be made by individuals who have experienced a "transformation of the heart." These personal and/or collective transformations need to be fostered by larger institutions in order to be sustainable.[26] When one considers the transformation experienced by local cadres, and its impact on the local villages they served, the question arises: To what extent can this transformation be sustained?

CONCLUSION

This six-year long project with women in China was successful in generating more egalitarian, respectful relations as seen in activities that broke new ground and challenged existing rigid, hierarchical structures. The women who were trained were interested in joining together to help one another and to meet local household and community needs, for example, in local micro-enterprise initiatives, and in groups to build alternative structures and networks, such as rural roads, wells, and libraries, to further women's needs and interests.

The Women's Federation cadres who participated in training activities and practicums raised their awareness of rural women and of women's mutual interests. They also drew from the lessons learned in the training, which stimulated improved morale, new perspectives and methods, and a greater energy for working at the grassroots with women who were no longer distanced from them. The activities and outcomes of the project can be framed as peacebuilding in that they changed relationships once characterized by tension and conflict and built capacity in individual participants and communities. They also initiated institutional change in that those ACWF cadres who applied the participatory methods learned in their work brought their experiences into the ACWF organization, a structure within the Communist Party. Although we do not know how the new ideas and practices were transferred to these bodies, nor do we know how much this was possible, we hope that some seeds were planted that will lead to greater equality between women and men at the grassroots, in the Women's Federation organizations, and in other government bodies.

NOTES

1. Johan Galtung, *Peace by Peaceful Means: Peace and Conflict, Development and Civilization* (London, England: Sage, 1996), 9.
2. Ibid., 31.
3. International Association for Humanitarian Policy and Conflict Research, "Empowerment: Women & Gender Issues: Women, Gender, & Peacebuilding Processes," 2009, accessed February 19, 2014, http://www.peacebuildinginitiative.org/index9aa5.html?pageId=1959.
4. Shun Hing Chan, "Beyond War and Men: Reconceptualizing Peace in Relation to the Everyday and Women," *Signs* 36.3 (2011): 524.
5. Ibid., 529–30.
6. Julie Drolet and Tuula Heinonen, "Gender Concepts and Controversies," in *International Social Development: Social Work Experiences and Perspectives*, ed. Tuula Heinonen and Julie Drolet (Halifax, NS and Winnipeg, MB: Fernwood, 2012).
7. The project, *Building Human Capacity—Social Work with Rural Women in China (2004–2010)*, was funded by the Canadian International Development Association (CIDA).
8. Maria Cheung and Tuula Heinonen, "Grassroots Change for Rural Women in China: Building Human Capacity," in *International Social Development: Social Work*

Experiences and Perspectives, ed. Tuula Heinonen and Julie Drolet (Halifax, NS and Winnipeg, MB: Fernwood, 2012).

9. For reference to Deng Xiaoping please refer to: Maria Cheung, Tuula Heinonen, and Meng Liu, "Gender Analysis of the Marginalization of Rural Women over the Life Span after the Initiation of Cultural Reforms in China," *Journal of Social Development Issues* 30.2 (2013): 59–77.

10. Ellen Judd, *The Chinese Women's Movement: Between State and Market* (Stanford, CA: Stanford University Press, 2002).

11. Ibid.

12. Jude Howell and Diane Mulligan, eds., *Gender and Civil Society: Transcending Boundaries* (London, England: Routledge, 2005).

13. Robert Chambers, *Participatory Workshops: A Sourcebook of 21 Sets of Ideas and Activities* (London, England: Earthscan, 2002).

14. Naila Kabeer, *Reversed Realities: Gender Hierarchies in Development Thought* (London, England: Verso, 1994).

15. N. Narayanasamy, *Participatory Rural Appraisal: Principles, Methods and Applications* (Los Angeles, CA: Sage, 2009).

16. For example, see Jack Rothman, "Three Models of Community Organization Practice," in *Strategies of Community Organization: A Book of Readings*, 2nd ed., ed. Fred M. Cox et al. (Itasca, IL: Peacock, 1974).

17. Cheung and Heinonen, "Grassroots Change."

18. Ibid.

19. Ervin Staub, "A World without Genocide: Prevention, Reconciliation and Creation of Peaceful Societies," *Journal of Social Issues* 69.1 (2013): 193.

20. Julia Anwar McHenry, "Rural Empowerment through the Arts: The Role of the Arts in Civic and Social Participation in the Mid West Region of Western Australia," *Journal of Rural Studies* 27.3 (2011).

21. Galtung, *Peaceful Means*, 1.

22. Stephen Kemmis, "Research for Praxis: Knowing Doing," *Pedagogy, Culture and Society* 18.1 (2010): 11.

23. Meng Liu, *A Collection of Stories in the China Project* (Beijing, China: Chinese Women's University, 2009), 20.

24. Malcolm Payne, *Humanistic Social Work: Core Principles in Practice* (Chicago, IL: Lyceum, 2011).

25. Michael Edwards and Gita Sen, "NGOs, Social Change and the Transformation of Human Relationships: A 21st-Century Civic Agenda," *Third World Quarterly* 21.1 (2000).

26. Ibid., 606.

BIBLIOGRAPHY

Anwar McHenry, Julia. "Rural Empowerment through the Arts: The Role of the Arts in Civic and Social Participation in the Mid West Region of Western Australia." *Journal of Rural Studies* 27.3 (2011): 245–53.

Chambers, Robert. *Participatory Workshops: A Sourcebook of 21 Sets of Ideas and Activities.* London, England: Earthscan, 2002.

Chan, Shun Hing. "Beyond War and Men: Reconceptualizing Peace in Relation to the Everyday and Women." *Signs* 36.3 (2011): 521–32.

Cheung, Maria and Tuula Heinonen. "Grassroots Change for Rural Women in China: Building Human Capacity." In *International Social Development: Social Work Experiences and Perspectives,* edited by Tuula Heinonen and Julie Drolet, 213–31. Halifax, NS and Winnipeg, MB: Fernwood, 2012.

Cheung, Maria, Tuula Heinonen, and Meng Liu. "Gender Analysis of the Marginalization of Rural Women over the Life Span after the Initiation of Cultural Reforms in China." *Journal of Social Development Issues* 30.2 (2013): 59–77.

Drolet, Julie and Tuula Heinonen. "Gender Concepts and Controversies." In *International Social Development: Social Work Experiences and Perspectives,* edited by Tuula Heinonen and Julie Drolet, 75–97. Halifax, NS and Winnipeg, MB: Fernwood, 2012.

Edwards, Michael and Gita Sen. "NGOs, Social Change and the Transformation of Human Relationships: A 21st-Century Civic Agenda." *Third World Quarterly* 21.1 (2000): 605–16.

Galtung, Johan. *Peace by Peaceful Means: Peace and Conflict, Development and Civilization.* London, England: Sage, 1996.

Howell, Jude and Diane Mulligan, eds. *Gender and Civil Society: Transcending Boundaries.* London, England: Routledge, 2005.

International Association for Humanitarian Policy and Conflict Research. "Empowerment: Women & Gender Issues: Women, Gender, & Peacebuilding Processes," 2009. Accessed February 19, 2014. http://www.peacebuildinginitiative.org/index9aa5.html?pageId=1959.

Judd, Ellen. *The Chinese Women's Movement: Between State and Market.* Stanford, CA: Stanford University Press, 2002.

Kabeer, Naila. *Reversed Realities: Gender Hierarchies in Development Thought.* London, England: Verso, 1994.

Kemmis, Stephen. "Research for Praxis: Knowing Doing." *Pedagogy, Culture & Society* 18.1 (2010): 9–27.

Liu, Meng. *A Collection of Stories of Growth in the China Project.* Beijing, China: Chinese Women's University, 2009.

Narayanasamy, N. *Participatory Rural Appraisal: Principles, Methods and Application.* Los Angeles, CA: Sage, 2009.

Payne, Malcolm. *Humanistic Social Work: Core Principles in Practice.* Chicago, IL: Lyceum, 2011.

Rothman, Jack. "Three Models of Community Organization Practice." In *Strategies of Community Organization: A Book of Readings*, 2nd ed., edited by Fred M. Cox, John L. Erlich, Jack Rothman, and John E. Tropman, 22–39. Itasca, IL: Peacock, 1974.

Staub, Ervin. "A World without Genocide: Prevention, Reconciliation and the Creation of Peaceful Societies." *Journal of Social Issues* 69.1 (2013): 180–99.

Chapter 7

The Role of Oromo Women in Peacemaking

Perspectives from an Indigenous System

Hamdesa Tuso

The concept of conflict resolution that uses negotiation and mediation has become common in North America during the last two-and-a-half decades and has been adopted at the international level.[1] From the perspective of developing societies (including the indigenous people in the Americas) who have been accustomed to a series of violent armed conflicts predicated on the interests and policies of the North, commencing with the fifteenth century, the evolution of an intellectual movement originating from the West whose basic tenets include concepts such as basic human needs,[2] conflict resolution through mediation, problem solving, and empowering the weaker party[3] is a very heartening and appealing development. In my view, the emergence of such an intellectual movement from the Western social and academic ecology should be greeted with a great sigh of relief and enthusiasm. However, in spite of the renewed interest by scholars and policymakers from the Western influential centers in the ideals of conflict resolution, we can safely state that the field of conflict resolution is far from enjoying a depth and breadth of theoretical and practical knowledge that allows it to interact with different cultures. As it stands now, literature relative to conflict resolution is based on a postindustrial, Western paradigm. This presents Western conflict resolution models with considerable limitations. While social conflict is a universal experience in human communities,[4] culture defines the social ethos, the "enemy," rules of engagement, taboos, sanctions of conflicts, and the frame of reference for their resolution.[5]

An example of this problem is third-party mediation, a Western method of conflict resolution. Third-party mediation is predicated on bringing externality and neutrality to the conflict situation. Other significant criteria associated

---

This chapter is a reprint, the original now not available. The original citation is:
Tuso, Hamdesa. "The Role of Women in Conflict Resolution: Perspectives from an Indigenous System." *A Leadership Journal: Women in Leadership—Sharing the Vision* 2.2 (1998): 29–43.

with the third-party mediation model are professionalism (the notion of expertise) and fairness.[6] These elements constitute the sources of legitimacy for the external intervener. Paul Wehr and John Paul Lederach, however, report that, based on their involvement in the negotiation to end the conflict in Central America during the 1980s, the *confianza* model was preferred over the North American-based third-party model.[7] According to these authors, the *confianza* model is predicated on trust and relationships, and the conflict groups in the above indicated case preferred insider, partial peacemakers rather than outsider, neutral mediators.[8] Reports are also coming from the experiences of indigenous peoples in North America that mediation in their cultural paradigm is radically different from the Western model relative to the issue of neutrality. Philmer Bluehouse and James Zion write:

> General American mediation uses the model of a neutral third person who empowers disputants and guides them to a resolution of their problems. In Navajo mediation, the *naat'aanii* is not quite neutral, and his or her guidance is more value-laden than that of the mediator in the American model.
>
> Peacemakers have strong personal values, which are the product of their language and rearing in the Navajo way. Those values are also the teachings of Navajo common law. A peacemaker, as a *naat'aanii*, is selected because of personal knowledge of Navajo values and morals and the demonstrated practice of them. Peacemakers teach values through prayer and a "lecture" to tell disputants what is right and wrong. Navajo peacemakers, unlike their American mediator counterparts, have an affirmative and interventionist role to teach parties how they have fallen out of harmony by distance from Navajo values.[9]

Furthermore, in the mediation of broader international disputes, evidence is emerging which indicates that cultural differences do influence the mediation process.[10]

Other social forces not unrelated to culture are pushing the need to embark on a line of inquiry regarding Western, neutral-party mediators. Three of these social forces are worth mentioning. First, many scholars and policymakers have called for the integration of cultural perspectives into the development of policy considerations. Major international organizations such as UNESCO, the UN, and the World Bank have legitimated this subject by convening major conferences on this critical area of development.[11] Second, contrary to the expectation that the end of the Cold War would reduce ethnic conflict around the world, ethnic conflict has proliferated since the collapse of the Berlin Wall in 1989, threatening the entire global system—which is predicated on a nation-state system.[12] Third is the fact that many ethnic groups, who have been in subordinate positions in the modern state system, are now asserting their basic rights; contained in this demand is the call for the restoration of their cultural institutions, including their system of conflict resolution, into the legal systems which affect their daily lives.[13]

This article is a preliminary attempt to contribute to filling this obvious gap in literature relative to the experiences of indigenous people with respect to social conflict and conflict resolution in the non-Western cultural systems. However, there is not much data on the subject of *indigenous* systems of *conflict resolution* from which one can draw information for the purpose comparative analysis.[14] Even anthropologists whose profession has invested an inordinate amount of time and energy in the study of *traditional* society have concentrated on searching for the *war-mongering* savages in developing societies. In the process they have neglected the peacemaking activities of such ethnic groups. In what could be considered an open confession, two anthropologists, Leslie Sponsel and Thomas Gregor, wrote: "In anthropology, until recently, conflict, aggression, and violence have claimed most of our attention; peace both interpersonal and intergroup have received relatively short shrift."[15]

Thus, we have to start with case studies. Of course, some may question the usefulness of case studies in the social sciences since they have limitations. However, case studies have been recognized for the unique opportunity they provide to researchers for the examination of a new subject from various dimensions.

On a personal level, I feel that, as one who originates from an indigenous system of social order, in addressing this topic, I may run the risk of being dismissed by some as an exilee who is "romantic about his 'tribal' past." Be that as it may, I hope this humble effort on my part will challenge others to take a serious interest in the subject of indigenous systems of conflict resolution, including the role of women in such processes.

CONFLICT RESOLUTION: PERSPECTIVES FROM THE INDIGENOUS CULTURES

The concept of indigenous identity and culture is complex. It is usually used to describe a broad range of ideas and systems. However, we can suggest that there are two major areas where this concept is commonly employed. The first is in reference to traditions and cultural systems which are non-Western. In this sense, all the cultures in Africa, Asia, and the Americas (i.e., the Indian cultural system)[16] can be classified as indigenous systems. Second, it is specifically used in reference to the populations around the world who have been marginalized culturally, economically, politically, and ideologically in the modern global system.[17]

Several definitions have been developed to characterize *marginalized* indigenous peoples around the world. Among the significant entities which have labored on this endeavor include: International Labor Organizations (ILOs), some indigenous organizations, scholars, and the United Nations (UN).[18] For our purpose, I will employ the working definition which has been adopted by the UN in 1982. It defines indigenous peoples as:

> People descended from those who originally inhabited a land at the time of conquest and domination by peoples of different ethnic origin who reduced them to a colonial situation;
>
> Cohesive societies who today wish to live more in conformity with their own continually adapting traditions than with those of the dominant (conquering) society;
>
> Societies which have been placed under the control of state structures which incorporate national, social, and cultural characteristics alien to theirs.[19]

Some analysts categorize indigenous peoples in the contemporary as being the fourth world on the already existing scale of classification relative to the level of development and industrialization.[20] Commonly, the *first world* category is used in identifying the Western nation-states, the *second world*, the former Soviet Union and its satellite states in Eastern Europe, and the *third world* encompasses those decolonized areas in Africa, Asia, the Middle East, and Latin America.[21] Thus, the *fourth world* represents those territories and nations that still remain under subjugation. The Oromo society belongs to the category of populations around the world who are stateless and, as such, are marginalized in the contemporary global system.

THE ROLE OF WOMEN IN "TRADITIONAL" SOCIETIES

I wish to suggest that women in developing societies play important roles in peacemaking. Because the subject of conflict resolution often limits the scope for the analysis of peacemaking to a "rational" dimension (i.e., negotiation and mediation), I wish to argue that our consideration should encompass a variety of rich activities which various segments undertake in order to ensure peace and justice in societies. Such rich activities may include playing supportive roles in some instances and undertaking pivotal roles in others. Such is the case with the women in Oromo society in the Horn of Africa.

OROMO WORLDVIEW

Worldview is a concept social scientists employ to describe an internalized body of values which shapes a society's meaning of life, its relations with the surrounding environment (human, natural, material, and spiritual), and its mores.[22] A society's worldview is constructed through the cultural lenses which people have developed through the years of socialization. They develop rituals to establish patterns of social behavior for the purpose of reinforcing the basic component of those worldviews. Several anthropological research accounts have shown that conflict prevention, management, and the aptitude of hostility or peaceful disposition toward fellow human beings had direct relevance to a society's worldviews and internalized value systems.[23]

In order to fully appreciate the Oromo indigenous system of conflict resolution and the critical role women play in it, we need to approach our analysis from the Oromo Perspective. The Oromo worldview is imbedded in their belief system. Contrary to the commonly held view among Westerners and Middle Eastern societies, the Oromos have a well-defined belief system.[24]

The Oromos are the largest national group in the entire region of the Horn of Africa (estimated to be about 30 million people). They are one the largest indigenous peoples on the African continent.[25] They constitute more than half of the population in contemporary Ethiopia (currently estimated to be about 52 million). Also, they are found in Kenya and Somalia. They belong to the large stock of the Cushitic family of people, of which the Oromos, Somalis, and Afars constitute the largest blocks (in the order in which they are listed).[26]

The following interrelated concepts constitute the basic Oromo belief system: (1) *Waaqa* (the universal creator); (2) *Ayaana* (a process through which *Waaqa* made all things); (3) *Shetna* (evil spirits which cause wrong); (4) *Chubu* (conscious acts to harm others); (5) *Ballessa* (transgression against others usually through omission); (6) *Kayyo* (a concept which describes a person's fullest life or lack of it); and (7) *Qitte* (equality among persons). In the Oromo worldview, conflict creates disharmony and poisons the relationships between *Waaqa* (the universal creator), *Lafaa* (the earth), humans, and other creatures. Thus, the Oromos believe that:

1. As much as possible, conflict should be prevented from occurring.
2. Once it occurs, everything should be done to prevent it from escalating.
3. All institutions should work together to manage conflict.
4. The ideological themes underpinning the processes of conflict resolution include:
   a. There is no conflict which cannot be resolved (the message is that relevant elements in the society should work hard until it is resolved).
   b. Pertinent facts must be unearthed before resolution to a conflict can be found.
   c. The goals of peacemaking must include the consummation of justice.
   d. While the individual parties must pay the price of causing conflict, conflict formation must be treated as a collective responsibility of the

family and community of the individuals who are responsible for causing the conflict in the first place.

e. The ultimate goal of conflict resolution is to make *arara* (reconciliation) of the parties. In the Oromo worldview, reconciliation is necessary so that the relationships between the supernatural, humans, and nature that have been damaged as the result of conflict should be repaired.[27]

WOMEN IN OROMO SOCIETY

For any person or group to intervene in a conflict situation with the purpose of resolving it, reality requires that the entity has the power to do so, and this power comes with status and resources.[28] Thus, it is relevant that we discuss, though briefly, the status of women in Oromo society.

Women in Oromo society have a special place.[29] They are considered the source of life, and as such, are treated as sacred (*woyyu*—partly divine) beings who have a special connection to *Waaqa* (God). In fact, in Oromo mythology, *Waaqa* has two beings below him: one called *Oglia* which is male and the second is *Atete* which is female.[30] Lambert Bartels, a European Catholic priest and anthropologist, who lived among Oromos and studied the Oromo belief system, made the following observation about the role of a woman:

> Matcha society (Matcha is a branch of the Oromo nation) has several roles of behavior which enshrine women's dignity as a source of life; (a) Matcha [Oromo] women are forbidden to kill; they should not even witness a killing; (b) Female animals which are not evidently barren or past bearing should not be killed, either for domestic use or for rituals; (c) This is even more the case if a girl or woman is killed, her fertility does not play a part at all. Far from being an honorable act, to kill a woman would be spoken of with horror.[31]

Oromo society can be classified as patrilineal, and men play prominent, heavy-handed roles. However, the society has made significant provisions in its legal and moral codes to ensure women's basic rights and protect them from negligence and physical abuse. For example, the basic rights of a woman are set out on the day of her marriage at the wedding. During the process of performing marriage rituals, someone representing her family will enunciate the basic rights of a woman in the new community (to become the mother of the community; one can become a member through child bearing or adoption), and protection from ill-treatment and negligence. If the new husband must discipline his wife,[32] he cannot do any harm to her physical well-being. If he breaks any of her bones, breaks her tooth, or spills her blood, he commits a crime equivalent to taking someone's life, and he and his family and community will be charged with *gumaa* (murder). In such events, the bride's family of birth and the community will press charges against the husband, family, and the entire community. Thus, on the wedding day, the family and community of the bridegroom, by virtue of the solemn pledge by which they undertake, accept the responsibility for the protection of the basic rights of the woman. Included in these rights is the prohibition against attacking her family and clan identity. The society will allow for disagreement between the husband and wife; however, the dispute and the verbal exchange between them should never cross over to her family or community. For example, the husband is strictly prohibited from insulting her family and community.

The Oromo system also provides for the economic basis for the woman. The bride is given property the day after her arrival. Also, she brings a lot of gifts (*gegaio*) from her family, relatives, and community on the day of the wedding. She is in charge of these properties as well as the property of her children until they are of marrying age.

Even in the area of her rights relative to engaging in extramarital affairs, which may be the most sensitive sphere with respect to husband and wife relations, the Oromo society makes relatively more liberal provisions to women than other societies. As with most traditional societies, the Oromo society is polygamous. Men are expected to engage in extramarital affairs. Likewise, women are allowed to have formally sanctioned lovers outside of marriage. It is perfectly acceptable that on the night when her lover wishes to come to her house, she would tell her husband her lover is coming.

THE ROLE OF OROMO WOMEN AS LEADERS IN CONFLICT RESOLUTION

As Walter Goldschmidt has suggested, we will examine the institutional roles which societies use in peacemaking.[33] Oromo use several institutions in making peace. Four such institutions are worth noting.

1. The *Gada* system: It is a political system which is based on generation-grade (comprised of five, each generation-grade rules for eight years) and five parties which rule for a period of 40 years. The *Gada* system may be one of the most studied African institutions. Reports and descriptions about the *Gada* institution go back in history commencing with the sixteenth century. The central attraction of the *Gada* system to Western travelers, diplomats, and scholars (particularly anthropologists) lies in its complexity and democratic features.[34] Thus, in some respects, the *Gada* system is the ultimate manifestation of the true national ethos with respect

to equality, justice, and peace for the framers of this institution have integrated the basics of conflict management into the political system.[35] Professor Asmarom Legesse, an authority on the *Gada* institution, captured this aspect of Oromo political philosophy when he wrote:

> *Gada* seems to be of the universals that bind the entire nation into a coherent system and give people a common political basis for understanding each other. It constitutes a shared political idiom.
>
> This, then, is the political vantage point from which we view the character of Oromo democracy. What is astonishing about this cultural tradition is how far the Oromos have gone to ensure that power does not fall in the hands of war chiefs and despots. They achieve this goal by creating a system of checks and balances that is at least as complex as the systems we find in the Western societies.[36]

2. *Kallu*: This is the religious institution that has been known to be present in all Oromo segments.[37] The main function of this institution is for the priests to serve as intermediaries between the divine, individuals, and the people as a whole in times of trouble. For example, when there is no rain, the community goes to the *Kallu* community for prayers, mediation, and predictions. Men or women can become priests in this religious system. However, the individuals who serve as *Kallu* are excluded from participating in the *Gada* system.[38] It seems this was done for the purpose of avoiding the concentration of power in the hands of a few. In fact, to some extent, it parallels the American doctrine of separation of church and state which has been enshrined in the American constitution. In Oromo society, there is no gender differentiation with respect to roles in the *Kallu* institution. The *Kallu* institution also plays an important role in peacemaking in the society.[39]
3. Eldership: Eldership is an institution which is predominant in most traditional societies.[40] It is the intellectual and moral backbone of such societies. Eldership is headed by competent, thoughtful, and respected individuals in the community. No one is born to eldership; one earns it through mastery of local tradition and cultural norms, and the quality of leadership one provides to the local community and beyond. Like other traditional societies, Oromos utilize eldership to resolve all manner of intra-Oromo disputes. As we will note later when discussing the role of Oromo women in mediating interethnic conflict, the institution of eldership is also used to address conflict which result from clashes between Oromos and other ethnic groups.
4. *Atete*: This is the fourth institution that one finds in Oromo society, though with considerable variations. It is a system organized and run by women for the purpose of empowering themselves and protecting their interests.

It is an institution which women use for resolving conflict among various groups.[41] Professor Paul Trevor William Baxter, a British anthropologist and an authority on Oromo culture, rendered the following description relative to *Atete*, as he observed it in the Arsie region:

> [*Atete*] is a meeting of women who assemble in order to discipline an erring male or female neighbor and later to celebrate their success in doing so in song, dance, prayer, blessing, and sacrifice is itself called *Atete*. The women at such meetings reiterate in their words and gestures the importance of both domestic and neighborhood concord and of fecundity—the former being, in part, a prerequisite for the latter because female fertility, like that of earth and the fertilizing rain, depends on a flow of prayers and blessings.
>
> The conclusion of each *Atete* I witnessed was marked by a casual, jocular, festal atmosphere, appropriate to a gathering of people who were well-known to each other. They were meetings of countrywomen. At each, one of the clearly expressed intentions of the participants was to celebrate the procreative importance of women and their contribution to the family as domestic and stock-caring labor. The tone was overwhelmingly and joyously woman.[42]
>
> *Atete* is distinctive in that it is the only public ritual in which women are the principal organizers, the active participants, and the congregation and of which the timing and staging is determined by them and at which they may decide a case that they have laid against a man.[43]

Oromo women most often take the role of activists in resolving social conflict. Women, as the voice of conscience and revered in the society as sacred (*woyyu*—partly divine), are situated in the social system to challenge the status quo. They raise consciousness and mobilize the attitudes of the society to take the necessary steps forward resolving the conflict at hand.

In Oromo society, men usually do not get involved in resolving intra-women disputes. For example, a grieved woman can call an *Atete*, and the women in the neighborhood usually respond; then she can put her case to the assembled women. Based on the evidence presented, they proceed to examining the complaints.[44]

In traditional Oromo settings, male-female conflicts are usually limited to domestic situations, for it is against societal norms for men to be in conflict with women outside of the immediate family. The exception is the conflict which occurs between the women and their outside male lovers. However, the most common male-female conflict is the one which involves husband and wife. In the case of grievances which a wife may level against her husband, she declares *Atete*, as describes in the above-presented description from Baxter's fieldwork. The basis for grievances which receive positive responses from the women are those which have been prescribed by the larger society. Three areas are worth mentioning: physical abuse; negligence; and improper treatment during the special periods in the woman's life cycle (i.e., pregnancy, suckling, or illness). Once a woman registers complaints on such grounds, and once the women in the neighborhood accept the allegation to be credible, they organize themselves as the *Atete* and march to the house of the husband and hang a *sinque* (a tall, thin wooden rod which women use as the symbol of their power and authority). Once that step is taken, the women will not depart until the concerned man submits and sends elders to make peace. Usually, their demands are met without resistance, wrongs are corrected, the resolution of the problem at hand is celebrated, and the man whose behavior was in question and his family are blessed and the process of conflict transformation is completed. Of such occasion, Baxter reported:

> The husband appeared apologetic and repentant and eager to please from the moment that *Atete* appeared. He found a sacrifice and a day was arranged for the *Atete* to return and celebrate. They did and the whole occasion had the air of a party, at which the husband played anxious host, rather than of a punishment.[45]

WOMEN'S PEACEMAKING ROLES IN INTRA-OROMO CONFLICT

When Oromos of different families in a community engage in a conflict which may lead to violence, all four institutions discussed in this chapter—the *Gada*, *Kallu*, eldership, and *Atete*—work in concert to stop the conflict from escalating and then to find some resolution through appropriate mechanisms, so that *arara* (reconciliation) may take place. The woman's role is very pivotal in halting the conflict immediately. They make distress calls (*uuu—uuu—uuu*) to all the neighborhoods in the surrounding area, organize themselves in the form of a human chain, physically enter between the conflicting parties, and lie on the ground. Women are the only group in the entire society who have such a status of being *woyyu* (sacred) with the authority to prevent violence and potential death. No one in Oromo society would pass over a chain of human bodies created by women and attack the other party, for no one would dare to attack women or disregard their will in such matters. Once the fighting is halted, the elders in the community approach the parties and initiate the peace process. In the case of a conflict that has cost human life, people who represent the *Gada* system also become involved in conjunction with elders. Under Oromo indigenous law, no one has the authority to rectify the loss of life (*guma*) without ratification by an authority of the *Gada* system. Also, those persons who are priests in the *Kallu* institution play an important role in exerting their moral authority in halting the conflict and moving the parties toward the road of peace and reconciliation.

Essentially, this process involves three major stages. Initially, when the leaders of various organizations become aware of the evolving conflict, they usually contact the women in the community who take the dramatic steps by sending the distress call (*uuu—uuu—uuu*). Next, the women organize themselves and physically intervene by forming a human chain and lying down on the ground between the conflicting parties. In effect, such dramatic actions by the women also puts pressure on the leaders of the three institutions (viz., the eldership, *Gada*, and *Kallu*) to move with some urgency in paying attention to the conflict at hand. Usually, this act will separate the conflicting parties. Finally, once the conflicting parties are separated and the fighting has stopped, the elders will commence their work of peacemaking. In case of loss of life as the result of the conflict, the *Gada* institution becomes involved.

OROMO WOMEN'S PEACEMAKING ROLE IN INTERETHNIC GROUP CONFLICT

A brief discussion of the Oromo's relationship with other ethnic groups helps clarifies the role of women in Oromo interethnic conflict.

The Oromos are ambivalent about war and peace when it comes to other ethnic groups. On the one hand, they have been known to act as fierce warriors in defending their basic rights.[46] On the other hand, there is a consistent pattern in Oromo history which shows that once the conflict at hand is over, they are willing to make peace and treat the former enemies as good neighbors or even as legitimate members of Oromo nationhood.[47] For example, after they prevailed over the Christian Abyssinians and Islamic forces led by the Afar and Somali coalition during a sixteenth century conflict, the Oromos accepted the two Abrahamic religions (Christianity and Islam), intermarried with them, and focused on cooperation and horizontal relationships which involved commerce and exchange of cultural habits as opposed to seeking domination and control.[48]

Women play critical roles as intermediaries between the Oromos and their neighbors. Taddesse Berisso, an Oromo anthropologist from the Guji area, wrote the following on this subject: "Among the Guji and their neighbors, it was a matter of mutual agreement between the groups through the intermediacy of women."[49]

A very interesting case showing how women became involved in an interethnic conflict has been reported by Professor John Hinnant from his fieldwork among the Oromo Gujis. In this case, both the Oromos and the

Sidamas (one of the ethnic groups which neighbor the Oromo country) sent five elderly women each to mediate in a particular conflict. Below, Hinnant presents the situation:

> When a battle had continued for three or four days, the old men on both sides decided that since many people were being killed and the crops needed tending and the children were starving, they should send old women to the other side to begin peace moves with the senior men there. They would send out five very old women. The five old women went to where the senior Sidama men were having a meeting called *songo*. They go and stand quietly until asked who they are. They say that Gujis are dying and that they are killing Sidamos who might even be their *soda* (in-laws). So they want to end the conflict. The Sidamas tell them to return to their country. The next day the Sidamo send five old women who say that the Sidamo agree with the Gujis and where should they make the appointment to kill the oxen and end the conflict? The Guji discuss and name a place and time. The Sidamo women go. The next day both sides come together and kill two oxen pouring blood on both sides of the boundary. Meanwhile, the warriors stand on both sides of the boundary, spears raised. The two sets of five women stand before them telling them to leave threats behind. The old men hold ends of a bone—any bone—and another breaks it. Then all eat the meat together as a sign of peace.[50]

WOMEN MAKING PEACE BETWEEN THE DIVINE AND THE HUMAN

In addition to playing a critical role in peacemaking, women play important roles in serving as intermediaries between the divine and the human. In particular, women organize themselves and pray for mercy and forgiveness in case of drought. Typically, they march, singing "*arrarro Rabio*" (Oh our God have mercy on us and give us rain), to the nearest river and plead with the Creator for rain. While by the river, they put (tap) grass on the water. Since women take their status as *woyyu* (sacred) very seriously, they undertake these sorts of activities of their own volition; they are not ordered by men in the community. In fact, men regard the women as the segment in society the universal Creator will give special recognition to, and as such, *Waaqa* is unlikely to ignore their petition for mercy and reconciliation.

The significance of this function of women relative to resolving social conflict lies in the fact that it is another set of activities full of symbolism and ritual which serve as another powerful source of legitimacy and reinforcement about the special roles women as *woyyu* (the sacred) play—their authority to speak out and lead in resolving social conflict.

CONCLUSION

I have argued that to the extent many indigenous cultural systems have invested more in resolution of social conflict through mediation than the West ever has, it is very important to include perspectives from such indigenous systems. I have further suggested that the field of conflict resolution, as it evolves, has an unparalleled opportunity to provide cultural parity. It is in this context that I have attempted to share with the readers of this book the experience of indigenous people in the Horn of Africa with respect to conflict resolution—particularly the role of women in conflict management and resolution. Research and oral tradition show that Oromo cosmology links all the creatures, human and nature, that are the creation of *Waaqa* (the supernatural), and therefore, all have the right to have fair treatment on this earth. In Oromo mythology women are considered *woyyu* (sacred—particularly divine) and as such command considerable respect in the society. This linkage of the origin and status of women to the divine gives them special status to provide leadership in the management and resolution of social conflict. In making this presentation, there was no claim that the Oromo women have been treated with equality in all respects, nor the suggestion that the Oromo system of conflict resolution is perfect. Simply stated, the effort has been to demonstrate that different societies have developed their own systems of conflict resolution, and it may be useful to study them and explore ways of incorporating rather than treating peoples in developing societies with disdain.

As we, as scholars, practitioners, activists, educators, and leaders for social change, justice, and peace, embark on a new road—the exploration into the field of conflict resolution—there are many difficult issues we have to confront honestly and constructively. I wish to highlight three. First, the area of indigenous conflict resolution is only beginning to blossom. Until recently, much of the material available was in the form of anecdotes or simple reference to the existence of these practices. Thus, what is needed is a disciplined methodological approach in describing and analyzing these systems. Second, in doing so, one may come across practices which may stand in contradiction to the current Western value system—particularly among the "more enlightened" humanist groups. Indeed, some practices which one may uncover on such a road of discovery could be in violation of basic human rights. Should we then avoid such practices in our studies or should we present them as part of historical processes in that social system and then share with such societies alternative practices which enhance human equality and dignity? Third, based on past experiences, paradigms which have not been rooted in cultures which are owned by the grassroots populace have failed dismally. The best examples are the modernization theory and the Marxist-Leninist model.[51] Is it not, then, reasonable to have some concerns that conflict resolution, as a new paradigm emerging from the post–Cold War West, might face the same fate?

NOTES

1. Robert A. Baruch Bush and Joseph P. Folger, *The Promise of Mediation: Responding to Conflict through Empowerment and Recognition* (San Francisco, CA: Jossey-Bass, 1994), 1–32; John W. Burton and Frank Dukes, *Conflict: Practices in Management, Settlement, and Resolution* (New York, NY: St. Martin's, 1990), 27–37; Christopher W. Moore, *The Mediation Process: Practical Strategies for Resolving Conflict*, 2nd ed. (San Francisco, CA: Jossey-Bass, 1996), 22–32. In fact, conflict resolution is becoming one of the fastest growing cottage industries around the world. It seems that the West, as the influential source of power and legitimacy, has once again set a new agenda and a new paradigm for the global community.

2. Roger A. Coate, *The Power of Human Needs in World Society*, ed. Jerel Rosate (Boulder, CO: Lynne Rienner, 1988); John W. Burton, ed., *Conflict: Human Needs Theory* (London, England: Palgrave Macmillan, 1990); Edward E. Azar, *The Management of Protracted Social Conflicts: Theory and Cases* (Hampshire, England: Dartmouth Publishing, 1990). John Burton, a leading intellectual figure in the field of conflict resolution, defines human needs theory as, "the notion of human needs that separates power theories from conflict resolution theories . . . . The idea that there may be more fundamental human needs that are inherent, needs that will be pursued by any means available including the risk to life, has emerged only in recent decades. The power of human needs has helped to redefine power [in] political thinking" (*Conflict Resolution: Its Language and Processes* [Lanham, MD: The Scarecrow Press, 1996], 30).

3. Bush and Folger, *The Promise of Mediation*; Sara Cobb, "Empowerment and Mediation: A Narrative Perspective," *Negotiation Journal* 9.3 (1993); James Laue and Gerald Cormick, "The Ethics of Intervention in Community Disputes," in *The Ethics of Social Intervention*, ed. Gordon Bermant, Herbert C. Kelman, and Donald P. Warwick (Washington, DC: Halsted Press, 1978).

4. Moore, *The Mediation Process*; Lewis A. Coser, *The Functions of Social Conflict: An Examination of the Concept of Social Conflict and its Use in Empirical Sociological Research* (New York, NY: Free Press, 1956).

5. Marc Howard Ross, *The Culture of Conflict: Interpretations and Interests in Comparative Perspective* (New Haven, CT: Yale University Press, 1993); John Paul Lederach, *Preparing for Peace: Conflict Transformation across Cultures* (Syracuse, NY: Syracuse University Press, 1995); George Peter Murdock, *Culture and Society: Twenty-Four Essays* (Pittsburgh, PA: University of Pittsburgh Press, 1965), 81–86, 140–50; Larry Samovar, Richard Porter, and Nemi Jain, *Understanding Intercultural Communication* (Belmont, CA: Wadsworth, 1981).

6. Ronald J. Fisher, "Third Party Consultation as a Method of Intergroup Conflict Resolution," *The Journal of Conflict Resolution Studies* 28.2 (1983).

7. Paul Wehr and John Paul Lederach, "Mediating Conflict in Central America," *Journal of Peace Research* 28.1 (1991).

8. Ibid.

9. Philmer Bluehouse and James W. Zion, "Hozhooji Naat'aanii: The Navajo Justice and Harmony Ceremony," *Conflict Resolution Quarterly* 10.4 (1993): 335.

10. Pierre Casse and Surinder Deol, *Managing Intercultural Negotiations: Guidelines for Trainers and Negotiators* (Washington, DC: SIETAR, 1985); Glen Fisher, *International Negotiation: A Cross-Cultural Perspective* (Yarmouth, ME: Intercultural Press, 1980).

11. Ismail Serageldin and June Taboroff, eds., *Culture and Development in Africa* (Washington, DC: The World Bank, 1994); Margareta von Troil, ed., *Changing Paradigms in Development—South, East and West: A Meeting of Minds in Africa* (Uppsala, Sweden: Scandinavian Institute of African Studies, 1993); Mamadou Dia, *Africa's Management in the 1990s and Beyond: Reconciling Indigenous and Transplanted Institutions* (Washington, DC: The World Bank, 1996).

12. Michael E. Brown, ed., *Ethnic Conflict and International Security* (Princeton, NJ: University of Princeton Press, 1993); Marina Ottaway, *Democratization and Ethnic Nationalism: Africa and Eastern European Experiences* (Washington, DC: Overseas Development Council, 1994); Rita Jalali and Seymour Martin Lipset, "Racial and Ethnic Conflicts: A Global Perspective," in *New World Politics: Power, Ethnicity, and Democracy*, ed. Demetrois Caraley, Robert L. Jervis, and Cerentha Harris (New York, NY: The Academy of Political Science, 1993); Chester A. Crocker, Fen Osler Hampson, and Pamela Aall, eds., *Managing Global Chaos: Sources of and Responses to International Conflict* (Washington, DC: United States Institute of Peace, 1996).

13. Diane LeResche, "Editor's Note," *Conflict Resolution Quarterly* 10.4 (1993); Emily Mansfield, "Balance and Harmony: Peacemaking in Coast Salish Tribes of the Pacific Northwest," *Conflict Resolution Quarterly* 10.4 (1993): 339–53; Franke Wilmer, "Domination and Resistance, Exclusion and Inclusion: Indigenous People's Quest for Peace and Justice," *Peace and Conflict Studies* 3.1 (1996). A case in point is the proposed declaration currently under consideration by the Organization of American States (OAS) to grant fundamental rights to the indigenous nations in all the states in the Americas. The document relative to this proposition contains sections relative to the need for incorporating the indigenous system of conflict resolution into the legal system which affects their affairs.

14. Note that this chapter is a reprint. Thankfully, much more work has been done in this area since this article was written—and much more needs to be done. Contemporary research about indigenous conflict resolution, indigenous feminism, the powerful contributions made by indigenous authors/academics to critical/feminist theory, and the expansion of research methodologies to incorporate indigenous and alternative worldviews continues to expand our understanding in this area.

15. Leslie E. Sponsel and Thomas Gregor, eds., *The Anthropology of Peace and Nonviolence* (Boulder, CO: Lynne Rienner, 1994), v.

16. Ali A. Mazrui, *Cultural Forces in World Politics* (London, England: James Curry, 1990); George B. N. Ayittey, *Indigenous African Institutions* (New York, NY: Transnational Publishers, 1991); Edward W. Said, *Culture and Imperialism* (New York, NY: Vintage Books, 1993); Dia, *Africa's Management in the 1990s and Beyond.*

17. Jillian Burger, *Report from the Frontier: The State of the World's Indigenous Peoples* (London, England: Zed Books, 1987); Franke Wilmer, *The Indigenous*

Voice in World Politics: Since Time Immemorial (Newbury Park, CA: Sage, 1993); Hector Diaz Polanco, *Indigenous Peoples in Latin America: The Quest for Self-Determination*, trans. Lucia Rayas (Boulder, CO: Westview, 1997).

18. For the definitions developed by ILO, indigenous organizations, and scholars, see Burger, *Report from the Frontier*, 6–11.

19. This is a summary of the UN definition relative to indigenous peoples. For the sake of convenience, I have borrowed the summarized text from Wilmer, "Domination and Resistance." For the full text of the UN Working Definition of Indigenous Peoples, see *UN Economic Social Council Commission on Human Rights, Preliminary Report on the Problem of Discrimination against Indigenous Populations* (UN Document E/CN.4/Sub.2/L.556, 1982, chapter 11).

20. Marc A. Sills and Glen T. Morris, *Indigenous Peoples' Politics: An Introduction*, vol. 1 (Denver, CO: Fourth World Centre, University of Colorado Denver, 1993); Wilmer, *The Indigenous Voice*.

21. Leslie Sklair, *Sociology of the Global System*, 2nd ed. (Baltimore, MD: Johns Hopkins University Press, 1995), 10–12; David Hulme and Mark M. Turner, *Sociology and Development: Theories, Policies, and Practices* (New York, NY: St. Martin's, 1990), 7–8; John Rapley, *Understanding Development: Theory and Practice in the Third World* (Boulder, CO: Lynne Rienner, 1996), 10–13.

22. Mary E. Clark, *Ariadne's Thread: The Search for New Modes of Thinking* (New York, NY: Palgrave Macmillan, 1989) 16–17.

23. Douglas P. Fry, "Maintaining Social Tranquility: Internal and External Loci of Aggression Control," in *The Anthropology of Peace and Nonviolence*, ed. Leslie E. Sponsel and Thomas Gregor (Boulder, CO: Lynne Rienner, 1994); Douglas Hollan, "Staying 'Cool' in Toraja: Informal Strategies for the Management of Anger and Hostility in a Nonviolent Society," *Ethos* 16.1 (1988): 52; Clayton A. Robarchek, "Ghosts and Witches: The Psychological Dynamics of Semai Peacefulness," in *The Anthropology of Peace and Nonviolence*, ed. Leslie E. Sponsel and Thomas Gregor (Boulder, CO: Lynne Rienner, 1994); Patricia Draper, "The Learning Environment for Aggression and Anti-Social Behavior among the !Kung," in *Learning Non-Aggression: The Experience of Non-literate Societies*, ed. Ashley Montagu (New York, NY: Oxford University Press, 1978); Carl W. O'Nell, "Hostility Management and the Control of Aggression in a Zapotec Community," *Aggressive Behavior* 7.4 (1981); Carl W. O'Nell, "Nonviolence and Personality Dispositions among the Zapotec: Paradox and Enigma," *Journal of Psychological Anthropology* 2.3 (1979); Carl W. O'Nell, "Primary and Secondary Effects of Violence Control among the Nonviolent Zapotec," *Anthropolgical Quarterly* 59.4 (1986).

24. Charles Fernand Rey, *In the Country of the Blue Nile* (London, England: Duckworth, 1927).

25. Paul Trever William Baxter, Jan Hultin, and Alessandra Triulzi, eds., *Being and Becoming Oromo: Historical and Anthropological Enquiries* (Lawrenceville, NY: The Red Sea Press, 1996), 7; Rey, *In the Country*, 39.

26. David D. Laitin and Said S. Samatar, *Somalia: A Nation in Search of a State* (Boulder, CO: Westview, 1987), 4–7.

27. John Hinnant, *Guji of Ethiopia*, vol. 1 and 2 (New Haven, CT: Human Relations Area Files, 1972), 35–38; Taddesse Berisso, "Traditional Warfare among the

Guji of Southern Ethiopia," MA thesis, Michigan State University, 1988, 22–25; Lambert Bartels, *Oromo Religion: Myths and Rites of the Western Oromo of Ethiopia—An Attempt to Understand* (Berlin, Germany: Dietrich Reimer, 1983), 91–112, 231–53. I have elaborated on this topic in "Indigenous Processes of Conflict Resolution in Oromo Society," in *Traditional Cures for Modern Conflicts: African "Medicine,"* ed. I. William Zartman (Boulder, CO: Lynne Rienner, 2000).

28. Joseph P. Folger, Marshall S. Poole, and Randall K. Stuttman, *Working through Conflict*, 3rd ed. (New York, NY: Longman, 1996), 95–126.

29. The data for this section comes mainly from three major southern Oromo "Federations": Arsie, Borana, and Guji. However, I have incorporated relevant information from the works which have been done on other Oromo groups. For example, Knutson's research on Shoa Oromos (Central Oromia) and Bartels' work on Wollenga (Western Oromia) were both very useful for my research; see Eric Karl Knutsson, *Authority and Change: A Study of the Kallu Institution among the Macha Galla of Ethiopia* (Göteborg, Sweden: Etnografiska Museet, 1967) and Bartels, *Oromo Religion*.

30. Rey, *In the Country*; George Wynn Bereton Huntingford, *The Galla of Ethiopia: The Kingdoms of Kafa and Janjero* (London, England: International African Institute, 1955), 76–77.

31. Bartels, *Oromo Religion*, 284.

32. Once again, it is necessary to point out that it is not my intention to validate this type of husband-wife relation (the notion that one party has exclusive rights to discipline the other party). However, it is significant to point out that in some societies where such limits have not been imposed by the societal values and marriage covenant, women get battered physically and abused psychologically. In the case of Oromo society, at least some clear limits were set relative to her physical safety and psychological welfare between the relevant parties, families, and communities. The relevant point here is the importance of worldview in curtailing abuse and violence against the members of the society.

33. Walter Goldschmidt, "Peacemaking and the Institutions of Peace in Tribal Societies," In *The Anthropology of Peace and Nonviolence*, ed. Leslie E. Sponsel and Thomas Gregor (Boulder, CO: Lynne Rienner, 1994).

34. Asmarom Legesse, *Gada: Three Approaches to the Study of African Society* (New York, NY: Free Press, 1973); Paul Trevor William Baxter, "Boran Age-Sets and Generation-Sets: Gada, a Puzzle?" In *Age, Generation and Time: Some Features of East African Age Organizations*, ed. Paul Trevor William Baxter and Uri Almagor (New York, NY: St. Martin's, 1978); John Hinnant, "The Gada System of the Guji of Southern Ethiopia," PhD diss., University of Chicago, 1977.

35. Based on our analysis of the *Gada* system and the way the conflict resolution features have been integrated into the political system, we can suggest tentatively that the *Gada* system resembles a model for which Professor John Burton has been advocating. See his conception of this type of model in "Conflict Resolution as a Political System," Working Paper No. 1, Centre for Conflict Analysis and Resolution, George Mason University, Fairfax, VA, 1988.

36. Asmarom Legesse, "Oromo Democracy," paper presented at a Conference on Oromo Revolution, Washington, DC, 1987, 2.

37. Knutsson, *Authority and Change*; Hinnant, *Guji of Ethiopia.*

38. Legesse, *Gada: Three Approaches.*

39. Knutsson, *Authority and Change.*

40. David Suzuki and Peter Knudtson, *Wisdom of the Elders: Sacred Native Stories of Nature* (New York, NY: Bantam Books, 1993); Ayittey, *Indigenous African Institutions*, 39–69.

41. Arsie is one of the largest branches in the Oromo nation. The Arsie branch used to be in one province known as Arrusie. The province was divided in 1960 by the government of the Emperor Haile Selassie's regime. The Arsie population is located in the southeast of the Oromo's country.

42. Professor Baxter correctly identifies various meanings associated with the concept of *Atete* in his article; see Paul Trevor William Baxter, "Atete in a Highland Arssi Neighborhood," *Northeast African Studies* 1.2 (1979). However, all of them confirm the special sacred authority for the female gender in Oromo society.

43. Ibid., 4–5.

44. Ibid.

45. Ibid., 5.

46. Mohammed Hassen, "The Oromo of Ethiopia, 1500–1820: With Special Emphasis on the Gibe Religion, PhD diss., University of London, 1983; Mohammed Hassen, *The Oromo of Ethiopia: A History, 1570–1860* (Cambridge, England: Cambridge University Press, 1990).

47. Berisso, "Traditional Warfare among the Guji."

48. Donald N. Levine, *Greater Ethiopia: The Evolution of a Multiethnic Society* (Chicago, IL: University of Chicago Press, 1974); Mohammed Hassen, "The Oromo Nation under Amhara Colonial Administration—Past and Present—And Oromo Resistance to Colonial Oppression," unpublished paper, 1981.

49. Berisso, "Traditional Warfare among the Guji," 41.

50. Hinnant, *Guji of Ethiopia*, 154–55.

51. Mitchell A. Seligson and John T. Passè-Smith, *Development and Underdevelopment: The Political Economy of Global Inequality* (Boulder, CO: Lynne Rienner, 1993); John Isbister, *Promises Not Kept: The Betrayal of Social Change in the Third World*, 3rd ed. (West Hartford, CT: Kumarian, 1995).

BIBLIOGRAPHY

Ayittey, George B. N. *Indigenous African Institutions*. New York, NY: Transnational Publishers, 1991.

Azar, Edward E. *The Management of Protracted Social Conflicts: Theory and Cases*. Hampshire, England: Dartmouth Publishing, 1990.

Bartels, Lambert. *Oromo Religion: Myths and Rites of the Western Oromo of Ethiopia—An Attempt to Understand*. Berlin, Germany: Dietrich Reimer, 1983.

Baxter, Paul Trevor William. "Boran Age-Sets and Generation-Sets: Gada, a Puzzle?" In *Age, Generation and Time: Some Features of East African Age Organizations*, edited by Paul Trevor William Baxter and Uri Almagor, 151–82. New York, NY: St. Martin's, 1978.

———. "Atete in a Highland Arssi Neighborhood." *Northeast African Studies* 1.2 (1979): 1–22.

Baxter, Paul Trevor William, Jan Hultin, and Alessandro Triulzi, eds. *Being and Becoming Oromo: Historical and Anthropological Enquiries*. Lawrenceville, NY: The Red Sea Press, 1996.

Berisso, Taddesse. "Traditional Warfare among the Guji of Southern Ethiopia." MA thesis, Michigan State University, 1988.

Bluehouse, Philmer and James W. Zion. "Hozhooji Naat'aanii: The Navajo Justice and Harmony Ceremony." *Conflict Resolution Quarterly* 10.4 (1993): 327–37.

Brown, Michael E., ed. *Ethnic Conflict and International Security*. Princeton, NJ: University of Princeton Press, 1993.

Burger, Julian. *Report from the Frontier: The State of the World's Indigenous Peoples*. London, England: Zed books, 1987.

Burton, John W., ed. *Conflict: Human Needs Theory*. London, England: Palgrave Macmillan, 1990.

———. "Conflict Resolution as a Political System." Working Paper No. 1. Centre for Conflict Analysis and Resolution. George Mason University, Fairfax, VA, 1988.

———. *Conflict Resolution: Its Language and Processes*. Lanham, MD: The Scarecrow Press, 1996.

Burton, John W. and Frank Dukes. *Conflict: Practices in Management, Settlement, and Resolution*. New York, NY: St. Martin's, 1990.

Bush, Robert A. Baruch and Joseph P. Folger. *The Promise of Mediation: Responding to Conflict through Empowerment and Recognition*. San Francisco, CA: Jossey-Bass, 1994.

Casse, Pierre and Surinder Deol. *Managing Intercultural Negotiations: Guidelines for Trainers and Negotiators*. Washington, DC: SIETAR, 1985.

Clark, Mary E. *Ariadne's Thread: The Search for New Modes of Thinking*. New York, NY: Palgrave Macmillan, 1989.

Coate, Roger A. *The Power of Human Needs in World Society*, edited by Jerel Rosate. Boulder, CO: Lynne Rienner, 1988.

Cobb, Sara. "Empowerment and Mediation: A Narrative Perspective." *Negotiation Journal* 9.3 (1993): 245–59.

Coser, Lewis A. *The Functions of Social Conflict: An Examination of the Concept of Social Conflict and its Use in Empirical Sociological Research*. New York, NY: Free Press, 1956.

Crocker, Chester A., Fen Osler Hampson, and Pamela Aall, eds. *Managing Global Chaos: Sources of and Responses to International Conflict*. Washington, DC: United States Institute of Peace, 1996.

Dia, Mamadou. *Africa's Management in the 1990s and Beyond: Reconciling Indigenous and Transplanted Institutions*. Washington, DC: The World Bank, 1996.

Draper, Patricia. "The Learning Environment for Aggression and Anti-Social Behavior among the !Kung." In *Learning Non-Aggression: The Experience of Non-literate Societies*, edited by Ashley Montagu, 31–53. New York, NY: Oxford University Press, 1978.

Fisher, Glen. *International Negotiation: A Cross-Cultural Perspective*. Yarmouth, ME: Intercultural Press, 1980.

Fisher, Ronald J. "Third Party Consultation as a Method of Intergroup Conflict Resolution." *The Journal of Conflict Resolution Studies* 28.2 (1983): 301–34.

Folger, Joseph P., Marshall S. Poole, and Randall K. Stuttman. *Working through Conflict*. 3rd ed. New York, NY: Longman, 1996.

Fry, Douglas P. "Maintaining Social Tranquility: Internal and External Loci of Aggression Control." In *The Anthropology of Peace and Nonviolence*, edited by Leslie E. Sponsel and Thomas Gregor, 133–54. Boulder, CO: Lynne Rienner, 1994.

Goldschmidt, Walter. "Peacemaking and the Institutions of Peace in Tribal Societies." In *The Anthropology of Peace and Nonviolence*, edited by Leslie E. Sponsel and Thomas Gregor, 109–32. Boulder, CO: Lynne Rienner, 1994.

Hassen, Mohammed. "The Oromo Nation under Amhara Colonial Administration—Past and Present—And Oromo Resistance to Colonial Oppression." Unpublished paper, 1981.

———. "The Oromo of Ethiopia, 1500–1820: With Special Emphasis on the Gibe Religion." PhD diss., University of London, 1983.

———. *The Oromo of Ethiopia: A History, 1570–1860*. Cambridge, England: Cambridge University Press, 1990.

Hinnant, John. *Guji of Ethiopia*. Vol. 1 and 2. New Haven, CT: Human Relations Area Files, 1972.

———. "The Gada System of the Guji of Southern Ethiopia." PhD diss., University of Chicago, 1977.

Hollan, Douglas. "Staying 'Cool' in Toraja: Informal Strategies for the Management of Anger and Hostility in a Nonviolent Society." *Ethos* 16.1 (1988): 52–72.

Hulme, David and Mark M. Turner. *Sociology and Development: Theories, Policies, and Practices*. New York, NY: St. Martin's, 1990.

Huntingford, George Wynn Bereton. *The Galla of Ethiopia: The Kingdoms of Kafa and Janjero*. London, England: International African Institute, 1955.

Isbister, John. *Promises Not Kept: The Betrayal of Social Change in the Third World*. 3rd ed. West Hartford, CT: Kumarian, 1995.

Jalali, Rita and Seymour Martin Lipset. "Racial and Ethnic Conflicts: A Global Perspective." In *New World Politics: Power, Ethnicity, and Democracy*, edited by Demetrois Caraley, Robert L. Jervis, and Cerentha Harris, 585–606. New York, NY: The Academy of Political Science, 1993.

Knutsson, Karl Eric. *Authority and Change: A Study of the Kallu Institution among the Macha Galla of Ethiopia*. Göteborg, Sweden: Etnografiska Museet, 1967.

Laitin, David D. and Said S. Samatar. *Somalia: A Nation in Search of a State*. Boulder, CO: Westview, 1987.

Laue, James and Gerald Cormick. "The Ethics of Intervention in Community Disputes." In *The Ethics of Social Intervention*, edited by Gordon Bermant, Herbert C. Kelman, and Donald P. Warwick, 205–32. Washington, DC: Halsted Press, 1978.

Lederach, John Paul. *Preparing for Peace: Conflict Transformation across Cultures*. Syracuse, NY: Syracuse University Press, 1995.

Legesse, Asmarom. *Gada: Three Approaches to the Study of African Society*. New York, NY: Free Press, 1973.

———. "Oromo Democracy." Paper presented at a Conference on Oromo Revolution, Washington, DC, 1987.

LeResche, Diane. "Editor's Note." *Conflict Resolution Quarterly* 10.4 (1993): 321–25.

Levine, Donald N. *Greater Ethiopia: The Evolution of a Multiethnic Society*. Chicago, IL: University of Chicago Press, 1974.

Mansfield, Emily. "Balance and Harmony: Peacemaking in Coast Salish Tribes of the Pacific Northwest." *Conflict Resolution Quarterly* 10.4 (1993): 339–53.

Mazrui, Ali A. *Cultural Forces in World Politics*. London, England: James Curry, 1990.

Moore, Christopher W. *The Mediation Process: Practical Strategies for Resolving Conflict*. 2nd ed. San Francisco, CA: Jossey-Bass, 1996.

Murdock, George Peter. *Culture and Society: Twenty-Four Essays*. Pittsburgh, PA: University of Pittsburgh Press, 1965.

O'Nell, Carl W. "Hostility Management and the Control of Aggression in a Zapotec Community." *Aggressive Behavior* 7.4 (1981): 351–66.

———. "Nonviolence and Personality Dispositions among the Zapotec: Paradox and Enigma." *Journal of Psychological Anthropology* 2.3 (1979): 301–22.

———. "Primary and Secondary Effects of Violence Control among the Nonviolent Zapotec." *Anthropolgical Quarterly* 59.4 (1986): 184–90.

Ottaway, Marina. *Democratization and Ethnic Nationalism: Africa and Eastern European Experiences*. Washington, DC: Overseas Development Council, 1994.

Polanco, Hector Diaz. *Indigenous Peoples in Latin America: The Quest for Self-Determination*. Translated by Lucia Rayas. Boulder, CO: Westview, 1997.

Rapley, John. *Understanding Development: Theory and Practice in the Third World*. Boulder, CO: Lynne Rienner, 1996.

Rey, Charles Fernand, Sir. *In the Country of the Blue Nile*. London, England: Duckworth, 1927.

Robarchek, Clayton A. "Ghosts and Witches: The Psychological Dynamics of Semai Peacefulness." In *The Anthropology of Peace and Nonviolence*, edited by Leslie E. Sponsel and Thomas Gregor, 183–96. Boulder, CO: Lynne Rienner, 1994.

Ross, Marc Howard. *The Culture of Conflict: Interpretations and Interests in Comparative Perspective*. New Haven, CT: Yale University Press, 1993.

Said, Edward W. *Culture and Imperialism*. New York, NY: Vintage, 1993.

Samovar, Larry, Richard Porter, and Nemi Jain. *Understanding Intercultural Communication*. Belmont, CA: Wadsworth, 1981.

Seligson, Mitchell A. and John T. Passè-Smith. *Development and Underdevelopment: The Political Economy of Global Inequality*. Boulder, CO: Lynne Rienner, 1993.

Serageldin, Ismail and June Taboroff, eds. *Culture and Development in Africa*. Washington, DC: The World Bank, 1994.

Sills, Marc A. and Glenn T. Morris. *Indigenous Peoples' Politics: An Introduction*. Vol. 1. Denver, CO: Fourth World Centre, University of Colorado Denver, 1993.

Sklair, Leslie. *Sociology of the Global System*. 2nd ed. Baltimore, MD: Johns Hopkins University Press, 1995.

Sponsel, Leslie E. and Thomas Gregor, eds. *The Anthropology of Peace and Nonviolence*. Boulder, CO: Lynne Rienner, 1994.

Suzuki, David and Peter Knudtson. *Wisdom of the Elders: Sacred Native Stories of Nature*. New York, NY: Bantam Books, 1993.

Tuso, Hamdesa. "Indigenous Processes of Conflict Resolution in Oromo Society." In *Traditional Cures for Modern Conflicts: African "Medicine,"* edited by I. William Zartman, 79–94. Boulder, CO: Lynne Rienner, 2000.

von Troil, Margareta, ed. *Changing Paradigms in Development—South, East and West: A Meeting of Minds in Africa.* Uppsala, Sweden: Scandinavian Institute of African Studies, 1993.

Wehr, Paul and John Paul Lederach. "Mediating Conflict in Central America." *Journal of Peace Research* 28.1 (1991): 85–98.

Wilmer, Franke. "Domination and Resistance, Exclusion and Inclusion: Indigenous People's Quest for Peace and Justice." *Peace and Conflict Studies* 3.1 (1996): 53–67.

———. *The Indigenous Voice in World Politics: Since Time Immemorial.* Newbury Park, CA: Sage, 1993.

Chapter 8

Remaining Human

Ukrainian Women's Experiences of Constructing "Normal Life" in the Gulag

Oksana Kis

In the mid-twentieth century tens of thousands of Ukrainians were sentenced to long-term imprisonment in Gulag camps, accused of political wrongdoings, so that in 1951 Ukrainians constituted one-fifth of the Gulag population, and remained the second most numerous ethnic group there.[1] The proportion of women among the Gulag detainees increased drastically during the same period—from 7.6 percent in 1941 to 26 percent in 1944. At the beginning of 1945 women constituted 30.6 percent of all Gulag prisoners, and their numbers continued to grow.[2] Young women from Western Ukraine sentenced to long-term confinement for real or alleged collaboration with the Ukrainian nationalist underground movement represented a large share of the female political convicts in the 1940s and 1950s.[3]

It was impossible to determine the exact number of people who went through the Gulag system from the late 1920s to the 1950s and how many actually survived. Scholars agreed that even the most accurate calculations are approximate, counting a total of about 25 to 30 million prisoners, of whom approximately 13.2 million detainees died while serving their sentences in camps and prisons.[4] Demographers of the Gulag do not provide these data disaggregated by the victims' gender, but it is clear that thousands of women survived the Gulag and managed to return to their "normal life" after many years in confinement. How was that possible? What helped them to hold on in the harshest living conditions, when their rights, resources, and opportunities were so extremely restricted? In spite of an impressive scope of research on the Gulag history and a sufficient pool of primary source materials available to scholars (archival documents, oral histories, memoirs, and autobiographies), Ukrainian women's lives in the Soviet concentration camps and prisons have not as yet been the primary focus of any historical anthropological research.[5]

This chapter will discuss how while living on the verge of death, suffering from severe hunger, inhumane living conditions, and an exhausting workload, Ukrainian women still found ways to defy the dehumanizing effects of camp regimes and to preserve their human, gender, and national identities. This study focuses on Ukrainian women's experiences of serving sentences in the Gulag camps and prisons from the mid-1940s, when the number of Ukrainian female political prisoners grew drastically until 1956, the beginning of the mass release and rehabilitation of political prisoners after the denouncement of Stalin's cult of personality. This research is based heavily on personal testimonies of Ukrainian female survivors of the Gulag (written memoirs, autobiographies, oral historical interviews, etc.). Women's narratives are analyzed to explore Ukrainian women's survival and accommodation strategies in these extraordinary circumstances, as well as forms of resistance to and transgression of the camp's regime resulting from women's specific gendered knowledge, skills, and everyday practices. The chapter will examine how women's gender-based knowledge, skills, and traditional practices equipped them with the necessary tools to create and to maintain a semblance of "normal life" where basic cultural values and social identities were preserved and performed. Their lives illuminate creative strategies of peaceful resistance to a harsh dehumanizing regime.

WOMEN IN THE GULAG: A GENERAL OVERVIEW OF LIVING CONDITIONS

A brief overview of the typical living conditions and regime in the camps where female political prisoners served their sentences is necessary to understand the extreme challenges women confronted on a daily basis in the Gulag.

Summarizing female survivors' personal testimonies, one can reconstruct a relatively accurate picture of everyday life in the camps. Women usually lived in wooden barracks, tents, or dugouts where up to a hundred persons were packed into one large room. Rows of two-story beds and a big plank table were the only furnishings.[6] Bedding was usually limited to a mattress (if there was any) made of straw or other dry natural materials (grass, leaves, etc.). The heating system consisted of an iron barrel adjusted to serve as an improvised wood stove located in the middle of the room. Because of poor insulation and primitive heating, it was very cold inside the barracks in the wintertime.[7] Detainees could not dry their wet outerwear and shoes after walking several kilometers in rain from their remote workplaces.[8] There was a serious problem with hygiene: on average women could take common baths two or three times per month, while their clothing was desinfected at high temperatures.[9] Women recalled a strong stench steaming from dirty bodies and clothes, as well as from festering wounds, to be intrinsic features of camp life.[10] In overcrowded barracks women also suffered from sleep deprivation, which further deteriorated their already poor health.[11] The situation was aggravated by lice and bed bugs attacking the inmates exhausted bodies at night,[12] and those itchy bites became easily infected sores, resulting in further health complications.

Female prisoners of the Gulag were considered universal workers so they were employed in all kinds of jobs, including physically demanding and hazardous ones (lumbering, earthmoving, construction of industrial plants and railroads, mining, etc.). Prisoners were stripped of most civic rights, therefore no protective norms of the Soviet Labour Code applied to them. "In the year 1951–1952 winter was unprecedentedly cold even for Norilsk. The temperature dropped (taking wind into account) to 74 degrees below freezing mark. The metals on the railroad were breaking apart because of that cold. Our duty was to replace the broken rails . . ."[13] In women's memoirs one can find numerous testimonies of injuries and casualties at work sites.[14]

In fact, the prisoners' work was merely severe exploitation of cheap human resources. For instance, in 1949 the level of mechanization of lumbering was 18 percent on average with the remaining work in the Gulag performed manually.[15] The Gulag economy was unprofitable: poor planning, mismanagement, corruption, and plundering wasted huge resources, and human resources above all.[16]

The prisoners food allowance was regulated by several Gulag bylaws related to the types of work performed; an actual portion depended on the prisoner's fulfillment of the established production rate ("the norm"). In general, the diet was poor, with critical lack of proteins and vitamins; often the ingredients were of bad quality and stale. By and large, inmates received insufficient, nonnutritious, low-grade food and suffered from hunger in most cases.[17]

As a result, prisoners suffered from diseases such as scurvy, dystrophia, nyctalopia, which were caused by the excessive work load and a severe Siberian climate combined with a poor diet. All female prisoners of the Gulag—even the healthy young ones—exhausted their physical resources soon after detention, and after a few years spent in camp their health was irreversebly undermined.

NATION AS IMAGINED AND REAL COMMUNITY: (RE)ESTABLISHING CONNECTIONS

National belonging and ethnic identity apparently played a significant role in the camps' informal social structures: inmates of the same ethnicity formed close circles/groups and maintained a certain distance from the rest. As Anne Applebaum pointed out, ethnic/national solidarity proved to be one of the most efficient strategies of survival in the Gulag.[18] Remarkably former Gulag inmates of different ethnic origins (Russians, Jews, Polish, Germans, etc.) refer in their memoirs to this fact, using Ukrainian or Baltic women's groups as exemplary cases of strong informal communities of compatriots providing their members with mutual support of all kinds.[19] Ukrainian women were seen as such a group held together with a number of common features.[20]

> We looked all the same, but we were different. There were women of different ethnic backgrounds: Latvians, Estonians, Germans, Russians, Koreans, Jews, but we Ukrainians constituted the majority. We were united by the same injustice, and we all were political prisoners who thought and believed in truth . . . We made groups on the national basis, despite the fact that we worked in different brigades. There were highly intelligent women among us, but there were also many regular peasant girls who self-sacrificially brought their health and youth on the altar of struggle for the justice.[21]

Staying together was the key factor in preserving presence of mind necessary to endure all the ordeals women had to deal with.

> Our unity, our readiness to help one another in a difficult moment, an awareness of our common fate, and the fact that we all are here for our common great idea of liberation struggle, a struggle against the barbaric tyranny—it helped us to live through all those horrors.[22]

Despite the gender segregation of prisoners and a strict prohibition of any contact, men and women felt an urge to communicate and did so. An illegal "post service" evolved in the Gulag. The internal secret correspondence played an important role in the detainees subculture: it helped to establish and to maintain contact with comrades, friends, or beloved ones, to share thoughts, memories, and dreams; it also facilitated circulation of important information among the inmates. There were various ways of secret messaging among prisoners, while washrooms and bathhouses served as main "post offices."[23] "We used to leave messages on small pieces of paper in hidden places. Many boys and girls maintained corrspondence with one another, the youth from Western Ukraine was very united."[24]

A little note of a few kind words, a postcard, or a small hand-made gift served as a token of women's moral support for their male counterparts, meant to prevent their despondency. Passing messages was a risky endeavor though.

> We have gotten lots of messages from men, because everybody wanted to get a warm woman's word. We exchanged letters with guys to hold up their spirit,

> but . . . sometimes you throw [message] successfully, but sometimes they catch you . . . If [the guards] find a message—you have to bear responsibility for that, they would punish you . . . One had to stay in a punishment cell for that, or they could deny you to write a letter [home], or they forbid to go to a kiosk. Those were three forms of punishment.[25]

In fact, the internal correspondence among the inmates helped them to (re)create a national micro-community, a kind of Ukrainian diaspora in the Gulag, so the prisoners could affiliate with and benefit from its moral and material support.

One of the aims of the Gulag system was the complete disintegration of a prisoner's personality. Inmates were systematically degraded and abused in different ways to break their psyche. In addition, due to the terrible living and work conditions, they found themselves on the verge of physical exhaustion, so that the basic instinct of survival was meant to take over any humanistic values, social norms, and cultural ideas. Complete isolation from the rest of society served that goal—pulled out from the familiar system of cultural axes, prisoners were expected to lose their basic points of reference and, as a result, became an easy-to-manipulate dull human mass with no moral principles whatsoever. Letters to and from home represented that last tiny thread which helped inmates to stay connected with their native culture and communities. For many prisoners it was a last chance to maintain that feeling of belonging.

> It is difficult to tell what it feels like for a a person who is in confinement for ten years . . . A human becomes indifferent to everything, it becomes barbarian. Letters were the only consolation and the only tiny bridge between us and our relatives.[26]

This is why in high security camps for political prisoners (*katorga*, where Ukrainians prevailed) correspondence was either severly restricted or banned altogether.

> Writing was strictly forbidden; it was even difficult to get a paper, a pencil, or ink. But we were looking for any possibility to contact the world all the time. In the monotony of our daily routine every news was like a light beam to strengthen us . . . But the connection to a native home and family was the most desirable . . . We girls were eager to get some information about our family members, relatives, about our towns or villages.[27]

Women's stories inform us about prisoners' will to find various ways to get around the restrictions and bans. Often camp civilian workers who sympathized with the detainees helped them to mail out their letters. The inmates' handmade postcards represent a peculiar type of Gulag art.[28] These were amateurish drawings featuring natural landscapes, flowers, children, boys and girls in love, the conventionalized horseshoe (traditional symbol of good luck).[29] Prisoners clearly preferred to visualize and share their memories and dreams about freedom and normal life, of which the beauty of nature and family happiness constituted essential elements.

Occasionally female political prisoners received parcels from home. Every parcel turned into a special event not only because of its material content; its special significance was related to a feeling of belonging to a family circle from which a woman had been taken.

> It was a real holiday when a parcel arrived. The entire barrack participated in that. A woman who received a gift unpacked it in front of everybody, and it must be said that everyone felt that care and tutelage of her relatives. Not only because there was something in the parcel, but we all had a feeling that [our families] remember us, they did not forget us yet and they are able to send us something.[30]

Another woman shared her experience.

> In the barrack there were many people who received parcels from home . . . They maintained a womanly guise, they lived with the interests of their families . . . and that gave them certain ground under their feet, as it usually is when one feels family care and support.[31]

Feelings of national belonging, shared misfortune, as well as a common dream for freedom created a strong sense of both an imagined and a real national community among Ukrainians in the Gulag camps. Correspondence within and beyond the Gulag was essential to restoring and maintaining the broken conectedness with a national collective.

RESTORING "NORMAL ORDER": STRUCTURING SPACE AND TIME IN CAMP

Female inmates found themselves in a situation that differed drastically from their usual daily lives. Living on the verge of death, Ukrainian women in the Gulag used their gendered knowledge and skills, as well as resourcefulness and mother wit to (re)create a semblance of "normalcy" in barracks.

A barrack did not remotely resemble any regular housing (neither a village cottage, nor a town apartment), but for the female inmates it was the only shelter they had. Guided by traditional ideas of how living space was supposed to be arranged and what a woman should do to keep it in proper order, prisoners showed enormous diligence creating and maintaining relative comfort inside and around the barracks.

> Girls from the Western Ukraine . . . The transformations that their industrious hands wrought in Hut Number 2, to which they had been assigned, were simply miraculous. The floor planking was polished to a gleaming yellow. The grazy windows, made of bits of broken glass glued together, sparkled like crystal. Green branches of dwarf pine embelished the corner posts of bunks, and straw pillows were touchingly draped with emboidered hand towels."[32]

In fact, barracks and the surrounding territory—no matter their actual condition—obtained a new meaning for the inmates; that place turned into a substitute home, to be treated as one's own habitable and well-attended place. Barracks turned into places of "collective privacy" from the regime. The camp administration actually had rather limited control over the detainees' lives in barracks, except for regular searches for prohibited items. Despite all the restrictions and bans, all kinds of forbidden activities took place in there.

Secret celebrations of religious holidays were some of those. Former female prisoners from other ethnic groups recall Ukrainian women attaching special significance to the celebration of Christmas and Easter. Women's memoirs from Gulag camps prove that these two holidays served as the major reference points in the prisoners' mental calendar. In fact, they provided structure for the whole year of detainees' otherwise extremely monotonous life in camps.

In spite of strict prohibition of any religious practices and lack of necessary religious objects, women showed exceptional purposefulness, assertiveness, and resourcefulness in preparing and carrying out those celebrations. They usually began accumulating foodstuffs well in advance, making a reserve of sugar, oil, and grains from small bits taken daily from their already scarce food rations. This collection was used later to cook something resembling holiday meals. Besides these "treats," women handmade other attributes of holidays from anything available (fabric and paper scraps, pieces of wood or wire, etc.). They aimed to conduct the celebration as close to the traditional scenario as possible, with major rituals and symbols in place.

> Easter was coming. A few days before that holiday all people in the barrack did not eat their evening portion of bread . . . On Saturday we made "cakes" of porridge. We invented Easter bread from regular bread. Easter eggs were made of clay and colored with paint . . . All that "beauty" was put on the table, cheered up with green branches, and everybody felt really in holiday mood then . . . Easter arrived. Everybody dressed up in whatever cloth people had from home, but everything was clean. The barracks were in order. We were prepared for the liturgy.[33]

The mass represented the apotheosis of a celebration when women (partially or in full) reconstructed the normal church liturgy performing the roles of priest, deacon, and choir.

> Everybody hurried to finish all the chores by noon. Then we were going to pray, or, as we called it, to attend a "divine service" . . .—a common prayer in one of the barracks . . . And to keep it in secret, we had to change barracks and goups every Sunday, so that our meetings did not draw attention of the administration. We prayed quietly in front of a locket or a little icon.[34]
>
> For that [common prayer] they penalized us, they threw us in the punishment cell, divested us of a right of correspondence. They were taking away beads, little icons, and the prayer books during the searches. But they were unable to take away our prayers."[35]

Paradoxically, under conditions of nearly total deprivation, the practice of common prayers and liturgies was a completely new experience for Ukrainian women: this was the first time the women had the opportunity to play central roles in Christian church rituals. Therefore, curiously enough, their new religious experience meant a kind of empowerment as it allowed women to access a sphere and activities previously reserved for men only. Former female prisoners recalled those moments with pride and excitement. What is more, following the customs of Christian holidays, women tried to avoid or to minimize hard work on that day. Remarkably, they were prepared to face penalties for refusing to work on the holiday; many times they openly confronted camp officials claiming their right to observe the tradition properly.[36]

For female prisoners these celebrations served as another avenue to maintain, perform, and represent their most significant social identities (gender, ethnic, and religious). As such, these practices challenged the totality of the regime's control on prisoners' bodies and minds. Reconstructing traditional ceremonies and performing corresponding ritual roles, women in fact maintained their connectedness to their native culture, and as a result, facilitated their loyalty to core cultural values and social norms of their distant native communities.

PERFORMING FEMINITY: TO BE A WOMAN NO MATTER WHAT

A main goal of the Soviet repressive machinery was suppression of the prisoners will to resist the totalitarian regime by eroding their personalities. Stripping prisoners of any attributes or markers of their social identities was another mechanism to achieve that goal. Women's awareness of their femininity being challenged or even endangered in the camps is noticeable in virtually every story. Women either expressed their grievance on losing their feminine features or described their efforts in sustaining them.

> A "zone" . . . was a kind of a massive human unit of female gender . . . We developed a new conditional reflex of gregariousness . . . but despite all that we remained humans of female gender.[37]

Mandatory use of dark color and baggy uniforms, banning any accessories or decorative elements, restricting access to means of hygiene, and other limitations served that goal. With bitterness women recalled their appearance in confinement:

> At every step they tried to persuade us that we are not human beings . . . We wear the men's clothing, the boots are too big.[38]
>
> We looked like exhausted human phantoms which did not resemble human beings.[39]
>
> Wearing shot through greatcoats and caps with ear flaps and soldiers' pants we looked like scarecrows, and not like girls.[40]

In spite of an absence of basic necessities and amenities, women did their best to take care of their bodies and appearance according to their concept of femininity. They hand-sewed underwear from scraps of fabric, made alterations and repaired clothing, decorated it with embroidery, did each other's hair, etc. One must not forget that many items necessary for such endeavors were prohibited in Gulag prisons and camps. The list included all kinds of needles, scissors, knives, as well as mirrors, cosmetics, and stationery, among others. But the will to remain women pushed female detainees to take risks, to break rules, to spend scarce free time to look feminine.

> When spring came, we took off our greatcoats. We started making skirts and blouses from those soldier clothes, and we turned into girls again! Only boots didn't really fit to such costume.[41]

Women did not do all that to please or attract men, as there was virtually no male population around to impress. It appears that maintaining their feminine look served another goal: it was one of those meaningful elements of their (bygone) "normal life," another point of reference helping women remember who they were and not dissolving in the melting pot of the Gulag. These practices should be understood as a form of a peaceful resistance to the Gulag totalitarian order.

TRADITIONAL WOMEN'S ACTIVITIES: EMBROIDERING AS SOCIAL NETWORKING

One might logically assume that female prisoners of the Gulag whose major goal was mere survival would not be willing to spend their remnants of time, energy, and extremely limited resources for anything but rest or sleep. The memoirs of former Ukrainian detainees testify to the opposite: not only did many women regularly engage in traditional women's pastimes, but they also took those activities very seriously, practicing them with true commitment.

One traditional women's activity, embroidering, acquired new meaning and special significance in camps and prisons. For Ukrainian women embroidery was an easily recognizable marker of Ukrainianness as well as a uniquely feminine way to manifest their gender identity.

In the context of Gulag realities traditional embroidering turned into a special craft because here it required remarkable skills, ingenuity and proficiency. Since needles and scissors were strictly prohibited for prisoners, women used fish bones for sewing and embroidering, while scraps of fabric and thread were obtained from worn out clothing. Embroidered items—of virtually no value aesthetically or pragmatically—gained special symbolic meaning in the context of prisoners' social life. Given to a fellow inmate, such an item served as a sign of a particular trust; it was a token of devoted friendship and lifelong bond between people of similar fate, a symbol of their common experience. Many former prisoners of the Gulag kept those memorabilia for the rest of their lives.[42]

> We girls state convicts . . . decided to give a little joy to our comrades in idea and struggle from the men's camp, so they could forget about the horrible reality for a moment and go to their homeland, to Ukraine in their imagination. Every girl found a scrap of fabric and embroidered a napkin with her initials in a corner. After a prayer, we sent our gifts . . . with one convoy guy (there were good people among them, too).[43]

In fact, the practice of exchanging embroidered gifts in confinement turned into a method of establishing, strengthening, and sustaining social ties; it contributed to the formation of a kind of sisterhood—a united Ukrainian women's community.

LAUGHING THROUGH TEARS: WOMEN'S LEISURE TIME

In their memoirs of the Gulag former female prisoners often mention the modest "forbidden pleasures" they secretly enjoyed in the camps. Singing Ukrainian folk songs was perhaps the most popular women's pastime, obtaining special significance in the camp context. In folk songs women found their consolation; group singing allowed women to release negative emotions and to develop a sense of unity and belonging to a group of common fate. Traditional folk songs reminded detainees of their beloved distant homeland. While singing they could both forget their real situation for a while and fantasize a better future.

> Young girls . . . sang songs with such nostalgia and sincerity which I am not able to describe . . . Girls sang whatever they knew from . . . They sang folk songs, and women from Galicia knew even the contemporary ones . . . Perhaps, in their imagination the singers in the embroidered shirts and their audience went to their unforgettable, inimitable, forever forcefully taken away [past] for a few moments.[44]

Group singing helped women pluck up their spirits in the most desperate circumstances. For instance, girls who participated in the uprising in the Norilsk camps in 1953 and were transferred to one of the high security camps (*katorga*) in Mordovia kept their presence of mind:

> Their term of detention has been extended, but they laughed . . . It was summer time, green around us . . . How could we not enjoy at least this scanty happiness we had in our lives? Every evening we gathered between the barracks in our zone and sang . . . The repertoire was endless. The entire camp used to gather at our evening concerts, some people sang along, while others' souls were flying over their native lands from where misfortune pulled them out.[45]

In fact, singing enabled women to restore and maintain a mental connection to their wider national collective in the camp and beyond, to remain a part of their native culture and remember their normal life in the past for the sake of their future. Folk songs served to manifest Ukrainian women's national identity and, at the same time, worked as peaceful resistance against the camp's regime of treating prisoners as emotionless slaves denying any enjoyment. Most importantly, group singing facilitated further consolidation of community.

In the 1940s to early 1950s any amateur talent activity was forbidden in the Gulag camps.[46] Nevertheless prisoners practiced all kinds of talent in secret. When despair and increasing despodency physically and emotionally plagued exhausted women, a bit of positive emotion from an improvised performance could help to keep one's presence of mind:

> The general mood was in decline. The number of conflicts was growing, people started to hate everything around them and one another, too. It was very sad—this atmosphere of mutual hostility in a common cage. I decided to relax somehow that tense situation . . . I announced that a circus performance will take place in the afternoon. One can always find people [to volunteer] so in two hours

> we opened a "stage" in the rear of barracks . . . The barracks were laughing, so the goal was achieved.[47]

Overwhelmed with strong emotions, writing poetry became one of the most popular creative activities among female detainees. Poets addressed different themes—from longing for loved ones and nostalgia for a homeland, dreams of freedom and happy life ever after, to various existential reflections on the meaning of life and Ukraine's destiny.

> Then many of our girls were writing poetry, mainly about their love of Ukraine and their longing for the homeland. So did I. It was qualified as "anti-Soviet propaganda by means of poetry of bourgeois-nationalist content."[48]

This activity was strictly prohibited, and the authors were severely penalized if any manuscript was found. "Poetry did not survive—they were our birthday gifts, recited orally or written on a hard-to-get scrap of paper, just to be destroyed straight away, or it was taken away during the next search."[49] Memories of Gulag survivors preserved innumerable examples of camp poetry: in their memories former female prisoners kept reciting poems of their fellow inmates learned by heart, thus bringing their legacy back to their native culture.[50]

Besides the unquestionable therapeutic effect of externalizing and verbalizing one's emotional burdens and grievous thoughts, this practice might have had another effect as it helped women to memorialize the most significant images from their normal life. These memories might have served as a life-saving beacon in the tumultuous disorienting experiences in the Gulag camps.

CONCLUSIONS

The majority of Ukrainian women sentenced to the Gulag in the 1940–1950s constituted a distinctive group of political prisoners. Residents of Western Ukraine—unlike many other female victims of Stalin's Great Terror in the 1930s—had not been indoctrinated by Soviet propaganda for two previous decades, so they were by no means loyal Soviet citizens. On the contrary, their nationalist political views strongly opposed the Communist ideology. They perceived the Soviet state as an oppressive system against which Ukrainian people should unite in their struggle for independence and freedom. Strong national awareness and understanding of their peoples' common destiny was one of the key factors contributing to solidarity among Ukrainian detainees in general and Ukrainian women in particular. Belonging to a cohesive national group in a camp as well as to the Ukrainian nation in a broader sense—as an imagined community—helped women to obtain all kinds of support necessary to survive in the Gulag. Regular correspondence with friends and relatives within and beyond the camps (despite all the restrictions) helped imprisoned women to sustain their connectedness to the national collective and to preserve their sense of humanity.

Women's gendered skills and knowledge were used to arrange their living space and time structure in the camps according to the traditional notion of a right and normal order. Examined practices of (re)constructing major elements of normal life in a camp context are considered as women's gendered strategies of survival in and resistance to the dehumanizing conditions of the Gulag. Otherwise trivial women's activities and practices (housekeeping, correspondence, sewing, embroidering, singing, as well as amateur poetry) proved to be relatively efficient tools to counteract devastating effects of the camp regime on prisoners' physical and mental state. In the camp context these activities acquired a new political meaning as they allowed women to preserve and perform their core social identities (gender, national, religious, political); they contributed to consolidation of a prisoners' community and developed a sense of solidarity among them, which in turn was a key factor for survival. These scraps of normal life contained significant points of reference (cultural values, social norms, and moral principles) reminding women who they were. These (forbidden but carried out) activities, in their nonviolent nature, could be interpreted as a form of a peaceful resistance to the destructive effects of the camp regime. In fact, the very totality of the Gulag system was undermined as women managed to create an invisible parallel reality, functioning according to life scripts of normalcy, hardly controlled by the Gulag authorities.

In studies on women's lives in the Gulag it is very important to focus not only on experiences related to women's victimhood or martyrdom, but to pay attention to forms of women's agency manifested in gendered practices of survival and accommodation, as well as their unique way of challenging and resisting the brutality of camp regime.

NOTES

1. Viktor Zemskov, "Gulag (instoriko-sotsiologicheskii aspect) (historical-sociological aspect)," *Sotsiologicheskie issledovania* no. 7 (1991): 3.

2. Galina Ivanova, "Gulag: gosudarstvo v gosudarstve" (Gulag: a state within the state), in *Sovetskoie obschestvo: vozniknovenie, razvitie, instoricjeskii final* (Soviet society: beginnings, development, and historical ending), ed. Yuriy Afanasiev, vol. 2 (Moscow: RGU, 1997), 216–17.

3. Oksana Kis, "National Femininity Used and Contested: Women's Participation in the National Guerrilla in Western Ukraine in the 1940–50s," *East/West: Journal of Ukrainian Studies*, forthcoming.

4. Anatolii Vishnevskii, "Obschee chislo repressirovanykh" (The total number of repressed people), *Demoskop* no. 313–14, 2007, accessed March 9, 2014.

http://demoscope.ru/weekly/2007/0313/tema05.php; Anatolii Vishnevskii, "Demograficheskie poteri ot repressii" (Demographical loss caused due to repressions), *Demoskop* no. 313–14, 2007, accessed March 9, 2014, http://demoscope.ru/weekly/2007/0313/tema06.php; Stephen Blyth, "The Dead of the Gulag: An Experiment in Statistical Investigation," *Journal of the Royal Statistical Society. Series C (Applied Statistics)* 44.3 (1995): 319.

5. For a detailed overview of existing scholarship and primary sources on women's experiences in the Gulag, see Oksana Kis, "Zhinochyi dosvid Gulagu: stan doslidzhen' ta dzherelni resursy v ukrainskomu konteksti" (Women's experiences of the Gulag: state of research and primary sources in the Ukrainian context), *Historians*, November 22, 2013, accessed March 9, 2014. http://historians.in.ua/index.php/doslidzhennya/943-oksana-kis-zhinochyy-dosvid-hulahu-stan-doslidzhen-ta-dzherelni-resursy-v-ukrayinskomu-konteksti-chastyna-i.

6. Eleanor Lipper, *Eleven Years in Soviet Prison Camps* (Chicago, IL: Regnery, 1951), 88.

7. *Neskorena berehynia: zhertvy moskovsko-komunistychnoho teroru XX stolittia* (Unsubdued berehynia: victims of the Moscow Communist terror in the 20th century), ed. Halyna Hordasevych and Yuriy Zaytsev (Lviv, Ukraine: Piramida, 2002), 133; other former prisoners also recall living in tents: Ivan Kryvutsky, *V namysti z koliuchogo drotu. Spohady zhinok vyazniv Gulagu, uchasnyts' noryl'skoho povstannia 1953 roku* (In the barbed wire necklace. Memoirs of women prisoners of the Gulag—participants of the Norilsk uprising in 1953) (Lviv, Ukraine: Manuskrypt, 2009), 209.

8. Hanna Pozniak-Skrypiuk, *Meni bulo 19: Avtobiohrafichna rozpovid* (I was 19: An autobiographical story) (Kyiv, Ukraine: Publishing House "Kyiv Mohyla Academy," 2001), 60.

9. *Neskorena berehynia*, 133; see also Halyna Kokhanska, Z *Ukrainoiu v sertsi: spomyny* (With Ukraine in my heart: memoirs) (Lviv, Ukraine: Litopys UPA, 2008), 258. No special ajustment of bathing time ever was made for menstruating women, neither were they provided with any hygienic products except for some scratchy cloth to be handwashed and reused (Ibid., 245).

10. *Neskorena berehynia*, 86–87.

11. Pozniak-Skrypiuk, *Meni bulo*, 44; Kokhanska, Z *Ukrainoiu*, 270–72.

12. *Neskorena berehynia*, 134; Anna Ivanytska also spoke on this issue: Anna Ivanytska, "Territory of Terror," Archive of the Memorial Museum of Totalitarian Regimes, collection 1, register 1, interview recorded in August 2009; see also Kokhanska, Z *Ukrainoiu*, 267.

13. Yefrosinia Kersnovskaia, Naskalnaia Zhyvopis' (Rock paintings) (Moscow, Russia: SP Kvardat, 1991), 337.

14. *Neskorena berehynia*, 134–35.

15. Ivanova, *Gulag*, 251.

16. Ibid., 240–43.

17. *Neskorena berehynia*, 124, 134; Kryvutsky, *V namysti*, 209.

18. Ann Applebaum, *Gulag: A History* (New York, NY: Anchor Books, 2003), 380.

19. Alexander Solzhenitsyn, *Arkhipelag Gulag, 1918–1956. Opyt khudozhestvennogo issledovamia* (Archipelago Gulag. Experiment in art studies), vol. 2 (Ekaterinburg, Russia: U-Faktoria, 2006), 211; Yevgenia Ginzburg, *Krutoi marshrut.*

Khronika vremen kulta lichnisti (Steep route. Chronicle of the times the cult of personality) (Moscow, Russia: Sovetskii Pisatel, 1990), 333–34; *Remembering the Darkness: Women in Soviet Prisons*, ed. and trans. Veronica Shapovalov (Lanham, MD: Rowman & Littlefield, 2001), 12.

20. Wally Schliess, "Christmas in Vorkuta," *Our Life* no. 1 (1957): 4.

21. *Neskorena berehynia*, 124.

22. Kryvutsky, *V namysti*, 150–51.

23. Nadia Surovtsova, Spohady (Memoirs) (Kyiv, Ukraine: Olena Teliha Publishing House, 1996), 239, 256, 273; Wally Schliess, "Post Service in Vorkuta," *Our Life* no. 11 (1956): 7.

24. *Neskorena berehynia*, 65.

25. Daria Husiak, "Territory of Terror," Archive of the Memorial Museum of Totalitarian Regimes, collection 1, register 1, interview recorded in June 2009.

26. Pozniak-Skrypiuk, *Meni bulo*, 96.

27. Schliess, "Post Service," 7.

28. Ukrainian museum holdings contain numerous examples of these artifacts, see *Virtual Museum of the Gulag*, accessed March 9, 2014, http://gulag-museum.org.ua.

29. Kateryna Peleshchyshyn, "Malodostidzheni aspekty tvorchosti vyazniv stalinskykh tiurem i taboriv" (Understudied aspects of creative art of prisoners of Stalin's camps and prisons), *Naukovi zapysky Lvivskoho istorychnoho muzeiu* 4.2 (1997).

30. Schliess, "Post Service," 7; a similar story was told by Volodymyra Kbryk-Senyk: *Neskorena berehynia*, 119.

31. Surovtsova, *Spohady* (Memoirs), 324.

32. Eugenia Ginzburg, Within the Whirlwind, trans. Ian Boland (New York, NY: Harcourt Brace Jovanovich, 1981), 84.

33. Kryvutsky, *V namysti*, 17.

34. Wally Schliess, "Sunday in Vorkuta," *Our Life* no. 9 (1956): 7.

35. Wally Schliess, "Prayer in Vorkuta," *Our Life* no. 10 (1956): 7.

36. Pozniak-Skrypiuk, *Meni bulo*, 45; similar stories could be found in many recollections, see for instance: Ihor Derevyany, "Velykden' za gratamy," *Den*, April 18, 2012; Kryvutsky, *V namysti*, 15–19.

37. Oksana Meshko, *"Ne vidstupliusia!" Do 100-richia Oksany Meshko* ("I won't give up!" 100 anniversary of Oksana Meshko), ed. Vasyl Ovsiyenko and Oles Serhiyenko (Kharkiv, Ukraine: Prava liudyny, 205), 41.

38. Pozniak-Skrypiuk, *Meni bulo*, 96.

39. Hanna Zayachkivska-Mykhalchuk, *Zaruchnytsia imperii: spohady politvyaznia* (A hostage of empire: memoirs of a political prisoner) (Lviv, Ukraine: PP Soroka, 2009), 73.

40. *Neskorena berehynia*, 96.

41. Pozniak-Skrypiuk, *Meni bulo*, 45.

42. One may find numerous examples of prisoners' embroidery in the Ukrainian museum collections, for more information see *Virtual Museum of the Gulag*, accessed March 9, 2014, http://www.gulag-museum.org.ua.

43. Kryvutsky, *V namysti*, 44–45.

44. Meshko, *Ne vidstupliusia*, 41, 59.

45. Zayachkivska-Mykhalchuk, *Zaruchnytsia imperii*, 160.

46. After Stalin's death and especially after the wave of camp uprisings in 1953–54, the camp regime was mitigated, so special "cultural-educational units" (CEU) were created in camps to engage prisoners in artistic activities for propaganda purposes. Applebaum, *Gulag*, 220–226.

47. Surovtsova, *Spohady*, 278.

48. Kryvutsky, *V namysti*, 202.

49. Meshko, *Ne vidstupliusia*, 41.

50. Bohdan Arey, *Invincible Spirit: Art and Poetry of Ukrainian Women Political Prisoners in the U.S.S.R.* (Baltimore, MD: Smoloskyp Publishers, 1977).

BIBLIOGRAPHY

Applebaum, Ann. *Gulag: A History*. New York, NY: Anchor Books, 2003.

Arey, Bohdan. *Invincible Spirit: Art and Poetry of Ukrainian Women Political Prisoners in the U.S.S.R.* Baltimore, MD: Smoloskyp Publishers, 1977.

Blyth, Stephen. "The Dead of the Gulag: An Experiment in Statistical Investigation." *Journal of the Royal Statistical Society. Series C (Applied Statistics)* 44.3 (1995): 307–21.

Derevyany, Ihor. "Velykden' za gratamy." *Den*, April 18, 2012.

Ginzburg, Eugenia. *Within the Whirlwind*. Translated by Ian Boland. New York, NY: Harcourt Brace Jovanovich, 1981.

Ginzburg, Yevgenia. *Krutoi marshrut. Khronika vremen kulta lichnisti* (Steep route. Chronicle of the times the cult of personality). Moscow, Russia: Sovetskii Pisatel, 1990.

Husiak, Daria. "Territory of Terror." Archive of the Memorial Museum of Totalitarian Regimes. Collection 1. Register 1. Interview recorded in June 2009.

Ivanova, Galina. "Gulag: gosudarstvo v gosudarstve" (Gulag: a state within the state). In *Sovetskoie obschestvo: vozniknovenie, razvitie, instoricjeskii final* (Soviet society: beginnings, development, and historical ending), edited by Yuriy Afanasiev. Vol. 2. Moscow, Russia: RGU, 1997.

Ivanytska, Anna. "Territory of Terror." Archive of the Memorial Museum of Totalitarian Regimes. Collection 1. Register 1. Interview recorded in August 2009.

Kersnovskaia, Yefrosinia. *Naskalnaia zhyvopis'* (Rock paintings). Moscow, Russia: SP Kvardat, 1991.

Kis, Oksana. "National Femininity Used and Contested: Women's Participation in the National Guerrilla in Western Ukraine in the 1940–50s." *East/West: Journal of Ukrainian Studies*, forthcoming.

———. "Zhinochyi dosvid Gulagu: stan doslidzhen' ta dzherelni resursy v ukrainskomu konteksti" (Women's experiences of the Gulag: state of research and primary sources in the Ukrainian context). *Historians*, November 22, 2013. Accessed March 9, 2014. http://historians.in.ua/index.php/doslidzhennya/943-oksana-kis-zhinochyy-dosvid-hulahu-stan-doslidzhen-ta-dzherelni-resursy-v-ukrayinskomu-konteksti-chastyna-i.

Kokhanska, Halyna. Z *Ukrainoiu v sertsi: spomyny* (With Ukraine in my heart: memoirs). Lviv, Ukraine: Litopys UPA, 2008.

Kryvutsky, Ivan. *V namysti z koliuchogo drotu. Spohady zhinok vyazniv Gulagu, uchasnyts' noryl'skoho povstannia 1953 roku* (In the barbed wire necklace. Memoirs of women prisoners of the Gulag—participants of the Norilsk uprising in 1953). Lviv, Ukraine: Manuskrypt, 2009.

Lipper, Eleanor. *Eleven Years in Soviet Prison Camps.* Chicago, IL: Regnery, 1951.

Meshko, Oksana. *"Ne vidstupliusia!" Do 100-richia Oksany Meshko* ("I won't give up!" 100 anniversary of Oksana Meshko), edited by Vasyl Ovsiyenko and Oles Serhiyenko. Kharkiv, Ukraine: Prava liudyny, 2005.

Neskorena berehynia: zhertvy moskovsko-komunistychnoho teroru XX stolittia (Unsubdued berehynia: victims of the Moscow Communist terror in the 20th century), edited by Halyna Hordasevych and Yuriy Zaytsev. Lviv, Ukraine: Piramida, 2002.

Peleshchyshyn, Kateryna. "Malodostidzheni aspekty tvorchosti vyazniv stalinskykh tiurem i taboriv" (Understudied aspects of creative art of prisoners of Stalin's camps and prisons). *Naukovi zapysky Lvivskoho istorychnoho muzeiu* 4.2 (1997): 57–70.

Pozniak-Skrypiuk, Hanna. *Meni bulo 19: Avtobiohrafichna rozpovid* (I was 19: An autobiographical story). Kyiv, Ukraine: Publishing House "Kyiv Mohyla Academy," 2001.

Remembering the Darkness: Women in Soviet Prisons. Edited and translated by Veronica Shapovalov. Lanham, MD: Rowman & Littlefield, 2001.

Schliess, Wally. "Christmas in Vorkuta." *Our Life* no. 1 (1957): 4.

———. "Post Service in Vorkuta." *Our Life* no. 11 (1956): 7.

———. "Prayer in Vorkuta." *Our Life* no. 10 (1956): 7.

———. "Sunday in Vorkuta." *Our Life* no. 9 (1956): 7.

Solzhenitsyn, Alexander. *Arkhipelag Gulag, 1918–1956. Opyt khudozhestvennogo issledovamia* (Archipelago Gulag, 1918–1956. Experiment in art studies). Vol. 2. Ekaterinburg, Russia: U-Faktoria, 2006.

Surovtsova, Nadia. *Spohady* (Memoirs). Kyiv, Ukraine: Olena Teliha Publishing House, 1996.

Vishnevskii, Anatolii. "Demograficheskie poteri ot repressii" (Demographical loss caused due to repressions). *Demoskop* no. 313–14, 2007. Accessed March 9, 2014. http://demoscope.ru/weekly/2007/0313/tema06.php.

———. "Obschee chislo repressirovanykh" (The total number of repressed people). *Demoskop* no. 313–14, 2007. Accessed March 9, 2014. http://demoscope.ru/weekly/2007/0313/tema05.php.

Zayachkivska-Mykhalchuk, Hanna. *Zaruchnytsia imperii: spohady politvyaznia* (A hostage of empire: memoirs of a political prisoner). Lviv, Ukraine: PP Soroka, 2009.

Zemskov, Viktor. "Gulag (instoriko-sotsiologicheskii aspect)" (historical-sociological aspect). *Sotsiologicheskie issledovania* no. 7 (1991): 3–16.

Chapter 9

One Step Forward, Two Steps Back?

Developing a Women's Peace Agenda in Post-Soviet Armenia and Azerbaijan[1]

Sinéad Walsh

The idea of a women's peace agenda has long been a source of tension within academic feminism. Lines have been drawn between those who favor an agenda that promotes the positive role of "feminine" qualities in peacebuilding and mediation processes, and those who believe that this risks essentializing women, undermining their capacity to perform a variety of roles in conflict and post-conflict settings and limiting feminist agency.[2] These debates have intensified in the aftermath of United Nations Security Council Resolution 1325, which was the product of an active feminist campaign in and outside the United Nations. Both as discourse and practice, the 1325 agenda focuses strongly on women as victims or as peacemakers.[3] Critics of this agenda argue that it reproduces conservative notions of gender and security, and that its top-down approach to women in conflict areas raises difficult questions about the relationship between feminism and imperialism.[4]

This chapter, which presents a case study on women and peacebuilding in Armenia and Azerbaijan, attempts to chart a path around these obstacles by paying close attention to the local processes of social and political transformation of which women's peace activism is a part. The first section, drawing on previous sociological and anthropological studies, argues that by adopting a more localized standpoint, feminists both in and outside of academia may be able to develop more appropriate ways of engaging in acts of solidarity with women affected by conflict.[5] The second part sketches the background to conflict and transition in the post-Soviet republics of Azerbaijan and Armenia. The remaining sections, based primarily on the author's fieldwork experiences in 2012 and 2013, argue that while women's peacebuilding initiatives may appear paradigmatic of the Women, Peace and Security agenda, they become open to an alternative reading when viewed in light of ongoing social and political developments. Furthermore, the discursive representation of women and peacebuilding—and related developments in the women's peace agenda—must be read against a complex web of power relations in which the value of gender is far from neutral.

THE INTERNATIONAL FRAMEWORK ON WOMEN, PEACE, AND SECURITY

The International Framework on Women, Peace and Security UNSCR 1325, adopted in October 2000, sets out a clear agenda on Women, Peace and Security, including: increasing women's participation in conflict resolution and peacebuilding, mainstreaming a gender perspective in United Nations peacekeeping operations, and protecting the rights of women and girls in conflict and post-conflict situations.[6] Contemporary discourse around the Resolution celebrates the peacemaking role played by some—though by no means all—women in places such as Northern Ireland and Liberia. These examples are used to support the practice of systematically engaging women in conflict resolution and peacebuilding in order to make a positive impact on international peace and security.[7] While this campaign initially targeted the UN Security Council, many have since questioned if and how individual member states implement the Resolution, particularly in the context of negotiations and post-conflict transition, and through the mechanisms of detailed National Action Plans.[8]

A key point to have emerged in this literature is that the implementation of a Women, Peace and Security agenda is rarely if ever effective without the support of women's civil society organizations. Therefore, while international organizations continue to lobby for change at an institutional level, there has also been recognition of the need to transmit an understanding of UNSCR 1325 to women's organizations in countries affected by and emerging from conflict.[9] The Resolution continues to be framed as a (welcome) tool for women's organizations to overcome barriers to participation, as a result of which some local women's groups have become targets for what Judy El-Bushra identifies as the "cultural essentialism" of the 1325 agenda.[10]

Another aspect of the Women, Peace and Security agenda that has been criticized in the literature is its perceived neutrality. A striking example of this is in the case of Iraq, where Nadje Al-Ali notes that some women's rights activists are reluctant to associate themselves with the Women, Peace and Security agenda for fear of aligning themselves with international occupation and increasing their marginalization.[11] Annika Björkdahl, looking at post-Dayton Bosnia-Herzegovina, succinctly argues that "gender is used relationally between competing forces—the international peacebuilding industry and local nationalists—as a tool to ensure the imposition of the values and norms inherent in the peacebuilding discourse and/or as a mechanism for local politicians to consolidate their domination of the private/domestic sphere."[12] Other research on the Balkan peace processes suggests that while certain actors outwardly conform to international expectations around gender and peace, adopting the relevant non-governmental organization (NGO) "buzzwords," they also subvert expectations by continuing to define peace and justice in their own way.[13]

In relation to the case study that follows, it is worth noting that the question of global/local feminism has been raised previously with regard to both Armenia and Azerbaijan, which became exposed to the influence of Western feminism after the fall of the Soviet Union.[14] The language of "peacebuilding," which is widely used by NGOs and the even more recent discourse on Women, Peace and Security, are easily read as the product of Western influence, and can be linked to programs implemented by international organizations, including the United Nations Development Fund for Women (UNIFEM) which promoted UNSCR 1325 in the Caucasus region up to 2006.[15] However, the language used by women's rights activists is also a reflection of their agency and strategic engagement with the discursive and practical tools offered by the "hegemonic model" of international feminism.[16]

This chapter does not present an exhaustive genealogy of women's peacebuilding in Armenia and Azerbaijan. It does, however, aim to highlight the disparity between the simplicity of the liberal "add women (to peace processes) and stir" formula and the broader transformations that are taking place in the region. It also portrays women's rights activists as complex actors with a flexible approach to the Women, Peace and Security agenda. However, as the overall political situation of both Armenia and Azerbaijan may be unfamiliar to many readers, I will first provide a brief overview of the conflict and transition process.

ARMENIA, AZERBAIJAN, AND THE CONFLICT OVER NAGORNO-KARABAKH

Armenia and Azerbaijan are situated at the confluence of three historically great powers—the Russian, Ottoman, and Persian empires. The two nations gained independence in 1918, but were incorporated into the Soviet Union in 1920. Both countries laid claim to the territory of Nagorno-Karabakh, which had an ethnic Armenian majority but was eventually assigned to Soviet Azerbaijan as an autonomous region.[17] In the 1980s, this latent conflict was once again politicized as nationalist movements emerged across the USSR and

Armenians in Nagorno-Karabakh demanded unification with Armenia. The war of 1988 to 1994 resulted in 20,000 fatalities and up to one million refugees and internally displaced people. This period of history was also marked by the cataclysmic dissolution of the Soviet Union in 1991, and the coming to power of the first democratic governments in both countries.[18]

Following a ceasefire agreement in 1994, the Organisation for Security and Cooperation in Europe (OSCE) was mandated to mediate a settlement. It established the so-called Minsk Group, now composed of Russian, French and American cochairs, to mediate between Azerbaijan and Armenia. While Karabakh itself has existed as a de facto state under Armenian patronage for 20 years, neither Karabakh Armenians nor the community of displaced Karabakh Azerbaijanis are formally represented in the negotiations. Both countries remain prepared for war and frequently engage in militarist and nationalist rhetoric.[19] In addition, expert groups have warned that the regular ceasefire breaches on both sides, which claim the lives of some 30 soldiers annually, could lead to the sudden re-escalation of the conflict.[20]

This situation of "no war, no peace" has been coterminous with the rise of autocratic political regimes and the demise of the democratic transition paradigm in the post-Soviet states.[21] As a result, civil society peacebuilders face increasing challenges emanating from the government level. Meanwhile, resolving the conflict over Nagorno-Karabakh or strengthening civil society in Armenia and Azerbaijan have never been a priority for the international community, in comparison with other conflict zones. Local NGOs, dependent on Western donors, have flitted between liberal concepts of human rights, democracy, and peacebuilding, creating a bricolage out of these concerns in an attempt to secure financial survival and to weave a shield against political repression. As a result they have variously been labeled as traitors, grant-eaters, and foreign agents by local politicians, and failed to gain the trust of the population at large—especially concerning peacebuilding.[22]

AN OVERVIEW OF WOMEN'S PEACE INITIATIVES

In spite of these challenges, women's peacebuilding has emerged as a distinct phenomenon in Armenia and Azerbaijan, as became clear to me during seven months of ethnographic fieldwork in the region. My research into how local women's organizations were responding to the Women, Peace and Security discourse brought me into contact with a dozen NGOs working in the sphere of women's rights and gender issues. Just over half of these had incorporated peacebuilding into their agenda, while others had at least some experience of transnational networking. The quotes used in this chapter are drawn from fifteen formal interviews with women's rights activists, which were used to supplement extensive participant observation at local events and cross-border meetings. Participants included experienced heads of NGOs as well as more recently recruited staff and volunteers. Throughout the research, particular attention was paid to the perspectives of women who were displaced during the conflict or are now living in the breakaway region or border areas.

It should be noted than in spite of many parallels, especially with regard to the post-Soviet legacy, Armenia and Azerbaijan are by no means uniform. They differ along ethnic, linguistic, and religious lines, as well as according to their present political and economic circumstances. Equally, there are tangible differences between NGOs within each country. However, as far as peacebuilding is concerned, the two sectors have been subject to similar influences and are engaged in a high level of transnational cooperation, which has a partially homogenizing effect. While differences remain in terms of how the two communities remember the war and imagine peace, outwardly their discourse conforms increasingly to the international Women, Peace and Security agenda. It should also be noted that outside of women's organizations, there are many women in the South Caucasus who play an active role in peacebuilding. However, this analysis pertains predominantly to women's collective activism for peace and security.

Women's NGOs began to emerge in Armenia and Azerbaijan toward the end of the Soviet period, and were shaped by both the war and political transition. Some women's groups were initially formed with the aim of extending women's traditional caring role to refugees, to those displaced and disabled by war, and to families deprived of the main breadwinner. Other organizations were more focused on political engagement, and on responding to liberal political and economic reforms, which stood to disadvantage women disproportionately by removing many of the safeguards and social protections that had existed under the Soviet Union. Some organizations did both, combining a strong position on the importance of supporting families and children with a demand for women's rights to be guaranteed at the political level. In either case, women were seen as playing a role that incorporated a strong sense of patriotism and national development.[23]

Within the first few years of transition, women's organizations became exposed to international women's networks and feminist discourse, including the participation of some women at the UN World Conference on Women in Beijing in 1995. The range of issues being addressed by women's NGOs both expanded and solidified during this period. Many organizations began dealing with issues such as domestic violence, human trafficking, and women's health. Some were also involved in capacity building programs focused on women's leadership, combining gender issues with democratization and often bringing together women from Armenia, Azerbaijan, and Georgia.

Some remained heavily engaged with communities affected by conflict, and began establishing links between women from Azerbaijan and Armenia. New organizations continued to form, including self-identified feminist collectives. A transnational women's network began to coalesce around a shared set of values including women's rights, peace, and democracy.

The existence of such initiatives outwardly conforms to the expectations of the international community regarding women's role in peacebuilding, and has been used as a foundation for introducing UNSCR 1325 among women's NGOs. However, local women have expressed ambivalence toward the Women, Peace and Security agenda. Earlier initiatives such as the Women's Peace Coalitions or the Caucasus Women's League, which advocated for women to play a more prominent role in peacebuilding, wound down within a few years, leaving the legacy of Women, Peace and Security discourse, but no formal structures uniting the women who had participated.[24] Many participants in interviews expressed doubt about the establishment of a women's peace movement, and some, such as this Azerbaijani activist, speculated that violence might reoccur before women could be mobilized en masse:

> If the war is re-started, for example, then there will be something about the decisions which women have to make, that they don't want their family members to get lost, so they might be united . . . that might be a topic which would bring fundamental change.[25]

Nevertheless, women's NGOs continue to cooperate with international NGOs in the sphere of women and peacebuilding, and are increasingly looking for ways to promote women's participation in the formal peace process, such as the development of National Action Plans on UNSCR 1325.

Many of the interviewees who participated in this research, knowing that I was particularly interested in Resolution 1325, spoke at length about the positive aspects of women's peacebuilding projects, and the changes these had heralded in their own lives and those of participants. While admitting that they had some concerns about the short-term prospects, they argued that this was a step-by-step process that was slowly gaining ground. However, others were less positive, and referred to UNSCR 1325 as a bureaucratic document which was relevant for some women's organizations, but not for women in general. Many were preoccupied with ongoing political developments in the region, expressing the fear of renewed warfare or internal political conflict. An Armenian activist stated that:

> You don't have these diplomatic relations and you still have closed borders . . . with Azerbaijan and with Turkey, so you feel that there is sort of—the conflict is not settled down until the end. So you live with this fear of war, fear of having the war once again, so that's even more terrible.[26]

Thus, while women's peacebuilding initiatives conform to the international discourse on Women, Peace, and Security, close observation reveals the a sub-text in which war and insecurity remain the dominant features of women's everyday lives, and peacebuilding can more accurately be read as a form of conflict prevention. Moreover, the presence of shared values is not synonymous with a shared understanding of the conflict or of the role of NGOs in conflict resolution.

WOMEN'S PEACE ACTIVISM IN BROADER PERSPECTIVE

While the scope of women's peacebuilding is gradually expanding from bigger cities to towns and villages around the region, concerns remain about the efficacy of peacebuilding within the broader context. NGOs may reach their goal of breaking down barriers between individual Armenians and Azerbaijanis and of raising awareness about the value of peace, but the two societies seem to be as embattled as ever. One interviewee, locating the crux of the issue in the geopolitical conflict between Russia, the United States and Turkey, described the false sense of progress within the peace process:

> We are doing like one step forward, two steps back; it's like the same mechanism, that there is an illusion that we are going on forward but no, we are stuck in the same place, actually. It isn't reality.[27]

Others expressed concern about the negative impact of the mass media's militaristic and nationalistic rhetoric on peacebuilding. Many described periods when civil society relations have undergone particular strain, including around the anniversaries of particular episodes in the conflict and during intense ceasefire violations.[28] It should be noted that relations between the peacebuilders themselves do not necessarily become more strained at these times—rather, it is often fear of public opinion and exposing inexperienced activists to retaliation from their communities that forces NGOs to weigh the benefits of peacebuilding against the risks.

The controversy surrounding different interpretations of the conflict leads to reluctance among many of those involved in peacebuilding initiatives to discuss some of the more sensitive issues under negotiation, such as the eventual political status of Nagorno-Karabakh, or return of refugees and displaced persons to their places of origin. While the two governments have conflicting views on these issues, so do many of the participants in peacebuilding projects, who must weigh their desire for peace between the two nations against their own reluctance to compromise on certain issues. The women involved in this study often practiced a strategic silence around some of the more sensitive issues, preferring to focus where possible on commonalities between communities.[29] In justifying this avoidance of "political" issues, a number of interviewees indicated that the gap between the negotiations process and civil society peacebuilding is too large to be overcome by grassroots activists alone. Even with the aid of UNSCR 1325, women's organizations are currently underprepared for resolving the outstanding issues in the Nagorno-Karabakh conflict. To expect it of them is, as feminist scholars have warned, creating an additional "peace burden" for women affected by conflict.[30]

Although it was common for women to refer to their organizations as "apolitical," a recurring theme throughout the fieldwork was women's criticism of corruption, injustice, and authoritarianism in their own countries. A number of activists asserted that while women's peacebuilding appeared to have little impact on the peace process, it could help to raise the level of democratic development across the region, starting at the community level. Women's NGOs were working in loose collaboration with a range of civil society organizations and independent media to create the conditions in which questions about gender, peace, and justice could be opened up for public debate and dialogue. Yet not all civil society activists or opposition politicians are in favor of peacebuilding, and some may call for democratization while supporting the government's hardline position in negotiations.[31] The task of creating a culture of peace, and the cooperation it entails between women and men, is a reminder that there is more to any women's peace agenda than a seat at the negotiation table.

Women's organizations mainly sought to portray themselves as neutral actors who were willing to cooperate with the state in developing new measures for women's participation. Yet at the same time, many of the activists who are involved in women's rights organizations also belong to opposition political parties or youth movements which challenge the legitimacy of the present governments and question their capacity to carry out structural reform. Several of the women I spoke to over the course of this research either supported or participated in a series of street protests in 2013, which challenged the outcome of presidential elections in both countries, as well as focusing on other domestic abuses such as military deaths and police violence in Azerbaijan or Armenia's decision to strengthen ties with Russia through the proposed Eurasian Customs Union. Opposition activists have been looking to protest movements in Turkey and Ukraine for examples of large-scale civil resistance against state corruption and the resurgence of Russian influence in the Black Sea region.

This raises some provocative questions about the Women, Peace and Security agenda and its relationship to political intransigence and the struggle for participatory democracy. Do women's organizations which seek dialogue with a corrupt or undemocratic state necessarily become co-opted by the political system? If progress is made on the implementation of UNSCR 1325, but the legitimacy of the political system is called into question, could the international agenda for Women, Peace and Security ultimately result in a backlash against women's organizations? The international community has a clear agenda around women's political participation, but the way forward may not be so obvious to activists who face daily choices about relying on the state as a partner in delivering peace and security. These choices are also bound up in the everyday contestation of gender politics at a local level.

REFLECTIONS ON PEACEBUILDING, FEMINISM, AND THE STATE

A positive aspect of UNSCR 1325 is that it offers legitimacy to women's activism and allows for the spread of multiple discourses on peace, security, and human rights. The work of women's NGOs encompasses a range of activities and ideas, but according to most interviewees, all of these branches stem from a common understanding of women's rights. In response to a question about this connection, one activist from Azerbaijan pointed out that as a result of the conflict:

> An enormous number of women were deprived of their living place . . . On that territory there were schools, hospitals, there were businesses where they worked. That means their right to work was taken away, their rights were taken away. That's why we absolutely don't distinguish [between women's rights and peacebuilding]; they're one and the same. We're taking practical steps towards regaining their rights.[32]

These organizations likewise deploy various discourses on gender, in which a complex understanding of "women" is continually weighed against their contemporary role in society. On the one hand, these women's rights defenders are well versed in terms of local laws and decision-making procedures, as well as international instruments such as the Convention to Eliminate All Forms of Discrimination Against Women (CEDAW) and the United Nations Resolutions on Women, Peace and Security. On the other hand, in the context of peacebuilding, a strong appeal is made to women's role in the family and in the community, as well as the particular troubles they went through during the war. Yet women who expressed this point of view did not hold to it rigidly. For example, one claimed:

> You know, I don't agree with all that "women suffer more"—they're also fighters, if you take a child away from its mother she will fight worse than a man, she

> will struggle even harder—so you know, you can't say that women don't have that warrior instinct, no, women have it too. But women think more about how to keep things smooth, how to keep the family together, how to create shelter.[33]

This viewpoint offers an important variation on maternalist discourses which have been known to present women as essentially nonviolent. Other interviewees gave examples of women who proved an exception to the idea of women's peacemaking identity, including female members of Parliament or politicians' wives, and they were quick to point out the suffering of men, including their own fathers and brothers, both during and after the war. Nevertheless, the dominant discourse which they had constructed about women's leadership appealed to a conservative national discourse which saw women's primary role as being in the home. It was important in the given context that women were seen as bridging the home and the public sphere rather than transgressing that particular boundary.

However, within some organizations and particularly among the younger generation of activists, there was a greater enthusiasm for exploring discourses around gender and sexuality, and experimenting with nontraditional forms of activism, such as flashmobs and social media campaigns. Among these organizations, there was a tendency for women to describe themselves as feminist, in spite of the prevalent discourse in post-Soviet societies which equates feminism with separatism, radicalism, or lesbianism. Yet outside of the narrow sphere of like-minded activists, this was an identity that many maintained a strategic silence about. Some activists were uncomfortable sharing feminist ideas with their parents, classmates, or colleagues. Often, when implementing peacebuilding projects at the community level, these organizations did not promote themselves as "feminist," although they did promote feminist values. There is a widespread view that a large part of society, particularly in rural areas, is too traditional to accept feminist discourse or a transformation in gender roles.

In Azerbaijan, women identifying as feminists approached awareness-raising in an almost organic way, framing their activism in terms of youth, education, and development, and avoiding overt politicization of gender. By investing young women and girls with a sense of civic duty and citizenship, they could develop their understanding of gender over time and provide access to information on matters such as sexual health and reproductive rights, which would be otherwise considered taboo. Similarly, the opportunity to participate in cross-border peacebuilding projects arose for younger women after they had been active in the organization for some time and adopted its values of peace, human rights, and women's empowerment. Women's NGOs in Armenia approached communities in a similar way, introducing the subjects of women's rights, leadership, and peacebuilding piece by piece. They also invited men to participate in early sessions, so that they could understand that it did not constitute a threat to their position in society.

However, some women's organizations in Armenia have achieved a high degree of visibility as feminist NGOs, which has had a serious impact on their security. Throughout the summer of 2013, women's organizations which were involved in the drafting of a law on gender equality became the subject of a homophobic propaganda campaign that presented gender equality as incommensurate with traditional Armenian values, equating the words "gender" and "gender-equality" with homosexuality and in turn pedophilia. This campaign included direct threats against named individuals and against the property of NGOs.[34] The campaign reflected the broader discourse on "traditional sexual orientation" and family values which is on the rise across the post-Soviet space. Women's rights activists saw this as being directly linked to political decision making, as the campaign against women's organizations was one in which the European Union was portrayed as a decadent and decaying society, while Russia was exalted as the defender of traditional family values. The coordinated attack on women's rights organizations melted away shortly after the Armenian government forwent an Association Agreement with the EU and announced its plans to join the Russian-led Eurasian Customs Union.[35]

The Armenian case is a paradigmatic example of how easily antifeminist and anti-gender discourse can be mobilized against women's organizations in contexts where the dominant cultural values are still bound to the existence of the patriarchal nation-state. Insofar as the state not only failed to adopt the law on gender equality but also was arguably complicit in putting women's rights activists at risk, it is questionable to what extent the state is a reliable partner in delivering peace and security for women. Regional initiatives creating a political/peacebuilding platform for women across the South Caucasus, however much they might appeal to traditional gender discourse, are therefore likely to maintain a high degree of separation from the development of state policy. In spite of the entry point provided by UNSCR 1325, the state may be more inclined to adapt to new norms on Women, Peace and Security by playing on more traditional gender roles—for example, by highlighting women's position as victims—and inserting its own ethno-territorial agenda into the discourse.

While the international feminist community can provide moral and technical support to women's NGOs in the region, they cannot confer legitimacy on them at the local level, nor spark a broader popular movement. In the current situation, the politics of gender must also be played out between women's organizations, the state, and other organizations working in the sphere of human rights, democracy, and conflict resolution. There is already much interplay between the two, and a growing awareness of gender issues in society. Yet it is also clear that many activists—including women's rights activists—understand feminism as something that happens in a marginal space, not as a fundamental part of the social transformation process. Bringing women's rights from the margins to the center of social transformation is an essential component of strengthening women's role in social and political change across the South Caucasus.

CONCLUSION

Both the discourse on Women, Peace and Security, and the practical agenda which accompanies it, consistently underrate the levels of social fragmentation and political instability in post-conflict and transitional contexts. Armenia and Azerbaijan represent a very specific scenario that challenges the liberal formula for women's participation by invoking not only protracted conflict and negotiations, but also governments that actively use war as a propaganda mechanism, two nations still divided over the past, a political entity which is unrecognized by the international system, and a fragmented opposition which increasingly frames its activities in terms of civil resistance rather than reform. Any attempt to provide a simplified understanding of women's roles in peace processes is subject to the criticism that women's collective activism is a complex phenomenon in which various actors adopt a range of subjectivities and approaches in their interactions at the level of state, civil society, and community.

The underlying potential for political instability and the very clear danger of gender becoming a battlefield for nationalist actors and civil society activists shows that in spite of international feminist intervention, women's rights activists—who are also peacebuilders—remain in a vulnerable position. A broader view of the political situation calls into question the strategy of relying on the state as a partner in delivering the Women, Peace and Security agenda. While women's organizations may make some inroads on state policies, they must also seek a balance between the co-opting influences of both national and international actors, and enact the results of this through daily practices of interaction with local communities and civil society. At a time when power and authority in the post-Soviet space are being reshaped in unexpected ways, the study of women's role in the process of social and political transformation can be expected to yield rich information about the politics of gender, peace, and security in a changing world.

NOTES

1. This chapter is based on ongoing PhD research which is funded by the Irish Research Council. Thank you to Gillian Wylie and Katie Sheehan for their generous

support and comments on earlier versions, and to all those who provided me with a warm welcome to the South Caucasus in 2012 and 2013. While this chapter draws on interviews and participant observation conducted in Armenia and Azerbaijan, the views expressed here are my own and should not be attributed to any organizations or activists in those countries.

2. Christine Sylvester, *Feminist International Relations: An Unfinished Journey* (Cambridge, MA: Cambridge University Press, 2002), 207–24; *contra* Betty Reardon, *Sexism and the War System* (Syracuse, NY: Syracuse University Press, 1996).

3. Nadine Puechguirbal, "Discourses on Gender, Patriarchy and Resolution 1325: A Textual Analysis of UN Documents," *International Peacebuilding* 17.2 (2010).

4. Diane Otto, "Power and Danger: Feminist Engagement with International Law through the UN Security Council," *Australian Feminist Law Journal*, vol. 32 (2010); Laura J. Shepherd, *Gender, Violence and Security: Discourse as Practice* (London, England: Zed Books, 2008).

5. Chandra Mohanty, *Feminism without Borders: Decolonizing Theory, Practicing Solidarity* (Durham, NC: Duke University Press, 2003); Caren Kaplan, "The Politics of Location as Transnational Feminist Critical Practice," in *Scattered Hegemonies: Postmodernity and Transnational Feminist Practices*, ed. Inderpal Grewal and Caren Kaplan (Minneapolis, MN: University of Minnesota Press, 1994).

6. United Nations Security Council, *United Nations Security Council Resolution 1325* [S/RES/1325], October 31, 2000, http://www.unfpa.org/women/docs/res_1325e.pdf.

7. Sanam Anderlini, *Women Building Peace: What They Do, Why It Matters* (Boulder, CO: Lynne Rienner, 2007), 81–83; Elisabeth Porter, *Peacebuilding: Women in International Perspective* (London, England: Routledge, 2007), 76.

8. Christine Bell and Catherine O'Rourke, "Peace Agreements or Pieces of Paper? The Impact of UNSCR 1325 on Peace Processes and their Agreements," *International and Comparative Law Quarterly* 59.4 (2010); Kara Ellerby, "(En)gendered Security? The Complexities of Women's Inclusion in Peace Processes," *International Interactions: Empirical and Theoretical Research in International Relations* 39.4 (2013); Fionnuala Ní Aoláin and Eilish Rooney, "Underenforcement and Intersectionality: Gendered Aspects of Transition for Women," *The International Journal of Transitional Justice* 1.3 (2007).

9. Carol Cohn, Helen Kinsella, and Sheri Gibbings, "Women, Peace and Security: Resolution 1325," *International Feminist Journal of Politics* 6.1 (2004).

10. Judy El-Bushra, "Feminism, Gender and Women's Peace Activism," *Development and Change* 38.1 (2007).

11. Nadje Al-Ali, "Reconstructing Gender: Iraqi Women between Dictatorship, War, Sanctions and Occupation," *Third World Quarterly* 26.4/5 (2005).

12. Annika Björkdahl, "A Gender-Just Peace? Exploring the Post-Dayton Peace Process in Bosnia," *Peace & Change* 37.2 (2012): 287.

13. Elissa Helms, "The Gender of Coffee: Women and Reconciliation Initiatives in Post-War Bosnia and Herzegovina," *Focaal—Journal of Global and Historical Anthropology*, vol. 57 (Summer 2010); Laura McLeod, "Experiences, Reflections and Learning: Feminist Organisations, Security Discourse and SCR 1325," in *Making*

Gender, Making War: Violence, Military and Peacekeeping Practices, ed. Annica Kronsell and Erika Svedberg (London, England: Routledge, 2012).

14. Nayereh Tohidi, "The Global-Local Intersection of Feminism in Muslim Societies: The Cases of Iran and Azerbaijan," *Social Research* 69.3 (2002); Armine Ishkanian, "Working at the Local-Global Intersection: The Challenges Facing Women in Armenia's Nongovernmental Organization Sector," in *Post-Soviet Women Encountering Transition: Nation Building, Economic Survival, and Civic Activism*, ed. Kathleen Kuehnast and Carol Nechemias (Washington, DC: Woodrow Wilson Center Press, 2004).

15. See, for example, accounts of the UNIFEM-led program Women for Conflict Prevention and Peacebuilding in the South Caucasus (2001–2006), some of which appear in the bulletins of the regional coalition Women for Peace, accessed March 7, 2014, http://www.gender-az.org/index_en.shtml?id_main=11&id_sub=29.

16. Chela Sandoval, *Methodology of the Oppressed* (Minneapolis, MN: University of Minnesota Press, 2000), 47–54.

17. Ronald G. Suny, *Transcaucasia, Nationalism and Social Change: Essays in the History of Armenia, Azerbaijan, and Georgia* (Ann Arbor, MI: University of Michigan Press, 1996).

18. Mark Beissinger, *Nationalist Mobilization and the Collapse of the Soviet State* (Cambridge, MA: Cambridge University Press, 2002), 186–90, 375–78; Thomas De Waal, *Black Garden: Armenia and Azerbaijan through Peace and War* (New York, NY: New York University Press, 2003).

19. Thomas De Waal, "Remaking the Nagorno-Karabakh Peace Process," *Survival: Global Politics and Strategy* 52.4 (2010).

20. International Crisis Group, "Armenia and Azerbaijan: A Season of Risks," Europe Briefing No. 71, September 26, 2013, accessed March 7, 2014, http://www.crisisgroup.org/en/regions/europe/south-caucasus/b071-armenia-and-azerbaijan-a-season-of-risks.aspx.

21. Thomas Carothers, "The End of the Transition Paradigm," *Journal of Democracy* 13.1 (2002).

22. Avaz Hasanov and Armine Ishkanian, "Bridging Divides: Civil Society Peacebuilding Initiatives," in *The Limits of Leadership: Elites and Societies in the Nagorny Karabakh Peace Process*, ed. Laurence Broers (London, England: Conciliation Resources, 2006); International Alert, *Advancing the Prospects for Peace: 20 Years of Civil Peacebuilding in the Context of the Nagorny Karabakh Conflict* (London, England: International Alert, 2013), 6–7.

23. Nora Dudwick, "Out of the Kitchen into the Cross-Fire: Women in Independent Armenia," in *Post-Soviet Women: from the Baltic to Central Asia*, ed. Mary Buckley (Cambridge, MA: Cambridge University Press, 1997); Mehrangiz Najafizadeh, "Women's Empowering Carework in Post-Soviet Azerbaijan," *Gender & Society* 17.2 (2003).

24. Natella Akaba, "The Peacebuilding Experience of the Caucasus Women's League," in *Mediation and Dialogue in the South Caucasus: A Reflection on 15 Years of Conflict Transformation Initiatives* (London, England: International Alert, 2012).

25. Author interview, Baku, October 2012.

26. Author interview, Yerevan, October 2013.

27. Author interview, Yerevan, October 2013.

28. Many interviewees also referred to the case of Ramil Safarov, an Azerbaijani soldier who was convicted of the murder of an Armenian solider during a NATO conference in Budapest in 2004. In 2012 he was extradited to Azerbaijan, where he received a presidential pardon. While not all Azerbaijanis supported this decision, the incident put a great deal of strain on the diplomatic and civil society level relationships between the countries, and caused Armenia to step up its own controversial rhetoric around the use of an airport in Nagorno-Karabakh.

29. The tactic of maintaining silence on sensitive or divisive issues is a feature of many women's peace initiatives. Cynthia Cockburn, *The Space Between Us: Negotiating Gender and National Identity During Conflict* (London, England: Zed Books, 1998), 262, cited in Helms, "The Gender of Coffee," 18.

30. Laura J. Shepherd, "Sex, Security and Superhero(in)es: From 1325 to 1820 and Beyond," *International Feminist Journal of Politics* 13.4 (2011).

31. LINKS: Dialogue, Analysis, Research, "Karabakh: The Big Debate," December 2, 2011, http://links-dar.org/2011/12/02/karabakh-the-big-debate/.

32. Author interview, Baku, November 2012.

33. Author interview, Baku, November 2012.

34. Women's Resource Centre Armenia, "Persecution and Threats Towards Women's Rights Defenders and Threat to Freedom of Association and Expression in Armenia," August 28, 2013, available at AWID, http://www.awid.org/Library/Persecution-and-threats-towards-women-s-rights-defenders-and-threat-to-freedom-of-association-and-expression-in-Armenia.

35. Author's field notes, Yerevan, September 2013.

BIBLIOGRAPHY

Akaba, Natella. "The Peacebuilding Experience of the Caucasus Women's League." In *Mediation and Dialogue in the South Caucasus: A Reflection on 15 Years of Conflict Transformation Initiatives*, edited by Batal Kobakhia, Jana Javakhishvili, Larisa Sotieva, and Juliet Schofield, 319–28. London, England: International Alert, 2012.

Al-Ali, Nadje. "Reconstructing Gender: Iraqi Women between Dictatorship, War, Sanctions and Occupation." *Third World Quarterly* 26.4/5 (2005): 739–58.

Anderlini, Sanam. *Women Building Peace: What They Do, Why It Matters*. Boulder, CO: Lynne Rienner, 2007.

Beissinger, Mark. *Nationalist Mobilization and the Collapse of the Soviet State*. Cambridge, MA: Cambridge University Press, 2002.

Bell, Christine and Catherine O'Rourke. "Peace Agreements or Pieces of Paper? The Impact of UNSCR 1325 on Peace Processes and their Agreements." *International and Comparative Law Quarterly* 59.4 (2010): 941–80.

Björkdahl, Annika. "A Gender-Just Peace? Exploring the Post-Dayton Peace Process in Bosnia." *Peace & Change* 37.2 (2012): 286–317.

Carothers, Thomas. "The End of the Transition Paradigm." *Journal of Democracy* 13.1 (2002): 5–20.

Cockburn, Cynthia. *The Space Between Us: Negotiating Gender and National Identity During Conflict.* London, England: Zed Books, 1998.

Cohn, Carol, Helen Kinsella, and Sheri Gibbings. "Women, Peace and Security: Resolution 1325." *International Feminist Journal of Politics* 6.1 (2004): 130–40.

De Waal, Thomas. *Black Garden: Armenia and Azerbaijan through Peace and War.* New York, NY: New York University Press, 2003.

———. "Remaking the Nagorno-Karabakh Peace Process." *Survival: Global Politics and Strategy* 52.4 (2010): 159–76.

Dudwick, Nora. "Out of the Kitchen into the Cross-Fire: Women in Independent Armenia." In *Post-Soviet Women: From the Baltic to Central Asia,* edited by Mary Buckley, 235–49. Cambridge, MA: Cambridge University Press, 1997.

El-Bushra, Judy. "Feminism, Gender and Women's Peace Activism." *Development and Change* 38.1 (2007): 131–47.

Ellerby, Kara. "(En)gendered Security? The Complexities of Women's Inclusion in Peace Processes." *International Interactions: Empirical and Theoretical Research in International Relations* 39.4 (2013): 435–60.

Hasanov, Avaz and Armine Ishkanian. "Bridging Divides: Civil Society Peacebuilding Initiatives." In *The Limits of Leadership: Elites and Societies in the Nagorny Karabakh Peace Process,* edited by Laurence Broers, 44–47. London, England: Conciliation Resources, 2006.

Helms, Elissa. "The Gender of Coffee: Women and Reconciliation Initiatives in Post-War Bosnia and Herzegovina." *Focaal—Journal of Global and Historical Anthropology,* vol. 57 (Summer 2010): 17–32.

International Alert. *Advancing the Prospects for Peace: 20 Years of Civil Peacebuilding in the Context of the Nagorny Karabakh Conflict.* London, England: International Alert, 2013.

International Crisis Group. "Armenia and Azerbaijan: A Season of Risks." Europe Briefing No. 71, September 26, 2013. Accessed March 7, 2014. http://www.crisisgroup.org/en/regions/europe/south-caucasus/b071-armenia-and-azerbaijan-a-season-of-risks.aspx.

Ishkanian, Armine. "Working at the Local-Global Intersection: The Challenges Facing Women in Armenia's Nongovernmental Organization Sector." In *Post-Soviet Women Encountering Transition: Nation Building, Economic Survival, and Civic Activism,* edited by Kathleen Kuehnast and Carol Nechemias, 262–87. Washington, DC: Woodrow Wilson Center Press, 2004.

Kaplan, Caren. "The Politics of Location as Transnational Feminist Critical Practice." In *Scattered Hegemonies: Postmodernity and Transnational Feminist Practices,* edited by Inderpal Grewal and Caren Kaplan, 137–52. Minneapolis, MN: University of Minnesota Press, 1994.

LiNKS: Dialogue, Analysis, Research. "Karabakh: The Big Debate," December 2, 2011. Available at http://links-dar.org/2011/12/02/karabakh-the-big-debate/.

McLeod, Laura. "Experiences, Reflections and Learning: Feminist Organisations, Security Discourse and SCR 1325." In *Making Gender, Making War: Violence,*

Military and Peacekeeping Practices, edited by Annica Kronsell and Erika Svedberg, 135–49. London, England: Routledge, 2012.

Mohanty, Chandra. *Feminism without Borders: Decolonizing Theory, Practicing Solidarity*. Durham, NC: Duke University Press, 2003.

Najafizadeh, Mehrangiz. "Women's Empowering Carework in Post-Soviet Azerbaijan." *Gender & Society* 17.2 (2003): 293–304.

Ní Aoláin, Fionnuala and Eilish Rooney. "Underenforcement and Intersectionality: Gendered Aspects of Transition for Women." *The International Journal of Transitional Justice* 1.3 (2007): 338–54.

Otto, Diane. "Power and Danger: Feminist Engagement with International Law through the UN Security Council." *Australian Feminist Law Journal*, vol. 32 (2010): 97–121.

Porter, Elisabeth. *Peacebuilding: Women in International Perspective*. London, England: Routledge, 2007.

Puechguirbal, Nadine. "Discourses on Gender, Patriarchy and Resolution 1325: A Textual Analysis of UN Documents." *International Peacebuilding* 17.2 (2010): 172–87.

Reardon, Betty. *Sexism and the War System*. Syracuse, NY: Syracuse University Press, 1996.

Sandoval, Chela. *Methodology of the Oppressed*. Minneapolis, MN: University of Minnesota Press, 2000.

Shepherd, Laura J. *Gender, Violence and Security: Discourse as Practice*. London, England: Zed Books, 2008.

———. "Sex, Security and Superhero(in)es: From 1325 to 1820 and Beyond." *International Feminist Journal of Politics* 13.4 (2011): 510–21.

Suny, Ronald G. *Transcaucasia, Nationalism and Social Change: Essays in the History of Armenia, Azerbaijan, and Georgia*. Ann Arbor, MI: University of Michigan Press, 1996.

Sylvester, Christine. *Feminist International Relations: An Unfinished Journey*. Cambridge, MA: Cambridge University Press, 2002.

Tohidi, Nayereh. "The Global-Local Intersection of Feminism in Muslim Societies: the Cases of Iran and Azerbaijan." *Social Research* 69.3 (2002): 851–87.

United Nations Security Council. *United Nations Security Council Resolution (UNSCR) 1325* [S/RES/1325], October 31, 2000. http://www.unfpa.org/women/docs/res_1325e.pdf.

Women for Peace. Bulletin No. 1–3 of the Regional South Caucasus Coalition, 2002–2004. *Azerbaijan Gender Information Center (ABIC)*. Accessed March 7, 2014. http://www.genderaz.org/index_en.shtml?id_main=11&id_sub=29.

Women's Resource Centre Armenia. "Persecution and Threats Towards Women's Rights Defenders and Threat to Freedom of Association and Expression in Armenia," August 28, 2013. Available at Association for Women in Development (AWID), http://www.awid.org/Library/Persecution-and-threats-towards-women-s-rights-defenders-and-threat-to-freedom-of-association-and-expression-in-Armenia.

Chapter 10

Black Tradeswomen Building

Toward Pragmatic Peacebuilding for Personal, Cultural, and Institutional Change

Roberta Hunte

Although women comprise 47 percent of the workforce in all occupations, they are only 2.6 percent of the workforce in construction and extraction careers.[1] White, non-Hispanic women make up 2 percent of construction workers, and Hispanic women make up 0.4 percent. African American represent 0.2 percent of the construction workforce, and Asian/Pacific Islander and American Indian/Alaska Native women constitute only 0.1 percent of all construction workers.[2] As these relatively low numbers suggest, the construction industry has been particularly resistant to women joining its ranks. The number of women has increased in many nontraditional occupations for women. For example, women comprise 15 percent of the military. The trades, however, have maintained low percentages of women employees since Executive Order 11246, which prohibited discrimination against women by federal contractors.

Ronald Reagan's presidency in 1980 stymied the tradeswomen's movement with his administration's affront to the affirmative action measures fought for by civil rights and women's rights activists.[3] His office removed the oversight of the inclusion of minority men and women into apprenticeship programs from the jurisdiction of the Equal Employment Opportunities Commission. He also gave industry boards control over their own compliance, thus severely limiting the effectiveness of antidiscrimination legislation.[4] In their report on the state of women in the trades 30 years after the Executive Order, Susan Moir, Meryl Thomson, and Christa Kelleher[5] note that the failure of institutional stakeholders to uphold antidiscrimination legislation fundamentally undercuts women's successful participation in the trades. Manifestations of sexism in the United States construction industry include slurs, derogatory language, wrongful termination, violence, a disregard for safety concerns, patronizing behavior on the job, a hostile work environment, stereotyping, lack of sanitary facilities, and accusations of reverse discrimination.[6]

I came to know and care about tradeswomen in 2008 when working as a career counselor for a pre-apprenticeship program, a training program to prepare women to apply for apprenticeships. Trades careers offer high wages that can support a family, and women's participation in these high wage careers ensures their economic security. In 2010 I began a narrative study with fifteen African American tradeswomen who shared their stories of addressing racism, sexism, and heterosexism in their careers, and their perseverance in the field.[7] The women, from different parts of the United States, worked as carpenters, laborers, cement masons, sprinkler fitters, electricians, contractors, and as technicians. Their careers spanned from six to more than thirty years in the industry. When I worked with them, the women were at different points in their work lives—in retirement, at mid-career, and recently having completed their journey-level accreditation. Journey-level workers have completed thousands of hours of academic and on the job training. They earn from 25 to 50 dollars per hour depending on the trade. The majority of the women interviewed completed formal apprenticeships. Apprenticeships are two to five year programs that combine on the job training and course work through recognized training centers. Apprenticeships are the gateway to becoming a licensed tradesperson.

My sample size is small, so the generalizability of these women's experiences is limited. However, their narratives highlight a continuum between individual acts to remain on the job site to more collective movements to shift institutional policies, practices, and procedures. Their efforts were not always consciously political. Women described their actions as being responsive to discrimination. Women shared with me the overt ways they worked to create an inclusive workplace for themselves and for others like them; for example, some of the women worked on policy advocacy at the local level and within their organizations to change harmful policies or practices. Women also talked about personal acts to overcome and transform prejudice, such as refusing to engage in bullying toward their colleagues even when those colleagues had harmed them. Their efforts had varied success due greatly to limited institutional commitment to women's inclusion on the job.

Marie Dugan's theory of the nested paradigm[8] asserts that conflict is systemic in nature, and that the agency of groups as they attempt conflict resolution strategies or initiatives to improve or advance their position, is embedded within subsystems of the larger system. The nested paradigm positions the actions of individual groups as part of subsystems that are "nested" within systems of overarching macro-system ideologies and institutions. Policies enacted by these systems affect the actions within the subsystem in direct and indirect ways. Using the theory of the nested paradigm, the issues of sexism, racism, and heterosexism are understood to be central factors contributing to the low retention of women in the trades. Relationships on and off the job contribute to, and can serve to mitigate these forms of oppression in the daily lives of tradeswomen. At the level of the subsystem, policies, practices, and procedures of apprenticeship programs, workplaces, and unions contribute to the on-the-ground experiences of tradeswomen, and directly and indirectly affect the issues of racism, sexism, and heterosexism that are present on the job, and are reflective of systemic oppressions throughout the United States.

John Paul Lederach[9] conceptualized peacebuilding efforts as also operating within a nested paradigm. Peacebuilding can be understood to operate at various levels of society with varying levels of efficacy based on one's position within the society and the strength of relationships between different levels of influence in the society. All efforts are affected by the ways institutional and cultural practices and ideologies support or negate these peacebuilding initiatives.

I am making a radical choice in applying peacebuilding to racial and gender conflict in the United States. Often, peacebuilding is discussed in postwar societies and within international contexts. It is not often used in the analysis of efforts to address chronic racial and gender conflicts, particularly in the United States. I am using the term *peacebuilding* to mean acts that seek to address and mitigate direct, institutional, and/or cultural violence. In terms of the experience of black tradeswomen, direct violence can be understood as acts that harm another person and can result in physical, emotional, or psychic harm. This includes sexual harassment and the threat of harm to targeted groups on the job.

Johan Galtung coined the term cultural violence[10] to mean cultural acts and ways of thinking that support the superiority of one identity group over another. In the trades, cultural violence includes racist, sexist, and homophobic jokes, slurs, language, and insults; derogatory representations of people of color, women, and queer people; negative assumptions about the competence, ability, and legitimacy of women and people of color to have these jobs; and hierarchical systems that privilege men, whiteness, and heterosexuality in the workplace. Cultural violence can be perpetuated as direct interpersonal violence, and more pervasively, within an organization and society. Institutional violence includes racist, sexist, and homophobic/transphobic practices that discriminate against women and people of color related to hiring, access to apprenticeships, inadequate job training, retention, and promotion. This also includes the failure of institutions to respond when allegations of racism, sexism, and homophobia are brought to light and the perpetuation of these behaviors by supervisors to subordinates and from peer to peer.

Tradeswomen report experiences of isolation, sexual harassment, endangerment, and poor training from male coworkers on the job.[11] Consistently, women report lower rates of apprenticeship completion than men. An especially high percentage of women leave carpentry apprenticeships—70 percent of women versus 53 percent of men—signifying the low rate of success for women in federally created and supervised construction apprenticeships.[12] Black women may be exposed to greater disrespect and slurs on the job due to their race and gender.[13]

I began to understand the individual and collective acts by black tradeswomen to address racism, sexism, and heterosexism within their workplaces and the broader industry as various peacebuilding efforts: their actions were acts of pragmatic peacebuilding that were both relationally and personally motivated. At times, this pragmatic peacebuilding was in partnership with other tradespeople and was connected to a broader movement for tradeswomen, people of color, and/or unions. Among the women I interviewed, however, their actions were less based on ideals of social justice, and more based on negotiating the real limitations of interpersonal, cultural, and institutional racism, sexism, and heterosexism when they emerged on and off the job site. Hence, their efforts must be understood as nested within a system that offered both opportunities for peace to emerge and a resistance to change. To make sense of these connections, women in the study were encouraged to discuss how they addressed the realities of racism, sexism, and heterosexism at personal, interpersonal, cultural, and institutional levels.

Pragmatic peacebuilding focuses on the day-to-day behaviors of individuals as they seek to address direct, cultural, and institutional violence as it manifests in their lives. Pragmatic peacebuilding efforts move on a continuum from working independently, to working with others, to working with institutions and cultural systems to change oppressive behaviors and attitudes. These efforts may be motivated by desires for larger systemic change, but the majority of the women interviewed did not initially describe themselves as activists or social change agents. When asked if they thought of themselves as activists, most participants answered, "No." After reflection, however, all of them said, "Yes." All interviewees had a desire for change in their positions on the jobsite and to improve their industry for other women and people of color. At times they were victims of racism, sexism, and homophobia. They developed strategies to work with resistant colleagues and to integrate themselves into the industry in order continue their careers while surviving various incidents. For all of the women this was not a smooth process. It was challenging and at times caused them to question whether continuing in the trades was worth it. At times they dealt with extreme isolation on the job, harassment, sexual objectification, extended periods of joblessness, and the disconcerting denial of injustices incurred in their workplaces. For some women survival has meant leaving the trades and returning when conditions improved.

ACTIONS FOR INSTITUTIONAL AND CULTURAL CHANGE

Some of the women interviewed agitated for institutional and cultural change within their organizations and the broader industry. Advocacy for racial and gender justice included two successful discrimination lawsuits against two apprenticeship training centers: five women spoke up about harassment and poor training they received on the jobsite, and two women became business owners and focused on hiring women and people of color. All of the women participated in networking among tradeswomen advocacy groups for moral support, relied on professional ties, and shared a common political agenda. Three women started their own advocacy efforts, and half of the women actively worked to shift the culture and policies of their workplaces and union. The tradeswomen's efforts were met with varying degrees of success in terms of broader change.

Kareema,[14] a cement mason and contractor, was the only study participant who successfully brought legal action against an institution for discrimination. She sued two training centers for practices that overtly discriminated against women. One center had not considered her application to their apprenticeship while the other had hiring practices that stipulated women apprentices could work only if they were specifically requested by a journeyman. No women were requested. While she did not receive any remuneration for her suits, Kareema's efforts created a platform for more women to enter the trades. The suits highlighted the discriminatory practices excluding women and forced unions to shift their behaviors. Suing remains only one component of changing the actual position of women on the job. It is illegal for employers to refuse to hire women based on their gender. However, black women repeatedly discussed the realities of racism and sexism as factors that interfered with steady employment in commercial construction.

Another strategy to increase the representation and success of women in the field has been for women to become contractors themselves and to hire women and people of color on their crews. In becoming the boss, Kareema used her status as a journeyperson and a signatory contractor with the union to bring more women into the trade. This strategy was an answer to the limited commitment on the part of the union to recruit women into apprenticeships, contractors' low investment in the long-term development of women as tradespeople, and the poor training practices that did not prepare female apprentices to become competent journey-level workers.

All of the tradeswomen participated in formal and informal tradeswomen's groups at different times in their careers. Shonda,[15] an electrician, helped start a pre-apprenticeship program for women. Sharla[16] served on the board for a tradeswomen's organization for 10 years. She also worked with other black tradeswomen to develop a pre-apprenticeship program focused on recruiting low-income people and people of color into the trades. A number of the women entered the trades through women-focused, pre-apprenticeship training programs. They used their affiliation with these programs to leverage work, as a platform for consciousness-raising among upcoming tradeswomen about how to navigate sexism on the job, and for public testimony for policy change to address discrimination. For example, Z,[17] a graduate of a women-focused pre-apprenticeship program and a carpenter, attributed a lot of her success in the trades to her long-term connection with her tradeswomen's organization. She said:

> I remember in 2008 . . . I had been off work for maybe a month or two and I just didn't have the money to buy my tools. Tradeswomen Gear Up[18] gave me the money to buy my tools. [In] all the discussion groups and the caucuses that I have been a part of, I've been able to get my story out.
>
> To this day, I still get approached by different people and they say, "I really appreciate the things that you've said. I feel like hearing the things from you and knowing what I know now is going to make my apprenticeship easier." When I'm not working and jobs are far between, Tradeswomen Gear Up puts me on the payroll. I appreciate it in so many ways. Had it not been for Tradeswomen, I probably wouldn't have made it through the trades as fast as I did.[19]

For Z, being involved with Tradeswomen Gear Up helped her leverage work, buy tools, build community, and share her story with others who were considering the trades. She, like all of the women who were heavily involved in tradeswomen's networks, needed the support of other tradeswomen at times in her career.

As part of her consciousness-raising efforts, Z regularly told the story of her career to groups of potential and existing tradeswomen. She also told her story to apprenticeship coordinators as a way of agitating for change, although at times when telling her experiences of racism and sexism other tradeswomen were resistant to her perspective. Z said:

> I'm always willing to tell my story in hopes that all the bad things that I went through, somebody else doesn't have to go through that. Or all the bad things I went through, people can realize their faults, realize their wrongs, and try to attempt to right their wrongs. I love telling my story, because my story is so different from everybody else's. A lot of people have the same experiences that I've had, but have dealt with them differently. I feel like the way I have dealt with mine is what makes my story unique.[20]

Telling her story was a form of catharsis and healing for Z. Though sometimes let down by her fellow white tradeswomen around their denial of the reality of racism on the job, she acknowledged that she still needed her fellow tradeswomen in the struggle for gender equality in the workplace.

Her story inspired others to enter the trades and helped to guide other women who encountered moments where they felt alone. She was fearless in her storytelling. Her experiences were particularly challenging to hear because she was in her late twenties when she began the trades, and at the time of this study was in her mid-thirties. She was a young black woman saying that equity in the trades was not changing for women of color in the same ways that they were for young white women.

Black women are involved in the broader tradeswomen's movement, and the women in this study acknowledged that this movement was important to them. However, they also acknowledged that membership in the broader movement could be difficult at times as white tradeswomen may not support shared leadership with black tradeswomen and may deny the current significance of racism within the trades. Racism is not a thing of the past. That said, black tradeswomen also noted that connections with white tradeswomen off the jobsite were important for pushing for political change at the institutional level, and networking for job prospects. At times, tradeswomen's organizations and their allies may be the only networks available for black tradeswomen.

Women discussed explicitly joining in antiracist and antisexist struggles within their institutions, with black trade unionists and other trade union affiliated groups. Seven of the tradeswomen were active in efforts to address racism and sexism in their unions, workplaces, and cities. These efforts were outside of their job duties and ordinary union involvement. They did so by leading diversity training within their institutions, educating themselves about systemic racism, becoming involved with tradespeople of color advocacy organizations, and bringing up issues of equity within their unions. They also worked with their employers to push management to learn about creating an inclusive workforce, advocating for people who had been victimized, and/or pushing organizations to take up antiracism and antisexism positions/efforts/ideologies to develop a more inclusive workplace. For some of the tradeswomen antiracism and antisexism efforts gave their presence in the trades a greater sense of purpose. This involvement also provided a sense of community and solidarity they may not have had at work.

Union involvement offered black women in this study the opportunity to be known in the union and to assume leadership roles. This had an impact on interpersonal relationships on the job, and fostered greater acceptance of black tradeswomen. Union advocacy groups focused on the needs of women and people of color and have fostered greater opportunities for marginalized groups within unions.

All of these efforts sought to mitigate institutional policies and practices, while also impacting cultural beliefs that devalued nontraditional workers. The women noted the impact of so few women and, depending on the region of the country, so few people of color on their job sites. This isolation at times hindered the efficacy of their efforts for change, yet women continued to engage in this work that proposed solutions and/or agitated for change. Women discussed the impact of the institutional structures that hindered them. At times these women could move the mountain of injustice or at least find ways to navigate around it. Sometimes, though, they had to walk away from the oppressive mountain entirely.

PERSONAL PEACEBUILDING

Racism, sexism, and homophobia can tear down one's sense of self-esteem. When individuals internalize these negative images of themselves as truth they inflict further harm on themselves and this can be transferred to others. This internalization of racist ideologies is part of structural oppression.[21] Resisting the internalization of oppressive ideologies is a component of personal positive peace. bell hooks[22] advocates for the development of a critical consciousness as a crucial component of positive self-esteem. Critical consciousness is the ability to be aware of one's environment and to act accordingly.[23] hooks said most black people were conscious of living in a racist world, however "critical consciousness is at work when we are able to utilize our knowledge of this reality in ways that circumvent racist exploitation and oppression."[24] She described positive self-esteem for black people as acknowledging the reality of racism in one's life, and working to challenge it. hooks[25] discussed black women's self-recovery as a key component of political liberation. She discusses self-recovery as the process of understanding the many ways that racism, classism, sexism, capitalism, and homophobia undermine a group's personal and collective self-determination, and recovery involves the application of this knowledge to work toward personal healing and wellness.

The tradeswomen interviewed said the cultivation of a positive self-concept that was independent of their workplace was necessary for them to continue in the industry and, despite resistance, to build positive relationships. A sense of purpose was a component of this self-concept participants discussed as necessary. They spoke of this sense of purpose as being "grounded" in why they were on the job. This was developed through knowing what they wanted to do and why they were doing it, and maintaining a commitment to that path. For example, Kareema's experiences as an apprentice caused her to develop a particular understanding of self-pride in the face of constant critique:

> I picked that up back in the day as an apprentice. You gotta have pride. They're not going to build up your self-esteem. They're gonna try to tear you down, put you down, and hammer you down on any level and every circumstance.

> My self-esteem has been maintained based on the pride that I know who my enemies are . . . It's all about the other person. It's the person who is actually administering the nonsense. You know, most of them are men, and some of them are women. I've seen women discriminate against other women. It's because their personal self-esteem and their personal growth is not there. So, you expect it. And you move on! I don't acknowledge those people. I didn't expect it any other way [laughing].[26]

As an apprentice Kareema came to understand the insults she encountered from men and women on jobsites as tactics to push her out of the trades. She developed a critical consciousness of the ways racism and sexism operated both in the trades and in broader society. In understanding this she maintained her sense of pride and was no longer surprised or thrown off when people behaved in racist and sexist ways toward her. This sense of pride and a keen understanding of her work environment helped her move past the hostility that coworkers expressed to deter her. Experiencing stigmatization helped Kareema understand the pervasiveness of racism and sexism on the job. It became something she expected. To withstand hostility she focused on building up her self-pride and the worthiness of her cause to advance other women of color in construction.

Other participants noted that experiencing adversity triggered commitment to self-worth. It was in those moments when they were faced with quitting or being pushed out of the trades that they relied on themselves to find the strength to continue. Self-esteem was necessary to navigate the challenges of getting into apprenticeships, getting hired, and staying in positions.

A number of the participants spoke of spirituality and the development of personal integrity as an important component of self-preservation and a positive self-concept. Shonda, an electrician, credited her spirituality as important in helping her navigate her workplace. She tried to "stay connected with who I really am as a spiritual being having this human experience."[27] She believed in reincarnation and said:

> In all environments you find people who are just limited in their ability. You know what I call them? I have this theory; it has to do with my reincarnation. When I find people who are just total assholes and don't get it and treat me like shit, I would always say "Okay this is their first time here." [Giggle] Then when I find people who are really evolved, "Okay they've been here a couple of times. Okay, they know what it takes to get out of here." That has been a survival tip for me.[28]

Shonda's spirituality offered her grace in dealing with personalities and situations throughout her career that have been challenging at best, and life threatening at worst. This spiritual distance supported Shonda to let go of negativity in the workplace, and maintain her personal value. She tried to model respectful behaviors and positive communication on the job. She did not want to have negativity come back to her because of her actions. This approach was a "survival tip"[29] for her. Her sense of grace allowed her to be an ally to people who harmed her in the past. A number of the women described helping people who initially harmed them. Their behaviors were acts of grace toward their colleagues, and a method of self-preservation. They recognized that working together was necessary to complete the job.

Similarly Veronica,[30] a utility worker, noted that personal integrity was a foundation of her moral compass when engaging with coworkers. She said there were times where male coworkers invited her to be a part of the group. Often she refused. At times, being a part of the group meant compromising on personal values that were important to her. Veronica said maintaining her personal value system was more important to her than being a part of the jobsite clique. Veronica said:

> There were times and points in my career where the guys were willing to embrace me, and like "invite me in." Then a few things happened. During some of those times, either part of being a part of them was dissing somebody else. I wouldn't be a part of it. So then that put me back on the outside.
>
> I used to bitch about that, and then I realized I made a choice. I could be a part of it. I empowered myself by saying, "I made a choice to be out here because I am not willing to sacrifice my integrity, or how I function in life in order to be a part of their group." . . . I am very okay standing on my own.[31]

Through these experiences Veronica consciously developed a personal awareness of her agency in relation to her coworkers. She recognized herself as someone who spoke against oppressive group-think in the workplace. Challenging oppressive group-think is necessary for a culture change to occur. She said: "Part of changing a culture, is getting people in there that will stand up and say, 'Hey! That's not okay!' It is so powerful, because that's what it takes."[32] Though Veronica and other tradeswomen in the study paid a price for speaking against oppression in the workplace, they remained true to their values. Their values of inclusion and respect for themselves and others were peacebuilding contributions toward industry change.

Other tradeswomen spoke about challenging off-color humor as a means of setting a hard boundary around themselves. Wanda Lou,[33] a riveter, said when men told sexist or racist jokes around her she would "set them straight." She said:

> You had a few prejudiced people. There's always going to be a few. I knew how to set them straight . . . If they said something to me, I knew how to answer them back . . . I did not allow them to tell me jokes.[34]

Each woman had to determine how she would deal with these comments. Interrupting or challenging these comments assisted in boundary setting, helping women avoid being taken advantage of by male coworkers, and interrupting interpersonal tactics of cultural violence.

Not every black tradeswomen has a critical consciousness or is actively working to address systemic racism and sexism in the industry. Some may be complicit with this system and may perpetuate harm toward others. The women interviewed shared pragmatic personal peacebuilding strategies including the development of a critical consciousness of how power and discrimination operated on the jobsite; a commitment to themselves and their self-worth; the development of a worldview that was unwilling to participate in interpersonal or cultural violence, and the cultivation of their ability to speak out against the discriminatory behaviors they witnessed. This internal peacebuilding is necessary to build the interpersonal relationships on and off the job that are needed to address issues of discrimination in tradeswomen's daily lives and to gather support for broader systemic change. These strategies employed short-term conflict resolution to address immediate issues, and they employed long-term internal peacebuilding strategies to mitigate systemic issues.

RELATIONSHIP BUILDING AS A NECESSARY COMPONENT

Tradeswomen acknowledged they could not succeed on the job without the building of relationships with peers, superiors, and subordinates. Some strategies used to build relationships were to focus on building allies on the job one at a time. Union involvement helped foster those individual relationships. Their long-term presence on the job could not happen without those who were willing to work with them, to stand up for them in the face of bullying and discrimination, to share skills and knowledge about the next job, and to include them in the network. Often this meant befriending people, men and women, who were overtly racist and/or sexist toward them initially. Constructive relationship building between superiors and subordinates protected and supported black women on the job. In terms of pragmatic peacebuilding tradeswomen used the building of relationships to support their professional survival and make way for opportunities.

As the second black woman electrician in her local union, Shonda had to navigate racial and gender stereotypes in every relationship she encountered. She said one-to-one she could connect with her white male coworkers. However, when a ring-leader led other men against her, their tactics were harder for her to surmount. She related some of her challenges with white male coworkers during her apprenticeship program:

> I feel like my lot through this program has been a one-on-one-meet. I have had such wonderful relationships with people. There have been folks who really wanted to kill me, and I have been able to persuade them . . . One-on-one I can get you. I can connect with you. They can see my value system, my work ethic.[35]

Relating her philosophy in working with white people, Shonda said she took each incident as it came. She did not think all white people were out to get her, though she was sensitive to signs of discriminatory behavior. Discrimination was familiar. In Shonda's experience, her presence challenged the white men she worked with to rethink some of their sexism and racism. Her openness to these men somewhat advanced their cultural awareness.

Shonda noted that her efforts meant that white men were open to her, but not necessarily more open to other black people and women. Her experience also brought up the question of whose responsibility it was to create a welcoming environment in the workplace. Shonda was responsible for winning over her colleagues. If she had not successfully done this she would have lost her job. This was not about her skill as an electrician, but rather her ability to soften hostile colleagues. Shonda noted that her relationship building was at the level of the individual. This did not necessarily mean systemic institutional change around workforce inclusion.

Construction requires a collaborative effort. As apprentices some of the women employed the strategy of walking onto jobsites and immediately assessing who was friendly toward them. They then tried to work with that journeyperson and learn as much as they could from him or her. This strategy was aimed to build a network of allies for tradeswomen on the job. However, one of the challenges of construction work is that people often move from job to job and are forced to create new relationships regularly on different job sites.

Shonda acknowledged she could not progress in her career without the white men who were willing to give her a chance on the job. She would not have lasted at different points in her career without her ally relationships with her union brothers. She said:

> If I did not have the [union] brothers I work with there is no way that I could stay there . . . When I started with this job my brothers took care of me. When my manager set me up for failure, to not complete my probationary period, they all wrote letters of my qualification. I had that as my support for my abilities. Against my supervisor! Yeah. It was big . . .
>
> These guys are really like family to me . . . We fight like siblings because we are truly brothers and sisters in this arena out here. That's kind of the beauty of being on a project where you have longevity. I've been at this location now for 19 years off and on.[36]

Shonda credited career longevity in the same place as having helped her build real relationships with her male coworkers. Though their relationships were not devoid of conflict, Shonda trusted her union coworkers to support her. This trust was proven when her coworkers stood up for her job in light of a hostile boss. She returned this ally behavior and stood up for them as well.

At times black tradesmen intentionally worked as allies with the black women in the study. They did this by hiring black tradeswomen, supporting their leadership, and sharing their knowledge as journeymen. They also worked with the black tradeswomen in their workplaces to challenge discrimination. At times, black women in the study experienced sexism from black men. In contrast, women appreciated the moments they were able to work in solidarity with black tradesmen.

In an environment where Veronica felt isolated as one of two women in her workplace, it was difficult for her to find colleagues who understood the combination of subtle and overt racist and sexist acts that occurred. She shared an example of how this solidarity network came into play in the light of oppressive acts. A noose was left in the locker of one of the black men working for a public utility company. In this instance, the employee's supervisor trivialized the incident by publicly laughing about what happened and treating the incident as a joke. The network of tradespeople of color on the job spread the word about the incident among each other. This "network of support"[37] offered Veronica some sense of community on the job. Though the supervisor minimized the significance of the noose incident, having a community of support around the targeted tradesman encouraged him to speak out about what happened.

The supervisor's treatment of this episode as a joke also gave the institutional message that there would be little recourse for the victim of this racist assault. At the time of that incident, the camaraderie among black people on the job was one of the few ways to highlight the egregious nature of the act. In the face of the institution's minimization of racism, group solidarity is a way to resist oppression. Solidarity did not result in holding the utility company accountable for addressing such racist behavior; however it did reinforce to Veronica that she and the other black people were supportive of each other.

To manage interpersonal relationships on the job black women employed some conflict resolution strategies that resulted in short and longer-term relationship building. This relationship building did not always mean that systemic changes to racism and sexism in the workplace were achieved. Rather these relationships served to counteract bias and to support their presence on the job. Without these strategies women said it would have been hard for them to continue in the industry. Strategies discussed ranged from clear boundary setting in regards to how close one allowed their workmates; limiting the types of jokes told around them; trying to educate coworkers about oppressive behaviors and equity issues; and speaking out when they were being mistreated. These pragmatic relationship strategies do not necessarily contribute to systemic peacebuilding, yet without them broader peacebuilding efforts would cease.

CONCLUSION

The stories from the black tradeswomen I interviewed highlight personal and institutional efforts toward peacebuilding. These efforts at the personal level are geared toward maintaining their self-esteem in the face of discrimination and mitigating the effects of oppression on their psyche. Women describe this personal peacebuilding as a way of helping them determine their own code of behavior that did not perpetuate the discriminatory behavior they experienced. This practice of pragmatic peacebuilding happened over time, and the women's ability to engage in these practices changed throughout their careers. At the relational level the tradeswomen I met worked collaboratively across racial and gender differences with coworkers. In having such limited numbers of black women on the job they have had to do this. At times they have been successful, and at times the hostility in the workplace was too much. Their interpersonal relationships were major contributors to their success. Tradeswomen also worked toward institutional and cultural change that addressed the systemic nature of racism and sexism in the workplace. These pragmatic peacebuilding efforts advocated for more inclusive policies, practices, and procedures and sought to increase the representation of women and people of color in the industry.

The women I interviewed cannot speak for all black tradeswomen. Their pragmatic actions have been in an effort to avoid, negotiate, challenge, and at times transform racist and sexist systems. As we theorize grassroots peacebuilding it is important to look at individuals who are directly squeezed by systemic issues. For black tradeswomen to survive in the industry, they have to engage with the issues of racism and sexism on the job throughout their careers. The particularly low numbers of black tradeswomen speaks to the difficult task of staying in this industry and the extent of the systemic impact of racism and sexism. It is not that peacebuilding efforts are not happening within chronic conflicts, like that of racism and sexism within the building trades. Rather, pragmatic peacebuilding acknowledges the interplay between individual actions to address systemic issues and the ways the efficacy of those actions may be supported or nullified by oppression. Given more institutional support pragmatic peacebuilding efforts can provide a framework for more comprehensive peacebuilding.

NOTES

1. National Women's Law Center calculations using Miriam King et al., Integrated Public Use Microdata Series, Current Population Survey 2013: Version 3.0, IPUMS-CPS: Minnesota Population Center (March 2013), available at http://cps.ipums.org/cps/index.shtml (Machine readable data).

2. Ibid.

3. Gunseli Berik and Cihan Bilginsoy, "Do Unions Help or Hinder Women in Training? Apprenticeship Programs in the United States," *Industrial Relations* 39.4 (2006).

4. Francine Moccio, *Live Wire: Women and Brotherhood in the Electrical Industry* (Philadelphia, PA: Temple University Press, 2009).

5. Susan Moir, Meryl Thomson, and Christa Kelleher, "Unfinished Business: Building Equality for Women in the Construction Trades," Scholar Works at UMass Boston: Labor Resource Center, 2011, accessed September 14, 2014, http://scholarworks.umb.edu/cgi/viewcontent.cgi?article=1004&context=lrc_pubs.

6. HASWIC Work Group, "Women in the Construction Workplace: Providing Equitable Safety and Health Protection," Occupational Safety and Health Administration's Advisory Committee on Construction Safety and Health, Department of Labor, 1999, accessed September 14, 2014, https://www.osha.gov/doc/accsh/haswicformal.html.

7. Roberta Hunte, "'My Walk Has Never Been Average': Black Tradeswomen Negotiating Intersections of Race and Gender in Long Term Careers in The United States' Building Trades" (PhD diss., University of Manitoba, 2012).

8. Marie Dugan, "A Nested Theory of Conflict," *Women in Leadership* 1.1 (1996).

9. John Paul Lederach, Building Peace: Sustainable Reconciliation in Divided Societies (Washington, DC: United States Institute of Peace, 2006).

10. Johan Galtung, "Cultural Violence," *Journal of Peace Research* 27.3 (1990).

11. Molly Martin, *Hard-Hatted Women: Life on the Job* (Seattle, WA: Seal Press, 1997).

12. Timothy Casey, "Still Excluded: There are Still Virtually No Women in the Federally Created and Supervised Apprenticeship System for the Skilled Construction Trades," *The Women's Legal Defense and Education Fund*, March 2013, accessed September 14, 2014, http://www.legalmomentum.org/resources/report-still-excluded.

13. Susan Eisenberg, *We'll Call You If We Need You: Experiences of Women Working Construction* (Ithaca, NY: ILR Press, 1998).

14. Kareima Ali asked that her real name be used in the dissertation. For other interviewees a pseudonym was used to protect anonymity. See Hunte, " 'My Walk Has Never Been Average.' "

15. Shonda is an electrician. She has been in the trades for thirty plus years. She has worked in the Northeast, Southeast, and Northwest United States. See ibid.

16. Sharla was a low voltage electrician. At the time of the study she had been in the trades for twelve years. She worked in the Northwest, Southwest, Northeast, Southeast, and Midwest United States. See ibid.

17. Z is a commercial carpenter who had worked in the trades for six years. She works in the Northwest. See ibid.

18. A pseudonym for a pre-apprenticeship program that Z was connected to. See Ibid.

19. Ibid., 246.

20. Ibid., 247.

21. Frans Fanon, *The Wretched of the Earth* (New York, NY: Grove Press, 1965).

22. bell hooks, *Rock My Soul: Black People and Self-Esteem* (New York, NY: Washington Square Press, 2003).

23. Nathaniel Branden, *The Six Pillars of Self-Esteem: The Definitive Work on Self-Esteem by the Leading Pioneer in the Field* (New York, NY: Bantam Books, 1994).

24. hooks, *Rock My Soul*, 70.

25. bell hooks, *Sisters of the Yam: Black Women and Self-Recovery* (Cambridge, MA: South End, 2005).

26. Hunte, " 'My Walk Has Never Been Average,' " 195.

27. Ibid., 199.

28. Ibid.

29. Ibid.

30. Veronica was a public utility worker and mill worker. She had been in the trades in Northwest. See ibid.

31. Ibid., 208.

32. Ibid., 209.

33. Wanda Lou was a riveter who worked in the shipyards for over thirty years. She was retired at the time of our conversation. She worked in the industry in the northwest. See ibid.

34. Ibid., 228.

35. Ibid., 221.

36. Ibid., 223.

37. Ibid., 226.

BIBLIOGRAPHY

Berik, Gunseli and Cihan Bilginsoy. "Do Unions Help or Hinder Women in Training? Apprenticeship Programs in the United States." *Industrial Relations* 39.4 (2001): 600–24.

Branden, Nathaniel. *The Six Pillars of Self-Esteem: The Definitive Work on Self-Esteem by the Leading Pioneer in the Field.* New York, NY: Bantam Books, 1994.

Casey, Timothy. "Still Excluded: There are Still Virtually No Women in the Federally Created and Supervised Apprenticeship System for the Skilled Construction Trades." *The Women's Legal Defense and Education Fund,* March 2013. Accessed September 15, 2014. http://www.legalmomentum.org/resources/report-still-excluded.

Dugan, Marie. "A Nested Theory of Conflict." *Women in Leadership* 1.1 (1996): 9–20.

Eisenberg, Susan. *We'll Call You if We Need You: Experiences of Women Working Construction.* Ithaca, NY: ILR Press, 1998.

Fanon, Frantz. *The Wretched of the Earth.* New York, NY: Grove Press, 1965.

Galtung, Johan. "Cultural Violence." *Journal of Peace Research* 27.3 (1990): 291–305.

Health and Safety of Women in Construction (HASWIC) Work Group. "Women in the Construction Workplace: Providing Equitable Safety and Health Protection." Occupational Safety and Health Administration's Advisory Committee on Construction Safety and Health, Department of Labor, 1999. Accessed September 14, 2014. https://www.osha.gov/doc/accsh/haswicformal.html.

hooks, bell. *Rock My Soul: Black People and Self-Esteem.* New York, NY: Washington Square Press, 2003.

———. *Sisters of the Yam: Black Women and Self-Recovery.* Cambridge, MA: South End, 2005.

Hunte, Roberta. "'My Walk Has Never Been Average': Black Tradeswomen Negotiating Intersections of Race and Gender in Long Term Careers in The United States' Building Trades." PhD diss., University of Manitoba, 2012.

Lederach, John Paul. *Building Peace: Sustainable Reconciliation in Divided Societies.* Washington, DC: United States Institute of Peace, 2006.

Martin, Molly. *Hard-Hatted Women: Life on the Job.* Seattle, WA: Seal Press, 1997.

Moccio, Francine. *Live Wire: Women and Brotherhood in the Electrical Industry.* Philadelphia, PA: Temple University Press, 2009.

Moir, Susan, Meryl Thomson, and Christa Kelleher. "Unfinished Business: Building Equality for Women in the Construction Trades." Scholar Works at UMass Boston: Labor Resource Center, 2011. Accessed September 14, 2014. http://scholarworks.umb.edu/cgi/viewcontent.cgi?article=1004&context=lrc_pubs.

National Women's Law Centre. "Underpaid & Overloaded: Women in Low-Wage jobs." Accessed April 29, 2015. http://www.nwic.org/sites/default/files/pdfs/final_nwlc_lowwagereport2014.pdf

Chapter 11

Karen Women Resettling in Canada

Exploring the Challenges of Transnational Networks for Peace

Anna Snyder

This chapter is based on a pilot study that explores the peacebuilding capacity of Karen women originally from Myanmar who have resettled in Canada. Some countries in the Global North develop conflict-refugee policy based on the assumption that diasporas will fuel the ongoing conflict rather than become part of the solution. Once the refugee leaves the camp, government perspectives shift from viewing the refugee as a passive victim to a potential security threat.[1] As such, government policy does not reflect the diversity of political views in diasporas or the capacity for diasporas to contribute to peace in their homelands. Nevertheless, research shows that some conflict diasporas have become transnational activists, playing key roles in peacemaking.[2] Moreover, recent studies indicate diasporas possess unique characteristics that could contribute to peacebuilding, such as their transnational networks.[3] However, little is known about the significance of refugees' transnational networks for peacework; in the Canadian context, I found government policy hindered the study of transnational networking because refugees without citizenship fear deportation and arrest if they talk about what might be considered political work.

This study builds on previous research highlighting the determination and success of three women's refugee organizations that developed the capacity to contribute to peacebuilding at local, national, and international levels.[4] Despite the overwhelming challenges of life in refugee camps, the Women's League of Burma (WLB), the Sudanese Women's Voice for Peace (SWVP), and the Tibetan Women's Association (TWA), with the assistance of governmental and non-governmental organizations (NGOs), formed transnational networks for positive social change. Each organization developed the capacity for transnational bridgebuilding, which I define as the capacity to build and sustain networks across geographical, social, and political boundaries with the aim of bringing about nonviolent social change. This study of Karen women explores transnational bridgebuilding capacity during the resettlement process in order to understand more fully how newcomers become transnational activists. My findings reinforce earlier conclusions that facilitating contact between women's organizations interested in conflict transformation in diaspora, refugee, and country of origin is of strategic importance for transnational grassroots peacebuilding. The Karen women in this study showed capacity for local peacemaking; however, without governmental or non-governmental support for nonviolent transnational activism, they exhibited little connection to or hope for conflict transformation efforts in their homeland.

GENDER, DIASPORAS, AND PEACEBUILDING

Focusing research on female diasporas explores new approaches to contemporary peacebuilding and facilitates deeper understanding of the capacity of female diasporas to become transnational activists. The growing research on diaspora peacebuilding tends to be gender blind. Yet scholars have documented several historical examples of women-in-exile leading peace efforts (e.g., in El Salvador and Cambodia).[5] Famously, the 2011 Nobel Peace Prize winner, Leymah Gbowee, relied on Liberian women in refugee camps in Ghana to pressure then president Charles Taylor and Liberian rebels at the Accra peace talks to finalize the agreement that ended the civil war in 2003.[6] Studying capacity for peacebuilding is important because some scholars maintain the decision to use nonviolent responses to conflict is linked to capacity building. For the purposes of this analysis, capacity building is defined as "the process of reinforcing the inherent capabilities and understandings of people related to the challenge of conflict in their context and to a philosophy oriented toward the generation of new, proactive, empowered action for desired change in those settings."[7] As such, a fundamental challenge of peacebuilding is changing the individuals' and the communities' belief that they are powerless to the sense that they have the power to effect change. My previous research showed that the three women's refugee organizations mentioned in the introduction developed capacity in three areas: (1) organizational strength—both transnational and local; (2) conflict resolution skills; and (3) leadership for social change. The Karen women in Winnipeg showed some capacity in all three areas.

Capacity to Lead Social Change: Empowerment

For women, developing peacebuilding capacity requires gender-based strategies tailored to contexts of political, economic, and social inequity at all levels from the individual to the structural level. Women's empowerment, defined as "altering relations of power . . . which constrain women's options and autonomy and adversely affect health and well-being," is considered a bottom-up rather than top-down progression.[8] In other words, women must be significant actors in the process, not simply recipients of improved outcomes. Inner transformation, a fundamental shift in perceptions, is essential to empowerment as is access to economic, social, and physical resources.[9] Moreover, culture is important for understanding choices; how women view access to new opportunities or resources that enhance the ability to make choices, is socially embedded.[10] At the structural level, addressing women's exclusion from decision making is thought to require adopting mechanisms and training to ensure the "mainstreaming" of gender issues in governments and international governmental organizations like the UN.[11] For example, UNSCR 1325 establishes a global mandate for women's inclusion in institutions and processes concerning issues of armed conflict and peace. A recent study of the national ceasefire process in Myanmar revealed that the handful of women already part of the political structure, were more likely to participate in the peace talks.[12]

Refugee women may experience "ambivalent empowerment"; that is, new alternatives open up at the same time as enormous limitations arise in the context of forced migration.[13] For example, Mary O'Kane maintains women-in-exile on the Thai/Burmese border created a gendered political space in the context of the patriarchal ethnic opposition movements.[14] My own research indicates that women-in-exile may become community leaders as a result of their empowerment work. Alex Butler came to a similar conclusion from his study of the TWA: "TWA spans culture and politics in a way which is unique within the exile community, and is therefore particularly well-placed to consciously contribute to, or even lead . . . both at the local and the global levels."[15] Assessing the capacity of refugees for self-organization shows the importance of cultural knowledge, relational networks such as the family and community, and survival skills.[16] However, constructed identities of refugee women as victims may obscure their capacity. Fariyal Ross-Sheriff's study illustrates how identifying Afghan women as passive victims of a brutal authoritarian regime obscured evidence of their community work.[17]

Capacity for Conflict Resolution

Diasporas contribute to peace and conflict resolution in their home countries in specific ways from: (1) civic-oriented nonpolitical activities, such as community development and business investments; (2) direct political involvement in the country of origin; to (3) advocacy and lobbying activities.[18] Direct political involvement is exemplified by the ethnic diasporic NGOs currently assisting with the nationwide ceasefire in Myanmar involving as many as 16 separate government negotiations with armed ethnic organizations.[19] Wolfram Zunzer maintains that the extent to which a diaspora can be "empowered to proactively work towards peace" depends on several factors including the motivation and resources for constructive engagement in the country of origin.[20] For example, training stakeholders and organizations in a variety of peacemaking skills can increase their capacity to participate in multitrack diplomacy.[21] Training in constitutional law, human rights, and conflict resolution empowered leaders of the WLB to advocate successfully for women's political inclusion at the constitutional convention of the Burmese government-in-exile; as a result, WLB began offering their own conflict resolution and leadership training in the camps.[22] Alternatively, recognizing and reinforcing peace capacities already embedded in the society may also increase the capacity to respond to conflict peacefully and transform violent structures.[23] Because women's power tends to be dispersed "outside of the bureaucratic structure of society,"[24] their conflict resolution efforts often go unrecognized, invisible to the public eye.

Collaboration that bridges divided communities indicates growing conflict resolution capacity. According to Giulia Sinatti, "Collaboration becomes an indicator of the ability and willingness of a particular diaspora group to discuss, negotiate and overcome ideological, ethnic or religious differences and cleavages that might be at the basis of conflict situations in the country of origin."[25] Moreover, collaboration is critical for building and maintaining activist networks. Transnational coalition building requires the ability to find common ground and set agendas, pinpoint values and decision-making systems that resonate broadly, build social infrastructure, and develop mechanisms or ways of resolving conflicts that arise within the networks.[26]

Capacity to Organize: Local and Transnational Networks

A key aspect of peacebuilding capacity is building and linking strategic social networks.[27] For diasporas, social networks are often transnational. Indeed, the transnational aspects of peacebuilding are thought to be unique to diasporas; the more diaspora organizations are transnational, the more likely they are to succeed in their interventions because of increased resources, capacities, and greater visibility.[28] In transnational social fields, "established structures of domination and exploitation are contested, altered and reconstructed"; class and political divisions in the homeland may be altered through resettlement, creating opportunities for positive social change in the new setting.[29] New forms of collaboration as well as new ideas, values, and norms, such as pluralism and democratic participation—also known as social remittances—may be transmitted transnationally.[30] Potentially, transnationalism impacts mono-dimensional identities that fuel intractable conflict. For example, Rudhramoorthy Cheran's research shows that Tamil diaspora have developed multiple identities and as a result, they do not necessarily identify themselves solely as Tamils.[31]

The organizational structure and strategic connections comprising transnational networks are important for diaspora mobilization.[32] John Paul Lederach's approach to strategic networking broadens the scope of relevant actors; he maintains linking key contacts at the grassroots level, the regional level, and ultimately the top government or leadership level maximizes societal involvement and, therefore, sustainable peace.[33] Likewise, Thomas Risse and Kathryn Sikkink highlight the importance of social movement alliances with governmental, non-governmental, and international governmental agencies for social change to occur through what they call "transnational advocacy networks."[34] Moreover, I found that local leadership of grassroots constituencies reinforces the legitimacy and effectiveness of the transnational network; for example, the TWA is a mass organization with 10,000 members with over 38 branches in India and abroad.[35] A comprehensive approach to strategic networking is relevant to this study because female activism is shaped by influence in their social, cultural, and economic context while access to political influence may be limited.[36]

KAREN WOMEN IN MYANMAR: BACKGROUND TO THE CONFLICT

Since its independence from Britain in 1948, Myanmar has experienced civil war. After independence, armed communist and ethnic groups challenged the government, maintaining they were underrepresented in the 1948 constitution. The autonomy promised to minority states was never granted. General Ne Win staged a coup in 1962 instituting authoritarian military rule and, in 1974, he suspended the constitution. His policy of "burmanisation" banned the teaching of ethnic minority languages, history and customs, and outlawed printing in any language other than Burmese. As the armed resistance increased, and the human rights abuses of the Burmese Army grew, hundreds of thousands fled their homes. Nonviolent opposition was crushed with brutal force in 1988 and the leader of the democratic movement, Aung San Suu Kyi, was placed under house arrest. Years of pressure to institute a new constitution culminated in a widely criticized referendum in 2008 and a constitution that reinforces military dominance. Since the 2010 parliamentary elections, the newly appointed president, Thein Sein, freed Aung San Suu Kyi, eased censorship, and released some 650 political prisoners. Sein has negotiated separate ceasefires with 16 ethnic armed organizations and is in the process of negotiating a nationwide ceasefire.

The Karen, a major ethnic group in Myanmar, have been involved in low-level insurgency and often brutal government counterinsurgency since 1949. The Karen national movement began in the late 1800s, an era when both the Christian missionaries and the British colonial administration facilitated the advancement of the Christian Karen. The Karen National Union (KNU), established in 1947, failed to reach agreement with the new independent government preferring a separate nation-state over participation in a federated Burma and, as such, in 1949 KNU began an armed insurgency. For about 50 years, KNU has acted as a government, controlling, in large part, areas of Karen state and neighboring provinces where many Karen live. The Christian, Sgaw Karen minority have dominated the leadership of the KNU, marginalizing the majority Buddhist, Pwo Karen; General Bo Mya was one such leader.[37] In 1992, the Burmese government, in an attempt to weaken the larger insurgent groups, identified 135 ethnic groups in Myanmar, further dividing the Karen. The government then granted local autonomy to smaller ethnic groups. Eventually, the Buddhist Karen mutinied, forming the Democratic Karen Benevolent Army (DKBA), their own militia, and allied with the Burmese military to seize the KNU military headquarters in Manerplaw in 1995. As such, Bo Mya/KNU lost control of the Karen "liberated zones" and lost touch with most non-Christian Karen communities.[38] In 2012, the KNU signed a ceasefire agreement with the government. They are currently participating in the nationwide ceasefire process.

Karen people have crossed the border into Thailand seeking asylum since the insurgency started in the late 1940s. When the KNU lost their military base in Manerplaw in the 1990s, large numbers of Karen sought refuge in the Thai/Burmese borderlands. The Karen fled military incursions, landmines, sexual violence, forced labor, burned villages, forced relocation, starvation, and of primary importance for some, a lack of education. As of 2014, 119,637 Karen refugees lived in seven refugee camps set up by the Thai government.[39] More than 115,000 Karen have been internally displaced.[40] The KNU runs the camps working with a coalition of international NGOs and the Thai Burma Border Consortium to deliver healthcare, food, education, housing and other services to Karen-in-exile. The Karen Women's Organization (KWO), a branch of KNU, delivers services specifically geared toward women's needs. Beginning in 2006–7 Western donor countries—Canada, United States, Australia, and Europe—began to accept Karen refugees for resettlement and by 2011, 30,000 Karen and other exiles from Burma had resettled in third countries abroad.[41] During that time, Canada resettled 810 refugees from Burma under the Immigration and Refugee Protection Act.

METHODOLOGY

After studying the experiences of refugee women in camps on the Thai/Burmese border in 2007, I followed up with a pilot study of Karen women-in-exile, resettled in Canada. My research assistant and interpreter, Marner Moo Sein, was the first Karen refugee to arrive in Winnipeg in 2004, sponsored by World University Service of Canada (WUSC). Like many first wave refugees, she had no reference group or community to welcome her, facilitate resettlement, or connect her to people or resources. With Marner Moo's assistance, I conducted five individual interviews and two focus groups using a mixture of closed and open-ended questions. Their names have not been changed at the request of all but one interviewee. The first four individual interviewees were selected based on their leadership of the KWO chapter in Winnipeg. KWO is a community-based organization of Karen women assisting with relief and economic development work in refugee camps on the Thai border and with internally displaced people inside Burma. Formed in 1949, with a membership of over 49,000 women, the KWO "encourages awareness of women's rights and promotes women's participation in community decision making and political processes."[42] However, the first focus group was selected based on the availability of community members *not* active in KWO. Because of the significance of "the first family" (Marner Moo, her sister, Mu Yeh Htoo, and their mother, Kay Seng, were the first family to immigrate to Winnipeg), the sisters comprised one of the focus groups and I interviewed the mother individually.

KAREN CAPACITY TO LEAD SOCIAL CHANGE: EMPOWERMENT

Change in Status: "Not like a Queen, but you feel special"

In the context of Canadian resettlement, a number of the young women employed by local refugee and immigrant NGOs have become leaders in the community. Empowered, they are developing the capacity to lead social change, which is essential for peacebuilding. In Karen culture, elders are highly respected by the community for their knowledge of social history, cosmology, ritual, ethics, and, historically, magic.[43] Traditionally, the headman, a religious and political leader, would make decisions important to the community, meaning men dominate decision making despite minimal sexual division of labor particularly in agricultural activities.[44] Sex and age are the most important criteria for determining social status.[45] However, in Winnipeg, the two young women are perceived as having the resources to help community members. Marner Moo and Mu Yeh Htoo, two young university educated women have experienced an increase in status in their community with which they are somewhat uncomfortable given cultural norms around age. Both maintain that the community sees them differently primarily because they attended university; they have more respect for them. Moreover, their language and cultural facility as founding community members as well as their employment with refugee social services agencies adds to their status. Marner Moo says every time Mu Yeh Htoo, her sister, goes to a birthday party or to church service, they treat her like she is a queen. Mu Yeh Htoo qualified, "not a Queen . . . but you feel special." Her hosts insist she sit on the couch; typically the best seats are given to visiting elders.[46]

Moreover, some of the women who took on leadership positions in the refugee camps continue to show leadership in the community. Tha Lay, a young woman with excellent English skills, developed income generation projects with local and global women's organizations in the refugee camp. In Winnipeg, she has worked as a neighborhood immigrant settlement worker and life skills coach; although she lacks university education, her employment places her in a leadership position. Christer Bell, Toe Paw, and Sar Lay, who all had leadership positions in the KWO, continue to lead KWO activities at the church, the center of the community. Christer Bell, formerly the national KWO secretary, now works in a nursery, assists settlement workers, and organizes activities for Karen youth. Toe Paw, currently the head of KWO Winnipeg, was a kindergarten teacher and KWO volunteer in the camps. Kay Seng, a former camp committee secretary, has partial employment as an online interpreter and teaches English as an Additional Language (EAL); she does not participate in KWO activities but her advice and assistance is much sought after. The interviews revealed a high level of volunteerism; almost every woman mentioned helping out other community members.

KAREN CAPACITY FOR CONFLICT RESOLUTION AND COLLABORATION

Change in Conflict and/or Problem-solving Process: "Saturdays and Sundays, the house is crowded"

Young Karen women are gaining the capacity to resolve conflicts nonviolently and collaborate, especially across divides in the community, which indicates the ability to build peace and the skill to lead. In Burma, elders and religious leaders would assist the community with conflict or problem solving; headmen, together with four elders or "old hearts", typically elderly men, developed consensus based on who speaks the most persuasively using

Karen axioms and proverbs.[47] Age and experience was more important than education level. From a cultural perspective, young people have to respect their elders; when an older person says something, the young person has to listen.[48] Senior family members would also be asked to assist with family conflict. At the village level, the KNU would also step in, particularly when there were issues related to theft, land use or adultery—usually criminal offenses.[49] This description is consistent with studies of traditional conflict resolution in the region that show mediators are more likely advisors, teachers, or spiritual leaders than neutral facilitators, and conflict intervention takes place in stages often beginning with parental consultation.[50]

In Winnipeg, contrary to tradition, the two young women are seen as leaders with the potential to resolve conflicts and/or find the resources to solve problems, indicating a potential shift in gender roles and expectations, even though community members still tend to call elders to calm situations and discuss how to resolve problems. A religious leader is always involved. Mu Yeh Htoo admits they seek advice from her mother, a former camp committee leader and community elder, first. However, unlike in the camps, Kay turns to her daughters for advice or refers community members to them. The community realizes the young women know English well and are aware that the community services jobs require networking, giving the young women access to valuable resources. Plus, Marner Moo says, they think that she knows better than they do; given all of these points, the community believes she might find a solution. The two sisters said that Karen people come to their offices, even if their problem has little to do with the services the NGO offers. For example, community members call Marner Moo if they are experiencing domestic violence or Mu Yeh Htoo for help filling out important forms. Mu Yeh Htoo said the Karen community does not call her so much at work but at home. They both said that on Saturdays and Sundays, it becomes crowded in the house with people requesting help. In the evening the phone rings constantly.

Collaboration: "They say that we don't love our people which is okay"

Resettlement in Winnipeg has brought together Karen communities who had little contact with each other in the remote refugee camps on the Thai/Myanmar border and who practiced different approaches to the conflict in Myanmar. Despite some tension in the community, Karen newcomers are forming bonds with each other, building bridges, working together, and cooperating with other agencies, another important aspect of peacebuilding capacity. The community tension appears to arise from the degree of political involvement in the ongoing conflicts in Myanmar which, according to Mu Yeh Htoo, are connected to the refugee camp from which they migrated.

There are literally two camps that relocated people to Winnipeg. One camp was populated by "ordinary people, they are farmers and grassroots people. They are not interested in politics at all, at least," Marner Moo said, "80 percent are not interested in politics." On the other hand, the sisters claim that people from the other refugee camp are very different, more likely to get involved with political support for the conflict parties. The community division, then, is marked by those who support the KWO and, in turn, the KNU and its political activities, and those who do not wish to be involved in politics anymore. However, Marner Moo and Mu Yeh Htoo maintain that they are able to bridge the community divide with friends on both sides.

Moreover, aspects of Karen identity appear to be shifting in importance, opening up space for nonviolent responses to the conflict and new multicultural identities. The shift is taking place in the context of ongoing dissension in the community over whether one can be a true Karen and not support the armed conflict. Marner Moo stated, "They say that we don't love our people which is okay. It is not that we don't love them, we don't want to get involved." Mu Yeh Htoo added "even though we don't donate it doesn't mean that we don't love or help peace in our country. We help in a different way." Fearing deportation if they were found participating in "political" activities, it was difficult to ascertain how free my informants felt to discuss their political activities. However, seven of the twelve interviewees made a point of saying they no longer wished to be involved in the conflict in Myanmar. For example, Toe Paw said she is going to become a Canadian citizen; she is in Canada now so she doesn't belong to Karen organizations in Myanmar anymore. She explained, "I'm so tired of running from Burmese troops . . . When you are in this country we do not have to worry about anything. In this country if you are a good person you will have good friends because the government is good unlike the government in Burma." In the Canadian context, volunteering to assist community members with their daily issues was a more important aspect of what it means to be Karen than supporting the fight for Karen sovereignty. Moreover, they are expanding their identities to include "Canadian" which bridges community divides.

KAREN CAPACITY FOR ORGANIZATION: LOCAL AND TRANSNATIONAL NETWORKS

Local Networks: "Karen people get together only at church."

The local Karen community showed a strong capacity for local community-building, for self-organization; as such, the Karen women also show peace-building capacity in this area. However, the local capacity for organization is far more significant than the transnational impacting the transnational bridgebuilding potential. Interviewees maintained the church was the center of the Karen community; Marner Moo went as far as to say that all of the community organizing takes place through the church. In Winnipeg, the City Church, founded in 2008 by Grant Memorial Baptist Church, is home to City Connections, a ministry to former refugees living in the Winnipeg core, and the church home for the Karen in Winnipeg.[51] According to Marner Moo, "They [the Karen] put their faith in God, they go to the Karen church a lot, they donate, they are involved a lot, especially young people who sing during the service." The Karen community celebrates special events and holidays at the church such as the Karen new year, children's birthday parties, and Thanksgiving. Informally, the Karen women also network locally by cooking and sharing food, usually at home and with friends, reinforcing cultural identity and community ties.

The KWO is largely active through the church. Christer Bell emphasized that the local chapter focuses on religion, not politics. Christer Bell claims they focus on religion because the Karen are Christian "everywhere we go." KWO keeps a communication network going with Karen families in Winnipeg. She maintains without their networking activities, the community will lose contact. Their goal is to preserve traditional Karen culture and to nurture parenting skills. The KWO visits families every week, "for services, worshiping and encouraging." It takes two years for the KWO to visit every single house. Toe Paw, chair of the KWO home visits committee, explained that every Sunday they have Karen services at City Church; then afterward, the KWO visits one or two of the families. Moreover, the KWO keeps an inventory of items needed in the community. Sar Lay, an active member of KWO, collects and coordinates information on what families need, especially furniture. Sar Lay joined the KWO in Winnipeg because when some families want to have ceremonies, they need elders like herself.

Transnational Networks: "I hope I do not upset you"

The personal transnational networks of the Karen women were quite active. Everyone I interviewed said they still had connections with family and friends in the camps in Thailand and some maintained connections in Burma as well. Several stayed in contact with Karen scattered around the world. They all talked about phone calls they initiated to or received from the camps; most used Skype, email, and Facebook to contact those living in cities. Many but not all interviewees sent remittances to individual family members in the camps for food, private education, or to pay fines for those caught working illegally; three of the women said remittances were no longer necessary. Some talked about the frustration or dread that they experienced knowing that callers would likely ask for money; the requests generated internal conflict because they are aware of the harsh circumstances in the camps. The focus group brought up concerns that monthly rations of rice and cooking oil have been cut.

Fearful of losing their permanent residency, the interviewees did not feel comfortable sharing openly the goals and activities of the women's transnational organizational networks; interviewees shared conflicting reports likely reflecting their security concerns. As such, the peacebuilding capacity of the women's organizational networks is unclear. The three current KWO leaders maintained that the Winnipeg chapter had little to no contact with KWO across Canada and the globe, repeating that they were a religious organization only. Toe Paw explained that they separated from KWO in Thailand because they no longer wish to support them financially. She was clearly upset by my questions because she said she did not know how to answer. She ended her interview with "I hope I do not upset you." However, those not involved in the KWO raised questions about local involvement in both the national and transnational KWO network. They were unclear as to whether the KWO now operated more as an NGO offering services to female refugees or as support for the KNU.[52] Additionally, a couple of the women mentioned that they donate and keep in contact with the church in the camps, donating money for bibles and hymnals to Kaw Thu Lei Baptist (KKBS). The KKBS is, however, an organization that studies show has been instrumental in the Karen nationalist struggle.[53] One of the interviewees was confident her donation to KBBS was used for conflict transformation but the others did not voice their opinions.

Tha Lay, the only woman with extensive experience working with transnational women's organizations, and who stayed in contact informally with her transnational organizational network, was also the only interviewee who expressed interest in peacebuilding in Myanmar. Significantly, she was the only interviewee who had worked and connected with the WLB, which is now taking leadership inside Myanmar to advocate for women's participation in the peace negotiations. In the camps, Tha Lay collaborated with foreigners on income generating projects for women and with the Women's Education for Advancement and Empowerment (WEAVE), an organization focused on empowering indigenous women. Tha Lay is currently working toward a BA in conflict resolution studies so she can return one day to Myanmar to help women. Tha Lay's interest in peacebuilding contrasted with interviewees who did not have a network of transnational women's organizations. Other interviewees openly discussed their mistrust of the current peace process which was reinforced, they said, by family and friends who told them that even the top female leader of KNU in exile did not support the current negotiations. Several interviewees referred to Karen news websites that covered ongoing human rights violations against the Karen by government soldiers. No one, except for Tha Lay, had heard of WLB's leadership in peacebuilding.

CONCLUSION

The Karen newcomers involved in my study are beginning to show the capacity to contribute to peacebuilding in their homeland; however, their transnational organizational networks are not yet mobilized for peace work. This data reinforces the conclusion from my earlier study of refugee women's organizations that contact with and support from governmental and nongovernmental organizations interested in peace is important for building grassroots refugee peacebuilding capacity. Unlike the refugee women's organizations in my previous research, the newcomers in Winnipeg had little to no contact with organizations encouraging women's participation in the political affairs of their country of origin. The interviewee with the most interest in conflict resolution in Myanmar was impacted by her experience working with transnational women's organizations. For the other Karen women in Winnipeg, political involvement was synonymous with support for the armed conflict; the interviewees were unaware of models of nonviolent grassroots participation as exhibited by the WLB or, for that matter, by KWO Thailand, and the peace negotiations seemed futile and remote. For the newcomers, government refugee policy reinforced the understanding of political activism as support for the armed conflict; complete dissociation from the conflict in Myanmar seemed the only secure route without Canadian citizenship and, from their perspective, the only route sanctioned by the Canadian government.

To some extent, the women exhibited the three aspects of transnational bridgebuilding: the capacity to lead social change, conflict resolution, and the capacity for both local and transnational networks. As such, the study reveals the potential for women's peacework in the context of resettlement while highlighting the need for further research on the impact of governmental and NGOs on the agency of refugee women and their transnational networks. The educated young women have developed community leadership capacity as well as skill in conflict resolution. Their leadership focuses primarily on serving the community and bridges political divides. Some of the younger women, then, experience empowerment and capacity building that could be resources for peacebuilding in their homeland. The older women who led programs in the camps continue to be active, volunteering to assist newcomers and organizing cultural activities for the community through the Karen church. They see themselves as serving the community, preserving Karen identity in the context of resettlement and ensuring the survival of the community. However, their transnational networks are largely personal, reinforced by remittances to family, friends and some organizations, with, as of yet, limited capacity for peacebuilding in Myanmar. Nevertheless, the study illustrates a variety of conflict-refugee responses, contradicting the dominant perception of conflict refugees as potential security threats. Further research is needed to understand the mobilizing factors for those refugees who chose transnational activism for peace in their homelands.

NOTES

1. Jennifer Hyndman and Wenona Giles, "Waiting for What? The Feminization of Asylum in Protracted Situations," *Gender, Place & Culture: A Journal of Feminist Geography* 18.3 (2011).

2. Päivi Pirkkalainen and Mahdi Abdile, "The Diaspora—Conflict—Peace—Nexus: A Literature Review," Working Paper No. 1, Diaspeace, 2009, accessed July 11, 2010, https://jyx.jyu.fi /dspace/bitstream/handle/123456789/36875/DIASPEACE_WP1.pdf?sequence=1; Wolfram Zunzer, "Diaspora Communities and Civil Conflict Transformation," Berghof Occasional Paper Nr. 26, Berghof Research Centre for Constructive Conflict Management, 2004, accessed May 5, 2011, http://citeseerx.ist.psu.edu/viewdoc/download?doi=10.1.1.126.9346&rep=rep1&type=pdf; Hazel Smith and Paul Stares, eds., *Diasporas in Conflict: Peace-Makers or Peace-Wreckers?* (Tokyo, Japan: United Nations University Press, 2007).

3. Giulia Sinatti, "Key Criteria of 'Good Practice' for Constructive Diaspora Engagement in Peacebuilding," Discussion Paper, African Diaspora Policy Centre, 2010: 19, accessed February 2, 2011, http://www.diaspora-centre.org.

4. Anna C. Snyder, "A Gendered Analysis of Refugee Transnational Bridgebuilding Capacity," in *Critical Aspects of Gender in Conflict Resolution, Peacebuilding, and Social Movements*, ed. Anna C. Snyder and Stephanie P. Stobbe (Bingley, England: Emerald Group, 2011).

5. Krishna Kumar and Hannah Baldwin, "Women's Organizations in Postconflict Cambodia," in *Women and Civil War: Impact, Organizations, and Action*, ed. Krishna Kumar (Boulder, CO: Lynne Rienner, 2001); Patricia Weiss Fagen and Sally W. Yudelman, "El Salvador and Guatemala: Refugee Camp and Repatriation Experiences," in *Women and Civil War: Impact, Organizations, and Action*, ed. Krishna Kumar (Boulder, CO: Lynne Rienner, 2001).

6. Leymah Gbowee, *Mighty Be Our Powers: How Sisterhood, Prayer, and Sex Changed a Nation at War* (New York, NY: Beast Books, 2013).

7. John Paul Lederach, *Building Peace: Sustainable Reconciliation in Divided Societies* (Washington, DC: United States Institute of Peace, 1997), 109.

8. Gita Sen, "Women's Empowerment and Human Rights: The Challenge to Policy," in *Population, the Complex Reality: A Report of the Population Summit of the World's Scientific Academies*, ed. Sir Francis Graham-Smith (Golden, CO: Fulcrum, 1994).

9. Amartya Sen, *Development as Freedom* (Oxford, England: Oxford University Press, 1999).

10. Naila Kabeer, "The Conditions and Consequences of Choice: Reflections on the Measurement of Women's Empowerment," Discussion Paper No. 108, United Nations Research Institute of Social Development, August 1999, accessed July 7, 2008, http://www.unrisd.org/UNRISD/website/document.nsf.

11. Caroline Moser and Annalise Moser, "Gender Mainstreaming Since Beijing: A Review of Success and Limitations in International Institutions," *Gender and Development* 13.2 (2005).

12. Salai Issac Khen and Muk Yin Haung Nyoi, "Looking at the Current Peace Process in Myanmar through a Gender Lens," Catalyzing Reflection Series, Bern, Switzerland: Swiss Peace, 2014, http:// www.swisspeace.ch/fileadmin/user.../Catalyzing_Reflections_1_2014.pdf.

13. Darini Rajasingham-Senanayake, "Ambivalent Empowerment: The Tragedy of Tamil Women in Conflict," in *Women, War and Peace in South Asia: Beyond Victimhood to Agency*, ed. Rita Manchanda (New Delhi, India: Sage, 2001).

14. Mary O'Kane "Gender, Borders and Transversality: The Emerging Women's Movement in the Burma-Thailand Borderlands," in *Gender, Conflict and Migration*, ed. Navnita Chadha Behera (New Delhi, India: Sage, 2006).

15. Alex Butler, *Feminism, Nationalism and Exiled Tibetan Women* (New Delhi, India: Kali for Women, 2003), 232.

16. Dorcas Grigg-Saito et al., "Building on the Strengths of a Cambodian Refugee Community through Community-Based Outreach," *Health Promotion Practice* 9.4 (2008); Frances Tomlinson and Sue Eagan, "From Marginalization to (Dis)Empowerment: Organizing Training and Employment Services to Refugees," *Human Relations* 55.8 (2002): 1019.

17. Fariyal Ross-Sheriff, "Afghan Women in Exile and Repatriation: Passive Victims or Social Actors," *Affilia: Journal of Women and Social Work* 21.2 (2006).

18. Pirkkalainen and Mahdi, "The Diaspora."

19. Ellen Paulley, "Peacebuilding in Myanmar," *MSC Currents* summer (2014): 3, accessed August 11, 2014, http://www.mscollege.ca/docs/currents/MSC_MSC_Currents_Spring_2014.pdf.

20. Zunzer, "Diaspora Communities," 42.

21. Kumar Rupesinghe, *Civil Wars, Civil Peace: An Introduction to Conflict Resolution* (London, England: Pluto, 1998).

22. Snyder, "A Gendered Analysis."

23. Mary B. Andersen, *Do No Harm: How Aid Can Support Peace—or War* (Boulder, CO: Lynne Rienner, 1999).

24. Rosemary Ridd and Helen Callaway, *Caught up in Conflict: Women's Responses to Political Strife* (London, England: Palgrave Macmillan, 1986), 2–4.

25. Sinatti, "Key Criteria."

26. Anna C. Snyder, *Setting the Agenda for Global Peace: Conflict and Consensus Building* (Aldershot, England: Ashgate, 2003).

27. Lederach, *Building Peace*.

28. Sinatti, "Key Criteria."

29. Patricia Landolt, Lilian Autler, and Sonia Baires, "From Hermano Lejano to Hermano Mayor: The Dialectics of Salvadoran Transnationalism," *Ethnic and Racial Studies* 22.2 (1999): 292.

30. Moses Naim, "The New Diaspora," *Foreign Policy* no. 131 (2002); Yossi Shain and Aharon Barth, "Diasporas and International Relations Theory," *International Organization* 57.3 (2003).

31. Rudhramoorthy Cheran, "Diaspora Circulation and Transnationalism as Agents for Change in the Post Conflict Zones of Sri Lanka," Policy Paper Submitted to the Berghof Foundation for Conflict Management, Berlin, Germany, 2004, accessed July 11, 2011, http://www.sangam.org/articles/view2/523.pdf.

32. Zunzer, "Diaspora Communities."

33. Lederach, *Building Peace.*

34. Thomas Risse and Kathryn Sikkink, "The Socialization of International Human Rights Norms into Domestic Practices: Introduction," in *The Power of Human Rights: International Norms and Domestic Change*, ed. Thomas Risse, Stephen C. Ropp, and Kathryn Sikkink (Cambridge, England: Cambridge University Press, 1999).

35. Snyder, "A Gendered Analysis."

36. Karen Sacks, *Caring By the Hour: Women, Work and Organizing at Duke Medical Center* (Urbana, IL: University of Illinois Press, 1988).

37. Ashley South, "Burma's Longest War: Anatomy of the Karen Conflict" *Transnational Institute*, March 28, 2011, accessed August 21, 2014, http://www.tni.org/briefing/burmas-longest-war-anatomy-karen-conflict; Jessica Harriden, "'Making a Name for Themselves': Karen Identity and the Politicization of Ethnicity in Burma," *The Journal of Burma Studies* vol. 7 (2002).

38. South, "Burma's Longest War."

39. Karen Refugee Committee, *Karen Refugee Committee Newsletter and Monthly Report, October, 2014*, last modified November 28, 2014, http://www.burmalibrary.org/docs20/KRCMR-2014-10.pdf.

40. Inge Brees, "Forced Displacement of Burmese People," *Forced Migration Review* no. 30 (2008).

41. Sang Kook Lee, "Scattered but Connected: Karen Refugees' Networking in and beyond the Thailand-Burma Borderland," *Asian and Pacific Migration Journal* 21.2 (2012).

42. Karen Women Organisation, "Karen Women Organisation—Who We Are," accessed December 17, 2014, http://www.karenwomen.org/about/.

43. Kirsten Ewers Andersen, "Deference for the Elders and Control over the Younger among the Karen in Thailand," *Folk* vol. 21–22 (1979/80).

44. Ananda Rajah, *Remaining Karen: A Study of Cultural Reproduction and the Maintenance of Identity* (Canberra, Australia: The Australian National University E-Press, 2008), accessed August 21, 2014, http://www.burmalibrary.org/docs6/Remaining_Karen.pdf.

45. Andersen, "Deference for the Elders."

46. Ibid.

47. Rajah, *Remaining Karen.*

48. Andersen, "Deference for the Elders."

49. Marner Moo Sein, email message to author, July 27, 2014.

50. David W. Augsburger, *Conflict Mediation across Cultures: Pathways and Patterns* (Louisville, KY: Westminster/John Knox, 1992); Stephanie P. Stobbe, "The Soukhouan Ritual: The Legacy of Lao Women in Conflict Resolution," in *Critical Aspects of Gender in Conflict Resolution, Peacebuilding, and Social Movements*, ed. Anna C. Snyder and Stephanie P. Stobbe (Bingley, England: Emerald Group, 2011).

51. City Church, "About Us," last modified December 20, 2010, http://citychurchwinnipeg.org/index.php/about-us.

52. Lee, "Scattered but Connected."

53. Ibid.

BIBLIOGRAPHY

Andersen, Kirsten Ewers. "Deference for the Elders and Control over the Younger among the Karen in Thailand." *Folk* vol. 21–22 (1979/80): 313–25.

Andersen, Mary B. *Do No Harm: How Aid Can Support Peace—or War.* Boulder, CO: Lynne Rienner, 1999.

Augsburger, David W. *Conflict Mediation across Cultures: Pathways and Patterns.* Louisville, KY: Westminster/John Knox, 1992.

Brees, Inge. "Forced Displacement of Burmese People." *Forced Migration Review* no. 30 (2008): 4–5.

Butler, Alex. *Feminism, Nationalism and Exiled Tibetan Women.* New Delhi, India: Kali for Women, 2003.

Cheran, Rudhramoorthy. "Diaspora Circulation and Transnationalism as Agents for Change in the Post Conflict Zones of Sri Lanka." Policy Paper Submitted to the Berghof Foundation for Conflict Management, Berlin, Germany, 2004. Accessed July 11, 2011. http://www.sangam.org/articles/view2/523.pdf.

City Church. "About Us." Last modified December 20, 2010. http://citychurchwinnipeg.org/index.php/about-us.

Fagen, Patricia Weiss and Sally W. Yudelman. "El Salvador and Guatemala: Refugee Camp and Repatriation Experiences." In *Women and Civil War: Impact, Organizations, and Action*, edited by Krishna Kumar, 79–96. Boulder, CO: Lynne Rienner, 2001.

Gbowee, Leymah. *Mighty Be Our Powers: How Sisterhood, Prayer, and Sex Changed a Nation at War.* New York, NY: Beast Books, 2013.

Grigg-Saito, Dorcas, Sheila Och, Sidney Liang, Robin Toof, and Linda Silka. "Building on the Strengths of a Cambodian Refugee Community through Community-Based Outreach." *Health Promotion Practice* 9.4 (2008): 415–25.

Harriden, Jessica. "'Making a Name for Themselves': Karen Identity and the Politicization of Ethnicity in Burma." *The Journal of Burma Studies* vol. 7 (2002): 81–144.

Hyndman, Jennifer and Wenona Giles. "Waiting for What? The Feminization of Asylum in Protracted Situations." *Gender, Place & Culture: A Journal of Feminist Geography* 18.3 (2011): 361–79.

Kabeer, Naila. "The Conditions and Consequences of Choice: Reflections on the Measurement of Women's Empowerment." Discussion Paper No. 108, United Nations Research Institute for Social Development, August 1999. Accessed July 7, 2008. http://www.unrisd.org/80256B3C005BCCF9/%28httpAuxPages%29/31EEF181BEC398A380256B67005B720A/$file/dp108.pdf.

Karen Refugee Committee. *Karen Refugee Committee Newsletter and Monthly Report, October 2014*. Last modified November 28, 2014. http://www.burmalibrary.org/docs20/KRCMR-2014-10.pdf.

Karen Women Organisation. "Karen Women Organisation—Who We Are." Accessed December 17, 2014. http://www.karenwomen.org/about/.

Khen, Salai Issac and Muk Yin Haung Nyoi. "Looking at the Current Peace Process in Myanmar through a Gender Lens." Catalyzing Reflection Series. Bern, Switzerland: Swiss Peace, 2014. http:// www.swisspeace.ch/fileadmin/user.../Catalyzing_Reflections_1_2014.pdf.

Kumar, Krishna and Hannah Baldwin. "Women's Organizations in Postconflict Cambodia." In *Women and Civil War: Impact, Organizations, and Action*, edited by Krishna Kumar, 129–48. Boulder, CO: Lynne Rienner, 2001.

Labman, Shauna. "Resettlement's Renaissance: A Cautionary Advocacy." *Refuge* 24.2 (2007): 35–47.

Landolt, Patricia, Lilian Autler, and Sonia Baires. "From Hermano Lejano to Hermano Mayor: The Dialectics of Salvadoran Transnationalism." *Ethnic and Racial Studies* 22.2 (1999): 290–315.

Lederach, John Paul. *Building Peace: Sustainable Reconciliation in Divided Societies*. Washington, DC: United States Institute of Peace, 1997.

Lee, Sang Kook. "Scattered but Connected: Karen Refugees' Networking in and beyond the Thailand-Burma Borderland." *Asian and Pacific Migration Journal* 21.2 (2012): 263–85.

Mohamoud, Abdullah A. "Diasporas: Untapped Potential for Peacebuilding in the Homelands." In *People Building Peace II: Successful Stories of Civil Society*, edited by Paul Van Tongeren, Malin Brenk, Marte Hellema, and Juliette Verhoeven, 339–47. Utrecht, Netherlands: European Centre for Conflict Prevention, 2006.

Moser, Caroline and Annalise Moser. "Gender Mainstreaming Since Beijing: A Review of Success and Limitations in International Institutions." *Gender & Development* 13.2 (2005):11–22.

Naim, Moses. "The New Diaspora." *Foreign Policy* no. 131 (2002): 95–96.

Ngulube, Mbongeni. "Africa: Diaspora as Dilemma." *All Africa*, July 17, 2013. Accessed August 22, 2014. http://allafrica.com/stories/201308061396.html.

O'Kane, Mary. "Gender, Borders and Transversality: The Emerging Women's Movement in the Burma-Thailand Borderlands." In *Gender, Conflict and Migration*, edited by Navnita Chadha Behera, 3–18. New Delhi, India: Sage, 2006.

Orjuela, Camilla. "Distant Warriors, Distant Peace Workers? Multiple Diaspora Roles in Sri Lanka's Violent Conflict." *Global Networks* 8.4 (2008): 436–52.

Paulley, Ellen. "Peacebuilding in Myanmar." *MSC Currents* Summer (2014): 3. Accessed August 11, 2014. http://www.mscollege.ca/docs/currents/MSC_MSC_Currents_Spring_2014.pdf.

Pirkkalainen, Päivi and Mahdi Abdile. "The Diaspora—Conflict—Peace—Nexus: A Literature Review." Working Paper No. 1, Diaspeace, 2009. Accessed July 11, 2010. https://jyx.jyu.fi/dspace/bitstream/handle/123456789/36875/DIASPEACE_WP1.pdf?sequence=1.

Rajah, Ananda. *Remaining Karen: A Study of Cultural Reproduction and the Maintenance of Identity.* Canberra, Australia: The Australian National University E-Press, 2008. Accessed August 21, 2014. http://www.burmalibrary.org/docs6/Remaining_Karen.pdf.

Rajasingham-Senanayake, Darini. "Ambivalent Empowerment: The Tragedy of Tamil Women in Conflict." In *Women, War and Peace in South Asia: Beyond Victimhood to Agency*, edited by Rita Manchanda. New Delhi, India: Sage, 2001.

Ridd, Rosemary and Helen Callaway. *Caught up in Conflict: Women's Responses to Political Strife*. London, England: Palgrave Macmillan, 1986.

Risse, Thomas and Kathryn Sikkink. "The Socialization of International Human Rights Norms into Domestic Practices: Introduction." In *The Power of Human Rights: International Norms and Domestic Change*, edited by Thomas Risse, Stephen C. Ropp, and Kathryn Sikkink, 1–38. Cambridge, England: Cambridge University Press, 1999.

Ross-Sheriff, Fariyal. "Afghan Women in Exile and Repatriation: Passive Victims or Social Actors." *Affilia: Journal of Women and Social Work* 21.2 (2006): 206–19.

Rupesinghe, Kumar. *Civil Wars, Civil Peace: An Introduction to Conflict Resolution.* London, England: Pluto, 1998.

Sacks, Karen. *Caring By the Hour: Women, Work and Organizing at Duke Medical Center*. Urbana, IL: University of Illinois Press, 1988.

Sen, Amartya. *Development as Freedom*. Oxford, England: Oxford University Press, 1999.

Sen, Gita. "Women's Empowerment and Human Rights: The Challenge to Policy." In *Population, the Complex Reality: A Report of the Population Summit of the World's Scientific Academies*, edited by Sir Francis Graham-Smith, 363–72. Golden, CO: Fulcrum, 1994.

Shain, Yossi and Aharon Barth. "Diasporas and International Relations Theory." *International Organization* 57.3 (2003): 449–79.

Sinatti, Giulia. "Key Criteria of 'Good Practice' for Constructive Diaspora Engagement in Peacebuilding." Discussion Paper, African Diaspora Policy Centre, 2010. Accessed February 2, 2011. http://www.diaspora-centre.org/DOCS/ADPC_Paper_June201.pdf.

Smith, Hazel and Paul Stares, eds. *Diasporas in Conflict: Peace-Makers or Peace-Wreckers?* Tokyo, Japan: United Nations University Press, 2007.

Snyder, Anna C. "A Gendered Analysis of Refugee Transnational Bridgebuildiing Capacity." In *Critical Aspects of Gender in Conflict Resolution, Peacebuilding, and Social Movements*, edited by Anna C. Snyder and Stephanie P. Stobbe, 13–44. Bingley, England: Emerald Group, 2011.

———. "Developing Refugee Peacebuilding Capacity: Women in Exile on the Thai/Burmese Border." In *Critical Issues in Peace and Conflict Studies*, edited by Thomas Matyók, Jessica Senehi, and Sean Byrne, 177–98. Lanham, MD: Lexington Books, 2011.

———. *Setting the Agenda for Global Peace: Conflict and Consensus Building.* Aldershot, England: Ashgate, 2003.

South, Ashley. "Burma's Longest War: Anatomy of the Karen Conflict." *Transnational Institute*, March 28, 2011. Accessed August 21, 2014. http://www.tni.org/briefing/burmas-longest-war-anatomy-karen-conflict.

Stobbe, Stephanie P. "The Soukhouan Ritual: The Legacy of Lao Women in Conflict Resolution." In *Critical Aspects of Gender in Conflict Resolution, Peacebuilding, and Social Movements*, edited by Anna C. Snyder and Stephanie P. Stobbe, 43–74. Bingley, England: Emerald Group, 2011.

Tomlinson, Frances and Sue Eagan. "From Marginalization to (Dis)Empowerment: Organizing Training and Employment Services to Refugees." *Human Relations* 55.8 (2002): 1019–43.

Worland, Shirley and Yvonne Darlington. "The Identity of Displaced Christian Karen in the Context of Resettlement: Threat or Opportunity?" *Asia Pacific Journal of Social Work and Development* 20.1 (2010): 16–28.

Zunzer, Wolfram. "Diaspora Communities and Civil Conflict Transformation." Berghof Occasional Paper Nr. 26, Berghof Research Centre for Constructive Conflict Management, 2004. Accessed May 5, 2011. http://citeseerx.ist.psu.edu/viewdoc/download?doi=10.1.1.126.9346&rep=rep1&type=pdf.

Chapter 12

"It's Not Just the Icing, It's the Glue"

Rural Women's Volunteering in Manitoba, Canada

Robin Neustaeter

Across the tall-grass prairie of south central Manitoba rural women contribute significant time, energy, knowledge, and skills by doing what needs to be done to improve their communities for their families, others, and themselves. Nearly 40 of these women took part in my doctoral research on rural women's community involvement. Women's community involvement has a significant impact on the well-being of their communities around the world. At the local level many women are involved in clubs, organizations, and associations to provide resources and services, and address inequalities. As Pearl, a research participant put it "if women didn't do it, nothing would get done for one thing. Women always seem to be looking out for their family and community. They want a thriving community for their children to live in and their families to come home to." According to Lena Dominelli "without women's work in the community, life as we know it could not exist."[1] However, women's volunteering experiences, challenges, and successes have been largely written out of the official history, leaving an incomplete picture of what really happened in our communities, societies, and nations.[2]

Using my research as a case study, this chapter tells the story of rural women's community involvement in South-Central Manitoba, Canada in order to discover and examine the dynamics, factors, and challenges of women's community involvement as they seek to address community needs and issues, or in other words, how rural women engage in local level peace and development.

SURVEYING THE FIELDS

To paint the unique and vibrant picture of rural women's volunteering, I will survey volunteering, women's community involvement, and rural and gender literature to help locate my case study within a larger thought and analysis context.

Volunteering is practiced around the globe in most societies by people motivated by their religion, spirituality, and values.[3] Volunteers contribute their time, energy, skills, and knowledge to charities, nonprofit organizations, and grassroots initiatives to deliver services and programs in their communities.[4] Through their participation and leadership, volunteers help create our communities. Many community organizations are dependent upon volunteers to deliver their services and programs to see the realization of their visions and mandates.[5] The United Nations *State of the World Volunteerism Report* highlights, "volunteerism is a basic expression of human relationships. It is about people's need to participate in their societies and to feel that they matter to others. We strongly believe that the social relationships intrinsic to volunteer work are critical to individual and community well-being."[6]

Volunteering has different names and manifests itself in different ways across the world,[7] yet in all places it is deeply rooted in "traditional beliefs and community practices."[8] Four key components of volunteerism are identified. First, volunteerism is an act of free will; second, it is for done for the public good; third, money is not a motivating factor, and; fourth, volunteerism can be done through an organization or directly between individuals not in one's household.[9] These proactive activities are "given freely to benefit another individual, group or organisation"[10] and require commitment of time and effort.[11]

As an act of free will, volunteering involves a degree of choice factoring in motivation, individual values, and social and cultural norms.[12] People may volunteer inspired by their religious, spiritual, communal, or individual values and ethics.[13] Volunteering is inherently a social endeavor. Not only do people often connect to volunteer work through their networks,[14] they also develop social ties, and a psychological sense of community with fellow volunteers and the community as a whole.[15]

Volunteering can be formal and informal. Formal volunteering happens through formal organizations and associated roles, such as board participation. Informal volunteering involves more general acts of caring or helping; for example, serving at community meals, driving neighbors to appointments, or visiting the elderly or ill. In contexts where there is a culture of involvement with formal organizations, volunteering may be considered to be more public and formal[16]; however, not all contexts have this type of culture of involvement. Limiting definitions of volunteering to formalized involvement risks eliminating the majority of volunteering which takes place around the world through informal local groups and associations.[17] Disqualifying "caring behaviors" from definitions of volunteering risks ignoring and devaluing significant caring volunteer work performed by women and men.

While men and women are typically equal in the amount of volunteering they do, the places they volunteer tend to be different.[18] "Men's volunteer work is typically in the 'public domain,' in civic and professional activities including serving on the boards of organizations. Conversely, women volunteers are found in the 'private domain,' helping others in need."[19] This public/male-private/female dichotomy reflects the greater patriarchal public/private gender divide. While volunteering can perpetuate gender roles,[20] it can also provide opportunities for women to challenge gender barriers.

Women's community involvement is often associated with the maternal and caring attributes socially and culturally ascribed to women in general and mothers in particular.[21] As such "women continue to mobilize around caring responsibilities."[22] In volunteering, women can use their roles as mothers and caregivers to their advantage, using their knowledge, skills, and authority to address community concerns.[23] Women's networks are an important source of motivation, resource, strategy, and support for their community involvement.[24] Networks are vital to women for contacting and connecting with other women to address their concerns, facilitate change, and provide support in balancing their responsibilities.[25]

Through volunteering in their communities, women contribute to the development and well-being of their communities:

> What tends to be ignored is the historical reality that women's work of feeding, rearing, and healing humans and of building and rebuilding households and communities under conditions of constant change—including war, environmental catastrophe, and continual push-pull migrations—produced resources and skills within women's cultures that have been critical not only to human *survival* but to human *development*.[26]

PEACE AND VOLUNTEERING

Volunteerism represents "an enormous reservoir of skills, energy and local knowledge for peace and development."[27] Many nongovernmental peace organizations are dependent upon volunteers to build awareness about peace and conflict issues and policies, advocate communities, leaders, and governments for decisions, actions, and policies that promote peace, and deliver education and programs in local communities. Yet the connections between peace and volunteerism go beyond volunteers in self-identified peace organizations. Many local community organizations that do not specifically identify with peace espouse ideals, values, and goals that contribute to building peace. Peace is more than the absence of conflict; it is addressing conflict with holistic, collaborative, nonviolent processes that focus on building relationships and understanding.[28] Peace is dynamic, not static; it is a process, a transformation.[29] A feminist concept of peace reflects positive peace—the absence of direct and structural violence and the presence of the ethics and practices of caring, interconnectedness, and social justice.[30] As such, volunteerism has a significant influence in creating peaceful societies, fostering ideas and values that promote peace and development across the globe.

> Above all, volunteerism is about the relationships that it can create and sustain among the citizens of a country. It generates a sense of social cohesion and helps to create resilience in confronting the issues . . . this cohesion and resilience are often the mainstay of a decent life for which all people strive. Volunteerism is an act of human solidarity, of empowerment and of active citizenship.[31]

Volunteering contributes significantly to individual and community peace and development by building social cohesion, resilience, solidarity, and social development and capital.[32]

WOMEN'S VOLUNTEERING IN CANADA

In Canada, women have long gathered with other women in response to various community needs and issues. This existed prior to European contact.[33] More recently, Statistics Canada reported that 48.2 percent of Canadian females over the age of 15 volunteer over one billion hours annually, an annual average of 158 hours.[34] In Manitoba, 52 percent of females over the age of 15 volunteer 34.7 million hours annually, an average of 132 hours per person.[35] Rural women's community involvement continues to have a significant role in strengthening their communities. Looking at the history of women's community involvement, Michael Welton highlights women's attention to "culture, education and health . . . the building blocks of any sustainable community life. *Women are quintessential community-builders*."[36] In the 1800s in Manitoba, many immigrant women reestablished their churches' ladies aid societies from their homelands to provide a venue for women's fellowship and raising funds for church and community needs.[37] In the late nineteenth and early twentieth centuries many women were involved in local community development based on their immediate community needs.

> Women's conception of community often reached far beyond their localities to encompass global issues of peace and justice. In their local sites, women purchased land for cemeteries, built library facilities, fought for better schools, created clubs to study child psychology, led efforts to provide garbage disposal, sewer systems, better mail service, provided restrooms for women in town and

> on the road, improved transportation, built playgrounds, tried to protect vulnerable working class women in the cities . . . and on and on.[38]

Rural women in Canada have significant knowledge and skills vital to the creation, implementation, and success of community programs and initiatives.[39] Coaching sports, fundraising, driving neighbors to appointments, organizing farmers markets or community gardens, advocating for family centers, foodbanks or women's shelters, or sitting on committees, boards, municipal councils or school boards, women are actively building community.

RURALITY AND GENDER

Developing a deeper appreciation for rural women's volunteering requires an understanding of the nuances of the sociocultural context, in particular the gender culture and ideologies in rural societies. In rural culture, masculinities and femininities are created and recreated in relationship to each other, changing social and economic conditions and policies, and media and mainstream culture.[40] Gender roles and ideologies inform the power relations in farming and rural communities, create challenges for many farm and rural women, and legitimize the subordination of women.[41] Emphasis is placed on harmonious social relationships, the collectivity of *gemeinshaft*, and the constructed homogeneity of rural communities that suppresses gender, class, and race conflicts[42] to maintain the rural idyll. "Romanticized narratives of rural life that legitimize the subordination of women"[43] limit women's ability to make individual choices, particularly when these choices may challenge gender roles. Farmwomen in Canada have been socialized to "take a back seat"[44] and be silent about their own emancipation because fighting for their own needs "would undermine the struggle of their farms and their communities."[45] Rural women often downplay the significance of their efforts in order to maintain the rural gendered idyll and avoid choices that challenge gender roles. Women use what are considered to be their feminine values to become agents of change to improve the lives of people.[46]

RURAL WOMEN: DOING WHAT NEEDS TO BE DONE

Between October 2012 and April 2013 I traveled across South-Central Manitoba meeting nearly 40 women in homes, libraries, restaurants, cafeterias, and offices to listen to their personal stories of being involved in their communities, including towns, villages, and a First Nations Reservation.

These women were or are involved in nearly 80 different community initiatives; 21 local chapters of provincial or national organizations; and eight religious or spiritual affiliations. The women range in age from 28 to 85. They are all seasoned community volunteers having been involved for at least five years, the longest period being more than 60 years. Some women have been involved with the same organization for nearly 60 years. They are single, married, mothers, grandmothers, great-grandmothers, teachers, accountants, councillors, retired, employed, social workers, nurses, business-owners, farmers, artists, historians, dreamers, advocates, and authors.

The mainly flat, lush prairie landscape is dotted with small cities, towns, villages, farms, and a First Nations Reservation. While the cultural makeup of the entire area is diverse, individual communities are to varying degrees ethnically mixed. Historically, the area was settled in more ethnic homogenous concentrations with distinct French, British, Russian-German Mennonite, and Ukrainian communities. Through immigration, some communities are experiencing increased cultural diversity. While English is the language of the majority, in education and business, French, Low-German, High-German, Russian, Ukrainian, Tagalog, Spanish, and Arabic are also spoken on the streets, in shops, and homes. For many people, churches and religion are a significant part of their lives. The area is predominantly Christian.

To clarify, this is my homeplace. I grew up and currently live in South-Central Manitoba, among the many community-active women, of which I am one. Growing up, I watched my mother, grandmother, aunts, and neighbour women dedicate countless hours and extensive energy to community improvement. Through my global travels, I witnessed women actively involved in their own communities, working for change in order to make their communities better. As a doctoral student my peace-curiosity led me to critically examine what women are doing in their own "backyards," to improve their communities and regions, including my own.

Women active in community-building often depend upon the support of political, economic, and religious institutions. As well, rural communities are known for the lack of anonymity. Thus, to ensure confidentiality and not put their involvement at risk, I've given the women who participated in this study pseudonyms. While this is a small portion of my study, my intent is to let the women tell their stories for the reader to hear and ponder.

The women shared countless, dynamic stories of community involvement. Often, women would interrupt themselves and saying things like, "Oh yeah, and then I did this . . ." and "Oh I completely forgot about the time that I . . ." to share another thing they did or something they want to do, what Maria, one study participant, referred to as her "someday plan." For many participants this was the first time anyone had asked them about their community involvement, noting that they had never stopped to think about it before. They were so busy doing the work. Some of the women shared that they appreciated the opportunity to reflect on what they had done, often while also raising a family and doing other work, for some on and off the farm. Looking on her notes listing everything she had done and is doing, Kathleen reflected, "I don't know how all this happened. How did I do all that I don't know? I just saw things and they called me and I went."

When I began this research process I sought a term broad enough to include all the different unpaid ways that I saw women formally and informally improving the social, cultural, and economic well-being of their communities, and common enough that the women would know what I meant without explanation. I didn't want to limit the focus to what is popularly considered volunteering. When I began talking about my research I used the term "community-building," which was usually met with blank stares. One evening my grandmother asked me about my research. When I explained it to her, "I'm looking at how women are making their communities better," she replied "Oh, I've been involved in my community for years," and shared countless personal stories spanning over 50 years. Thus "community involvement" became my term of choice. Here, community involvement and volunteering will be used interchangeably.

My "what do you call it?" conundrum prompted me to ask the women "Do you have a name for what you do in your community?" Their responses were revealing. Some women simply said they had no name for it—reflecting the "tradition without a name."[47] Several women stated it's just who they are. Somewhat jokingly, Jackie said, "Nope, some people tell me I'm crazy . . . but to put a name on it, I don't know, it's just who I am." Simone reflected, "for me personally it just came naturally. It's natural." Being involved is just how she is, noted Georgia, "For me being a woman in the community and being involved in the community is just how I carry myself out on a daily basis, right. It's, you know, it goes down to, you know, saying hello to the lady in the grocery store and asking them how they are," later adding "I don't know if I have a name for it because I will probably do anything if I see value in it." To Lena, it meant "You are just doing your thing." Margaret said, "I just be." Considering that some women had no name for their involvement or consider their involvement to be just who they are suggests that the naturalness and taken-for-granted-ness is so everyday as to be considered ordinary and mundane, not extraordinary to the extent that it should be distinguished by a name. This natural, ordinary character highlights sociocultural and community values and expectations of volunteering: "It's just the way *we* are." It is assumed. Debra recounted a childhood memory growing up in rural Manitoba.

> 'Cause that is just what you did. It was part of what, who you were. If you belonged to the community, even if you didn't want to necessarily, like back

> when I was growing up there was fall suppers all the time . . . Everybody contributed, you know, it just was. And the women had their role and the men had their role. So my grandfathers would have done more of what the men do and the women would have done what the women do . . . a lot of the fundraising and the cooking at any of those events. And they brought food and it was just what you did. Whether it was a dance, a fall supper, a New Year's—whatever, you brought food. It was part of being community. If somebody died then automatically you brought food to the house and you brought food to the hall, you know, because they would need food for the funeral. It just, it wasn't even questioned should you do that. It was just what you did.

Other terms women had for their involvement, included service, help, responsibility, entrepreneur, social entrepreneur, advocate, activist, and "volunteer." The latter was the most common term. Service reflects a religious ethic of serving others. Responsibility, referred to the caring responsibilities women feel toward people and the civic responsibility they felt toward their communities. Reflecting on her sense of civic responsibility, Maria recalled a pivotal conversation she had with her husband.

> I think I was talking about the church and I said, "Why don't they?" And he said, "There's no 'they'." He said, "There's no 'they,'" and I thought that was something that just stuck in my mind. He probably wouldn't ever remember having said it but it's something people say all the time, like, "Why don't they get these roads fixed up?" or "Why don't they. . ." Well you know there's a town council that you can run to go on and get those roads fixed and learn that there's not always money for it, but you know. But I think that's something that I've always thought about. I believe that it is my responsibility to do what I can—to use the abilities I have to make things work. I really believe there is no "they" there is only "us."

Belinda has two names for her involvement: "I would call it advocacy, you know, I would call it advocacy, asking for what you need, but I don't know if anybody was to ask me what I was doing with that I would say that I was a volunteer . . . I think people are put off with words like advocacy, it sounds like you are fighting." Private and public names for one's community involvement indicate that women must strategically choose how they identify their activities to ensure they do not damage their public reputation and ally networks. Name or no name, what they chose to call or not call their community involvement is a choice factoring personal and community values, motivations, and strategies.

Seeing a need, such as gaps in local services, resources, or opportunities in their communities prompts women to fill in the missing pieces. Helena matter-of-factly stated, "It was just something that needs to be done. If you want it done then you are going to have to do it." Along the same lines, Fiona said, "I see a need and think there has to be a way of solving that problem." For some women it is also about addressing inequalities, social justice, and deeper transformation. For example, Belinda shared the following thoughts.

> It always has been a bit about the underdog, about inequities. Like, if I think there is something that is not fair, you know, a little bit of that Robin Hood and Maid Marion thing. Like, how there is the rich, the people that have, don't even know the problems that the have-nots are facing. They simply do not know. And I guess that I would consider that some of the work that I get to do as being a bit of a bridge to that. So that the people that are the haves can understand actually what is happening for the others.

The work of volunteers contributes significantly to the local economy, as Mia noted, "Women's volunteer labour subsidizes the economy," while Margaret pointed out, "Women's community involvement is important; we can't afford to pay for all the services." Volunteers are crucial to a community's survival, as Suzette noted, "If people don't care for a town it will die." Gail highlighted "a lot of vital important community services are run by volunteers, volunteers are connected with other volunteers, volunteers keep the town going." Volunteering is significant to community development and well-being, as well as families, Wanda observed: "I think there are a lot of things that wouldn't be happening in our world if it wasn't for people being involved. I often think of it as volunteer jobs. Volunteer work creates huge plusses in our society . . . How do you develop community without getting involved in it? Community is what makes our world. It's really important for family structure, for child development."

Women's volunteering manifests itself in formal and informal ways as reflected in the earlier definitions from the literature. In their interviews, women noted their formal involvement in organizations and the various roles they've held, including leadership roles. They also noted their informal volunteering or "helping." Wendy distinguished her volunteering by saying, "My community involvement is not formal like starting a food bank; my community work is helping." Helena pointed out, "There are a lot of people who volunteer and don't even consider what they are doing as volunteering."

Women discussed various influences on their community involvement, including family and spouses; upbringing; values and beliefs; disabilities; responsibilities such as work, family, farm; gender; and, motherhood. Upbringing and family were significant in Debra's memory recounted above. Some women completely dismissed gender, while others identified it in overt and latent ways. Maria clarified, "My husband is a bigger influence; being a woman may have influenced the kind of things I did." On the influence of gender in community involvement, Mia speculated, "Probably being a woman had something to do with the value I placed on family. I mean I hope that if I was a man that I would do it. I don't know. I kind of see men and women as being pretty equal in needing to be involved with other people." While women may more naturally be nurturers, this role should also extend to men, argued Wendy. "Women are the connectors in a community, women have a sense of the community's pulse, women do it more naturally given our nurturing roles, important for women to be involved in community and invite men too, not just to coach hockey." Kathleen identified patriarchy's gender dichotomy as limiting both men and women, saying, "Women and men both are locked into cultural gender roles which would mean each missed opportunities for career and nurturing family."

Gender determines legitimate volunteer roles and activities women can perform. Joan, the first woman municipal councillor for her community, pointed out, "In the community I think it was always just done by men so it was always just expected that the men would do it . . . and being secretary well that's okay because that's a woman's job. Men don't take notes." She added, "Women aren't stupid. It goes back to a lot of that old thinking, right? Women should be in the home, bake your cookies, bake your pies, belong to the United Church Women, that's kind of the attitude that we're trying to get away from and it's slowly changing." Several other women shared similar sentiments. For example Barbara reflected, "I think a lot of women do wonderful work. I think they still contribute to what they are told to contribute to. They don't break out of that and say, 'Oh we need this!' It's still I think quite difficult. I think some of them are working quietly at that, but it's always surprising to me how long change takes." Both women noted that gender roles are changing, slowly.

The social aspect of volunteering is a motivation and benefit for the women. Bea is involved simply because, "My bottom line is that I love people." Being involved is "a great way to meet neighbours and people in the community," noted Lois. It's a chance to create relationships; it's also a social outlet. Sonia admitted that she's always "amazed at what different personalities and unique gifts can do together." Lena observed that having the right kind of people together could be the difference between an initiative being a success, challenge, or a flop. Connecting with like-minded women through volunteering is a coping strategy and a source of encouragement for women challenged by sociocultural norms and values. Tanya recalled, "There are other women like me and not necessarily living all that close to me but relatively close to me, who share some of my views, my world view, and that is a very comforting feeling. And then you also have more confidence in being yourself in your own community."

Women's community work is often not recognized or translated into community leadership, decision making, or power. Regarding where she sees women's community involvement happening and what women are doing Belinda observed, "Its community building. Women are doing that part, not on city council but every day," adding "It's not the streets, it's not the sidewalks because no one would want to live here if it's shitty, if all that other stuff wasn't happening, but all that other stuff is happening because of women, and still, though, primarily leaders in the churches are men. The women do all the grunt work." The "Old Boys Club" is a challenge Pam described: "They do not shut down the work women do, but I get the sense that there's so much more we would be able to do if there weren't men in authority who would shut us down. So the fight to do something that's very progressive in a community is not worth it because there's an Old Boys' Club there that will not see that through," adding "You can have all the ideas in the world and until a man says it's good, it's not relevant and is trivialized. And, that's sad, that's very sad." Echoing this point Stacey commented, "Being a woman here is frustrating, patriarchy, women not respected as they should be because they are women. They are seen as emotional, not strategic thinkers, not left-brained." In order to have their issues heard, several women admitted to having men front their issue, as Barbara seemed to confess. "It's more challenging to get attention and I have actually stooped to having a man front some issues because then they will be heard. So I'm not above that in getting things done. It is simply because the issues that I work on are not the sort of grabbing ideas that the powers that be will pay attention to." Barbara's strategy highlights challenges women face when their issues aren't the priority of the decision-makers and money-holders. Many women lamented that they have to make themselves visible and prove themselves to be heard. The Old Boys' Club, the silencing of women, and devaluing women's issues are sociocultural control mechanisms to maintain gender, culture and power. Despite these challenges the women persevere.

Mothers in particular expressed wanting to create more opportunities for their children.

The majority of participants were mothers; some were grandmothers. One was a great-grandmother. Motherhood motivated women to improve their communities for their children by providing opportunities and resources for their kids, such as play structures and recreation programs. Simone clarified, "We do it for our kids. We always want more for our kids, the best. Really, I don't know why else I would be on all these committees." Georgia echoed, "I have kids, and I wanna, and we live in a remote area, and I want to provide lots of opportunities for my kids."

Community involvement is also a way moms teach and role model their values to their children. Georgia's involvement is a way "to be a good mother, set a good example for my kids." For Belinda being involved is a chance for her to show her daughter what a woman can do in society, that she can make a change. Many moms involve their children in their community work. When Simone's son told her he wanted a skatepark she said, "Okay, let's try but you need to help." She noted, "My kids are involved in everything I'm involved in and I just bring them and I think it's a good way for them to learn that you know what you gotta give back to your community. If you want something you gotta work for it."

Several women acknowledged that being a woman presented them the culturally legitimate option of being the stay-at-home parent, in a two-parent household, which granted them the time, energy, and flexibility to be involved in their community. For example, Kathleen shared, "Probably, the fact that I had the luxury staying . . . being a stay-at-home mom gave me that option." After recounting all her involvements Mia chuckled, "That is why I am staying at home. I won't be able to do all that." In rural areas where the traditional gender roles are still prevalent, mothers typically stay home with their children. There is a concern that women will have less time for volunteering when they move into the workforce, reducing volunteers to maintain the work of the existing community organizations. Mia observed, "Around here it's getting very difficult. I see in the country here the ones who are working and they have their own farm. They . . . it's tricky already and if they have kids, they are not able to volunteer anymore. That is why we have a shortage, like in every group." Studies show that as women move into the labor force, volunteer rates remain stable; however women often change how they volunteer.[48]

It's important for women to be involved, share their perspectives and skills, noted all the participants, as Joan emphasized, "Women also have their experiences to bring to the table, a whole new perspective that men sometimes don't see, and after all we are half the population or half the gender so why wouldn't we be involved?" Mia feels that, "Women are the main community makers, community builders." Similarly, Holly believes, "Women keep the community alive, are the backbone of the community." Women are always ready to be involved, noted Pearl half-jokingly, "Men need a motivation . . . they are good once you get them started, whereas women—you don't have to get them started. They are usually going."

CONCLUSION

As I write, many women around South-Central Manitoba and around the world are volunteering in community clubs, organizations, and associations, in formal and informal ways to ensure that the needs of their families and communities are met and issues are addressed, "that their communities thrive and are great places to come home to" as Pearl stated. Despite barriers, including gender, fueled by their motivations, women choose to commit significant time, energy, skills, and knowledge to the well-being of their communities. Regarding the significance of women's community involvement Belinda declared, "I mean, without it I cannot imagine how the community would be . . . without that, without it. It's not just the icing it's the glue. It's not just the icing keeping, holding the community together, it's really the glue."

NOTES

1. Lena Dominelli, "Women in the Community: Feminist Principles and Organising in Community Work," *Community Development Journal* 30.2 (1995): 133.
2. Dominelli, "Women in the Community"; Shulameit Reinharz, "Women as Competent Community Builders: The Other Side of the Coin," *Issues in Mental Health Nursing* 5.1–4 (1983).
3. United Nations Volunteers, *State of the World's Volunteerism Report, 2011: Universal Values for Global Well-Being* (New York, NY: United Nations Volunteers, 2011).
4. Mirielle Vézina and Susan Crompton, *Volunteering in Canada* (Ottawa, ON: Statistics Canada, 2012).
5. Ibid.
6. United Nations Volunteers, *Volunteerism Report*, xx.
7. Ibid.
8. Ibid., 2.
9. International Labour Organisation, *Manual on the Measurement of Volunteer Work* (Geneva, Switzerland: International Labour Organisation, 2011), 11.
10. John Wilson, "Volunteering," *Annual Review of Sociology* 26.1 (2000): 215.
11. Ibid., 216.
12. Allen M. Omoto and Mark Snyder, "Considerations of Community: The Context and Process of Volunteerism," *American Behavioral Scientist* 45.5 (2002).
13. Vezina and Crompton, *Volunteering in Canada*; John Wilson and Marc Musick, "Who Cares? Toward an Integrated Theory of Volunteer Work," *American Sociological Review* 62.5 (1997).
14. Vézina and Crompton, *Volunteering in Canada.*
15. Omoto and Snyder, "Considerations of Community."
16. Wilson, "Volunteering," 216.
17. United Nations Volunteers, *Volunteerism Report*, 35.
18. Ibid., 36.
19. Ibid., 10.
20. Ibid.
21. Nancy Chodorow, *The Reproduction of Mothering: Psychoanalysis and the Sociology of Gender* (Los Angeles, CA: University of California Press, 1978); Linda Forcey, "Women as Peacemakers: Contested Terrain for Feminist Peace Studies," *Peace & Change* 16.4 (1991); Sara Ruddick, *Maternal Thinking: Toward a Politics of Peace* (Boston, MA: Beacon, 1989).

22. Dominelli, "Women in the Community," 82.

23. Ibid.; Celene Krauss, "Challenging Power: Toxic Waste Protests and the Politicization of White, Working Class Women," in *Community Activism and Feminist Politics: Organizing Across Race, Class, and Gender*, ed. Nancy A. Naples (New York, NY: Routledge, 1998).

24. Dominelli "Women in the Community"; Krauss, "Challenging Power"; Cynthia Cockburn, *From Where We Stand: War, Women's Activism & Feminist Analysis* (London, England: Zed Books, 2007).

25. Krauss, "Challenging Power"; Reinharz, "Community Builders."

26. Elise Boulding, "Feminist Inventions in the Art of Peacemaking," *Peace & Change* 20.4 (1995): 410.

27. United Nations Volunteers, *Volunteerism Report*, 3.

28. Ian M. Harris and Mary Lee Morrison, *Peace Education*, 2nd ed. (Jefferson, NC: McFarland, 2003); Betty Reardon, "Feminist Concepts of Peace and Security," in *A Reader in Peace Studies*, ed. Paul Smoker, Ruth Davies, and Barbara Munske (Oxford, England: Pergamon Press, 2010).

29. Betty Reardon, *Sexism and the War System* (Syracuse, NY: Syracuse University Press, 1985); Jo Vellacott, "Dynamic Peace and the Practicality of Pacifism," in *Patterns of Conflict, Paths to Peace*, ed. Larry J. Fisk and John L. Schellenberg (Peterborough, ON: Broadview Press, 2000), 203.

30. Johan Galtung, "Violence, Peace, and Peace Research," *Journal of Peace Research* 6.3 (1969); Birgit Brock-Utne, *Feminist Perspectives on Peace and Peace Education* (New York, NY: Permagon Press, 1989); Betty Reardon, *Women and Peace: Feminist Visions of Global Security* (Albany, NY: State University of New York Press, 1993); Anna Snyder, "Ambivalent Empowerment: Refugee Women and Sustainable Peacebuilding on the Thai/Burmese Border," paper presented at the International Peace Research Association Conference, University of Leuven, Belgium, July 15–19, 2008.

31. United Nations Volunteers, *Volunteerism Report*, 92.

32. Ibid.

33. Kim Anderson and Bonita Lawrence, eds. *Strong Women Stories: Native Vision and Community* (Toronto, ON: Sumach Press, 2006); Marlene Epp, *Mennonite Women in Canada: A History* (Winnipeg, MB: University of Manitoba Press, 2008); Gloria Neufeld Redekop, *The Work of Their Hands: Mennonite Women's Societies in Canada* (Waterloo, ON: Wilfrid Laurier University Press, 1996); Jo-Anne Weir, "*Undan Snjobreidunni* (What Lies Beneath the Snow): Revealing the Contributions of Icelandic Pioneer Women to Adult Education in Manitoba 1875–1914." (MA thesis, University of Manitoba, 2007); Michael R. Welton, "Amateurs Out to Change the World: A Retrospective on Community Development," *Convergence* 28.2 (1995).

34. Statistics Canada, Social and Aboriginal Statistics Division, *Caring Canadians, Involved Canadians: Tables Report 2010*, no. 89-649-X — 2011001 (Ottawa, ON: Statistics Canada, 2012), 27.

35. Ibid., 34.

36. Welton, "Amateurs Out to Change the World." Emphasis added.

37. Redekopp, *The Work of Their Hands*; Weir, "What Lies Beneath the Snow."

38. Welton, "Amateurs Out to Change the World," para. 14.

39. Rebecca Sutherns, Marilou McPhedron, and Margaret Haworth-Brockman, *Rural, Remote and Northern Women's Health: Policy and Research Directions—Summary Report* (Ottawa, ON: Centres of Excellence for Women's Health, 2004).

40. Berit Brandth, "Rural Masculinity in Transition: Gender Images in Tractor Advertisements," *Journal of Rural Studies* 11.2 (1995); Berit Brandth and Marit S. Haugen, "Text, Body, and Tools: Changing Meditations of Rural Masculinity," *Men and Masculinities* 8.2 (2005); Hugh Campbell and Michael M. Bell, "The Question of Rural Masculinities," *Rural Sociology* 65.4 (2000); Ian Coldwell, "Masculinities in the Rural and the Agricultural: A Literature Review," *Sociologia Ruralis* 50.2 (2010).

41. Berit Brandth, "On the Relationship between Feminism and Farm Women," *Agriculture and Human Values* 19.2 (2002); Berit Brandth and Marit S. Haugen, "Rural Women, Feminism and the Politics of Identity," *Sociologia Ruralis* 37.3 (1997); Barbara Heather et al., "Women's Gendered Identities and the Restructuring of Rural Alberta," *Sociologia Ruralis* 45.1–2 (2005); Gloria J. Leckie, "Female Farmers in Canada and the Gender Relations of a Restructuring Agricultural System," *The Canadian Geographer* 37.3 (1993); Jo Little "Rural Geography: Rural Gender Identity and the Performance of Masculinity and Femininity in the Countryside," *Progress in Human Geography* 26.5 (2002); Nancy Naples, "Contradictions in Agrarian Ideology: Restructuring Gender, Race Ethnicity, and Class," *Rural Sociology* 59.1 (1994); Caroline E. Sachs, *Gendered Fields: Rural Women, Agriculture and Environment* (Boulder, CO: Westview, 1996); Sally Shortall, "Power Analysis and Farm Wives: An Empirical Study of the Power Relationships Affecting Women on Irish Farms," *Sociologia Ruralis* 32.4 (1992); Elizabeth K. Teather, "Farm Women in Canada, New Zealand and Australia Redefine Their Rurality," *Journal of Rural Studies* 12.1 (1996); Elizabeth Kenworthy Teather, "The Double Bind: Being Female and Being Rural: A comparative Study of Australia, New Zealand and Canada," *Rural Society* 8.3 (1998).

42. Naples, "Contradictions."

43. Brandth, "Feminism and Farm Women," 107.

44. Ella Haley, "Getting Our Act Together: The Ontario Farm Women's Movement," in *Women and Social Change: Feminist Activism in Canada*, ed. Jeri .D. Wine and Janice Ristock (Toronto, ON: Lorimer, 1991).

45. Heather et al., "Women's Gendered Identities," 90.

46. Teather, "Redefine Rurality"; Teather, "Double Bind."

47. Mary F. Belenky, Lynn A. Bond, and Jacqueline S. Weinstock, *A Tradition that has No Name: Nurturing the Development of People, Families, and Communities* (New York, NY: Basic Books, 1997), 12.

48. Wilson, "Volunteering," 217.

BIBLIOGRAPHY

Anderson, Kim and Bonita Lawrence, eds. *Strong Women Stories: Native Vision and Community Survival.* Toronto, ON: Sumach Press, 2006.

Belenky, Mary F., Lynne A. Bond, and Jacqueline S. Weinstock. *A Tradition that has No Name: Nurturing the Development of People, Families, and Communities.* New York, NY: Basic Books, 1997.

Boulding, Elise. "Feminist Inventions in the Art of Peacemaking." *Peace & Change* 20.4 (1995): 408–38.

Brandth, Berit. "On the Relationship between Feminism and Farm Women." *Agriculture and Human Values* 19.2 (2002): 107–17.

———. "Rural Masculinity in Transition: Gender Images in Tractor Advertisements." *Journal of Rural Studies* 11.2 (1995): 121–33.

Brandth, Berit and Marit S. Haugen. "Rural Women, Feminism and the Politics of Identity." *Sociologia Ruralis* 37.3 (1997): 325–44.

———. "Text, Body, and Tools: Changing Meditations of Rural Masculinity." *Men and Masculinities* 8.2 (2005): 148–63.

Brock-Utne, Birgit. *Feminist Perspectives on Peace and Peace Education.* New York, NY: Permagon Press, 1989.

Campbell, Hugh and Michael M. Bell. "The Question of Rural Masculinities." *Rural Sociology* 65.4 (2000): 532–46.

Chodorow, Nancy. *The Reproduction of Mothering: Psychoanalysis and the Sociology of Gender.* Los Angeles, CA: University of California Press, 1978.

Cockburn, Cynthia. *From Where We Stand: War, Women's Activism & Feminist Analysis.* London, England: Zed Books, 2007.

Coldwell, Ian. "Masculinities in the Rural and the Agricultural: A Literature Review." *Sociologia Ruralis* 50.2 (2010): 171–96.

Dominelli, Lena. "Women in the Community: Feminist Principles and Organising in Community Work." *Community Development Journal* 30.2 (1995): 133–43.

Epp, Marlene. *Mennonite Women in Canada: A History.* Winnipeg, MB: University of Manitoba Press, 2008.

Forcey, Linda. "Women as Peacemakers: Contested Terrain for Feminist Peace Studies." *Peace & Change* 16.4 (1991): 331–54.

Galtung, Johann. "Violence, Peace, and Peace Research." *Journal of Peace Research* 6.3 (1969): 167–91.

Haley, Ella. "Getting Our Act Together: The Ontario Farm Women's Movement." In *Women and Social Change: Feminist Activism in Canada*, edited by Jeri D. Wine and Janice L. Ristock, 169–83. Toronto, ON: Lorimer, 1991.

Harris, Ian M. and Mary Lee Morrison. *Peace Education.* 2nd ed. Jefferson, NC: McFarland, 2003.

Heather, Barbara, Lynn Skillen, Jennifer Young, and Theresa Vladicka. "Women's Gendered Identities and the Restructuring of Rural Alberta." *Sociologia Ruralis* 45.1–2 (2005): 86–97.

International Labour Organisation. *Manual on the Measurement of Volunteer Work.* Geneva, Switzerland: International Labour Organisation, 2011.

Krauss, Celene. "Challenging Power: Toxic Waste Protests and the Politicization of White, Working Class Women." In *Community Activism and Feminist Politics: Organizing Across Race, Class, and Gender*, edited by Nancy A. Naples, 129–50. New York, NY: Routledge, 1998.

Leckie, Gloria J. "Female Farmers in Canada and the Gender Relations of a Restructuring Agricultural System." *The Canadian Geographer* 37.3 (1993): 212–30.

Little, Jo. "Rural Geography: Rural Gender Identity and the Performance of Masculinity and Femininity in the Countryside." *Progress in Human Geography* 26.5 (2000): 665–70.

Naples, Nancy A. "Contradictions in Agrarian Ideology: Restructuring Gender, Race Ethnicity, and Class." *Rural Sociology* 59.1 (1994): 110–35.

Omoto, Allen M. and Mark Snyder. "Considerations of Community: The Context and Process of Volunteerism." *American Behavioral Scientist* 45.5 (2002): 846–67.

Reardon, Betty. "Feminist Concepts of Peace and Security." In *A Reader in Peace Studies*, edited by Paul Smoker, Ruth Davies, and Barbara Munske, 136–43. Oxford, England: Pergamon Press, 2010.

———. *Sexism and the War System.* Syracuse, NY: Syracuse University Press, 1985.

———. *Women and Peace: Feminist Visions of Global Security.* Albany, NY: State University of New York Press, 1993.

Redekop, Gloria Neufeld. *The Work of Their Hands: Mennonite Women's Societies in Canada.* Waterloo, ON: Wilfrid Laurier University Press, 1996.

Reinharz, Shulamit. "Women as Competent Community Builders: The Other Side of the Coin." *Issues in Mental Health Nursing* 5.1–4 (1983): 19–43.

Ruddick, Sara. *Maternal Thinking: Toward a Politics of Peace.* Boston, MA: Beacon, 1989.

Sachs, Caroline E. *Gendered Fields: Rural Women, Agriculture, and Environment.* Boulder, CO: Westview, 1996.

Shortall, Sally. "Power Analysis and Farm Wives: An Empirical Study of the Power Relationships Affecting Women on Irish Farms." *Sociologia Ruralis* 32.4 (1992): 431–51.

Snyder, Anna. "Ambivalent Empowerment: Refugee Women and Sustainable Peacebuilding on the Thai/Burmese Border." Paper presented at the International Peace Research Association Conference, University of Leuven, Belgium, July 15–19, 2008.

Statistics Canada. Social and Aboriginal Statistics Division. *Caring Canadians, Involved Canadians: Tables Report 2010*, no. 89-649-X — 2011001. Ottawa, ON: Statistics Canada, 2012.

Sutherns, Rebecca, Marilou McPhedron, and Margaret Haworth-Brockman. *Rural, Remote and Northern Women's Health: Policy and Research Directions—Summary Report.* Ottawa, ON: Centres of Excellence for Women's Health, 2004.

Teather, Elizabeth Kenworthy. "Farm Women in Canada, New Zealand and Australia Redefine their Rurality." *Journal of Rural Studies* 12.1 (1996): 1–14.

———. "The Double Bind: Being Female and Being Rural: A Comparative Study of Australia, New Zealand and Canada." *Rural Society* 8.3 (1998): 209–21.

United Nations Volunteers. *State of the World's Volunteerism Report, 2011: Universal Values for Global Well-Being.* New York, NY: United Nations Volunteers, 2011.

Vellacott, Jo. "Dynamic Peace and the Practicality of Pacifism." In *Patterns of Conflict, Paths to Peace*, edited by Larry J. Fisk and John L. Schellenberg, 202–05. Peterborough, ON: Broadview Press, 2000.

Vézina, Mirielle and Susan Crompton. *Volunteering in Canada*. Ottawa, ON: Statistics Canada, 2012.

Weir, Jo-Anne. "*Undan Snjobreidunni* (What Lies Beneath the Snow): Revealing the Contributions of Icelandic Pioneer Women to Adult Education in Manitoba 1875–1914." MA thesis, University of Manitoba, 2007.

Welton, Michael R. "Amateurs Out to Change the World: A Retrospective on Community Development." *Convergence* 28.2 (1995): 49–62.

Wilson, John. "Volunteering." *Annual Review of Sociology* 26.1 (2000): 215–40.

Wilson, John and Marc Musick. "Who Cares? Toward an Integrated Theory of Volunteer Work." *American Sociological Review* 62.5 (1997): 694–713.

Chapter 13

Militarization and Gender in Israel

Galia Golan

Many changes have occurred in recent years with regard to the status of women in Israel in general and the effects of militarization on gender in particular.[1] The present chapter attempts to update the picture as well as point to often contradictory as well as disturbing recent trends. Therefore, I shall focus on the changes that have occurred, that is, what is new, the results of these changes, and the reactions or responses to them (primarily among women). I shall not deal with the Palestinian minority in Israel, for whom militarization has quite different effects, including the effects related to gender. This topic has been addressed elsewhere and warrants far greater attention than I can accord in this short chapter.[2] Another caveat is that even within Jewish Israeli society there are vast differences of class, ethnicity, and so on, which do produce differences and refinements in the way militarization affects each of them, some of which may impact on gender.[3] These will be referred to only slightly in the following analysis.

BACKGROUND—THE LONG ESTABLISHED EFFECTS OF MILITARIZATION ON GENDER

That Israel is a militarized society is not in question. As a society which since even its prestate days has been involved in armed conflict, with bursts of wars, terror attacks, armed incursions, uprisings, and rocket attacks, that is, both low and high intensity conflict, the central concern of the country has been "security." Not only the precarious nature of Israel's position in the region at its creation but also due to Jewish history over centuries (and particularly because of the Holocaust), security for Israeli Jews tends to be defined as "survival," physical survival that rests only upon the primarily military capacity to meet what is perceived as an ever present threat to the country's very existence. It is easy enough to see how this affects gender roles, namely the traditional division between public and private, the male protector, the female nurturer—the latter bearing children and supporting the protector (be he son or husband),[4] the value accorded to the male child (clearly apparent in the school system from an early age and most directly by the army itself via its presence in high school programs) who will grow up to play a critical role in the survival of the society, and the central role of the military—meaning all things and persons connected with it. Thus, serving in the military carries with it not only the function of masculine identity formation but it also provides glorification as warrior/hero serving the collective, in what may be deemed the epitome of citizenship.[5] And for those who make the military a career for at least part of their lives, this will also accord them benefits and privileges once they retire in the political realm (which is often dependent upon those with military experience and expertise) as well as the business world, the media, and even the area of education—in which all of their presumed expertise in organization and command are thought to provide an advantage. This not only accounts for priority in political office, executive positions, media attention and the like, but it also involves the prominence of values and methods acquired and honed in the military as well as the glorification of these same values and methods. Aside from the obvious dangers and risks when this occurs in the political arena, as it does in a country involved in conflict such as Israel, it is also disturbing when, for example, the Israeli army offers retiring senior officers courses in school management, assisting them to "parachute" into jobs as school principals.

How, you may ask, does this affect gender? Why doesn't the same work for women,[6] since Israel is in fact one of the few countries that has an obligatory military service for women as well as men at age 18? One reason is that the above values, emphasized and developed by the military, are those stereotypically and popularly associated with masculine qualities: courage, boldness, strength, rationality, and the like, in stark contrast to those associated with women such as emotionality, empathy, and softness. Thus, high ranking women veterans (who in any case are very, very few in number) are rarely viewed the same way as their male colleagues, primarily because of the different (or perceived as different) tasks they pursued during their military service. The important point is indeed what happens within the army—particularly important both because of the centrality of the army in a society in conflict but also because the (ostensibly) universal draft means that for Israelis the army is an expected, "natural" step from adolescence to adulthood. In other words, the three years that men serve in the army and the two that women serve have a socialization effect of some importance.[7] While these young people arrive to the army with gender roles developed over the years, the army provides, at the least, a fortifying if not defining influence on recruits. Aside from the fact that far fewer women are drafted than men (it is relatively easy for a girl to opt out on the basis of religion;[8] and married women, pregnant women or single mothers are not drafted at all), women serve less time and do virtually no reserve duty. Moreover, they are still found primarily in clerical or support positions as distinct from combat positions, and, more importantly, they are viewed as "weaker"; they are subject to sexual harassment, and, for those who remain in the professional army, they experience discrimination in promotions. As a patriarchal institution, even the changes that have taken place over recent years have not altered the basic attitudes with regard to the superiority of "masculine" (warrior) over "feminine" virtues or with regard to just what these virtues are, regardless of the gender of those demonstrating them (as we shall see below).[9]

Beyond the role of the army in a militarized society, there are also the accompanying effects of violence, and in the Israeli case, the use of violence in the occupied territories spilling over into Israeli society. Creating or at the least contributing to a culture of violence, this spillover is reflected in part in the high rate of family violence, murders of wives or girlfriends, and possibly even contributing to the rising violence in the schools as well as to the spread of firearms among civilians.[10] Yet these matters, like so many other issues including gender equality, are subordinate to the far more salient and important issue of the Israeli concept of security.

CHANGED FACTORS AND CIRCUMSTANCES

Four major changes have taken place in recent years, some of them connected: change in population attitudes toward the Israeli Defense Force (IDF); globalization; women in combat positions; and religious inroads in the IDF. The Israeli army held an extraordinary place in the hearts of Israelis for many years, related both to the fact of an ongoing conflict, that is, the sense of the collective effort of a "people's army" to defend the country (the IDF stands for Israel *Defense* Forces, the name given to the army when the state was created) and also to the whole ethos of the "new" manly Jew as distinct from the "weak" Jew of the diaspora.[11] This pride in the army was strengthened by the 1956 blitz of the Egyptian army in Sinai and, especially, by the unexpected three-front six-day victory in the 1967 war. Cracks in the overconfidence in the IDF began to appear with the 1973 war when Israel was not only caught by surprise (a failure of army intelligence) but also fared quite poorly in the first days of the war, a period in which the chief of staff as well as the government also lied to the public regarding the situation on the battlefield. Despite what turned into a decisive military victory for Israel in the end, popular protests emerged after the war and the resultant Commission of Inquiry laid the blame for the surprise and unpreparedness on the military echelon, bringing about the resignation of the IDF chief of staff and other military personnel changes.[12] A further blow came with the first Lebanon War of 1982, not because of any military failures but, rather, because this was the first time the public perceived the war as one of "choice" for Israel. Israeli society became split over the necessity of the war once it was understood that the move into Lebanon was not just another border action (against the Palestinian Liberation Organization [PLO], contingents there) but a move on Beirut (and battles with the Syrian army in Lebanon). For the first time in Israel's history, there were large, even massive demonstrations against the war while "our soldiers" were still fighting there. Indeed the major peace movement hesitated, for this reason, to demonstrate, and when it did finally go to the streets it was careful to have soldiers (reservists) returning from the front as speakers, for the sake of legitimacy. It should, perhaps, be pointed out here, that this very movement, Peace Now, Israel's first and only mass peace movement, was created in 1978 with an open letter signed by 148 "reserve officers and soldiers from combat units," a motif employed in order to gain legitimacy within the public, indeed prompting mainstream support for just this reason. That this was a deliberate exploitation of the public trust in the military—that is the male military—was demonstrated by the refusal of the group to include the signature of the one woman among the initiators (who had been a lieutenant when she did her obligatory service).[13] The use of military motifs was typical of many peace groups that emerged over the years, a natural phenomenon for a militarized society perhaps, and an exclusion of women from public representation that was only gradually altered over the years.

The 1982 Lebanon War[14] prompted massive demonstrations and the eventual appointment of a Commission of Inquiry (regarding the role of the IDF in the Lebanese Christian massacre of Palestinians in the two refugee camps, Sabra and Chatilla). In the case of this commission, blame was placed on the political echelon, in particular the Minister of Defense, retired General Ariel Sharon, but there was also public criticism of military actions. Though small in number, refusals of some reservists (in a new group called Yesh Gvul)[15] and even of individual regular army officers to carry out orders, marked a turning point in what was previously an almost monolithic view of military service as a sacred cow. Over the ensuing years, Israeli society was to see more criticism of the army and a larger, mainstream group of reservists refusing to serve in the occupied territories as well as conscientious objectors among would-be recruits. At the same time, also reflecting the loss of blind faith in the army, parents became much more involved in their children's military service—in part because of a new generation of children whose parents had served, partly because of greater openness on the part of the army, though the army occasionally saw this as interference and sought to strike a balance.

Yet, the army's importance remained, even if more open to outside criticism and involvement. Neither the decline in prestige nor the greater involvement of families changed the gender aspects of the military and the notion of gender roles it projected. For example, in the massive social justice protest of the summer of 2011, there were occasional demands to curb the defense budget in favor of social needs, but a recurrent theme in the protest, expressed repeatedly by a male leader (chair of the National Students Union), was that as "soldiers and reservists" "we" deserve a decent standard of living. In one fell swoop women (and Arab citizens) were excluded from this valued group of those contributing to society. Though the intention may have been to infer that a large segment of qualified men were receiving benefits without contributing, namely, ultraorthodox men (who were automatically exempted), the comment was typical of many of the (male) protestors: "look at our contribution, we deserve something in return" or more theoretically, the epitome of citizenship—IDF reserve duty—should carry rewards. The involvement of the family in the military service of their children also served to maintain—rather than change—the gender division. Elevation or emphasis upon the importance of family in connection with the military did not move the family out of the private into the public sphere but rather strengthened the traditional role of the family, associated with women, as nurturing, providing warmth, and emotional support.[16] Moreover, even this involvement was gendered, with the men providing criticism and expertise (based on their own past service) for the benefit of their children-soldiers, while the women provided the traditional caring, home-cooked food, warm clothing, and so on.

A second major change was the linking of the Israeli economy to globalization, beginning in the 1980s. Privatization and the gradual dismantling of the welfare state brought in a neoliberal economy, and capitalist values of individualism and free competition, along with materialism and consumerism. Several phenomena resulted with regard to the military: as individualism replaced the former collective ethos, more individualistic motivation for serving in the IDF appeared among certain sectors of the population. Other sectors opted for careers in the burgeoning private sector, which was during a time of increased dependence upon technology in the military. All of these were to affect the character of the IDF with significant ramifications with regard to gender. For example, Orna Sasson-Levy examined the hypothesis that the decline in the collectivist ethos would result in the "devaluing" of the militaristic, masculine warrior concept at the base of the perceived hegemonic status of men.[17] Studying the motivation for serving, Sasson-Levy found that rather than a devaluation (or to combat it), "militarized masculinity" was simply accorded a more individualistic form by those serving in the army.

The collective self-sacrificing hero, defender of society motivating ethos was replaced, Sasson found, by the stoic, self-disciplined, cool (as in unemotional), individual fighter for whom battle was also "thrilling."[18] Thus, the "new" warrior ethos was no less "masculine" in its virtues or description (though it had other ramifications discussed by Sasson-Levy).

While globalization did not incur a devaluation that might have affected gender relations, it did affect recruitment in a different, more prosaic way, and in a way impacted gender. For many in the middle class, educated (Ashkenazi) elites, the burgeoning private sector was a greater draw than a far less lucrative career in the regular army or even extended service.[19] While this did not change the postretirement advantages enjoyed by those who did remain in the army, it did leave gaps in the recruitment pool. Into these gaps came women and religious men. Thus, a major change occurred over the past two decades for women's positions in the army. In addition to the openings or demand created by male shifts to the private sector, there was also the greater demand for "quality" personnel as a result of increased technology-related needs, a trend apparent in most advanced militaries.[20] This corresponded with a campaign by liberal feminists in Israel for equal rights and roles for women in the IDF, which also included combat. The breakthrough came with a precedent-setting decision by the High Court in 1995, which commanded the Air Force to permit women to join the pilot training course.[21] Basing its judgment on the principle of equality, the Court ordered the IDF to institute any adjustments necessary for women to serve in such a role. Not long after, in 2000, the law regulating national security service was amended to allow for women to serve in all positions of the army. The IDF interpreted this to mean that women could serve in some combat positions on a voluntary basis (only), but it did precipitate the opening of a total of 90 percent of all positions to women, including 10 percent of combat positions.[22] The length of women's and men's obligatory service was not equalized, but women in certain positions did require longer service and, perhaps more significantly, training for many positions was to be conducted jointly. However, in fact, only three percent of women drafted serve in combat positions,[23] and perhaps more to the point, none of the changes in the nature of women's service, including many noncombat command positions, have significantly changed the stereotypical gender attitudes (nor the amount of sexual harassment). On the contrary, Sasson-Levy in her groundbreaking study of gender in the IDF found that women who served in previously "male" positions adopted male models of behavior (such as lowering their voices in giving commands, dressing in certain ways, etc.) and seemed even to internalize the disdain for women's weakness. The negative epithet "women" to describe soft or weak behavior not only has persisted among the men but is also employed by women.[24]

The "estrangement of the middle class from the army," as Yagil Levy puts it, and the resultant gap in personnel, especially "quality" personnel, led to the fourth major change. Not only were women moving into new positions but also, and in large number, religiously observant men. The once almost totally secular officer corps, especially at the higher ranks, was rapidly being replaced by religious Jews, primarily associated with what is called the national (or Zionist) religious community (as distinct from the ultraorthodox), many of whom were graduates from yeshivas (and settlements) in the West Bank as well as Israel proper. This community is not only one of the fastest growing groups in Israeli society, but also a group that has been steadily becoming more fundamentalist, that is, religiously observant, over the years, to the point of allying with parts of the still more religious ultraorthodox. From the beginning of the changes regarding women's military service, there was opposition from this group, but with increasing numbers of the religious men remaining in the army, there has been a marked shift in the role of the Military Rabbinate and demands for religious observance in the army. The principal demand, which has increasingly been granted, is for separation between men and women. This gained public attention—and anger—on more than one occasion when religious soldiers left the hall when women (soldier) singers appeared in an official army program. An order by the Head of the IDF Personnel Division, General Orna Barbivai (herself the first women to achieve this high position) expressly forbidding such behavior met with resistance, such as, for example, the February 2012 resignation of the Rabbi-officer serving the Israeli Air Force.[25]

Thus, the patriarchal nature of the army has now been compounded and strengthened by the influx of this other patriarchy. In fact, the issue of separating men and women in public, even official events and (public) transportation, has become a major issue in Israel with a distinct blurring of the military and civilian spheres. While one might view the religious move into (some might say takeover of) the army as a further sign of the militarization of Israeli society, it would appear to be, rather, a sign of the greater religiosity of an already militarized society.[26] Yet this development, an apparent contradiction to the trend toward greater gender equality both in the army and in Israeli society, can be expected to contribute further to the militarization of Israeli society given the strong link between these religious groups and militaristic *policies* (settlement building, continuing the occupation). Their religious beliefs tie them to territorial domination (sentiments such as "eretz Israel" constitutes God-given lands to Abraham) while their political beliefs are based on the conviction that Israel is fated to live by the sword ("Arabs/Islam will never accept Israel in the region"). And as they take control of the sword, gender will be further affected through the influence of the army. Thus, the swing toward greater religiosity in Israel may be seen as still another change impacting on militarization, with the accompanying effects on gender.

Another change is simply the greater militarization of Israeli society through the still greater encroachment not only of the IDF itself but also of support for the army and for the occupation, introduced by the Ministry of Education under the Netanyahu government. As if the traditional military visits and activities in the school system, mainly during the last two years of high school, were not enough, there are new, additional obligatory school programs. These include visits (usually led by settlers) to Jewish historic sites and settlements in the occupied territories including the controversial Silwan area of East Jerusalem. Bonuses of various types were given to schools with high percentages of graduates joining combat units, and other programs to boost patriotism and military service. These have had the effect of augmenting (still further) the perceived importance of security and the centrality of the army—with all their accompanying gender related influence and ramifications, in the education system itself. To these may be added the fear campaign conducted by the Netanyahu government with regard both to the threat of a "second holocaust" from Iran and the threat to Israel's survival from the "de-legitimization" campaign abroad. This manipulation of the public's emotions is designed to heighten nationalism as a bond (or diversion) for a society torn by many social and economic rifts, thereby strengthening loyalty to the present government and support for whatever militarist policies it deems necessary—all of which add to the importance of security with all its incumbent gender aspects.

There have, of course, been other changes in Israeli society over the same period, such as demographic changes, electoral shifts, and fluctuations in the peace process. To some degree, and in various ways, these changes too have had some effect on militarization or on gender but the four changes addressed above constitute the *major* changes with regard to the link between militarization and gender, more specifically the negative effects of militarization on gender. Not only has the security ethos remained, along with the traditional and stereotypical gender roles reinforced by the army, but also the enhanced role of religion and its link to the army has raised this to an alarming level with the threat of overlapping and mutually reinforcing patriarchies.

RESPONSES

The changes that have occurred over the past years, and their effects on gender, have prompted a number of reactions and developments that may be seen as responses primarily by women, inside Israeli society. Women's organizations and women's peace groups (including joint groups with Palestinian women) have long sought to provide a voice for women and to change gender relations, but those that we might see in connection with militarization could fall into three categories: (1) those perpetuating the gender effects; (2) those seeking to change the gender effects by engendering, from inside; and (3) those rejecting militarism explicitly and thoroughly. These might be associated with conservative, liberal, and radical feminist approaches, respectively, although not all of those involved are feminists and those who are might well object to such categorizations altogether. The three categories loosely consist of the Four Mothers movement and *Machsom* Watch (Checkpoint Watch) in the first category; Inclusive Security and Women in International Security (WIIS) Israeli chapters, the groups promoting UN Security Council resolution 1325 (e.g., the Center for Women in Public Life [CWIPL]) and *Itach/Ma'aki* in the second category, and New Profile and conscientious objectors in the third.[27]

The Four Mothers group was in fact a mixed gender peace group pressing for Israeli withdrawal from Lebanon (in the 1990s) but it was created by a group of women, mothers of soldiers serving in Lebanon. A similar group, Parents Against Silence, had preceded them in the early days of the Lebanon War. This earlier group was often called Mothers Against Silence because the association with family ("Parents" Against Silence) led to the assumption that they were mainly mothers. In both cases, the idea was to use the female associated family motif, in the case of the Four Mothers—directly. Legitimacy of their protest was thus achieved by associating themselves with those fighting (similar in a way to the Peace Now and later ex-military protests). But in the case of the Four Mothers (so named for the biblical "mothers" Rachel, Leah, Rebecca, and Sarah), this also was a protest that far from threatening the male gender role expressly maintained the traditional women's role as mother. Thus, their approach was not a critical view of the necessity or strategy of the war—as would be expected from male protestors, but rather a plea based on emotions, emphasizing the caring mother. *Machsom* Watch, which was formed by women during the second Intifada, does not use a women or mother motif. However, the role they were intended to play, initially, was indeed a perpetuation of the traditional role of women in a war situation. The task for which they formed themselves was to try to moderate (i.e., soften, the behavior of Israeli soldiers at the checkpoints in the occupied territories). This was to be done simply by the women's very presence at these checkpoints, often without any direct intervention by them in the work of the soldiers. The fact that most of the women were elderly or at least not particularly young added to this "mother is watching you" effect, while their abstention from expressing any political views added to the less threatening (in terms of gender roles) nature of their actions, as in the case of the Four Mothers. This changed in time, as they took on a far more active, interventionist role, but they continued to view their gender as merely a tool, namely, an unthreatening means of gaining access.[28] In a related activity, there was also a brief period in which men volunteered for the checkpoints, but they did so as reservists actually joining the young recruits manning these posts, therefore fulfilling a different type of function, in a different (military) framework based on their experience and expertise, appropriate, one might say, to their gender.

A second type of women's activities designed to change the militarist nature of Israeli policies and society was one that sought to bring women, and with them a gender perspective, into national decision making on matters of peace and security. In adopting this goal, most of these generally already existing feminist groups based their demands on UNSC resolution 1325 (adopted in 2000 and calling for involvement of women in national deliberations on peace and war). Groups such as *Isha l'Isha* (Women to Women), *Itach/Ma'aki* (With You), the Israeli part of the now defunct International Women's Commission for a Just and Sustainable Palestinian-Israel Peace (IWC), the Israeli branches of the American-based Inclusive Security (renamed *Dvora*) and WIIS, plus a newer CWIPL all advocated and worked for greater inclusion of women in security matters, peace talks, and related deliberations. Some of these groups also sought to formulate and promulgate a gendered perspective on such matters. There were many differences within the groups themselves over such issues as descriptive or substantive representation, such as "numbers versus content." Is it enough to demand that there be women, or should the demand be for feminist women, those who would see themselves as representing women's interests and possessing a feminist consciousness? (At the urging of some of these groups, the Israeli law adopting 1325 had changed the original wording to call for inclusion of women from all parts of society but this was meant to ensure that women from marginalized or weakened segments of society would be included, unrelated to their ideology). Yet the issue of content extended also to the question of political views—should one push for or accept the inclusion of right-wing women, who presumably would support militarist policies? There was also the question of just which decision-making bodies should be targeted for the application of 1325. This question arose when *Itach/Ma'aki*, a radical feminist group of women lawyers, decided to petition the Supreme Court to include women in the newly appointed Turkle Commission. The Commission had been created by the government to examine Israel's behavior with regard to the 2010 Gaza Flotilla incident in which the IDF had killed nine activists aboard the Turkish vessel Marmara when the flotilla tried to break the Israeli siege on Gaza. Since the women of the group had objected to the Israeli military action itself, and there was also concern that the Commission would whitewash the whole affair, there were those who said people on the left, including women, should not be a party to the exercise. Nonetheless, this was the first opportunity for a real challenge in the High Court on 1325, and *Itach/Ma'aki* won their case. In the end, however, the government claimed, apparently truthfully, that not even one woman could be found to agree to serve on the Commission.

Even within these groups, there were feminist voices that argued that women should only struggle for a role in peace talks and decisions of that nature, but not for participation or equality in security organs (such as the army or the security services, and the like). Yet the latter were in fact among the goals of groups like WIIS and Inclusive Security, and they were subjected to criticism on the grounds that women's participation—even with the goal of challenging militarization—must be selective, to the exclusion of serving the very institutions that are the instruments of militarization. This was an old argument among Israeli feminists, and one generally ignored by groups like the IWC and CWIPL. These groups preferred to undertake a gendered analysis of, and proposals for, the issues central to the security/peace discourse in the country. Such an endeavor, it was hoped, would provide a basis for women's contribution, whether it be through direct participation or through injection of new, gendered thinking for policymakers. Since many of the same feminist women were involved in all or most of these (second category) groups simultaneously, the basic objective was generally common to them all, namely to alter (if not eliminate) the militarism of the (male) decision-making elite in Israel by introducing their "different" voice, per resolution 1325.

The third category consisted of, mainly, women challenging militarism directly, by total rejection of the security discourse and institutions, and active resistance to them. The organized effort is conducted by New Profile, an organization created by a group of feminist women and men in 1998. Describing themselves as primarily an educational organ, the organization's goals are said to be "the development of a truly civic society in Israel . . . to end conscription, to legalize men's right to conscientious objection, to demilitarize education . . . [to end] the exploitation of and injury to women [and other groups] caused by militarization, to achieve the radical reduction of the role of the military in Israel's social structure."[29] Pitting themselves against the mainstream Israeli discourse and security ethos, their major thrust has been to educate the public, and especially young people, on the "discriminatory and antidemocratic" nature of conscription and military service, which favors the male—actually the Jewish male—and perpetuates war by imbuing a "militarized consciousness." The group became most notable for its support of conscientious objectors in their hundreds, and, in particular, young women seeking exemption from military service, no longer on religious grounds. The army was at a loss over how to deal with this new phenomenon, and a lively debate—and police investigation of New Profile—occurred, while some young women conscientious objectors spent time in jail. A case that gained media attention in 2005 was that of Idan Halili who refused to serve on feminist grounds, stating that the military was an inherently patriarchal institution. Supported by New Profile, she nonetheless was imprisoned for refusing to serve.[30]

CONCLUSIONS

Aside from these more or less organized women's responses to militarism in recent years, there has been a much broader and more highly publicized reaction to the religious attempts to marginalize (physically) and exclude women in the army. The fact that this reaction has come almost equally from men as well as women strongly suggests that the real issue for many is not women's rights or patriarchy in any sphere but rather the increases in the power of the fundamentalist religious community in the country, now reaching into the holy of holies, the IDF. Suddenly new voices are championing women's roles in the army and the need for women's participation at every level, as heard, for example, from a long list of retired generals.[31] Welcome as these voices may be, they by no means address the fundamental issues of militarism, or the effects of militarism on gender, including the central role the IDF plays in this. Ironically, thanks to the militaristic nature of Israeli society and the continued centrality of the IDF as an institution, advocacy by this group—ex-generals, our security experts and heroes—is likely to draw far greater attention than that of the various feminist activists, though just what kind of change it will engender (literally) is by no means certain.

NOTES

1. See the earlier, Galia Golan, "Militarization and Gender in Israel," *Women's Studies International Forum* 5.6 (1987).

2. Working Group on the Status of Palestinian Women Citizens of Israel, "NGO Alternative Pre-Sessional Report on Israel's Implementation of the UN Convention on All Forms of Discrimination Against Women (CEDAW)," January 21, 2005; Nadira Shalhoub-Kevorkian, "Racism, Militarization, and Policing: Police Reactions to Violence against Palestinian Women in Israel," *Social Identities* 10.2 (2004); Isha L'Isha, "On Violence: Women in the Economy of War—Personal Witnesses" (Hebrew), unpublished document, Haifa, Israel, 2005; Sarai Aharoni, "The Influence of the State of War on the Lives of Israeli Women—A Gender Anaysis," unpublished paper (Haifa, Israel: Isha L'Isha), August 11, 2006; Manar Hasan, "The Politics of Honor: Patriarchy, the State, and the Murder of Women in the Name of Family Honor," *Journal of Israeli History: Politics, Society, Culture* 21.1–2 (2002).

3. Some of these matters are treated in more detail in Orna Sasson-Levy, "Military, Masculinity, and Citizenship: Tensions and Contradictions in the Experience of Blue-Collar Soldiers," *Identities: Global Studies in Culture and Power* 10.1 (2003); Galia Golan, "Women and Political Reform in Israel," in *Women in the Middle East and North Africa: Agents of Change*, ed. Fatima Sadiqi and Moha Ennaji (London, England: Routledge, 2011).

4. Hannah Herzog, "Homefront and Battlefront: The Status of Jewish and Palestinian Women in Israel," *Israel Studies* 3.1 (1998).

5. Cynthia Enloe, *Does Khaki Become You* (London, England: Pandora, 1988); Carole Pateman, *The Disorder of Women: Democracy, Feminism and Political Theory* (Palo Alto, CA: Stanford University Press, 1989); Anne Phillips, *Democracy and Difference* (University Park, PA: Pennsylvania State University Press, 1993); Ruth Lister, *Citizenship: Feminist Perspectives* (New York, NY: New York University Press, 1977).

6. Or, we might ask, other "out groups" such as blue-collar, lower class male soldiers or new immigrants, for example. See Sasson-Levy, "Military, Masculinity, and Citizenship."

7. Most women and many men avoid service primarily for "religious" reasons, and members of the Arab minority are not obliged to serve. Both the length of service for men and for women along with the religious exemptions from service are undergoing reform at the time of this writing.

8. Only women are allowed exemption as conscientious objectors or for reasons of "religious family lifestyle." Male "religious" exemption has applied for those in various categories of religious studies.

9. Orna Sasson-Levy, "Feminism and Military Gender Practices: Israeli Women Soldiers in 'Masculine' Roles," *Sociological Inquiry* 7.3 (2003). The opening of combat positions to women (on a voluntary basis) has not changed the disproportionate numbers of women in clerical rather than combat positions.

10. For an interesting analysis of the gender effects of the growing private security sector in Israel, see Rela Mazali, "The Gun on the Kitchen Table," in *Sexed Pistols: The Gendered Impacts of Small Arms and Light Weapons*, ed. Vanessa Farr, Henry Myrttinen, and Albrecht Schnabel (Tokyo, Japan and New York, NY: United Nations University Press, 2009).

11. There were political reasons for the joining of terms, one of which was Ben Gurion's wish to associate the new name with the prestate *Haganah* (Defense) forces as distinct from its right-wing rival groups, the Etzel and Lehi. For discussion of these concepts behind the formation of the IDF, see Herzog, "Homefront and Battlefront"; Sasson-Levy, "Feminism and Military Gender Practices"; Barcuh Kimmerling, *The Invention and Decline of Israeliness* (Berkeley, CA: University of California Press, 2001).

12. The failure to implicate the political echelon was considered a mistake by many, but deservedly or not, the military took the brunt of the blame for years to come.

13. Yuli Tamir, who went on to become one of the leaders of the movement, later became a member of Knesset and ultimately Minister of Education. In the Knesset she cosponsored the adoption into law of UNSC resolution 1325. Women actually

were dominant in the leadership of the movement over the years, though rarely given public attention.

14. The "active" part of the war ended in 1984 when the IDF retreated to a position in southern Lebanon where occasional fighting continued. Full withdrawal came only in May 2000.

15. Translation: "There is a border [limit]," which carries a double meaning since the word *gvul* in Hebrew means both border and limit.

16. Herzog, "Homefront and Battlefront."

17. Orna Sasson-Levy, "Individual Bodies, Collective State Interests: The Case of Israeli Combat Soldiers," *Men and Masculinities* 10.3 (2008).

18. This is my simplification, and just one aspect of Sasson-Levy's far more complex and multifaceted analysis.

19. Yagil Levy, "Social Convertability and Militarism: Evaluations of the Development of Military-Society Relations in Israel," *Journal of Political and Military Sociology* 31.1 (2003).

20. Daphna Izraeli, "Gendering Military Service in the Israeli Defense Forces," *Israel Social Science Research* 12.1 (1997). Religious men refers to those associated with what is known as the national-religious sector as distinct from ultrareligious men, who generally did not serve in the army.

21. Israel Supreme Court—*Bagatz* 4541/94 Alice Miller v. The Minister of Defense, 1995.

22. In time the separate Women's Corps was disbanded and its commander position converted into an advisor to the Chief of Staff on the Status of Women. This was viewed as a positive step toward the integration of women.

23. Efrat Cohen, "Controlled Integration," *Israel Defense*, August 4, 2011, accessed June 14, 2013, http://www.israeldefense.com/?CategoryID=411&ArticleID=544.

24. Orna Sasson-Levy, "Constructing Identities at the Margins: Masculinity and Citizenship in the Israeli Army," *Sociological Quarterly* 43.3 (2002).

25. *Ha'aretz*, February 15, 2012, called this "Battle of the Rabbis."

26. In a poll conducted by the Guttman Institute Avi Hai Foundation in January 2012 consisting of over 2,000 face-to-face interviews of Jewish Israelis, 80 percent said they believed in God (Y-Net, January 28, 2012). "Apart from the fact that four out of five Israeli Jews believe in God, the study's findings revealed that 77 percent are convinced that the world is guided by an 'extraordinary force,' 72 percent believe that praying can improve a person's situation, 67 percent are convinced that the Jews are the chosen people and 65 percent think Torah and *mitzvot* [good deeds] are a divine order" (Y-Net, January 28, 2012).

27. The Israeli Coalition of Women for Peace could be in this category as a radical feminist peace organization but it does not directly challenge militarism as such or the draft.

28. For a feminist analysis of *Machsom Watch*, see Hagar Kotef and Merav Amir, "(En)Gendering Checkpoints: Checkpoint Watch and the Repercussions of Intervention," *Signs* 32.4 (2007).

29. Haggith Gor and Rela Mizrahi, "Militarism and Education from a Feminist Perspective: The Case of Israel," Centre of Critical Feminist Pedagogy, 2007,

accessed June 14, 2013, http://www.criticalpedagogy.org.il/english/critfemlibrary/articles/MilitarismandEducationFeministPerspective/tabid/303/Default.aspx; see also War Resisters International. "The Precarious Position of War Resisters in Israel," 2013, accessed June 14, 2013, http://wri-irg.org.

30. Ruth Hiller and Sergely Sandler, "A Matter of Conscience: Militarism and Conscientious Objection in Israel," in *Peace, Justice, and Jews: Reclaiming Our Tradition*, ed. Murray Polner and Stephan Merken (New York, NY: Bunim and Bannigan, 2007).

31. *Ha'aretz*, November 14, 2011.

BIBLIOGRAPHY

Aharoni, Sarai. "The Influence of the State of War on the Lives of Israeli Women—A Gender Anaysis." Unpublished paper. Haifa, Israel: Isha L'Isha, August 11, 2006.

Cohen, Efrat. "Controlled Integration." *Israel Defense*, August 4, 2011. Accessed June 14, 2013. http://www.israeldefense.com/?CategoryID=411&ArticleID=544.

Enloe, Cynthia H. *Does Khaki Become You? The Militarization of Women's Lives*. London, England: Pandora, 1988.

Golan, Galia. "Militarization and Gender in Israel." *Women's Studies International Forum* 5.6 (1987): 581–86.

———. "Women and Political Reform in Israel." In *Women in the Middle East and North Africa: Agents of Change*, edited by Fatima Sadiqi and Moha Ennaji, 62–78. London, England: Routledge, 2011.

Gor, Haggith and Rela Mizrahi, "Militarism and Education from a Feminist Perspective: The Case of Israel." Centre of Critical Feminist Pedagogy, 2007. Accessed June 14, 2013. http://www.criticalpedagogy.org.il/english/critfemlibrary/articles/MilitarismandEducationFeministPerspective/tabid/303/Default.aspx.

Hasan, Manar. "The Politics of Honor: Patriarchy, the State, and the Murder of Women in the Name of Family Honor." *Journal of Israeli History: Politics, Society, Culture* 21.1–2 (2002): 1–37.

Herzog, Hannah. "Homefront and Battlefront: The Status of Jewish and Palestinian Women in Israel." *Israel Studies* 3.1 (1998): 61–84.

Hiller, Ruth and Sergely Sandler. "A Matter of Conscience: Militarism and Conscientious Objection in Israel." In *Peace, Justice, and Jews: Reclaiming Our Tradition*, edited by Murray Polner and Stephan Merken, 207–14. New York, NY: Bunim and Bannigan, 2007.

Izraeli, Daphna. "Gendering Military Service in the Israeli Defense Forces." *Israel Social Science Research* 12.1 (1997): 129–66.

Kimmerling, Barcuh. *The Invention and Decline of Israeliness*. Berkeley, CA: University of California Press, 2001.

Kotef, Hagar and Merav Amir. "(En)Gendering Checkpoints: Checkpoint Watch and the Repercussions of Intervention." *Signs* 32.4 (2007): 974–96.

Levy, Yagil. "Social Convertability and Militarism: Evaluations of the Development of Military-Society Relations in Israel." *Journal of Political and Military Sociology* 31.1 (2003): 71–96.

L'Isha, Isha. "On Violence: Women in the Economy of War—Personal Witnesses" (Hebrew). Unpublished document. Haifa, Israel, 2005.

Lister, Ruth. *Citizenship: Feminist Perspectives.* New York, NY: New York University Press, 1977.

Mazali, Rela. "The Gun on the Kitchen Table." In *Sexed Pistols: The Gendered Impacts of Small Arms and Light Weapons*, edited by Vanessa Farr, Henry Myrttinen, and Albrecht Schnabel, 246–89. Tokyo, Japan and New York, NY: United Nations University Press, 2009.

Pateman, Carole. *The Disorder of Women: Democracy, Feminism and Political Theory*. Palo Alto, CA: Stanford University Press, 1989.

Phillips, Anne. *Democracy and Difference.* University Park, PA: Pennsylvania State University Press, 1993.

Sasson-Levy, Orna. "Constructing Identities at the Margins: Masculinity and Citizenship in the Israeli Army." *Sociological Quarterly* 43.3 (2002): 357–83.

———. "Feminism and Military Gender Practices: Israeli Women Soldiers in 'Masculine' Roles." *Sociological Inquiry* 7.3 (2003): 440–65.

———. "Individual Bodies, Collective State Interests: The Case of Israeli Combat Soldiers." *Men and Masculinities* 10.3 (2008): 296–321.

———. "Military, Masculinity, and Citizenship: Tensions and Contradictions in the Experience of Blue-Collar Soldiers." *Identities: Global Studies in Culture and Power* 10.1 (2003): 319–45.

Shalhoub-Kevorkian, Nadira. "Racism, Militarization, and Policing: Police Reactions to Violence against Palestinian Women in Israel." *Social Identities* 10.2 (2004): 171–94.

War Resisters International. "The Precarious Position of War Resisters in Israel," 2013. Accessed June 14, 2013. http://www.wri-irg.org/node/600.

Working Group on the Status of Palestinian Women Citizens of Israel. "NGO Alternative Pre-Sessional Report on Israel's Implementation of the UN Convention on All Forms of Discrimination Against Women (CEDAW)," January 21, 2005.

Chapter 14

Women at the Peace Table

The Gender Dynamics of Peace Negotiations

Monica McWilliams

Where violence and conflict have become the norm, negotiating an agreement built on peace and justice can be a challenging prospect for those involved. Since 2000, with the introduction of Security Council Resolutions on women, peace, and security, the United Nations has asserted that the environment enabling peace agreements become more inclusive of women and that gender perspectives be taken into account throughout the peacebuilding process.[1] This chapter draws on examples from the Northern Ireland peace process to show the changes that took place when a group of women moved out of the political activism of civic society to become engaged in the more formal politics of peace negotiations. The women activists grasped the opportunities of the "constitutional moment" to frame gender-specific interests within the new constitutional framework of the 1998 Belfast/Good Friday Agreement. They built on skills honed through years of activism to form the Women's Coalition, a political party that was involved in the multiparty peace negotiations, and became signatories to the peace agreement. However, in the transitional space that opens up following a peace agreement, what gets resourced and implemented often falls short of what was promised. Despite its success in the negotiating process, enforcing the proposals on women's interests in the aftermath proved to be the most difficult task. Where a democratic deficit exists, with women continuing to be excluded from political participation, those who have struggled to build a new society will ask for whom was the reconstruction meant. For a genuinely transformative process to take place, women's interests must not be left in the "aspirational/to do" list but instead form a central part of the "constitutional" and legislative guarantees for the new society.

WOMEN PARTICIPATING AT THE TABLE: NOT JUST A "PRESENCE"?

There are now international standards in place to ensure that the promotion of gender equality is an essential part of peacebuilding.[2] These standards have also demanded the inclusion of women from the outset, leading to a more comprehensive understanding of security in post-conflict societies.[3] The experience in Northern Ireland, where the Women's Coalition was founded, is illustrative of both the inclusion of women participants in peace negotiations and the inclusion of gender equality issues in the final peace agreement. The formation of the Coalition, six weeks before the elections to the peace talks, was the outcome of intense discussion by women activists from a variety of backgrounds who, during the exclusively male pre-negotiation phase, had come to realize that unless women formed themselves into a political party the talks on the future of Northern Ireland would be heavily influenced by a different kind of gender dynamics.

A transitional space was opened up by the Republican and Loyalist cease-fires that set the scene for peace negotiations in 1996.[4] A new electoral system designed to include the political representation of smaller, predominantly loyalist, parties provided the impetus for women to build on their preexisting networks to form their own political party. The Women's Coalition party, with its roots in civic society, succeeded in getting an electoral mandate for its two delegates, leading to their direct involvement in the multiparty peace negotiations. The Coalition was formed to highlight the underrepresentation of women at the party political level in Northern Ireland and to ensure that equality and human rights would be an integral part of the peace negotiations.[5] By getting elected to the peace talks on this agenda, the women in the Coalition exerted their autonomy and engaged as peace negotiators in their own right.[6]

Given that fewer than 10 percent of peace negotiators are women, and only 3 percent of women are signatories to international peace agreements, the UN believes that augmenting the number of women at the peace table should remain a priority.[7] In a meeting with the Northern Ireland peace negotiators, President Nelson Mandela noted that before the talks with the South African government could take place, he had insisted that half of all the negotiating teams had to be female. This is in keeping with the view that "an inclusive peace will not be realised without women's presence and perspective at the table."[8]

But moving from the margins of participatory democracy to mainstream political deliberations has been critiqued more negatively, seeing this merely as the incorporation of women's presence into formal processes. In response to this, Fionnuala Ní Áolain believes that although presence by itself "may not fundamentally reshape women's engagement in transitional justice processes or shape outcomes . . . it remains a necessary first step to forward-looking transformation for women."[9] There are gendered dimensions to all aspects of political, economic, and social construction, so gender equality and women's participation requires focused attention throughout the substantive negotiations and especially in the implementation phase of peace agreements. Catherine O'Rourke's recent analysis of UN documents furthers this argument by interpreting the participation of women in the peace and security agenda from five different perspectives: first, participation as seen through the lens of representation (the importance of "presence"); second, participation as deliberation (those most affected by conflict being involved in reflective and thoughtful outcomes); third, participation through inclusion (women's specific needs being addressed); fourth, participation requiring women's expertise (on gender-specific concerns) and fifth, participation providing role models (showing how women can perform these tasks).[10] Tangible evidence exists to show that if one, or more, is built into the framework for peace, the better the outcomes.[11]

Effectiveness of peace processes also requires that they should be built on the widest base of experience. Thus, they need to take into account women's diverse experiences before, during, and post conflict. Failure to do so can lead to an impoverished understanding of peace and security. As Donald Steinberg explains, if governments want to know whether justice and security sector reforms are working, they need to ask the women who are the eyes, ears, and consciences of the communities to which the fighters are returning.[12] Women can also provide security personnel with many of the best ideas and the most reliable information because their families' safety depends on it. As Ruth Jacobson notes even if the activism is not widely acknowledged as political, "the way in which women have set about rebuilding their lives so that their children do not have to experience the same horrors is unmistakably transformative."[13]

UTILIZING S DIFFERENT SKILL BASE IN PEACE NEGOTIATIONS

Peace negotiations also need a great deal of nurturing especially since so many agreements fail during the first five years.[14] John Paul Lederach argues that it can take a society the same amount of years to come out of conflict as the duration of the conflict itself.[15] In such a scenario, peacebuilding requires patience and persistence and an understanding that progress can be precarious. Whether women bring this "added value" to the "mix" of conflict transformation is a question that has exercised academics, peace activists, the global women's movement, and international agencies. Kofi Annan agrees with the importance of "greater consultation with and involvement in peace processes of important voices of civil society, especially those of women, who are often neglected during negotiations."[16] However, if civic actors are expected to make their contribution through representative participation and consultative mechanisms rather than as direct participants in peace accords, what difference does it make when they become directly involved?[17]

As UN Secretary General, Kofi Annan recognized that successful negotiations required the involvement of individuals who could test the public thermometer for political accommodation, dismantle rumors and maintain dialogue at times of crisis. Women community leaders attain these skills through mediating local disputes and by opening up dialogue across divided lines during conflict. There has been a growing acceptance of the need to incorporate these skills into the task of peacekeeping and reconstruction following conflict.[18]

In the Northern Ireland process, the Women's Coalition made a leap from Track Two (indirect involvement through civic society) to Track One Diplomacy (direct participation in formal high level negotiations). Anthony Wanis-St. John and Darren Kew's comments are pertinent to this contextual shift: "viewed from the shoes of negotiators and mediators, civil society participation at peace negotiations can be predicted to disturb the already murky waters of multi-party negotiations."[19] In swimming in these murky waters, the Women's Coalition moved from the margins to the mainstream. In becoming more directly involved in the male-dominated polity, the women delegates were initially regarded as an unwelcome intrusion.[20] Where the polity has thrived on adversarialism and triumphalism, in pursuing a peace agreement women activists may be seen as participating in an elusive quest.[21] However, given the adversarial nature of mainstream politics, there is often not just one peace process going on but instead a whole range of processes in which women play an active part and without their role, lasting change is highly unlikely.[22]

FACILITATING A CONSTRUCTIVE ENVIRONMENT FOR NEGOTIATIONS

Given the overt hostility of some politicians, ensuring women's voices are heard during peace negotiations can be a difficult task. The antagonism and sexism directed at members of the Women's Coalition in Northern Ireland has been documented as an example of this hostility.[23] Targeting abuse at women in leadership positions is a deliberate tactic employed by male politicians across a range of conflict societies.[24] Women who have been singled out for attack report how their denigration was intentionally designed to diminish their credibility in public life.[25] A gender-specific lens has been applied to the objectification and degradation of women during violent conflict.[26] However, much less attention has been paid to the ways in which abusive insults are used strategically to keep women out of public life and to diminish their positions of leadership. This has to be publically challenged if the social/political transformation in post-conflict societies is to be meaningful.

Due to the enmity between the parties, the Women's Coalition paid attention to the process and sought ways to achieve consensus in the tense atmosphere of negotiations. Unlike the majority of parties at the table, the Women's Coalition was a bicommunal party with membership crossing the nationalist/unionist divide, which enabled its members to have a much wider engagement with others at the table. In the Northern Ireland context, most of the delegates were strangers to each other exemplified by a party leader in his refusal to sit next to an individual he considered to be "a warlord." Seating arrangements can be contentious at peace talks especially where parties feel aggrieved at being placed next to those perceived to have caused serious harm. But placing adversaries alphabetically next to each other can also encourage exchanges between previous protagonists. Reverting to non-alphabetic seating arrangements in the aftermath of the peace agreement can be indicative of the larger parties' nostalgia to return to the "status quo."[27]

Since the Coalition's aim was to build an inclusive negotiating process, it opened up back channels to parties affiliated to armed groups. However it was more often censured than accepted as it was perceived to be "talking to terrorists." Despite the opposition, the Coalition continued to nurture contacts with both republican and loyalist ex-combatants. It maintained the dialogue when these groups were excluded from the talks, following breaches of their cease-fires, and entered the prison to engage with those who had become skeptical of the process.[28] These examples should exhort policymakers to recognize that women's perspectives, women's agency, and particularly women's ways of promoting peace do make a difference in conflict resolution, and conflict transformation.[29]

INCLUDING A GENDER PERSPECTIVE ON THE SUBSTANTIVE AGENDA

Negotiating agreement in such conflict zones provides several challenges particularly from a gender perspective: first, creating a process that is inclusive of women; second, ensuring proposals for sustainable peace include women's interests; and third, ensuring the commitments in the agreement on women's issues are implemented. From a gender perspective, the process and the substance of negotiations are interdependent. Achieving substantive commitments on women's rights and ensuring that women's interests are contained in the plans for transformative change requires an inclusive process and vice versa. In the forging of the Belfast Agreement, Beatrix Campbell reflects positively on the role of the Northern Ireland Women's Coalition in this regard.[30]

In relation to substantive proposals, the Coalition ensured the establishment of a civic forum that would act in an advisory capacity to the legislative assembly on economic, social, and cultural issues. The Civic Forum also provided a role for civil society actors to advise on, and measure the performance of, the new democratic institutions. However, the Forum's influence was short-lived as the political parties regarded it as surplus to their new power sharing arrangements and suspended its operation two years after its formation. Other substantive proposals in the peace agreement addressed the needs of victims and had the Women's Coalition not been present at the negotiations, these provisions would have been absent from the final agreement. Providing resources for victims was not a key priority for some of the other parties; their concerns focused mainly on constitutional matters and institutional change. But social justice has to be prioritized if peace agreements are to gain a sense of allegiance among those most affected by the conflict. This was apparent in the subsequent referendum on the peace agreement where it was widely acknowledged that had the Belfast/Good Friday Agreement been silent on the issue of victims, there might not have been such a successful outcome.[31]

The Women's Coalition also ensured that the agreement made provision for "young people affected by the troubles" which included the development of special community-based initiatives based on international best practice.[32] In insisting on such clauses, the Coalition was conscious that post-conflict rebuilding had to include a societal transition. For young men, the role models had been the paramilitaries and the vanguard fighters perceived to be the standard bearers in their local communities but in a post-conflict situation this would have to be radically changed. The term post-conflict may be a misnomer since it assumes an element of restoring people to a position that previously existed. But what most people seek is societal transformation based on respect for human rights standards that may never have previously existed. These are the challenges for men and women alike in adjusting to life after war. Local and international actors need to be able to respond to such challenges otherwise a transition that accords full citizenship, social justice, and empowerment for all will not occur but finding champions to support these can be problematic.

CHAMPIONING GENDER-SPECIFIC CLAUSES

On gender-specific interests, the Women's Coalition proposed a separate clause affirming "the right of women to full and equal political participation."[33]

While this was an important aspiration, it has not been legally enforced in the implementation process nor has the British government exerted any influence in making it obligatory for local parties as part of the process of electoral reform. Where peace agreements phrase the gender-related provisions at a level of generality, this can lead to no further action at the implementation phase. For example, while there may be references in peace agreements to the participation of women in executive, legislative, or judicial bodies, there is rarely reference to quotas or a commitment to 50/50 gender balance in such bodies within a specified time frame. Agreements often fall short on measures that ensure implementation as well as sanctions for noncompliance.

Kate Fearon argues that proposals to address gender-specific concerns in peace agreements require political leadership and effective oversight so leaving the responsibility to the participants was misguided.[34] Despite the UN Security Council Resolutions, creating a political climate that endorses women's equal political participation as an outcome of peace agreements remains a significant challenge.[35] Given this scenario, electoral reforms are needed to increase the proportion of women in politics particularly in post-conflict situations.[36] In the Northern Ireland context, the Women's Coalition was unsuccessful in getting an election based on the "list" system added to the agenda. This proved beneficial in Scotland and Scandinavian countries, leading to a critical mass (over 30 percent) of women in these legislatures.[37] In Northern Ireland the major political parties were reluctant to retain the "list" system and insisted on a return to the status quo. This meant that the pluralism and diversity that had helped to create the agreement were frittered away.[38]

THE ROLE OF OVERSIGHT IN CHAMPIONING COMMITMENTS

The problem remains that in the aftermath of an agreement, most parties prefer to return to the customary "top-down" processes; where local communities—especially women—are typically excluded and women, despite their activity in informal peace processes, remain largely absent from the implementation. Christine Chinkin draws attention to this huge gap between community-based processes and the official negotiation processes of peace settlements, which UN Resolution 1325 has not been able to bridge.[39] For this reason, women challenging the status quo and entering public life require champions to affirm their roles and to ensure that their rights are enforced.[40] Since it is at the implementation stage of peace accords that the foundations for a future society are set, more women need be included in policy making at this level. If this is not achieved, the good practice that exists at the community level will not be developed.[41]

Donald Steinberg acknowledges that his experience in drafting the Angolan peace agreement in the mid-1990s taught him that any agreement, perceived to be gender neural, is inherently discriminatory against women.[42] In Angola, the exclusion of women was notable with 40 men and no women present. Nothing in the commission members' backgrounds as military commanders provided them with special insights into girls' education, mother-child healthcare, or related concerns. From this experience, Steinberg argues that the silencing of women's voices in peace negotiations means that issues such as sexual abuses by government and rebel forces and the rebuilding of social services and girls' education get short shrift. The result is that such agreements are far less likely to succeed since the process is viewed as serving the interests of the warring parties rather than the people.[43] In every situation women have argued that human rights relating to women, including health, education, political rights, and equality should be recognized. However, following peace agreements, the focus is on the removal of arms and the disbandment of armies or paramilitary groups rather than on these issues.

Simultaneously, women in local communities compete for resources against projects for the reintegration of prisoners. In the trade-offs on demilitarization and disarmament, women negotiators have little to bargain with.[44] When issues are prioritized for implementation, it is the militarists who win out while the women's interests get marginalized. The gain in normalizing society by standing down armed groups is important but making provision for health, education, and housing is also crucial. The international monitoring bodies established to deal with no recurrence of violence, have paid scant attention to these needs as articulated by women on the front line.[45]

MAKING PUBLIC THE PRIVATE HARMS

Despite the impact of violent conflict on the lives of women and girls being highlighted by the UN Security Council Resolutions, in places like Northern Ireland there has been less focus on this issue. During the conflict, higher femicide rates have been recorded due to the availability of legally held weapons together with high levels of domestic violence.[46] While the decommissioning of illegal weapons was a contentious issue in the political negotiations, the retention of legally held personal protection weapons did not form part of the security sector reforms post conflict.[47]

Reflecting on the discourse on legal and illegally held weapons in post-conflict situations, Shelley Anderson calls for an examination of the links between this "private" violence and the "public" violence of armed conflict:

> The attitudes and values that give rise to the former lay the groundwork for the latter. Both are rooted in mind sets where domination, control and beliefs in certain group's superiority and others' inferiority are central. A mind set that permits and justifies the use of physical or psychological force by a "superior" against an "inferior" cannot be safely relegated to one corner of life, such as the home, or certain personal relationships. It will become a part of public life.[48]

There is some recognition of the gendered harms suffered by women and girls, including sexual and other violence throughout the conflict and the need to end impunity for these crimes but there is less recognition of the importance of reconfiguring gender relations in the post-conflict society, leaving this as a priority and concern for women. As Marie Smyth notes, what is needed is "demilitarisation at a cultural and ideological level."[49] Although women have, on rare occasions, emerged empowered from the experience of war, it is more usual to find women losing what has been a hard-won autonomy once war ends. Cynthia Cockburn phrases this in stark terms:

> The civil society rebuilt after war or tyranny seldom reflects women's visions or rewards their energies. The space that momentarily opens up for change is not often used to secure genuine and lasting gender transformations. Effort may be put into healing enmity by reshaping ethnic and national relations, but gender and class relations are usually allowed to revert to the status quo ante . . . Instead of the skills and confidence forged by some women by the furnace of war being turned to advantage, the old sexual division of labour is reconstituted, in the family, and in the labour force.[50]

The establishment of an implementation or validation committee, inclusive of political parties and civic society, could have counteracted the nostalgia for the status quo.[51]

Despite the peace agreements' specific proposals, there have still been no special measures and no enforcement mechanisms to ensure that the commitments for women's rights and equality were met. A paradigm shift is essential if gender justice is to be understood as an important feature of democratization in a deeply conservative society. The lessons from Northern Ireland as from elsewhere are that gender-specific proposals should move from being aspirational clauses to become institutional guarantees with benchmarks, timetables and indicators similar to those for security sector reform or prisoner releases.

CONCLUSION

If women are absent from peace negotiations then much-needed "social services justice" (care for victims, education, health, and well-being) will also be absent in post-conflict societies.[52] This would have been the case in Northern Ireland had the Women's Coalition not been present in the peace talks. The clauses on children and young people, education, and community development would have been missing and victims' needs would have been ignored. Promoting a role for participatory democracy through a civic forum and introducing electoral reform should also be seen as a necessary part of the democratization process. Reflecting on the contribution of the Women's Coalition, the international chairperson of the peace talks stated "the emergence of women as a political force was a significant factor in achieving the Agreement."[53]

The Women's Coalition was aware that any silence in the peace agreement about the position of women would perpetuate and institutionalize the marginalization of women in the transitional political process. It would also have allowed those tasked with implementation, including international agencies, to commence their mandates without reference to how their operations impact differentially upon women and men. However, if the post-conflict phase becomes narrowed to security sector reforms then transitional justice measures such as proposals for affirmative action and temporary special measures will get lost. Without strong enforcement mechanisms, women will disappear from the process. Robust language in a peace agreement that promotes gender equality and women's participation needs to be backed by specific responsibility and an allocation of resources to facilitate implementation. Unless entrenchment mechanisms are in place, the progress in advancing women's interests in achieving long-term workable solutions will remain precarious.

The involvement of women in peace processes opens up a space for political transformation but this space needs to be sustained. It requires the support of political leaders. If there is no political will to encourage the wider participation of women, the ownership of an agreement can become fragmented. What gets prioritized or placed in the archives will also determine who and what were important to the process. Women's contribution to peace talks shows what can be delivered but much more needs to be done for women to maintain a central role in rebuilding their societies.

NOTES

1. UN Security Council, *United Nations Security Council Resolution (UNSCR) 1325* [S/RES/1325], October 31, 2000; UN Security Council, *UNSCR 1820* [S/RES/1820], June 19, 2008; UN Security Council, *UNSCR 1888* [S/RES/1888], September 30, 2009; UN Security Council, *UNSCR 1889* [S/RES/1889], October 5, 2009; all available at http://www.un.org/en/peacekeeping/issues/women/wps.shtml.

2. United Nations, *Beijing Declaration and Platform for Action,* adopted at the *Fourth World Conference on Women*, October 27, 1995, available at http://www1.

umn.edu/humanrts/instree/e5dplw.htm#four; International Labour Office, "Outcome of the Special Session of the General Assembly—Women 2000: Gender Equality, Development and Peace for the Twenty-First Century," 2000, available at http://www.ilo.org/public/english/standards/relm/gb/docs/gb279/pdf/esp-4.pdf; *UNSCR 1325*.

3. Fionnuala Ní Aoláin, Dina F. Haynes, and Naomi Cahn, *On the Frontlines: Gender, War and the Post Conflict Process* (Oxford, England: Oxford University Press, 2011).

4. The region itself has been contested since the 1922 division of the island of Ireland, resulting in the southern Republic of Ireland (Ireland) and the north-eastern corner (constituted as Northern Ireland) remaining within the United Kingdom. The predominance of a politics of identity saw a Protestant/Unionist/Loyalist majority reflected in one party rule for 50 years. The Catholic/Nationalist/Republican population, holding aspirations toward a united Ireland, formed a substantial minority that was both marginalized and alienated. Violence erupted in 1968 resulting in the British Army patrolling the streets and the reemergence of militant republicanism and loyalist paramilitaries. The outcome was the consolidation of divided ethnic/political identities and increasing residential segregation.

5. The Women's Coalition succeeded in getting women elected to the Multi-Party Peace Talks, to the Forum for Dialogue and Understanding, to local councils and to the first Northern Ireland Legislative Assembly. In 2006 it stood down the formal structures of the Coalition.

6. Fionnuala Ní Aoláin, "Advancing Feminist Positioning in the Field of Transitional Justice," *International Journal of Transitional Justice* 6.3 (2012). In this article Fionnuala Ní Aoláin comments on how the focus of Transitional Justice has been on the role of women as victims rather than as autonomous agents of change and the need to change this discourse to take more account of the latter.

7. UNIFEM, *UNIFEM Annual Report 2009-2010*, July 13, 2010, p. 3, accessed December 10, 2013, http://.unwomen.org.sg/annual%20reports/Annual%20Report.

8. The Kvinna till Kvinna Foundation, *Make Room for Peace: A Guide to Women's Participation in Peace Processes*, 2011, available at http://www.peacewomen.org/node/90331.

9. Ní Aoláin, "Advancing Feminist Positioning."

10. Catherine O'Rourke, "'Walking the Halls of Power'? Understanding Women's Participation in International Peace and Security," *Melbourne Journal of International Law* 15.1 (2014).

11. Elisabeth Porter, *Peacebuilding: Women in International Perspectives* (New York, NY and London, England: Routledge, 2007), 41.

12. Donald Steinberg, "The Role of Men in Engendered Peacebuilding," *Building Peace* no. 3 (2014), accessed December 10, 2013, http://buildingpeaceforum.com.

13. Ruth Jacobson, "Women 'After' Wars," in *Women & Wars: Contested Histories, Uncertain Futures*, ed. Carol Cohn (Cambridge, England: Polity Press, 2013), 240.

14. Examples are Angola and Central African Republic, among others.

15. John Paul Lederach, *Building Peace: Sustainable Reconciliation in Divided Societies* (Washington, DC: United States Institute of Peace, 1997).

16. UN Secretary General, *A More Secure World: Our Shared Responsibility*, Report of the Secretary General's High-level Panel on Threats, Challenges and Change (New York, NY: United Nations, 2004), 38.

17. Anthony Wanis-St. John and Darren Kew, "Civil Society and Peace Negotiations: Confronting Exclusion," *International Negotiation* 13.1 (2008): 21.

18. UN Secretary General, *A More Secure World.*

19. Wanis-St John and Kew, "Civil Society and Peace Negotiations."

20. Kate Fearon, *Women's Work: The Story of the Northern Ireland Women's Coalition* (Belfast, Northern Ireland: Blackstaff Press, 1999). The book provides a more extensive discussion on why its election poster: "Wave Goodbye to Dinosaurs" caused such mirth as well as some considerable controversy.

21. This term is used by Norman Porter in his book *The Elusive Quest: Reconciliation in Northern Ireland* (Belfast, Northern Ireland: Blackstaff Press, 2003).

22. The Northern Ireland process benefited from having a concentration of feminist and community activists who were established "agents of change" within the community but when the peace talks were declared they moved to become more formal players in the process.

23. Avila Kilmurray and Monica McWilliams, "Struggling for Peace: How Women in Northern Ireland Challenged the Status Quo," *Solutions* 2.2 (2011), accessed June 16, 2014, http://www.thesolutionsjournal.com/node/893.

24. The Kvinna till Kvinna Foundation, *Equal Power—Lasting Peace: Obstacles for Women's Participation in Peace Processes*, 2012, Available at http://www.equalpowerlastingpeace.org/resource/equal-power-lasting-peace-2012/.

25. Labels such as "whore" and "witch" were highlighted by women from Armenia and Azerbaijan, reported by The Kvinna till Kvinna Foundation in *Equal Power Lasting Peace.*

26. Monica McWilliams, "Violence against Women in Societies Under Stress," in *Rethinking Violence against Women*, ed. Rebecca Emerson Dobash and Russell P. Dobash (London, England: Sage, 1998).

27. When the New Assembly was formed after the Peace Talks the alphabetical arrangement was dropped as the larger parties wished to return to the status quo and be seated on opposite sides of the Chamber. This proved to be a regressive step as parties reversed to adversarial behavior with opposing sides facing each other.

28. At a tense stage of the peace talks, the Women's Coalition visited the Maze high security prison at the request of one of the parties. The women who went to the prison agreed to sit down with paramilitary prisoners and to be locked in a mobile hut for the duration of the visit.

29. Swanee Hunt and Kemi Ogunsanya, "Women Waging Peace: Making Women Visible," *Conflict Trends* no. 3 (2003): 46.

30. Beatrix Campbell, *Agreement! The State, Conflict and Change in Northern Ireland* (London, England: Lawrence and Wishart, 2008).

31. During the Referendum following the Belfast/Good Friday Agreement, there was a public outcry on prisoner releases. However, the provisions for victims helped to increase the vote of those in favor—71 percent—of the agreement.

32. British-Irish Council, *The Agreement: Agreement Reached in the Multi-Party Negotiations*, 1998, available at http://cain.ulst.ac.uk/events/peace/docs/agreement.pdf, 18, para. 12.

33. Ibid., 16. The clause on women's political participation was based on the equality provisions of the Guatemalan peace agreement.

34. Kate Fearon, "Gender and Peace in Northern Ireland," in *A Farewell to Arms? From "Long War" to Long Peace in Northern Ireland*, ed. Michael Cox, Adrian Guelke, and Fiona Stephen (Manchester, England: Manchester University Press, 2000), 157.

35. The political participation of women has become an issue not just for post-conflict societies. For example, governments such as those in France and the Republic of Ireland are bringing forward legislative proposals to increase the proportion of women selected.

36. In Northern Ireland the election to the peace talks was based on a list system and the top 10 parties achieving the most votes in the electoral list were invited by the two governments to attend the peace negotiations. Women were more comfortable with this electoral system as they perceived themselves to be standing for the party and not as individuals in a single constituency. The list system was particularly beneficial to women given their safety and security concerns. More women are encouraged to come forward for the party list system, in comparison to standing alone as a party candidate in a constitueny. The benefits of the various systems for women should be taken into account when decisions are made on electoral reform in post-conflict societies.

37. This proposal was not just an alternative to the single constituency system but would have added to it. It was still seen as unacceptable to the Unionist parties in particular and received little support in the negotiations. It is currently under consideration in relation to electoral reform in the Republic of Ireland.

38. The Women's Coalition won two seats to the first assembly but lost these at the next election. Had the list system been retained it is predicted that the life span of the three smaller parties, the NIWC, the PUP and the UDP would have been longer. None of these parties currently hold seats in the Northern Ireland Assembly.

39. Christine Chinkin, "Peace Processes, Post-Conflict Security and Women's Human Rights: the International Context Considered," paper delivered to the 9th Torkel Opsahl Memorial Lecture (Belfast, Northern Ireland, December 2004), 6.

40. What is significant, in terms of female political participation, is the fact that, although numbers elected to the Assembly have increased marginally from 13 percent in 1999 to 17 percent in 2012, this has not been accompanied by greater representation in substantive decision making.

41. Jacklyn Cock, "Closing the Circle: Toward a Gendered Understanding of War and Peace," in *Women and War: Gender Identity and Activism in Times of Conflict*, ed. Joyce P. Kaufman and Kristen P. Williams (Sterling, VA: Kumarian, 2010).

42. Steinberg, "The Role of Men."

43. Chinkin, "Peace Processes." Examples include Sierra Leone, Liberia, the Democratic Republic of Congo, Afghanistan and East Timor.

44. European Union and Irish diaspora funds totaling 1.6 million have been allocated for the reintegration of ex-combatants.

45. In Ní Aoláin, Haynes, and Cahn, *On the Frontlines*, this theme is further expanded.

46. Joan McKiernan and Monica McWilliams, "The Impact of Political Conflict on Women's Lives," in *Gender Relations in Public and Private: New Research Perspectives*, ed. Lydia Morris and E. Stina Lyon (London, England: Palgrave Macmillan, 1996). Femicide is where men use these guns to kill their spouses or female partners in intimate relationships. Figures for incidents of domestic violence have risen steadily, from 6,727 in 1996 to over 17,000 by 2011.

47. There are 134,000 legally held small arms with one person in 17.6 holding a shotgun certificate.

48. Shelley Anderson quoted in Marie Smyth, "The Process of Demilitarization and the Reversibility of the Peace Process in Northern Ireland," *Terrorism and Political Violence* 16.3 (2004): 548.

49. Ibid.

50. Cynthia Cockburn, "The Gendered Dynamics of Armed Conflict and Political Violence," in *Victims, Perpetrators or Actors? Gender, Armed Conflict and Political Violence*, ed. Caroline Moser and Fiona Clark (London, England: Zed Books, 2001).

51. In December 2003, when briefing the Council of Europe on the role of women in the Northern Ireland peace process, the Department of Foreign Affairs declared that the benefits of involving women in conflict resolution to be "clearly evident in Northern Ireland, where women played and continue to play a pivotal role in building peace and are essential contributors to the on-going process." Despite this recognition the British and Irish governments have made no attempt to ensure the inclusion of more women in the implementation process.

52. Naomi Cahn, Dina Haynes, and Fionnuala Ní Aoláin, "Returning Home: Women in Post-Conflict Societies," *University of Baltimore Law Review* 39.3 (2010): 369.

53. George Mitchell, *Making Peace* (New York, NY: Knopf, 1999), 44.

BIBLIOGRAPHY

British-Irish Council, *The Agreement: Agreement Reached in the Multi-Party Negotiations*, 1998, available at http://cain.ulst.ac.uk/events/peace/docs/agreement.pdf.

Cahn, Naomi, Dina Haynes, and Fionnuala Ní Aoláin. "Returning Home: Women in Post-Conflict Societies." *University of Baltimore Law Review* 39.3 (2010): 339–69.

Campbell, Beatrix. *Agreement! The State, Conflict and Change in Northern Ireland*. London, England: Lawrence and Wishart, 2008.

Chinkin, Christine. "Peace Processes, Post-Conflict Security and Women's Human Rights: The International Context Considered." Paper delivered to the 9th Torkel Opsahl Memorial Lecture. Belfast, Northern Ireland, December 2004.

Cock, Jacklyn. "Closing the Circle: Toward a Gendered Understanding of War and Peace." In *Women and War: Gender Identity and Activism in Times of Conflict*, edited by Joyce P. Kaufman and Kristen P. Williams. Sterling, VA: Kumarian, 2010.

Cockburn, Cynthia. "The Gendered Dynamics of Armed Conflict and Political Violence." In *Victims, Perpetrators or Actors? Gender, Armed Conflict and Political Violence*, edited by Caroline Moser and Fiona Clark, 13–29. London, England: Zed Books, 2001.

Fearon, Kate. "Gender and Peace in Northern Ireland." In *A Farewell to Arms? From "Long War" to Long Peace in Northern Ireland*, edited by Michael Cox, Adrian Guelke, and Fiona Stephen, 153–64. Manchester, England: Manchester University Press, 2000.

———. *Women's Work: The Story of the Northern Ireland Women's Coalition*. Belfast, Northern Ireland: Blackstaff Press, 1999.

Hunt, Swanee and Kemi Ogunsanya. "Women Waging Peace: Making Women Visible." *Conflict Trends* no. 3 (2003): 44–46.

International Labour Office. "Outcome of the Special Session of the General Assembly—Women 2000: Gender Equality, Development and Peace for the Twenty-First Century," June 5–9, 2000, available at http://www.ilo.org/public/english/standards/relm/gb/docs/gb279/pdf/esp-4.pdf.

Jacobson, Ruth. "Women 'After' Wars." In *Women & Wars: Contested Histories, Uncertain Futures*, edited by Carol Cohn, 215–42. Cambridge, England: Polity Press, 2013.

Kilmurray, Avila and Monica McWilliams. "Struggling for Peace: How Women in Northern Ireland Challenged the Status Quo." *Solutions* 2.2 (2011). Accessed June 16, 2014. http://www.thesolutionsjournal.com/node/893.

Lederach, John Paul. *Building Peace: Sustainable Reconciliation in Divided Societies*. Washington, DC: United States Institute of Peace, 1997.

McKiernan, Joan and Monica McWilliams. "The Impact of Political Conflict on Women's Lives." In *Gender Relations in Public and Private: New Research Perspectives*, edited by Lydia Morris and E. Stina Lyon, 56–75. London, England: Palgrave Macmillan, 1996.

McWilliams, Monica. "Violence against Women in Societies under Stress." In *Rethinking Violence against Women*, edited by Rebecca Emerson Dobash and Russell P. Dobash, 111–40. London, England: Sage, 1998.

Mitchell, George. *Making Peace*. New York, NY: Knopf, 1999.

Ní Aoláin, Fionnuala, Dina F. Haynes, and Naomi Cahn. *On the Frontlines: Gender, War and the Post Conflict Process*. Oxford, England: Oxford University Press, 2011.

Ní Aoláin, Fionnuala. "Advancing Feminist Positioning in the Field of Transitional Justice." *International Journal of Transitional Justice* 6.3 (2012): 1–24.

O'Rourke, Catherine. "'Walking the Halls of Power?' Understanding Women's Participation in International Peace and Security." *Melbourne Journal of International Law* 15.1 (2014): 128–54.

Porter, Elisabeth. *Peacebuilding: Women in International Perspectives*. New York, NY and London, England: Routledge, 2007.

Porter, Norman. *The Elusive Quest: Reconciliation in Northern Ireland*. Belfast, Northern Ireland: Blackstaff Press, 2003.

Smyth, Marie. "The Process of Demilitarization and the Reversibility of the Peace Process in Northern Ireland." *Terrorism and Political Violence* 16.3 (2004): 544–66.

Steinberg, Donald. "The Role of Men in Engendered Peacebuilding." *Building Peace* no. 3 (2014): 30–32. Accessed December 10, 2013. http://buildingpeaceforum.com.

The Kvinna till Kvinna Foundation. *Equal Power—Lasting Peace: Obstacles for Women's Participation in Peace Processes*, 2012. Available at http://www.equalpowerlastingpeace.org/resource/equal-power-lasting-peace-2012/.

———. *Make Room for Peace: A Guide to Women's Participation in Peace Processes*, 2011. Available at http://www.peacewomen.org/node/90331.

UN Development Fund for Women (UNIFEM). *UNIFEM Annual Report 2009-2010*. July 13, 2010. Accessed December 10, 2013. http://.unwomen.org.sg/annual%20reports/Annual%20Report.

United Nations. *Beijing Declaration and Platform for Action,* adopted at the *Fourth World Conference on Women*. October 27, 1995, available at http://www1.umn.edu/humanrts/instree/e5dplw.htm#four.

UN Security Council. *United Nations Security Council Resolution (UNSCR) 1325* [S/RES/1325], October 31, 2000, http://www.un.org/en/peacekeeping/issues/women/wps.shtml.

———. *UNSCR 1820* [S/RES/1820], June 19, 2008, http://www.un.org/en/peacekeeping/issues/women/wps.shtml.

———. *UNSCR 1888* [S/RES/1888], September 30, 2009, http://www.un.org/en/peacekeeping/issues/women/wps.shtml.

———. *UNSCR 1889* [S/RES/1889], October 5, 2009, http://www.un.org/en/peacekeeping/issues/women/wps.shtml.

UN Secretary General. *A More Secure World: Our Shared Responsibility*. Report of the Secretary General's High-level Panel on Threats, Challenges and Change. New York, NY: United Nations, 2004.

Wanis-St. John, Anthony and Darren Kew. "Civil Society and Peace Negotiations: Confronting Exclusion." *International Negotiation* 13.1 (2008): 11–36.

Chapter 15

(Re)Examining Women's Role in Peacebuilding

Assessing the Impact of the International Fund for Ireland (IFI) and the European Union (EU) PEACE III Funding on Women's Role in Community Development, Peacebuilding, and Reconciliation in Northern Ireland and the Border Counties

Patlee Creary and Sean Byrne

Internationally funded peace and reconciliation initiatives have received their fair share of criticism and praise for the kind of peace that they engender as part of the liberal democratic peacebuilding model. On the positive side, internationally funded peacebuilding signals the necessary intervention of a third party that commands enough resources and support to facilitate and underwrite the process of rebuilding cooperation and trust.[1] On the other hand, the process of facilitating internationally funded peacebuilding work has been subject to criticism about the kind of peace being created and the structural impact on local societies who are expected to train-up and adopt an imposed expectation for post-conflict recovery.[2] The nature of liberal peacebuilding is changing—there are indications that the process is moving from a once highly externally driven, statist orientation toward a more emancipatory approach concerned with welfare, empathy, and free engagement with local groups.[3] However, one aspect of the liberal peacebuilding dynamic that remains relatively underdeveloped and underexplored is the role that grassroots women play in grounding the emerging emancipatory claims of liberal peacebuilding.

In this chapter, we provide some rationalizations for a reexamination of women's role in peacebuilding by highlighting the perceptions and experiences of some women peacebuilders who participated in Northern Ireland's post-accord peacebuilding process at the grassroots levels. These women were interviewed as part of a larger study on the impact of the IFI and the EU PEACE III funding, which was undertaken by the second author during the summer of 2010. The women either administered or benefited from IFI and/or PEACE III funding as part of a grassroots or bottom-up civil society approach to achieving Northern Ireland's post-conflict transformation. Their perspectives suggest that conflict transformation is in reality a process of structural transformation that addresses not only the locally lived intrastate conflict scenario. It is also a process of societal and personal transformation that reflects the gradual imbuing of feminist values into liberal peacebuilding models. The extent of the achievement of these feminist values that associate peacebuilding with personal and social transformation in a post-peace accord scenario are nevertheless very heavily dependent on the level of confidence that can be created by all the peace-interested parties to the post-peace accord recovery process.

To be sure, the liberal peacebuilding funding structure imposes some limitations on the lay actor's ability to claim human agency.[4] It also elevates the risks to women by imposing direct and hidden political and structural arrangements that contribute to the further marginalization of women and women's voices in peace processes.[5] In this chapter, we take the position that if we look at the issue of liberal peacebuilding from women's perspectives on the value and role of international peacebuilding funding, we see that feminist values are being mainstreamed by IFI and PEACE III funding strategies. The funding frameworks' contemporary focus on conflict transformation places relationships and the development of civil society values at the forefront of the post-accord peacebuilding process.[6] In doing so, they have heralded the inclusion of gendered understandings and feminist values in the state-building process. There are some that may argue that the incorporation of feminist values is token, since the narrative of masculinity and femininity has not changed.[7] This analysis reveals that cultivating human agency by developing the capacity and confidence among participants to engage in the process of social engineering to promote peace could be a useful starting point for everyday women to begin to challenge established gendered narratives about conflict and peace.

METHODOLOGY

This chapter examines the responses of 36 women peacebuilders who shared their perspectives on peace and reconciliation funding in interviews with the second author during the summer of 2010. The women are leaders of various community groups, funding administrators, and funding agency community development officers in Derry and the Border Counties who administered or received funding from the IFI and/or PEACE III. The second author conducted in-depth, semi-structured interviews with each participant who was asked questions about her views on the peace process and community work, her experiences with IFI and EU funding structures, the progress of peace and reconciliation strategies, and about her hopes and fears for the future of Northern Ireland.

For this study, the women's responses were subject to detailed inductive analysis that resulted in themes emerging from the data related to grassroots and civil society empowerment, the role of women, and funding impact on community and relationship building. The data is presented by *restorying* aspects of the narrative data to establish sequences and causal links among ideas.[8] Fictitious names are used to protect the identity of the respondents. Where necessary, statements that identify projects have been deleted from the featured responses.

WOMEN'S PERCEPTIONS ABOUT INTERNATIONALLY FUNDED CIVIL SOCIETY PEACEBUILDING IN NORTHERN IRELAND

Ireland's traditional androcentric view of political power ignores the role of women in civil society.[9] Civil society represents a critical mass of energy and will to promote, engage, or undermine a peace process. It can act effectively as a means of transmitting and entrenching prevailing norms, and it functions as a means of disaggregating and challenging existing behavior and practices by pushing new issues onto public agendas.[10] Liberal peacebuilding in Northern Ireland was focused to a great extent on the cultivation of civil society, particularly through grassroots involvement as a means of achieving conflict transformation.[11] However, women's everyday peacebuilding roles in the Northern Ireland process were ignored or downplayed in favor of highlighting their efforts to affect the wider post-accord negotiation and power-sharing processes.[12] In doing so, women's peacebuilding value was reduced to understandings of their direct political and negotiated impact on the post-conflict landscape. By attempting to empower grassroots citizen groups a broad network of peacebuilding organizations are empowered to influence the political process through other methods than post-conflict negotiations.[13] The result is a multitrack approach to building peace that attempts to be elicitive of the needs of the local population, while using a systems approach that draws in and engages actors from different levels of the peacebuilding spectrum.[14] The liberal approach to peacebuilding remains viable only to the extent that it facilitates such a hybrid approach to peace that values the participation of local actors, yet uses grassroots, middle level, and upper level actors in a form of negotiated hybridity.[15]

Unfortunately, the arguments for civil society engagement, bottom-up approaches, and negotiated hybridity for peacebuilding do not attend to the role that a gendered analysis plays in understanding the real value of civil society as a counterweight to state institutions and as a bulwark for peace work. There are several studies that highlight the role that women have played in Northern Ireland's peace process. Kate Fearon,[16] Avila Kilmurray and Monica McWilliams,[17] and Margaret Ward,[18] for example, speak to the progress that women have made in achieving a place at the post-accord negotiating table and their organized activism prior to and after the Belfast/ Good Friday Agreement (GFA). Tahnya Donaghy[19] and Linda Connolly[20] address some of the lesser-attended-to issues that affect women's activism on the whole during the period of the Troubles, noting that the Northern Ireland Women's Coalition (NIWC) is only a small part of the contributions that Northern Irish women have made to catalyzing and grounding the peace process.

Yet there is room to expand our understanding about how the experiences of Northern Ireland's grassroots women contribute to peacebuilding claims, particularly in light of some views held by women in our study that alternative approaches to the state-centric model were perceived by some in the political process as threatening. Lilith, a project director with the IFI, explains it this way:

> One of the disappointments with the GFA was the ambition to create a civic forum in Northern Ireland, which never happened because there were very strong political voices who saw it as a threat and who would be deeply concerned about an act of civic society. This is going back to the gatekeepers in power and leadership.

There was also a view that there is a significant grassroots contribution to building durable peace that cannot be achieved through organized, state-centered political processes, even if they are led by women. Ruth, a project director with the EU, explains the situation this way:

> The NIWC was a big part of the peace settlement, and some of the women would have been involved in some kind of grassroots women's groups. The NIWC did some very good work; but they were very much about the agreement and Stormont negotiations and stuff, which was very different from the work being done by the community based women's sector. Over the years there's been lots of tension and debate about the prevailing feminist ethos; but especially here in the North, most of the community development has happened because of the community-based women's sector.

Northern Ireland's traditional androcentric view of political power ignores the role of women in civil society.[21]

Valuing Women's Voices and Experiences to Build Peace

Ho-Won Jeong[22] argues that because women experience conflict and violence in different ways than men, they are in a position to appreciate the value of peace better through their vulnerability to the structure of violence and deprivation. The goals of peace, he posits, are enhanced and intertwined with the feminist agenda through a commitment to the "removal of privileged systems for the few and the rejection of coercive power in human interaction."[23] For Elise Boulding,[24] although women are disproportionately impacted by structural inequalities, they can orient themselves to a social or humanist feminist agenda that is focused on the development of a civil society movement. Women's participation in civil society is the transformation of their political claims for empowerment in a system that has ignored their inner voices.[25] Their engagement in peace work is symbolic of the informal roles that they may choose to play in peacebuilding because their connectedness to the conflict creates relationships of trust.[26]

Often the conflict at hand is not the direct violence that the GFA attempts to address. Elisabeth explains it this way:

> We did some cross-Border research on women and their mental health issues. The Troubles were not necessarily the first issues women identified. What emerged was a lack of proper education, no access to maternity education, unaffordable holiday childcare, juggling work life balance, a general lack of support, abusive relationships . . . For marginalized communities like minorities, single parents, women living in areas of disadvantage, older women, these are the issues that are paramount. This is what peacebuilding should be about . . . Sometimes the electoral process is not necessarily enough.

As Elizabeth suggests, policymakers need to create necessary policy measures to meet women's real basic needs.

With these issues in mind, many of the women in this study expressed concerns about the future of programs that attended to the issues that affect women, which were not directly related to the post-accord peace process. Lois, for example, a community group leader, worried that "the end of all that funding is really going to adversely impact women in Northern Ireland and Southern Ireland through job loss, loss of programs, and health problems. Because of that, women are going to take steps backwards from public life." Women's voices and their participation in political mobilization, consciousness-raising, and popular education is a strong supporter of democratization and other qualitative, nonmaterial aspects of development goals that cannot be achieved through top down strategies.[27]

At the same time it would be disingenuous to assume that women's roles in conflict have been wholly peaceable. Ruth Jacobson,[28] for example, challenges the idea of women naturally assuming the peacemaking role in the Northern Ireland conflict. She points out that while it may be assumed that women had a proportionately higher stake in securing an eventual political settlement to end armed conflict during the Troubles, the ways in which women constructed their identities have not always been conducive to peace. She highlights that while only few women have exercised their agency to actually inflict violence, considerably larger numbers have invoked their role as mothers seeing "our children's future" as a reason to act in support of activities that have a "virtual certainty of provoking violence," such as Orange Order or Sinn Fein marches through contested areas.[29] There are also emerging media reports that detail the willing and active involvement of women like Dolours and Marian Price in the Provisional Irish Republican Army bombings during the period of the Troubles.[30] In socially conservative Northern Ireland, Republican and Loyalist women served mainly in support roles and rarely as combatants in active service units. Some of the respondents in our study presented some challenging views on this dual identity that women take on in their communities; yet their common sentiment was that one could be a cultural participant and supporter of one's immediate community and still peacefully coexist with others.

The value of their community-level activism was to reach out to out-groups and to teach people within their own in-groups that they could build relationships together. A significant tool for accomplishing this was through the sharing of their experiences of the Troubles. Veronica, a community group leader explains the phenomenon of women's divergent roles and stories of Northern Ireland conflict experiences as follows:

> The stories of women from the Troubles are stories of women as ex-combatants and women involved in community development in their areas. These voices are very important. One side of the story is that it is men who do the fighting and it's the women who do the tidying up and trying to put family, community, and neighborhoods back together and pick up the pieces. Our project facilitates women sharing all of their experiences. It is opening up a process of thinking more healthily about life and about this place and the people and their histories. So it's about seeing through the other's eyes, the others perspective; it's about giving different perspectives.

Consequently, women took on multiple roles as mother, soldier, worker and more, and had different perspectives about the conflict.

Veronica's point is a relevant reminder of the value of including women's lived experiences, memories, and stories, which help to create intercultural and cross-community bonds through shared identities along multiple lines, such as gender, parenthood, or shared values into peacebuilding and reconciliation processes.[31] The effortlessness of such storied interactions can be taken for granted as Allyssa McCabe and Lynn Bliss note that informal interactions generate spontaneous stories, which in turn generate more spontaneous stories.[32] When people tell stories of their personal experiences, they generate an understanding that permeates perceived differences such as culture, gender, class, ethnicity, or religion, to the extent that the teller and listener can identify with each other, define a common social identity, create shared knowledge, help to negotiate power relations, and educate new community members transculturally.[33] Sharing personal stories helps to acknowledge change, loss, and trauma; to rehumanize those that have been dehumanized by change, conflict, and loss; and to help people reconstruct their sense of identity.[34] Sharing stories and memories are a profound way in which individuals can "master" their environment.[35]

However, the confidence to take these steps is an issue for many community peacebuilders in our study, as Frances, a community group leader explains:

> Finding our voice and gaining a bit of confidence is the challenge because as Protestants, we had no confidence at all in engaging with wider society.

Where the confidence is achieved, the impact is phenomenal. Abigail related this story about the impact of sharing women and men's experiences of the conflict:

> I remember sharing what it was like being a policeman's wife, and I talked about my husband and how he lost his arm and how I never opened the door without constantly being in a state of uneasiness and almost trauma wondering when they would come to the door and shoot my husband. Or not allowing my children to open the door.
>
> And when I told this story, somebody who would have cheered in his own community for taking down a policeman or army person, said it never even occurred to them that there might be families around the police. He said: "I saw them as legitimate targets, never even thought about a wife or children or the mothers or fathers" . . . We've brought in ex-British soldiers who would sit in the room and say to somebody who might have been hurt in Bloody Sunday or somewhere else, who would say: "I joined the army because there was no employment, no hope, nothing. I left secondary school without qualifications, I was thrown into the army, and I didn't know what I was coming into. I had no idea"—.

> So the heart of our project is rehumanizing. People are suffering. They need to feel a sense of justice that they might not get from the courts. They need for their loss to be understood.

Sharing their stories brings the point home that Protestant and Catholic women have real feelings, and hopes and dreams for the future.

Lilith offers one explanation of why there is more ease and impact with having these participative projects at a smaller, local, community-based level. She had this to say about one project:

> Women tend to sometimes talk about very painful and very personal things, and when you are doing our activity, your head is down and you can make a comment and keep your head down and you can throw that comment out and then it's entirely up to the other people in that group whether they want to pick it up. So it's not confrontational. The vast majority of times the things that are discussed or thrown into the conversation are being dealt with by the group, so in a way part of that relationship-building and moving forward has been completely uncontrolled.

The women share painful experiences in their stories that build their resiliency and their relationships with each other.

(RE)EXAMINING GENDERED UNDERSTANDINGS AND FEMINIST VALUES IN CIVIL SOCIETY PEACEBUILDING

Essentially, as explained by Dennis Sandole, if conflict transformation is to encompass the full array of processes, approaches, and stages needed to move a complex conflict toward more sustainable, peaceful relationships, "civil society inclusion in the intervention ensures that some degree of attention will be paid to the fractured relationships as well as the underlying causes and conditions of why relationships regress into self-stimulating/self-perpetuating violent conflicts."[36] This idea is not lost on any of our respondents who expressed consensus that IFI and PEACE III funding helped to jumpstart processes of interaction and community-building that significantly changed their relationship with others. Civil society, "that arena of uncoerced collective action around shared interests, purposes and values, which embraces a diversity of spaces, actors and institutional forms, has varying degrees of formality, autonomy and power and is distinct from other institutional forms like the family, state, and market," is part and parcel of the liberal peacebuilding governmentality because it serves the purpose of implementing aspects of the liberal peacebuilding agenda.[37] Economic assistance to shore up or create civil society functions as a means of curating organic peacebuilding assets by treating people as local sociocultural resources that are matched with externally provided socioeconomic resources.[38] The civil society focus is therefore necessarily centered on how grassroots, everyday citizens are able to influence peacebuilding processes. The women is this study share the perspective that international economic assistance has provided them with the resources needed to build their capacity and confidence to take on peacebuilding roles within their social spheres.

The takeaway is that both women and men who experience higher levels of vulnerability to structural violence are in a position to better understand the limitations of a state-building focus and to support the creation of civil society as a means of conflict resolution and transformation that seeks solutions beyond the masculinized presentation of the state-centric political system that excludes people's needs and voices. Ingrid Sandole-Staroste uses the concept of gender mainstreaming in conflict resolution to make this point, arguing that "gender mainstreaming" makes visible the conditions that create the conflict and for building cooperative relationships.[39] Gender mainstreaming brings to the fore the generally taken-for-granted power and policy arrangements that exclude the nonelite, marginalized, and disempowered members of a society from the conflict resolution process. Its incorporation into peacebuilding naturally brings focus to those elements of society that would contribute alternative voices and paths to peace that can provide durable and lasting solutions.

The reality is, however, that in general peacebuilding praxis and discourse, gendered understandings, and acknowledgment of gender consciousness are still taboo to the extent that few scholars and practitioners have gone to the appropriate lengths to credit or understand the role and value of gender mainstreaming to peacebuilding.[40] In reality, gendered understandings that lend to the mixing of feminist values with the goals of peace at the state level through organized political participation have become subject to Gramsci's notion of *transformiso*—it is co-opted by elites and used to retain control and reify a hierarchical arrangement focused on state-building.[41] Women and official women's movements are often co-opted into existing male, elite-driven peace processes with little positive outcome for the mainstreaming of women's voices and issues.[42] Locally driven, community-based participation becomes a lesser valued component reflected in structurally hierarchical terms like "grassroots" and "bottom-up." This can be seen as a positive or negative outcome, depending on one's position pertaining to the value of the state and one's notions of peace and security.

Feminist theory offers no coherent, unitary position on this dilemma. On the one hand liberal feminists would commend the incorporation of civil society into peacebuilding processes as an emancipatory move for women as well as for other marginalized groups, such as LGBTTQ citizens or ethnic minorities. Civil society movements are therefore critical because they create social capital and act as a space for conducting values of civility and are therefore highly complementary to the state.[43] As such, women have an important role to play in civil society and getting more of them actively involved in it would have the effect of increasing women's participation in political processes, policy dialogue, advocacy, and protests that help to make governments and state structures more responsive to the needs of all citizens.[44] The NIWC stands out as an example of organic civil society growth and how the cultivation of conservative feminist values can impact peace processes. However, concentration on women's roles in peacebuilding as chiefly dependent on them gaining a seat at the negotiating table reduces the value that women bring to peace processes in the daily interactions at the grassroots level. On the other hand, a more radical feminist approach would be concerned with the nature of the system in which women find themselves operating, and their role in reifying and perpetuating a hierarchical state system that is itself the producer of conflict and insecurity. The issue then is not the inclusive, voluntary, and community-building counterweight to institutions that civil society provides.[45] Rather, it is the global patriarchic metanarrative that women's involvement is used to strengthen. Cynthia Enloe, for example, argues that getting more women involved in democratization is not the same as inviting women to reinterpret politics by drawing on their own experiences as women.[46] Women's inability to define the problem or conflict "looks to many locally engaged women like abstract do-gooding with minimal connection to the battles for a decent life in their households and their communities."[47] As a result, broad issues of equality and human rights can never be fully incorporated and women's issues can never be fully mainstreamed.[48]

The concept of human agency presumes that individuals possess enough knowledge to make structural rules and schemas work to his or her benefit.[49] The cultivation of agency for women in Northern Ireland may be embodied in the feelings of empowerment and their potential for transformative change that is derived from participation in grassroots, post-accord civil society movements. The findings of this study do not reflect that these local women see themselves as engaging in "abstract do-gooding." Instead they see themselves as gaining the capacity and confidence to raise their voices and work within their families and communities to build peace through new relationships. In doing so, they are realizing the feminist values that undercut an emancipatory peacebuilding process, even though they did not sit at the negotiating table or direct the peace process.

CONCLUSION

The women in this study articulate a common perception that IFI and EU funding has gone a long way in giving them the confidence to engage in a critical understanding of their role as citizens, neighbors, and peacebuilders. The IFI and PEACE III funding have helped to create new prospects for these Northern Irish women by moving them from being reactive to political processes and acted upon by conflictants. They are coming to see themselves, even within the structural limitations of the funding framework, as proactive and sufficiently empowered to make a difference within their own spheres of influence. As a result, participation in internationally funded post-accord peacebuilding has created conditions for knowledge, learning, and empowerment toward fostering their claims of agency in Northern Ireland's peace process. Our participants' perspectives on their role in community development, peacebuilding and reconciliation paint a picture of promise for the changing role of women in Northern Ireland's peacebuilding process. Unlike the highly respected NIWC and other aspects of the civil rights movement that initiated some high profile changes but withered away over time, women are now able to present themselves as change agents within their own sphere of influence. In doing so, they signal a commitment to the values of a civil society and they have entrenched themselves as part of a sustainable local peace structure that is more likely to remain when international funding ends.

The question of women's role in Northern Ireland's post-peace accord is ripe for further research and discussion that will go further in rethinking women's role in post-accord peacebuilding and the reassessment of gendered understandings of peace, the state, and civil society. The stories, experiences, and memories of women's vulnerability to direct and indirect violence during and after the Troubles have guided a willingness to be part of a civil society process that stands in valid contrast to the state-centric system; yet at the same time it remains in support of the humanist aims of the post-peace accord process. These grassroots women may not be operating from positions of public office, achieving popular votes, or challenging the system from within, as the NIWC did during its heyday in the 1990s. They are instead imbuing feminist values into the peace process through everyday activities that highlight and mainstream the inner voices of society.

ACKNOWLEDGMENTS

The authors thank Brian Creary, Tom Boudreau, and Jessica Senehi for commenting on various drafts of this chapter. The research for this chapter was supported by a three-year research grant from the Social Sciences and Humanities Research Council of Canada.

NOTES

1. John Paul Lederach, *Building Peace: Sustainable Reconciliation in Divided Societies* (Washington, DC: United States Institute of Peace, 1997).

2. Roger Mac Ginty, *No War, No Peace: The Rejuvenation of Stalled Peace Processes and Peace Accords* (New York, NY: Palgrave Macmillan, 2008).

3. Oliver P. Richmond, "Becoming Liberal, Unbecoming Liberalism: Liberal-Local Hybridity Via the Everyday as a Response to the Paradoxes of Liberal Peacebuilding," *Journal of Intervention and Statebuilding* 3.3 (2009); Chuck Thiessen, "Emancipatory Peacebuilding: Critical Responses to (Neo)Liberal Trends," in *Critical Issues in Peace and Conflict Studies: Theory, Practice, and Pedagogy*, ed. Thomas Matyók, Jessica Senehi, and Sean Byrne (Lanham, MD: Lexington, 2011).

4. Patlee Creary and Sean Byrne, "Peace with Strings Attached: Exploring Reflections of Structure and Agency in Northern Ireland Peacebuilding Funding," *Journal of Peacebuilding* 2.1 (2014).

5. Mac Ginty, *No War, No Peace*; Susan Evangelista, "Inner Voices and Outer Positions: Women in Peacemaking," *Social Alternatives* 16.2 (1997); Margaret Ward, "Finding a Place: Women and the Irish Peace Process," *Race and Class* 37.1 (1997).

6. Sandra Buchanan, "Transforming Conflict in Northern Ireland and the Border Counties: Some Lessons from the Peace Programmes on Valuing Participatory Democracy," *Irish Political Studies* 23.3 (2008); Sean Byrne, Cynthia Irvin, and Eyob Fissuh, "The Perceptions of Economic Assistance in Northern Ireland and its Role in the Peace Process," in *Handbook of Conflict Analysis and Resolution*, ed. Dennis J. D. Sandole et al. (New York, NY: Routledge, 2011).

7. For example, Cynthia Enloe, *Bananas, Beaches and Bases: Making Feminist Sense of International Politics* (Berkeley, CA: University of California Press, 2000).

8. John W. Creswell, *Qualitative Inquiry & Research Design: Choosing Among Five Approaches*, 2nd ed. (London, England: Sage, 2007).

9. Evangelista, "Inner Voices."

10. Robert W. Cox, "Gramsci, Hegemony, and International Relations," in *International Relations Theory*, 4th ed., ed. Paul R. Viotti and Mark V. Kauppi (New York, NY: Longman, 2010).

11. Buchanan, "Transforming Conflict."

12. For example, Avila Kilmurray and Monica McWilliams, "Struggling for Peace: How Women in Northern Ireland Challenged the Status Quo," *Solutions* 2.2 (2011), accessed May 13, 2014, www.thesolutionsjournal.com/node/893.

13. Bruce Hemmer et al., "Putting the 'Up' in Bottom-Up Peacebuilding: Broadening the Concept of International Negotiations, *International Negotiation* 11.1 (2006).

14. John Paul Lederach, *Preparing for Peace: Conflict Transformation across Cultures* (New York, NY: Syracuse University Press, 1995); Louise Diamond and John McDonald, *Multi-Track Diplomacy: A Systems Approach to Peace*, 3rd ed. (West Hartford, CT: Kumarian, 1996); Tristan Anne Borer, John Darby, and Siobhan McEvoy-Levy, *Peacebuilding after Peace Accords: The Challenges of Violence, Truth and Youth* (Notre Dame, IN: University of Notre Dame Press, 2006).

15. Timothy Donais, "Empowerment or Imposition? Dilemmas of Local Ownership in Post-Conflict Peacebuilding Processes," *Peace and Change* 34.1 (2009); Richmond, "Becoming Liberal"; and Michael Pugh, "The Political Economy of Peacebuilding: A Critical Theory Perspective," *International Journal of Peace Studies* 10.2 (2005).

16. Kate Fearon, "Northern Ireland's Women's Coalition: Institutionalizing a Political Voice and Ensuring Representation," *Conciliation Resources* no. 13 (2002), accessed May 10, 2014, http://www.c-r.org/accord-article/northern-ireland%E2%80%99s-women%E2%80%99s-coalition-institutionalising-political-voice-and-ensuring.

17. Kilmurray and McWilliams, "Struggling for Peace."

18. Ward, "Finding a Place."

19. Tahnya Barnett Donaghy, "Women's Contribution to the Northern Ireland Peace Agreement," *Canadian Women's Studies* 22.2 (2003).

20. Linda Connolly, "Feminist Politics and the Peace Process," *Capital and Class* 23.3 (1999).

21. Evangelista, "Inner Voices."

22. Ho-Won Jeong, *Peace and Conflict Studies: An Introduction* (Burlington, MA: Ashgate, 2000), 83.

23. Ibid.

24. Elise Boulding, *Cultures of Peace: The Hidden Side of History* (Syracuse, NY: Syracuse University Press, 2000), 108.

25. Ibid.; Evangelista, "Inner Voices."

26. Johannes M. Botes, "Informal Roles," in *Conflict: From Analysis to Intervention*, ed. Sandra Cheldelin, Daniel Druckman, and Larissa Fast (New York, NY: Lexington, 2003).

27. Boulding, *Cultures of Peace.*

28. Ruth Jacobson, "Women and Peace in Northern Ireland: A Complicated Relationship," in *States of Conflict: Gender, Violence and Resistance*, ed. Susie Jacobs, Ruth Jacobson, and Jennifer Marchbank (New York, NY: Zed Books, 2000).

29. Ibid., 181.

30. Patrick Sawer and Bob Graham, "'Republicanism is Part of Our DNA,' Says IRA Bomber Dolours Price," *Telegraph*, September 23, 2012, accessed May 13, 2014, http://www.telegraph.co.uk/news/uknews/northernireland/9560100/Republicanism-is-part-of-our-DNA-says-IRA-bomber-Dolours-Price.html.

31. Jessica Senehi, "Storytelling and Peace," in *The Oxford International Encyclopedia of Peace*, ed. Nigel Young (Oxford, England: Oxford University Press, 2010).

32. Allyssa McCabe and Lynn S. Bliss, *Patterns in Narrative Discourse: A Multicultural, Life Span Approach* (Boston, MA: Allyn & Bacon, 2003).

33. Jessica Senehi, "Constructive Storytelling in Intercommunal Conflicts: Building Community, Building Peace," in *Reconcilable Differences: Turning Points in Ethnopolitical Conflicts*, ed. Sean Byrne and Cynthia L. Irvin (West Hartford, CT: Kumarian, 2000); Jessica Senehi, "The Role of Constructive, Transcultural Storytelling in Ethnopolitical Conflict Transformation in Northern Ireland," in *Regional and Ethnic Conflicts: Perspectives from the Front Lines*, ed. Judy Carter, George E. Irani, and Vamik D. Volkan (Upper Saddle River, NJ: Pearson Prentice Hall, 2008).

34. Kenneth V. Hardy and Tracey A. Laszloffy, *Teens Who Hurt: Clinical Interventions to Break the Cycle of Adolescent Violence* (New York, NY: Guildford Press, 2005); Linda Watkins-Goffman, *Understanding Cultural Narratives: Exploring Identity and the Multicultural Experience* (Ann Arbor, MI: University of Michigan Press, 2006).

35. Michael Toolan, *Narrative: A Critical Linguistic Introduction*, 2nd ed. (New York, NY: Routledge, 2001).

36. Dennis J. D. Sandole, *Peacebuilding: Preventing Violent Conflict in a Complex World* (Malden, MA: Polity Press, 2010), 55.

37. Roger Mac Ginty and Andrew Williams, *Conflict and Development* (London, England: Routledge, 2009), 82.

38. John Paul Lederach, *Building Peace*; Christine Barnes, "Weaving the Web: Civil-Society Roles in Working with Conflict and Building Peace," in *People Building Peace II: Successful Stories of Civil Society*, ed. Paul van Tongeren et al. (London, England: Lynne Rienner, 2005); Roger Mac Ginty, *International Peacebuilding and Local Resistance: Hybrid Forms of Peace* (New York, NY: Palgrave Macmillan, 2011); Thania Paffenholz, "Civil Socieity and Peacebuiding," in Civil *Socieity and Peacebuilding: A Critical Assessment*, ed. Thania Paffenholz (London, England: Lynne Rienner, 2010); Mark Duffield, "Social Reconstruction and the Radicalization of Development: Aid as a Relation of Global Liberal Governance," *Development and Change* 33.5 (2002); Christine Bell, "Human Rights, Peace Agreements, and Conflict Resolution: Negotiating Justice in Northern Ireland," in *Human Rights and Conflict: Exploring the Links between Rights, Law, and Peacebuilding*, ed. Julie A. Mertus and Jeffrey W. Helsing (Washington, DC: United States Institute of Peace, 2006).

39. Ingrid Sandole-Staroste, "Gender Mainstreaming: A Valuable Tool in Building Sustainable Peace," in *Handbook of Conflict Analysis and Resolution*, ed. Dennis J. D. Sandole et al. (New York, NY: Routledge, 2011).

40. Ibid., 236.

41. Cox, "Gramsci," 218.

42. Ward, "Finding a Place"; Richmond, "Becoming Liberal."

43. Barnes, "Weaving the Web," 9.

44. Boulding, *Cultures of Peace*.

45. Mac Ginty and Williams, *Conflict and Development*.

46. Enloe, *Bananas, Beaches, and Bases*.

47. Ibid., 15.

48. Connolly, "Feminist Politics."

49. William H. Sewell Jr., "A Theory of Structure: Duality, Agency and Transformation," *American Journal of Sociology* 98.1 (1992): 1–29.

BIBLIOGRAPHY

Barnes, Cathrine. "Weaving the Web: Civil-Society Roles in Working with Conflict and Building Peace." In *People Building Peace II: Successful Stories of Civil Society*, edited by Paul van Tongeren, Malin Brenk, Marte Hellema, and Juliette Verhoeven, 7–24. London, England: Lynne Rienner, 2005.

Bell, Christine. "Human Rights, Peace Agreements, and Conflict Resolution: Negotiating Justice in Northern Ireland." In *Human Rights and Conflict: Exploring the Links between Rights, Law, and Peacebuilding*, edited by Julie A. Mertus and Jeffrey W. Helsing, 345–74. Washington, DC: United States Institute of Peace, 2006.

Borer, Tristan Anne, John Darby, and Siobhan McEvoy-Levy. *Peacebuilding after Peace Accords: The Challenges of Violence, Truth, and Youth*. Notre Dame, IN: University of Notre Dame Press, 2006.

Botes, Johannes M. "Informal Roles." In *Conflict: From Analysis to Intervention*, edited by Sandra Cheldelin, Daniel Druckman, and Larissa Fast, 210–19. New York, NY: Lexington, 2003.

Boulding, Elise. *Cultures of Peace: The Hidden Side of History*. Syracuse, NY: Syracuse University Press, 2000.

Buchanan, Sandra. "Transforming Conflict in Northern Ireland and the Border Counties: Some Lessons from the Peace Programmes on Valuing Participatory Democracy." *Irish Political Studies* 23.3 (2008): 387–401.

Byrne, Sean, Cynthia Irvin, and Eyob Fissuh. "The Perception of Economic Assistance in Northern Ireland and Its Role in the Peace Process." In *Handbook of Conflict Analysis and Resolution*, edited by Dennis J. D. Sandole, Sean Byrne, Ingrid Sandole-Staroste, and Jessica Senehi, 475–94. New York, NY: Routledge, 2011.

Connolly, Linda. "Feminist Politics and the Peace Process." *Capital and Class* 23.3 (1999): 145–59.

Cox, Robert W. "Gramsci, Hegemony, and International Relations." In *International Relations Theory*, 4th ed., edited by Paul R. Viotti and Mark V. Kauppi, 215–25. New York, NY: Longman, 2010.

Creary, Patlee and Sean Byrne. "Peace with Strings Attached: Exploring Reflections of Structure and Agency in Northern Ireland Peacebuilding Funding." *Journal of Peacebuilding* 2.1 (2014): 62–84.

Creswell, John W. *Qualitiative Inquiry & Research Design: Choosing Among Five Approaches*. 2nd ed. London, England: Sage, 2007.

Diamond, Louise and John McDonald. *Multi-Track Diplomacy: A Systems Approach to Peace*. 3rd ed. West Hartford, CT: Kumarian, 1996.

Donaghy, Tahnya Barnett. "Women's Contribution to the Northern Ireland Peace Agreement." *Canadian Women's Studies* 22.2 (2003): 83–87.

Donais, Timothy. "Empowerment or Imposition? Dilemmas of Local Ownership in Post-Conflict Peacebuilding Processes." *Peace and Change* 34.1 (2009): 3–26.

Duffield, Mark. "Social Reconstruction and the Radicalization of Development: Aid as a Relation of Global Liberal Governance." *Development and Change* 33.5 (2002): 1049–71.

Enloe, Cynthia. *Bananas, Beaches and Bases: Making Feminist Sense of International Politics*. Berkeley, CA: University of California Press, 2000.

Evangelista, Susan. "Inner Voices and Outer Positions: Women in Peacemaking." *Social Alternatives* 16.2 (1997): 38–41.

Fearon, Kate. "Northern Ireland's Women's Coalition: Institutionalizing a Political Voice and Ensuring Representation." *Conciliation Resources* no. 13 (2002): 78–81. Accessed May 10, 2014. http://www.c-r.org/accord-article/

northern-ireland%E2%80%99s-women%E2%80%99s-coalition-institutionalising-political-voice-and-ensuring.

Hardy, Kenneth V. and Tracey A. Laszloffy. *Teens Who Hurt: Clinical Interventions to Break the Cycle of Adolescent Violence.* New York, NY: Guildford Press, 2005.

Hemmer, Bruce, Paula Garb, Marlett Phillips, and John L. Graham. "Putting the 'Up' in Bottom-Up Peacebuilding: Broadening the Concept of Peace Negotiations." *International Negotiation* 11.1 (2006): 129–62.

Jacobson, Ruth. "Women and Peace in Northern Ireland: A Complicated Relationship." In *States of Conflict: Gender, Violence and Resistance,* edited by Susie Jacobs, Ruth Jacobson, and Jennifer Marchbank, 179–98. New York, NY: Zed Books, 2000.

Jeong, Ho-Won. *Peace and Conflict Studies: An Introduction.* Burlington, MA: Ashgate, 2000.

Kilmurray, Avila and Monica McWilliams. "Struggling for Peace: How Women in Northern Ireland Challenged the Status Quo." *Solutions* 2.2 (2011). Accessed May 13, 2014. www.thesolutionsjournal.com/node/893.

Lederach, John Paul. *Building Peace: Sustainable Reconciliation in Divided Societies.* Washington, DC: United States Institute of Peace, 1997.

———. *Preparing for Peace: Conflict Transformation across Cultures.* New York, NY: Syracuse University Press, 1995.

Mac Ginty, Roger. *International Peacebuilding and Local Resistance: Hybrid Forms of Peace.* New York, NY: Palgrave Macmillan, 2011.

———. *No War, No Peace: The Rejuvenation of Stalled Peace Processes and Peace Accords.* New York, NY: Palgrave Macmillan, 2008.

Mac Ginty, Roger and Andrew Williams. *Conflict and Development.* London, England: Routledge, 2009.

McCabe, Allyssa and Lynn S. Bliss. *Patterns in Narrative Discourse: A Multicultural, Life Span Approach.* Boston, MA: Allyn & Bacon, 2003.

Paffenholz, Thania. "Civil Society and Peacebuilding." In *Civil Society and Peacebuilding: A Critical Assessment,* edited by Thania Paffenholz, 43–64. London, England: Lynne Rienner, 2010.

Pugh, Michael. "The Political Economy of Peacebuilding: A Critical Theory Perspective." *International Journal of Peace Studies* 10.2 (2005): 23–42.

Richmond, Oliver P. "Becoming Liberal, Unbecoming Liberalism: Liberal-Local Hybridity Via the Everyday as a Response to the Paradoxes of Liberal Peacebuilding." *Journal of Intervention and Statebuilding* 3.3 (2009): 324–44.

Sandole, Dennis J. D. *Peacebuilding: Preventing Violent Conflict in a Complex World.* Malden, MA: Polity Press, 2010.

Sandole-Staroste, Ingrid. "Gender Mainstreaming: A Valuable Tool in Building Sustainable Peace." In *Handbook of Conflict Analysis and Resolution,* edited by Dennis J. D. Sandole, Sean Byrne, Ingrid Sandole-Staroste, and Jessica Senehi, 226–40. London, England: Routledge, 2011.

Sawer, Patrick and Bob Graham. "'Republicanism is Part of Our DNA,' Says IRA Bomber Dolours Price." *Telegraph,* September 23, 2012. Accessed May 13, 2014.

http://www.telegraph.co.uk/news/uknews/northernireland/9560100/Republican-ism-is-part-of-our-DNA-says-IRA-bomber-Dolours-Price.html.

Senehi, Jessica. "The Role of Constructive, Transcultural Storytelling in Ethnopolitical Conflict Transformation in Northern Ireland." In *Regional and Ethnic Conflicts: Perspectives From the Front Lines*, edited by Judy Carter, George E. Irani, and Vamik D. Volkan, 227–37. Upper Saddle River, NJ: Prentice Hall, 2008.

———. "Constructive Storytelling in Intercommunal Conflicts: Building Community, Building Peace." In *Reconcilable Differences: Turning Points in Ethnopolitical Conflicts*, edited by Sean Byrne and Cynthia L. Irvin, 96–114. West Hartford, CT: Kumarian, 2000.

———. "Storytelling and Peace." In *The Oxford International Encyclopedia of Peace*, edited by Nigel Young. Oxford, England: Oxford University Press, 2010.

Sewell Jr., William H. "A Theory of Structure: Duality, Agency and Transformation." *American Journal of Sociology* 98.1 (1992): 1–29.

Thiessen, Chuck. "Emancipatory Peacebuilding: Critical Responses to (Neo)Liberal Trends." In *Critical Issues in Peace and Conflict Studies: Theory, Practice, and Pedagogy*, edited by Thomas Matyók, Jessica Senehi, and Sean Byrne, 115–42. Lanham, MD: Lexington, 2011.

Toolan, Michael J. *Narrative: A Critical Linguistic Introduction*. 2nd ed. New York, NY: Routledge, 2001.

Ward, Margaret. "Finding a Place: Women and the Irish Peace Process." *Race and Class* 37.1 (1995): 41–50.

Watkins-Goffman, Linda. *Understanding Cultural Narratives: Exploring Identity and the Multicultural Experience*. Ann Arbor, MI: University of Michigan Press, 2006.

Chapter 16

Women Peacekeepers

Gender Discourses on "Equal but Different" Among Irish Peacekeepers

Shirley Graham

Despite repeated calls by the United Nations Security Council (UNSC) to member states to increase the total of women peacekeepers they are sending to mission areas, the numbers still remain at only three percent of military personnel globally.[1] Influenced by women's activism and feminist scholarship on the gendered nature of war, and the requirement for Peace Support Operations (PSOs) to reflect gender needs, the UNSC adopted Resolution 1325 on Women, Peace and Security,[2] which obliges member states to include a gender perspective in the planning and practice of peacekeeping, and to increase the numbers of women peacekeepers in all jobs and ranks including senior decision-making positions.[3] United Nations Security Council Resolution 1325 (UNSCR 1325) argues that the current global security environment needs more women peacekeepers to support the needs of civilian women and girls caught up in conflict.

In 2009, UN Secretary General Ban Ki-moon launched a campaign to increase the numbers of female peacekeepers to 10 percent in military units and 20 percent in police units by 2014.[4] However, 14 years since its adoption the resolution has had little impact on either the numbers of women in peacekeeping missions or the inclusion of civilian/gender perspectives within the planning and practice of missions.[5] Recent reports link this lack of action to an absence of understanding among member states about UNSCR 1325 (often interpreted as about increasing the numbers of women peacekeepers only with little understanding as to why this is important or why including a gender perspective into missions is necessary).[6] For example, there is a gap in data and analysis about women's participation in national security institutions and how the prevalence of social norms and biases perpetuate gender inequalities within the security sector.

Motivated by this lack of action, I set out to explore the gendering processes within a military institution, in this case the Irish Defence Forces (DF), which position women and men in particular roles, formally and informally, and which can support or inhibit women's access to PSO positions. The study reveals a multiplicity of contradictory discourses operating simultaneously on topics such as sexuality, caregiving, protection, and culture. It also uncovers muted discourses with transformative potential that could lead to the empowerment of women peacekeepers by equalizing gender relations within a mission context.

The study adopted a feminist theoretical approach influenced by Cynthia Enloe's research on gender and militarism and her groundbreaking questions: where are the women; which women are there; what are they doing; and what do they think about being there?[7] Following Enloe's lead, I became curious about the conditions of women peacekeeper's lives and set out to pay close attention to how gender is created and re-created through patriarchal structures and systems, revealed through the discourses drawn on by peacekeepers' within their narratives.

United Nations reports[8] outline how the presence of women peacekeepers can make positive differences to missions: by building trust between troops and the local community, providing access to civilian women; role-modeling gender equality and challenging gender stereotypes, through their jobs, tasks and ranks; and by having a constructive influence on social relations among troops. However, feminist scholars argue that increasing the numbers of women does not necessarily translate into better outcomes[9] because gender balancing is complex and research on gender quotas has revealed mixed results.[10] They claim that "the assumption that adding women mitigates concerns about gender stereotypes in the security sector is untested, as the mere presence of women does not necessarily change military gender hierarchies and the militarized culture within the security institutions."[11] My study set out to test these assumptions and theories about women's influence on a mission. It did this by using post-positivist qualitative research methods: semi-structured interviews with 28 members of the DF (women and men); participant observation of a mission camp in Kosovo; and attendance at military training courses on gender and culture. I taped the interviews and looked for repeating themes and subthemes within participants' narratives. I then used interpretive discourse analysis to reveal the meaning repertoires within the narratives and to explore how the military institutions position women and men in certain peacekeeping scenarios, as well as how women and men position each other.

In relation to women's inclusion into the ranks of the DF, a dominant discourse within the organization revealed through the interviewing process, is that women are "equal but different." Therefore, the study used this dominant discourse on gender as a lens through which to analyze the findings. I set out to explore what "equal but different" means in practical terms, and how this discourse plays itself out in the different situations in which peacekeepers find themselves. I was also keen to draw connections between discourses and women's opportunities to take part in a wide variety of jobs, tasks, and missions, access promotions, and ultimately their likelihood to be retained within the organization.

METHODOLOGY

The research participants had varying degrees of peacekeeping experience. Some were senior officers with 30 years of service and others were junior ranks with only one or two missions behind them. From the interview transcripts I identified key words and phrases, while connecting theoretical concepts written about in the literature with the peacekeepers' own experiences of peacekeeping and gender. My aim was to "identify the particular perspective, angle or point of view from which the main themes were represented."[12] Through my feminist lens I was continually asking a series of questions: What do women bring to a mission? Is a mixed-gender peacekeeping mission received differently than a male-only team by the host community or by other PSO militaries? What are the costs to women soldiers for being part of a minority group in the peacekeeping setting? Does the presence of women enable an inclusion of different voices and perspectives in peacekeeping? How does the "equal but different" discourse operate to position women and men within specific gender roles within the mission? Through these questions I sought to explore theories about women's visibility on a mission: whether their presence is highlighted and promoted through their jobs and tasks or whether they are expected to behave and look the same as men by blending in,[13] whether their presence fosters greater trust and confidence among civilians, and whether women provide legitimacy for a mission by virtue of being women.[14] These questions also consider if women and men peacekeepers are seen as equals by civilians as well as by soldiers from other Troop Contributing Countries (TCCs) and the implications of this for the mission outcome. By asking these questions the study reveals how women are positioned within and without their own culture and discusses which gender norms are being tested by women's inclusion in a PSO.

The overarching themes emanating from the narratives were: culture, caregiving, protection, divisions of labor, segregation of facilities, and sexuality. I pulled out extracts from participant accounts to illuminate particular recurring themes and the multiple discourses operating simultaneously in different contexts. Some of these discourses were subtle or muted and others were powerful or dominant. Discourses can be understood as vessels that contain certain ideologies contributing to the creation and production of collective attitudes and behaviors.[15] To identify discourses I looked for the representation of a specific part of the world, and how it was represented from a particular perspective.[16] For example, themes such as culture and caregiving were open to a range of different perspectives, representations, and discourses. On the theme of culture within the host nation of a PSO, the country's culture and gender relations are discursively differentiated depending on who is speaking and from what perspective they are sharing their experience or ideas. Therefore, my aim was to deconstruct dominant discourses to reveal invisible structures of power, and social and political control that lead to dominance and exclusion.[17]

Dominant discourses are those meaning repertoires that are taken-for-granted or considered "normal" or "natural" within a given community or society. Dominant discourses refer to how some ways of making meaning become mainstream in a particular order of discourse while others are marginal, oppositional, or alternative.[18] As such, dominant discourses are those that are operating as truths or knowledges within an institution. They are not powerful on their own; they become powerful when used on a daily basis by commanding individuals and institutions.[19] The dissemination of dominant discourses by those in elite positions within institutions can result in inequalities and injustices in wider society.[20] Therefore, discourse analysis can be useful in exposing the ways institutions create dominant discourses to exclude certain groups, such as women, by leading the majority of people to think about specific jobs, tasks, and roles in society as belonging to men.[21] For example, there are widely circulated discourses that position women who soldier as "unnatural." There are discourses that use differentials in physical strength between women and men as an exclusionary mechanism for women accessing militaries; even though there are wide differentials in strength among men as well as among women and men, and physical strength is not a key component of many jobs in today's multidimensional PSOs. There are discourses that position women as disrupters of all-male team cohesion and exclude women from certain missions, jobs, or tasks. On their own, or used together, these discourses can discourage women from accessing militaries. Therefore, discourse analysis has the ability to make visible the interconnectedness of things, and this can enable individuals to become aware of exactly how they are being dominated or oppressed. By seeing the oppression they can make efforts to liberate themselves.[22] Analyzing how the participants within this study position each other within certain discourses reveals their relationship to one another and whether they are competing with, dominating, or complementing each other in the different PSO scenarios in which they find themselves.

STUDY FINDINGS

I divided my findings into three sections: Discourses on What Women Bring to Missions; Discourses on Inhibitors to Women Accessing Missions; and Alternative Discourses with Transformative Potential. As there is not the space in this chapter to explore each of these sections in detail, I will give a brief overview of some of the dominant discourses. The diagram below gives an outline of the main themes drawn on by the participants and some of the contradictory discourses within each of the themes (depending on whether they are drawn on by a man or a woman).

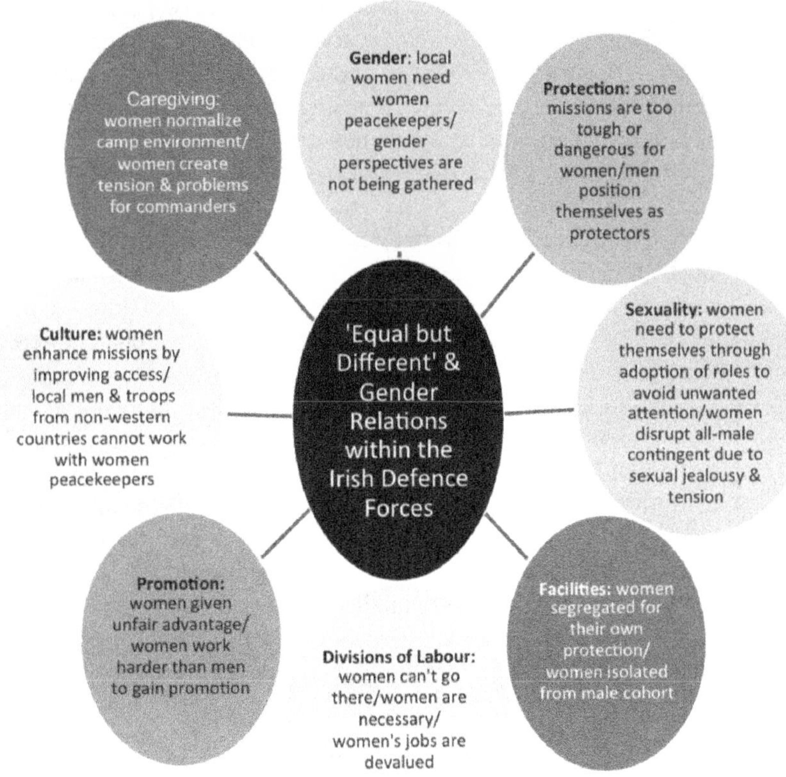

Figure 16.1 Diagram representing the "Equal but Different" discourse and its contradictory sub-discourses all operating at the same time in different contexts on a mission. *Source*: Author

What Do Women Peacekeepers Bring to a Mission?

The findings reveal discourses that position women as bringing a new energy to peacekeeping missions with their diversity of experience and knowledge. Both women and men peacekeepers draw on discourses that position women as necessary because they can search civilian women at checkpoints, gather different types of intelligence, and communicate with civilian women on sensitive issues such as sexual violence. The discourses reveal that a mixed peacekeeping mission is received differently to a male-only operation; when women peacekeepers are recognized by their gender, they can elicit surprise, creating opportunities for connection and dialogue between peacekeepers and civilians. However, while women peacekeepers can have better and important access to civilian women in a host country, there was no evidence in the findings that civilian women's differing experiences and perspectives on war and peace were either being gathered or valued by peacekeepers.

Male participants positioned women peacekeepers as benefiting a mission predominantly in their care-giving roles to the men themselves. For example, men stated that women normalize the camp environment; that the presence of even a few women can reduce tension among men by diffusing the all-male, testosterone-fueled atmosphere; that women provide empathy and listen to men's concerns "like a wife away from home"; and that women galvanize men into performing to higher standards physically and mentally "as few men want to be outdone by women." These findings link with the theory that women must fit into male-dominated institutions in a way that does not draw too much attention to them or disrupt the masculine status quo.[23] Power relations depend upon sustaining certain notions of what it is to be male or female, masculine or feminine, and the appropriate roles associated with each. In men's accounts femininities are associated with empathy and care. Women are positioned as the embodiment of home for men and act as reminders of where they belong and who is waiting for them. Women are positioned as complementary to men, and whose positive influence may diffuse tensions between and among men, thereby confirming the theory that women are perceived to be calming[24] and that gender categories become an organizing device.[25] Femininities are seen as beneficial to the provision of normal life *within* the camp, while masculinities are associated with instrumental peacekeeping work *outside* the camp.[26]

What Are the Inhibitors to Women's Inclusion on Missions?

Within this section of the research a series of contradictory discourses were revealed. While the discourses drawn on by women and men participants often overlapped on certain topics, there were also contradictions relating to their differing positions, experiences, and perspectives. What follows is a map of some of the different discourses that highlight the complexities around women's inclusion in the military and peacekeeping missions.

Discourses on Military Culture

Peace Support Operations are multinational and therefore bring military personnel into close proximity of each other, illuminating working styles, values, and attitudes. Gender is an organizing device used to draw boundaries and maintain cultural differences between nations and TCCs.[27] For example, the discourse "foreign male soldiers cannot work with Irish women peacekeepers" reveals how women become the symbolic markers of culture and difference among troops on a mission. It also illuminates how women's presence allows Irish male peacekeepers to be both masculine males (protectors) and ethnically differentiated (nonsexist). In these discourses women belong to the nation and are linked to men via the nation's military and must be protected from the other soldier and nation. This discourse dualistically positions Western and non-Western peacekeepers along a continuum as nonsexist and sexist in their attitudes toward women. The discourse reveals a tension between different types of masculinities performed within the PSO context. These differences are most visible between the warrior and peacekeeping models of masculinity that prevail in particular cultures and nations.[28]

There is a clear delineation between women's and men's narratives on the subject of working with peacekeepers from other countries and they reveal how "equal but different" gets played out in the field to position and reposition women depending on the culture of their peacekeeping peers. The women focus on how their presence "surprises" soldiers from some TCCs while the men's discourses focus on how these "other soldiers can't work with women." The first position is not seen as particularly problematic, but the second one is extremely so. Discourses that position the other male as the problem who cannot be trusted may operate to exclude women from certain tasks or missions. The military would be positioning these soldiers as privileged over their own women officers if they shift women's access to missions or tasks specifically because of the discourse "some male soldiers can't work with women." Rather than transforming the sexist attitudes of those male peacekeepers it is women who will have to shift to accommodate them. Differences among militaries therefore need to be understood in terms of the relationships between masculinities as much as between masculinities and femininities and the impact these cultural truths have on women's positioning within a PSO. If the discourse "other male peacekeepers cannot be trusted" takes root, it has the power to position women in designated women-friendly spheres away from military men and maintain both hegemonic masculinities and cultural and gender stereotypes.

Discourses on Host Nation Culture

On the subject of host nation culture there is a notable shift in the discourse over time from "women cannot go there" to "women are necessary" on a mission. However, some male peacekeepers still consider the culture of the host country and traditional gender roles within those countries as inhibitors to women's access to certain jobs or missions. The rationale is that civilian men from certain cultures, such as fundamentalist, traditional, or tribal ones will not communicate with women peacekeepers. For example, Irish women officers serving in Lebanon in the 1980–90s were advised to take a step back and to let their male peers or subordinates deal with local men. Women themselves said that while they occasionally had difficulty dealing with local men, the military uniform, and their role as peacekeepers gives them status and respect among civilians, both women and men. While they respect cultural differences they don't think those differences should curtail their access to the jobs they have been trained to perform.

Divisions of Labor

The participant accounts revealed discourses on how certain jobs and tasks become gendered within the work setting and that few women reach the most senior ranks (to date only three women have reached the rank of Lieutenant Colonel in the DF).[29] These discourses reflect Helena Carreiras'[30] theory that the ways masculinities and femininities are performed and valued by the military is revealed through the gendering of specific tasks and jobs and through discourses on gender roles within specific contexts. Some women peacekeepers voice concerns that UNSCR 1325 may position them in essentialized women's roles such as caring, listening, and working predominantly with civilian women rather than in more active soldiering tasks and operational duties. These discourses reveal a tension between the roles the UN want women soldiers to take on, the roles the women soldiers themselves would like to take on, and the roles the local women in post-conflict countries would like the women soldiers to take on.

In research conducted by Cynthia Cockburn, women working in NGOs in Bosnia-Herzegovina[31] argued that the majority of civilians are in favor of more women soldiers being present on a mission, and that it is important for these women to be represented at all levels of seniority because if they are not respected inside the military they are not likely to be respected by the local community. Civilians in these situations also want women to retain their femininity, bringing with them their concerns and interests as women, and for some women to be given a civil-military brief and responsibility for liaising with women's groups.[32] These civilian women asserted that they cannot get their needs met if military women are not available to them in these capacities. However, some women peacekeepers are concerned that UNSCR 1325 will ghettoize women soldiers into women/civilian-facing jobs that they may not be suited to doing or that may become devalued as feminized jobs within a mission,which has happened previously.

Research conducted by Lt. Col. Maureen O'Brien of the DF identifies a devaluing of jobs associated with the feminine. The example cited is the appointment of the Pay Officer on a mission, which is a task frequently done by women and has become unpopular with men.[33] In her research, concerns were raised by women soldiers in the DF that the civil-military coordination job (known as CIMIC, which interfaces between the military component of a mission and the human rights, political, humanitarian or developmental components) might become feminized and devalued, and have an impact on women's worth in the military institution, limiting their access to a breadth of jobs and experiences, thereby creating barriers to promotion opportunities. While currently more men than women are taking up CIMIC roles in the DF, an important concern is raised, that if more women are recruited specifically to fulfill women-facing tasks, the military would deepen gender stereotypes by homogenizing women and corralling them all together in women-friendly jobs. These discourses could create policies that force women into jobs that are not suitable for their individual set of competencies and place an unrealistic pressure on them to transform gender issues in the post-conflict situation. Women peacekeepers also raised a concern that UNSCR 1325 could create a backlash toward them if military men think that the military is becoming too feminized or if they believe that women are being promoted or sent on certain missions instead of them because of their gender.

While the discourses outlined are informally circulating among peacekeepers, they do have the power to influence formal policy and practice as they are often taken for granted within society. Therefore, how a military interprets and responds to UNSCR 1325 will impact discourses concerning the resolution and women's inclusion in PSOs. Highlighting the minority status of women in the military and UN peacekeeping missions without balancing it with understandings of gender stereotypes or dominant discourses that operate to exclude women from powerful roles in society could push women into taking jobs that they would not have chosen otherwise. This could further impact women's positioning as tokens or the perception that they are only suitable for certain tasks or jobs within the military.

What Are the Opportunities?

Throughout the study it was important to me as a feminist researcher to uncover discourses with transformative potential, ones that could genuinely equalize gender relations within a mission. Depending on the context of a PSO and its mandate, peacekeepers perform a variety of tasks which call on a multitude of gender performances including being capable and authoritative as well as sensitive and compassionate. So, I looked for discourses that position women in multiple roles not only in their socialized role as caregivers to male peers or civilian women, but within a variety of jobs, tasks, and missions suiting their particular skill sets and interests. Alternative discourses reveal all those in-between spaces, where muted ideas and attitudes can take root, and if supported, could eventually disrupt dominant discourses. Some of the transformative and emancipatory discourses revealed in the participants' accounts position women as: fitter than some men; competent and capable leaders; and equals with civilian and military men. These accounts reveal how gender identities are not fixed, but are constantly changing. Other discourses with transformative potential include: buddies protect regardless of gender; the importance of integrating without adopting the gender norms or culture of the host nation; how gender inequalities within the host nation need to be addressed as well as gender inequalities within militaries; and discourses on women as role models and as the leaders and protectors of their troops. These discourses move away from gender stereotyping and the gendering of specific jobs or roles in a PSO.

The presence of women soldiers, if they are positioned in multiple ranks, roles, jobs and tasks, can challenge the notion of women as homogenous, as victims, or as powerless, thereby eroding the gender stereotyping that positions women and men differently and unequally on issues of war and peace. The development of the "women are protectors" discourse, although muted, challenges the dominant discourse "men are protectors" and critiques gender binaries that position women as victims and men as their protectors in the peace/war dichotomy. The expansion of these protective discourses to include women as protectors alongside the discourse on cultural relations with host nations (i.e., integrate without adopting cultural or gender norms) could lead to a new discourse on the inclusion of women in missions (i.e., add women and transform).

Unequal power relations and gender norms are being challenged by women's presence as peacekeepers. In particular, senior male officers are positioning some women in jobs and tasks that they had previously been discouraged from participating in due to cultural norms in host nations or because they were perceived as too tough for women. These findings confirm the theory that the presence of women can have positive effects on an institution's attitude toward gender equality and that presence may create cracks in the institutional façade.[34] These cracks may create opportunities for new perspectives and approaches to peacekeeping as well as new codes of conduct in relation to women's human rights.

CONCLUSION

The findings in my study reveal that the "equal but different" discourse positions women as equal to men and a necessary component of today's multidimensional PSOs. Meanwhile, the different axis sets women apart, which while this may enhance their access to certain jobs and missions, it can also create barriers to particular jobs and experiences necessary for promotion and retention. The UN and all security institutions involved in peacekeeping must challenge discourses that undermine women's right to be included in PSOs within a diversity of jobs and ranks, if agencies want to erode barriers to women's inclusion and to increase their numbers. A plan of action to include gender perspectives in a mission must adopt an agenda-setting approach to gender mainstreaming. This approach would consider the desired impacts likely to flow from specific practices and policies. Security institutions then need to wholeheartedly engage with these reforms to enable gender-equal outcomes.

While UNSCR 1325 is clearly not only a numbers game, numbers are important. The military is male dominated which gives men control over how the military and peacekeeping is organized, strategized, what is prioritized, and what is minimized. Women absent or underrepresented in the military means they will not have influence over agendas and how things are done. The first step in any modern military taking the needs of women in post-conflict situations seriously is to take the needs of women within their own ranks seriously. This is not likely to happen if the numbers remain low and women are seen by civilians and other TCCs as being in token positions within missions.

The discourses in the research suggest that while the military culture in the DF has transformed somewhat to incorporate women among its ranks it needs further changes to take place if it is to incorporate women as fully equal members. Women are not just an adjunct to men on a PSO. Men need to understand the value of women to a mission beyond their care-giving roles. Multiple positioning of women peacekeepers within a mission, especially within decision-making and leadership roles, will demonstrate to civilian women in fragile post-conflict situations that the UN and national militaries take gender equality seriously, and that they acknowledge the empowerment of women as a necessary step toward the creation of a just and peaceful society.

NOTES

1. United Nations DPKO, "Mandates and the Legal Basis for Peacekeeping," accessed November 2014, http://www.un.org/en/peacekeeping/operations/pkmandates.shtml.

2. UNSCR 1325 (New York, NY: United Nations, October 31, 2000), http://www.un.org/en/ga/search/view_doc.asp?symbol=S/RES/1325%282000%29.

3. UNSCR 1325 specifically calls for the Secretary General to seek to expand the role and contribution of women in field-based operations, and especially among military observers, civilian police, human rights, and humanitarian personnel. The resolution also calls for a willingness to incorporate a gender perspective into peacekeeping operations, and urges the Secretary General to ensure that, where appropriate, field operations include a gender component.

4. Sabrina Karim and Kyle Beardsley, "Female Peacekeepers and Gender Balancing: Token Gestures or Informed Policymaking?" *International Interactions: Empirical and Theoretical Research in International Relations* 39.4 (2013).

5. Sahana Dharmapuri, "Not Just a Numbers Game: Increasing Women's Participation in UN Peacekeeping," *Providing for Peacekeeping* no. 4 (New York, NY: International Peace Institute, 2013); Anita Schjølset, "Data on Women's Participation in NATO Forces and Operations," *International Interactions: Empirical and Theoretical Research in International Relations* 39.4 (2013).

6. Dharmapuri, "Not Just a Numbers Game."

7. Cynthia Enloe, *Maneuvers: The International Politics of Militarizing Women's Lives* (Berkeley, CA: University of California Press, 2000), 294.

8. United Nations DPKO, "Women in Peacekeeping," accessed December 2014, http://www.un.org/en/peacekeeping/issues/women/womeninpk.shtml; United Nations Commission on the Status of Women, *Women in International Decision-Making: Participation of Women in Political Life and Decision-Making*, Report of the Secretary-General, March 15–April 4, 1995, http://www.un.org/documents/ecosoc/cn6/1995/ecn61995-12.htm.

9. Sheila Jeffreys, "Double Jeopardy: Women, the US Military and the War in Iraq," *Women's Studies International Forum* 30.1 (2007); Kathleen M. Jennings, "Protecting Whom? Approaches to Sexual Exploitation and Abuse in UN Peacekeeping Operations," Fafo-report (Oslo, Norway: Allkopi AS, 2008), 36; Olivera Simic, "Does the Presence of Women Really Matter? Towards Combating Male Sexual Violence in Peacekeeping Operations," *International Peacekeeping* 17.2 (2010).

10. Lisa Baldez, "The Pros and Cons of Gender Quota Laws: What Happens When You Kick Men Out and Let Women In?" *Politics & Gender* 2.1 (2006); Rikil R. Bhavnani, "Do Electoral Quotas Work after They Are Withdrawn? Evidence from a Natural Experiment in India," *American Political Science Review* 103.1 (2009); Miki Caul, "Political Parties and the Adoption of Candidate Gender Quotas: A Cross-National Analysis," *Journal of Politics* 63.4 (2001); Li-Ju Chen, "Do Gender Quotas Influence Women's Representation and Policies?" *The European Journal of Comparative Economics* 7.1 (2010); Drude Dahlerup, "Gender Quotas—Controversial But Trendy," *International Feminist Journal of Politics* 10.3 (2008); Drude Dahlerup and Lenita Freidenvall, "Quotas as a 'Fast Track' to Equal Representation for Women," *International Feminist Journal of Politics* 7.1 (2005); Mona Lena Krook, *Quotas for Women in Politics: Gender and Candidate Selection Reform Worldwide* (New York, NY: Oxford University Press, 2010); Aili Mari Tripp and Alice Kang, "The Global Impact of Quotas: On the Fast Track to Increased Female Legislative Representation," *Comparative Political Studies* 41.3 (2008).

11. Karim and Beardsley, "Female Peacekeepers and Gender Balancing," 466.

12. Norman Fairclough, *Analysing Discourse: Textual Analysis for Social Research* (London, England and New York, NY: Routledge, 2003), 129.

13. Enloe, *Maneuvers*; Annica Kronsell, "Methods for Studying Silences: Gender Analysis in Institutions of Hegemonic Masculinity," in *Feminist Methodologies for International Relations*, ed. Brooke A. Ackerly, Maria Stern, and Jacqui True (Cambridge, England: Cambridge University Press, 2006).

14. Donna Bridges and Debbie Horsfall, "Increasing Operational Effectiveness in UN Peacekeeping: Toward a Gender-Balanced Force," *Armed Forces & Society* 36.1(2009); Annica Kronsell and Erika Svedberg, eds., *Making Gender, Making War: Violence, Military and Peacekeeping Practices* (New York, NY and Oxon, England: Routledge, 2012); Dyan Mazurana, "Do Women Matter in Peacekeeping? Women in Police, Military and Civilian Peacekeeping," *Canadian Woman Studies* 22.2 (2003); Simic, "Does the Presence of Women Really Matter?"

15. Paul Baker et al., "A Useful Methodological Synergy? Combining Critical Discourse Analysis and Corpus Linguistics to Examine Discourses of Refugees and Asylum Seekers in the UK Press," *Discourse and Society* 19.3 (2008).

16. Fairclough, *Analysing Discourse.*

17. Andrea H. Tapia, Lynette Kvasny, and Julio Angel Ortiz, "A Critical Discourse Analysis of Three US Municipal Wireless Network Initiatives for Enhancing Social Inclusion," *Telematics and Informatics* 28.3 (2011).

18. Norman Fairclough, *Discourse and Social Change* (Cambridge, England: Polity Press, 2000).

19. Baker et al., "A Useful Methodological Synergy?"

20. Elaine Burroughs, "Irish Institutional Discourses of Illegal Immigration: A Critical Discourse Analysis Approach," PhD diss., National University of Ireland, 2012.

21. Peter Burnham et al., *Research Methods in Politics*, 2nd ed. (London, England: Sage, 2008).

22. Ruth Wodak and Michael Meyer, *Methods of Critical Discourse Analysis* (London, England: Sage, 2009); Anne B. Ryan, "Discourse: Some Considerations for the Reflective Practitioner," in *The Reflective Practitioner*, ed. Tony Walsh (Maynooth, Ireland: MACE, 2011).

23. Torunn Laugen Haaland, "Friendly War Fighters and Invisible Women: Perceptions of Gender and Masculinities in the Norwegian Armed Forces on Missions Abroad," in *Making Gender, Making War: Violence, Military and Peacekeeping Practices*, ed. Annica Kronsell and Erika Svedberg (New York, NY and Oxon, England: Routledge, 2012).

24. Gerald J. DeGroot, "A Few Good Women: Gender Stereotypes, the Military and Peacekeeping," *Women and International Peacekeeping* 8.2 (2002).

25. Helena Carreiras, "Gendered Culture in Peacekeeping Operations," *International Peacekeeping* 17.4 (2010).

26. Joshua S. Goldstein, *War and Gender: How Gender Shapes the War System and Vice Versa* (Cambridge, England: Cambridge University Press, 2001).

27. Carreiras, "Gendered Culture in Peacekeeping Operations."

28. Sandra Whitworth, *Men, Militarism and UN Peacekeeping: A Gendered Analysis* (Boulder, CO: Lynne Rienner, 2004).

29. Irish Independent Newspapers, "More Women in Defence Forces Urged," January 1, 2014, http://www.independent.ie/irish-news/more-women-in-defence-forces-urged-29879882.html.

30. Carreiras, "Gendered Culture in Peacekeeping Operations."

31. Cynthia Cockburn, "The Continuum of Violence: A Gender Perspective on War and Peace," in *Sites of Violence: Gender and Conflict Zones*, ed. Wenona Giles and Jennifer Hyndman (Berkeley, CA: University of California Press, 2004).

32. Cynthia Cockburn and Meliha Hubic, "Gender and the Peacekeeping Military: A View from Bosnian Women's Organisations," in *The Postwar Moment: Militaries, Masculinities and International Peacekeeping*, ed. Cynthia Cockburn and Dubravaka Zarkov (London, England: Lawrence &Wishart, 2002), 114.

33. Maureen O'Brien, "UNSCR 1325: Just Add Women and Stir—A Recipe for Gender Stereotyping in Peacekeeping Operations?" in *Building a Better Future: Contributions by the Irish Defence Forces*, ed. Tony Walsh (Maynooth, Ireland: MACE, 2012).

34. Ryan, "Discourse."

35. Kronsell, "Studying Silences."

BIBLIOGRAPHY

Baker, Paul, Costas Gabrielatos, Majid Khosravinik, Michał Krzyżanowski, Tony McEnery and Ruth Wodak. "A Useful Methodological Synergy? Combining Critical Discourse Analysis and Corpus Linguistics to Examine Discourses of Refugees and Asylum Seekers in the UK Press." *Discourse and Society* 19.3 (2008): 273–306.

Baldez, Lisa. "The Pros and Cons of Gender Quota Laws: What Happens When You Kick Men Out and Let Women In?" *Politics & Gender* 2.1 (2006): 102–09.

Bhavnani, Rikil R. "Do Electoral Quotas Work after They Are Withdrawn? Evidence from a Natural Experiment in India." *American Political Science Review* 103.1 (2009): 23–35.

Bridges, Donna and Debbie Horsfall. "Increasing Operational Effectiveness in UN Peacekeeping: Toward a Gender-Balanced Force." *Armed Forces & Society* 36.1 (2009): 120–30.

Burnham, Peter, Karin Gilland Lutz, Wyn Grant, and Zig Layton-Henry. *Research Methods in Politics*. 2nd ed. London, England: Sage, 2008.

Burroughs, Elaine. "Irish Institutional Discourses of Illegal Immigration: A Critical Discourse Analysis Approach." PhD diss., National University of Ireland, 2012.

Carreiras, Helena. "Gendered Culture in Peacekeeping Operations." *International Peacekeeping* 17.4 (2010): 471–85.

Caul, Miki. "Political Parties and the Adoption of Candidate Gender Quotas: A Cross-National Analysis." *The Journal of Politics* 63.4 (2001): 1214–29.

Chen, Li-Ju. "Do Gender Quotas Influence Women's Representation and Policies?" *The European Journal of Comparative Economics* 7.1 (2010): 13–60.

Cockburn, Cynthia. "The Continuum of Violence: A Gender Perspective on War and Peace." In *Sites of Violence: Gender and Conflict Zones*, edited by Wenona

Giles and Jennifer Hyndman, 24–44. Berkeley, CA: University of California Press, 2004.

Cockburn, Cynthia and Meliha Hubic. "Gender and the Peacekeeping Military: A View from Bosnian Women's Organisations." In *The Postwar Moment: Militaries, Masculinities and International Peacekeeping*, edited by Cynthia Cockburn and Dubravaka Zarkov, 103–21. London, England: Lawrence &Wishart, 2002.

Dahlerup, Drude. "Gender Quotas—Controversial But Trendy." *International Feminist Journal of Politics* 10.3 (2008): 322–28.

Dahlerup, Drude and Lenita Freidenvall. "Quotas as a 'Fast Track' to Equal Representation for Women." *International Feminist Journal of Politics* 7.1 (2005): 26–48.

DeGroot, Gerard J. "A Few Good Women: Gender Stereotypes, the Military and Peacekeeping." *Women and International Peacekeeping* 8.2 (2002): 23–38.

Dharmapuri, Sahana. "Not Just a Numbers Game: Increasing Women's Participation in UN Peacekeeping." *Providing for Peacekeeping* no. 4. New York, NY: International Peace Institute, 2013.

Enloe, Cynthia. *Maneuvers: The International Politics of Militarizing Women's Lives*. Berkeley, CA: University of California Press, 2000.

Fairclough, Norman. *Analysing Discourse: Textual Analysis for Social Research*. London, England and New York, NY: Routledge, 2003.

———. *Discourse and Social Change*. Cambridge, England: Polity Press, 2000.

Irish Independent Newspapers. "More Women in Defence Forces Urged," January 1, 2014. http://www.independent.ie/irish-news/more-women-in-defence-forces-urged-29879882.html.

Goldstein, Joshua S. *War and Gender: How Gender Shapes the War System and Vice Versa*. Cambridge, England: Cambridge University Press, 2001.

Haaland, Torunn Laugen. "Friendly War Fighters and Invisible Women: Perceptions of Gender and Masculinities in the Norwegian Armed Forces on Missions Abroad." In *Making Gender, Making War: Violence, Military and Peacekeeping Practices*, edited by Annica Kronsell and Erika Svedberg, 63–75. New York, NY and Oxon, England: Routledge, 2012.

Jeffreys, Sheila. "Double Jeopardy: Women, the US Military and the War in Iraq." *Women's Studies International Forum* 30.1 (2007): 16–25.

Jennings, Kathleen M. *Protecting Whom? Approaches to Sexual Exploitation and Abuse in UN Peacekeeping Operations*. Fafo-report. Oslo, Norway: Allkopi AS, 2008.

Karim, Sabrina and Kyle Beardsley. "Female Peacekeepers and Gender Balancing: Token Gestures or Informed Policymaking?" *International Interactions: Empirical and Theoretical Research in International Relations* 39.4 (2013): 461–88.

Kronsell, Annica. "Methods for Studying Silences: Gender Analysis in Institutions of Hegemonic Masculinity." In *Feminist Methodologies for International Relations*, edited by Brooke A. Ackerly, Maria Stern, and Jacqui True, 108–28. Cambridge, England: Cambridge University Press, 2006.

Kronsell, Annica and Erika Svedberg, eds. *Making Gender, Making War: Violence, Military and Peacekeeping Practices*. New York, NY and Oxon, England: Routledge, 2012.

Krook, Mona Lena. *Quotas for Women in Politics: Gender and Candidate Selection Reform Worldwide*. New York, NY: Oxford University Press, 2010.

Mazurana, Dyan. "Do Women Matter in Peacekeeping? Women in Police, Military and Civilian Peacekeeping." *Canadian Woman Studies* 22.2 (2003): 64–71.

O'Brien, Maureen. "UNSCR 1325: Just Add Women and Stir—A Recipe for Gender Stereotyping in Peacekeeping Operations?" In *Building a Better Future: Contributions by the Irish Defence Forces*, edited by Tony Walsh, 179–96. Maynooth, Ireland: MACE, 2012.

Ryan, Anne B. "Discourse: Some Considerations for the Reflective Practitioner." In *The Reflective Practitioner*, edited by Tony Walsh. Maynooth, Ireland: MACE, 2011.

Schjølset, Anita. "Data on Women's Participation in NATO Forces and Operations." *International Interactions: Empirical and Theoretical Research in International Relations* 39.4 (2013): 575–87.

Simic, Olivera. "Does the Presence of Women Really Matter? Towards Combating Male Sexual Violence in Peacekeeping Operations." *International Peacekeeping* 17.2 (2010): 188–99.

Tapia, Andrea H., Lynette Kvasny, and Julio Angel Ortiz. "A Critical Discourse Analysis of Three US Municipal Wireless Network Initiatives for Enhancing Social Inclusion." *Telematics and Informatics* 28.3 (2011): 215–26.

Tripp, Aili Mari and Alice Kang. "The Global Impact of Quotas: On the Fast Track to Increased Female Legislative Representation." *Comparative Political Studies* 41.3 (2008): 338–61.

United Nations Department for Peacekeeping Operations (DPKO). "Mandates and the Legal Basis for Peacekeeping." Accessed November 2014. http://www.un.org/en/peacekeeping/operations/pkmandates.shtml.

———. "Women in Peacekeeping." Accessed December 2014. http://www.un.org/en/peacekeeping/issues/women/womeninpk.shtml

United Nations Security Council Resolution (UNSCR) 1325. New York, NY: United Nations, October 31, 2000. http://www.un.org/en/ga/search/view_doc.asp?symbol=S/RES/1325%282000%29.

United Nations Commission on the Status of Women. *Women in International Decision-Making: Participation of Women in Political Life and Decision-Making*. Report of the Secretary-General, March 15–April 4, 1995. http://www.un.org/documents/ecosoc/cn6/1995/ecn61995-12.htm.

Whitworth, Sandra. *Men, Militarism and UN Peacekeeping: A Gendered Analysis*. Boulder, CO: Lynne Rienner, 2004.

Wodak, Ruth and Michael Meyer, eds. *Methods of Critical Discourse Analysis*. London, England: Sage, 2009.

PART II

PEACE EDUCATION

Chapter 17

Peace Studies and Feminism

Debates, Linkages, and Intersections[1]

Lisa McLean and María Lucía Zapata

Despite the important institutional and academic developments in women's rights and gender equality, peacebuilding remains an area where gender analyses are insufficient. From peace negotiations, peacekeeping interventions, peace research, and concrete grassroots initiatives, gender is often a marginal topic. This chapter analyzes the connections between feminism and Peace Studies and their contributions to our understanding of violence, conflict, and peace. The first section presents the evolution of feminist approaches in relation to war and peace. The second considers the ways that feminist theories compliment the theoretical foundation of Peace Studies and peacebuilding. This is followed by an examination of the contributions of critical theories, such as anticolonial and grassroots peacebuilding theories that challenge colonialist assumptions in both feminism and Peace Studies. From these critical perspectives we consider the practical applications of these theories for peace scholarship.

PEACE STUDIES AND FEMINISM: THE EVOLUTION OF A PARTNERSHIP

As an interdisciplinary field, the objective of Peace Studies is to understand the causes and effects of war and violence, and to develop better approaches for building peace. Influenced by Western disciplines such as Political Science and International Relations, Peace Studies made the state and the international community its main focus of analysis.[2] Within Peace Studies, peacebuilding refers to those initiatives and processes used to promote peace, including mechanisms and structures necessary to tackle the emergence of violence.[3] Although the concept was initially coined in 1975 by Norwegian sociologist Johan Galtung, it was in 1991 with the UN's *An Agenda for Peace* that the term gained significance. According to *An Agenda*, peacebuilding was designed as a mechanism to operate after a peace agreement was reached, to create the structures and institutions to avoid relapse into violence and to support the implementation of the agreement.[4]

Despite the relevance of this initial definition, various scholars and practitioners insist that peacebuilding practices should not be limited to post-conflict settings. Lisa Schirch and Manjrika Sewak assert that peacebuilding "seeks to prevent, reduce, transform and help people recover from violence in all forms, even structural violence that has not yet led to massive civil unrest."[5] In addition, John Paul Lederach states that peacebuilding "encompasses, generates and sustain[s]" different processes needed to transform conflict to more sustainable peaceful relations.[6] These definitions highlight three important characteristics of contemporary approaches to peacebuilding. First, peacebuilding must operate before, during, and after peace negotiations. Second, in addition to the state, a broad array of actors working in different levels of society, are responsible for peacebuilding activities. Third, the role of peacebuilding is to transform conflict not by the use of power but through the strengthening of human relations.

After the Cold War ended and intrastate violence devastated countries like Rwanda and the former Yugoslavia, new perspectives in Peace Studies and peacebuilding emerged. Enriched with postcolonial, feminist, and post-structural debates, as well as with contributions from scholars and practitioners from the Global South, Peace Studies broadened its perspectives. New areas of research emerged, and new debates provided alternative perspectives in the analysis of peace, violence, and conflict.[7] It is in this context that research on the effects of violence on women's lives, as well as their contributions and struggles in peacebuilding began to command the attention of scholars and practitioners.

According to Elisabeth Porter, literature on women, war, and peace usually focuses on the effects of war and violence on women; peacemaking and peacekeeping processes; and the design and implementation of transitional justice mechanisms such as disarmament, demobilization, and reintegration.[8] Feminist scholars assert that to better understand gender dynamics in the context of war and peacebuilding, traditional analyses centered on the state need to be deconstructed. By asking "where are the women," these scholars seek to understand how war affects women and how it shapes their peacebuilding efforts.

Feminist scholarship has developed three theoretical approaches to the issues of gender, war, and peace.[9] The first is the essentialist approach. This approach states that women are peace oriented, whereas men are inclined to violence and war. In its most basic form, and based on biological factors, essentialist theorists argue that women are born to be caring, peaceful, and have the natural skill for consensus building.[10] Socialization theories later complemented the biological approach by arguing that in addition to biology, women are socialized in "relational thinking," allowing them to prioritize relationships over competitive and violent behavior.

Essentialist theory has concrete and contradictory consequences for understanding peacebuilding. On one hand, women's image as caring mothers allows them to approach powerful men in a nonthreatening way, but there is also the risk that they won't be taken as seriously as political actors. The case of Liberia illustrates this point. Women from different social and religious backgrounds led a peacebuilding initiative that forced both the government and the rebels to negotiate after a protracted and violent conflict that affected the country for more than five years. The women, however, were excluded from the negotiation table, ultimately undermining their important contributions in their struggle for an end to the violence.[11]

Many contemporary feminist theorists strongly reject the essentialist framework. They claim that it is a simplistic approach that perpetuates unchangeable visions of society that reinforce stereotypes of peace as feminine and militarism as masculine, ignoring the multiple roles men and women adopt in society.[12] Essentialism relies on "simple binary oppositions" and does not reflect the influence that social and cultural structures, as well as individual agency have in shaping gender roles.[13] Moreover, as an analytical framework, essentialism has been used to preserve social inequality by perpetuating unchangeable roles between men and women.[14]

Standpoint feminism is the second central theoretical approach to the study of gender and conflict. This view emphasizes people's experience in war and peace and the roles assigned to men and women. Cynthia Enloe coined the term "gendered phases of war" to illustrate how war affects the politics of marriage, property, sexuality, parenting, and women's access to employment.[15] Moreover, she highlights that for the military to successfully wage war, it must manipulate the understanding of the concepts of femininity and masculinity.[16] For instance, women are often singled out as victims as if they are a homogenous group, ignoring their individual agency and initiative that developed according to their experiences during war. Indeed, Enloe states that war not only affects women and men differently, but also women as individuals develop a variety of responses to conflict as war progresses.[17]

Social structures also define specific roles for women within peacebuilding initiatives. Women are usually expected to be strong community peacebuilders, but not political decision makers or active players in peace negotiations. In addition, women often find more obstacles to organize and develop their own initiatives.[18] Women who are the sole providers in their household face the dilemma to choose between participating in peacebuilding initiatives or to protect and care for their families. This dilemma is more acute in the context of intense violence. In many cases, survival may take priority over peacebuilding.[19] Safety is another major obstacle for women. Women can be targets, not only because of their leadership, but because their individual or group empowerment can be perceived as a direct challenge to traditional patriarchal structures. Perhaps one of the main obstacles women peacebuilders face is that their opinions and contributions are often ignored and minimized.

Neither men nor women are homogenous groups with a unified voice. Men and women are influenced by a variety of factors such as political identities and social and economic background. Within war and peace scenarios, women and men take a variety of roles, including the role of the soldier or the role of peacebuilder, many of which go far beyond predefined stereotypes of victims or passive actors. Although standpoint feminism responds to the gaps of essentialism, neither of these perspectives challenge the theoretical foundation of peacebuilding or its understanding of gender, conflict, and peace. Each fail in challenging the stereotypes of masculinity and femininity, thus contributing to the perpetuation of dominant ideas and practices that exclude women from the political arena.

Despite these criticisms, the essentialist and standpoint frameworks are the rule in international institutions. Based on the analysis of United Nations documents, Hilary Charlesworth identifies several elements that characterize the UN's institutional understanding of women and peace. First, there is an assumption that women are more vulnerable than men but, nevertheless, they are better in the implementation of peacebuilding initiatives. The UN also highlights the need to include women in peace negotiations, although it is not clear whether it is because of their skills and understanding of the conflict or just to keep a formal balance during peace negotiations. Finally, in the UN documents there is a tendency to equate "gender" with women only, without considering how the term is a social construct that includes men.[20]

As a reaction to the criticisms of both essentialist and standpoint feminist perspectives, post-structuralist debates propose a different approach. They require a careful analysis of the dynamics between gender and power and the connections between gender, war, and peace.[21] Post-structuralist feminists argue that women's identities are both self and socially constructed within their context and cannot be reduced to a single truth or ideal.[22] This approach acknowledges the diversity of women's responses to conflict and peace, while "valu[ing] women's lived experiences as a crucial and legitimate form of knowledge."[23] Thus, post-structuralist feminists challenge deep-rooted concepts in gender and peacebuilding, and are critical of strict peacebuilding models that do not consider the context of conflict and its social, political, and cultural particularities. In the context of Peace Studies, post-structuralism represents a change of lenses from a general understanding of war and peace with no gender considerations to an analysis of what Tarja Väyrynen calls the "gendered micropractices of power," that highlight the need to understand how gender is present in the various manifestations of violence and how it influences the construction of peace.[24]

Each of these theoretical perspectives focuses on gender dynamics in conflict and affirms that women's experiences, and contributions to war and peace, are worth studying. That said, a scholar's adherence to one or the other of these feminist perspectives will have a significant impact on their analysis of conflict and peace. Awareness of one's own feminist perspective, as a scholar or practitioner, is essential as it directly influences how an individual understands gender dynamics and the role of women and men in perpetuating war or pursuing peace. Nevertheless, this chapter privileges post-structural feminism as a comprehensive approach that better responds to the challenges that men and women from different social and cultural locations face in experiences of conflict and violence. In the following section we explore the potential as well as the challenges of incorporating a gender perspective in Peace Studies in general, and in peacebuilding in particular.

PEACE STUDIES AND FEMINISM: STRENGTHS AND POSSIBILITIES

Feminist theorists have contributed much scholarship to the analysis of conflict regarding the ways that women are affected by conflict, and the ways that women engage with structures and institutions to promote both peace and conflict. The study of peace and conflict through a gendered or feminist lens allows researchers to ask questions previously unasked, and learn about the gendered dynamics that lead to conflict, occur during conflict, and persist post-conflict.[25] These analyses are critical for uncovering the gendered impact of conflict, as well as examples of agency and strength that exist in communities that are commonly overlooked by traditional approaches to the study of conflict. In this section we highlight the connection between Peace Studies and feminist approaches by focusing on two main areas: peace research and peacebuilding practice.

Catia Confortini suggests that Peace Studies and feminism have much in common and the cooperation between those disciplines is both needed and desirable.[26] Each encourages critical approaches to look at power relations and related conflicts, and focus on identity and human needs. Additionally, they acknowledge the importance of relationships, diversity, and interdependence as well as the importance of historical and cultural differences. Despite this, Peace Studies, as the discipline is commonly framed, remains deficient, failing to properly explore and integrate the role of gender in the social construction of violence and peacebuilding.

Theorists such as Galtung consider gender identity to merely be one of many variables to approach cultural violence. Feminists, on the other hand, argue that gender is not just another variable; it represents a "symbolic process or system" that is the foundation for other processes and systems to operate.[27] Thus, our understanding of the world is based on gendered dichotomies that play an important role in the production and reproduction of power and our understanding of conflict, defining as well our approaches to peace and violence.[28] In this context, gender analysis strengthens Peace Studies by highlighting, questioning, and deconstructing the relations of power that are central to these systems.

A core concept in peacebuilding is the recognition of not only obvious, direct forms of violence, but also the acknowledgment that violence also exists in the margins, and is built into the structures of society. The pursuit of social justice, or *positive* peace, involves addressing physical acts of violence, conflict, and war, as well as the structural inequalities and injustices resulting from unequal access to resources and power.[29] These theories push academics and practitioners to move their focus beyond state-level acts of violence and brinksmanship to the more insidious ways that conflict is sown among and between people, and to critique the structures that allow these forms of violence to flourish.

The concept of structural violence easily lends itself to a feminist analysis of violence and conflict, as well as a more feminist conception of "peace." Feminist examinations of conflict help reveal the violence that is sometimes invisible such as racism, sexism, poverty, and colonialism that are hidden "within the hegemony of ordinariness . . . in the mundane details of everyday life."[30] These forms of oppression are created through gender relations of power and are embedded within various aspects of social organization, including language.[31] Though there are many feminist theories and viewpoints, a feminist conception of "peace" would likely echo Galtung's concept of positive peace, namely, a condition of social justice where there is an absence of both physical violence and the oppressive structures that perpetuate inequality.

To this end, feminist scholars use the theory of intersectionality to explore how aspects of a person's social location, such as their gender, race, class, sexual orientation, and religion among others, inform both their personal experiences as well as their own understanding of their experience. Intersectionality theory explains how the various aspects of a person's identity can either provide them with access to social status and power, or conversely, how theses aspects can limit access to power. A power imbalance can manifest itself as structural violence when it results in harm or unequal life chances to those who lack power.[32] From a feminist perspective, the theory of structural violence helps explain what injustice is, while intersectionality theory explains, through its analysis of the power dynamics related to identity, how injustice is created and experienced.

Used together, these theories provide a basis to understand the underlying gender dynamics in conflict and the interlocking systems that perpetuate gender violence. Gender violence manifests in a variety of ways in different locations and cultural contexts. Microlevel acts of individualized violence are connected with macro-level structural violence and are experienced as social and economic inequality.[33] In conflict and post-conflict situations, women face a variety of abuses including physical violence, sexual violence, and abduction, abuses that are further exacerbated by social and economic inequality. While gender violence and inequality may not be the direct cause of war, it can be a source of insecurity that leads to, or perpetuates, conflict.[34] All people are affected by gender inequality, either through direct experiences of oppression, or indirectly through the destabilizing effect of injustice in a system.

An analysis of the experiences of women who are exposed to direct and structural violence allows for an understanding of the impact of conflict on human security.[35] For both women and men, conflict threatens or restricts access to basic needs including food and shelter, as well as economic and personal security, though these forms of insecurity are, themselves, gendered. Gendered power dynamics and expectations related to behavior and ways of being contribute to the direct and structural violence women experience during and after conflict. By focusing on state-level conceptions of security, conflict, and peace, the reality of everyday violence perpetrated against marginalized groups, including women, is often overlooked, even when these forms of violence escalate as peace processes are underway.[36] Analyses of state security miss these critical areas where conflict and injustice are preserved in structures and enacted against a population when the construction of the "human" in human security is so narrow as to only include the perspectives of a privileged few.[37]

Addressing both direct and structural violence is essential to building a culture of peace. The silence in research and policy making regarding this topic contributes to the power structures that allow these practices and injustices to continue. Oppression experienced by women through direct and structural violence, along with a culture of silence regarding these issues, can lead to disenfranchisement and the internalization of oppression.[38] Addressing these issues in research and practice contributes to the goal of positive peace and social justice.

MOVING TOWARD A TRULY "INTERDISCIPLINARY" APPROACH: FEMINIST AND ANTI-COLONIAL CONTRIBUTIONS

Due to the interdisciplinary nature of the field, Peace Studies draws scholars and theories from a variety of disciplines. Feminist voices and perspectives have long been a part of Peace Studies, and have informed the development of both theory and practice. Despite this, there remains continued concern that while gender analyses are accepted and welcomed within the field, they have not been fully integrated into theoretical and practical approaches to conflict resolution and remain the purview of specifically "feminist" researchers and practitioners.[39] Feminist theories are not only significant for those wishing to study gender violence and conflict, they also direct attention to latent power structures including racism and colonialism that form the basis of conflict and oppression.

Anticolonial and feminist theories have articulated ways that the practice of research and scholarship can serve to perpetuate structural violence through the use of colonizing narratives and unequal power relations, which place researchers and practitioners in privileged positions relative to the subjects of their inquiries. Many peace theorists have integrated grassroots, anticolonial, and indigenous peacebuilding theories into their approaches to the study of conflict and conflict resolution in order to mitigate the deleterious effect of colonizing narratives such as the assumption of universality of the researcher's perspective or worldview.[40] These scholars decolonize their theory and practice by challenging the liberal peace paradigm and other approaches to conflict resolution that are built on the assumptions of Western universality and Western superiority.

Conflict transformation and grassroots peacebuilding approaches are gaining significant attention among peacebuilding theorists and practitioners, mainly as a critical response to the implicitly colonialist dimension of the dominant liberal peace paradigm. Conflict transformation is an approach to conflict analysis and intervention that aims not only to respond to the day-to-day manifestations of conflict, but also to build structures that can support a vision of sustainable peace in the long term.[41]

Within Peace Studies and conflict resolution, theorists such as Oliver Richmond assert that contemporary peacebuilding and peacekeeping initiatives respond to a Western model that privilege "democratization, the rule of law, human rights, free and globalized markets and neo-liberal development," but ignore local processes, actors, and approaches that are pivotal for better analyses and interventions in peacebuilding.[42] Roland Paris asserts that current peacebuilding models resemble colonial interventions that were based on the perceived "duty to 'civilize' dependent populations and territories."[43] These theorists argue that a particular set of Western liberal values is often imposed via international peacebuilding and peacekeeping operations without considering if the country desires, or is ready for, such interventions.

Grassroots peacebuilding theories must be interdisciplinary in order to disrupt these narrow conceptions of peacebuilding that support dominant Western social structures, such as the liberal peace model, in order to address the roots of conflict and meet the needs of marginalized populations. Approaches such as conflict transformation and Alternative Dispute Resolution (ADR) focus on rebuilding relationships and are situated at the grassroots level with the aim of building sustainable peace and social justice.[44] These initiatives are intended to support, rather than replace or impose upon the work that is already being done by local organizations in the development and implementation of peacebuilding projects.

The focus on grassroots models of peacebuilding in peace literature follows an important tenet of current feminist theory that holds that outsiders are not the "experts" in a community, and that change must be driven from within. Audre Lorde shook mainstream white feminism with her analysis of the underlying racism in the movement in her essay, *The Master's Tools Will Never Dismantle the Master's House*.[45] Western scholars and practitioners of peacebuilding are similarly confronted with the realization that their practice, rooted in their own culture and worldview, has significant colonialist implications, and can, indeed, be quite harmful, rather than helpful. Dominant social structures will by nature support the status quo and maintain the power imbalance that is at the root of all structural violence.[46] To counter the colonialist narrative, the processes and even language of peace must be conceived at the grassroots level, grounded in the experiences of those affected by conflict.

As a movement, feminism has a long and painful history in confronting the racist and colonialist implications of its academic foundation and practice. Critical theories within feminism have called out the oppressive structures and beliefs that are supported by mainstream feminists that contribute to the further marginalization of numerous populations. These theories speak to the same prejudices and challenges that are embedded within the liberal-peace model of peacebuilding and conflict resolution, and can be used to further inform a decolonized peacebuilding practice.

Critical theories in feminism problematize the erasure of difference in mainstream feminist analyses of violence and oppression. While women around the world are faced with a variety of oppressions, it is a mistake to assume that women ascribe similar meanings to their experiences. One of the tendencies of Western feminist scholarship is the imagining of women as a category of analysis, united in the common oppression of patriarchal institutions and systems.[47] The assumption of commonality or universality of oppression based on gender "is problematic, based as it is on the assumption that the categories of race and class have to be invisible for gender to be visible."[48] It is context, history, meaning, and the intersection of different aspects of identity that lend significance to women's experiences.[49] Rather than uniting women in the cause of eliminating gendered violence, the notion of the universal experience of oppression erases the specificities of the experiences of marginalized women, and hides the various structures that work in concert to oppress women and men around the world.

A belief in the universality of oppression may lead to a binary understanding of the world where Western women have the agency and capacity to resist oppression, whereas women in other countries or places do not.[50] These assumptions promote a reductive understanding of identity, meaning, and agency and are not conducive to a deep, thoughtful analysis of power structures or methods of resistance.[51] These assumptions may also contribute to the idea that Western women are positioned to "save" or "liberate" the passive Third World victim of oppression, denying their agency and historical and ongoing activism.[52] While these subtle acts of colonialism may be cloaked in good intentions and the desire for empowerment, they serve to sustain the structures that promote conflict, oppression, and marginalization.

Women are not passive recipients of oppression and violence, but actively resist oppression and engage in peacebuilding. Gendered dynamics shape both the context of conflict and violence, as well as the meanings associated with gender roles and the construction of identity.[53] Recognition of women's agency, despite or due to experiences of trauma, leads one to complicate their view of so-called vulnerable populations. They are not merely victims requiring services, nor warriors without emotional or psychological needs. They are community activists, frontline workers, mothers, wives, negotiators, and a host of other identities, all of whom are affected by violence and conflict in different ways, and who work to promote change within their communities.

These key feminist contributions to the study of conflict and violence can further help shape Peace Studies and peacebuilding as holistic, interdisciplinary endeavors that consider the gendered consequences of violence, as well as the power structures that allow injustices to persist over time. These analyses influenced by feminist and anticolonial theories are not only significant for studying the specific impact of violence on women, but should be integrated into the foundation of scholarly and practical applications. The focus on structural violence, as well as the recognition of the knowledge and agency of those affected by conflict and oppression, allows peacebuilders to address the colonial and oppressive narratives that can seep into the methodological framework of research and practice.

METHODOLOGIES FOR EMPOWERMENT: "PEACEFUL" APPROACHES TO RESEARCH

Utilizing a combination of feminist, anticolonial, and peace scholarship is helpful in positioning oneself as a researcher who is focused on empowerment. To be a student, scholar, or practitioner of Peace Studies, one must make a conscious and consistent effort to consider the ways that their worldview and biases shape their work in the field, and how they may have unforeseen consequences for those whom they are purporting to help. Recognizing the implicitly imperialist undercurrents of perspectives and assumptions can be seen as personally threatening, yet this process has the potential to "invigorat[e] and transfor[m] the practice of feminist theory and research" and lends significance and depth to scholarship.[54] Grounding scholarship in methodologies that elevate the importance of empowerment and voice is central to this process.

Methodologies such as feminist, anticolonial theories, participatory action research, and narrative inquiry strive to be in tune with issues surrounding power, voice, and inequality in the construction of knowledge and research. The idea of the "objective researcher" is questioned, in favor of acknowledging the social construction of knowledge and the biases and assumptions that are implicit in the worldviews of the researcher and researched.[55] In a scholar-activist approach, as seen in Lederach's elicitive model, "cross-cultural and cross-experience exchanges" can lead to mutual learning through empowerment and respect.[56] A feminist methodology aims to consider power dynamics and the social location of both the participants and the researcher with the ultimate goal of confronting inequality and oppression.[57] This approach not only favors the voices of the participants, but also connects the study with the importance of storytelling to Peace Studies.[58]

Central to a mutual learning approach is the inclusion of participants in the creation of knowledge. This is achieved by showing respect for the participants' knowledge and perspective, and ensuring that their voices are accurately interpreted and represented. An important contribution of feminist methodology is the acknowledgment that the researcher has a particular worldview or epistemology that may not be shared by those participating in the research.[59] This recognition ultimately shapes the questions asked, what is understood as "fact" or "knowledge," along with conclusions drawn from the research. Storytelling and critical reflection, as well as sharing and owning knowledge with the participants, can form a collaborative approach that minimizes misperception and misrepresentation.[60] This approach allows the researcher to conceive of themselves as a student or learner, rather than expert, and the participants as "theorists of their own everyday lives."[61]

Participatory Action Research (PAR) is another research methodology that involves the community in the process of knowledge creation. Unlike traditional research methodologies, PAR ensures that communities and scholars work together to analyze the reality of the community and design concrete actions toward change and transformation.[62] As a methodological approach, PAR encourages settings where relationships are created and nurtured, empowering people to actively participate in decision-making processes. As a result, participants feel more committed to a process because they own it from its inception.

Methods such as narrative inquiry allow the researcher to capture the complexity of the participant's experiences and their perceptions of the challenges and strengths that exist in their communities. The focus of feminist and anticolonial methodologies involves elevating respect for the participant's voice, rather than the researcher's interpretation of their story. The researcher conducts their analysis of these stories and statements, and evaluates this interpretation in consultation with the participants.[63] This is a holistic approach that promotes an emancipatory, empowering experience as a part of participation in research, rather than a disinterested gathering of "facts."[64] These methods and methodologies connect the process of conducting research with critical theories such as feminism and anticolonial theory that inform the practice and interrogate the oppressive structures that contribute to conflict. These approaches and methodologies will not eliminate the oppressive qualities of cross-cultural study, though, if utilized deftly, they may mitigate some of the impact of a power imbalance.

CONCLUSION: PURSUING PEACE THROUGH FEMINIST ANALYSES OF CONFLICT

"Mainstreaming" feminist and anticolonial theories and methodologies into the theoretical framework of Peace Studies and peacebuilding is a way for scholars and practitioners to live the practice in pursuit of not only peace for some, but *positive* peace for all. These perspectives can be highly complementary to each other and assist in identifying the outcomes related to conflict, as well as the structures that promote conflict and allow it to persist, often undetected or unrecognized over long periods. These structures and forms of violence persist, in part, due to unrecognized privilege and power structures that benefit the few over the many.

Students of Peace Studies can confront these oppressive structures by making a conscious effort to incorporate perspectives that are outside their own in their analysis of conflict and violence. Consideration of the way that conflict affects women and marginalized populations, as well as acknowledgment of their own experiences and agency, is part of this approach. Incorporating, or "mainstreaming" feminist and anticolonial theories and methodologies for research into the foundation of *all* analyses of conflict and peacebuilding, regardless of whether or not the subject of inquiry is overtly related to gender, would focus peace research on social justice, and the complexities of oppression. Through these means, scholars can develop theories and practical approaches for the transformation and resolution of conflict, while maintaining their focus on positive peace, peace for all.

NOTES

1. Portions of this paper have been drawn from Lisa McLean's unpublished Master's thesis, 2013.
2. Craig Zelizer and Valerie Oliphant, Introduction to *Integrated Peacebuilding: Innovative Approaches to Transforming Conflict*, ed. Craig Zelizer (Boulder, CO: Westview, 2013), 4.
3. Thania Paffenholz, ed. *Civil Society and Peacebuilding: A Critical Assessment* (Boulder, CO: Lynne Rienner), 44.
4. Boutros Boutros-Ghali, "Agenda for Peace: Preventive Diplomacy, Peacemaking and Peace-Keeping" (New York, NY: United Nations, 1992).
5. Lisa Schirch and Manjrika Sewak, "Women: Using the Gender Lens," in *People Building Peace II: Successful Stories of Civil Society*, ed. Paul van Tongeren et al. (Boulder, CO: Lynne Rienner, 2005), 98.
6. John Paul Lederach, *Building Peace: Sustainable Reconciliation in Divided Societies* (Washington, DC: United States Institute of Peace, 1997), 20.
7. Zelizer, *Integrated Peacebuilding*, 4.
8. Elizabeth J. Porter, *Peacebuilding: Women in International Perspective*, vol. 60 of *Routledge Advances in International Relations and Politics* (New York, NY: Routledge, 2007).
9. Tarja Väyrynen, "Gender and Peacebuilding," in *Palgrave Advances in Peacebuilding: Critical Developments and Approaches*, ed. Oliver P. Richmond (New York, NY: Palgrave Macmillan, 2010).
10. Ibid., 142.
11. John Paul Lederach and Angela Jill Lederach, *When Blood and Bones Cry Out: Journeys through the Soundscape of Healing and Reconciliation* (Brisbane, Australia: University of Queensland Press, 2010), 30.
12. Väyrynen, "Gender and Peacebuilding," 142.
13. Ibid., 143.
14. Hilary Charlesworth, "Are Women Peaceful? Reflections on the Role of Women in Peace-Building," *Feminist Legal Studies* 16.3 (2008): 349.
15. Cynthia Enloe, *Nimo's War, Emma's War: Making Feminist Sense of the Iraq War* (Berkley, CA: University of California Press, 2010), 5.
16. Ibid.

17. Ibid.

18. Väyrynen, "Gender and Peacebuilding," 143–44.

19. Lederach, *Building Peace*, 42.

20. Charlesworth, "Are Women Peaceful?" 351.

21. Väyrynen, "Gender and Peacebuilding."

22. Christine Sylvester, *Feminist International Relations: An Unfinished Journey* (New York, NY: Cambridge University Press, 2002), 177.

23. Tami Amanda Jacoby, *Women in Zones of Conflict: Power and Resistance in Israel* (Kingston, ON: McGill-Queen's University Press, 2005), 22–23.

24. Väyrynen, "Gender and Peacebuilding," 145.

25. Enloe, *Nimo's War, Emma's War*, 8–9.

26. Catia C. Confortini, "Galtung, Violence, and Gender: The Case for a Peace Studies/Feminism Alliance," *Peace & Change* 31.3 (2006).

27. Ibid., 339.

28. Ibid., 333.

29. Johan Galtung, "Violence, Peace, and Peace Research," *Journal of Peace Research* 6.3 (1969).

30. Sally Engle Merry, *Gender Violence: A Cultural Perspective* (Malden, MA: Wiley-Blackwell, 2009), 5.

31. Confortini, "Galtung, Violence, and Gender," 356.

32. Galtung, "Violence, Peace, and Peace Research"; Barbara H. Chasin, *Inequality and Violence in the United States: Casualties of Capitalism*, 2nd ed. (Amherst, MA: Humanity Books, 2004).

33. Merry, *Gender Violence*, 2, 19.

34. Ghada Moussa, "Gender Aspects of Human Security," *International Social Science Journal* 59.1 (2008): 81.

35. Betty A. Reardon, "Women and Human Security: A Feminist Framework and Critique of the Prevailing Patriarchal Security System," in *The Gender Imperative: Human Security vs State Security*, ed. Betty A. Reardon and Asha Hans (New York, NY: Routledge, 2010), 11.

36. Gabrielle Eva Carol Groves, Bernadette P. Resurreccion, and Phillippe Doneys, "Keeping the Peace is Not Enough: Human Security and Gender-based Violence during the Transitional Period of Timor-Leste," *Journal of Social Issues in Southeast Asia* 24.2 (2009).

37. Natasha Marhia, "Some Humans are More *Human* than Others: Troubling the 'Human' in Human Security from a Critical Feminist Perspective," *Security Dialogue* 44.1 (2013).

38. Merry, *Gender Violence*, 22.

39. Ingrid Sandole-Staroste, "Gender Mainstreaming: A Valuable Tool in Building Sustainable Peace," in *Handbook of Conflict Analysis and Resolution*, ed. Dennis J. D. Sandole et al. (New York, NY: Routledge, 2011), 235.

40. Polly O. Walker, "Decolonizing Conflict Resolution: Addressing the Ontological Violence of Westernization," *Cooperation and Conflict: Journal of the Nordic International Studies Association* 43.2 (2004); Roger Mac Ginty, "Indigenous Peace-Making Versus the Liberal Peace," *Cooperation and Conflict: Journal of the Nordic International Studies Association* 43.2 (2008).

41. John Paul Lederach, *Preparing for Peace: Conflict Transformation across Cultures* (Syracuse, NY: Syracuse University Press, 1995).

42. Oliver P. Richmond, "The Problem of Peace: Understanding the 'Liberal Peace,'" *Conflict, Security & Development* 6.3 (2006): 292.

43. Roland Paris, *At War's End: Building Peace after Civil Conflict* (Cambridge, England: Cambridge University Press, 2004), 637.

44. Mac Ginty, *Indigenous Peace-Making*.

45. Audre Lorde, *Sister Outsider: Essays and Speeches by Audre Lorde* (Berkeley, CA: Crossing Press, 1984).

46. Mary B. Anderson, *Do No Harm: How Aid can Support Peace or War* (Boulder, CO: Lynne Rienner, 1999).

47. Chandra Talpade Mohanty, *Feminism without Borders: Decolonizing Theory, Practicing Solidarity* (Durham, NC: Duke University Press, 2003), 22; Merry, *Gender Violence*, 15.

48. Mohanty, *Feminism without Borders*, 107.

49. Merry, *Gender Violence*, 13.

50. Mohanty, *Feminism without Borders*, 31.

51. Ibid.

52. Melanie Butler, "Canadian Women and the (Re)production of Women in Afghanistan," *Cambridge Review of International Affairs* 22.2 (2009).

53. Enloe, *Nimo's War, Emma's War*, 57–58.

54. Sharlene Hesse-Biber, Christina Gilmartin, and Robin Lydenberg, Introduction to *Feminist Approaches to Theory and Methodology*, ed. Sharlene Hesse-Biber, Christina Gilmartin, and Robin Lydenberg (New York, NY: Oxford University Press, 1999), 5.

55. Andrew C. Okolie, "Toward an Anti-racist Research Framework: The Case for Interventive In-depth Interviewing," in *Critical Issues in Anti-Racist Research Methodologies*, ed. George J. Sefa Dei and Gurpreet Singh Johal (New York, NY: Peter Lang, 2005), 242.

56. Lederach, *Preparing for Peace*, 67.

57. Brooke Ackerly and Jacqui True, *Doing Feminist Research in Political and Social Science* (London, England: Palgrave Macmillan, 2010), 2.

58. Jessica Senehi, "Building Peace: Storytelling to Transform Conflicts Constructively," in *Handbook of Conflict Analysis and Resolution*, ed. Dennis J. D. Sandole et al. (New York, NY: Routledge, 2011).

59. Ackerly and True, *Doing Feminist Research*, 25.

60. Karen Max, "Anti-colonial Research: Working as an Ally with Aboriginal Peoples," in *Critical Issues in Anti-Racist Research Methodologies*, ed. George J. Sefa Dei and Gurpreet Singh Johal (New York, NY: Peter Lang, 2005), 87; Ackerly and True, *Doing Feminist Research*, 257.

61. George J. Sefa Dei, Introduction to *Critical Issues in Anti-Racist Research Methodologies*, ed. George J. Sefa Dei and Gurpreet Singh Johal (New York, NY: Peter Lang, 2005), 5–6.

62. Davydd J. Greenwood and Morten Levin, Introduction to *Action Research: Social Research for Social Change* (Thousand Oaks, CA: Sage, 2007).

63. Ackerly and True, *Doing Feminist Research*, 189.

64. Okolie, *Anti-racist Research Framework*, 249.

BIBLIOGRAPHY

Ackerly, Brooke and Jacqui True. *Doing Feminist Research in Political and Social Science*. London, England: Palgrave Macmillan, 2010.

Anderson, Mary B. *Do No Harm: How Aid can Support Peace or War*. Boulder, CO: Lynne Rienner, 1999.

Butler, Melanie. "Canadian Women and the (Re)production of Women in Afghanistan." *Cambridge Review of International Affairs* 22.2 (2009): 217–34.

Charlesworth, Hilary. "Are Women Peaceful? Reflections on the Role of Women in Peace-Building." *Femist Legal Studies* 16.3 (2008): 347–61.

Chasin, Barbara H. *Inequality and Violence in the United States: Casualties of Capitalism.* 2nd ed. Amherst, MA: Humanity Books, 2004.

Confortini, Catia C. "Galtung, Violence, and Gender: The Case for a Peace Studies/ Feminism Alliance." *Peace & Change* 31.3 (2006): 333–67.

Dei, George J. Sefa. Introduction to *Critical Issues in Anti-Racist Research Methodologies*, edited by George J. Sefa Dei and Gurpreet Singh Johal, 1–27. New York, NY: Peter Lang, 2005.

Enloe, Cynthia. *Nimo's War, Emma's War: Making Feminist Sense of the Iraq War*. Berkeley, CA: University of California Press, 2010.

Galtung, Johan. "Violence, Peace, and Peace Research." *Journal of Peace Research* 6.3 (1969): 167–91.

Ghali, Boutros Boutros. "An Agenda for Peace: Preventive Diplomacy, Peacemaking and Peace-Keeping." New York, NY: United Nations, 1992.

Greenwood, Davydd J. and Morten Levin. Introduction to *Action Research: Social Research for Social Change*. Thousand Oaks, CA: Sage, 2007.

Groves, Gabrielle Eva Carol, Bernadette P. Resurreccion, and Phillippe Doneys. "Keeping the Peace is Not Enough: Human Security and Gender-based Violence during the Transitional Period of Timor-Leste." *Journal of Social Issues in Southeast Asia* 24.2 (2009): 186–210.

Hesse-Biber, Sharlene, Christina Gilmartin, and Robin Lydenberg. Introduction to *Feminist Approaches to Theory and Methodology: An Interdisciplinary Reader*, edited by Sharlene Hesse-Biber, Christina Gilmartin, and Robin Lydenberg, 1–14. New York, NY: Oxford University Press, 1999.

Jacoby, Tami Amanda. *Women in Zones of Conflict: Power and Resistance in Israel.* Kingston, ON: McGill-Queen's University Press, 2005.

Lederach, John Paul. *Building Peace: Sustainable Reconciliation in Divided Societies*. Washington, DC: United States Institute of Peace, 1997.

———. *Preparing for Peace: Conflict Transformation across Cultures*. Syracuse, NY: Syracuse University Press, 1995.

Lederach, John Paul and Angela Jill Lederach. *When Blood and Bones Cry Out: Journeys through the Soundscape of Healing and Reconciliation*. Brisbane, Australia: University of Queensland Press, 2010.

Lorde, Audre. *Sister Outsider: Essays and Speeches by Audre Lorde*. Berkeley, CA: Crossing Press, 1984.

Mac Ginty, Roger. "Indigenous Peace-Making Versus the Liberal Peace." *Cooperation and Conflict: Journal of the Nordic International Studies Association* 43.2 (2008): 139–63.

Marhia, Natasha. "Some Humans are more *Human* than Others: Troubling the 'Human' in Human Security from a Critical Feminist Perspective." *Security Dialogue* 44.1 (2013): 19–35.

Max, Karen. "Anti-colonial Research: Working as an Ally with Aboriginal Peoples." In *Critical Issues in Anti-Racist Research Methodologies*, edited by George J. Sefa Dei and Gurpreet Singh Johal, 79–94. New York, NY: Peter Lang, 2005.

Merry, Sally Engle. *Gender Violence: A Cultural Perspective*. Malden, MA: Wiley-Blackwell, 2009.

Mohanty, Chandra Talpade. *Feminism without Borders: Decolonizing Theory, Practicing Solidarity*. Durham, NC: Duke University Press, 2003.

Moussa, Ghada. "Gender Aspects of Human Security." *International Social Science Journal* 59.1 (2008): 81–100.

Okolie, Andrew C. "Toward an Anti-racist Research Framework: The Case for Interventive In-depth Interviewing." In *Critical Issues in Anti-Racist Research Methodologies*, edited by George J. Sefa Dei and Gurpreet Singh Johal, 241–67. New York, NY: Peter Lang, 2005.

Paffenholz, Thania, ed. *Civil Society and Peacebuilding: A Critical Assessment*. Boulder, CO: Lynne Rienner, 2010.

Paris, Roland. *At War's End: Building Peace after Civil Conflict*. Cambridge, England: Cambridge University Press, 2004.

Porter, Elizabeth J. *Peacebuilding: Women in International Perspective*, vol. 60 of *Routledge Advances in International Relations and Global Politics*. New York, NY: Routledge, 2007.

Reardon, Betty A. "Women and Human Security: A Feminist Framework and Critique of the Prevailing Patriarchal Security System." In *The Gender Imperative: Human Security vs State Security*, edited by Betty A. Reardon and Asha Hans, 7–37. New York, NY: Routledge, 2010.

Richmond, Oliver P. "The Problem of Peace: Understanding the 'Liberal Peace.'" *Conflict, Security & Development* 6.3 (2006): 291–314.

Sandole-Staroste, Ingrid. "Gender Mainstreaming: A Valuable Tool in Building Sustainable Peace." In *Handbook of Conflict Analysis and Resolution*, edited by Dennis J. D. Sandole, Sean Byrne, Ingrid Sandole-Staroste, and Jessica Senehi, 226–40. New York, NY: Routledge, 2011.

Schirch, Lisa and Manjrika Sewak. "Women: Using the Gender Lens." In *People Building Peace II: Successful Stories of Civil Society*, edited by Paul van Tongeren, Malin Brenk, Marte Hellema, and Juliette Verhoeven, 97–107. Boulder, CO: Lynne Rienner, 2005.

Senehi, Jessica. "Building Peace: Storytelling to Transform Conflicts Constructively." In *Handbook of Conflict Analysis and Resolution*, edited by Dennis J. D. Sandole, Sean Byrne, Ingrid Sandole-Staroste, and Jessica Senehi, 201–14. New York, NY: Routledge, 2011.

Sylvester, Christine. *Feminist International Relations: An Unfinished Journey*. New York, NY: Cambridge University Press, 2002.

Väyrynen, Tarja. "Gender and Peacebuilding." In *Palgrave Advances in Peacebuilding: Critical Developments and Approaches*, edited by Oliver P. Richmond, 137–53. New York, NY: Palgrave Macmillan, 2010.

Walker, Polly O. "Decolonizing Conflict Resolution: Addressing the Ontological Violence of Westernization." *Cooperation and Conflict: Journal of the Nordic International Studies Association* 43.2 (2004): 527–49.

Zelizer, Craig and Valerie Oliphant. Introduction to *Integrated Peacebuilding: Innovative Approaches to Transforming Conflict*, edited by Craig Zelizer, 3–30. Boulder, CO: Westview, 2013.

Chapter 18

Cultural Violence and Gender

Peacebuilding via Peace Education

Katerina Standish

Sustainable peace requires a civilization to forge and maintain long-term nonviolent relationships.[1] These relationships need to be fostered and fed at all levels of society from the agents of the state to the individual child. What Johan Galtung terms positive peace—equitable and harmonious relationships—is much more than a cessation of violence (negative peace) but a constructive societal configuration where conflict is resolved nonviolently and facets of culture that legitimize violence are eradicated.[2]

Peacebuilding refers to both intervention strategies that attempt to lessen the impact of violence through problem-solving policies and the academic field that analyzes and theorizes peacebuilding from both liberal and critical perspectives.[3] While a variety of ideological positions exist within peacebuilding literature, recent scholars have taken a critical turn and examined the role of power in peacebuilding.[4] This has resulted in a bifurcated analytical platform in peacebuilding—programs that illuminate the ineffectiveness of social systems (social paradigm critique) and programs interested in resolving social dilemmas (problem solving). Peace education is a form of peacebuilding that straddles both positions—social critique and problem solving. As both an ideological and instrumental pursuit, peace education teaches us how to recognize violence, act nonviolently and work toward positive peace.[5] Because all human behaviors are gendered—containing differing expectations of behavior for the sexes—peace education is well-positioned to address forms of cultural violence that relate to gender (discrimination, hierarchy, violence against women) because education, as a form of secondary socialization, helps to create society; a society socialized toward gender equality delegitimizes gender-based violence (GBV) and does not tolerate violence against women and girls (VAW).[6] The following chapter explores the concepts of cultural violence, GBV and strategies that struggle against these and other forms of social/cultural violence—peacebuilding and peace education.

CULTURAL VIOLENCE

Violence can be direct (physical), indirect (structural) or cultural (symbolic),[7] and individuals, institutions, or societies perpetrate violence.[8] Some forms of violence are considered the result of violent agents and other types of violence may be the consequence of social inequalities or discrimination. When someone uses force against someone else it is a form of direct violence whereas institutionalized discrimination based on age, sex, gender, race, or ability is considered a form of indirect violence. Cultural violence is a form of violence that makes other incarnations of harm possible and colors the morality of an act "from red/wrong to green/right or at least to yellow/acceptable."[9] With the exception of mental pathologies, most forms of direct and indirect violence can be rooted in the emblematic spheres of culture including: religion, science, language, media, and education. Put simply, cultural violence can make other forms of violence permissible.

Galtung's theory of cultural violence requires investigating cultural elements to "show how [they] can, empirically or potentially, be used to legitimize direct or structural violence."[10] In cultural violence—all of which is symbolic—cultural facets can act to legitimize direct and structural violence using symbols, narratives, imagery and censorship—a deliberate erasure of information.[11] When we look for cultural violence in society we need to ask "does this cultural aspect lead to physical or structural violence?" And when we find incarnations of cultural violence we can assume that at least some parts of society hold, perform, and transmit those values to others.

GENDER AND GENDER-BASED VIOLENCE DURING CONFLICT

Gender is a socially constructed[12] behavioral expectation of the sexes.[13] Because gender refers to communal understandings and constructions of behavior based on sex—it is "deeply embedded in systems of kinship, religion, warfare and nationalism."[14] And, although gender is something that is socially transmitted it is more than something that we humans learn, "it is something that we *do*"[15] as a cultural act (italics in original).[16]

GBV[17] is aggression that targets individuals from a particular gender,[18] either individually or in groups.[19] GBV exists in many facets of daily living and is present in pre-conflict, in-conflict, post-conflict and tranquil nations. There is a critical connection between gender[20] and conflict (especially violent conflict) because conflict is a highly gendered social activity.[21] The expressions and expectations of gender during conflict are simplified and mobilized[22] to motivate men and women into so-called natural roles (warrior male, victim female) and even if this acts to make gender more visible it may also "leave it unquestioned."[23] Leaving gender unquestioned makes many forms of cultural violence invisible, making direct and indirect incarnations of violence permissible.

Equality is difficult—in nontraditional cultures inequality is seen as unequal access to power and status for men and women[24] and in more "traditional" cultures gendered forms of cultural violence become "customary"—rooted in history and myth and using folklore as a rationale to subordinate women.[25] One common rationale for the subordination of women is the ideology of nationalism—the imagined and entitled autonomy of a people.[26] Nationalism has both civic and ethnic incarnations but both are tied to twentieth century notions of self-determination.[27] Self-determination is an ideal that each distinct people should be able to self-govern and indeed, proposes that each group or nation should have his or her own country. Nationalism, as a social and cultural force, is highly gendered,[28] intrinsically linked to notions of manhood[29] and routinely supportive of stereotypes that prescribe manly behavior for men while simultaneously limiting women's full participation in society.[30]

Females experience violence (direct, indirect and cultural) in every culture in the world but during conflict there are particular expectations of maleness or femaleness that have lead numerous scholars to point out that regardless of whatever gender norms existed pre-conflict, during conflict gender becomes essentialized[31]—women become symbols to protect and men become warriors to protect them.[32] This communal "nationalist" or "ethnic" solidarity transfers a political identity to a whole group of people (*ethnie*) who become conceptualized as an extended family.[33] Because most GBV happens in the home when the "nation" becomes an extension of the home this means that intervening to stop GBV can involve much cultural resistance—changing how gender is performed in society means addressing the symbolic foundations of gender identity and, under stress, those foundations become very fortified.

Militarized Masculinity, Patriarchy and Gender

In both military and paramilitary groups gender categories become powerful constructs[34] affecting the social and political status of women.[35] In organized aggression (either national, ethnic, or insurgent) masculinity can become militarized[36] "hyper-masculine, hegemonic . . . [a] stoic, strong, and emotionless warrior, who is willing to engage in violence when ordered to."[37] Militarized masculinity refers to the social construction of maleness, manhood, manliness, and power for men as well as the femininity, womanliness, powerlessness, and subordination of women to manly (soldier) men. Militaries are a form of patriarchy and despite numerous instances of women warriors, fighters and paramilitaries,[38] militaries (and paramilitaries) remain bastions of male privilege and prestige.

Patriarchies are cultures that hold men (generally older men) in dominant hierarchal positions over younger males and females.[39] Male and masculine supremacies in social, economic, political, and cultural spheres of life are incarnations of patriarchy and often include traditional practices that are harmful for women and girls because females are considered "less valuable" in society.[40] Modern human rights standards delegitimize "traditional" cultural practices that subordinate women and perceive resistance to the "universality" of human rights as a way to maintain "patriarchal privileges."[41] Although the scope of this chapter does not allow for an in-depth exploration of the connection between patriarchy and gendered forms of violence, it can be said that women's social subordination in both "human-rights-based" and "traditional" societies "has historically been exacerbated by the obstacles women face in gaining literacy, reproductive control, health care, and both economic and political agency."[42] When women are considered less than men it is a form of control and discrimination that relies upon complex cultural constructs. Because sexism "like racism is a belief system rooted in a worldview that [assigns] varying levels of worth to different groups of human beings"[43] then facing sexism means changing culture. Changing less to equal, for everyone, means making visible facets of culture that may legitimize gendered subservience. As a social project, such cultural transformation is incomplete in every country in the world.

The term patriarchy can be considered a *carte blanche* declaration that overall (and all over) women are the victims of cultural subordination. This is untrue. That there are patriarchal structures (should one be struggling to imagine one perhaps a picture of most of the attendees at the latest G20 summit would suffice) is not under review here but it should be mentioned that there are many global incarnations of gender equality and multiple instances of genuine local female power (e.g., the clan mothers in the Iroquois Confederacy). This chapter examines the connection between the role of cultural violence and gender as a symbolic support for concrete disadvantages and particular social incarnations of power and powerlessness based on gender. The next section illuminates the art and act of peacebuilding and the importance of gender in building peace.

PEACEBUILDING

Peacebuilding can be conceived of as actions (programs or projects) and intentions (ideas and initiatives) that are fashioned to cease or modify violent conflict.[44] The majority of peacebuilding enterprises are ideologically liberal (holding the assumption that human society can be somehow improved), designed in the Global North for use in the Global South[45] and are used in a post-conflict setting (often after events of mass violence).

Temporality, Spatiality and Performance in Peacebuilding

Peacebuilding occurs along a continuum of conflict and peace. Traditionally utilized in post-conflict settings—after peacemaking and peacekeeping—peacebuilding is becoming increasingly correlated with the prevention of hostility and societal transformation.[46] While traditional peacebuilding was interested in processes that supported the economic recovery, political reconciliation, and security reform of post-conflict states, contemporary peacebuilding prioritizes social outcomes valid in tranquil nations as well.[47]

Building peace is not solely the work of societies that have recently emerged from violent conflict but "entails building the political conditions for a sustainable, democratic peace" in any nation.[48] The time of peace is anytime,[49] before, during, or after conflict, and more and more is it perceived that peacebuilding is a preventive project that aims to counter violence before it begins.[50] The place of peace is anywhere: spaces exist (in person and in cyber-space) for individuals, groups, and nations to occupy[51] in ways that foster vibrant and creative social spaces of engagement and support the creation of institutional, mediatory, and resolutory processes.[52] Peace can be done in any setting and by anyone. We mostly act in ways we have been conditioned to behave and how we perform[53] life and interact with one another[54] become ways of living and being that are examples for others.

In this way, peacebuilding is conceptualized as something that happens in an array of conflict temporalities—taking place in both contemporary and utopian time—something that exists in a variety of spatial incarnations (relational spaces), and something that is performed (not just imagined but done) in a variety of social locations and involving diverse actors.

Peacebuilding and Gender

Post-conflict peacebuilding, like all components of society, is a gendered pursuit. Despite the recognition that gender impacts both the experiences of conflict (and post-conflict development) women continue to hold a marginalized position in peace processes, reconstruction, transitional justice, and decision making.[55] Until conventional peacebuilding models incorporate and implement full "gender mainstreaming" peacebuilding proposals routinely duplicate existing gender inequalities.

> This situation points to the need to explore the ways in which (re) building peace may (re) construct gendered forms of domination, injustice and insecurity in transitional societies, rather than empowering women (and marginalized men) to achieve political, economic and social transformation in the aftermath of war.[56]

Post-conflict peacebuilding that ignores how gender impacts human needs are inconsiderate and can make existing emancipatory pursuits more difficult to realize.

A peacebuilding initiative is an intervention—an action, taken by an outside agent that introduces elements that impose either values or configurations to affect change.[57] An intervention is a transformative tool or technique that either contributes to empowerment or decreases aggression.[58]

> The challenge for contemporary peacebuilders is not only to understand how the construction of hierarchical gender roles and identities is entangled in conflict—in its emergence, escalation, de-escalation and settlement—but also how to make use of the transformative potential of peacebuilding processes . . . in ways that contest rather than reaffirm gendered inequalities and exclusions.[59]

Interventions that do not take gender into account often face the possibility that the "change" they affect will result in harm to women.

POST-CONFLICT FEMINIST RESPONSES

There are (during conflict), four feminist responses to GBV: universal rights responses, women as peacemaker's responses, diversity responses, and critical responses. The first incarnation utilizes various multilateral and international instruments such as the UN Gender mainstreaming platform[60] or the Convention for the Elimination of All Forms of Discrimination Against Women[61] to support the full incorporation of women into peacebuilding, social justice, and security. These rights-based approaches maintain that women must have full and meaningful participation in all social spheres—particularly in pre- and post-conflict settings.[62] The second approach utilizes the female propensity for care[63] and building positive reciprocal relationships.[64] This approach posits that women are socialized into more nurturing, protective, and maternal behavior and that adding "women's voices and experiences to peace processes and postwar institutions"[65] will result in the "nurturing of peaceful relationships and in militarism being challenged, making peace more likely to be sustainable."[66] The third response highlights the global diversity of female understandings and the importance of recognizing the differences that exist—not only between the genders—but also among women themselves.[67] Women of color, women in the developing world, and women who identify with the experience of domination and discrimination critique the singular standpoint of the "feminine peacemaker" construction and suggest exploring the role of gender from multiple standpoints.[68] A fourth position regarding the role of gender and building peace can be termed critical because it posits that the mere addition of women to peace processes does not challenge the hegemonies of liberal peacebuilding adequately; "while the UN has embraced gender mainstreaming in peacekeeping missions, it has also silenced more radical questions that feminists have raised such as the deployment of peacekeeping forces and performances of militarized masculinities in post-conflict settings."[69]

These feminist responses show how critical it is to illuminate gender when seeking to contribute to positive peace. For peacebuilders, making gender visible means recognizing that female experiences are critical to understanding how, where, and when building peace should occur. We are becoming more aware that conflict zones are particularly dangerous places to be women[70] and we need to understand that making gender visible delegitimizes the othering[71] of women based on their gender to make relational spaces for all genders.

PEACE EDUCATION

A fundamental form of peacebuilding, peace education is geared toward the identification of violence, learning and utilizing nonviolent alternatives and strategizing peace. It is a critical component of building peace. Peace education encompasses a number of different practices and pursuits that foster peaceful behavior, attitudes and values,[72] and it can occur anywhere along the conflict and peace continuum.[73] Peace education utilizes learning to instill values and attitudes in participants and educands.[74] Peace education is an academic subfield of PACS that locates forms of violence in schools and utilizes both formal and informal learning to investigate and transform negative attitudes and beliefs about others.[75] Practitioners of peace education use organized learning to share methods of nonviolent conflict resolution and other peace-abilities such as respect for the environment, gender equality, and nonviolent social, cultural, and political transformation.[76]

Transmission Belts

Education is a forum for the intergenerational transmission of values, attitudes, and beliefs.[77] Schools are transmission belts[78]—cultural institutions that allocate collective ideals and principles using pedagogical constructs that reflect social standards. "Although the transmission of values is a universal phenomenon, there may be culture-specific differences in degree, content and process of transmission. Every culture offers specific developmental niches and socialization practices for the transmission of values."[79] Humans are cultural creatures who mostly acquire their knowledge and understandings from others, socially.[80] Education systems are sites of secondary socialization—places where we learn to be human and interact in society.

Peace Education as Peacebuilding

Education does not simply "bank" information into humans—depositing information uncritically—it also occupies a social space that demonstrates ways of being and living.[81] Educations that reproduce the values and ideals of "dominant" groups transmit cultural capital to students that can lead to the reproduction of social inequalities and perpetuate forms of gendered marginalization.[82] The difference between "normal" or "common" education and peace education lies in the purpose of its curricula and the method of pedagogy. Normal schoolings serve the existing needs of society preparing the next generation of voters, workers, participants, and perpetuators. Peace education is optimistic, transformative, and geared toward human rights, sustainability, responsibility, and positive peace (harmonious relations).[83] Peace education is a form of transformational pedagogy—focused on changing social mores and values. Because schools are social institutions they are often locations where cultural disparities lead to disadvantages; peace education recognizes that schools can be sites of indirect violence and involves vision, commitment, and the courage to transform patterns of cultural (and gendered) dominance.[84]

Although some perceive that patriarchy is no longer a hegemonic social structure,[85] identity norms continue to impact the experiences and opportunities of individuals because of their gender. Peace education, because it espouses gendered equality (the notion that women, girls, and persons with sexual/gender identity-differences are fully human and should not be considered less worthy because of their gender) can contribute to the transformation of gendered norms without directly addressing patriarchal privilege.[86] Put bluntly, gendered cultural constructs are maintained by both men and women and their reproduction contains both active and passive activities that are duplicated in the home, schools, and greater society.[87] It is not sufficient to say that sustaining male privilege and female subordination are projects of one gender to the detriment of the other; all members of society participate (to some extent) in maintaining gendered forms of cultural violence or they simply would not be there.

Peace education is a form of education that begins with the notion that all humans deserve respect, dignity, and the basic rights of life regardless of individual identity and that we can both teach and learn the abilities of peace. The so-called normal education is a meritocracy that results in outcomes that are often the result of life outside of school. Because our educations can directly impact our life chances in society it is critical that we work toward educations that destabilize the roots of cultural violence in the classroom.

Peace Education Curricula

There are formal and nonformal incarnations of peace education. Most contain some reference to the value of peace and encompass methodologies that investigate violence—in direct, indirect, and cultural forms—in order to empower individuals to both locate acts of violence in the self and society and work actively—and nonviolently—when looking to engage and transform negative social aspects. Importantly, although formal education is a form of socialization that is both institutional and frequently the result of national or state initiatives, peace education works at the individual level. Peace education, when in mainstream (formal) curriculum may be perceived as something that impacts society *en masse* but in practice, peace education, in all of its forms, works at transforming society from the individual up. Despite psycho-ecological constructs of human structures that locate cultural attitudes and beliefs in macrosystems—ecologies of human development held by the greater society,[88] peace education is about empowering individuals to locate, encompass, and transform their inner ecosystems—peace education works on transforming cultural violence in the individual.

Critical Peace Education

Some observers imagine that because peace education is offered in a variety of settings for diverse populations, peace education lacks a concrete definition—because it applies to everything, it ends up being nothing.[89] Critics of peace education comment that programs are often temporary (Montessori Education), utilized in single (often post-conflict) cultural settings (Unity-Based Peace Education in Bosnia-Herzegovina), or that peace education programs have a limited impact on the sensibilities of the greater culture (Seeds of Peace, Project Children).

With global attention often captured by top tier (diplomatic and governmental) negotiations and peace processes, programs that focus on individual transformation can be considered less significant. However, this is one of the great strengths of peace education, "as a strategy it depends upon millions of students being educated who first transform their inner hearts and minds and then must in turn work to transform violence."[90] As peace education triumphs at the individual level it imparts values and outlooks in students that eventually come to compose collective society. Peace education aims to affect social change and transform violence into nonviolence; as an agent of peace, each student becomes an obstacle to violence escalation because peace educands have the tools, skills, attitudes, and awareness to assess situations appropriately and act nonviolently to build relationships and transform conflict. Simply put, peace education aims to plant peace in the individual and then grow peace in society.

Nonetheless, it cannot be denied that there is no single peace education curriculum and no one format for its delivery. Peace education used in post-conflict settings is not suitable for usage in intractable conflict and, likewise, peace education geared toward social transformation in tranquil nations will likely not include content specifically geared toward post-conflict reconstruction or resolving identity politics. However, programs that involve organized learning that impart the values of social harmony, equanimous government, conscious inclusivity, relationship building, and nonviolent cooperation are peace educations.

There are educative curricula being taught in informal settings and institutional locations that are mobilizing and manifesting the values of peace education but are not called peace education. A single example is the Kaupapa Māori, *Te Whāriki* Early Childhood Education (ECE) Curriculum currently being utilized in New Zealand. The values imparted in *Te Whāriki* ECE include respect for self and others.

Self-Respect

This value relates to how educators foster and support building confidence and personal fortitude in individual students so that they perceive that they are worthy of thoughtfulness and respect, as are others. To realize this, three dimensions of learning are emphasized:

1. Empowerment: Children can be empowered to learn at an individual and a group level, which demonstrates collective empowerment within the school environment. It is important to encourage responsible decision making on an individual level, and responsibility for collective decision making on a group level, for the well-being of the whole school community. While group activities should always be encouraged, it is also important to make solitary time for reading, reflecting, and learning in order to cultivate a positive and productive sense of independence and empowerment. Empowerment is increased as a child's independence and responsibilities increase when, for example, by learning to get help for themselves and for others if they are in a dangerous situation. Children's self-esteem should be nurtured and developed by the educators by fostering an appreciation for individuality and creativity by encouraging children's unique talents and interests.

2. *Imagination:* Creativity is an important aspect of learning and experimentation as it cultivates a greater understanding of concepts, language, and expression. Imagination opens the child's mind to different methods of thinking about and solving problems. Educators should encourage children to make sense of the natural world and their environment through language and artistic, expressive means. Art fosters a link between culture, language, and learning. Formal education systems and teaching methods should be tailored to foster a child's imagination including spontaneous play and expressiveness by including alternative forms of learning in the curriculum, such as dance, songs, art, poems, plays, and movement as a form of communication. Movement increases a child's locomotor, non-locomotor, and physical manipulation skills that are vital in holistic education.

3. *Cognitive Development*: Creativity in learning fosters critical and creative thinking, which are vital components in balanced and holistic education. Cognitively, children should be encouraged to develop their familiarity with the physical world through methods of objective and subjective learning. Objectively children should be educated to observe and classify various objects through developing the language skills to differentiate between size, shape, color, and function. Subjectively children should be provided with opportunities to explore the natural world, use their imagination in problem solving and to read pictures for their explicit or implicit meaning, and therefore develop an appreciation for art and the human depiction of nature. A comprehensive, balanced, and holistic education increases skills in memory retention, reasoning, and problem solving.

Respect for Others

This value relates to the child in the community. In order to be able to exemplify respect toward self and others in a confident and consistent manner, educators and parents must value the rights of children as individuals. An understanding and an appreciation for diversity in culture and spirituality is vital in order to teach children to appreciate and value their own culture and spirituality. To realize this, four dimensions of learning are emphasized:

1. Collaboration: Collaborative learning is a vital component when learning to live and work with others. Educators should foster an inclusive environment that encourages students to find collaborative solutions to problems through group decision making. A supportive, active learning environment is conducive to finding creative solutions to problems and creating an atmosphere of questioning and discovery. Within a multicultural environment, collaborative learning helps to curb social and identity-based stereotypes at a very young age reducing societal prejudice and increasing tolerance. Children should also be exposed to the various cultures (through the arts, plays and music) that are represented in the community in order to foster a positive perception and understanding of all others within the community increasing a comprehensive sense of belonging and social responsibility.

2. Conflict Resolution: Conflict and disagreements are a natural part of the human experience and children should be made aware of the normality of this occurrence. Educators should explicitly demonstrate the triviality of accepting a difference in viewpoint in a nonviolent and non-offensive manner. Skills in active listening, reasoning, and articulation of thoughts, feelings, and logic (through the correct use of language) are gradually developed when resolving conflict. The school needs to form a consistent and standardized method of intervening in various forms of disputes, so as not to confuse students with the logic behind various disciplinary actions. Conflict resolution skills help sustain friendships by teaching students to compromise, by fostering the ability to voice one's own opinion assertively, and to disagree with others in a non-offensive and respectful manner.

3. Developing Responsibility, Empathy, and Consideration: Caring for others stimulates connectivity and sharing and communicating with others, with empathy, helps children take responsibility for their decisions. Learning to empathize with the needs of others fosters emotional intelligence in a child and an appreciation of the feelings and attitudes of others. Responsibility entails developing respect for rules, elders, and authority within the schooling environment. It is important to acknowledge that mistakes can and will be made on a regular basis in a schooling environment, however, the ability to take responsibility for them and to take steps toward correcting the mistake is an important ethical characteristic that should be encouraged.

4. Appreciating the Environment: Appreciating and respecting the environment and all organisms, which coexist within it, is a component of moral and ethical education, which can be encouraged during field expeditions, observations at art class, or in science class. Practical environmental action learning includes caring for the environment through cleaning, gardening, and recycling. It is important for children to develop a sense of appreciation and respect for nature because sustainable practices result in building peace. Environmental education involves fostering values of respect for the environment (and the creatures who dwell within it), while facilitating the ability to appreciate the environment—its observable characteristics and many changes.

Educative curricula such as the *Te Whāriki* ECE being taught in New Zealand are not called peace education. Upon further investigation it is evident that content supported in the curriculum are congruent with the objectives and normative values of educating for peace. Further muddying the peace education critique may be the realization that peace education—a term that applies to everything and therefore nothing—also includes educations that do not call themselves peace education.

One additional critical perspective is offered by Robert Mizzi[91] who reminds us that peace educations, like existing educations, run the risk of supporting heterosexism or the practice and belief that only relationships between opposite-sexes (heterosexuality) are legitimate. "This, in turn, causes policies, curricula, conversations, and day-to-day practices that render sexual/ gender minorities invisible, subversive, and deviant. An example of heterosexism . . . would be the assumption that all students in a post-secondary peace education classroom identify and practice heterosexuality."[92] Mizzi perceives that peace education needs to be an inclusive project that challenges heteronormativity (the assumption that cross-sex relationships are normal and other forms of relationships are deviant) so that all forms of gender hegemony are investigated and transformed. As Betty Reardon has remarked, "learning to achieve . . . gender justice and human equality [is] integral to the establishment of a culture of peace."[93] For peace educators, proposing curricula and utilizing peace pedagogies needs to include an understanding that gender hegemonies may be culturally reproduced so that peace education considers the many incarnations and experiences of gender—not solely heterosexuality. Additionally, Mizzi[94] makes the connection between gendered (heteronormative) nationalism[95] (strong man, weak woman) and the marginalization of sexual/gender identity differences and reminds us that future peace educations must be culturally sensitive and gender-inclusive[96] because the project of building peace is connected to global citizenship,[97] social justice, and human rights for all.[98]

CONCLUSIONS

Ian Harris, a major voice in the field, perceives that peace education is still marginalized in global pedagogy[99] but when the components of existing educations (e.g., *Te Whāriki* ECE in New Zealand) are analyzed we may find that that although curricula are not called peace education they may still be educating for peace. Peace education is a peacebuilding pursuit that can be introduced in any social temporality and in every cultural space in order to contribute to new peace performances in society. The ongoing project of gender equality and global cultural-sensitivity to persons who inhabit sexual/gender identity difference is part of the work of educating for peace. As Suzanne Pharr, remarks "to eliminate one oppression successfully, a movement has to include work to eliminate them all."[100] For peace educators hoping to change worldviews (cultural violence) that legitimize GBV it is necessary to investigate our curricula and peace pedagogies to be certain we are contributing to positive peace—full, equanimous, and harmonious civilizations—and making VAW and other minorities intolerable.

NOTES

1. John Paul Lederach, *Building Peace: Sustainable Reconciliation in Divided Societies* (Washington, DC: United States Institute of Peace, 2006).
2. Johan Galtung, *Peace by Peaceful Means: Peace and Conflict, Development and Civilization* (London, England: Sage, 1996).
3. Roger Mac Ginty, *Routledge Handbook of Peacebuilding* (London, England: Routledge, 2013).
4. Michael Pugh, "The Problem-Solving and Critical Paradigms," in *Routledge Handbook of Peacebuilding*, ed. Roger Mac Ginty (London, England: Routledge, 2013).
5. Ian Harris and Mary Lee Morrison, *Peace Education*, 3rd ed. (Jefferson, NC: McFarland, 2013).
6. Katerina Standish, "Understanding Cultural Violence and Gender: Honour Killings; Dowry Murder; the Zina Ordinance; and Blood Feuds," *Journal of Gender Studies* 23.2 (2013).
7. Johan Galtung "Cultural Violence," *Journal of Peace Research* 27.3 (1990).
8. Elizabeth K. Englander, *Understanding Violence* (Mahwah, NJ: Lawrence Erlbaum Associates, 1997).
9. Galtung, *Cultural*, 292.
10. Ibid., 296.
11. Ibid.
12. Karen Heimer and Candace Kruttschnitt, *Gender and Crime: Patterns in Victimization and Offending* (New York, NY: New York University, 2006).
13. Judith M. Bennet, *History Matters: Patriarchy and the Challenge of Feminism* (Philadelphia, PA: University of Pennsylvania Press, 2006).
14. Sally Engle Merry, *Human Rights and Gender Violence* (Chicago, IL: University of Chicago Press, 2006), 2.

15. Maria O'Reilly, "Gender and Peacebuilding," in *Routledge Handbook of Peacebuilding*, ed. Roger Mac Ginty (London, England: Routledge, 2013), 59.

16. Judith Butler, *Excitable Speech: A Politics of the Performative* (New York, NY: Routledge 1997).

17. Øystein Gullvåg Holter, "A Theory of Gendercide," in *Gendercide and Genocide*, ed. Adam Jones (Nashville, TN: Vanderbilt University Press, 2004).

18. Adam Jones ed., *Gendercide and Genocide* (Nashville, TN: Vanderbilt University Press, 2004).

19. Geraldine Terry and Joanna Hoare, *Gender-Based Violence* (Oxford, England: Oxfam GB, 2007).

20. O'Reilly, *Gender and Peacebuilding*.

21. Joshua S. Goldstein, *War and Gender* (Cambridge, MA: Cambridge University Press, 2001).

22. Elise Boulding, *Cultures of Peace: The Hidden Side of History* (New York, NY: Syracuse University Press, 2000).

23. Cynthia Cockburn, "The Gendered Dynamics of Armed Conflict and Political Violence," in *Victims, Perpetrators or Actors? Gender, Armed Conflict and Political Violence*, ed. Caroline Moser and Fiona Clark (New York, NY: Zed Book, 2001), 14.

24. Merry, *Human*.

25. Radhika Coomaraswamy and Lisa Kios, "Violence Against Women," in *Women and International Human Rights Law*, ed. Kelly D. Askin and Dorean M. Koenig (Ardsley, NY: Transnational Publishers, 1999).

26. Benedict Anderson, *Imagined Communities* (London, England: Verso, 2006).

27. Margaret MacMillan, *Paris 1919: Six Months That Changed the World* (New York, NY: Random House, 2003).

28. Nira Yuval-Davis, *Gender and Nation* (London, England: Sage, 1997).

29. Tami A. Jacoby, *Gendered Nationalism and Palestinian Citizenship* (Toronto, ON: York University Press, 1996).

30. Cynthia Enloe, *Bananas, Beaches and Bases: Making Feminist Sense of International Politics* (Berkeley, CA: University of California Press, 2000).

31. Ibid.

32. Mary Caprioli, "Primed for Violence The Role of Gender Inequality in Predicting Internal Conflict," *International Studies Quarterly* 49.1 (2005).

33. Jack D. Eller, *From Culture to Ethnicity to Conflict* (Ann Arbor, MI: The University of Michigan Press, 1999).

34. Enloe, *Bananas*.

35. Sandra Whitworth, *Men, Militarism, and UN Peacekeeping: A Gendered Analysis* (London, England: Lynne Rienner, 2004).

36. Ibid.

37. Hayley Lopes, "Militarized Masculinity in Peacekeeping Operations: An Obstacle to Gender Mainstreaming," Background Paper, Canadian Department of Foreign Affairs and International Trade, 2011, accessed December 13, 2013, http://peacebuild.ca/Lopes%20website%20ready.pdf, 2–3.

38. Jacoby, *Gendered*.

39. Merry, *Human*.

40. Enloe, *Bananas*, xiv.

41. Merry, *Human*, 14.

42. Standish, "Understanding," 3.

43. Birgit Brock-Utne, *Educating for Peace: A Feminist Perspective* (New York, NY: Pergamon Press, 1985), 75.

44. Mac Ginty, *Handbook.*

45. Roger Mac Ginty and Oliver Richmond, *The Liberal Peace and Post-War Reconstruction: Myth or Reality*? (London, England: Routledge, 2009).

46. Boutros Boutros-Ghali, *An Agenda for Peace* (New York, NY: United Nations, 1995).

47. Nicole Ball, "The Challenge of Rebuilding War-Torn Societies," in *Turbulent Peace: The Challenge of Managing International Conflict*, ed. Chester A. Crocker, Fen Osler Hampson, and Pamela R. Aall (Washington, DC: United States Institute of Peace).

48. Eva Bertram, "Reinventing Governments: The Promise and Perils of United Nations Peace Building," *The Journal of Conflict Resolution* 39.3 (1995): 388.

49. Gavriel Salomon and Edward Cairns, *Handbook on Peace Education* (New York, NY: Psychology Press, 2010).

50. Halvard Vike, "Utopian Time and Contemporary Time: Temporal Dimensions of Planning and Reform in the Norwegian Welfare State," in *Elusive Promises: Planning in the Contemporary World*, ed. Simone Abram and Gisa Weszkalnys (New York, NY: Berghahn Books, 2013).

51. Lederach, *Building*.

52. Walter Nicholls, Byron Miller, and Justin Beaumont, *Spaces of Contention: Spatialities and Social Movements* (Farnham, England: Ashgate, 2013).

53. Butler, *Excitable*.

54. Louise Diamond and John McDonald, *Multi-Track Diplomacy* (West Hartford, CT: Kumarian, 1996).

55. O'Reilly, *Gender*.

56. Ibid., 57.

57. Patricia M. Fabiano et al., "Engaging Men as Social Justice Allies in Evading Violence Against Women: Evidence for a Social Norms Approach," *Journal of American College Health* 52.3 (2003).

58. Sofia Gruskin, "Violence Prevention: Bringing Health and Human Rights Together," *Health and Human Rights* 6.2 (2003).

59. O'Reilly, *Gender*, 61.

60. Security Council Resolution 1325, United Nations Security Council, October 31, 2000, accessed December 13, 2013, http://www.un.org/womenwatch/osagi/wps/.

61. UN General Assembly, *Convention on the Elimination of all Forms of Discrimination Against Women*, December 18, 1979, accessed December 12, 2013, http://www.un.org/womenwatch/daw/cedaw/.

62. O'Reilly, *Gender*.

63. Nel Noddings, *Peace Education: How We Come to Love and Hate War* (New York, NY: Cambridge University Press, 2012).

64. Brock-Utne, *Educating*.

65. Boulding, *Cultures*.

66. O'Reilly, *Gender*, 63.

67. Nira Yuval-Davis, "Intersectionality and Feminist Politics," *European Journal of Women's Studies* 13.3 (2006).

68. O'Reilly, *Gender*.

69. Ibid., 64.

70. Anne Betts-Fetherston, "Voices from Warzones: Implications for Training," in *A Future for Peacekeeping?* ed. Edward Moxon-Browne (Basingstoke, England: Palgrave Macmillan, 1998).

71. Emanuel Levinas, *Totality and Infinity*, trans. Alphonso Lingis (Pittsburgh, PA: Duquesne University Press, 1969).

72. Ian Harris, "History of Peace Education," in *Handbook on Peace Education*, ed. Gavriel Salomon and Ed Cairns (New York, NY: Psychology Press, 2010).

73. Salomon and Cairns, *Handbook.*

74. Noddings, *Peace*.

75. Monisha Bajaj, *Encyclopedia of Peace Education* (Charlotte, NC: Information Age Publishing, 2008).

76. Boulding, *Cultures*.

77. Vamik Volkan, *Killing in the Name of Identity: A Study of Bloody Conflicts* (Charlottesville, VA: Pitchstone, 2006).

78. Ute Schönpflug, "Intergenerational Transmission of Values: The Role of Transmission Belts," *Journal of Cross-Cultural Psychology* 32.2 (2001).

79. Isabelle Albert, Gisela Trommsdorf, and Lieke Wisnubrata, "Intergenerational Transmission of Values in Different Cultural Contexts: A Study in Germany and Indonesia," (Manuscript Submitted to the Proceedings of the 18th International Congress of the International Association for Cross-Cultural Psychology, Isle of Spetses, Greece, 2006), 221.

80. Jeffrey C. Alexander and Kenneth Thompson, *A Contemporary Introduction to Sociology: Culture and Society in Transition*, 2nd ed. (Boulder, CO: Paradigm, 2011).

81. Paulo Freire, *Pedagogy of the Oppressed: 30th Anniversary Edition* (New York, NY: Continuum, 2001).

82. Pierre Bourdieu, "Cultural Reproduction and Social Reproduction," in *Power and Ideology in Education*, ed. Jerome Karabel and A. H. Halsey (New York, NY: Oxford University Press, 1977).

83. Clive Harber and Noriko Sakade, "Schooling for Violence and Peace: How Does Peace Education Differ from 'Normal' Schooling?" *Journal of Peace Education* 6.2 (2009).

84. Candace Carter and Salosha Vandeyar, "Peace Education in Conflict and Post-conflict Societies: Comparative Perspectives," in *Peace Education in Conflict and Post-conflict Societies Comparative perspectives*, ed. Claire McGlynn et al. (New York, NY: Palgrave Macmillan, 2009).

85. Slavoj Žižek, *Living in the End Times* (New York, NY: Verso, 2011).

86. Betty Reardon, *Education for a Culture of Peace in a Gender Perspective* (Paris, France: The Teacher's Library/UNESCO Publishing, 2001).

87. Annika Takala, "Feminist Perspectives on Peace Education," *Journal of Peace Education* 28.2 (1991).

88. Urie Bronfenbrenner, *The Ecology of Human Development: Experiments by Nature and Design* (Cambridge, MA: Harvard University Press, 1979).

89. Gavriel Salomon, "Comment: What is Peace Education?" *Journal of Peace Education* 1.1 (2004).

90. Harris and Morrision, *Peace*, 31.

91. Robert Mizzi, "Let's Get This Straightened Out: Finding a Place and Presence for Sexual/Gender Identity Difference in Peace Education," *Journal of Peace Education* 6.2 (2010).

92. Ibid., 141.

93. Reardon, *Education*, 34.

94. Mizzi, "Let's."

95. Jacoby, *Gendered.*

96. Reardon, *Education.*

97. Felisa Tibbits, "Human Rights Education," in *Encyclopedia of Peace Education*, ed. Monisha Bajaj (Charlotte, NC: Information Age Publishing, 2008).

98. Lynn Davies, "Global Citizenship Education," in *Encyclopedia of Peace Education*, ed. Monisha Bajaj (Charlotte, NC: Information Age Publishing, 2008).

99. Harris, "History."

100. Suzanne Pharr, *Homophobia: A Weapon of Sexism* (Berkeley, CA: Chardon Press, 1997), 53.

BIBLIOGRAPHY

Albert, Isabelle, Gisela Trommsdorff, and Lieke Wisnubrata. "Intergenerational Transmission of Values in Different Cultural Contexts: A Study in Germany and Indonesia." Manuscript Submitted to the Proceedings of the 18th International Congress of the International Association for Cross-Cultural Psychology, Isle of Spetses, Greece, 2006.

Alexander, Jeffrey C. and Kenneth Thompson. *A Contemporary Introduction to Sociology: Culture and Society in Transition.* 2nd ed. Boulder, CO: Paradigm, 2011.

Anderson, Benedict. *Imagined Communities.* London, England: Verso, 2006.

Bajaj, Monisha. *Encyclopedia of Peace Education.* Charlotte, NC: Information Age Publishing, 2008.

Ball, Nicole. "The Challenge of Rebuilding War-Torn Societies." In *Turbulent Peace: The Challenge of Managing International Conflict*, edited by Chester A. Crocker, Fen Osler Hampson, and Pamela R. Aall, 719–36. Washington, DC: United States Institute of Peace, 2003.

Bennet, Judith. M. *History Matters: Patriarchy and the Challenge of Feminism.* Philadelphia, PA: University of Pennsylvania Press, 2006.

Bertram, Eva. "Reinventing Governments: The Promise and Perils of United Nations Peace Building." *The Journal of Conflict Resolution* 39.3 (1995): 388–89.

Betts-Fetherston, Anne. "Voices from Warzones: Implications for Training." In *A Future for Peacekeeping?* Edited by Edward Moxon-Browne, 159–175. Basingstoke, England: Palgrave Macmillan, 1998.

Boulding, Elise. *Cultures of Peace: The Hidden Side of History*. New York, NY: Syracuse University Press, 2000.

Bourdieu, Pierre. "Cultural Reproduction and Social Reproduction." In *Power and Ideology in Education*, edited by Jerome Karabel and A. H. Halsey, 487–511. New York, NY: Oxford University Press, 1977.

Boutros-Ghali, Boutros. *An Agenda for Peace*. New York, NY: United Nations, 1995.

Brock-Utne, Birgit. *Educating for Peace: A Feminist Perspective*. New York, NY: Pergamon Press, 1985.

Bronfenbrenner, Urie. *The Ecology of Human Development: Experiments by Nature and Design*. Cambridge, MA: Harvard University Press, 1979.

Butler, Judith. *Excitable Speech: A Politics of the Performative*. New York, NY: Routledge, 1997.

Caprioli, Mary. "Primed for Violence The Role of Gender Inequality in Predicting Internal Conflict." *International Studies Quarterly* 49.1 (2005): 161–78.

Carter, Candace and Salosha Vandeyar. "Peace Education in Conflict and Post-Conflict Societies: Comparative Perspectives." In *Peace Education in Conflict and Post-Conflict Societies: Comparative Perspectives*, edited by Claire McGlynn, Michael Zembylas, Zvi Bekerman, and Tony Gallagher, 247–61. New York, NY: Palgrave Macmillan, 2009.

Coomaraswamy, Radhika and Lisa Kios. "Violence Against Women." In *Women and International Human Rights Law*, edited by Kelly D. Askin and Dorean M. Koenig, 177–217. Ardsley, NY: Transnational Publishers, 1999.

Cockburn, Cynthia. "The Gendered Dynamics of Armed Conflict and Political Violence." In *Victims, Perpetrators or Actors? Gender, Armed Conflict and Political Violence*, edited by Caroline Moser and Fiona Clark, 13–29. New York, NY: Zed Books, 2001.

Davies, Lynn. "Global Citizenship Education." In *Encyclopedia of Peace Education*, edited by Monisha Bajaj, 109–14. Charlotte, NC: Information Age Publishing, 2008.

Diamond, Louise and John McDonald. *Multi-Track Diplomacy*. West Hartford, CT: Kumarian, 1996.

Eller, Jack D. *From Culture to Ethnicity to Conflict*. Ann Arbor, MI: The University of Michigan Press, 1999.

Englander, Elizabeth K. *Understanding Violence*. Mahwah, NJ: Lawrence Erlbaum Associates, 1997.

Enloe, Cynthia. *Bananas, Beaches and Bases: Making Feminist Sense of International Politics*. Berkeley, CA: University of California Press, 2000.

Fabiano, Patricia M., Wesley Perkins, Alan Berkowitz, Jeff Linkenback, and Christopher Stark. "Engaging Men as Social Justice Allies in Evading Violence Against Women: Evidence for a Social Norms Approach." *Journal of American College Health* 52.3 (2003): 105–12.

Freire, Paulo. *Pedagogy of the Oppressed: 30th Anniversary Edition*. New York, NY: Continuum, 2001.

Galtung, Johan. "Cultural Violence." *Journal of Peace Research* 27.3 (1990): 291–305.

———. *Peace by Peaceful Means: Peace and Conflict, Development and Civilization*. London, England: Sage, 1996.

Goldstein, Joshua S. *War and Gender*. Cambridge, MA: Cambridge University Press, 2001.

Gruskin, Sofia. "Violence Prevention: Bringing Health and Human Rights Together." *Health and Human Rights* 6.2 (2003): 1–10.

Gullvåg Holter, Øystein. "A Theory of Gendercide." In *Gendercide and Genocide*, edited by Adam Jones, 62–97. Nashville, TN: Vanderbilt University Press, 2004.

Harber, Clive and Noriko Sakade. "Schooling for Violence and Peace: How Does Peace Education Differ from 'Normal' Schooling?" *Journal of Peace Education* 6.2 (2009): 171–87.

Harris, Ian. "History of Peace Education." In *Handbook on Peace Education*, edited by Gavriel Salomon and Ed Cairns, 11–20. New York, NY: Psychology Press, 2010.

Harris, Ian and Mary Lee Morrison. *Peace Education*. 3rd ed. Jefferson, NC: McFarland, 2013.

Heimer, Karen and Candace Kruttschnitt. *Gender and Crime: Patterns in Victimization and Offending*. New York, NY: New York University, 2006.

Jacoby, Tami A. *Gendered Nationalism and Palestinian Citizenship*. Toronto, ON: York University Press, 1996.

Jones, Adam, ed. *Gendercide and Genocide*. Nashville, TN: Vanderbilt University Press, 2004.

Lederach, Jean Paul. *Building Peace: Sustainable Reconciliation in Divided Societies*. Washington, DC: United States Institute of Peace. 2006.

Levinas, Emanuel. *Totality and Infinity*. Translated by Alphonso Lingis. Pittsburgh, PA: Duquesne University Press, 1969.

Lopes, Hayley. "Militarized Masculinity in Peacekeeping Operations: An Obstacle to Gender Mainstreaming." Background Paper, Canadian Department of Foreign Affairs and International Trade, 2011. Accessed December 13, 2013. http://peacebuild.ca/Lopes%20website%20ready.pdf.

Mac Ginty, Roger. *Routledge Handbook of Peacebuilding*. London, England: Routledge, 2013.

Mac Ginty, Roger and Oliver Richmond. *The Liberal Peace and Post-War Reconstruction: Myth or Reality*? London, England: Routledge, 2009.

MacMillan, Margaret. *Paris 1919: Six Months That Changed the World*. New York, NY: Random House, 2003.

Merry, Sally Engle. *Human Rights and Gender Violence*. Chicago, IL: University of Chicago Press, 2006.

Mizzi, Robert. "Let's Get This Straightened Out: Finding a Place and Presence for Sexual/Gender Identity Difference in Peace Education." *Journal of Peace Education* 6.2 (2010): 139–56.

Nicholls, Walter, Byron Miller, and Justin Beaumont. *Spaces of Contention: Spatialities and Social Movements*. Farnham, England: Ashgate, 2013.

Noddings, Nel. *Peace Education: How We Come to Love and Hate War*. New York, NY: Cambridge University Press, 2012.

O'Reilly, Maria. "Gender and Peacebuilding." In *Routledge Handbook of Peacebuilding*, edited by Roger Mac Ginty, 57–68. London, England: Routledge, 2013.

Pharr, Suzanne. *Homophobia: A Weapon of Sexism*. Berkeley, CA: Chardon Press, 1997.

Pugh, Michael. "The Problem-Solving and Critical Paradigms." In *Routledge Handbook of Peacebuilding*, edited by Roger Mac Ginty, 11–24. London, England: Routledge, 2013.

Reardon, Betty. *Education for a Culture of Peace in a Gender Perspective*. Paris, France: The Teacher's Library/UNESCO Publishing, 2001.

Salomon, Gavriel. "Comment: What is Peace Education?" *Journal of Peace Education* 1.1 (2004): 123–27.

Saloman, Gavriel and Edward Cairns. *Handbook on Peace Education*. New York, NY: Psychology Press, 2010.

Schönpflug, Ute. "Intergenerational Transmission of Values: The Role of Transmission Belts." *Journal of Cross-Cultural Psychology* 32.2 (2001): 174–85.

Security Council Resolution 1325. United Nations Security Council, October 31, 2000. Accessed December 13, 2013. http://www.un.org/womenwatch/osagi/wps/.

Standish, Katerina. "Understanding Cultural Violence and Gender: Honour Killings; Dowry Murder; the Zina Ordinance; and Blood Feuds," *Journal of Gender Studies* 23.2 (2013): 111–24.

Takala, Annika. "Feminist Perspectives on Peace Education." *Journal of Peace Education* 28.2 (1991): 231–35.

Terry, Geraldine and Joanna Hoare. *Gender-Based Violence*. Oxford, England: Oxfam GB, 2007.

Tibbits, Felisa. "Human Rights Education." In *Encyclopedia of Peace Education*, edited by Monisha Bajaj, 99–108. Charlotte, NC: Information Age Publishing, 2008.

UN General Assembly. *Convention on the Elimination of all Forms of Discrimination Against Women*, December 18, 1979. Accessed December 12, 2013. http://www.un.org/womenwatch/daw/cedaw/.

Vike, Halvard. "Utopian Time and Contemporary Time: Temporal Dimensions of Planning and Reform in the Norwegian Welfare State." In *Elusive Promises: Planning in the Contemporary World*, edited by Simone Abram and Gisa Weszkalnys, 35–56. New York, NY: Berghahn Books, 2013.

Volkan, Vamik. *Killing in the Name of Identity: A Study of Bloody Conflicts*. Charlottesville, VA: Pitchstone, 2006.

Whitworth, Sandra. *Men, Militarism, and UN Peacekeeping: A Gendered Analysis*. London, England: Lynne Rienner, 2004.

Yuval-Davis, Nira. *Gender and Nation*. London, England: Sage, 1997.

———. "Intersectionality and Feminist Politics." *European Journal of Women's Studies* 13.3 (2006): 193–209.

Žižek, Slavoj. *Living in the End Times*. New York, NY: Verso, 2011.

Chapter 19

Peacebuilding without Western Saviors?

An Approach to Teaching African Gender and Sexuality Politics to American students

Robin L. Turner

What words or phrases first come to mind when you think of Africa?

Natural resources. Hot. Lion King. Elephants. Diverse. Blood diamonds. AIDS. Misunderstood. Marginalized. Cradle of Humankind. Africa doesn't make sense.

. . . When you think of African women?

Subordinate. Enslaved. Dominated. Family-oriented. Uneducated. Baskets on heads. Rape. Empowered. Barriers to independence. Subaltern of the subaltern. Carrying babies in slings.

. . . When you think of African men?

Nelson Mandela. Soldier. Patriarch. Chauvinist. Chiefs. Loincloth and spear. Uneducated.

. . . When you think of African queers?

African queer? Illegal. Hunted. Is "queer" pejorative? Not discussed.

January 2014 class discussion

Most American students have had few direct encounters with African peoples or places. Their impressions of Africa are thus heavily influenced by popular media, which tends to present the continent as a distant and very different country with undifferentiated masses of suffering dark peoples and awe-inspiring endangered wildlife.[1] Frequently critiqued for its ahistorical, decontextualized emphasis on catastrophe, conflict, disease, and violence, Western media coverage of Africa also highlights gendered injustices such as female genital cutting, homophobia, and sexual violence.[2] This coverage often flattens Africa's complex and varied reality, creating the impression that all women have been cut, raped, or are HIV-positive, that queerness is uniformly condemned, and that there is little internal contestation because gender and sexuality-based oppression are culturally rooted. At present, as during the colonial past, popular representations portray African people as different, less civilized, and in need of Western rescue.[3] These misrepresentations render Africans profoundly other, deny African subjectivity, and erase the long, complex, violent entanglement of Africa, Europe, and the Americas.

It is easy to understand why many American college students believe that African women, transgender people, and same-gender-loving people are particularly oppressed and that African men are particularly sexist as the quotations in the chapter epigraph suggest.[4] These preconceptions can hinder student participation in efforts to end gender and sexuality-inflected violence in Africa and elsewhere; however, caring, empathetic American students are often ill-prepared to work with the people they want to help. In this context, African studies courses that assist students to decolonize their minds are important peacebuilding interventions.[5] Thoughtful critical engagement with African realities, perspectives, and histories can engender greater recognition and respect for the full humanity of all people that is an essential component of peacebuilding at home or abroad.

African same-gender-loving people, transgender people, and women undoubtedly suffer from oppressive practices, policies, and laws that are said to be justified by culture, tradition, and/or religion, as do same-gender-loving people, transgender people, and women in North America, Western Europe, and elsewhere. African gender and sexuality politics do not exist in isolation but in a complex relationship to past and present global currents: gendered ideologies, policies, and practices have crossed the Atlantic and Indian Oceans and the Mediterranean and Red Seas for centuries. The brutal physical, epistemic, and structural violence entailed in Western "discoveries" of African places, in the slave trade and in colonialism, continues to affect Western peoples' perceptions of Africa, to influence interactions between Western and African polities, and to shape beliefs, policies, and practices across the Atlantic.[6] "A radical questioning or permanent suspicion regarding the humanity" of Africans and other "colonized and racialized peoples" continues to infuse the present.[7]

This chapter details the pedagogical strategies I have used to teach undergraduate students at Butler University about gender and sexuality politics in Africa. A small teaching-focused university in Indianapolis, Indiana, Butler has a student body comprised principally of young adults from the American Midwest who have had little direct contact with African people but often have a strong desire to help suffering people in Indianapolis and elsewhere. The university's Indianapolis Community Requirement and service-oriented campus groups reinforce this helping orientation.

The upper-level gender and sexuality politics in Africa seminar helps students develop "the conceptual tools and background knowledge to think, talk, and write intelligently about gender, sex, and sexuality politics in Africa and elsewhere . . . [to] strengthen [their] analytical skills, and [to] make [them] better equipped to critically engage with Western representations of other places" as the syllabus states through a collective consideration of gender, sexuality, and politics that takes variation, context, history, and agency seriously. My aims in teaching this seminar are broadly decolonial: I seek to foster "responsibility and the willingness to take many perspectives, particularly the perspectives and points of view of those whose very existence is questioned and produced as insignificant."[8] Understanding that it is essential to practice these principles in the seminar, I treat all participants with respect, instruct students to use inclusive language, and facilitate the collective development of ground rules. The remainder of this chapter elaborates on pedagogical strategies I use to accomplish these objectives: directly confronting the question of representation, creating a shared vocabulary, encouraging critical engagement, and highlighting African voices and initiatives.

CONFRONTING REPRESENTATIONS

Believing that it is essential to confront how African people and places are and have been seen, I start every Africa-focused course by eliciting students' preconceptions, encouraging openness to other perspectives, and placing contemporary (mis)representations in historical context. Seminar participants shared and discussed the words and phrases in the chapter epigraph during our first session in spring 2014. Prior to this session, I emailed the students and asked them to jot down what the words or phrases "Africa," "African woman," "African man," and "African queer" brought to mind; to ask two other people they knew to do the same and share their thoughts; and to bring the results to class. The message also stated, "There are no right or wrong answers" and indicated that respondents would not be identified. After we had developed ground rules, the students shared the material they collected, and we had an open discussion of the collected jottings. I use this participatory activity to bring common ideas about Africa and Africans into the classroom for discussion and critique and to clear the ground for rigorous intellectual inquiry by directly confronting these potential hindrances. In noting that it makes little sense to talk of Africa or of Asia as these huge continents are internally diverse, for example, a student reminded us that broad generalizations about Africa are unlikely to be valid.

The well-known TED talk "The Danger of a Single Story," by the Nigerian-born writer Chimamanda Ngozi Adichie also serves to identify and destabilize student preconceptions and to invite critical inquiry and openness to diverse perspectives.[9] Adichie effectively challenges othering preconceptions of Africa by naming them, "Her [Adichie's American college roommate] default position toward me, as an African, was a kind of patronizing, well-meaning pity . . . In this single story there was no possibility of Africans being similar to her in any way, no possibility of feelings more complex than pity, no possibility of a connection as human equals"; by describing her middle-class Nigerian childhood; and by humorously reversing the gaze, ". . . a student told me that it was such a shame that Nigerian men were physical abusers like the father character in my novel. I told him that I had just read a novel called *American Psycho* . . . and that it was such a shame that young Americans were serial murderers." Adichie also directly addresses the global politics of representation by arguing that power shapes narrative representations in multiple ways, influencing not only whether people are exposed to multiple representations of a place or a singular representation ("a single story") but also what sort of narratives are disseminated and by whom. Power, she states, is "the ability not just to tell the story of another person, but to make it the definitive story of that person."

It is equally important to place contemporary representations in historical context and to encourage intersectional consideration of gender/sexuality politics in Africa and elsewhere.[10] I want seminar participants to understand that gender, sexuality, and race are co-constitutive—they are formed with and through one another—and to think about gender and sexuality in relation to other political, economical, and social forces rather than examining gender and sexuality politics in isolation. "The careful analysis of represented sexualities helps to explain the meanings of race, the persistence of stereotypes, the reproduction of gender and the operation of power," as Desiree Lewis writes in "Representing African Sexualities."[11] Our initial consideration of representation thus closes with discussion of a text that adopts this approach. Desiree Lewis's transatlantic intersectional analysis of colonial and post-colonial representations of black men and women spurred a lively discussion on the two occasions I have assigned it.[12] This text highlights the ways in which misunderstandings and misrepresentations of African people's genders and sexualities are deeply entangled with violence.

CREATING A SHARED VOCABULARY

Creating a common vocabulary is crucial to enabling all participants to share their ideas, perspectives, and questions in an interdisciplinary seminar that engages with political science, gender and queer studies, and African studies from a decolonial perspective. We build this conceptual vocabulary throughout the first several weeks of the semester. The ground rules and preconceptions activities encourage participants to attend to our language, to think about words and what they signify, and to speak with care. A student's desire to show respect for all persons led her to question whether "queer" was pejorative and whether it was a word lesbian, gay, bisexual, transgender, and intersex Africans would apply to themselves in January 2014, for example. The representation texts provide a set of common reference points such as the "single story" and initiate dialogue about race, bodies, and sexualities. While research suggests that many white American students actively avoid talking about race, Lewis' essay invites us to address these oft-avoided topics by demonstrating the continued salience of raced, gendered bodily representations.[13] We need to talk about bodies, race, and sex to make sense of the extended display of southern African Sarah (Sartjie) Baartman as the "Hottentot Venus," of other representations of African people, and of support for and resistance to "reactionary constructions of sexuality" in African postcolonies.[14]

The seminar builds a shared conceptual framework for thinking and talking about gender, sex, and sexuality in African contexts through successive discussions of texts that define, critique, and apply important gender studies concepts and that present examples, ethnographic descriptions, or personal narratives to ground the discussion. Anne Fausto-Sterling's "Dueling Dualisms," for example, traces how our understandings of gender, sex, and sexual identity have changed over time, highlights the social nature of sex assignment, and advocates a constructivist approach to these concepts.[15] Fausto-Sterling writes, "Labeling someone a man or a woman is a social decision. We may use scientific knowledge to help us make the decision, but only our beliefs about gender—not science—can define our sex."[16] Seminar participants then discuss work by Ugandan intersex activist Julius Kaggwa and about the South African athlete Caster Semenya in light of Fausto-Sterling's intervention.[17] These works draw our attention to the difficulties confronting people whose bodies defy the male/female binary and identify the multiple forces driving sex/gender politics in Uganda, in South Africa, and in Africa more generally. Kaggwa highlights how both discursive avoidance of sex—"in my tribe of Baganda in Uganda, sex cannot be bluntly called 'sex'"—and poverty shape the lived experiences of African intersex people. South Africans' support for Semenya, whom international sports officials subjected to "sex verification testing," shows that non-gender-normative Africans are not always marginalized.[18] Seminar discussions of masculinities and femininities draw from students' experiences and from Jordanna Matlon and Pumla Gqola's work on African masculinities, while works by Oyěwùmí, Oyèrónké and Bibi Bakare-Yusuf encourage students to consider how well and to what the extent concepts developed in Western contexts help us understand other places.[19] In addition to building a shared vocabulary and conceptual framework, these discussions assist participants to continue developing a nuanced understanding of how local, national, transnational, and global forces shape gender and sexuality politics in Africa and elsewhere.

ENCOURAGING CRITICAL ENGAGEMENT

Building students' critical faculties is an essential aspect of decolonial pedagogy: decolonizing our minds requires questioning what is often taken for granted. Seminar participants engage in critical thought and inquiry as we identify and question our preconceptions, look closely at visual and textual representations of Africans, work with concepts, and discuss assigned texts. Student-driven activities that foster critical engagement are equally important components of the seminar.[20] I describe student media presentations and student-led discussions and provide illustrative examples below.

The media presentation activity involves students in critical analysis of contemporary media and helps them to identify connections between course material and current events. Each student identifies a short topical media clipping such as a video, newscast, or song; presents the clipping to the class and facilitates a short discussion; and writes an essay analyzing the clipping in light of the assigned texts once during the semester.

The first two examples address sex work, transactional sex, and HIV/AIDS in sub-Saharan Africa in light of Marc Epprecht's *Heterosexual Africa* and Mark Hunter's article, "The Materiality of Everyday Sex."[21] A spring 2012 student presented a portion of a documentary about Melvin, a young Kenyan who has relied upon sex work to support himself and his younger sister since their parents died of HIV/AIDS.[22] The presenter highlighted how the video illustrates the effects of the "assumptions and silences that are present in the discussion of African sexuality" on Africans with nonnormative sexualities and how silence regarding same-sex sexualities facilitates the spread of HIV/AIDS while noting we should not treat Melvin's story as *the* story of African men who have sex with men. "Not all of these men would identify the way that Melvin does or are economically forced to engage in transactional sex," she wrote.

Another presenter showed part of an interview with an HIV-positive young woman from a Western Cape township to complement Mark Hunter's ethnographic analysis of transactional sex in northern KwaZulu Natal Province, South Africa.[23] The student wrote, "The clip showed [an interview with] a young woman who had several boyfriends who she relied on for both subsistence and material goods . . .. The young woman describes her life growing up and soon became involved in relationships with older men after receiving pressure from her family. She was expected to bring home food or some sort of material goods in order to provide for herself and her family." As the student noted, the circumstances shaping this woman's decisions closely mirrored the forces Hunter highlights: need for basic necessities, desire for luxuries, and lack of education and employment. Hunter argues "close association between sex and gifts . . . is a central factor driving multiple-partnered sexual relationships" and HIV infections, and contends that men's "privileged economic position," "masculinist discourses," and "the agency of women" jointly result in transactional sex.[24] The presentation sparked a discussion about women's agency in this context, about which the presenter commented "While women may have access to more power, it [transactional sex] is still putting men in a position of superiority since men provide the resources or materials that women need." She concluded, "While this media clip was significant in gaining an individual's perspective towards transactional sex and understanding how it works, it is important to consider the fact that she was from a different area in South Africa . . . Her experience may be different considering a different set of cultural practices and a different upbringing . . . Transactional sex among young girls and older men does contribute to the spread of HIV/AIDS; however, it is not the only factor that needs to be explored."

The final media presentation example is drawn from a session on sexual violence in South Africa. The assigned readings addressed so-called curative rape—the sexual assault of individuals with nonnormative sexualities or gender presentations in order to "correct" their behavior—the events surrounding the 2006 rape trial of former deputy president (and now president) Jacob Zuma, and the broader context surrounding sexual violence in South Africa.[25] The presenter showed a video about a court action launched by Sonke Gender Justice to challenge disparaging comments about Zuma's accuser.[26] "Julius Malema, the ANC Youth League President at the time, told Cape Town students that the woman who accused Zuma of rape actually enjoyed the sex, quoting cultural norms like 'staying for breakfast' and 'asking for taxi fare' as evidence," as the student wrote. The student encouraged us to consider "gender-based violence and patriarchal rhetoric that informs rape culture as part of a larger system of African women's oppression," highlighted the connections between the video and session texts, and raised several critical questions:

> The readings (and Suttner (2009)) discussed the complexities of gender-based violence in South Africa, using Zuma's trial as both evidence of structural challenges to women's equality and as a contingent place to trace contemporary insecurities relating to gender and sex. The importance of the video lies in the public outcry against Malema's comments regarding the rape survivor, Fezeka (Khwezi), and Sonke's understanding of sexist rhetoric as part of a larger

> patriarchal system that obstructs gender equality and justice. Questions that may come out of this media text include: what are the roles of men in contemporary struggles for gender equality and justice? Considering the past, how can Africans (particularly South Africans in this context) make gender equality and justice a physical reality as opposed to constitutional rhetoric? Also, how does language, the media, and the representation of women allow us (or prohibit us) to realize the potential of gender equality and justice?

Media presentations advance the seminar's principal pedagogical objectives: most students present interesting, current, and relevant videos that spark lively discussions and write thoughtful analyses that employ relevant concepts and consider the contexts in which differently situated African people experience oppression and exercise agency. In those instances where the clipping or the presenter's questions have reinforced broad stereotypes about undifferentiated Africans, other students have critiqued those stereotypes or articulated more nuanced perspectives during the discussion.

Student-led sessions direct our attention to the issues and questions in which students are most interested and build their capacities to facilitate nonviolent communication. As leaders, students facilitate a 35–45 minute discussion that addresses the issues they see as most important and encourages all participants to share their views and then write a reflective essay on the experience. The guidelines for this peer-guided learning activity state, "Your objective will be to assist your classmates to understand, analyze, and respond to the assigned texts by sharing your perspective, asking questions, and presenting relevant audiovisual material." I require each presenter to send his or her plans to me at least a day in advance and design the remainder of each session to complement the class leader's approach.

One student leader facilitated our spring 2014 discussion of the previously mentioned Caster Semenya case. Organizing her portion of the session around five issues—athlete versus activist, femininity and sports, sex determination testing, intersectionality, and politics—the leader displayed several different images of Semenya, showed a short video of a track race in which Semenya competed, and asked a series of open-ended questions that elicited participants' perspectives on these issues, the Semenya case, and the readings. In her reflection, the leader wrote,

> I realized that what I wanted my fellow students to learn from the reading was not necessarily the point. That was my subconscious objective: for them to learn what I had learned. The reality, however, is that the dialogue created is the true learning. When people parse out their own thoughts, they are learning. That is part of the reason that I framed my portion of the class in terms of questions. It allowed me to show what I had personally learned while allowing space for others to contribute as well.

Our second leader facilitated a discussion of Xavier Livermon's article, "Queer(y)ing Freedom: Black Queer Visibilities in Postapartheid South Africa."[27] Accompanied by a video about Cheaters, a popular radio show discussed in the article, this student invited us to consider the relationship between culture and politics in South Africa and the United States, to talk about how black queers use Cheaters to think about the relationship between blackness and queerness, and to discuss how South Africa's apartheid past affects contemporary cultural politics. The second leader wrote, "my actual experience far surpassed my preconceived notions of how the class would go . . .. there was thought-provoking, substantive discussion for each question I posed. In fact, the discussions we had were so lengthy that I did not even get a chance to present my final two questions."

These reflections suggest that student-led sessions encourage students to think about how people learn and to think about and try to create the conditions for open discussion, thereby preparing students to participate in collaborative peacebuilding dialogues. The activity can also build students' facilitation confidence and competence. Both presenters asked questions that fostered critical analysis, encouraged attention to context and agency, and consistently showed respect for Caster Semenya and the other individuals we discussed.

HIGHLIGHTING AFRICAN VOICES AND INITIATIVES

Believing that recognition and respect for the agency of all people is a fundamental requisite for peacebuilding, I view the recent resurgence of neocolonial savior discourses that suggest African children, women, and LGBTI-Q people need to be rescued by more liberated Westerners as a major hindrance to constructive engagement.[28] As Gayatri Spivak famously contended, expressions such as "white men are saving brown women from brown men," not only other brown people, thereby (re)producing hierarchical and racialized distinctions, but also render expressions and actions that do not fit into these narratives incomprehensible: savior narratives entail "the asymmetrical obliteration of the trace of that Other in its precarious Subject-ivity."[29] Close engagement with essays, films, creative texts, and scholarly publications that document Africans writing, speaking, and acting for themselves and that place contemporary struggles in historical and global context help counter these narratives by directing participants' attention to the differing ways in which African men, women, transgender/gender queer and intersex people describe their circumstances, make sense of their experiences, and work individually and collectively for change. The pedagogical aim in highlighting African voices is neither to provide an essentializing celebratory Afro-optimistic counter-narrative nor to discount analyses and interventions by non-Africans like myself but rather to foster serious and critical consideration of the perspectives, priorities, and strategies of those seminar participants who might want to help.

Heeding African perspectives on same-sex sexuality politics, for example, not only provides insider perspectives but also directs seminar participants' attention to past and present Western contributions to so-called African homophobia.[30] The films *Difficult Love* and *Call Me Kuchu*, and selections from the *Queer African Reader* grounded our discussion of same-sex sexuality politics.[31] These texts inform us that European colonial powers enacted many of the homophobic policies in place today; depict the joys, sorrows, and struggles of same-gender loving people in South Africa and Uganda; and provide a glimpse of the varied ways in which African politicians, journalists, religious leaders, and non-LGBTI-Q people perceive same-sex sexualities. *Call Me Kuchu* and the *Queer African Reader* highlight how alliances between American and African fundamentalist Christian evangelicals, many African politicians' heteropatriarchal nationalist discourse, transnational LGBTI groups' context-insensitive advocacy, and Western governments' interventions have contributed to resurgent "African homophobia." Seminar discussions of these issues gained heightened salience in 2014 due to their temporal coincidence with the widely publicized passage of the Same Sex Marriage Prohibition Act in Nigeria and the Anti-Homosexuality Act in Uganda; the consequent suspension or cancellation of foreign aid to Uganda from Denmark, Norway, Sweden, and the World Bank; and increased mobilization around African LGBTI-Q issues inside and outside the continent. Considering the interconnections between LGBTI-Q politics over time and across places shifts the impetus from saving other people to considering our roles in collective local, national, and global sexuality struggles.

Highlighting local perspectives and initiatives fosters a non-Orientalist approach to female genital cutting/mutilation (henceforth FGC/M), a harmful gendered practice now most widely practiced in the Horn of Africa and in West Africa. FGC/M encompasses a range of practices from "symbolic circumcision"—the nicking or pricking of the genitals—to excision and infibulation—the "narrowing of the vaginal orifice by cutting and bringing together the labia minora and/or the labia majora to create a type of seal."[32] FGC/M is often performed upon infants, children, and adolescents who are not yet capable of granting informed consent, who have not been asked whether they wish to be cut, or who decide while subject to considerable familial and social pressure, and it can have serious adverse health consequences for cut girls, women, and their children.[33] At present, 27 of the 29 countries in which FGC/M is most prevalent are in Africa, and more than 85 percent of girls and women in Somalia, Guinea, Djibouti, Egypt, Eritrea, Mali, Sierra Leone, and Sudan have been cut.[34]

FGC/M understandably has drawn attention, concern, and efforts to eradicate these practices across the globe. However, Western depictions of FGC/M and anti-FGC/M activism have been critiqued for "contribut[ing] to promoting a racist culture grounded in unequal power relations."[35] Western FGC/M discourses can reinforce the beliefs that African and Middle Eastern peoples are backward, non-Western women are passive, and Western women are relatively free. To counter these misrepresentations and foster critical inquiry, I assign texts that present African and Africanist perspectives on genital cutting. Critiquing Western fascination with cutting and presenting context-specific analyses of cutting practices and anti-cutting initiatives, these texts document variation in cutting prevalence and practices within and across Kenya, Senegal, South Africa, and Sudan; highlight local and national contestation over cutting; and bring male genital cutting into the conversation.[36] Considering male genital cutting has provoked discussion of why some cutting practices receive more opprobrium and encouraged participants to view FGC/M as one of many gendered cutting/mutilation practices across the globe. Examining the forces propelling continued FGC/M in some places despite anti-cutting interventions and anti-FGC/M laws serves to highlight strategic challenges confronting those trying to change or eradicate violent practices. In summary, highlighting African perspectives and initiatives regarding genital cutting/mutilation encourages a less othering approach to this violent practice.

CONCLUSION

This chapter has called attention to epistemic and other forms of violence to which African people are subject and contended that peacebuilding requires the decolonization of would-be-participants' minds. I have argued that popular (mis)representations of Africans have left many Americans ill-prepared to contribute to peacebuilding initiatives in the continent. Dominant representations and discourses foster a colonial mindset, one oriented to saving oppressed African girls, women, and LGBTI-Q people rather than working in partnership with African girls and boys, men and women, and transgender, intersex, and gender-queer people to address the violence from which all of us suffer and in which we are all implicated. This seminar seeks not only to increase participants' knowledge of gender/sexuality politics in Africa, but also to engender greater respect and recognition of the agency, initiatives, and perspectives of marginalized people in Africa and elsewhere by directly addressing participants' preconceptions and popular (mis)representations, building a shared conceptual vocabulary, using student-directed activities to build participants' critical faculties, and calling attention to affected peoples' perspectives and initiatives.

While this chapter has focused specifically on teaching African gender/sexuality politics in America, the pedagogical strategies described have relevance beyond American-African peacebuilding initiatives. Decolonial pedagogies are likely to be useful wherever people subject to violence have been misrepresented and misrecognized, and girls and women, non-gender normative people, and non-heterosexual people have been subject to epistemic, structural, and physical violence across the globe. Context-sensitive pedagogical interventions can assist us to better address the complex entanglements among gender, sexuality, and other socio-cultural-political constructs in violence and in peace.

NOTES

1. Binyavanga Wainaina, "How to Write About Africa. Some Tips: Sunsets and Starvation Are Good," *Granta*, no. 92 (2005); Jo Ellen Fair, "War, Famine, and Poverty: Race in the Construction of Africa's Media Image," *Journal of Communication Inquiry* 17.2 (1993).

2. For example Thabo Mbeki, "When Is Good News Bad News?" *ANC Today* 4.39, October 1–7, 2004, http://www.anc.org.za/docs/anctoday/2004/at39.htm; Desiree Lewis, "Representing African Sexualities," in *African Sexualities: A Reader*, ed. Sylvia Tamale (Oxford, England: Pambazuka Press, 2011).

I use "West" and "Western" throughout this chapter to concisely refer to Western Europe and North America while recognizing the co-constitutive character of "the West" and its others: Africa, Asia, the Orient, the Middle East.

3. Peyi Soyinka-Airewele and Rita Kiki Edozie, "Reframing Contemporary Africa: Beyond Global Imaginaries," in *Reframing Contemporary Africa: Politics, Economics, and Culture in the Global Era*, ed. Peyi Soyinka-Airewele and Rita Kiki Edozie (Washington, DC: CQ Press, 2009); Kathryn Mathers, "Mr. Kristof, I Presume? Saving Africa in the Footsteps of Nicholas Kristof," *Transitions* 107.1 (2012); Fair, "War, Famine, and Poverty."

4. I use "same-gender-loving" to refer to the broad range of non-heterosexual identities and LGBTI-Q (lesbian, gay, bisexual, transgender, intersex—queer) to refer to all people with nonnormative gender or sexual identities throughout this chapter.

5. Ngũgĩ wa Thiong'o, *Decolonising the Mind: The Politics of Language in African Literature* (London, England: James Currey, 1986).

6. Peyi Soyinka-Airewele, "Colonial Legacies: Ghosts, Gulags, and the Silenced Traumas of Empire, in *Reframing Contemporary Africa: Politics, Economics, and Culture in the Global Era*, ed. Peyi Soyinka-Airewele and Rita Kiki Edozie (Washington, DC: CQ Press, 2009).

7. Nelson Maldonado-Torres, "On the Coloniality of Being," *Cultural Studies* 21.2–3 (2007): 245, 49.

8. Ibid., 262. Also see Ramón Grosfoguel, "The Epistemic Decolonial Turn," *Cultural Studies* 21.2–3 (2007); Aníbal Quijano, "Coloniality and Modernity/Rationality," *Cultural Studies* 21.2–3 (2007).

9. Chimamanda Ngozi Adichie, "The Danger of a Single Story," filmed July 2009, TED video, 18:49, posted 2009. http://www.ted.com/talks/lang/eng/chimamanda_adichie_the_danger_of_a_single_story.html.

10. Kimberlé Crenshaw, "Demarginalizing the Intersection of Race and Sex: A Black Feminist Critique of Antidiscrimination Doctrine, Feminist Theory and Antiracist Politics," *The University of Chicago Legal Forum* (1989); Kimberlé Crenshaw, "Mapping the Margins: Intersectionality, Identity Politics, and Violence against Women of Color," *Stanford Law Review* 43.6 (1991); Sumi Cho, Kimberlé Williams Crenshaw, and Leslie McCall, "Toward a Field of Intersectionality Studies: Theory, Applications, and Praxis," *Signs* 38.4 (2013).

11. Lewis, "Representing African Sexualities," 202.

12. *Heterosexual Africa*? which I used as a core text in spring 2012, could also serve these pedagogical objectives; Marc Epprecht, *Heterosexual Africa? The History of an Idea from the Age of Exploration to the Age of AIDS*, New African Histories Series (Athens, OH: Ohio University Press, 2008).

13. Evan P. Apfelbaum, Michael I. Norton, and Samuel R. Sommers, "Racial Color Blindness: Emergence, Practice, and Implications," *Current Directions in Psychological Science* 21.3 (2012).

14. Lewis, "Representing African Sexualities," 213.

15. Anne Fausto-Sterling, "Dualing Dualisms," in *Sex, Gender, and Sexuality: The New Basics*, ed. Abby L. Ferber, Kimberly Holcomb, and Tre Wentling (New York, NY: Oxford University Press, 2009); Excerpted from Anne Fausto-Sterling, *Sexing the Body: Gender Politics and the Construction of Sexuality* (New York, NY: Basic Books, 2000).

16. Ibid., 7.

17. Julius Kaggwa, "Intersex: The Forgotten Constituency," in *African Sexualities: A Reader*, ed. Sylvia Tamale (Oxford, England: Pambazuka Press, 2011); Julius Kaggwa, "The Struggle for Intersex Rights in Africa," in *Queer African Reader*, ed. Sokari Ekine and Hakima Abbas (Oxford, England: Pambazuka Press, 2013), 203–08; Brenna Munro, "Caster Semenya: Gods and Monsters," *Safundi: The Journal of South African and American Studies* 11.4 (2011).

18. Kaggwa, "The Struggle for Intersex Rights in Africa," 204.

19. Jordanna Matlon, "*Il Est Garçon*: Marginal Abidjanais Masculinity and the Politics of Representation," *Poetics* 39.5 (2011); Pumla Dineo Gqola, "'A Woman Cannot Marry a Boy': Rescue, Spectacle and Transitional Xhosa Masculinities," in *From Boys to Men: Social Constructions of Masculinity in Contemporary Society*, ed. Tamara Shefer et al. (Cape Town, South Africa: UCT Press, 2007); Oyèrónkẹ́ Oyěwùmí, "Conceptualising Gender: Eurocentric Foundations of Feminist Concepts and the Challenge of African Epistemologies," in *African Gender Scholarship: Concepts, Methodologies, and Paradigms*, ed. Signe Arnfred (Dakar, Senegal: CODESRIA, 2004); Bibi Bakare-Yusuf, "'Yorubas Don't Do Gender': A Critical Review of Oyeronke Oyewumi's *The Invention of Women: Making an African Sense of Western Gender Discourses*," in *African Gender Scholarship: Concepts Methodologies, and Paradigms*, ed. Signe Arnfred (Dakar, Senegal: CODESRIA, 2004).

20. The media presentation discussion is adapted from Robin L. Turner, "Media Presentations as a Strategy for Teaching African Politics," *African Politics Conference Group Newsletter*, September 2013.

21. Mark Hunter, "The Materiality of Everyday Sex: Thinking Beyond 'Prostitution,'" *African Studies* 61.1 (2002).

22. "A Gay Kenyan's Struggle to Survive: Melvin and His Sister," *The Guardian*, March 18, 2011, http://youtu.be/JKnb8WOSTvo.

23. "Siyayinqoba Beat It! Episode 6: Intergenerational Sex," 5:43, South Africa, Community Media Trust, 2008, http://youtu.be/gPwNP2GpYwA.

24. Hunter, "The Materiality of Everyday Sex," 100–1.

25. Zanele Muholi, "Thinking through Lesbian Rape," *Agenda: Empowering Women for Gender Equity* 18.61 (2004); Jane Bennett, "Challenges Were Many: The One in Nine Campaign, South Africa," in *Changing Their World: Challenges and Practices of Women's Movements*, ed. Srilatha Batliwala (Toronto, ON, Mexico City, Mexico, and Cape Town, South Africa: AWID, 2008); One in Nine Campaign, "Five Years of Exile and Injustice: Fezeka (Khwezi) Still in Exile after Accusing Zuma of Rape" (Johannesburg, South Africa: One in Nine Campaign, 2011); Dean Peacock and Bafana Khumalo, "'Bring Me My Machine Gun': Contesting Patriarchy and Rape Culture in the Wake of the Jacob Zuma Rape Trial," paper presented at *Politicizing Masculinities: Beyond the Personal*, Dakar, Senegal, October 2007.

26. Sonke Gender Justice is a South Africa-based organization that works toward gender equality with African men and boys; "Sonke Gender Justice Takes Julius Malema to the Equality Court," YouTube video, posted by "Helen Alexander," February 24, 2010. http://youtu.be/T8cHMcYGTDM.

27. Xavier Livermon, "Queer(y)ing Freedom: Black Queer Visibilities in Post-apartheid South Africa," *GLQ-A Journal of Lesbian and Gay Studies*, 18.2–3 (2012).

28. See Mathers, "Mr. Kristof, I Presume?"

29 Gayatri Spivak, "Can the Subaltern Speak?" in *Marxism and the Interpretation of Culture*, ed. Cary Nelson and Lawrence Grossberg (London, England: Macmillan, 1988), 296, 81.

30. Sibongile Ndashe, "The Single Story of 'African Homophobia' is Dangerous for LGBTI Activism," in *Queer African Reader*, ed. Sokari Ekine and Hakima Abbas (Oxford, England: Pambazuka Press, 2013).

31. Zanele Muholi and Peter Goldsmid, *Difficult Love* (South Africa: SABC, 2010), http://www.imdb.com/video/wab/vi3128728089; Katherine Fairfax Wright and Malika Zouhali-Worrall, *Call Me Kuchu* (Los Angeles, CA: Cinedigm Entertainment, 2012); Ekine Sokari and Hakima Abbas, eds., *Queer African Reader* (Oxford, England: Pambazuka Press, 2013).

32. UNICEF, *Female Genital Mutilation/Cutting: A Statistical Overview and Exploration of the Dynamics of Change* (New York, NY: UNICEF, 2013), 7.

33. Ibid.; WHO, *Eliminating Female Genital Mutilation: An Interagency Statement—UNAIDS, UNDP, UNECA, UNESCO, UNFPA, UNHCHR, UNHCR, UNICEF, UNIFEM, WHO* (Geneva, Switzerland: WHO, 2008).

34. UNICEF, *Female Genital Mutilation/Cutting.*

35. Chima Korieh, "'Other' Bodies: Western Feminism, Race, and Representation in Female Circumcision Discourse," in *Female Circumcision and the Politics of Knowledge: African Women in Imperialist Discourses*, ed. Obioma Nnaemeka (Westport, CT: Praeger, 2005).

36. Ibid.; Liselott Dellenborg, "A Reflection on the Cultural Meanings of Female Circumcision: Experiences from Fieldwork in Casamance, Southern Senegal," in *Re-Thinking Sexualities in Africa*, ed. Signe Arnfred (Uppsala, Sweden: Nordiska Afrikainstitutet, 2004); Asha Mohamud, Samson Radeny, and Karin Ringheim, "Community-Based Efforts to End Female Genital Mutilation in Kenya: Raising Awareness and Organizing Alternative Rites of Passage," in *Female Circumcision: Multicultural Perspectives*, ed. Rogaia Mustafa Abusharaf (Philadelphia, PA: University of Pennsylvania Press, 2006); Gqola, "'A Woman Cannot Marry a Boy'"; Ellen Gruenbaum, "Feminist Activism for the Abolition of FGC in Sudan," *Journal of Middle East Women's Studies*, 1.2 (2011); Sami A. Aldeeb Abu-Sahlieh, "Male and Female Circumcision: The Myth of the Difference," in *Female Circumcision: Multicultural Perspectives*, ed. Rogaia Mustafa Abusharaf (Philidelphia, PA: University of Pennsylvania Press, 2006).

BIBLIOGRAPHY

"A Gay Kenyan's Struggle to Survive: Melvin and His Sister." *The Guardian*, March 18, 2011. http://youtu.be/JKnb8WOSTvo.

Abu-Sahlieh, Sami A Aldeeb. "Male and Female Circumcision: The Myth of the Difference." In *Female Circumcision: Multicultural Perspectives*, edited by Rogaia Mustafa Abusharaf, 47–72. Philadelphia, PA: University of Pennsylvania Press, 2006.

Adichie, Chimamanda Ngozi. "The Danger of a Single Story." Filmed July 2009. TED video, 18:49. Posted 2009. http://www.ted.com/talks/lang/eng/chimamanda_adichie_the_danger_of_a_single_story.html.

Apfelbaum, Evan P., Michael I. Norton, and Samuel R. Sommers. "Racial Color Blindness: Emergence, Practice, and Implications." *Current Directions in Psychological Science* 21.3 (2012): 205–09.

Bakare-Yusuf, Bibi. "'Yorubas Don't Do Gender': A Critical Review of Oyeronke Oyewumi's *The Invention of Women: Making an African Sense of Western Gender Discourses*." In *African Gender Scholarship: Concepts, Methodologies, and Paradigms*, edited by Signe Arnfred, 61–81. Dakar, Senegal: Council for the Development of Social Science Research in Africa (CODESRIA), 2004.

Bennett, Jane. "Challenges Were Many: The One in Nine Campaign, South Africa." In *Changing Their World: Challenges and Practices of Women's Movements*, edited by Srilatha Batliwala, 48–50. Toronto, ON, Mexico City, Mexico, and Cape Town, South Africa: Association for Women's Rights in Development (AWID), 2008.

Cho, Sumi, Kimberlé Williams Crenshaw, and Leslie McCall. "Toward a Field of Intersectionality Studies: Theory, Applications, and Praxis." *Signs* 38.4 (2013): 785–810.

Crenshaw, Kimberlé. "Demarginalizing the Intersection of Race and Sex: A Black Feminist Critique of Antidiscrimination Doctrine, Feminist Theory and Antiracist Politics." *University of Chicago Legal Forum* (1989): 139–67.

———. "Mapping the Margins: Intersectionality, Identity Politics, and Violence against Women of Color." *Stanford Law Review* 43.6 (1991): 1241–99.

Dellenborg, Liselott. "A Reflection on the Cultural Meanings of Female Circumcision: Experiences from Fieldwork in Casamance, Southern Senegal." In *Re-Thinking Sexualities in Africa*, edited by Signe Arnfred, 79–94. Uppsala, Sweden: Nordiska Afrikainstitutet, 2004.

Ekine, Sokari and Hakima Abbas, eds. *Queer African Reader*. Oxford, England: Pambazuka Press, 2013.

Epprecht, Marc. *Heterosexual Africa? The History of an Idea from the Age of Exploration to the Age of AIDS*. New African Histories Series. Athens, OH: Ohio University Press, 2008.

Fair, Jo Ellen. "War, Famine, and Poverty: Race in the Construction of Africa's Media Image." *Journal of Communication Inquiry* 17.2 (1993): 5–22.

Fausto-Sterling, Anne. "Dualing Dualisms." In *Sex, Gender, and Sexuality: The New Basics*, edited by Abby L. Ferber, Kimberly Holcomb, and Tre Wentling, 6–21. New York, NY: Oxford University Press, 2009.

———. *Sexing the Body: Gender Politics and the Construction of Sexuality*. New York, NY: Basic Books, 2000.

Gqola, Pumla Dineo. "'A Woman Cannot Marry a Boy': Rescue, Spectacle and Transitional Xhosa Masculinities." In *From Boys to Men: Social Constructions of Masculinity in Contemporary Society*, edited by Tamara Shefer, Kopano Ratele, Anna Strebel, Nokuthula Shabalala, and Rosemarie Buikema, 145–59. Cape Town, South Africa: UCT Press, 2007.

Grosfoguel, Ramón. "The Epistemic Decolonial Turn." *Cultural Studies* 21.2–3 (2007): 211–23.

Gruenbaum, Ellen. "Feminist Activism for the Abolition of FGC in Sudan." *Journal of Middle East Women's Studies* 1.2 (2011): 89–111.

Hunter, Mark. "The Materiality of Everyday Sex: Thinking Beyond 'Prostitution.'" *African Studies* 61.1 (2002): 99–120.

Kaggwa, Julius. "Intersex: The Forgotten Constituency." In *African Sexualities: A Reader*, edited by Sylvia Tamale, 231–34. Oxford, England: Pambazuka Press, 2011.

———. "The Struggle for Intersex Rights in Africa." In *Queer African Reader*, edited by Sokari Ekine and Hakima Abbas, 203–08. Oxford, England: Pambazuka Press, 2013.

Korieh, Chima. "'Other' Bodies: Western Feminism, Race, and Representation in Female Circumcision Discourse." In *Female Circumcision and the Politics of Knowledge: African Women in Imperialist Discourses*, edited by Obioma Nnaemeka, 111–32. Westport, CT: Praeger, 2005.

Lewis, Desiree. "Representing African Sexualities." In *African Sexualities: A Reader*, edited by Sylvia Tamale, 199–216. Oxford, England: Pambazuka Press, 2011.

Livermon, Xavier. "Queer(y)ing Freedom: Black Queer Visibilities in Postapartheid South Africa." *GLQ-A Journal of Lesbian and Gay Studies* 18.2–3 (2012): 297–323.

Maldonado-Torres, Nelson. "On the Coloniality of Being." *Cultural Studies* 21.2–3 (2007): 240–70.

Mathers, Kathryn. "Mr. Kristof, I Presume? Saving Africa in the Footsteps of Nicholas Kristof." *Transitions* 107.1 (2012): 14–31.

Matlon, Jordanna. "*Il Est Garçon*: Marginal Abidjanais Masculinity and the Politics of Representation." *Poetics* 39.5 (2011): 380–406.

Mbeki, Thabo. "When Is Good News Bad News?" *ANC Today* 4.39, October 1–7, 2004. http://www.anc.org.za/docs/anctoday/2004/at39.htm.

Mohamud, Asha, Samson Radeny, and Karin Ringheim. "Community-Based Efforts to End Female Genital Mutilation in Kenya: Raising Awareness and Organizing Alternative Rites of Passage." In *Female Circumcision: Multicultural Perspectives*, edited by Rogaia Mustafa Abusharaf, 75–103. Philadelphia, PA: University of Pennsylvania Press, 2006.

Muholi, Zanele. "Thinking through Lesbian Rape." *Agenda: Empowering Women for Gender Equity* 18.61 (2004): 116–25.

Muholi, Zanele and Peter Goldsmid. *Difficult Love*. South Africa: South African Broadcasting Corporation (SABC), 2010. http://www.imdb.com/video/wab/vi3128728089, 2010.

Munro, Brenna. "Caster Semenya: Gods and Monsters." *Safundi: The Journal of South African and American Studies* 11.4 (2011): 383–96.

Ndashe, Sibongile. "The Single Story of 'African Homophobia' Is Dangerous for LGBTI Activism." In *Queer African Reader*, edited by Sokari Ekine and Hakima Abbas, 155–64. Oxford, England: Pambazuka Press, 2013.

One in Nine Campaign. "Five Years of Exile and Injustice: Fezeka (Khwezi) Still in Exile after Accusing Zuma of Rape." Johannesburg, South Africa: One in Nine Campaign, 2011.

Oyěwùmí, Oyèrónké. "Conceptualising Gender: Eurocentric Foundations of Feminist Concepts and the Challenge of African Epistemologies." In *African Gender Scholarship: Concepts, Methodologies, and Paradigms*, edited by Signe Arnfred. Dakar, 1–8, Senegal: CODESRIA, 2004.

Peacock, Dean, and Bafana Khumalo. "'Bring Me My Machine Gun': Contesting Patriarchy and Rape Culture in the Wake of the Jacob Zuma Rape Trial." Paper presented at *Politicizing Masculinities: Beyond the Personal*, Dakar, Senegal, October 2007.

Quijano, Aníbal. "Coloniality and Modernity/Rationality." *Cultural Studies* 21.2–3 (2007): 168–78.

"Siyayinqoba Beat It! Episode 6: Intergenerational Sex." 5:43. South Africa: Community Media Trust, 2008. http://youtu.be/gPwNP2GpYwA.

"Sonke Gender Justice Takes Julius Malema to the Equality Court." YouTube video. Posted by "Helen Alexander," February 24, 2010. http://www.youtube.com/watch?v=T8cHMcYGTDM.

Soyinka-Airewele, Peyi. "Colonial Legacies: Ghosts, Gulags, and the Silenced Traumas of Empire." In *Reframing Contemporary Africa: Politics, Economics, and Culture in the Global Era*, edited by Peyi Soyinka-Airewele and Rita Kiki Edozie, 100–30. Washington, DC: CQ Press, 2009.

Soyinka-Airewele, Peyi and Rita Kiki Edozie. "Reframing Contemporary Africa: Beyond Global Imaginaries." In *Reframing Contemporary Africa: Politics, Economics, and Culture in the Global Era*, edited by Peyi Soyinka-Airewele and Rita Kiki Edozie, 4–33. Washington, DC: CQ Press, 2009.

Spivak, Gayatri. "Can the Subaltern Speak?" In *Marxism and the Interpretation of Culture*, edited by Cary Nelson and Lawrence Grossberg, 271–316. London, England: Macmillan, 1988.

Thiong'o, Ngũgĩ wa. *Decolonising the Mind: The Politics of Language in African Literature*. London, England: James Currey, 1986.

Turner, Robin L. "Media Presentations as a Strategy for Teaching African Politics." *African Politics Conference Group Newsletter*, 7–8, September 2013.

United Nations Children's Fund (UNICEF). *Female Genital Mutilation/Cutting: A Statistical Overview and Exploration of the Dynamics of Change*. New York, NY: UNICEF, 2013.

Wainaina, Binyavanga. "How to Write About Africa. Some Tips: Sunsets and Starvation Are Good." *Granta*, no. 92 (2005): 91–97.

World Health Organization (WHO). *Eliminating Female Genital Mutilation: An Interagency Statement—UNAIDS, UNDP, UNECA, UNESCO, UNFPA, UNHCHR, UNHCR, UNICEF, UNIFEM, WHO*. Geneva, Switzerland: WHO, 2008.

Wright, Katherine Fairfax and Malika Zouhali-Worrall. *Call Me Kuchu*. Los Angeles, CA: Cinedigm Entertainment, 2012.

PART III

MOVING FORWARD

Chapter 20

Gender, Violence, and Dehumanization

No Peace with Patriarchy

Franke Wilmer

One question about gender and war sure to ignite debate is "would the world be as violent if women were in charge, if women ran the world?" Violence is, after all, the problem that gives rise to the need for peacebuilding. After momentary discomfort, most students, almost apologetically, and avoiding an essentialist position, say, "well of course it would be, women are just like men."

Today, students of gender studies know that it is more complicated. It's not about women or men "running things"; it's about how societies masculinize boys to conform to behavior that affirms their identity as men and girls to a feminine identity that will sustain patriarchy. Patriarchy is a system of power relations, including the power to construct patriarchal gendered identities and reproduce them over time. Shifting the focus to gender suggests that the problem is not literally the domination of women by men, but the ideology of patriarchy that produces and reproduces identities and power relations that sustain and defend patriarchy. The problem is that political behavior and political institutions are masculinized. Masculine identity is not given; it is constructed specifically to elevate and naturalize patriarchal norms—domination, control, and fear.

"First we should get rid of patriarchy," says 2003 Nobel Peace Prize recipient and former Iranian judge, and now human rights advocate, Shirin Ebadi, "then we will see what problems Islam has with women. We need to fight patriarchy," she says, "not men."[1] That patriarchy privileges a particular idea of masculinity does not mean that it necessarily or only privileges men and marginalizes women. Indeed, men who reject masculine socialization are also marginalized, disciplined, punished, and risk becoming the targets of violence as are women who reject patriarchal feminine socialization.

As an ideology that naturalizes domination, control, and fear, patriarchy structures power as a dichotomous hierarchy of oppositional categories stemming from dominance by the masculine over the feminine: men over women (literally), public over private, reason over emotion, individual freedom over obligations of relationship, and war over peace. Feminists often criticize dichotomous hierarchies as a product of patriarchal epistemology.[2] The assertion that there are "women's human rights," for example, obscures the "male-as-norm" assumption of the broader category of human rights. Differences in reproductive functions really make no difference in terms of rights; men and women both want and expect respect for bodily integrity and respect for bodily integrity is a human right. When trapped within the gendered ideology of patriarchal domination, neither men nor women can achieve full respect for their humanity, for their existence and dignity as human beings.

So the question should be, would a world run by men and women, freed from the entrapment of patriarchal gendered identities be as violent as the one we now live in? Is the path to dismantling patriarchy and liberating all of us from the ideology of patriarchy also the path to less violence, and more sustainable peace as the norm? That is the question examined in this chapter. Sustainable peace and stable institutions require not only de-patriarchalized women's participation in peace processes, but also the dismantling of institutional patriarchal practices and norms and the involvement of de-patriarchalized men as well as women in peace processes and post-conflict capacity building.

PATRIARCHY AS A POLITICAL PROBLEM

Patriarchy kills. Patriarchy is the ideological foundation of a social system that naturalizes domination, control, and fear, and socializes men to carry out and sustain that system through force, violence, and intimidation, and women to enable and reproduce men to do so. Our present world order—economically, politically, and socially—including relations between states as well as the structure of the state itself, is grounded in patriarchal norms. From the "wounded manhood" that fuels militarization and war, to the 40 percent of women worldwide who were killed by an intimate partner, and the one-third of the world's women who have been sexually or physically assaulted by a current or former partner, patriarchy kills publicly and privately in genocides, epidemics of violence, atrocities, and sexualized criminal behavior.[3] According to the United Nations, "women aged 15–44 are more at risk from rape and domestic violence than from cancer, car accidents, war and malaria."[4]

Patriarchy is antiliberal, immoral, and unethical.[5] When viewed only as "the dominance of women by men," it is easily misunderstood as an injustice that can be remedied by electing more women heads of state, increasing the number of women visible and present in roles previously reserved for men, eliminating inequalities of status between men and women. But the "dominance of women by men" view does not address the underlying cause of inequalities—the patriarchal paradigm of domination, control, and fear to which men and women are socialized. It also overlooks entirely the role of patriarchalized women in sustaining patriarchy, as well as the possibility of patriarchalized women and men carrying out acts of violence against feminized men, and the role of patriarchal ideology in producing and rationalizing hate and violence toward gay, lesbian, and transgender people. Without dismantling patriarchal ideology, the women most likely to rise to positions of influence or become heads of state will be those who are more, rather than less or not at all, patriarchalized.

Patriarchy is antiliberal because liberalism rests on the twin pillars of justice and liberty. Liberty for some is not justice; unequal liberties are unjust. Patriarchy is the metanarrative of domination that makes all other forms of domination possible. Domination and liberalism cannot coexist. Gerda Lerner argues that patriarchy prefigured and enabled the development of slavery, based on the belief that bodies and their labor can be treated politically, economically, and legally as property. "Women's sexuality and reproductive potential," Lerner says, "became a commodity to be exchanged or acquired for the service of the family."[6] Patriarchy rests on a system of hierarchical property rights ranging from a distribution of wealth and power to a narrowing ruling class at the top, and down to a bottom that excludes the largest number of people not only by denying them access to basic needs of dignified human existence, but also sovereignty over their own body and labor.

What might be called the first stage of liberalization—the overthrow of monarchs and the establishment of more decentered rule by men of property—was actually the overthrow of rule of the fathers by their sons. This replaced the literal rule by fathers with a "fraternal patriarchy," as Carole Pateman calls it.[7] A second liberal revolution is therefore necessary to overthrow fraternal patriarchy if liberalism grounded in the codependent ideals of justice and liberty—or equal liberty—is to be realized.

Patriarchy is immoral because domination is immoral and because, as when it manifests as slavery, it is predicated on moral exclusion. Moral exclusion occurs when one group affords its own members moral reciprocity while excluding non-group members from the same moral regard. "Others" are regarded, at best, as having a diminished humanity or diminished entitlement to treatment as moral equals. At worst, they are dehumanized. Sheryl WuDunn and Nicholas Kristof assert that women's worldwide oppression is the great moral issue of the twenty-first century, like the defeat of totalitarianism in the twentieth and the ending of the slave trade in the nineteenth. Indeed, they view the oppression of women as "twenty-first century slavery."[8]

In their recent book on the cultural and political evolution of patriarchy and its tension with liberal democracy, Carol Gilligan and David Richards, make the argument that connection and relationality are what make ethical and moral reasoning possible. Connection and relationality are realized through sexual intimacy, which under patriarchy is ruptured and traumatized:

> If one can justify shutting down the forms of sexual intimacy through which human beings experience loving connection, care, and mutual responsiveness, one is well on the way to shutting down the psychological basis for ethical reasoning and experience, making the acceptance of stereotypes that dehumanize and thus rationalize atrocity.[9]

Patriarchy actually *impairs* our capacity for moral and ethical reasoning. Viewing all systems of domination—race, economic class, gender, religion, ethnicity, totalitarianism—as enabled by underlying patriarchal ideology explains why these systems keep rearing their ugly heads, even in liberal democracies where patriarchal norms have not been confronted and transformed. It also reveals, in relief, sites of resistance. Before turning to some of those, however, a brief description of how these dynamics play out in the sexualized political violence in the Democratic Republic of Congo will illustrate many of the previous points.

RAPE, TORTURE, WAR, AND PRISON

A study published in June 2011 found that over one thousand women per day were being raped in the Democratic Republic of Congo.[10] The use of rape in war as a form of torture and terror is not new. Revelations about the victims including more men and perpetrators including more women are. That same year, two brothers were captured as they attempted to leave the country seeking safety in neighboring Uganda after their parents were murdered in the eastern region of the DR Congo. Their captors, six men armed with guns, machetes, and sticks raped and left them unconscious in the forest.[11] The younger brother was so badly injured he needed surgery. A report published in the Journal of the American Medical Association estimates that as many as 23.6 percent of men from eastern regions have suffered some kind of sexual violence.[12] A 36-year-old mother traveling by bicycle in the same area of DR Congo was stopped by "bandits":

> "When I saw women, I thought I was saved," she recalls. Not so. The women were armed and dressed in military uniform. They argued with the men in the group over who would "have" Marie. The women won.

> "They asked why I was here doing business while they were starving," she remembers. "They told me I was fat, and that I'd stay with them in the forest until I become thin." One started to push her fingers inside Marie. Another tried to introduce her hand. The women continued to psychologically and physically abuse Marie for four days. She was forced to imitate sexual pleasure as they assaulted her. By the fourth day she was bleeding so much that the women gave up. They wanted to kill her, but the men in the group argued with them. Finally, after nine days, the militia let her go.[13]

One study of human rights abuses in eastern Congo found that 40 percent of the women and 10 percent of the men surveyed in 1000 households reported being subjected to sexual violence perpetrated by women.[14]

As Gilligan and Richards show, it is true that women are better positioned to resist patriarchal socialization, and they are socialized at a later time in their emotional development, but they do not escape it. Patriarchy is a shared social order. Patriarchy functions "normally" in times of peace to sustain a social order of hierarchical domination, but in the environment of war or armed violence, it is heightened and intensified. Patriarchal domination and submission are also reproduced in the prison environment evidenced by sexual violence committed by men against other men. As one former prisoner put it:

> In prison, the concentration of the patriarchy pathology is on *steroids*—even tho' there are no women in men's prisons. Not as prisoners anyway. No need really, cause patriarchy is also homophobia and heterosexism, so it finds expression in this way. Whether thru predation or hate outright, ill vibrations play out against gays or transgender prisoners as, invariably, they are referred to as "punk," "faggots," "bitches," etc.[15]

These disturbing anecdotes illustrate that women as well as men can be perpetrators *because* they are both socialized to patriarchal norms. They also show that both men and women can be victimized because victims are sexualized as feminine (or feminized) in a system of hierarchical *gendered* domination.

SITES OF RESISTANCE AND STRUGGLE

Once one realizes how pervasive and naturalized patriarchal norms are and how deeply they penetrate and structure our social order, sites of resistance also become more apparent. Feminisms (there are many rich debates and categories of feminism) have long been defined as sites of resistance to patriarchy, but resistance occurs wherever people resist domination or seek to replace domination and control with partnership and symbiosis.[16]

In deepening my own understanding of patriarchy as causal to domination and violence, I came to a new understanding of my earlier work as engaging sites of resistance and struggle grounded in a more fundamental resistance to and struggle with patriarchy—Indigenous peoples' struggle for justice locally and globally, and the dehumanizing violence of the Yugoslav wars in the 1990s.

Many Indigenous cultures are far less patriarchal than modern societies or not patriarchal at all. Indigenous peoples generally live in small-scale communities and are descendants of the first inhabitants of an area that has since been subjected to the domination of political institutions built by European settlers in what are now settler states. Tim Coulter of the Indian Law Resource Center says Indigenous peoples are "American Indians and people like that."[17]

Indigenous cultures generally view the earth as holistic, feminine, and sacred, a strong indicator of a non-patriarchal ideology. They also view their relationship with the earth and its resources as a codependent and symbiotic partnership. When Western imperialists and colonizing settlers and later, anthropologists, encountered Indigenous cultures, they interpreted their observations through the lens of their own patriarchal values. This often led to misinterpretation about the structure of gender and gender relations among Indigenous peoples.

The Haudenosaunnee (Iroquois) Grand Council provides an example. The Council is made up of men who serve in the roles of council member (chief) and faith keeper (who oversees the chief). At first, this may look like a patriarchal system, but each chief and faith keeper is associated with a sponsoring Clan Mother. In fact, the faith keepers' role is to inform Clan Mothers if and when chiefs fail to conduct themselves in a manner that reflects the "good mind" of a leader. A good-minded leader takes into consideration the impact of decisions on the whole community, appreciates the need for compromise and conciliation, and approaches decision making with these values in mind.

Many traditional Indigenous peoples refer to their communities and their relationship to all "living beings" in terms of "relations" or using the metaphor of "all my relations." It is the basis for Indigenous ethics, both within the community and between the community and its natural surroundings or what Westerners would call the environment and natural resources. This is consistent with the relationality that Gilligan and Richards claim is the basis for non-patriarchal ethical and moral reasoning. As holistically earth-centric and regarding the femininity of the earth as sacred, Indigenous worldviews directly threatened the patriarchal order brought by Europeans.

It should be noted that there is tremendous diversity across Indigenous cultures; indeed, one of the features that distinguish Indigenous from Western/European cultures is that they value diversity and cultural distinctiveness and resist homogenization and totalization. There are debates among anthropologists and Indigenous scholars about commonalities and differences among Indigenous cultures in terms of social structure, gender relations, and the construction of gender identity.[18] But in December 1992 Indigenous leaders from all over the world spoke at the Opening Ceremonies of the United Nations International Year of Indigenous Peoples and all spoke of their common values—earth-centric, human interdependency with the natural world, and of the earth as a metaphoric mother figure to humans and all living beings.[19]

Understanding the depth of patriarchal penetration into the foundation of the dominant social order today also prompted a rethinking of my earlier work drawing on psychoanalytic theory as an explanatory tool for understanding identity conflicts and violence.[20] Psychoanalytic theory, particularly feminist interpretations, suggests that a psychic split in early emotional development creates a vulnerability to the development of identities prone to moral exclusion and moral exclusionary behavior.[21]

Feminist psychologists like Dorothy Dinnerstein and Nancy Chodorow point to absent fathers and ruptured or at least conflicted infant-parent relationships with an earlier impact on boys (early childhood as gender identity begins to develop) than girls (adolescence as differentiation from the mother becomes important in identity development) as a root cause.[22] It was Carol Gilligan, whose widely influential work on differences in the moral reasoning of boys and girls, working with David Richards on the question of patriarchy's progressive entrenchment in Western culture from ancient Rome to the fraternal liberalism of democracies in the West today who make the explicit link to patriarchy and its psychic effect on moral development.[23]

Women's movements in general and women's (and other) peace movements specifically have long recognized their struggle as one against masculinized violence and this was true in former Yugoslavia as well.[24] But like the DR Congo, women like Biljana Plavšić could be found in high profile leadership positions advocating for the dehumanization of the enemy, and men were also victims of dehumanizing sexualized violence in the prisoner camps, though overwhelmingly the perpetrators were men and victims were women, elderly, and children.[25] The question remains, why, from the perspective of psychoanalytic explanations, do certain conflicts descend rapidly into pathological violence with a high incidence of sexualized torture and genocide, and others do not? This has important implications for finding paths to stable peace in the aftermath of conflict as well as preventing conflicts from becoming pathologized in the first place.

To some extent, earlier psychoanalytic theories applied to the question of political violence implicated not only the absent father but also the gender of early childhood and infancy caretakers—usually breastfeeding mothers—as problematic. In this account, male anxiety associated with identity development seems difficult to mitigate, almost inevitably so. In many Indigenous communities, uncles, grandfathers, and male relatives generally are involved in the caretaking of young boys at a very young age, almost as soon as they can walk. Infants and children are frequently in the company of a large extended family and experience physical intimacy and affection from a large number of adults of both sexes. Does the opportunity for close and affectionate relationships between boys and men at an early age explain differences between some Indigenous and modern societies in the proneness to large-scale, collective, and pathologically violent "othering?"

Viewing these cases and psychoanalytic theory's insight into identity conflict through the lens of a deeper patriarchal explanation opened new possibilities for resolving some of the unanswered questions. If patriarchy has developed in connection with the notion of private property, as many suggest, and if patriarchy is an underlying, permissive causal factor in explaining violence in personal as well as intergroup relations, then perhaps patriarchy is "thicker" and "thinner" in different sociocultural settings. If patriarchy can deepen as a cultural foundation over time, as Gilligan and Richards' work suggests, then it can also vary by degree across historical time and cultural space. From the perspective of peacebuilding, if patriarchy varies in this way, can it be engineered or made to vary? Can it be lessened? Can it even be dismantled?

THE EMOTIONAL PROBLEM OF PATRIARCHY

In his article "Liberal Democracy and the Problem of Patriarchy," David Richards asks why is it so difficult to see what is before our eyes, our common humanity? Rather than asking how do we gain the capacity to care, how do we develop a capacity for mutual understanding, how do we learn to take the point of view of the other or to overcome the pursuit of self-interest, we are prompted to ask: how do we loose the capacity to care: what inhibits our ability to empathize with others and read their intentions, what stunts our desire to cooperate with others, and, more painfully, how do we lose the capacity to love?[26]

Overlaying the Richards and Gilligan argument that patriarchal socialization blinds us to our common humanity revealed sites of resistance in my previous research. It was there in Indigenous resistance to European imperialism and assimilation—and othering Indigenous cultures as "backward" and "primitive." It was there in the individual and collective psychic fractures that enabled patriarchal leaders to mobilize and provoke dehumanizing violence in former Yugoslavia. It is there in every attempt to remedy, reveal, and resist the injuries of social domination over social justice. Unknowingly, unwittingly, theorists of liberal democracy planted the seeds of the inevitable struggle between liberation and patriarchal control. There can be no peace without justice, and there can be no justice without dismantling the patriarchal foundations of contemporary sociopolitical order/s.

Patriarchy naturalizes domination. No democracy will be stable and sustainable without confronting this fact. How does it damage the psyche in ways that produce and reproduce domination, control, and fear *as if they were the normal human condition?* This is the question tackled by Gilligan and Richards as they trace the transformation of the Roman Republic into the Roman Empire, and the cultural and normative penetration of patriarchal violence—and resistances to it—in religion, psychology, the arts, and politics.

In their account, the first move is to rupture the connection between reason and emotion through trauma and loss of intimacy. In a later essay addressing the tension between liberalism and patriarchy, Richards recounts recent research on the emotion-reason split from neurobiology, evolutionary anthropology, and research on infant cognitive and emotional development. All findings turn on its head the notion of a split as the original condition of the psyche and show that, to the contrary, humans are "hard-wired to connect mind and body, emotion and thought."[27] Says Richards:

> We are by nature homo empathicus rather than homo lupus. Cooperation is wired into our nervous system, and our brains light up more brightly when we opt for cooperative rather than competitive strategies—the same area of the brain lit up by chocolate.[28]

That hard wiring *should* give rise to the development of empathetic connection and relationality—our common humanity. Instead, patriarchy relies on rending that connection, leading to dissociation, which in turn enables the production and reproduction of hierarchies of domination, exclusion, and marginalization within the family, community, the state, and in enmity in intergroup and interstate relations that seem "natural." Dissociation, says Gilligan and Richards, makes "intolerance possible and appealing" by destroying the relational intelligence that gives us the capacity for "loving connection, care, and mutual responsiveness."[29] Connection, care, and reciprocity provide the psychological foundation for moral and ethical reasoning. Destroying them makes the acceptance of stereotypes that dehumanize and rationalize atrocity possible.

What follows from traumatic loss of emotional intimacy is "a shutting down of the very sources of our relational intelligence and imagination, including ethical intelligence" and produces a "psychology that requires enemies, and the disassociation makes it easier to dehumanize them and thus to rationalize unjust violence against them."[30] Since patriarchal dissociation undermines the capacity for intimate and real relationships as well as ethical reasoning, it produces individuals and societies characterized by *an underlying propensity to violence* (as Gilligan and Richards call it). This propensity to violence is enacted in varying degrees through hierarchies of dominance and subordination, privilege and marginalization, and dehumanization based on moral exclusion. What my previous work in the former Yugoslavia suggests is that the propensity to violence produced by patriarchy can be mobilized when two additional variables are present: a sense of collective trauma, and leaders willing to exploit it by mobilizing people to act out patriarchal violence.

NO STABLE, SUSTAINABLE PEACE WITH PATRIARCHY

The argument thus far is that underlying all other causes of violence is the patriarchal system built on and sustained by the ideology and practice of domination as the natural order of things, fear, and control. In looking for the causes of violence, we are like fish swimming around looking for water—but actually the water is not exactly what we are looking for—we are looking for what's in the water that is making us sick. It is polluted and it is the pollution we are looking for—polluted by patriarchy. We need to take Confucius's advice and start by naming the problem. In 2000 the UN Security Council adopted a landmark resolution linking women's participation in peacebuilding to achieving sustainable peace and security in the aftermath of conflict. Resolution 1325 reaffirms

> . . . the important role of women in the prevention and resolution of conflicts and in peace-building, and stressing the importance of their equal participation and full involvement in all efforts for the maintenance and promotion of peace and security, and the need to increase their role in decision-making with regard to conflict prevention and resolution.[31]

The resolution also calls on (state and non-state) actors to "incorporate gender perspectives in all United Nations peace and security efforts" and take

> . . . special measures to protect women and girls from gender-based violence, particularly rape and other forms of sexual abuse, in armed conflict.[32]

But we must recognize that ensuring women's participation in peacebuilding and protecting women and girls from gender-based violence in armed conflict will not be enough. Incorporating "gender perspectives" in all peace and security efforts begins to get at the problem—but it does not name it. We are looking at the symptoms and effects as if they are the problem. Protecting women and advancing their equal status is a slow path that fails to make the connection between patriarchy and the marginalization of women in the first place. If it did, we would begin to see how it functions more broadly and deeply to naturalize all forms of domination and especially sexuality, not just gender and gender categories.

Instead of measuring the "progress" in women's status, what if we were to begin by assessing indicators of patriarchy and devise a more comprehensive commitment to and project aimed at dismantling patriarchy? A partial list of patriarchal indicators could include: proportion of women, gay, and lesbian political and business leaders; a gender wage gap; levels of violence against women and antigay violence; gay rights legislation; legal status of and social regard for children born out of wedlock; legal status of reproductive rights; education of girls/women; women's earnings as a percent of men's if not 100; incest, child sexual abuse; gender-neutrality of property and inheritance rights.

The idea of peace here includes justice and equal liberty. Peace conceived as the absence of armed conflict does not address the necessity of building sustainable, stable, legitimate institutions that do not perpetuate domination, control and fear but instead promote an understanding of citizenship grounded in an ethic of connection and recognition of common humanity. Given the violent history of state-formation, any society that does not develop these kinds of institutions is always at risk of conflict—the propensity to violence is there to the extent that patriarchy functions as a system of social order.

PATRIARCHY AND PEACEBUILDING

If patriarchy produces and reproduces a propensity to violence and conflict, then dismantling it is a precondition for sustainable and stable peace. Would the world be more peaceful and less violent if women were in charge? Well, yes, if they are depatriarchalized women; and depatriarchalized men too. Resistance is crucial, but transforming the struggle into a symbiotic partnership will require widespread consciousness-raising among both men and women. No democracy will be stable without confronting and transforming patriarchy.

Recent research on norm diffusion suggests that both top-down and bottom-up approaches to norm transmission play a role in normative transformation.[33] Tackling improvement in the indicators is important, but success ultimately rests on the ability to confront not only the symptoms, but also the system of domination. If patriarchy is antiliberal, then liberalism is also anti-patriarchal. Liberalism creates the opportunity to engage in activism that changes both institutional and normative foundations of patriarchy. Indeed, the domination, fear, and control perpetrated by patriarchy are inherently and incessantly in conflict with liberal democracy.

Peace is grounded in the notion of a social contract among equals to guarantee themselves freedom from domination, the ability as equals to regulate themselves, and to undertake collective action to achieve collective goods. Under a patriarchal social system, it is a contract among men. War is the dissolution of that contract. Peacemaking in the aftermath of armed conflict requires the reconstruction of the contract—but if it is reconstructed in patriarchal terms, that peace made will not be stable. Liberalism has enabled struggles of resistance to prevail—ending slavery, enfranchising women, and prohibiting discrimination. Evidence of past success is no guarantee of its continuation and justice delayed enables continued injury.

Perhaps no norm has done more to perpetuate the psychic dissociation—the separation between reason and emotion that makes moral exclusion, hierarchy, and differences that divide us seem natural—than the norm of "self-interested behavior." Self-interest is dissociation and is the ultimate barrier to recognition of our common humanity. A non-patriarchal social order must be based not on a self-interested conception of citizenship—"What's in it for me?"—but on the interchangeability of citizens. In contemporary political theory, Rawls captures the problem with the "veil of ignorance" metaphor viewed from the "original position," that is, before knowing what one's attributes and life circumstances are.[34] If anyone can be excluded from equal opportunity, then I can be excluded; if anyone earn $1 million less over their working lifetime because of their gender, then I can: if anyone can be the target of warrantless surveillance, then I can be; if anyone can become the target of a drone assassination, then I can be. Behind the "veil of ignorance," we are all potentially situated as those situated most unjustly on the other side. Self-interest is not a guide to good choices because all selves are potentially the worst off self.

This is an argument for the irrationality of self-interest. But it does not remedy what Gilligan and Richards identify as the underlying psychic injury that prevents us from understanding and valuing as an ethical position, our interchangeability—the dissociation that ruptures connection and makes it impossible to perceive our common humanity. There are three strategies for addressing the underlying problem: support resistance; promote human rights; reconcile through public discourse.

Supporting resistance means supporting activism, academic freedom, social movements, and supporting resisters. What are the alternatives to patriarchy? *Everything else that does not rely on domination, control, and fear is an alternative to patriarchy.* Supporting resistance means fearlessly defending and protecting the right of dissent. All ideas, including bad ones, maybe especially bad ones, must be tolerated in public discourse. When bad ideas go underground, they cannot be challenged or confronted. Confront anything and anyone that promotes and naturalizes domination, control, fear, and violence—anything that validates dissociation. Research, report, and publicize resistance as Gilligan and Richards do.

Promoting human rights is also an effective strategy. Human rights are the rights of all humans, the rights that, when deprived of them or when acting as perpetrators violating them, our humanity is diminished. Women and men are both entitled to protection of their physical integrity. Differences in gender and culture do not alter the rights of human beings. As Gilligan and Richards acknowledge:

> Our convictions have led us to do something Rome never did, namely, to end slavery and to aspire to respect all religions and to treat people of color and women as democratic equals. We have come far but remain deeply flawed in our democracy, as basic rights of intimate life are in political peril, issues of racial and gender inequality persist, and economic inequality worsens.[35]

Finally, patriarchy can be transformed by addressing the underlying problem of dissociation by engaging in relationship, affirming connection, reconciling historical injury and its present effects. Truth commissions are one way of engaging in this kind of reconciliation. Our capacity for connection is impaired by patriarchal socialization, the traumatic loss of intimacy, and its emotional consequences. Violence and conflict are effects of the patriarchal propensity to rationalize violence by stereotyping and dehumanization. The remedy is to restore connection where it has been damaged or obstructed. In South Africa, Archbishop Tutu popularized the concept of *Ubuntu*—an Nguni Bantu word meaning "human-ness"—but which as a broader philosophical basis for reconciliation means "my humanity is realized through my relationship with others." Not only "others like me" but also "others not like me."[36] In the terminology of moral exclusion, our tendency is to regard others "like me" as moral equals; the truly moral community is one of moral equality among individuals who are different.

There are thousands of ethnic or communal groups living in just under 200 states, and of course men and women living together in all societies. In understanding the importance of not only healing or restoring justice to the victim of an historical injury (or any injury caused by domination, control, and fear) but also healing both the perpetrator and victim, I find the metaphor of family therapy useful. It assumes that there has been some injurious, dysfunctional experience that injured a weaker member of the family—like a historically marginalized minority or women in a patriarchal society. Does restoring the victim to wholeness require that the perpetrator acknowledge responsibility and engage in reconciliation including, possibly, an apology (which is really an acknowledgment of responsibility)? No, I argue. The victim can be treated and restored independently of any involvement by the perpetrator. Most therapists would agree. Perpetrators are often dead, have abandoned the family, or in denial they simply refuse to participate in the victim's healing process. Victims can be restored to wholeness; they can recover lost or suppressed personal power without the perpetrator's participation.

What cannot be restored or made whole is the *relationship*. The individuals, the family system, cannot become fully mutually supportive emotionally without the active participation of all members affected (and this generally means all family members). This is what a democracy requires—it is not enough to be a room full of healed and empowered individual citizens—we must have connection. Violence, especially intergroup and/or dehumanizing violence, is only possible because the fundamental capacity for identifying the self with the universal self, the connected, relational self, to see one's selfhood in the self of the other, has been ruptured if not destroyed by patriarchal socialization.

Therefore, if we are to prevent future rounds of violence, patriarchal socialization must be dismantled, displaced by socialization that affirms connection and common humanity. Liberal democracy focused on the dual political virtues of individual liberty and social justice (or just "equal liberty"), depends on the capacity to repair the psychic damage of patriarchal socialization.

NOTES

1. Shirin Ebadi, speech at the 2004 World Social Forum, Mumbai, India, January 16, 2004.

2. V. Spike Peterson, *Gendered States: Feminist (Re)Visions of International Relations Theory* (Boulder, CO: Lynne Rienner, 1992).

3. "WHO Study: Third of Women Suffer Domestic Violence," *World Health Organization*, June 20, 2013, accessed March 10, 2014, http://bigstory.ap.org/article/who-third-women-suffer-domestic-violence.

4. Maria Cheng, "Ending Violence Against Women and Girls," *The Big Story*, June 20, 2013, accessed March 21, 2014, http://bigstory.ap.org/article/who-third-women-suffer-domestic-violence.

5. Carol Gilligan and David A. J. Richards, *The Deepening Darkness: Patriarchy, Resistance, and Democracy's Future* (Cambridge, England: Cambridge University Press, 2009); Nicholas D. Kristof and Sheryl WuDunn, *Half the Sky: Turning Oppression into Opportunity for Women Worldwide* (New York, NY: Knopf, 2009); David A. J. Richards, "Liberal Democracy and the Problem of Patriarchy," *Israel Law Review* 46.2 (2013): 169–91.

6. Gerda Lerner, *The Creation of Patriarchy* (Oxford, England: Oxford University Press, 1986), 77.

7. Carole Pateman, *The Sexual Contract* (Stanford, CA: Stanford University Press, 1988), 1–4.

8. Kristof and WuDunn, *Half the Sky*, 17.

9. Gilligan and Richards, *Deepening Darkness*, 115.

10. Jo Adetunji, "Forty-Eight Women Raped Every Hour in Congo, Study Finds," *The Guardian*, May 12, 2011, accessed March 8, 2014, http://www.theguardian.com/world/2011/may/12/48-women-raped-hour-congo.

11. IRIN, "DRC-Uganda: Male Sexual Abuse Survivors Living on the Margins," *UN Office for Coordination of Humanitarian Affairs*, 2011, accessed March 7, 2014, http://www.irinnews.org/fr/report/93399/drc-uganda-male-sexual-abuse-survivors-living-on-the-margins.

12. IRIN, "DRC-Uganda."

13. Jessica Hatcher, "Congo's Forgotten Curse: Epidemic of Female-on-Female Rape," *Time Magazine*, December 3, 2013, accessed March 9, 2014, http://world.time.com/2013/12/03/congos-forgotten-curse-epidemic-of-female-on-female-rape/.

14. Hatcher, "Congo's Forgotten Curse."

15. Sanyika Shakur, "The Pathology of Patriarchy: A Search for Clues at the Scene of the Crime," *Prison Focus* no. 39 (2013), accessed March 10, 2014, http://www.prisons.org/documents/CPF-39.pdf.

16. Susan Faludi, *Backlash: The Undeclared War Against American Women* (New York, NY: Vintage, 1991); Sylvia Walby, *Theorizing Patriarchy* (Hoboken, NJ: Blackwell, 1990); Marilyn French, *The War Against Women* (New York, NY: Summit, 1992); Lerner, *The Creation of Patriarchy*; Pateman, *The Sexual Contract*.

17. Personal conversation with Tim Coulter, June 14, 1998.

18. Will Roscoe, *The Zuni Man-Woman* (Albuquerque, NM: University of New Mexico Press, 1991); Franke Wilmer, *The Indigenous Voice in World Politics: Since Time Immemorial* (Thousand Oaks, CA: Sage, 1993); Sue Ellen Jacobs, Wesley Thomas, and Sabine Lang, *Two-Spirit People: Native American Gender Identity, Sexuality, and Spirituality* (Chicago, IL: University of Illinois Press, 1997); Cora J. Voyageur and Brian Calliou, "Various Shades of Red: Diversity within Canada's Indigenous Community," *London Journal of Canadian Studies* vol. 16 (2000/2001): 109–22.

19. Elsa Stamatopoulou, "Indigenous Peoples and the United Nations: Human Rights as a Developing Dynamic," *Human Rights Quarterly* 16.1 (1994): 58–81.

20. Franke Wilmer, *The Social Construction of Man, the State, and War: Conflict, Violence, and Identity in Former Yugoslavia* (New York, NY: Routledge, 2003).

21. Melanie Klein, *Love, Guilt, and Reparation and Other Words 1921–1945*, vol. 1 of *The Writings of Melanie Klein*, ed. Roger Money-Kyrle (New York, NY: Free Press, 2002); C. Fred Alford, *Melanie Klein and Critical Social Theory: An Account of Politics, Art, and Reason Based on Her Psychoanalytic Theory* (New Haven, CT: Yale University Press, 2001); Wilmer, *The Social Construction*.

22. Nancy Chodorow, *The Reproduction of Mothering: Psychoanalysis and the Sociology of Gender* (Berkeley, CA: University of California Press, 1978); Dorothy Dinnerstein, *The Mermaid and the Minotaur* (New York, NY: Random House, 1999).

23. Gilligan and Richards, *The Deepening Darkness*.

24. Wilmer, *The Social Construction*.

25. Ibid.

26. David A. J. Richards, "Liberal Democracy," 10.
27. Ibid., 174.
28. Ibid., 2.
29. Gilligan and Richards, *The Deepening Darkness*, 115.
30. Ibid., 117.
31. United Nations Security Council, *Resolution 1325*, adopted October 31, 2000, accessed March 12, 2014, http://www.un.org/en/ga/search/view_doc.asp?symbol=S/RES/1325%282000%29.
32. Ibid.
33. Margaret E. Keck and Kathryn Sikkink, *Activists Beyond Borders: Advocacy Networks in International Politics* (Ithaca, NY: Cornell University Press, 1998); Thomas Risse-Kappen, Stephen C. Ropp, and Kathryn Sikkink, *The Power of Human Rights: International Norms and Domestic Change* (Cambridge, England: Cambridge University Press, 1999); Pamela Martin and Franke Wilmer, "Transnational Normative Struggles and Globalization: The Case of Indigenous Peoples in Bolivia and Ecuador," *Globalizations* 5.4 (2008), 583–98.
34. John Rawls, *A Theory of Justice* (Cambridge, England: Belknap, 1971).
35. Gilligan and Richards, *The Deepening Darkness*, 11.
36. Battle, Michael, *Ubuntu: I In You and You In Me*, forward by Desmond Tutu (Nashville, TN: Abingdon, 2009).

BIBLIOGRAPHY

Adetunji, Jo. "Forty-Eight Women Raped Every Hour in Congo, Study Finds." *The Guardian*, May 12, 2011. Accessed March 8, 2014. http://www.theguardian.com/world/2011/may/12/48-women-raped-hour-congo.

Alford, C. Fred. *Melanie Klein and Critical Social Theory: An Account of Politics, Art, and Reason Based on Her Psychoanalytic Theory*. New Haven, CT: Yale University Press, 2001.

Battle, Michael. *Ubuntu: I In You and You In Me*. Forward by Desmond Tutu. Nashville, TN: Abingdon, 2009.

Cheng, Maria. "Ending Violence Against Women and Girls." *The Big Story*, June 20, 2013. Accessed March 21, 2014, http://bigstory.ap.org/article/who-third-women-suffer-domestic-violence.

Chodorow, Nancy. *The Reproduction of Mothering: Psychoanalysis and the Sociology of Gender*. Berkeley, CA: University of California Press, 1978.

———. *Feminism and Psychoanalytic Theory*. New Haven, CT and London, England: Yale University Press, 1989.

Dinnerstein, Dorothy. *The Mermaid and the Minotaur*. New York, NY: Random House, 1999.

Ebadi, Shirin. Speech at the 2004 World Social Forum, Mumbai, India, January 16, 2004.

"Ending Violence Against Women and Girls." *United Nations*. Accessed March 21, 2014. http://www.un.org/en/globalissues/briefingpapers/endviol/.

Faludi, Susan. *Backlash: The Undeclared War Against American Women.* New York, NY: Vintage, 1991.

French, Marilyn. *The War Against Women.* New York, NY: Summit, 1992.

Gilligan, Carol and David A. J. Richards. *The Deepening Darkness: Patriarchy, Resistance, and Democracy's Future.* Cambridge, England: Cambridge University Press, 2009.

Gilligan, Carol. *In a Different Voice*. Cambridge, England: Harvard University Press, 1982.

Hatcher, Jessica. "Congo's Forgotten Curse: Epidemic of Female-on-Female Rape." *Time Magazine*, December 3, 2013. Accessed March 9, 2014. http://world.time.com/2013/12/03/congos-forgotten-curse-epidemic-of-female-on-female-rape/.

IRIN. "DRC-Uganda: Male Sexual Abuse Survivors Living on the Margins." *UN Office for Coordination of Humanitarian Affairs*, 2011. Accessed March 7, 2014. http://www.irinnews.org/fr/report/93399/drc-uganda-male-sexual-abuse-survivors-living-on-the-margins.

Jacobs, Sue Ellen, Wesley Thomas, and Sabine Lang. *Two-Spirit People: Native American Gender Identity, Sexuality, and Spirituality.* Chicago, IL: University of Illinois Press, 1997.

Keck, Margaret E. and Kathryn Sikkink. *Activists Beyond Borders: Advocacy Networks in International Politics.* Ithaca, NY: Cornell University Press, 1998.

Klein, Melanie. *Love, Guilt, and Reparation and Other Words 1921–1945*. Vol. 1 of *The Writings of Melanie Klein*, edited by Roger Money-Kyrle. New York, NY: Free Press, 2002.

Kristof, Nicholas D. and Sheryl WuDunn. *Half the Sky: Turning Oppression into Opportunity for Women Worldwide.* New York, NY: Knopf, 2009.

Lerner, Gerda. *The Creation of Patriarchy.* Oxford, England: Oxford University Press, 1986.

Martin, Pamela and Franke Wilmer. "Transnational Normative Struggles and Globalization: The Case of Indigenous Peoples in Bolivia and Ecuador." *Globalizations* 5.4 (2008): 583–98.

Pateman, Carole. *The Sexual Contract.* Stanford, CA: Stanford University Press, 1988.

Peterson, V. Spike, ed. *Gendered States: Feminist (Re)Visions of International Relations Theory.* Boulder, CO: Lynne Rienner Publishers, 1992.

Rawls, John. *A Theory of Justice.* Cambridge, England: Belknap, 1971.

Richards, David A. J. "Liberal Democracy and the Problem of Patriarchy." *Israel Law Review* 46.2 (2013): 169–91.

Risse-Kappen, Thomas, Stephen C. Ropp, and Kathryn Sikkink. *The Power of Human Rights: International Norms and Domestic Change*. Cambridge, England: Cambridge University Press, 1999.

Roscoe, Will. *The Zuni Man-Woman.* Albuquerque, NM: University of New Mexico Press, 1991.

Shakur, Sanyika. "The Pathology of Patriarchy: A Search for Clues at the Scene of the Crime." *Prison Focus* no. 39 (2013). Accessed March 10, 2014. http://www.prisons.org/documents/CPF-39.pdf.

Stamatopoulou, Elsa. "Indigenous Peoples and the United Nations: Human Rights as a Developing Dynamic." *Human Rights Quarterly* 16.1 (1994): 58–81.

United Nations Security Council. *Resolution 1325*. Adopted October 31, 2000. Accessed March 12, 2014. http://www.un.org/en/ga/search/view_doc.asp?symbol=S/RES/1325%282000%29.

Voyageur, Cora J. and Brian Calliou. "Various Shades of Red: Diversity within Canada's Indigenous Community." *London Journal of Canadian Studies* vol. 16 (2000/2001): 109–22.

Walby, Sylvia. *Theorizing Patriarchy*. Hoboken, NJ: Blackwell, 1990.

"WHO Study: Third of Women Suffer Domestic Violence." *World Health Organization*, June 20, 2013. Accessed March 10, 2014. http://bigstory.ap.org/article/who-third-women-suffer-domestic-violence.

Wilmer, Franke. *The Indigenous Voice in World Politics: Since Time Immemorial*. Thousand Oaks, CA: Sage, 1993.

———. *The Social Construction of Man, the State, and War: Conflict, Violence, and Identity in Former Yugoslavia*. New York, NY: Routledge, 2003.

Chapter 21

Queer Theory and Peace and Conflict Studies

Some Critical Reflections

Robert C. Mizzi and Sean Byrne

A number of recent studies articulate the need for the Peace and Conflict Studies (PACS) field to continue to include issues and people on the margins of society in the plurality of peacebuilding.[1] Johan Galtung (2009) points out how the "transdisciplinary" nature of PACS in terms of theory building and practice[2] deconstructs direct, cultural, and structural (invisible violence in systems and institutions) violence to empower people to build a positive peace (social justice) for all citizens.[3] Those critical of the Western model of "liberal peacebuilding" state that the model often leaves people out of the peace process altogether and point toward prompt reconsideration in light of this exclusion practice.[4] For example, people with disabilities; lesbian, gay, bisexual, transgender, or queer people (LGBTQ); youth; women; and the elderly are often excluded from the peace processes and practices that confront continuous acts of violence and hate crimes directed against these social groups.[5] The intersection of gender, race, sexuality, and class in the socialization process, and its engagement with dominant oppressive patriarchal power, ensures that certain values relegate particular groups (such as those listed above) to the social periphery. Concomitantly, this marginalization process shapes people's daily life experiences and provides little room for social emancipation.[6] The effects of this marginalization process by dominant patriarchal power often means, in practical terms, unbalanced power structures with little or no representation of marginal voices, and for those marginalized, feelings of low self-worth and the development of unhelpful coping mechanisms. Clearly, as much as positive peace is a promising ideology, it remains a forgotten or distant concept for certain groups excluded from peace processes.

This chapter provides some rationale and direction toward a more inclusive peacebuilding process. It explores the potential of queer theory in adding to diversity in theory building, research, pedagogy, and praxis in the PACS field, and vice versa. Although queer theory largely focuses on deconstructing sexuality and gender categories in a social hierarchy, such as analyzing the effects of normative gender roles on the lives of people with same-sex sexual and/or gender nonconforming desires, there are tenets to queer theory that advance Galtung's assertion to deconstruct violence and build a positive peace for *all* citizens.[7] As Robert Mizzi points out, in a comparative view there is similarity between peace movements and gay and lesbian liberation movements, which may be enough to form a "same-sex marriage" between the two theoretical frameworks.[8] We hope to perform such a marriage through this chapter, and conceptualize implications for *all* activists and educators, regardless of their sexual orientation or gender identity. We begin this chapter with an explanation of queer theory and PACS as distinct theoretical frameworks. We then highlight new insights that may be useful when reconceptualizing both theoretical frameworks in relation to one another. The question that drives this comparative analysis is: What are the tenets of queer theory and PACS that may be useful toward advancing notions of positive peace (social justice)? In a time of dynamic and radical changes around queer issues in social organizing, and the pervasive nature of conflict and violence, this chapter offers critical perspectives toward the reconceptualization of necessary peacebuilding processes.

QUEER THEORY

The term "queer theory" appeared in queer lexicon by way of de Lauretis's work on deconstructing gay and lesbian identities.[9] As de Lauretis states, queer theory "conveys a double emphasis—on the conceptual and speculative work involved in discourse production and on the necessary critical work of deconstructing our own discourses and their constructed silence."[10] Deconstructing discourse is a key theme in this work, as queer activisms (rooted in feminism) highlight the prevalence of *hetero*sexism, which uses values, understandings, and practices that favor cross-sex relationships, and *hetero*patriarchy that purports heterosexual masculinity as superior and dominant to expressions of femininity (e.g., effeminate males). Queer theory challenges dominant social hierarchies and values and disrupts altogether the social construction of male/female and hetero/homo as fixed and stable categories.[11] The acronym "LGBTQ," for example, creates identity-categorizations that limit fluid, nonbinary conceptualizations of sex, sexuality, and gender.

The use of the term "queer" represents a significant political shift. Historically, it is a term that was used to name and shame queerness, people who engage in same-sex sexual practices and/or do not subscribe to strict, traditional male/female gender roles. Over the past few decades, "queer" has been reclaimed by activists and scholars to pushback against the violent use of language, re-shift the balance of power, and position the term as a preferable and useful term to challenge heterosexism and heteropatriarchy. Although the term remains controversial both internal and external to queer communities due to its troubling historical use, the term is growing worldwide as a symbol of reclamation and inclusion. Queer theory comprises several key intellectual engagements to understand human relationships, gender diversity, and power. Generally speaking, these engagements are based on the following intersecting concepts: sexual regulation, performativity, and heteronormativity.

Sexual Regulation

Michel Foucault's work highlights the hegemonic practice of institutionalized systems using identity-categories (for example, a "homosexual" identity) to shame, regulate, and eradicate same-sex sexual behavior.[12] Science, medicine, and religion are institutions that Foucault names that cause women and men to "confess" their shameful same-sex sexual practices when they stray from the pro-creationist, gendered expectations to engage only in cross-sex sexual practices. Women and men who engage in same-sex sexual practices must be willing to accept punishment and adhere to a regime that will "correct" the "deviant" behavior. Foucault's work indicates that sexuality is a political marker, whereby institutions work to regulate sexuality according to what is considered "acceptable" social norms. Through this work on sexual regulation emerges the potential for discourse to resist dominant understandings and restrictions of sex, sexuality, and gender. An example of this sexual regulation process is the use of electroshock therapy in psychiatric hospitals as a means to "punish" and "correct" homosexual desires among gay men.[13]

Performativity

The notion of "performativity" stems from a position of resistance to queer oppression, which is widely considered a second intellectual engagement that is a part of queer theory. Judith Butler critiques the social construction of gender, whereby men and women adhere to rigid social roles and rules of masculinity and femininity in order to gain acceptance into society.[14] These roles and rules cause difficulty for people who do not subscribe to such normative definitions of gender to gain agency and autonomy. Butler states that gender then becomes "performative," which means that people "perform" their gender according to these social rules and roles.[15] Through performativity, attention is drawn to how gender becomes a concept that is socially constructed, which makes gender fluid and not fixed. An example that Butler puts forth to "trouble" gender is situated within a gay and lesbian social context.[16] Butler highlights how parody and fantasy disrupt normative constructions of gender through drag performances. Drag performances destabilize the notion of what constitutes a "female" identity in order to expose a set of social relations (i.e., normative expectations of masculine and feminine behaviors).[17] Through the use of parody, drag performances reveal aspects of a normatively gendered experience, rather than a whole female identity, that are portrayed and made intelligible for heterosexual understanding.[18] Significantly, drag becomes a parody of the masculine and feminine mechanisms and practices that construct and bind gender.[19] When subjects disturb such binding practices around (gender) identity, they then open up radical possibilities that break from the constraints of social regulation.[20] As Butler states, "gender proves to be performative, that is, constituting the identity it is purported to be. In this sense, gender is always a doing, though not a doing by a subject who might be said to preexist the deed."[21] Butler comes to argue that there can be no gender identity since it is always "doing" and remains in flux.[22]

Heteronormativity

A third intellectual engagement that is considered a part of queer theory is Michael Warner's work on heteronormativity.[23] Warner states that "a whole field of social relations becomes intelligible as heterosexuality, and this privatized sexual culture bestows on its sexual practices a sense of rightness and normalcy. This sense of rightness–embedded in things and not just in sex–is referred to as heteronormativity."[24] In other words, heterosexuality becomes embedded into everyday understandings and psyches as the "norm" in which to base operations, with little space to explore differences in sex, sexuality, and gender. For example, a discussion on different forms of family violence that excludes the possibility of violence toward and within families with same-sex partners would be a heteronormative predisposition. In this instance, teaching practices, support systems, curricula, policies, mandates, and communications are all structured along heteronormative lines, which make it difficult for people to learn about how to address violence within/toward same-sex parent families and to think creatively about other non-normative constructions of "family."

These three elements of sexual regulation, performativity, and heteronormativity are considered hallmarks of queer theory. Analyzing social problems from each of these perspectives may produce new lines of thinking into the origins of these problems as well as some of the possible solutions. For example, the recent intensification of globalization has now prompted queer theory to adopt a transnational perspective, where there is acknowledgment that sexuality and gender are constructed differently everywhere and has become influenced by global "gay rights" movements that employ Western-oriented "LGBTQ" language.[25] Also, at the front of recent queer scholarship is an analysis of organizations that operate on rigid principles of heteropatriarchy, such as the Canadian military,[26] and a reconceptualization of ways to make them more queer-friendly.

PEACE AND CONFLICT STUDIES

Peace and Conflict Studies (PACS) is the fusion of conflict analysis and resolution, social justice, conflict transformation, human rights, restorative justice, reconciliation, and peace studies and assists us in understanding the deep roots of social conflict. It also provides some direction into the appropriate innovative processes that can be utilized to creatively intervene and transform human relationships and social structures while deconstructing patriarchy and militarization. The following sections outline some of the key components and future direction of PACS including some selected recent debates in the field.

Alternative or Appropriate Dispute Resolution and Peace Studies

Historically, traditional mechanisms of negative peace (the absence of war) such as diplomacy, elite negotiations, and international law by powerful states and international organizations were used to manage conflict at the global level.[27] At the same time these processes were in place a broad plethora of grassroots social movements emerged in the 1960s in Europe and North America to protest the balance of terror of nuclear weapons and Mutually Assured Destruction (MAD), violence against women, the denial of African-American civil rights in the United States, student protest movements against the Vietnam War, and inequality in France, the United States and Northern Ireland. These mainly nonviolent movements sought to transform society from a culture of violence to a culture of peace. As a result of local people's distrust of the state, alternative and/or appropriate dispute resolution (ADR) processes were developed and employed to emancipate local communities.

Subsequently, alternative or ADR processes of mediation, negotiation and arbitration began to emerge in university law schools as the credentialing and professionalization of practitioners in the field became more tied to court annexed mediation.[28] Peace Studies programs also appeared on undergraduate and graduate campuses as scholars and students struggled to understand the important social issues of their time—and how to address them.

Conflict Analysis and Resolution

Conflict Analysis and Resolution (CAR) undergraduate and graduate programs analyze the emergence and escalation of deep-rooted, destructive conflicts, and how they can be resolved.[29] John Burton and Edward Azar distinguish between values, interests, and needs by arguing that denial of people's basic human needs (security, identity, self-esteem, and freedom, etc.) would escalate conflict and only the satisfaction of those needs would resolve or prevent social conflicts.[30] They argue that human needs were universal across cultures, which can be found at interpersonal (between individuals), intergroup (between groups), and global (between nations) levels. They contended that a problem-solving process could assist people in need to analyze the roots of conflict in comparison to the actualization of meeting human needs as a means to devise sustainable solutions and end protracted conflict.

"Interactive problem-solving" largely takes place at the intergroup level as middle-level professionals such as doctors, teachers, lawyers, and so forth come together to discuss the underlying causes of protracted ethnic conflicts in a process facilitated by a knowledgeable third party.[31] The idea is that over time problem-solving or dialogue group participants can build trust and a common understanding of the dynamics of their conflicts as well as culturally relevant solutions to resolve them, and transmit new knowledge to decision-makers, and to the grassroots.[32]

Conflict Transformation

Conflict Transformation advocates believe that relationships have to be built and rebuilt and that structures need to be changed over time to ensure peace processes are sustainable and involve the whole society in its transformation to a just, peaceful, and inclusive society.[33] Building a culture of peace necessitates cocreating a long-term holistic system that includes all internal and external stakeholders to forge a sustainable infrastructure for peace.[34] Such a peacebuilding process implies coordinating resources, training, structure, process, and evaluation of the transformative process into an "integrated framework."[35]

Reconciliation and forgiveness processes where truth, justice, mercy, and peace intersect to build relationships are necessary to build a sustainable peace.[36] Reconciliation processes such as the national Truth and Reconciliation Commissions in El Salvador and South Africa and local peacemaking processes provide critical contexts and spaces for protagonists and survivors of conflict and violence to come together and for the former to seek forgiveness from the latter so that together they can heal from the trauma of past violence. "Chosen traumas" and "chosen glories" are often used by unscrupulous leaders in the process of "the transgenerational transmission" of trauma or glory so that the seeds are sown for the next escalation of violence.[37]

Peace and Conflict Studies

Peace and Conflict Studies (PACS) teachers, students, and scholars focus on critical issues and innovative and creative intervention processes to build positive peace (social justice) and to address direct, cultural, and structural violence. For example, peace activists in local cultural contexts empower women within patriarchal societies to change behaviors and promote a social justice frame around global human rights laws.[38] Global human rights laws protect the rights of the individual within a diverse and complex world. Real peace cannot be forged for nations or ethnic groups emerging from violent wars unless there is social justice that addresses group trauma, poverty, environmental issues, oppressive structures, and people's needs among others.[39]

Peace educators seek to build a pluralistic and diverse civil society among adults and children, across cultures, classes, and genders. For example, the Waldorf and Montessori peace education methods integrate children's abilities and interests with nature and peacebuilding activities.[40] "Constructive storytelling" processes and approaches also play a role in educating children cross-culturally, and in empowering adults transitioning out of violent ethnic conflicts to deal with traumatic past events.[41] Storytelling is a low-tech process and it is the way that children learn about the world from adults.[42] As Jessica Senehi articulates, anyone can tell a story and the human voice is inextinguishable as the process of constructive (compared to destructive) storytelling is both nonviolent and inclusive.[43] Mahatma Gandhi and Dr. Martin Luther King Jr. lived lives that demonstrated the power of principled (compared to pragmatic) nonviolence in confronting social injustice where the practitioner in a state of pure inner peace, works lovingly with the protagonist to find the truth (social justice) together.[44]

Peacebuilding involves a multitrack, multimodal, multidimensional, and primarily external intervention process that is conceptually and practically steeped in Western liberal practices that include human rights, democracy, the rule of law, liberal development, and a free-market economy.[45] However, peacebuilding also includes bringing young people, disabled people, elderly citizens, LGBTQ citizens, and women into the decision-making process as well as including indigenous peoples and their traditional processes of restorative justice and peacemaking within peacebuilding efforts to cocreate new systems and structures within a pluralistic and tolerant civil society.[46]

QUEERING PEACE/PEACING QUEER

When we reflect on these theoretical frameworks, we observe two similarities that may be of use to scholars and researchers. First, both frameworks rely on metanarratives, which are neither hierarchical nor in competition with each other. The presence of these metanarratives indicates how both frameworks evolved over time to critique different social institutions and arrangements, and as a means to end marginalizing and violent processes; thereby, promoting equity and justice. These metanarratives work in tandem with each other, reshaping and reforming perceptions of identity, power, and knowledge according to social context.

Second, the encouragement of voice as a means for human emancipation is at the core for both frameworks. Both frameworks reconceptualize social hierarchies to highlight specific groups that suffer negative consequences when they do not fit in with the status quo. As a means to achieve an inclusive society, both frameworks call for human dialogue, such as sharing experiences, deconstructing and dismantling dominant systems of power, and promoting cultural values that do not fit normative categories of what is (not) "acceptable" in society. It is through this emphasis on voice, and the challenging and restructuring of power relations, that justice and peace can be achieved.

Pointedly, we live in an interdependent global village where inclusivity of all perspectives grounds us in a synergistic, flexible, and pragmatic way. "Everyday peacemakers" work at all levels to build connections and transform relations weaving together stories of peacemaking as "hybridity and hybridization" of local and outside peacebuilding approaches, which allows for creating realistic methods that incorporate a plethora of voices into the creation of a just peace.[47] Creating critical spaces for people to come together and describe their experiences and identities is an essential component of a pluralistic democracy, and in maintaining and forging human rights and a positive peace with "transcultural constructive storytelling" at the heart of peacemaking and peace education since it empowers people to "discover and share knowledge."[48]

We see tremendous potential for both theoretical frameworks when pinned together. First, queer theory stands to benefit from a strengthened inclusion of ally perspectives that are a part of PACS. Allies can navigate through dominant systems that structure hetero/homo binaries and help create change from within such systems. Although queer theory is useful at deconstructing social systems that relegate queerness to the periphery, an inclusion of ally perspectives would indicate how such systems affect us all, are violent in their construction, and that the heteropatriarchial nature of these systems can be challenged from the participation of allies that work in conjunction with

LGBTQ people. Embedded in this ally work, and related queer activisms, can be PACS's focus on reconciliation and forgiveness processes where there is consideration of such notions as justice and peace. For example, a Truth and Reconciliation Commission formed on the basis of exploring the persecution of LGBTQ people might be useful in working through this peace process.

Of significance here is the idea that the construction of gender identities holds masculine notions of competition and hierarchy as more sacred values by society than feminine values of caring and compassion.[49] The use of violence to achieve order within the state and to maintain the state's projection of power reinforces the masculine values in a dominant (hetero)patriarchy, and a realpolitik self-help anarchic security system.[50] Consequently, "sex typed" individuals are influenced by gender when they filter information and carry their "gender schemata" into different conflict contexts.[51] Anita Taylor and Judi Beinstein Miller call for a radical reconceptualization that "allows for more than two genders" (e.g., androgyny and sexual orientation).[52] John Stephens warns, for example, that the ADR mediation process fails to change the structural roots of male domination residing in ownership of property and a "power over" social order that promotes an "ethics of rights" rather than an "ethics of care."[53] Instead he articulates that feminist and gender issues can be more appropriately dealt with by peace studies because it addresses direct, cultural, and structural violence that includes anti-LGBTQ violence and victimization, and hate crimes.[54] Thus, men and women, LGBTQ and heterosexuals, and children and adults have to create "new partnerships" to work together to create egalitarian relationships and a just society.[55]

Second, PACS stands to benefit from queer theory by promoting inclusion on the basis of more than simply listing "sexual orientation" and "gender identity" within calls for antiviolence activism. Queer theory can be helpful in deconstructing heteronormative understandings of peace and nonviolence, determining what kinds of "performative" discourses exist in PACS, and conceptualizing how violence acts as a form of (homo)sexual regulation. Peace may be understood then as being a fluid concept, where peace includes diverse identities and ideas that are constantly being re-formed to adjust to changing societies, rather than a fixed state of nonviolence determined by a larger authority figure. For example, exploring notions of gender-based violence through a queer theory lens may highlight how gender and sexuality are fluid and interconnected and that violence occurs in macro- and micro-levels to screen out sexuality and gender difference. Women and men may both experience harsh consequences if they do not subscribe to fixed gender role expectations.

What remains in the future for research that utilizes both frameworks? One direction may be located in the very nature of queer activism, which throughout history and around the globe remains a nonviolent movement. The world to date has not witnessed bloodshed committed by LGBTQ people as a means to demand equal rights and fair treatment. On the contrary, there have been significant acts of violence toward LGBTQ people as a perceived means to suppress and eradicate sexuality and gender difference. Research into why queer activism remains nonviolent, and at times, in solidarity with other marginalized groups (even with those who struggle with accepting queerness), might be of use to both queer theory and PACS. Also of use may be research into how PACS may become more queer-inclusive, especially when researching matters relating to identity-difference and identity-expression. Given that peace education has been marked as a heteronormative pedagogy,[56] researching efforts to trouble such heteronormativity can help steer things around so that attempts to end violence are inclusive and relevant to *all* lives. Both research approaches may shed further light on the mechanics of violence in order to build peaceful and peace-filled societies.

CONCLUSION

The recent challenge to civil and human rights by President Vladimir Putin evidenced by the arrest and detention of Pussy Riot feminist punk rock band members, the violence directed against the LGBTQ community in Russia that led to international protest against the Sochi Winter Olympic Games, and the controversial antihomosexuality law ("Kill the Gays" bill) in Uganda are illustrative of recent global examples of direct and indirect violence directed against LGBTQ people. Until the components of patriarchy in the "private policy individual sphere" and the "public policy-collective battering sphere" are removed the battering of women, nations, and LGBTQ people globally will continue unabated.[57]

In sum, this chapter reviewed and espoused the main tenets of queer theory and PACS as a theoretical framework. This analysis indicates how despite the different orientations, there are similar perspectives, such as the deconstruction of social norms and a re-shift in power relations in light of marginalized peoples' experiences. Queer theory reminds us of fixed binaries that create and sustain social hierarchies, such as hetero/homo, white/black, male/female, and adult/child, which has given little room to explore differences in human lives outside of this binary. PACS's focus on constructive storytelling, reconciliation, and positive peace demonstrates the importance of coming to shared understanding and achieving some degree of forgiveness, especially for LGBTQ people who have suffered tremendous loss of life, family, status and resource as a result of transphobic and homophobic violence. Queer reactions to this violence continue to consist of peaceful protests, expressions of love, and nonviolent actions worldwide. PACS researchers and scholars can indeed find a place and presence in this peacebuilding process.

NOTES

1. Louis Kriesberg and Bruce Dayton, *Constructive Conflicts: From Escalation to Resolution* (Lanham, MD: Rowman & Littlefield, 2002); Jessica Senehi and Sean Byrne, "Where Do We Go From Here?" in *Critical Issues in Peace and Conflict Studies*, ed. Thomas Matyók, Jessica Senehi, and Sean Byrne (Lanham, MD: Lexington, 2011); Sean Byrne and Jessica Senehi, "Revisiting the CAR Field," in *Handbook of Conflict Analysis and Resolution*, ed. Dennis Sandole et al. (London, England: Routledge, 2009); Charles Webel and Johan Galtung, eds. *Handbook of Peace and Conflict Studies* (London, England: Routledge, 2009).

2. Johan Galtung, "Towards a Conflictology: A Quest for Trans-Disciplinarity," in *Handbook of Conflict Analysis and Resolution*, ed. Dennis Sandole et al. (London, England: Routledge, 2009).

3. Johan Galtung, *Peace by Peaceful Means* (Los Angeles, CA: Sage, 1996).

4. Roger MacGinty, *No War, No Peace: The Rejuvenation of Stalled Peace Processes and Peace Accords* (Basingstoke, England: Palgrave Macmillan, 2008); Roger MacGinty, *International Peacebuilding and Local Resistance: Hybrid Forms of Peace* (Basingstoke, England: Palgrave Macmillan, 2012); Oliver Richmond, "A Genealogy of Peace and Conflict Theory," in *Palgrave Advances in Peacebuilding: Critical Developments and Approaches*, ed. Oliver Richmond (New York, NY: Palgrave Macmillan, 2010).

5. Roger MacGinty and Andrew Williams, *Peace and Development* (London, England: Routledge, 2009).

6. Margaret Anderson and Patricia Hill Collins, *Race, Class and Gender: An Anthology* (Scarborough, ON: Cengage Learning, 2012); bell hooks, *Yearning: Race, Gender, and Cultural Politics* (Boston, MA: South End, 1990); Sean Byrne and Jessica Senehi, *Violence: Analysis, Intervention and Prevention* (Athens, OH: Ohio University Press, 2012).

7. Galtung, "Towards a Conflictology."

8. Robert C. Mizzi, "Let's Get this Straightened Out: Finding a Place and Presence for Sexual/Gender Identity-Difference in Peace Education," *Journal of Peace Education* 7.2 (2010).

9. Teresa de Lauretis, "Queer Theory: Lesbian and Gay Sexualities," *Differences: A Journal of Feminist Cultural Studies* 3.2 (1991).

10. Ibid., iv.

11. Ibid.

12. Michel Foucault, *The History of Sexuality: An Introduction* (Harmondsworth, England: Penguin, 1978).

13. Jennifer Terry, *An American Obsession: Science, Medicine and Homosexuality in Modern Society* (Chicago, IL: University of Chicago Press, 1999).

14. Judith Butler, *Gender Trouble: Feminism and the Subversion of Identity* (Rev. ed.) (New York, NY: Routledge, 1999).

15. Ibid.

16. Ibid.

17. Ibid.

18. Ibid.
19. Ibid.
20. Ibid.
21. Ibid., 33.
22. Ibid.
23. Michael Warner, *Publics and Counter-Publics* (New York, NY: Zone, 2002).
24. Ibid., 194.
25. Gayatri Gopinath, *Impossible Desires: Queer Diasporas and South Asian Public Cultures* (Durham, NC: Duke University Press, 2005).
26. Robert C. Mizzi. "Uncovering Rainbow (Dis)connections: An Exploration of Sexual and Gender Diversity in the Canadian Forces and Implications for Post-Conflict Reconstruction Training," in *Learning Gendered Militarism in Canada: A Lifelong Pedagogy of Acceptance and Resistance*, ed. Nancy Taber (Edmonton, AB: University of Alberta Press, forthcoming).
27. David Barash and Charles Webel, *Peace and Conflict Studies* (Thousand Oaks, CA: Sage, 2002).
28. Louis Kriesberg, Stuart Thorson, and Terri Northrup, eds., *Intractable Conflicts and Their Transformation* (Syracuse, NY: Syracuse University Press, 1989).
29. Kriesberg and Dayton, *Constructive Conflicts.*
30. John Burton, *Violence Explained: The Sources of Conflict, Violence, and Crime and Their Prevention* (Manchester, England: Manchester University Press, 1997).
31. Ron Fisher, ed. *Paving the Way: Contributions of Interactive Conflict Resolution to Peacemaking* (Lanham, MD: Lexington Books, 2005).
32. Herb Kelman, "Group Processes in the Resolution of International Conflicts: Experiences from the Israeli-Palestinian Case," *The American Psychologist* 52.3 (1997).
33. John Paul Lederach, *Preparing for Peace: Conflict Transformation across Cultures* (Syracuse, NY: Syracuse University Press, 1995).
34. John Paul Lederach, *Building Peace: Sustainable Reconciliation in Divided Societies* (Washington, DC: United States Institute of Peace, 1997).
35. Ibid.
36. Ibid., 28.
37. Vamik Volkan, *Bloodlines: From Ethnic Pride to Ethnic Terrorism* (Boulder, CO: Lynne Rienner, 1998).
38. Sally Engle Merry, *Human Rights and Gender Violence: Translating International Law into Local Justice* (Chicago, IL: University of Chicago Press, 2006).
39. Margot Hurlbert, ed., *Pursuing Justice: An Introduction to Justice Studies* (Winnipeg, MB: Fernwood, 2011).
40. Elise Boulding, *Cultures of Peace: The Hidden Side of History* (Syracuse, NY: Syracuse University Press, 2000), 117.
41. Jessica Senehi, "Constructive Storytelling: A Peace Process," *Peace and Conflict Studies* 9.2 (2002); Jessica Senehi, "Storytelling to Transform Conflicts Constructively," in *Handbook of Conflict Analysis and Resolution*, ed. Dennis Sandole et al. (London, England: Routledge, 2009).
42. Jessica Senehi, "The Role of Constructive, Transcultural Storytelling in Ethnopolitical Conflict Transformation in Northern Ireland," in *Regional and Ethnic*

Conflicts: Perspectives from the Front Lines, ed. George Irani, Vamik Volkan, and Judy Carter (New York, NY: Prentice Hall, 2009).

43. Jessica Senehi, "Constructive Storytelling in Inter-communal Conflicts: Building Community, Building Peace," in *Reconciliable Differences: Turning Points in Ethnopolitical Conflict*, ed. Sean Byrne et al. (West Hartford, CT: Kumarian, 2000).

44. Barash and Webel, *Peace and Conflict Studies*, 519.

45. Chuck Thiessen, *Local Ownership of Peacebuilding in Afghanistan: Shouldering Responsibility for Sustainable Peace and Development* (Lanham, MD: Lexington, 2014), 12.

46. Brian Rice, Jill Oakes, and Roderick Riewe, *Seeing the World With Aboriginal Eyes* (Winnipeg, MB: University of Manitoba Press, 2005); Brian Rice, "People of the Longhouse," in *Handbook of Conflict Analysis and Resolution*, ed. Dennis Sandole et al. (London, England: Routledge, 2009).

47. MacGinty, *International Peacebuilding*.

48. Jessica Senehi, "Constructive Storytelling: A Peace Process."

49. Ho-Won Jeong, *Peace and Conflict Studies: An Introduction* (London, England: Ashgate, 2000).

50. Ibid.

51. Anita Taylor and Judi Beinstein Miller, "Introduction: The Necessity of Seeing Gender in Conflict," in *Conflict and Gender*, ed. Anita Taylor and Judi Beinstein Miller (New York, NY: Hampton, 1994), 10.

52. Ibid., 12.

53. John Stephens, "Gender Conflict: Connecting Feminist Theory and Conflict Resolution Theory and Practice," in *Conflict and Gender*, ed. Anita Taylor and Judi Beinstein Miller (New York, NY: Hampton, 1994), 225.

54. Ibid., 226.

55. Elise Boulding, *Cultures of Peace*.

56. Mizzi, "Let's Get This Straightened Out."

57. Larry Tifft and Lyn Markham, "Battering Women and Battering Central Americans: A Peacemaking Synthesis," in *Criminology as Peace-Making*, ed. Harold Pepinsky and Richard Quinney (Bloomington, IN: Indiana University Press, 1991).

BIBLIOGRAPHY

Anderson, Margaret and Patricia Hill Collins. *Race, Class and Gender: An Anthology*. Scarborough, ON: Cengage Learning, 2012.

Barash, David and Charles Webel. *Peace and Conflict Studies*. Thousand Oaks, CA: Sage, 2002.

Boulding, Elise. *Cultures of Peace: The Hidden Side of History*. Syracuse, NY: Syracuse University Press, 2000.

Burton, John. *Violence Explained: The Sources of Conflict, Violence, and Crime and Their Prevention*. Manchester, England: Manchester University Press, 1997.

Butler, Judith. *Gender Trouble: Feminism and the Subversion of Identity* (Rev. ed.). New York, NY: Routledge, 1999.

Byrne, Sean and Jessica Senehi. "Revisiting the CAR Field." In *Handbook of Conflict Analysis and Resolution*, edited by Dennis Sandole, Sean Byrne, Ingrid Sandole-Staroste, and Jessica Senehi, 525–30. London, England: Routledge, 2009.

———. *Violence: Analysis, Intervention and Prevention*. Athens, OH: Ohio University Press, 2012.

Darby, John. *The Effects of Violence on Peace Processes*. Washington, DC: United States Institute of Peace, 2001.

de Lauretis, Teresa. "Queer Theory: Lesbian and Gay Sexualities." *Differences: A Journal of Feminist Cultural Studies* 3.2 (1991): iii–xviii.

Fisher, Ron, ed. *Paving the Way: Contributions of Interactive Conflict Resolution to Peacemaking*. Lanham, MD: Lexington, 2005.

Foucault, Michel. *The History of Sexuality: An Introduction.* Harmondsworth, England: Penguin, 1978.

Galtung, Johan. *Peace by Peaceful Means*. Los Angeles, CA: Sage, 1996.

———. "Towards a Conflictology: A Quest for Trans-Disciplinarity." In *Handbook of Conflict Analysis and Resolution*, edited by Dennis Sandole, Sean Byrne, Ingrid Sandole-Staroste, and Jessica Senehi, 511–24. London, England: Routledge, 2009.

Gopinath, Gayatri. *Impossible Desires: Queer Diasporas and South Asian Public Cultures*. Durham, NC: Duke University Press, 2005.

hooks, bell. *Yearning: Race, Gender, and Cultural Politics*. Boston, MA: South End, 1990.

Hurlbert, Margot, ed. *Pursuing Justice: An Introduction to Justice Studies*. Winnipeg, MB: Fernwood, 2011.

Jeong, Ho-Won. *Peace and Conflict Studies: An Introduction.* London, England: Ashgate, 2000.

———. *Peacebuilding in Postconflict Societies: Strategy and Process*. Boulder, CO: Lynne Rienner, 2005.

Kelman, Herb. "Group Processes in the Resolution of International Conflicts: Experiences from the Israeli-Palestinian Case." *The American Psychologist* 52.3 (1997): 212–20.

Kemp, Graham and Douglas Fry, eds. *Keeping the Peace: Conflict Resolution and Peaceful Societies Around the World*. London, England: Routledge, 2003.

Kriesberg, Louis and Bruce Dayton. *Constructive Conflicts: From Escalation to Resolution.* Lanham, MD: Rowman & Littlefield, 2002.

Kriesberg, Louis, Stuart Thorson, and Terri Northrup, eds. *Intractable Conflicts and their Transformation.* Syracuse, NY: Syracuse University Press, 1989.

Lederach, John Paul. *Building Peace: Sustainable Reconciliation in Divided Societies.* Washington, DC: United States Institute of Peace, 1997.

———. *Preparing for Peace: Conflict Transformation across Cultures.* Syracuse, NY: Syracuse University Press, 1995.

MacGinty, Roger. *International Peacebuilding and Local Resistance: Hybrid Forms of Peace*. Basingstoke, England: Palgrave Macmillan, 2011.

———. *No War, No Peace: The Rejuvenation of Stalled Peace Processes and Peace Accords*. Basingstoke, England: Palgrave Macmillan, 2008.

MacGinty, Roger and Andrew Williams. *Peace and Development*. London, England: Routledge, 2009.

Matyók, Thomas, Jessica Senehi, and Sean Byrne, eds. *Critical Issues in Peace and Conflict Studies: Theory, Practice, and Pedagogy*. Lanham, MD: Lexington, 2011.

Merry, Sally Engle. *Human Rights and Gender Violence: Translating International Law into Local Justice*. Chicago, IL: University of Chicago Press, 2006.

Mizzi, Robert C. "Let's Get This Straightened Out: Finding a Place and Presence for Sexual/Gender Identity-Difference in Peace Education." *Journal of Peace Education* 7.2 (2010): 139–56.

———. "Uncovering Rainbow (Dis)connections: An Exploration of Sexual and Gender Diversity in the Canadian Forces and Implications for Post-Conflict Reconstruction Training." In *Learning Gendered Militarism in Canada: A Lifelong Pedagogy of Acceptance and Resistance*, edited by Nancy Taber. Edmonton, AB: University of Alberta Press, forthcoming.

Redekop, Vern Neufeld. *From Violence to Blessing: How An Understanding of Deep Rooted Conflict Can Open Paths to Reconciliation*. Toronto, ON: Novalis, 2002.

Rice, Brian. "People of the Longhouse." In *Handbook of Conflict Analysis and Resolution*, edited by Dennis Sandole, Sean Byrne, Ingrid Sandole-Staroste, and Jessica Senehi, 409–19. London, England: Routledge, 2009.

Rice, Brian, Jill Oakes, and Roderick Riewe. *Seeing the World With Aboriginal Eyes*. Winnipeg, MB: University of Manitoba Press, 2005.

Richmond, Oliver. "A Genealogy of Peace and Conflict Theory." In *Palgrave Advances in Peacebuilding: Critical Developments and Approaches*, edited by Oliver Richmond, 14–40. New York, NY: Palgrave Macmillan, 2010.

Ross, Marc Howard. *The Management of Conflicts: Interpretations and Interests in Comparative Perspectives*. New Haven, CT: Yale University Press, 1993.

Ross, Marc Howard and Jay Rothman, eds. *Theory and Practice in Ethnic Conflict Management: Theorizing Success and Failure*. New York, NY: St. Martin's, 1999.

Said, Abdul Aziz, Nathan C. Funk, and Ayse S. Kadayifci. *Peace and Conflict Resolution in Islam: Precept and Practice*. Lanham, MD: University Press of America, 2001.

Sandole, Dennis, Sean Byrne, Ingrid Sandole-Staroste, and Jessica Senehi, eds. *Handbook of Conflict Analysis and Resolution*. London, England: Routledge, 2009.

Senehi, Jessica. "Constructive Storytelling: A Peace Process." *Peace and Conflict Studies* 9.2 (2002): 41–63.

———. "Constructive Storytelling in Inter-communal Conflicts: Building Community, Building Peace." In *Reconciliable Differences: Turning Points in Ethnopolitical Conflict*, edited by Sean Byrne, Cynthia Irvin, Paul Dixon, Brian Polkinghorn, and Jessica Senehi, 96–114. West Hartford, CT: Kumarian, 2000.

———. "Storytelling to Transform Conflicts Constructively." In *Handbook of Conflict Analysis and Resolution*, edited by Dennis Sandole, Sean Byrne, Ingrid Sandole-Staroste, and Jessica Senehi, 199–212. London, England: Routledge, 2009.

———. "The Role of Constructive, Transcultural Storytelling in Ethnopolitical Conflict Transformation in Northern Ireland." In *Regional and Ethnic Conflicts: Perspectives from the Front Lines*, edited by George Irani, Vamik Volkan, and Judy Carter, 227–37. New York, NY: Prentice Hall, 2009.

Senehi, Jessica and Sean Byrne. "Where Do We Go From Here?" In *Critical Issues in Peace and Conflict Studies*, edited by Thomas Matyók, Jessica Senehi, and Sean Byrne, 397–404. Lanham, MD: Lexington, 2011.

Smock, David. *Interfaith Dialogue and Peacebuilding*. Washington, DC: United States Institute of Peace, 2002.

Stephens, John. "Gender Conflict: Connecting Feminist Theory and Conflict Resolution Theory and Practice." In *Conflict and Gender*, edited by Anita Taylor and Judi Beinstein Miller, 217–35. New York, NY: Hampton, 1994.

Taylor, Anita and Judi Beinstein Miller. "Introduction: The Necessity of Seeing Gender in Conflict." In *Conflict and Gender*, edited by Anita Taylor and Judi Beinstein Miller, 1–17. New York, NY: Hampton, 1994.

Terry, Jennifer. *An American Obsession: Science, Medicine and Homosexuality in Modern Society*. Chicago, IL: University of Chicago Press, 1999.

Thiessen, Chuck. *Local Ownership of Peacebuilding in Afghanistan: Shouldering Responsibility for Sustainable Peace and Development*. Lanham, MD: Lexington, 2014.

Tifft, Larry and Lyn Markham. "Battering Women and Battering Central Americans: A Peacemaking Synthesis." In *Criminology as Peace-Making*, edited by Harold Pepinsky and Richard Quinney, 138–39. Bloomington, IN: Indiana University Press, 1991.

van Der Merwe, Hugo and Audrey Chapman. *Truth and Reconciliation in South Africa: Did the TRC Deliver?* Philadelphia, PA: University of Pennsylvania Press, 2008.

van Tongeren, Paul, Malin Brenk, Marte Hellema, and Juliette Verhoeven, eds. *People Building Peace II: Successful Stories of Civil Society*. Boulder, CO: Lynne Rienner, 2005.

Volkan, Vamik. *Bloodlines: From Ethnic Pride to Ethnic Terrorism*. Boulder, CO: Lynne Rienner, 1998.

Warner, Michael. *Publics and Counter-Publics*. New York, NY: Zone, 2002.

Webel, Charles and Johan Galtung, eds. *Handbook of Peace and Conflict Studies*. London, England: Routledge, 2009.

Chapter 22

(Dis)ability, Gender, and Peacebuilding

Natural Absences Present but Invisible

Maureen Flaherty and Nancy Hansen

As a discipline, Peace and Conflict Studies (PACS) looks toward inclusive means of building a more peaceful world. This requires looking at theories and practice—praxis—forward movement, to create what Elise Boulding[1] called a "culture of peace." But what does a culture of peace look like? Who decides? Indeed, who is included in the discussion?

Building peace and the culture that will sustain it is an ongoing process. Our own work with people who have lived through trauma and abuse has led us to understand that in order to move ahead toward a more peaceful, inclusive world, it is vital to have some kind of vision of the direction in which one intends to move.[2] How will we know when we get there? What will be the signs? What do we need to do to get there? What are the pieces present now upon which we can build? What next small steps are necessary to propel us forward? In therapy or counseling, these are solution-focused steps that facilitate a process toward a positive end goal.[3] Peace scholars John Paul Lederach and Elise Boulding also write about a shared vision being important in building cultures of peace.[4]

The field of PACS, like most disciplines, historically was led by male voices,[5] though that has changed slowly since the 1980s.[6] In the process of change, the consideration of gender, and inclusion of women in peacebuilding processes, particularly at the grassroots, has become a requirement of most development projects. Writers in this book add new perspectives related to gender and peacebuilding, including the reality that the conversations around gender and social inclusion have been largely heteronormative. Robert Mizzi and Sean Byrne among others in this volume address this area more directly.

This chapter adds yet another perspective for consideration. We write about the imperative of consciously engaging and ensuring people with disabilities are integral participants in the discussion/processes of building inclusive, peaceful societies. We contend that along with gender considerations, development approaches must add a disability lens—to assure that disabled persons are involved in discussions that impact them, and processes related to the community-building/peacebuilding include the perspectives of individuals with a variety of disabilities. People with disabilities must be contributors to these processes, not just recipients for consideration. Representatives from multiple intersections of health and well-being support the possibility of a growing, developing, substantial peace. Unfortunately literature related to disabilities and peacebuilding is limited.[7]

We are feminists, and also women with disabilities, one with visible challenges and the other with a disability that is not as visible. We have both had to confront external as well as internalized oppression/stigma to have our voices heard, to be considered contributors to society, and not just users of services. We are both active in our multiple communities. We write not as representatives of people with disabilities, but as scholars coming from our own places of knowledge and continued learning. We also want to be represented by others with similar perspectives at any table when decisions about what we need and what we can contribute are being discussed.

Nancy teaches graduate courses in Disability Studies. She has a lifelong visible disability and is acutely aware of inclusion and exclusion in many different forms. Maureen has a usually invisible disability and teaches graduate courses in PACS. She observed early on that PACS scholars, including herself, often neglect to address the subject of "disability" in PACS the same way that many used to treat gender in PACS—just combined with "people," either invisible, or as those who might need services post-conflict. This might be called "ableism," just as assumptions about gender might be called "sexism," a not-so-mild version of misogyny. Our approach follows a progression from discussions with other people with disabilities through the work of a variety of peace scholars such as Janie Leatherman who considers the ways women and men are impacted differentially in conflict situations. We examined the work of Cynthia Enloe who interrogates the different experiences of women and war,[8] and Betty Reardon who opened early conversations about the different impacts of war and peace on women.[9] We considered the cost of ableism not only in post-conflict reconstruction, but in everyday attempts at building and living in a peaceful, just society, where all people's needs are met.

Uncovering and addressing the reality of gender inequality provided a gift to all humans—even those who have lived so far with the privilege that has come with being recognized and respected. The civil rights movement in the United States particularly in the 1960s highlighted the need to challenge racism. Also in the 1960s, the second wave of feminism normalized the need to identify the connections between gender and power and the need to address inequality. Since, humans have been prompted to address other inequalities within our world—inequities connected to power and race, economic status, physical and intellectual ability, age,[10] and even location. The intersection of these "categories" of people requires further scrutiny as to the distribution of power, accessibility to resources, and inclusion as full members in civil society.

With a gendered perspective on John Burton's human needs theory[11] and the international acknowledgment of basic human rights,[12] of which social inclusion is a staple, people are challenged to see and acknowledge the disparities in treatment of people throughout the world. Arthur Blaser, Angeliki Kanavou and Samuel Schleier argue that the continued focus on negative peace ("not war") in Peace Studies and the tendency to assess situations using a deficit model, for example, equating disability with ill health, further adds to discrimination and stands in the way of building peaceful societies.[13] Indeed the special issue in which they wrote acknowledged the difficulty of finding scholars who are writing in this area.[14]

As we introduce the topic of ability mainstreaming in PACS, we first consider who constitutes the population of people with disabilities, then examine the intersections of gender and disability. We look at everyday community-building and peacebuilding and peacebuilding considerations post-conflict. We conclude with considerations for peacebuilding and PACS going forward.

WHAT DO WE KNOW ABOUT PEOPLE WITH DISABILITIES?

Who Are People with Disabilities?

> The World Health Organization (WHO) estimates that fifteen percent of any population is made up of persons with disabilities, with potentially higher proportions in communities that have fled war or natural disasters. Based on this, as many as 6.5 million of the world's 43.51 million people displaced by conflict have disabilities.[15]

Dan Goodley notes "Disability affects us all, transcending class, nation and wealth. The notion of TAB—Temporarily Abled Bodied—recognizes that many people will at some point become disabled,"[16] challenged to fully participate in their social lives.

"Disability is complex, dynamic, multidimensional, and contested."[17] The 2011 World Report on Disability has adopted a bio-psycho-social approach to disability, stating, "[D]isability is the umbrella term for impairments, activity limitations and participation restrictions, referring to the negative aspects of the interaction between an individual (with a health condition) and that individual's contextual factors (environmental and personal factors)."[18] This same report notes that more than one billion people in the world live with or experience some sort of disability themselves and of these, two hundred million experience difficulties in daily functioning.[19] This is the world's largest minority.[20] People with disabilities include but are not limited to people who are impacted by violent conflict. People with disabilities are found worldwide at all ages and stage of life. The Disability Rights Fund adds that 80 percent of people with disabilities live in developing countries where they make up 20 percent of the poorest of the poor.[21]

Physical health is relative and fluctuates for all humans whatever their physical condition and abilities. In Canada, 10 disability types are identified: seeing, hearing, mobility, flexibility, dexterity, pain, learning, developmental, mental/psychological, and memory.[22] The WHO's International Classification of Functioning, Disability and Health (ICF) and the social model of disability describe disability as a challenge that "arises out of the interaction between functional limitations and an unaccommodating environment."[23] Limitations to a person's involvement or participation in the world are contingent not only to the individual's bodily functions or "impairments," but also on environmental factors and personal factors including choice. It is not about a deficit in an individual or group of people, but rather the incompatibility or inability of the environment to accommodate or meet physiological and/or psychological needs of the individual or group.

The World Bank describes mental health as "a state of complete mental well-being including social, spiritual, cognitive and emotional aspects."[24] Mental illness on the other hand is "a disorder of the cognition (thinking) and/or the emotions (mood) as defined by the standard diagnostic systems such as the American Psychiatric Association's Diagnostic and Statistical Manual, 4th Edition (DSM IV)."[25] The World Bank also notes that, on average, 1–3 percent of every population experiences a psychiatric disorder at some point in their lives. This number usually increases during and post-conflict with Post Traumatic Stress Disorder (PTSD) and other conflict-related stress in addition to challenges not considered to be a psychiatric disorder such as sleeplessness, and accompanying hyper-vigilance, feelings of hopelessness and such experienced by at least 30 to 40 percent of the rest of the population. In addition to the many active combatants who experience PTSD and other mental illnesses,[26] 50 to 70 percent of refugees have been found to experience acute clinical depression and PTSD. Children are the most impacted by conflict with often long-term impact of shocks to their development including their still-developing neurological systems.[27]

A medical model sees disability as the impairment of individual functions; the more recent socio-contextual approaches consider the nature of social interactions of people in different contexts or environments. Using a socio-contextual approach or framework, disability is seen as a social construct and empowerment is dependent partially on the right to live in a barrier-free environment.[28] This approach seems to resonate for peacebuilders already using a feminist lens.

"BASIC" STRUCTURAL VIOLENCE AND DISABILITY: THE INTERSECTION OF GENDER AND DISABILITY

Johan Galtung, early and foundational peace scholar, wrote about structural violence as being the inequitable social arrangements that privilege one group of people above another.[29] Structural violence is experienced in social conditions that support and/or allow inadequate housing, inequitable health care services, improper nourishment, unsafe living conditions, poor access to meaningful work and other conditions that privilege one or more groups of people over others. Poverty and disability are often intertwined. The WHO cites persons with disabilities as being "among the poorest of the poor."[30] "More than a billion people in the world, one in seven, have a disability. Eighty percent of people with disabilities live in developing countries, and they make up 20 percent of the poorest of the poor, living on less than one dollar a day."[31] These conditions are everyday challenges, not contingent upon extraordinary circumstances.

Access to education is a strong correlate to better health and social inclusion among other human rights, yet more than 90 percent of children with disabilities in developing countries do not have access to education.[32] The United Nations Educational, Scientific and Cultural Organization (UNESCO) suggests that girls with disabilities are even more underserved than boys and the double discrimination related to ability and gender often spans across both cultures and levels of development.[33]

The intersection of age, gender, education, and other factors influences who is most at risk to violence. Both men and women with disabilities are more vulnerable to violence and abuse than others, often because of necessary reliance for some assistance or caregiving by someone who may have more physical or mental power at a given time. Indeed, Douglas Brownridge states, "It is common in the literature to see very high estimates of violence against persons with disabilities, such as being 50 percent more likely to encounter abuse than the rest of the population . . . or having two to five times the likelihood of abuse compared to nondisabled persons."[34] Each person has his or her own challenges; however, the prevalence of females with disabilities is reportedly 60 percent higher than males.[35]

Women and children with disabilities experience violence at even more alarming rates than men.[36] Children with disabilities are almost four times more likely than other children to experience physical and sexual abuse while women with disabilities are three times more likely to experience these kinds of abuse than their non-disabled sisters.[37] Sometimes this abuse is disability-specific as, for example, "Purposefully not toileting, bathing, feeding, or hydrating a woman; sabotaging assistive services (e.g. unplugging the battery pack to a scooter); beating, strangling, or withholding medication; sexual abuse and exploitation; verbal and emotional abuse; and so on."[38] These conditions are unfortunately everyday occurrences globally. More extraordinary, natural disasters such as tsunamis and earthquakes challenge infrastructures and resources of even the best prepared and appointed societies, and they devastate those already strained and challenged. Consider the added conditions of armed conflict and it is clear that ability is another factor that influences the constraints, challenges and impact on people identified as men, women, two-spirited people, and people of varying ages, stages, and abilities in life.[39]

DISABILITY POST-CONFLICT OR NATURAL DISASTER

Prior to Haiti's earthquake (which occurred on January 12, 2010), people with disabilities in Haiti had few available services. The earthquake itself increased the numbers of disabled Haitians exponentially, leaving people across the age spectrum with new disabilities including spinal cord and brain injuries, amputations, and multiple fractures not to mention PTSD related to the horrors of living through the experience and from losing everything including family and other loved ones.[40] Unfortunately, contrary to a plea from medical practitioners immediately on site following this disaster[41] little consideration was given to including those most directly impacted in the rebuilding of the country. It appears there was an assumption that other specialized organizations would "look after" people with disabilities as if they were entirely separate from the rest of the population.

For every child killed in conflict, three are disabled or permanently injured.[42] Dyan Mazurana and Khristopher Carlson estimate that in addition to the more than two million children killed and 14 million children displaced due to armed conflicts between 1996 and 2006, six million were permanently disabled or otherwise physically injured. This statistic does not include the many, many children who have been emotionally and sexually injured and traumatized.[43] These statistics do not include children forced into marriage and/or left with a legacy of HIV/AIDS. There is very little information on what happens for people with intellectual disabilities in any of these situations.[44]

Even in the best of circumstances, people with disabilities have less access to healthcare resources than those without disabilities, and often have unmet healthcare needs.[45] While people with disabilities are among the most vulnerable in times of conflict and emergency, they are also the least likely to be consulted or involved in planning post-conflict. They might be included in a survey, and referred to a "special" agency, or given special aid or assistance, particularly at the grassroots level by people who know them, but when planning for resource utilization or community capacity building, disabled people are seldom invited or included at the table. Assuming that disability is going to be present whether it is acknowledged at first instance, the natural, logical assumption should be that people will always have to contend with or rather accommodate or deal with disabilities as a matter of course.

Perhaps a different way of looking at the world is needed. Just as we see peace as much more than "not war," Peace Studies must now open to a more holistic understanding of what health and well-being involve, working from a place other than non-disabled as the norm. Perhaps we should consider the human body as something in constant flux with adaptation being socially constructed. Being human involves constant adjusting to physical, mental, social, emotional needs, varying in circumstances and spaces. Western society has yet to develop a level of comfort with the rich messiness that constitutes humanity.[46]

EVERYDAY PEACEBUILDING AND DISABILITY

Elise Boulding described conditions for cultures of peace[47] that are also reflected in the WHO's Determinants of Health.[48] These factors include education, socioeconomic status, social support networks, physical environment including access to healthy and safe food, water, sanitation, and proximity to health care facilities. Health, in all of its facets is mostly social, not individual in its essence. Gender is also a variable.

The UN Convention on the Rights of Persons with Disabilities acknowledges that equality means and requires the removal of barriers that prevent people with disabilities from participating in all aspects of the development of societies—societies that include them/us fully.[49] Like the WHO, psychologist Abraham Maslow,[50] and peace scholar John Burton [51] acknowledge that basic needs for people are not only food, clothing, shelter, physical safety, but also inclusion in a community where the individual is valued and as productive as possible. That means more than "being taken care of."

The lens through which we perceive the world is extremely important. Must we always see people as either or? It is time to take a different approach. "She is a strong person *and* she is disabled."[52] "He is a veteran—and he is a person with a disability." When we consider the complexities of humans and the many ways that lives intersect (sometimes in spite of ourselves), it is much harder to think of another human being as "other."

Gender mainstreaming is a term and concept that came about as a result of the Platform for Action at the United Nations Fourth World Conference on Women in Beijing in 1995. People involved realized that in order to address inequalities between men and women, the impact of any policy or program must be considered from the perspective of each of these two genders. So, more than looking at inequalities, or adding a component of gender to any project, gender issues were to be situated at the center of policy decisions, plans, budgeting, institutional processes etc. Gender mainstreaming means bringing the expertise and experience of women and men to every stage of policy making, planning and decision making.[53] This is not so much about including women equally in number but rather equally in contribution, noting that contributions of men's and women's experience and knowledge would be different.

It is long past time for post-conflict societies, or any kind of community-building venture, to mainstream disability considerations along with gender and other considerations of power inequity locations, just as, for example, the UN Convention on the Rights of Persons with Disabilities focuses on a "holistic" approach to any development or redevelopment work.[54]

WHAT NEEDS TO HAPPEN GOING FORWARD: BUILDING AN INCLUSIVE, PEACEFUL WORLD

Inclusion is not a given in the day-to-day "not war" reality of the developed world. The UN Convention on the Rights of People with Disabilities and its Optional Protocol was adopted in December 2006. At the time there were a significant 82 signatories to the Convention and one ratification.[55] When natural disasters and conflicts occur, it seems that policymakers make expedient service-related decisions based on the assumption that they and those closest to them will never need the services. Disability services are often seen as "extra"—a waste of resources for the less deserving, the less worthy. What would happen if policies were made with the knowledge that all of us at some time will not be fully able-bodied? Even when accessible and inclusive services designed with people with disabilities have priority legislation, such as with the UN's Convention on the Rights of People with Disabilities, there is no actual follow-through and thus far no penalties for noncompliance.

When disasters happen, people with disabilities are often left behind, individuals and communities having made no provision to attend to their needs, and few facilities are prepared to meet their needs.[56] Frequently redevelopment plans do not take into account the need for accessible toilets, ramps, washing stations, and other necessities which cost approximately 2 percent more when built rather than added after.

This is not "us" and "them." We are not talking about "other." It is "we." We have to get over the fear of disability. There must be a component that recognizes disability as natural just as is size, hair color. We are no longer content to be remote and disassociated from the markers of everyday life.[57] We have to start seeing with an accessibility, (dis)ability lens, as with race and gender. Ability crosses race, class, and gender—the intersections move and change and we never know when one is going to subsume the other. There must be natural space acknowledged for all.

Going forward, many steps can be taken using already existing resources, particularly when it comes to education. First, we must all be educated in and have conversations about what disability really is. Why is a disabled person considered "unhealthy"? Is this a way of categorizing and socially distancing people?

Conferences related to best practices in Peace Studies and Development Studies are common practice. Is disability anywhere near the discussion for these events? Disability is no longer an add-on or afterthought. We must bring disability out of the shadows.

If an individual does not think he or she is personally affected by disability at a given moment, then it is even more important to consider what it means to be a good ally.[58] Part of ally work is assisting people to empowerment which includes realizing their full potential and participating as fully as this potential allows in building and rebuilding civil society.[59]

Considering people differently going forward means seeing the intersection of many facets that are integral to people. The acknowledgment of these facets must be for the purpose of increasing people's development and involvement in civil society. After all, a community is made up of its members and the health of a community is reliant upon the health and well-being of each member. We like the way activist Catherine Frazee writes about the interconnectedness of us all, how our lives must be connected. She says, "Dignity is social. It doesn't come from inside of me. It comes from others, always, in relation to me."[60]

NOTES

1. Elise Boulding, *Cultures of Peace: The Hidden Side of History* (New York, NY: Syracuse University Press, 2000).

2. John Paul Lederach, *Preparing for Peace: Conflict Transformation across Cultures* (New York, NY: Syracuse University Press, 1995).

3. Barry L. Duncan and Scott D. Miller, *The Heroic Client: Doing Client-Directed Outcome-Informed Therapy* (San Francisco, CA: Jossey-Bass, 2000).

4. John Paul Lederach, *Building Peace: Sustainable Reconciliation in Divided Societies* (Washington, DC: United States Institute of Peace, 1997); John Paul

Lederach, *The Moral Imagination: The Art and Soul of Building Peace* (New York, NY: Oxford University Press, 2005); Boulding, *Cultures of Peace.*

5. For a cursory glance at some of those voices, see David J. Dunn, *The First Fifty Years of Peace Research: A Survey and Interpretation* (Burlington, VT: Ashgate, 2005).

In Louis Kriesburg's review of the growing field, there are a few more women's names though they remain far outnumbered by males. See Louis Kriesberg, "Contemporary Conflict Resolution Applications," in *Leashing the Dogs of War: Conflict Management in a Divided World*, ed. Chester A. Crocker, Fen Osler Hampson, and Pamela R. Aall (Washington, DC: United States Institute of Peace Press, 2007).

6. See for example the work of Betty Reardon, *Educating for a Culture of Peace in a Gender Perspective* (Paris, France: UNESCO, 2001); Cynthia Enloe, *Bananas, Beaches and Bases: Making Feminist Sense of International Politics*, updated ed. (Berkely, CA: University of California Press, 2000); and Peggy Chinn, *Peace and Power: Creative Leadership for Building Community*, 6th ed. (Mississauga, ON: Jones and Bartlett, 2004) as among the earlier female peace writers who continue their work today.

7. See Arthur W. Blaser, Angeliki Kanavou, and Samuel Schleier, "The Peace Studies/Disability Studies Nexus," *Peace Studies Journal* 6.4 (2013) and Gregor Wolbring, "From Peace Studies to Disability Studies," introduction to *Peace Studies Journal* 6.4 (2013) for a summary of the very little that was found when searching for peacebuilding articles including disability.

8. Enloe, *Bananas, Beaches and Bases.*

9. Reardon, *Educating for a Culture of Peace*; Cynthia Enloe, *Nimo's War, Emma's War: Making Feminist Sense Out of the Iraq War* (Berkely, CA: University of California Press, 2010).

10. Joey Sprague, *Feminist Methodologies for the Critical Researcher: Bridging Differences* (New York, NY: AltaMira, 2005).

11. John Burton, *Conflict: Human Needs Theory* (London, England: Macmillan, 1990).

12. United Nations Office of the High Commissioner for Human Rights, *Women's Rights Are Human Rights: Special Issue* (New York, NY and Geneva Switzerland: United Nations, 2000).

13. Blaser, Kanavou and Schleier, "The Peace Studies/Disability Studies Nexus."

14. Wolbring, "From Peace Studies to Disability Studies."

15. Women's Refugee Commission, "Disabilities Among Refugees and Conflict-Affected Populations," June 2008, accessed November 14, 2014, https://womensrefugeecommission.org/resources/document/609.

16. Dan Goodley, *Disability Studies: An Interdisciplinary Approach* (London, England: Sage, 2011).

17. World Health Organization, "World Report on Disability 2011," 2011, accessed December 30, 2014, http://www.who.int/disabilities/world_report/2011/en/.

18. Ibid.

19. Ibid.

20. World Health Organization, "Disability and Health Fact Sheet No. 352," December 2014, accessed December 26, 2014, http://www.who.int/mediacentre/factsheets/fs352/en/.

21. Disability Rights Fund, "Impact," accessed December 26, 2014, www.disabilityrightsfund.org/impact.

22. Statistics Canada, "Canadian Survey on Disability, 2012," Government of Canada, accessed November 20, 2014, www.statcan.gc.ca/daily-quotidien/131203/dq131203a-eng.htm.

23. Daniel Mont and Mitchell Loeb, "Beyond DALYs: Developing Indicators to Assess the Impact of Public Health Interventions on the Lives of People With Disabilities," Social Protection Discussion Paper No. SP 0815 (Washington, DC: The World Bank, 2008), 2.

24. Jane Wilbur, "What the Global Disability Report Means for the WASH Sector," *WaterAid*, 2011, accessed November 14, 2014, http://www.susana.org/_resources/documents/default/2-1309-reportwhattheglobalreportondisabilitymeansforthewash-sector1.pdf.

25. The World Bank, "Mental Health and Conflict," *Social Development Notes: Conflict Prevention & Reconstruction* no. 13 (2003).

26. Charles Milliken, Jennifer Auchterlonie, and Charles Hoge, "Longitudinal Assessment of Mental Health Problems Among Active and Reserve Component Soldiers Returning from the Iraq War," *Jounal of the American Medical Association* 298.18 (2007).

27. The World Bank, "Mental Health and Conflict."

28. Konstantina Daviki et al., *Discrimination Generated by the Intersection of Gender and Disability*, Directorate-General for Internal Policies: Citizens' Rights and Constitutional Affairs, European Parliament (Brussels, Belgium: European Union, 2013), 8.

29. Johan Galtung, "Violence, Peace, and Peace Research," *Journal of Peace Research* 6.3 (1969): 167–91.

30. Mont and Loeb, "Beyond DALYs."

31. Disability Rights Fund, *One in Seven: How One Billion People are Redefining the Global Movement for Human Rights* (Boston, MA: Disability Rights Fund, 2013).

32. UNESCO, "The Right to Education for Persons with Disabilities: Towards Inclusion," accessed December 30, 2014, www.unesco.org/education/efa/know_sharing/flagship_initiatives/persons_disabilities.shtml.

33. Harilyn Rousso, "Education for All: A Gender and Disability Perspective," background paper prepared for the Education for All (EFA) Global Monitoring Report 2003/4, *Gender and Education for All: The Leap to Equality*, UNESCO, 2003, accessed February 3, 2015, http://unesdoc.unesco.org/images/0014/001469/146931e.pdf.

34. Douglas A. Brownridge, "Partner Violence Against Women with Disabillties: Prevalence, Risk, and Explanations," *Violence Against Women* 12.9 (2011): 805.

35. Wilbur, "What the Global Disability Report Means."

36. Chrystal C. Barranati and Francis K. Yuen, "Intimate Partner Violence and Women with Disabilities: Toward Bringing Visibility to an Unrecognized Population," *Journal of Social Work in Disability and Rehabilitation* 7.2 (2008): 115.

37. Disability Rights Fund, "One in Seven," 8.

38. Barranati and Yuen, "Intimate Partner Violence," 119.

39. Janie L. Leatherman, *Sexual Violence and Armed Conflict* (Cambridge, England: Polity Press, 2011).

40. Lisa I. Iezzoni and Laurence J. Ronan, "Disability Legacy of the Haitian Earthquake," *Annals of Internal Medicine* 152.12 (2010).

41. Ibid.

42. UNESCO, "The Right to Education."

43. Dyan Mazurana and Khristopher Carlson, "The Girl Child and Armed Conflict: Recognizing and Addressing Grave Violations of Girls' Human Rights," United Nations Division for the Advancement of Women, Expert Group Meeting, Florence, Italy, September 25–28, 2006.

44. Brigitte Rohwerder, "Intellectual Disabilities, Violent Conflict and Humanitarian Assistance: Advocacy of the Forgotten," *Disability and Society* 28.6 (2013).

45. World Health Organization, "Disability and Health Fact Sheet No. 352." This same fact sheet noted that a recent survey found that in developed countries between 35 and 50 percent of people with mental illness do not receive proper care for their illness. This number shoots to between 76 and 85 percent in developing countries.

46. Ato Quayson, *Aesthetic Nervousness: Disability and the Crisis of Representation* (New York, NY: Columbia University Press, 2007).

47. Boulding, *Cultures of Peace.*

48. World Health Organization, "Health Impact Assessment (HIA)," 2014, accessed December 30, 2014, www.who.int/hia/en/.

49. United Nations, "Convention on the Rights of Persons With Disabilities" (A/RED/62/127), *United Nations Enable: Development and Human Rights for All*, accessed December 26, 2014, www.un.org/disabilities/default.asp?=259.

50. Abraham H. Maslow, *Motivation and Personality* (New York, NY: Harper and Row, 1954).

51. Burton, *Conflict: Human Needs Theory.*

52. Annie Delin, "Buried in the Footnotes: The Absence of Disabled People in the Collective Memory of Our Past," in *Museums, Society, Inequality*, ed. Richard Sandell (London, England: Routledge, 2002).

53. Sarah Murison, "Elements of a Gender Mainstreaming Strategy: A Fourteen-point Framework," *The Capacity Development Group Inc.: Analysis, Learning and Change Management for Diversity and Gender Equality* (2004).

54. United Nations, "Convention on the Rights of Persons With Disabilities."

55. Ibid.

56. United Nations Enable, "Disability, Natural Disasters and Emergency Situations," accessed December 30, 2014, www.un.org/disabilities/default.asp?id=1546.

57. Nancy Hansen and Chris Philo, "The Normality of Doing things Differently: Bodies, Spaces and Disability Geography." *Tijdschrift voor Economische en Social Geografie* (Royal Dutch Geographical Society) 98.4 (2007).

58. Ann Bishop, *Becoming an Ally: Breaking through the Cycle of Oppression in People*, 2nd ed. (Halifax, NS: Fernwood, 2000).

59. Edward W. Schwerin, *Mediation, Citizen Empowerment, and Transformational Politics* (Westport, CT: Praeger, 1995).

60. Catherine Frazee, "There Can Be Dignity in All States of Life," *The Ottawa Citizen*, October 14, 2014.

BIBLIOGRAPHY

Barranati, Chrysral C. R. and Francis K. O. Yuen. "Intimate Partner Violence and Women with Disabilities: Toward Bringing Visibility to an Unrecognized Population." *Journal of Social Work in Disability and Rehabilitation* 7.2 (2008): 115–30.

Bishop, Ann. *Becoming an Ally: Breaking Through the Cycle of Oppression in People.* 2nd ed. Halifax, NS: Fernwood, 2000.

Blaser, Arthur W., Angeliki Kanavou, and Samuel Schleier. "The Peace Studies/ Disability Studies Nexus." *Peace Studies Journal* 6.4 (2013): 6–21.

Boulding, Elise. *Cultures of Peace: The Hidden Side of History.* New York, NY: Syracuse University Press, 2000.

Brownridge, Douglas A. "Partner Violence Against Women with Disabillties: Prevalence, Risk, and Explanations." *Violence Against Women* 12.9 (2011): 805–22.

Burton, John. *Conflict: Human Needs Theory.* London, England: Macmillan, 1990.

Chinn, Peggy L. *Peace and Power: Creative Leadership for Building Community.* 6th ed. Mississauga, ON: Jones and Bartlett, 2004.

Daviki, Konstantina, Claire Marzo, Elisa Narminio, and Maria Arvanitidou. *Discrimination Generated by the Intersection of Gender and Disability.* Directorate-General for Internal Policies: Citizens' Rights and Constitutional Affairs, European Parliament, Brussels, Belgium: European Union, 2013.

Delin, Annie. "Buried in the Footnotes: The Absence of Disabled People in the Collective Imagery of Our Past." In *Museums, Society, Inequality,* edited by Richard Sandell, 84–97. London, England: Routledge, 2002.

Disability Rights Fund. "Impact." Accessed December 26, 2014. www.disabilityrightsfund.org/impact.

———. *One in Seven: How One Billion People are Redefining the Global Movement for Human Rights.* Boston, MA: Disability Rights Fund, 2013.

Duncan, Barry L. and Scott D. Miller. *The Heroic Client: Doing Client-Directed Outcome-Informed Therapy.* San Francisco, CA: Jossey-Bass, 2000.

Dunn, David J. *The First Fifty Years of Peace Research: A Survey and Interpretation.* Burlington, VT: Ashgate, 2005.

Enloe, Cynthia. *Bananas, Beaches and Bases: Making Feminist Sense of International Politics.* Updated ed. Berkely, CA: University of California Press, 2000.

———. *Nimo's War, Emma's War: Making Feminist Sense Out of the Iraq War.* Berkely, CA: University of California Press, 2010.

Frazee, Catherine. "There Can Be Dignity in All States of Life." *The Ottawa Citizen,* October 14, 2014.

Galtung, Johan. "Violence, Peace, and Peace Research." *Journal of Peace Research* 6.3 (1969): 167–91.

Goodley, Dan. *Disability Studies: An Interdisciplinary Approach.* London, England: Sage, 2011.

Hansen, Nancy and Chris Philo. "The Normality of Doing Things Differently: Bodies, Spaces and Disability Geography." *Tijdschrift voor Economische en Social Geografie* (Royal Dutch Geographical Society) 98.4 (2007): 493–506.

Iezzoni, Lisa I. and Laurence J. Ronan. "Disability Legacy of the Haitian Earthquake." *Annals of Internal Medicine* 152.12 (2010): 812–14.

Kriesberg, Louis. "Contemporary Conflict Resolution Applications." In *Leashing the Dogs of War: Conflict Management in a Divided World*, edited by Chester A. Crocker, Fen Osler Hampson, and Pamela R. Aall, 455–76 . Washington, DC: United States Institute of Peace, 2007.

Leatherman, Janie L. *Sexual Violence and Armed Conflict*. Cambridge, England: Polity Press, 2011.

Lederach, John Paul. *Building Peace: Sustainable Reconciliation in Divided Societies*. Washington, DC: United States Institute of Peace, 1997.

———. *Preparing for Peace: Conflict Transformation across Cultures*. New York, NY: Syracuse University Press, 1995.

———. *The Moral Imagination: The Art and Soul of Building Peace*. New York, NY: Oxford University Press, 2005.

Maslow, Abraham H. *Motivation and Personality*. New York, NY: Harper and Row, 1954.

Mazurana, Dyan and Khristopher Carlson. "The Girl Child and Armed Conflict: Recognizing and Addressing Grave Violations of Girls' Human Rights." United Nations Division for the Advancement of Women. Expert Group Meeting, Florence, Italy, September 25–28, 2006.

Milliken, Charles, Jennifer Auchterlonie, and Charles Hoge. "Longitudinal Assessment of Mental Health Problems Among Active and Reserve Component Soldiers Returning from the Iraq War." *Jounal of the American Medical Association* 298.18 (2007): 2141–48.

Mont, Daniel and Mitchell Loeb. "Beyond DALYs: Developing Indicators to Assess the Impact of Public Health Interventions on the Lives of People With Disabilities." Social Protection Discussion Paper No. SP 0815. Washington, DC: The World Bank, 2008.

Murison, Sarah. "Elements of a Gender Mainstreaming Strategy: A Fourteen-Point Framework." *The Capacity Development Group Inc.: Analysis, Learning and Change Management for Diversity and Gender Equality* (2004): 1–10.

Quayson, Ato. *Aesthetic Nervousness: Disability and the Crisis of Representation*. New York, NY: Columbia University Press, 2007.

Reardon, Betty. *Education for a Culture of Peace in a Gender Perspective*. Paris, France: UNESCO, 2001.

Rohwerder, Brigitte. "Intellectual Disabilities, Violent Conflict and Humanitarian Assistance: Advocacy of the Forgotten." *Disability and Society* 28.6 (2013): 770–83.

Rousso, Harilyn. "Education for All: A Gender and Disability Perspective." Background paper prepared for the Education for All (EFA) Global Monitoring Report 2003/4, *Gender and Education for All: The Leap to Equality*. UNESCO, 2003. Accessed February 3, 2015. http://unesdoc.unesco.org/images/0014/001469/146931e.pdf.

Schwerin, Edward W. *Mediation, Citizen Empowerment, and Transformational Politics*. Westport, CT: Praeger, 1995.

Sprague, Joey. *Feminist Methodologies for the Critical Researcher: Bridging Differences*. New York, NY: AltaMira, 2005.

Statistics Canada. "Canadian Survey on Disability, 2012." Government of Canada. Accessed Novemer 20, 2014. www.statcan.gc.ca/daily-quotidien/131203/dq131203a-eng.htm.

The World Bank. "Mental Health and Conflict." *Social Development Notes: Conflict Prevention & Reconstruction* no. 13 (2003): 1–4.

UNESCO. "The Right to Education for Persons with Disabilities: Towards Inclusion." Accessed December 30, 2014. www.unesco.org/education/efa/know_sharing/flagship_initiatives/persons_disabilities.shtml.

United Nations. "Convention on the Rights of Persons With Disabilities" (A/RED/62/127). *United Nations Enable: Development and Human Rights for All.* Accessed December 26, 2014. www.un.org/disabilities/default.asp?id=259.

United Nations Enable. "Disability, Natural Disasters and Emergency Situations." Accessed December 30, 2014. www.un.org/disabilities/default.asp?id=1546.

United Nations Office of the High Commissioner for Human Rights. *Women's Rights are Human Rights: Special Issue.* New York, NY and Geneva, Switzerland: United Nations, 2000.

Wilbur, Jane. "What the Global Disability Report Means for the WASH Sector." *WaterAid,* 2011. Accessed November 14, 2014. http://www.susana.org/_resources/documents/default/2-1309-reportwhattheglobalreportondisabilitymeansforthewashsector1.pdf.

Wolbring, Gregor. "From Peace Studies to Disability Studies." Introduction to *Peace Studies Journal* 6.4 (2013): 2–5.

Women's Refugee Commission. "Disabilities among Refugees and Conflict-Affected Populations," June 2008. Accessed November 14, 2014. https://womensrefugeecommission.org/resources/document/609.

World Health Organization. "Disability and Health Fact Sheet No. 352," December 2014. Accessed December 26, 2014. http://www.who.int/mediacentre/factsheets/fs352/en/.

———. "Health Impact Assessment (HIA)," 2014. Accessed December 30, 2014. www.who.int/hia/en/.

———. "World Report on Disability 2011," 2011. Accessed December 30, 2014. http://www.who.int/disabilities/world_report/2011/en/.

Chapter 23

Getting It Right

Some Advice from Feminist Methodologists[1]

Joey Sprague

When you are working with communities seeking to make their lives less difficult, there is an extra impetus to "get it right." Dorothy Smith[2] argues that professional sociologists should recognize that scholarship developed in real world contexts can have scientific value but the observation about the pressure to get it right applies equally to activists.

Social scientists have a fairly good track record for getting some things right. They have helped us understand a great deal about social processes, the regularization of social practices into social structures, and the impact of social structures and interpersonal relationships on human understanding and action. Social scientists have helped us to understand some of what works and what doesn't work in the general project of making the world a better place.

However, feminists and other critical scholars have generated a rich literature showing just how wrong social scientists have been at times and I believe the ultimate source of the error has been unquestioned assumptions about how to best create knowledge. In my view, an important aspect of "getting it right" is about the link one is making between an epistemology—a theory of what knowledge is—and a methodology, a way of collecting and interpreting evidence. Whether we are paying attention or not, how we develop an understanding about the world is premised on our assumptions about what makes for a competent knower, what the underlying characteristics of the known are, and what the process of knowing entails. First I will summarize our epistemological choices and make a case that the safest choice would be a hybrid of two of them. Then I will briefly discuss what that choice implies for how knowers should proceed in building valid knowledge.

EPISTEMOLOGICAL CHOICES

To wildly oversimplify, there are four basic sets of assumptions about the knower, the known, and the process of knowing currently in circulation: Positivism, Post-Modernism, Critical Realism, and Standpoint Theory. The first two are false choices in that they conflict with the findings of social science and its ultimate purpose.

Positivist approaches assume that the objective world is governed by discoverable rules and the knower gains access to those rules by minimizing the role of subjective judgment through the use of quantitative procedures for collecting and analyzing data. However social science research shows that knowing cannot be the objective, unbiased, ahistorical process Positivism represents. In order to perceive, the researcher must use some framework to carve up the continuity of lived experience to identify objects or facts to investigate.[3] Further, in order to test any hypothesis, a researcher must maintain a set of other assumptions, for example, about the reliability of the measures, the comprehensiveness of the causal model, and so on. Flaws in any of these other assumptions are alternative explanations for observed outcomes. Even the notion that science is pure hypothesis testing is belied by the actual practice of scientists. If a test of the research hypothesis fails to achieve the expected results, the scientist does not necessarily reject that hypothesis but rather can and often does tinker with the background assumptions (e.g., maybe a measure is flawed), arriving at a way to make sense of the data while maintaining the original thought or expectation. A thread running through all three of these points is that the knower operates under assumptions that express a specific culture. Science is not value-neutral[4] and an epistemology that ignores subjectivity is not tenable.

The other false epistemological choice is the one generated in the arguments of strong social constructivist or Postmodern thought. Proponents of this approach argue that any order or perceived regularity in phenomena is not "out there" in the empirical world. Rather, we give order to our perceptions through the application of a cultural framework.[5] The object of knowledge, that which appears to us as the truth, is merely the creation of the very process that "discovers" it.[6] Rather than a process of discovery, social science knowledge is an important way that power works in our era. Social scientists generate and feed discourses that circulate through our daily lives, prompting us to construct certain forms of self-awareness and to discipline ourselves toward a socially constructed standard of normality. We have learned to see ourselves, for example, in terms of our position in a distribution of scores on intelligence and aptitude tests, our behaviors in terms of their appropriateness for our gender, and the degree to which our consumption patterns communicate positions of social status.

While it is consistent with sociological understanding to say that knowledge is socially created, saying that something is socially constructed does not imply it is not real. We know, for example, that the belief in dichotomous gender is socially constructed yet it increases our ability to predict vulnerability to rape and domestic violence and level of income, which are all very real social facts. Second, the fundamental justification of social science is that it produces knowledge about people and groups that can inform human action. Intentional action is premised on an analysis of what is and what might be. When analyses of experiences are considered mere texts or the narrative of one individual, no better or worse than any contrasting narrative, the potential for supporting meaningful social action is eroded.[7] Donna Haraway coined a term that aptly communicates the impact: "epistemological electro-shock therapy."[8]

Realistic Choices

The choice between a blind trust in the facts, uninfluenced by the knower, and a radical rejection of them, denying the known, is a false choice, one that would be rejected by many of those who believe in science and/or social constructionism. There are two general approaches to epistemology that take as a given that knowledge is socially constructed without rejecting the possibility of developing knowledge at all: Critical Realism and Standpoint Theory.

Critical Realist epistemology, like Positivism, holds that the world exists independently of our thinking about it and it is knowable. Critical Realists, however, have developed a more complex understanding of the nature of the known. For them, reality exists in three nested domains: the empirical, the actual, and the real.[9] What we can observe and measure in the *empirical* domain does not capture all that exists at that moment, the domain of the *actual*, which in turn is the product of the mechanisms of underlying structures in the domain of the *real*.

The underlying structures in the domain of the real occur in different layers so that when we talk about causes of a phenomenon as physical or biological or chemical or economic or political or ideological, we are talking about the mechanisms of different structures that typically work in complex interactions with one another. Institutions, for example, are not just the outcome of economical, political, or ideological mechanisms but rather all of these, and probably others.[10] Both natural and social systems tend to be dynamic and changing products of complex and at times conflicting forces. Thus any statement about the causes is incomplete and our explanations are about probabilities.

Like postmodernists, Critical Realists see knowledge as a social product. The individual knower is shaped by historically specific discourses of culture and science. The key knower is not an individual but a loosely integrated collection of networks of scholars who often disagree, thus pushing the process of knowledge-building forward through a continual quest for further information and better understandings.[11] Even if we will never be able to develop a perfect knowledge of the world, Critical Realists believe that through scientific practices and the application of human rationality we can approximate the underlying causal mechanisms generating phenomena.[12]

Critical Realists recognize that the relationship between knower and known is socially and culturally organized but every knower operating within the same network of discourses seems to have the same potential access to the known. Yet, a key intellectual contribution of sociological scholarship has been to demonstrate that systems of social relations organizing gender, class, and race are particularly important in shaping our opportunities and constraints, our perceptions, and our stakes in social life. The epistemology that does take the impact of systematic differences in social location of knowers into account is Standpoint Theory.

Standpoint epistemology argues that all knowledge is constructed from a specific position and that what a knower can observe is shaped by the location from which that knower's inquiry begins. To illustrate the contrasts in the kinds of knowledge that are accessible by beginning from distinct standpoints, Nancy Hartsock uses the example of varying ways political scientists have developed a conceptualization of power.[13] The predominant notion of power in political science, Hartsock says, has been developed by taking the standpoint of capitalists. Capitalists are removed from the concrete circumstances involved in producing goods and services, including their relationship with workers. Capitalists engage with the political economy through exchanges in markets. Beginning from the experience and interests of capitalists, Hartsock argues, provides resources for understanding power as a "commodity" that a person has more or less of, something that can be exchanged, taken, or given away.

On the other hand, scholars who begin from the practical experience of workers have access to resources that allow them to foreground the operation of power in the capitalist/worker relationship. Workers must sell their labor to capitalists, do their work in coordination with the labor of other workers, and earn wages that are lower than the market value of the goods that they produce. The workers' standpoint offers resources for understanding power as a relationship of domination in which one party, by virtue of their control over wealth, is able to take advantage of and extract compliance from the other. Beginning an analysis from the standpoint of workers allows one to conceptualize power as a relationship of domination, a conceptualization that Hartsock represents as "power over."

However, Hartsock argues, there is a third construction of power, one that becomes available by beginning from the standpoint of women. The sexual division of labor in Western societies makes women responsible for domestic labor in the home, doing the work of transforming commodities into food, clothing, and other things that meet peoples' needs. Beginning from the position of those who do this work of nurturing makes it possible to develop a notion of power as a capacity or potential, as in the word "empower." Hartsock argues that the standpoint of women offers unique resources for developing the notion of power as "power to."

Standpoint Epistemology helps us understand some systematic biases in mainstream accounts of social structures and social processes. For example, in spite of the fact that gender researchers have been demonstrating for more than 30 years the centrality of gender in shaping nearly every dimension of human social life, there are still areas in sociology in which the dominant discourses fail to take gender into account. Yet, scholars examining these areas using gender as an analytic framework reveal challenges to predominant organizing assumptions. Joan Acker shows that the tendency to ignore gender in conventional class analyses hides the degree to which "non-responsibility" for reproduction of people is a central feature of how capitalist corporations and economies operate.[14] Similarly, prevailing conceptualizations of globalization emphasize the transnational activities of dominant economic actors, particularly men. Manisha Desai, beginning from the standpoint of women in countries of the Global South, reveals a much bigger and potentially more democratic version of "globalization on the ground," including cross-national entrepreneurial and social justice work done by women.[15]

Critical Realism contributes a sophisticated model of the nature of the *known*, one that researchers should keep in mind in making sense of the data. However, Standpoint Theory offers a more complex model of the nature of the *knower*, understanding that knowers are occupants of varying social locations, especially those organized by social relations of gender, race, class, and nation. To maximize our chances of getting it right, we need to take these perspectives into account.

CRITICALLY SEEKING REALITY

Feminist sociologists have developed a rich literature on the methodological implications of standpoint epistemology. While it includes many thoughtful and creative innovations, there are some troubling stereotypes as well. One is that feminist methodology means transferring control over knowledge to research subjects. Another is that researchers who are "insiders," that is, members of marginalized groups, will produce better knowledge about those groups. Taking a critical look at each reveals that such simple transfers of authority are inadequate responses to the problems associated with researcher power.

The Problems with "Handing Over Authority"

Some contend that standpoint epistemology implies that researchers should give all control over knowledge creation to those being studied. The researcher should serve as the mere conduit, the holder of the microphone, to "give voice" to research subjects.[16] This position sounds democratic and open on a superficial level but, considered more carefully, has at least four shortcomings.

First, it fails to take into account how and where research subjects already have some power, such as providing access, deciding what to reveal, how to tell their stories, and which response to select in a survey. In fact, the less vested interest potential informants have in a project, the more power they have in the process. Second, it ignores situations in which the researched have even more power than the researcher. Those who interview subjects who occupy positions of political or social power report that they have no trouble communicating their perspective and enforcing their own agenda even when it conflicts with the researcher's goals. Third, it is insensitive to the selection biases built into implementing this strategy. Members of any social category—white women, people of color, immigrants from Mexico, and so on—are very diverse in experience and opinion. How do researchers choose which among their informants appropriately speaks for their group? What kind of selection bias comes into play in their choices? Finally, to the degree that our informants are deprived of access to more critical discourses, the effort to simply and uncritically report subjects' narratives can give priority to hegemonic discourses over critical ones.[17]

As Miriam Glucksmann[18] observes, those who want to simply transfer authority to subjects of research have tended to confuse the empowerment of those we study in the process of doing research with real social empowerment. We would never make this error, she maintains, if we were thinking of women interviewing men (or, I would add, if we were thinking of Blacks interviewing Whites, or researchers from the working class interviewing the wealthy).

Another unfortunate stereotype is the idea that standpoint epistemology implies we should grant authority based on the social identity of the researcher, for example, their gender, race, or national origin. Some say that researchers should not study people over whom they have social privilege: only women can study women, only Blacks can study Blacks, and so on. Others would merely assume that researchers who are members of the social category they are studying will develop more valid knowledge than will researchers who are not of that group.

Yet, there is a broad consensus among contemporary feminist theorists that multiple relations of domination interact in shaping life chances and consciousness.[19] That is, how gender works depends on an individual's class and race/ethnicity; how race/ethnicity works varies across different combinations of class and gender, and so on. The idea of an insider advantage seems inconsistent with the implications of these intersectional arguments. It is also contradicted by the reflections of researchers regarding their experiences on the ground.[20] Sharing some aspect of identity, say, gender or race, with the researched does not assure "common experiences or interests."

Commonalities in life experience can enhance empathy. For example, to the extent that women confront similar normative expectations, struggle with discrimination based on their sex, and deal with similar interpersonal issues in their relations with men and children, there is the possibility that they can identify with the struggles of other women, even across divisions of race, class, or nation. However, when the investigator differs from the investigated in other significant dimensions of social inequality, researchers' assumptions of shared identity can be an exercise in self-deception. Further, while some cultural nuances may be better observed by an insider, some may be more accessible to a person who did not grow up within the discourses dominating that culture.[21] What the insider shares with group members—cultural assumptions, shared social practices and history—can easily slip into the taken-for-granted. Yet, taking things for granted is the bane of good social research. David Morgan said it well: "The obvious deserves at least as much attention from the sociologist as the extraordinary. It is also more difficult to recognize."[22] Each investigator embodies attributes that constitute a set of advantages and obstacles.

Beyond the question of exactly who is and who is not an insider in any particular situation, an idealization of insider-only research has troubling political implications. After all, much of the history of social science is a classic case of insider-only research, of men who feel that they should study only men. As a rule, those men have not focused on undermining patriarchy.[23] If privileged researchers avoid studying disadvantaged groups, that omission serves to sustain their own hegemony.[24] If Whites do not study Blacks, if men ignore the lives and experiences of women, if the affluent do not seek to understand the actual circumstances of the poor, we will have returned to the bad old days when the privileged could easily justify ignoring the lives and perspectives of the oppressed.

Both the idea that the knowledge of the oppressed is better than the knowledge of the oppressor and the belief that the insider researcher has privileged access to knowledge are a misreading of the argument of standpoint epistemology as advanced by its key developers. Hartsock says that a standpoint is "achieved rather than obvious, a mediated rather than immediate understanding."[25] Smith describes a standpoint as a place from which to begin an inquiry and proposes a methodology for how researchers can begin from a social location other than the one they regularly occupy.[26] Sandra Harding talks about that location in terms of the array of resources available in a specific context, including an embodied location in a specific time and place, interests emerging from and in relation to that location, access to discourses through which to interpret one's interests, and position in a social organization of the production of legitimate knowledge.[27] It cannot be stated too baldly: *a standpoint is not how people think.* A standpoint is a social location from which to construct an understanding.

REALIST STANDPOINT EPISTEMOLOGY ON GETTING IT RIGHT

What does all of this imply for how we should build knowledge? In this section I propose four provisional guidelines for how we might implement any method with more caution about the distorting effects power can have on the kind of knowledge we produce.

1. Work from the Standpoint of the Disadvantaged

A flourishing of new analytic frames and avenues of research has followed the increasing diversity of the academy. Many of those who have changed our understanding of basic social phenomena like work, family, health, violence, politics, race/ethnicity, demographic patterns, and criminology have been women; some have been scholars of color or from the working class. However, *some have been privileged white men.* The transformations in social science knowledge have occurred *not because of the changing identity of the scholars, but because scholars have been shifting the standpoints from which they develop scholarship.* Change has come when knowers have taken previously marginalized standpoints as the gateway for developing questions, collecting evidence, and developing interpretations.

For example, the data on the frequency of sexual violence changed when scholars stopped restricting it to reports of "rape" because the prevailing conceptualization at the time excluded from the count sexual contact within marriage or unwanted sex with an acquaintance. Rather than asking women if they had been raped, Diana Russell created a measure of sexual behaviors based on women's desires and preferences.[28] Similarly, to understand why poor kids are more likely to fail in school, Allison Griffith asked the mothers of elementary school children about all the work they did in relationship to their kids going to school.[29] In the process she learned how the organization of educational institutions makes time and resource demands on parents that put poor and working class kids at a serious disadvantage but that teachers and administrators blame parents for kids' failures instead of the class biases in the institution's expectations and practices.

Working from the standpoint of the disadvantaged does not preclude studying the powerful. Rather, it involves problematizing power and advantage, asking about the mechanisms that sustain privilege and about the consequences of privilege for the broader society. One way for those with privilege to proceed is to analyze the circumstances and practices that support their privilege, for example, by examining their own biography from the standpoint of those over whom they have privilege.[30] The important point is that knowledge has changed in critical directions when knowers have mounted their inquiries into some aspect of the social by beginning from the situations of women, people of color, the poor, and other socially marginalized categories.

2. Ground Interpretations in Interests and Experience

Those at the downside of social hierarchies have some epistemological advantages. Their daily practices and the constraints within which they struggle are the basic stuff of how social power and domination work. They have little material or ideological interest in continuing those forms of social organization that place them at serious disadvantage, and so less reason to deny the flaws and injustices embedded in them. As outsiders in relation to official knowledge construction, they may have experiences that allow them to detect the gap between their lives and the conceptual frameworks that are distributed to make sense of them.[31]

The workings of cultural power mean that members of oppressed groups are less likely to encounter an analysis that identifies their situation as unjust. Thus, the marginalized may not directly challenge mainstream notions about their lives. However taking their situations into account in interpreting their reports can enhance insight. Operating from this premise, Marjorie DeVault rejected the standard practice of "correcting" hesitations, gaps, and tag questions ("you know?"), instead using these speech patterns as potential indicators that the mainstream conceptualizations were not adequate to describe their experience.[32]

Taking into account the interests and experience of women in a society that routinely devalues them led Linda Carli to challenge the prevailing stereotype in the research literature of women's speech as systematically tentative thus communicating to others that they were not to be heeded. Rather than assigning blame to women for the devaluation of their speech, Carli asked whether those tentative speech patterns were a strategy for dealing with relative powerlessness in particular gendered interactions; her experimental findings suggest this is the case.[33]

Researchers should also ask about the degree to which their own material interests and experiences shape their priorities and assumptions. White researchers assuming race is not significant in their projects, men assuming gender is irrelevant, and heterosexuals assuming the social organization of sexuality is not in play invite error by failing to take into account the limitations of operating from a standpoint of privilege.

3. Maintain a Strategically Diverse Discourse

The complexity of causal processes and the biases and blind spots in the standpoint of researchers mean that critical scholars should consider how they might compensate. The feminist movement has learned this lesson firsthand. Racial and class privilege has allowed white feminists to dominate the discourse on feminism. Feminists of color have struggled since the 1970s to demonstrate the theoretical and empirical salience of the racial and class diversity among women and how social processes and policies had differential impacts depending how race and class interacted with gender.[34] Over time this dialogue has become a central organizer of feminist discourse.[35] While often uncomfortable and sometimes even heated, this cross-race dialogue has been invaluable for the development of feminist knowledge on all sides, sharpening our thinking, broadening our scope, and increasing our rigor.

Wise researchers will construct and maintain dialogue with others occupying contrasting social locations. We can diversify our dialogue in several ways. First, researchers, themselves, comprise people in varying social locations depending on their gender, class, race, ethnicity, sexuality, disability, immigrant status, and so on. They can thus build dialogues across these differences. Second, researchers can attend to the discourses of everyday actors, particularly those at the bottom of social hierarchies. Some qualitative researchers have demonstrated that popular culture forms like blues music, poetry, novels, folk wisdom, and graffiti are also venues through which people can reflect on their experience and share their analyses with others.[36]

Finally, researchers can maintain dialogue with members of groups actively struggling for social justice. In the process of mobilizing, such groups develop analyses of their situation and alternative or even counter-hegemonic discourses. Much of what we think of as critical scholarship today can trace its origins to a social movement. For example, even though gender inequality has long existed in Western history, the whole idea of sex/gender being a distinct social system emerged in the 1970s as a result of the women's movement.[37] Women started coming together to analyze their lives, and scholars began taking their analyses seriously.

Knowledge constructed from multiple standpoints can, and in an unjust society will, sometimes be conflicting.[38] Whether and, more importantly, under what conditions the analyses developed from contrasting standpoints are commensurable is an empirical question—an exciting and crucial question. Taking contrasting standpoints seriously and working to understand the sources of, and if possible to reconcile, differences among them is the heart of what critical scholarship can contribute to social understanding.

4. Create Knowledge That Empowers the Disadvantaged

Most feminists writing about power and research have focused on the actual process and products of research, and Diane Wolf suggests that this is because processes and products are easier to do something about than researchers' social power.[39] However, the reason we have to be worried about systematic biases toward the worldview and interests of the privileged in the knowledge we produce is that we exist in an unequal society. The very need to ensure that research subjects have voice and are taken seriously as analysts of their lives, is the outcome of social power. People need to claim that they can speak with authority only when they are silenced; part of being privileged is being able to assume that one has authority.[40]

The inequality between the researcher and the subjects of research is usually grounded in the material—it is based in social structures, organizing opportunities and costs by gender, class, race, nation, and so on. Kamala Visweswaran argues that the key question is not whether a researcher can do a better job of representing people than they themselves can. Rather, it is "whether we can be accountable to people's own struggles for self-representation and self-determination" in the way we do our research.[41]

Self-representation requires self-determination. As long as we live in a social world that sorts men and women, whites and people of color, rich and poor, the West and the rest into such differing social locations, imposing a logic that creates conflicts in interest (so that for some to "win," others have to lose), that controls the flow of information and ideas to ensure the hegemony of the dominant, and that blocks so many from active legitimate participation in the production of knowledge, we cannot have a fully free and inclusive discourse about what is and what should be. The interests of critical researchers in valid knowledge should lead them to value social justice.

CONCLUSION

The work of building understanding about social processes is more than a personal career choice. Social scientists do not have to look far back into history for examples showing how the analyses we produce become part of circulating discourses in which the consequences of being wrong can be damaging to people's lives. Thus all of us who seek to understand social processes should pay close attention to the assumptions underlying our methodological choices and how we might do what we do differently if we intentionally take Realist Standpoint Epistemology into account.

Critical Realism calls us to recognize that the world we are trying to understand is more complicated than it might seem to be, certainly more complicated than Positivist approaches tend to represent it. Standpoint Epistemology asserts that like the known, the knower is also more complex than is usually represented. Particularly, the model of scholarship we have been trained in may be inadequate to the task of producing unbiased knowledge. We need to explore the degree to which prevailing ways of posing questions, looking for evidence and drawing conclusions can be expressing the interests and experiences of the privileged as against those over whom they have privilege.

Critical Realism should lead us to realize how much we depend on the criticism of peers to identify the limitations in our practices; that is, the identification of valid claims to truth is a highly collaborative enterprise. Standpoint Epistemology advises us to widen the circle of the critique and collaboration by exposing our truth claims to people who exist in very different social locations than do most researchers. Critical Realism warns that the world is changing and thus changeable. Standpoint Epistemology gives us guidance on how to make the most useful contributions to those who want to take informed intentional action to guide social change.

In a democratic society, or at least one that aims to be democratic, being a producer of knowledge entails making a contribution—either by omission or by commission—to the collective imagination about the kind of future we can have and how to achieve our shared values. Let us work together to increase our ability to get it right.

NOTES

1. Portions of the material in this chapter originally appeared in Joey Sprague, *Feminist Methodologies for Critical Researchers* (Walnut Creek, CA: AltaMira Press, 2005).

2. Dorothy E. Smith, *Institutional Ethnography: A Sociology for People* (Walnut Creek, CA: AltaMira, 2005), 141.

3. Dorothy E. Smith, *The Conceptual Practices of Power: A Feminist Sociology of Knowledge* (Boston, MA: Northeastern University Press, 1990).

4. Linda Alcoff, "Justifying Feminist Social Science," in *Feminism and Science*, ed. Nancy Tuana (Bloomington, IN: Indiana University Press, 1989).

5. C.f., Patricia T. Clough, "On the Bank of Deconstructing Sociology: Critical Reading of Dorothy Smith's Standpoint Epistemology," *The Sociological Quarterly* 34.1 (1993).

6. Michel Foucault, *Power/Knowledge: Selected Interviews and Other Writings, 1972–1977*, 1st American ed., ed. Collin Gordon (New York, NY: Pantheon Books, 1980); Donna Haraway, "Situated Knowledges: The Science Question in Feminism and the Privilege of Partial Perspective," *Feminist Studies* 14.3 (1988).

7. Frances E. Mascia-Lees, Patricia Sharpe, and Colleen Ballerino Cohen, "The Postmodern Turn in Anthropology: Cautions from a Feminist Perspective," *Signs: Journal of Women in Culture and Society* 15.1 (1989).

8. Haraway, "Situated Knowledges," 578.

9. Andrew Collier, *Critical Realism: An Introduction to Roy Bhaskar's Philosophy* (London, England, New York, NY: Verso, 1994); Jon Frauley and Frank Pearce, eds., *Critical Realism and the Social Sciences: Heterodox Elaborations* (Toronto, ON: University of Toronto Press, 2007).

10. Collier, *Critical Realism*; Christopher Norris, Roy Bhaskar, and Julian Baggini, "The New Realism," *The Philosophers' Magazine* no. 8 (1999).

11. Sylvia Walby, "Against Epistemological Chasms: The Science Question in Feminism Revisited," *Signs: Journal of Women and Culture in Society* 26.2 (2001).

12. Norris, Bhaskar, and Baggini, "The New Realism."

13. Nancy C. M. Hartsock, *Money, Sex, and Power: Toward a Feminist Historical Materialism* (New York, NY: Longman, 1983).

14. Joan Acker, *Class Questions, Feminist Answers*, ed. Judith Howard, Barbara Risman, and Joey Sprague (Lanham, MD, Boulder, CO, New York, NY, Toronto, ON, and Oxford, England: Rowman & Littlefield, 2005).

15. Manisha Desai, *Gender and the Politics of Possibilities: Rethinking Globalization* (Lanham, MD: Rowman & Littlefield, 2009).

16. c.f., Michal McCall and Judith Wittner, "The Good News About Life Histories," in *Cultural Studies and Symbolic Interaction*, ed. Howard Becker and Michal McCall (Chicago, IL: University of Chicago Press, 1990); Rosanna Hertz, ed., *Reflexivity and Voice* (Thousand Oaks, CA: Sage, 1997).

17. Miriam Glucksmann, "The Work of Knowledge and the Knowledge of Women's Work," in *Researching Women's Lives from a Feminist Perspective*, ed. Mary Maynard and June Purvis (Abingdon, England and New York, NY: Taylor & Francis, 1994).

18. Ibid.; Suruchi Thapar-Björkert, "Negotiating Otherness: Dilemmas for a Non-Western Researcher in the Indian Sub-Continent," *Journal of Gender Studies* 8.1 (1999).

19. See, for example, Patricia Hill Collins, *Black Feminist Thought: Knowledge, Consciousness, and the Politics of Empowerment*, 2nd ed. (New York, NY: Routledge, 2000); Evelyn Nakano Glenn, "From Servitude to Service Work: Historical Continuities in the Racial Division of Paid Reproductive Labor," *Signs: Journal of Women in Culture and Society* 18.1 (1992).

20. For example, Josephine Beoku-Betts, "When Black Is Not Enough: Doing Field Research among Gullah Women," *NWSA Journal* 6.3 (1994); Jane Ribbens,

"Interviewing—An 'Unnatural Situation,'" *Women's Studies International Forum* 12.6 (1989); Patricia Zavella, "Feminist Insider Dilemmas: Constructing Ethnic Identity with Chicana Informants," in *Feminist Dilemmas in Fieldwork*, ed. Diane L. Wolf (Boulder, CO: Westview, 1996).

21. Margery Wolf, *A Thrice-Told Tale: Feminism, Postmodernism, and Ethnographic Responsibility* (Stanford, CA: Stanford University Press, 1992), 5–6.

22. David Morgan, "Men, Masculinity, and the Process of Sociological Inquiry," in *Doing Feminist Research*, ed. Helen Roberts (London, England and New York, NY: Routledge and Kegan Paul, 1981), 88.

23. Mascia-Lees, Sharpe, and Ballerino Cohen, "The Postmodern Turn in Anthropology."

24. Rosalind Edwards, "Connecting Method and Epistemology: A White Woman Interviewing Black Women," *Women's Studies International Forum* 13.5 (1990).

25. Hartsock, *Money, Sex, and Power*, 132.

26. Smith, *Institutional Ethnography*; Smith, *The Conceptual Practices of Power*.

27. Sandra G. Harding, *Is Science Multicultural? Postcolonialisms, Feminisms, and Epistemologies* (Bloomington, IN: Indiana University Press, 1998).

28. Diana Russell, *Sexual Exploitation* (Newbury Park, CA: Sage, 1984).

29. Allison Griffith, "Mothering, Schooling, and Children's Development," in *Knowledge, Experience, and Ruling Relations: Studies in the Social Organization of Knowledge*, ed. Marie Campbell and Ann Manicom (Toronto, ON: University of Toronto Press, 1995).

30. Sandra Harding, *Whose Science? Whose Knowledge? Thinking from Women's Lives* (Ithaca, NY: Cornell University Press, 1991).

31. Collins, *Black Feminist Thought*.

32. Marjorie L. DeVault, "Talking and Listening from Women's Standpoint: Feminist Strategies for Interviewing and Analysis," *Social Problems* 37.1 (1990).

33. Linda L. Carli, "Gender, Language, and Influence," *Journal of Personality and Social Psychology* 59.5 (1990).

34. Delia D. Aguilar, "Tracing the Roots of Intersectionality," *MRZine*, December 4, 2012.

35. Mascia-Lees, Sharpe, and Ballerino Cohen, "The Postmodernist Turn in Anthropology."

36. See, for example, Bettina Aptheker, *Tapestries of Everyday Life: Women's Work, Women's Consciousness, and the Meaning of Daily Experience* (Amherst, MA: University of Massachusetts Press, 1989); Ann Arnett Ferguson, *Bad Boys: Public Schools in the Making of Black Masculinity* (Ann Arbor, MI: University of Michigan Press, 2000).

37. Sandra Harding, "Why Has the Sex/Gender System Become Visible Only Now?" In *Discovering Reality: Feminist Perspectives on Epistemology, Metaphysics, Methodology, and Philosophy of Science*, ed. Sandra Harding and Merrill B. Hintikka (New York, NY, Boston, MA, Dordrecht, Netherlands, London, England, and Moscow, Russia: Kluwer Academic Publishers, 1983).

38. Kum-Kum Bhavnani, "Empowerment and Social Research: Some Comments," *Text & Talk: An Interdisciplinary Journal of Language, Discourse & Communication Studies* 8.1–2 (1988).

39. Diane L. Wolf, "Situating Feminist Dilemmas in Fieldwork," in *Feminist Dilemmas in Fieldwork*, ed. Diane L. Wolf (Boulder, CO: Westview, 1996).

40. Bat-Ami Bar On, "Marginality and Epistemic Privilege," in *Feminist Epistemologies*, ed. Linda Alcoff and Elizabeth Potter (New York, NY: Routledge, 1993).

41. Kamala Visweswaran, "Defining Feminist Ethnography," *Inscriptions* 3.4 (1988): 39.

BIBLIOGRAPHY

Acker, Joan. *Class Questions, Feminist Answers.* The Gender Lens Series, edited by Judith Howard, Barbara Risman, and Joey Sprague. Lanham, MD, Boulder, CO, New York, NY, Toronto, ON, and Oxford, England: Rowman & Littlefield, 2005.

Aguilar, Delia D. "Tracing the Roots of Intersectionality." *MRZine*, December 4, 2012.

Alcoff, Linda. "Justifying Feminist Social Science." In *Feminism and Science*, edited by Nancy Tuana, 85–103. Bloomington, IN: Indiana University Press, 1989.

Aptheker, Bettina. *Tapestries of Everyday Life: Women's Work, Women's Consciousness, and the Meaning of Daily Experience.* Amherst, MA: University of Massachusetts Press, 1989.

Bar On, Bat-Ami. "Marginality and Epistemic Privilege." In *Feminist Epistemologies*, edited by Linda Alcoff and Elizabeth Potter, 83–100. New York, NY: Routledge, 1993.

Beoku-Betts, Josephine. "When Black Is Not Enough: Doing Field Research among Gullah Women." *NWSA Journal* 6.3 (1994): 413–33.

Bhavnani, Kum-Kum. "Empowerment and Social Research: Some Comments." *Text & Talk: An Interdisciplianry Journal of Language, Discourse & Communication Studies* 8.1–2 (1988): 41–50.

Carli, Linda L. "Gender, Language, and Influence." *Journal of Personality and Social Psychology* 59.5 (1990): 941–51.

Clough, Patricia T. "On the Bank of Deconstructing Sociology: Critical Reading of Dorothy Smith's Standpoint Epistemology." *The Sociological Quarterly* 34.1 (1993): 169–82.

Collier, Andrew. *Critical Realism: An Introduction to Roy Bhaskar's Philosophy.* London, England, New York, NY: Verso, 1994.

Collins, Patricia Hill. *Black Feminist Thought: Knowledge, Consciousness, and the Politics of Empowerment.* 2nd ed. New York, NY: Routledge, 2000.

Desai, Manisha. *Gender and the Politics of Possibilities: Rethinking Globalization.* Lanham, MD: Rowman & Littlefield, 2009.

DeVault, Marjorie L. "Talking and Listening from Women's Standpoint: Feminist Strategies for Interviewing and Analysis." *Social Problems* 37.1 (1990): 96–116.

Edwards, Rosalind. "Connecting Method and Epistemology: A White Woman Interviewing Black Women." *Women's Studies International Forum* 13.5 (1990): 477–90.

Ferguson, Ann Arnett. *Bad Boys: Public Schools in the Making of Black Masculinity.* Ann Arbor, MI: University of Michigan Press, 2001.

Foucault, Michel. *Power/Knowledge: Selected Interviews and Other Writings, 1972–1977.* 1st American ed. Edited by Colin Gordon. New York, NY: Pantheon Books, 1980.

Frauley, Jon and Frank Pearce, eds. *Critical Realism and the Social Sciences: Heterodox Elaborations.* Toronto, ON: University of Toronto Press, 2007.

Glenn, Evelyn Nakano. "From Servitude to Service Work: Historical Continuities in the Racial Division of Paid Reproductive Labor." *Signs: Journal of Women in Culture and Society* 18.1 (1992): 1–43.

Glucksmann, Miriam. "The Work of Knowledge and the Knowledge of Women's Work." In *Researching Women's Lives from a Feminist Perspective,* edited by Mary Maynard and June Purvis, 149–65. Abingdon, England and New York, NY: Taylor & Francis, 1994.

Griffith, Allison. "Mothering, Schooling, and Children's Development." In *Knowledge, Experience, and Ruling Relations: Studies in the Social Organization of Knowledge,* edited by Marie Campbell and Ann Manicom, 108–21. Toronto, ON: University of Toronto Press, 1995.

Haraway, Donna. "Situated Knowledges: The Science Question in Feminism and the Privilege of Partial Perspective." *Feminist Studies* 14.3 (1988): 575–99.

Harding, Sandra. *Is Science Multicultural? Postcolonialisms, Feminisms, and Epistemologies.* Bloomington, IN: Indiana University Press, 1998.

———. *Whose Science? Whose Knowledge? Thinking from Women's Lives.* Ithaca, NY: Cornell University Press, 1991.

———. "Why Has the Sex/Gender System Become Visible Only Now?" In *Discovering Reality: Feminist Perspectives on Epistemology, Metaphysics, Methodology, and Philosophy of Science,* edited by Sandra Harding and Merrill B. Hintikka, 311–24. New York, NY, Boston, MA, Dordrecht, Netherlands, London, England, and Moscow, Russia: Kluwer Academic Publishers, 1983.

Hartsock, Nancy C. M. *Money, Sex, and Power: Toward a Feminist Historical Materialism.* New York, NY: Longman, 1983.

Hertz, Rosanna, ed. *Reflexivity and Voice.* Thousand Oaks, CA: Sage, 1997.

Mascia-Lees, Frances E., Patricia Sharpe, and Colleen Ballerino Cohen. "The Postmodern Turn in Anthropology: Cautions from a Feminist Perspective." *Signs: Journal of Women in Culture and Society* 15.1 (1989): 7–33.

McCall, Michal and Judith Wittner. "The Good News About Life Histories." In *Cultural Studies and Symbolic Interaction,* edited by Howard S. Becker and Michal McCall, 46–89. Chicago, IL: University of Chicago Press, 1990.

Morgan, David. "Men, Masculinity, and the Process of Sociological Inquiry." In *Doing Feminist Research,* edited by Helen Roberts, 83–113. London, England and New York, NY: Routledge & Kegan Paul, 1981.

Norris, Christopher, Roy Bhaskar, and Julian Baggini. "The New Realism." *The Philosophers' Magazine* no. 8 (1999): 48–50.

Ribbens, Jane. "Interviewing—An 'Unnatural Situation.' " *Women's Studies International Forum* 12.6 (1989): 579–92.

Russell, Diana. *Sexual Exploitation.* Newbury Park, CA: Sage, 1984.

Smith, Dorothy E. *Institutional Ethnography: A Sociology for People.* Walnut Creek, CA: AltaMira, 2005.

———. *The Conceptual Practices of Power: A Feminist Sociology of Knowledge.* Boston, MA: Northeastern University Press, 1990.

Sprague, Joey. *Feminist Methodologies for Critical Researchers.* Walnut Creek, CA: AltaMira Press: Rowman & Littlefield, 2005.

Thapar-Björkert, Suruchi. "Negotiating Otherness: Dilemmas for a Non-Western Researcher in the Indian Sub-Continent." *Journal of Gender Studies* 8.1 (1999): 7–69.

Visweswaran, Kamala. "Defining Feminist Ethnography." *Inscriptions* 3.4 (1988): 27–44.

Walby, Sylvia. "Against Epistemological Chasms: The Science Question in Feminism Revisited." *Signs: Journal of Women in Culture and Society* 26.2 (2001): 485–509.

Wolf, Diane L. "Situating Feminist Dilemmas in Fieldwork." In *Feminist Dilemmas in Fieldwork*, edited by Diane L. Wolf, 1–55. Boulder, CO: Westview, 1996.

Wolf, Margery. *A Thrice-Told Tale: Feminism, Postmodernism, and Ethnographic Responsibility*. Stanford, CA: Stanford University Press, 1992.

Zavella, Patricia. "Feminist Insider Dilemmas: Constructing Ethnic Identity with Chicana Informants." In *Feminist Dilemmas in Fieldwork*, edited by Diane L. Wolf, 139–59. Boulder, CO: Westview, 1996.

Index

Adichie, Chimamanda Ngozi (Nigerian), 323–24
Afghanistan, 17, 22;
backlash, 17;
hostility toward foreign intervention, 25;
King Zahir Shah (1964), 19;
Pashtuns, 21;
Soviet invasion (1979), 19–20;
2004 Constitution, 22;
U. S. military invasion (2002), 20, 21.
See also Afghan women
Afghan women, 17–18, 25;
Burqa, 21;
collaboration, 26;
education, 26, 27;
framed as men's enemy, 28;
gender rights and human rights, 27;
history, 19;
illiteracy, 19–20;
international interventions, 23;
Kabul, 23;
need to localize change, 29;
objectified, 20;
security raids, 27;
state violence, 20;
two-tier system, 23;
violence encouraged, 28;
westernization, 24, 29
Africa, 321;
African perspectives, 330;
Africans, 326;
African voices, 329–30;
Americans ill-prepared to engage, 322;
false impressions, 321, 322;
few direct American encounters, 321;
influence of media, 321;
perception of, 321–22
African gender and sexual politics, 322, 323;
common ideas about, 323;
female genital cutting, 330–31;
historical context, 323;
importance to American students, 323;
intersex people, 325;
media, 328;
narratives, 324;
sexual violence, 327;
subject to epistemic violence, 331–32
A.I.D.s, 40, 46, 326–27;
Mark Hunter, 326–27
Annan, Kofi (UN Sec't General), 231–32, 240n16
anthropologists, 101
anti-war movement. *See* peace movement

Armenia and Azerbaijan (Post-Soviet), 139;
fear of renewed warfare, 144;
fieldwork (2012–2013), by Sinéad Walsh, 139ff;
global/local, 141;
local women's ambivalence, 144;
mass media rhetoric, 145;
nationalistic rhetoric, 145;
one step forward, two steps back, 145;
politicalization, 146;
transnational cooperation, 143
Arthur V. Mauro Centre for Peace and Justice, xi
Association of Widows of Genocide (AEVGA), 38

Beirut, 216
Berlin Wall, 100
Black Tradeswomen (construction industry), 157;
addressing discrimination, 160;
building relationships, 167–71;
consciousness-raising, 162;
coworker relations, 166;
derogatory representations, 159;
discrimination, 158;
heterosexism, 159;
institutional and cultural change, 161, 170;
isolation, 159;
male allies, 169;
non-traditional workers, 163;
pragmatic actions, 170;
racism, 158, 163, 169;
sexism, 158, 159, 163;
spirituality and grace,165;
stereotypes, 167
Bonga (Ethiopia), 69
Boulding, Elise, 375, 383n1

Canada, 175, 184;
volunteering history, 198–99
Canadian women (rural), 195;
community, 196–97;
compared to men, 197;
doctoral research by Robin Neustaeter, 195–212;
gender, 199, 207;
motivation, 196;
peace, 197–98;
rurality, 200–206;
stay-at-home, 206;
women's involvement, 195;
women volunteering, 196
capacity development. *See* Karen women
capitalism, 395
Castro, Fidel, 5
China, 83;
See also Rural Women in China
China Women's Federations (ACWF), 84, 85;
cadres, 87;
carries out policies, 85;
funu zhuren, 85;
hierarchy, 93;
not always trusted or supported, 86;
participation, 87–88;
transformation, 93–94, 95–96
Chodorow, Nancy, 347
civilians, 217
Civil Rights Movement, 5, 11, 376
civil society, 365
CNVA. *See* Committee for Non-Violent Action
Cold War, 100, 282
colonialism, 102;
attitudes, 289, 290
Committee for Nonviolent Action (CNVA), 5
community, xiv;
self-respect, 309
conflict, xiii;
confienza, 100;
ethnic, 35–36;
neutrality, 99;
pre-conflict, 301;
post-conflict, 84, 150, 283, 301;
resolution, 54, 79, 99, 288;

restoration of resolution, 100, 101;
social, 99, 364;
status quo, 78.
See also gender; Peace and Conflict Studies
conflict resolution, 101;
indigenous, 111;
rationalization, 102.
See also Oromo women
creativity, 309;
cognitive development, 309;
imagination, 309
critical realism, 393–94
Cuba, 5
cultural violence, 300;
symbolic, 300.
See also cultural violence and gender
cultural violence and gender, 299;
feminist responses, 305;
harmful interventions, 304;
mere addition of women, 305;
peacebuilding and gender, 303;
post-conflict, 303, 304;
sustainable peace, 299.
See also peacebuilding

decolonizing our minds, 326
Deming, Barbara, 3–16;
biography 5–6;
exploitation and domination, 6;
lesbian, 6;
theorist of non-violence, 4.
See also peace movement
democratic society, 402
Deng Xiaoping, 85
Derry and Border Counties (Ireland). *See* women's role in peacebuilding
Disability Studies, 376
Disabled People, 376;
access to education, 379;
contested field, 377;
Disability Rights Fund, 378;
disability services, 382;
environmental accommodation, 378;
fear, 383;
impacted by violent conflict, 378;
inclusivity, 382;
not just recipients, 376;
people with disabilities, 375–76;
perspective, 381;
population, 377;
post-conflict, 380;
poverty, 378, 379;
UN Convention (2006) on the Rights of Persons with Disabilities, 382.
See also Peace and Conflict Studies

Ebadi, Shirin (Iranian), 341
Enloe, Cynthia, 264, 274n7
environment. *See* peace education
equality. *See* gender
imposed, 18
Ethiopia, 69;
fieldwork ethnographic project, 69–70, 78;
kinship, 72;
peacemaking systems 71–72;
spiritual authority, 72

family therapy, 353
feminism, xvi, 11;
feminist nonviolence, 8–9;
peace, 4;
second wave, 376–77;
UNSCR 1325, 147
feminists, 36, 376;
critical of social scientists, 391, 402;
empower disadvantaged, 401;
epistemological choices, 391, 392–93;
methodologies, 391;
psychologists, 347;
value social justice, 401.
See also peace studies and feminism
Fourth World, 102

gacaca (community trials), 42
Galtung, Johan, 77, 81n20–22, 96n1–2, 93, 97n21, 159, 171n10;

founder, 281–82, 379;
Peace and Conflict Study, 359;
positive peace, 299;
structural violence, 379, 385n29.
See also cultural violence
Gandhi, 5
gender, 19, 301;
all human behavior, 299;
analysis insufficient, 281;
class, xv, 397;
complexity, 148;
cultural violence, 299;
deeply embedded, 300;
demonstrating traditional, 282;
differences within, 213;
dualistic, 11;
dynamic, xiv;
education, 77;
effects of militarization, 213;
equality, 84, 230, 231, 264, 301;
ethnicity, xv;
foundational source, 3;
gendered harms, 237;
heteronormative, 375;
inequality, 79, 263, 376;
Israeli army, 217;
job gendering, 270;
justice, 73;
kyriarchy, 299;
male exclusiveness, 230;
mainstreaming, 382;
manipulated by militarism, 283;
marginal topic, 281;
militarism, 264;
notions challenged, 94;
not neutral, 140;
and organized violence, 56, 65n24;
peacekeepers, 263;
perspective, 233;
politics of, 150;
positive peace, 84;
racial ethnicity, 397;
rights, 29;
sexuality, 148;
socially transmitted, 300;
specific interests, 234–35;
strategies, 177.
See also Canadian women; queer theory
genocidal rape, 39;
Bernadette's experience, 39–47;
Rosa's experience, 39–47;
victims hide their experience, 40.
See also rape
globalization:
connected to local, 17–18
grassroots, 364, 375
Gulag, 121;
1940–1950s, 132.
See also Ukrainian women

Haiti (2010 earthquake), 280
Harris, Ian, 311–12
Healing of Life Wounds (HLW, 1995), 35, 43, 46–47, 48;
combines western and non-western theories and practices, 38;
Dr. Simon Gasibire, 38, 48, 50;
study by Uwibereyeho King, 38, 51
heteronormativity, 362–63;
Michael Warner, 362;
predisposed narrative, 362;
rightness and normalcy, 362.
See also queer theory
heteropatriarchy. *See* queer theory
hierarchy. *See* patriarchy
HLW. *See* Healing of Life Wounds
hooks, bell, 6–7, 12nn23–24
human needs universal, 364
human rights, 353, 377
Hutu, 35;
males, 37

Iddir (voluntary associations), 75–77, 79;
and women, 76
identity, xv, 19;
child soldiers, 58;
Tamil, 179
India, 63–64

indigenous people, 99, 100, 101, 111;
gender identity, 147;
how they view the earth, 346.
See also conflict resolution
intersections. *See* peace studies and feminism
Iraq, 23
Irish Defense Forces (DF), 264, 271
Islam, 22
Israel, 216;
exclusion of women, 216;
militarized society, 219;
Peace Now (1978), 216
Israeli Defense Force (IDF), 215;
Lebanon War, 216;
parents involvement, 217;
patriarchal, 217;
reserve duty, 217
Israeli women, 213;
challenging militarism, 223;
combat, 215, 218;
differences, 213;
impact of globalization, 215;
marginalized in the army, 224;
militarized masculinity, 217, 226n17;
Palestinians, 213;
reactions, 213, 221;
recent trends, 213;
religion, 215, 219;
status, 213;
study by Galia Golan, 213–228;
working for peace, 222–23

Jews, 215

kabechino (peace-making system), 73, 78, 79
Kaffa (society), 69;
history of success, 73;
informal justice, 73;
justice administered, 71;
land disputes, 74;
layout, 71;
oral tradition, 71;
society transformed, 77;
spirituality, 74–75;
treatment of women, 71
Karen women (Myanmar), 175;
active networks, 185;
background, 179;
capacity building, 176;
capacity for organization, 184–85;
capacity to lead social change, 181–82;
diasporas, 175–76, 178;
empowerment, 181–82;
fear of deportation, 175;
importance of support, 187;
local/global, 184;
networking, 185–86;
NGOs, 175, 178, 183, 187;
power dispersed, 178;
recipients of actors, 177;
refugee organizations, 175, 177;
resettlement in Canada, 175ff;
resettlement in Winnipeg, 183;
seeking asylum, 180;
study of Anna Snyder, 175–94;
transnational capacity, 176, 188
kebele (local government), 69
Ki-moon, Ban (U. N. Sec't General, 2009), 263
Kosovo (1999), xiii, 23

Lauretis, Teresa de, 369n9;
See also queer theory
Lederach, John Paul, 61, 66nn61–66, 100, 112nn7–8, 159, 171n9, 231, 239n15, 312n1;
peacebuilding, 282, 293n6;
peace scholar, 375, 383nn2–4
LGBTI-Q, 329–30
Liberia, 53;
coup d'état, 53;
gender-based violence, 57;
Patriotic Front, 53;
rehumanizing, 59
Liberian Civil War, 53;
Charles Taylor, 53;
child soldiers, 54, 58–59;

Comprehensive Peace Agreement (Accra), 54, 56;
women's response, 54.
See also LWMAP
Liberian Truth and Reconciliation Commission (LTRC), 57
Liberian Women's Mass Action for Peace (LWMAP), 56, 62;
cultural context, 62;
effectiveness, 58;
formation (Monrovia), 55;
hair-cutting ritual, 59;
holistic approach, 61–62;
irony in success, 57;
long-term change, 63;
peace practitioners, 60;
reconciliation, 59;
sex strike, 55;
subverts notions of gender, 57;
white tee-shirts, 55–56;
women totally marginated, 61
LWMAP. *See* Liberian Women's Mass Action for Peace
Lyttle, Brad, 6

Manitoba (Canada). *See* Canadian women
Mano River Union Women's Network (MAWOPNET), 55;
See also LWMAP
masculinity, 301;
militarized, 302
Matcha (society). *See* Oromo women
mediation, 100;
influenced by culture, 100;
influenced by social forces, 100–101;
role of women, 101;
third-party, 99.
See also conflict
methodology, 391;
See also feminists
multiple communities, 376
Muste, A. J., 6
myth, 71;
Oromo, 110

negotiation. *See* conflict
nonviolence, 9–10;
how it works, 10;
radical, 9;
relationships, 299;
truth, 11
Northern Ireland, 229–30;
aftermath of agreement, 235;
diplomacy, 232;
facilitation good environment, 232–33;
feminicide, 236;
male-dominated policy, 232;
peace negotiations (1996), 229;
politics of peace, (1998), 229;
social services justice, 238;
sustaining transformation, 238;
under-represented, 230;
women participating, 230;
Women's Coalition, 229, 230, 232, 238

oppression, 290
Oromo, 105;
Atete, 106–7, 108;
Eldership, 106;
Gada system, 105–6, 109;
institutional roles, 105;
Kallu (religion), 106, 108;
three stages of conflict, 109.
See also Oromo women
Oromo women, 99, 102;
basic rights, 104;
conflict, 103;
economic basis, 105;
Horn of Africa, 102;
inter-ethnic group conflict, 109;
intermediation, 110;
leaders in conflict resolution, 105–8;
role in internal conflict, 109;
status, 104;
worldview, 102–4

pacifists, 5
PACS. *See* Peace and Conflict Studies

Palestinian Liberation Organization (PLO), 216
patriarchy, xvi, 4, 7, 368;
absent fathers, 347;
absent from indigenous cultures, 346;
anti-liberal, 343;
both genders socialized, 345;
carte blanche, 302;
contribution to violence, 341–42;
dehumanizing violence, 346;
dismantling, 351;
domination, control, and fear, 342;
emotional problem, 348;
exclusion, 343;
hierarchy, 342;
ideological formation, 342;
immoral, 343;
impairs reasoning, 344;
instability, 351;
instituted, 73;
marginalizes women, 351;
masculinization, 341;
narratives, 343;
naturalizes domination, 349;
no peace, 349;
norms, 342, 345;
patriarchy, not men, 341;
pernicious, 342;
pollutant, 350;
psychic damage, 354;
reason and emotion divided, 349;
rends connections, 349;
resistance, 352;
rhetoric, 327;
underlining violence, 350;
undermines real relations, 349;
values, 346
Peace and Conflict Studies, xiii, xv;
ability mainstreaming, 377;
ADR (Appropriate Dispute Resolution), 363, 367;
CAR (Conflict Analysis Resolution), 364;
conflict transformation, 364;
cultures of peace, 375;
deficient in terms of gender, 286;
disabilities, 376;
future queer activism, 367–68;
gender, xvi;
heteronormative pedagogy, 368;
human dialogue, 366;
inclusivity, 366, 375;
interdependency, 366;
intervention, 363;
Johan Galtung, 359, 369nn2–3;
LGBTQ, 359–60, 363;
metanarratives, 366;
need for queer theory, 359–60;
paucities, 377;
peacebuilding, 359;
poverty, 365;
purpose, 281;
queer theory, 367;
reconciliation, 364;
roots of social conflict, 363;
storytelling, 366;
structures changing, 364;
teachers and students, 365;
theoretical framework, 368;
Truth and Reconciliation Commissions, 364;
women empowered, 365.
See also queer theory
peacebuilding, xiii, 24, 365;
academic field, 299;
actors other than government, 282;
applied to social and gender conflict, 159;
current models, 288;
defined, 303;
by U. N., 282;
described, 3;
dialogues, 329;
disability, 381;
everyday, 381;
feminist, 6–7;
gender analysis insufficient, 281;
gender-based, 17–18;
grassroots, 54, 245;
holistic, xv;

identity, 286;
imposed from without, 245;
includes justice and liberty, 350;
innovative, 54;
international, 245;
Karen women, 175;
lessons from Liberia, 61;
LGBTQ, 365;
liberal, 245–46, 247;
patriarchy, 349–50;
peace education, 305, 306–7, 309;
performance, 303;
personal, 164, 170;
positive peace, 294n32;
post-conflict, 303;
problem solving, 299;
re-defined, 282;
re-examining women's role, 245–56;
social paradigm critique, 299;
spaciality, 303;
temporality, 303;
without Western saviors, 321;
women, xiv, 145;
workplace, 160.
See also Oromo women; women; women's role in peacebuilding
peace education, 305;
appreciating the environment, 310;
collaboration, 310;
conflict resolution, 310;
critics, 307, 311;
developing responsibility, 310;
no single curriculum, 308;
still marginalized, 311;
transmission belts, 306.
See also creativity; peacebuilding
peacekeepers. *See* women peacekeepers
Peace Movement, 4, 11;
See also queer theory
peace studies and feminism, 281;
anti-colonial, 288;
conflict transformation, 288;
connections, 281–98;
empowerment, 291;
feminist rejection of essentialism, 283;
feminists, 285–89;
feminist theories, 288;
gender, 286;
grassroots, 288, 289;
history, 281–85;
imposing liberal values, 289;
including participants, 291;
interdisciplinary, 288;
methodology, 291;
mutual learning, 291;
outsiders not the experts, 289;
Participatory Action Research (PAR), 292, 295n62;
positive peace for all, 292;
power relations, 285–86;
racism, 289;
scholarship, 281;
self-bias, 291;
social construction of knowledge, 291;
storytelling, 291;
strengths and possibilities, 285;
theorists, 285, 289;
theory, 281
Peace Support Operations (PSO), 263, 266, 271, 272;
women excluded, 273
performativity, 361–62;
disrupting normative construction, 362;
Judith Butler, 361;
opening up new possibilities, 362;
performing genders, 361;
social construction of gender, 361, 362.
See also queer theory
positivism, 392
postcolonial, 282
post-modernism, 392
Post Traumatic Stress Disorder (PTSD), 378
poverty, 7
Pussy Riot, 368
Putin, Vladimir, 368

Queer Studies. *See* African gender and sexual politics

queer theory, xvi;
advancing peace, 360;
challenges fixed and stable hierarchies. 360;
challenges hierarchy, 360;
deconstructing sexuality, 360;
heteropatriarchy, 360;
LGBTQ, 367;
liberation movements, 360;
name and shame, 360–62;
normative gender roles, 360;
same-sex desire, 360;
symbol of inclusion, 362;
three elements of sexual regulation, 361–63

racism, 6
rape, 35, 49;
genocidal, 35, 38, 39;
inadequate aid, 37;
lack of support, 35;
lasting impact, 47;
legal response insufficient, 37;
stigma, 36;
unstudied, 37;
war, 345;
wartime, 35–36;
weapon of war, 36.
See also Liberian Civil War
Reagan, Ronald, 157–58
Reardon, Betty, xvii, xviii, 3, 376
Rural Women in China, 83;
building social capital, 90–91;
conflict reduced, 89;
expressing themselves, 91;
labour, 90;
men dominate, 92;
oppression, 85;
project of Cheung and Heinonen, 83–85;
trust and respect from ACF cadres, 88, 95;
women's centres, 92.
See also ACWF
Rwanda, 35;
Kinyarwanda language, 39

San Francisco to Moscow Walk for Peace, 5
San Sun Kyi. *See* Karen women
satyagraha, 10
security, 287
segregation, 7
sexism, 8
sexual regulation, 361;
Michel Foucault, 361;
political sexuality, 361;
shame and punishment, 361.
See also queer theory
social processes, 391;
regularized, 391
social scientists, 391;
damaging, 402
Stalin (cult), 122
Standpoint Epistemology, 396;
contrasting locations, 400;
disadvantaged, 398–99;
experience, 399;
insiders, 396–97;
multiple, 401;
researcher, 396–97;
research subjects, 396
Standpoint Theory, 393, 394–95
Sudanese Women's Voice for Peace (SWVP), 175

Taliban, 19, 26;
fundamentalism, 21;
1996 takeover, 20
Tibetan Women's Association (TWA), 175, 177
Tree of Frustration, 59;
Mothers at the Tree, 62
truth commissioners, 353
Tutsi, 35;
women, 37

Ukrainian women, 121;
correspondence, 125;
diaspora within the Gulag, 125;
disorientation, 132;
embroidering, 130;
general overview, 122–23;

group singing, 131;
history of imprisonment, 121–22;
internal communications, 125;
leisure time, 130–31;
life in barracks, 127;
living space, 132;
nationalism and patriotism, 126;
opposed Communism, 132;
performing femininity, 128–29;
poetry, 132;
poor health, 123;
prison alienation, 125;
social structure, 124;
solidarity, 124;
subverting brutality, 133;
traditional activities, 130;
ways around restriction, 125
UN. *See* United Nation
United Nations, 60, 101;
advantages of women, 264;
Agenda for Peace (1991), 282;
engaging women in peace activities, 140;
explaining ineffectiveness, 140;
more inclusive of women, 221, 230;
participation (Catherine O'Rourke), 231;
question of neutrality, 140;
Security Council Resolution 1325 (UNSCR 1325), 139, 147, 235, 350;
UNESCO, 100, 379;
WHO, 377, 379;
World Conference on Women (Beijing, 1995), 143, 382;
See also Kofi Annan; Ban Ki-moon
United Nations Security Council. *See* women peacekeepers
United States (U.S.), 5;
drones, 28;
legitimizing war and invasion, 17–18.
See also Afghanistan
US. *See* United States

Vietnam, 6
violence, 8, 11;
built into society, 286;
most at risk, 379;
not limited, 57;
perpetuated, 300;
structural, 78;
women exposed, 287

war, 7–8
War Resister's League, 5
women, 99;
access restricted, 77;
becoming symbols, 301;
developing societies, 102;
discrimination, 73, 77;
equal but different, 264, 273;
excluded, 3;
frontiers of war, 57;
inclusion, 84;
injustice and corruption, 146;
issues, 86;
NGOs, 149;
nonviolent essentialism, 148;
peace, 83, 145;
peacebuilders, 246;
perpetrators, 345;
role in rebuilding, 238;
subjects of peace, objects of violence, 17–18;
unable to be elders, 73;
victimhood, 56, 61;
violence by, 345;
and war, 62, 145.
See also Canadian women; Israeli women; mediation; Ukrainian women; working women
women peacekeepers (Irish), 263;
contradictory discourses, 268, 269;
dominant discourses, 266;
domination and oppression, 266;
feminist approach, 264;
host nation culture, 270;
male peacekeepers, 269;

military culture, 269;
multiple roles, 272;
national security institutions, 263;
needs of civilian workers, 263;
restricted to care-giving roles, 273;
still few in number, 263;
study by Shirley Graham, 263–73;
women soldiers, 272
Women's League of Burma (WLB), 175
women's role in peacebuilding, 245;
basic needs, 249;
bottom-up approach, 246, 248;
empowerment, 249, 254;
feminist values, 246;
gendered understanding, 252–54;
hidden structures, 246;
inter- and cross-cultural bonds, 251;
motivations, 250;
multiple roles, 250;
need for further research, 255;
NIWC (Northern Ireland Women's Coalition), 248, 255;
Northern Ireland, 247;
seen as a threat, 248;
sharing stories, 252;
social engineering, 246;
study described, 247;
valuing women, 249–50;
women ignored in civil society, 247.
See also peacebuilding
Women Strike for Peace, 5
woreda (administrative divisions), 69
working women. *See* Black Tradeswomen
World Bank, 100, 378

Contributor Biographies

Elham Atashi is an Assistant Professor in the Program on Justice and Peace Studies at Georgetown University. She has published on issues relating to transitional justice, collective memory, truth telling, community peacebuilding, and reconciliation processes. Dr. Atashi works extensively as a practitioner providing peace education to youth from conflict zones, and as a dialogue facilitator in transitional justice and peacebuilding workshops focusing on Northern Ireland, Rwanda, the Middle East and Afghanistan.

Sean Byrne is a Professor of Peace and Conflict Studies (PACS), and with Jessica Senehi, founding director of the PACS Ph.D. Program in 2006, and the Arthur V. Mauro Centre for Peace and Justice at St. Paul's College at the University of Manitoba in 2003. He is a cofounder with Jessica Senehi, University of Manitoba, and Dean Peachey and Brian Rice of the University of Winnipeg, and Anna Snyder of Menno Simons College of the Joint M.A. program in PACS in 2010. He is a recipient of three teaching awards. He is author and coauthor of over eighty peer reviewed articles and book chapters, and he is author, coauthor and coeditor of eight books. The Social Sciences and Humanities Research Council of Canada, Human Resources and Skills Development Canada, and the United States Institute of Peace have funded his research. His current research interests include ethnic conflict and peacebuilding, children and war, the role of economic aid and peacebuilding, women and peacebuilding, global peacemaking, the deconstruction of the liberal peacebuilding paradigm, critical issues and human rights in PACS, nonviolent social action, and third party intervention. He was a consultant to the special advisor to the Irish Taoiseach on the decommissioning of weapons in Northern Ireland. He is a consultant on the Northern Ireland peace process to the Senior Advisor for Europe and Eurasia at the U.S. Senate Foreign Relations Committee.

Maria Cheung is an Associate Professor of University of Manitoba Faculty of Social Work. She is also Research Affiliate, and Advisory Board member of the Centre for Human Rights Research at the University of Manitoba. She directed a CIDA six-year China Project on gender equality and protection of human rights from 2004–2010. Dr. Cheung's present research focuses on human rights and spiritual minorities, and on newcomer experiences.

Celia Cook-Huffman is an educator and training consultant. She is a Professor of Peace and Conflict Studies at Juniata College where she holds the W. Clay and Kathryn Burkholder Professorship in Conflict Resolution. She is also the Associate Director of the Baker Institute for Peace and Conflict Studies and Director of Baker Mediation Services. Her background combines peace studies with specialized training and education in conflict transformation, nonviolence, gender, and mediation.

Patlee Creary is a PhD Candidate in Peace and Conflict Studies at the University of Manitoba. She is a native of Jamaica, former military officer, and current Wu Graduate Scholar. Her Social Sciences and Humanities Council-funded dissertation research is focused on the role of the military in peacebuilding, specifically how military personnel mediate their roles and identities in peace operations and how peacekeeper experiences could inform international peacebuilding strategies. She has also coauthored peer-reviewed journal articles on peacebuilding in Northern Ireland.

Federica De Sisto is a research associate at the Institute of International Integration Studies, Trinity College, Ireland. Advocate of the need for greater interaction between theory and practice of development and proponent thereof, she has worked as consultant for international and community-based organizations on human rights and conflict resolution projects in Ethiopia, South Africa, Peru, Bangladesh and recently Nigeria. Federica has also lectured in several universities in Europe, Africa and North America.

Maureen P. Flaherty is an Assistant Professor in Peace and Conflict Studies at the University of Manitoba. She has spent more than thirty years as a front-line social worker, then therapist, consultant and educator specializing in crisis and trauma recovery and intimate partner abuse. Her work in education and community development has taken her to areas of Canada, Ukraine, and Russia. Her research interests include gendered perspectives in interpersonal violence, narrative, visioning, and community development, and post-conflict community-building focused on rebuilding agency through healing and inclusion. She is the author of *Peacebuilding with Women in Ukraine: Using Narrative to Envision a Common Future* (2012), and a coeditor of *Peace On Earth: The Role of Religion in Peace and Conflict Studies* (2014).

Galia Golan is Darwin Professor of Soviet and East European Studies, emerita, Hebrew University of Jerusalem, founder and former chair of Lafer Center for Gender and Women's Studies and former chair, Department of Political Science. She is a founding executive member of Bat Shalom and the Jerusalem Link (a joint Israeli and Palestinian Venture for Peace); executive member International Commission for a Just and Sustainable Palestinian-Israeli Peace. Feminist and peace activist, she is currently Professor of Government, Interdisciplinary Center, Herzliya; author of ten books, most on Soviet foreign policy; latest: *Israeli Peacemaking Since 1967: Factors Behind the Breakthroughs and Failures*, Routledge, 2014) and coeditor with Walid Salem, *Non-State Actors in the Middle East: Factors for Peace and Democracy*, Routledge, 2013.

Shirley Graham is an independent consultant advising on issues relating to women, peace, and security. Based in Ireland, she has worked on a number of cross-border projects assessing the legacy of the conflict and its impact on women's lives. She has an MA in International Relations and a Doctoral Degree in Adult and Community Education. She is currently working on a book about women peacekeepers based on findings from her PhD thesis *Equal but Different: Gender Discourses in the Social Relations of Irish Peacekeepers & Possibilities for Transformation.*

Nancy Hansen is Director of the Interdisciplinary Master's Program in Disability Studies at the University of Manitoba. Nancy obtained her PhD from the University of Glasgow. Her thesis examined the impact of education and social policy on the employment experiences of women with physical disabilities. Nancy's post-doctoral research also at University of Glasgow examined women with disabilities' access to primary health care. Nancy received an Einstein Research Fellowship examining Disability Studies and the Legacy of Nazi Eugenics. She is past president of the Canadian Disability Studies Association (CDSA). In June 2006, she was awarded Ireland Canada University Foundation Sprott Asset Management Scholarship to examine the history of people with disabilities in Ireland. Her research interests include disability history (eugenics and bioethics), geography of disability, disabled women's issues, and disability and the media.

Tuula Heinonen is a Professor with the Faculty of Social Work, University of Manitoba. She holds a Doctorate of Philosophy from the Institute of Development Studies, University of Sussex, UK and a Master of Social Work from McGill University. Dr. Heinonen's research interests explore health and well-being, gender in rural China, health dimensions and determinants, arts-informed qualitative research, refugee and immigrant services and needs, international community development and health, and gender and newcomer settlement in Manitoba.

Roberta Hunte is an Assistant Professor in Black Studies and Women, Gender and Sexuality Studies at Portland State University. Her doctoral work from the University of Manitoba is focused on black women and long-term careers in construction. She likes to bring her work to the stage and film through ethnographic theater productions. Her current play *My Walk Has Never Been Average,* coauthored with Bonnie Ratner, showcases the narratives of black women from her thesis and brings them to a wider audience. Roberta appreciates laughter, and a good story.

Régine Uwibereyeho King is an Assistant Professor in the Faculty of Social Work, University of Manitoba. Her research interests include mental health and cross-cultural mental health interventions for survivors of organized violence, including refugees and those who continue to live where violence occurred. Dr. King is committed to human rights, social justice, and healthy communities.

Oksana Kis, historian and anthropologist, is a Senior Research Fellow at the Institute of Ethnology, National Academy of Sciences of Ukraine (in Lviv). Her book,*Women in Ukrainian Traditional Culture in the second half of the 19th and early 20th centuries* (in Ukrainian) was published in Lviv in 2008 (2nd edition 2012). Dr. Kis is one of the editors of *ASPASIA: The International Yearbook of Central, Eastern, and Southeastern European Women's and Gender History* (Berghahn Books) and an editor in chief for the *Ukraina Moderna* web-site. Dr. Kis is a Director of the Lviv Resarch Center "Woman and Society" (NGO), President of the Ukrainian Association for Research in Women's History and a cofounder of the Ukrainian Oral History Association. Her current research focuses on the Ukrainian women's everyday lives and experiences in extraordinary historical circumstances in the Soviet Ukraine. Since 2003 Dr. Kis occasionally teaches courses at the universities in Ukraine and internationally.

Angela J. Lederach is a PhD student in Anthropology and Peace Studies at the University of Notre Dame. Her current research explores grassroots peacebuilding efforts in northern Colombia with a specific focus on youth, gender, and race. She has previously worked in West Africa, the Philippines, and Central America. She is a coauthor of the book, *When Blood* *and Bones Cry Out: Journeys through the Soundscape of Healing and Reconciliation.*

Thomas Matyók is an Associate Professor and Chair of the Department of Peace and Conflict Studies at the University of North Carolina at Greensboro. His research interests include the role of religion in peacebuilding, civil-military cooperation, peace and stability operations, and conflict analysis, and the education and training of peacebuilding actors. He possesses substantial knowledge of international conflict management, and organizational conflict transformational processes. Thomas was a Visiting Research Professor at the U.S. Army Peacekeeping and Stability Operations Institute (2013–2014) where he continues as a Senior Fellow (2014–2016) He was also a Distinguished Visiting Professor at the U.S. Army War College (2015). Thomas is the coeditor of *Critical Issues in Peace and Conflict Studies: Theory. Practice, and Pedagogy* (2011) and *Peace On Earth: The Role of Religion in Peace and Conflict Studies* (2014).

Lisa McLean is a PhD student at the School for Conflict Analysis and Resolution (S-CAR) at George Mason University, and holds a Master of Arts in Peace and Conflict Studies from the University of Manitoba. Lisa previously worked for the Canadian federal government and is currently employed as a Dean's Fellow for the Center for the Study of Gender and Conflict at S-CAR. As a part of her Master's degree, Lisa studied the challenges faced by newcomer women in Winnipeg, Manitoba, as well as the ways that newcomer women pursue positive social change by engaging in community-building activities. Lisa's current research interests include gender and conflict, gender-based violence, reproductive justice, security, and immigration and refugee-related issues.

Monica McWilliams is a Professor of Women's Studies in the Transitional Justice Institute at the University of Ulster. She is currently an Oversight Commissioner for prison reform and was, formerly, the Chief Commissioner of the Northern Ireland Human Rights Commission. As a Member of the Legislative Assembly (MLA), she represented the Northern Ireland Women's Coalition and was a participant in the multiparty peace talks, leading to the 1998 Belfast/Good Friday Agreement. She has a range of publications on the impact of political conflict on women's lives and assists international agencies working in this field.

Robert C. Mizzi is an Assistant Professor in the Faculty of Education at the University of Manitoba. He has published over thirty-five chapters, articles and reviews in journals and books, such as the *Journal of Homosexuality* and

Journal of Peace Education. He has also published three books that focus on education and social development, including the edited book *Breaking Free: Sexual Diversity and Change in Emerging* Nations (QPI Publications/ Lambda Foundation). Robert is a Research Associate for the Arthur V. Mauro Centre for Peace and Justice (University of Manitoba) and Perspectives Editor (Adult Education) for the journal *New Horizons in Adult Education and Human Resource Development*. For more information on Robert's background, please visit www.robertmizzi.com.

Robin Neustaeter is a doctoral student in Peace and Conflict Studies at the University of Manitoba, researcher, as well as a community educator and organiser. Her research examines women, community development, peacebuilding, and the everyday in rural contexts and cultures. Her professional experience includes peace and democracy researcher, research assistant, international program manager, sessional instructor in the West Indies and Canada, English as an Additional Language instructor, community educator in community development, peace, women's leadership and family literacy, and research assistant. She's also an artist and active volunteer.

Anna Snyder is an Associate Professor in conflict resolution studies at Menno Simons College an affiliate of University of Winnipeg and Canadian Mennonite University. Her work in her 2011 coedited book, *Critical Issues of Gender in Conflict Resolution, Peacebuilding, and Social Movements* focuses on the peacebuilding capacity of refugee women's organizations in Burma, Tibet, and Sudan. Her research builds on her expertise in women's peace organizations; Dr. Snyder's book *Setting the Agenda for Global Peace: Conflict and Consensus Building* looks at transnational women's peace networks. A practitioner, she trained political parties in conflict resolution in Myanmar on behalf of the Council for Democracy for Burma in 2013. Her coauthored chapter in the Aboriginal Healing Foundation's *From Truth to Reconciliation* (2008) arose from her practice in Indigenous/non-Indigenous reconciliation and resulted in an invitation to organize reconciliation events at Canada's Truth and Reconciliation Commission (2010) on Aboriginal Residential Schools.

Joey Sprague, Professor in Sociology at the University of Kansas, explores the ways that gender, class, and race shape knowledge, from public discourse to the social organization of the academy. Recent publications include "Economic Sociology vs. Real Life: the Case of Grocery Shopping." (with Shelley Koch, *American Journal of Economics and Sociology*, 2014), "The Standpoint of Art/Criticism: Cindy Sherman as Feminist Artist?" (with Jessica

Sprague-Jones, *Sociological Inquiry,* 2011) and "Research and reporting on the development of sex in fetuses: Gendered from the start." (with Molly Dingel, *Public Understanding of Science*, 2010). The second edition of her book, *Feminist Methodologies for Critical Researchers: Bridging Differences* (Rowman & Littlefield, 2005), is scheduled to appear in 2015. She teaches feminist theory, feminist methodology, sociology of knowledge, and social psychology. She is Executive Officer of Sociologists for Women in Society and coeditor of *The Gender Lens* book series (Rowman & Littlefield).

Katerina Standish obtained her PhD from the Peace and Conflict Studies program at the University of Manitoba and is a Lecturer at the National Centre for Peace and Conflict Studies at the University of Otago. She is interested in cultural violence, gender, education, peace curriculum, and narratives in ethnic conflict. Her previous publications include content related to cultural violence and gender, cultural violence and education.

Robin L. Turner is an Assistant Professor of political science at Butler University in Indianapolis, Indiana. Her teaching and scholarship span multiple fields, including development studies, tourism studies, and gender studies as well as political science. Focusing principally on state-society relations and political economy in southern Africa, Robin examines the interplay between state policies and local practices over time and analyzes how past and present ways of structuring property and authority shape local political economies and influence constructions of identity. Her work has appeared in the *Journal of Modern African Studies, Africa Spectrum, Development and Change*, and the *Journal of Wildlife Law and Policy.*

Hamdesa Tuso is a faculty member of the Peace and Conflict Studies program of University of Manitoba. Before joining the University of Manitoba, Hamdesa was Associate Professor of Conflict Resolution at the Department of Conflict Analysis and Resolution at Nova Southeastern University. Prior to that, he taught at the Conflict Resolution programs of Antioch University and George Mason University. His areas of interest include indigenous processes of conflict resolution, nationalism, ethnicity and conflict, organizational conflicts, theories of social conflict, human rights and human security. During 2006/2007, he was selected as the Distinguished Visiting Esau Professor of Conflict Resolution Studies, Menno Simons College, University of Winnipeg, Canada. He is the founder of the Oromo Studies Association (OSA). In 2004, he founded the Africa Working Group (AWG) of which he is currently the director. He is coeditor of *Peace on Earth: The Role of Religion in Peace and Conflict Studies,* Lexington Books (2014).

Sinéad Walsh is a Government of Ireland Postgraduate Research Scholar at Trinity College Dublin (2012–2015). Her doctoral dissertation considers the peacemaking aspect of women's activism in Armenia and Azerbaijan, emphasizing creative tensions between this and the international discourse on Women, Peace, and Security. Her main research interests are gender, civil society, and conflict in the former Soviet Union. She is also interested in comparative peace processes, drawing in particular on her research experience in post-conflict Northern Ireland.

Franke Wilmer is a Full Professor of Political Science and International Relations at Montana State University in Bozeman, MT. She teaches courses on international relations, international law, international relations theory, human rights, and the politics of war and peace She has written on the subjects of human rights, indigenous peoples political activism, the psychology of political violence, and feminist IR. Her third book, *Human Rights in International Relations*, will be published with Lynne Rienner in February 2015. She is the former chair of the Montana Human Rights Commission and a served four terms in the Montana House of Representatives.

María Lucía Zapata is a lawyer from Bogotá, Colombia, and is a PhD Candidate in Peace and Conflict Studies at the University of Manitoba following a MA in International Peace Studies from the University of Notre Dame. Maria Lucia has extensive experience in peacebuilding, conflict transformation and restorative justice in Colombia, Canada, and the Philippines. Her main research interests are grassroots peacebuilding and postliberal peace.